Flash® Professional CS5 Bible

Flash® Professional CS5 Bible

Todd Perkins

WILEY

Wiley Publishing, Inc.

Flash® Professional CS5 Bible

Published by
Wiley Publishing, Inc.
111 River St.
Hoboken, NJ 07030-5774
www.wiley.com
Copyright © 2010 by Wiley Publishing, Inc., Indianapolis, Indiana

Library of Congress Control Number: 2010929311

ISBN: 978-0-470-60228-7

Manufactured in the United States of America

10 9 8 7 6 5 4 3 2 1

Published by Wiley Publishing, Inc., Indianapolis, Indiana
Published simultaneously in Canada

For general information on our other products and services or to obtain technical support, please contact our Customer Care Department within the U.S. at 877-762-2974, outside the U.S. at 317-572-3993 or fax 317-572-4002.

Wiley also publishes its books in a variety of electronic formats. Some content that appears in print may not be available in electronic books.

About the Author

As a lifelong fan of animation, Todd's childhood dream was to become a cartoonist. In 2000, Todd had an opportunity to create his first Web site, and at the time, Flash was a popular tool for doing so. He quickly fell in love with Flash, and a few years later got a job as a Flash designer at a graphic design company. After gaining real-world experience using Flash to develop Web sites, Todd decided to become a Flash consultant, using his skills to help others master Flash. Since then, Todd has written several books, including *Flash CS3 Hands on Training, ActionScript 3.0 in Flash CS3 Hands on Training, Nintendo Wii Flash Game Creator's Guide,* and *Search Engine Optimization for Flash.* He has also recorded a vast array of video titles about Flash and ActionScript for Lynda.com, including *Flash CS5 Essential Training, ActionScript 3.0 in Flash CS4 for Designers, Object Oriented Programming in ActionScript 3.0,* and several others. Todd also speaks at conferences, trains in classrooms, and has taught Flash to employees in several major organizations including Disney, Boeing, and *Los Angeles Times.* Todd also loves to create Flash applications and games, and has created Web sites and apps for clients, such as Chris Orwig and Douglas Kirkland.

When Todd is not teaching Flash or creating Flash applications, he enjoys playing video games, and spending quality time with his wife and son in southern California.

Credits

Preface

In 1997, Macromedia acquired a small Web graphics program, FutureSplash, from a company named FutureWave. FutureSplash was a quirky little program with the astounding capability to generate compact, vector-based graphics and animations for delivery over the Web. With Macromedia's embrace, Flash blossomed. In 2005, Adobe Systems, Inc. acquired Macromedia and, in three short years, has successfully integrated Flash into their family of powerhouse graphics, video, and design software. Not only has the Flash platform obtained ubiquity, but Flash content is now more easily created across a wide range of professional software applications. The Flash Player plug-in ships with most major browsers and operating systems. Flash graphics appear not only all over the Web, but also on television and movie screens, on phones, on kiosks, and even in art galleries.

As the Web-surfing public and the development community have continued to demand more of Flash, Adobe has delivered. After Creative Suite 3 was released, Adobe went out into the world and sat with people using its programs to see what they used, what they needed, and how the next generation of Creative Suite tools could support daily workflow and specialize tasks more effectively. The result is a release that promotes expressiveness and enhances efficiency while encouraging best practices in development — a functional and an inspiring combination that has earned rave reviews from visual designers and code-oriented developers at all levels.

The Flash CS5 Professional interface is consistent with other Creative Suite 5 (CS5) products; it has tool options and other editing features contained in streamlined panels and lots of important changes to the authoring environment. The Mac interface is nearly 100 percent identical to the Windows interface, with support for docked panels, tabbed panels, and enhancements to the coding environments in Flash CS5 and Dreamweaver CS5.

Flash movies can communicate directly with server-side scripts and programs, using standard URL-encoded variables, XML-formatted structures, Web services, or powerhouse data transfers from Flash Remoting–enabled servers. Sounds can be imported and exported as MP3 audio for high-quality music on the Web at the smallest file sizes. Flash Player 10 supports nearly every Web file format you'll ever come across. Loading of JPEG, PNG, GIF, MP3, FLV, AAC, and H.264 video content streamlines production and maintenance of dynamic high-volume media sites. The updated FLVPlayback component and the addition of custom tools, custom effects, and behaviors offer Flash users of all skill levels some exciting possibilities. Evidence of the dominance of the Flash format can be found in the wide range of third-party developers creating applications that output to the Flash movie format (.swf files). Flash has fulfilled its promise of becoming the central application for generating interactive content for delivery on the Web; the potential only seems to expand as more developers tap into the data-handling power of Flash and its increasingly sophisticated graphics capabilities as it continues to grow beyond the computer screen.

Is there any other Flash book for you?

Adobe Flash CS5 Professional Bible is the most comprehensive and exhaustive reference on Flash. It helps you get started on your first day with the program and will still be a valuable resource when you've attained mastery of the program. When you're looking for clues on how to integrate Flash with other programs so that you can deliver unique and compelling content in the Flash format, you'll know where to turn. We've put significant effort into this edition, updating all ActionScript content to use ActionScript 3.0, the most recent version of the ActionScript language available in Flash Player 9 or higher.

Flash is not just a single tool. You can think of Flash as a multitasking application. It's an illustration program, an image/sound/video editor, an animation machine, and a scripting engine, all rolled into one. In this book, we look at each of these uses of Flash and explain how all the features work together.

To address advanced scripting topics and more server-side development issues, Roger Braunstein, Mims Wright, Josh Noble, and Joey Lott have written the *ActionScript 3 Bible* (Wiley, 2007) to fully address advanced use of the ActionScript 3.0 scripting language. If you're already adept at creating animation and basic interactive interfaces in Flash and you want to expand your knowledge of more complex coding techniques, you may want to compare the table of contents in this book with that of *ActionScript Bible* to determine which book covers the topics you're most interested in.

How to Get the Most Out of This Book

Here are some things to know so you can get the most out of this book:

First, to indicate that you need to select a command from a menu, the menu and command are separated by an arrow symbol. For example, if we tell you to select the default workspace layout from the Flash application menu, the instructions will say to choose Window ➪ Workspace ➪ Essentials.

Parts I and II of the book are entirely dedicated to project planning and getting familiar with the Flash interface. Parts III and IV explain how to generate animation and integrate other media files into your Flash movies. Parts V through VIIgradually introduce you to the power of ActionScript and show you how to take advantage of Flash components to quickly create dynamic applications that support live data. Although this book was written to take a beginner by the hand, starting from page one, you can also use it as a reference. Use the index and the table of contents to find what you're looking for, and just go there, or jump in anywhere. If you already know Flash and want to get some details on sound, for example, just go to any of the chapters in Part IV, "Integrating Media Files with Flash."

This is a real-world production book: We've worked hard to ensure that our lessons, examples, and explanations are based on professional conventions. The CD-ROM that accompanies this book contains many of the source Flash project files (.fla), with original artwork and ActionScript for the examples and lessons in the book. You can also find sample video files to encode with Flash video!

Icons: What Do They Mean?

Although the icons are pretty standard and self-explanatory (they have their names written on them!), here's a brief explanation of what they are and what they mean.

Tip

Tips offer you extra information that further explains a given topic or technique, often suggesting alternatives or workarounds to a listed procedure. ■

Note

Notes provide supplementary information to the text, shedding light on background processes or miscellaneous options that aren't crucial to the basic understanding of the material. ■

Caution

When you see the Caution icon, make sure you're following along closely to the tips and techniques being discussed. Some external applications may not work exactly the same with Flash on different operating systems and some workflows have inherent risks or drawbacks. ■

Cross-Reference

If you want to find related information to a given topic in another chapter, look for the Cross-Reference icons. ■

New Feature

The New Feature icons point out differences between Flash 8 and previous versions of Flash. ■

Web Resource

For related information, resources, or software available online, look for the Web Resource icons. ■

On the CD-ROM

This icon indicates that the CD-ROM contains a related file and points you to the folder location. ■

How This Book Is Organized

This book has been written in a format that gives you access to need-to-know information very easily in every section (or part) of the book. If you are completely new to Flash, then you'll want to read Parts I through VI. After you have developed a familiarity with the Flash interface and the new drawing and effects tools, you can proceed to Parts VII and VII. We've included step-by-step descriptions of real Flash projects to help you "leap" from the intro topics to the advanced topics. These sections of the book guide you through the production process, helping you apply ActionScript and production techniques that may be new to you.

If you've already used Flash, then you may want to review the changes to the Flash CS5 interface in Part I, and then jump right into other specific parts to learn more about animation, ActionScript, creating artwork and content in other applications, integrating Flash with HTML, and using Flash to publish iPhone applications. There are many new features and workflow enhancements for new and experienced users alike in every section of the book, so even if you've done a lot of work in Flash, it's worth scanning each part for an introduction to new tools and techniques.

Part I: An Introduction to Flash Web Production

The first part of this book explores the Flash file format and how Flash CS5 fits into the evolution of the program (Chapter 1), explains the context in which Flash movies interact on the Web (Chapter 2), and gives an overview of multimedia planning and some specific techniques and suggestions that will make your Flash project development less painful and more productive (Chapter 3).

Part II: Mastering the Flash Environment

This part gives you all the information you need to feel comfortable in the Flash CS5 authoring environment. Get an introduction to, and some tips for, customizing the Flash UI (Chapter 4). Learn where to find your drawing tools and how to use them efficiently (Chapter 5), and then discover all the ways that Flash helps you to organize and optimize project assets (Chapter 6). Learn key color concepts relevant to multimedia production and find out why Flash has the best color tools yet (Chapter 7). Jump into using text-editing tools and see how to get the best-looking type and the smallest file sizes in your Flash projects (Chapter 8). Finally, learn how to modify text and graphics to get the most out of your Flash artwork (Chapter 9).

Part III: Creating Animation and Effects

After you've learned how to find your way around the Flash interface and how to create static graphics, you can learn to make things move and how to work with different symbol types to optimize your animation workflow (Chapter 10). Then, add polish and pizzazz with Flash filter effects and blend modes (Chapter 11).

Part IV: Integrating Media Files with Flash

Now that you're fluent in the Flash workspace, take your projects to the next level by adding sound, special graphics, and video assets. In Chapter 12, you learn the basics of digital sound, and how to import, optimize, and export high-quality sound for different types of projects. Chapter 13 gives you an overview of how to bring vector or raster artwork from other programs into Flash and how to protect image quality while optimizing your Flash movies. Chapter 14 introduces the exciting video features of Flash CS5 and the new Adobe Media Encoder CS5 application, including the use of the high-quality AVC/H.264 video codec and adding ActionScript cue points without writing ActionScript code.

Part V: Adding Basic Interactivity to Flash Movies

Learn how to start using Flash actions to create interactive and responsive presentations. Get oriented in the Flash CS5 Actions panel and fundamental ActionScript in your movies (Chapter 15). Use ActionScript in Flash movies to control internal elements on multiple timelines, such as nested Movie Clips (Chapter 16). Finally, use Flash CS5 to create your first full application (Chapter 17).

Part VI: Distributing Flash Movies

You need to learn how to export (or publish) your Flash presentations to the .swf file format for use in an HTML document, or within presentations in other formats. Chapter 18 details options in the Flash CS5 Publish settings, and provides tips for optimizing your Flash movies in order to achieve smaller file sizes for faster download performance. If you prefer to hand-code your HTML, read Chapter 19, which describes how to use the <embed> and <object> tags and how to create plug-in detection systems for your Flash movies using the SWFObject JavaScript library. If you want to find out how to create a Flash stand-alone projector, or use the Flash stand-alone player, check out Chapter 20. Learn how to publish cross-platform applications using Adobe AIR in Chapter 21. In Chapter 22, use Flash to create iPhone applications and learn how to get those apps on your iPhone and in the App Store.

Getting in Touch

Check Appendix B to learn more about this book's various contributors and guest experts, including URLs of their work and contact information for people who don't mind being contacted directly by our readers.

For quality concerns or issues with the CD-ROM, you can call the Wiley Customer Care phone number: (877) 762-2974. Outside the United States, call 1 (317) 572-3994, or contact Wiley Customer Service by e-mail at techsupdum@wiley.com. Wiley Publishing, Inc. will provide technical support only for CD-ROM installation and other general quality-control items; for technical support on the applications themselves, consult the program's vendor.

Adobe Wants to Help You

Adobe has created a Feature Request and Bug Report form to make it easier to process suggestions and requests from Flash users. If you have an idea or feature request for the next version or you find a bug that prevents you from doing your work, let the folks at Adobe know. You can find the online form at www.adobe.com/support/email/wishform.

The simple fact is this: If more users request a specific feature or improvement, it's more likely that Adobe will implement it.

Regardless of your geographic location, you always have access to the global Flash community for support and the latest information through the Adobe online forums at www.adobe.com/cfusion/webforums/forum/index.cfm?forumid=15.

For inspiration and motivation check out the Site of the Day, weekly features, and case studies at www.adobe.com/showcase.

Acknowledgments

This book would not have been possible without the dedication and talent of many people. Although much of the content in this edition has changed to reflect changes in the tools, there is also a good deal of content from dedicated contributors that has been carried over from the previous edition. We are always grateful for the added breadth and depth the tutorials from our guest experts bring to the content. First and foremost, we would like to thank the Flash development community. In our combined experiences in research and multimedia production, we haven't seen another community that has been so open, friendly, and willing to share advanced tips and techniques. It has been gratifying to be involved as the community keeps expanding and to see the innovators in the first wave of Flash development become mentors to a whole new generation. Thank you all for continuing to inspire and challenge audiences and each other with the possibilities for Flash.

I would like to thank everyone at Wiley Publishing who supported us as we researched and revised, week after week. A *Flash Bible* production team can't steer itself — our gratitude goes to Aaron Black, the acquisitions editor, and Beth Taylor, the project editor. Zachary Szukala, the technical editor, was instrumental in helping me keep our material honest and effective.

Of course, this book about Flash wouldn't even exist without the hard work of the people at Adobe who make it all possible. Many thanks to the developers, engineers, and support staff at Adobe, especially Jay Armstrong, for answering so many of my questions. I am also indebted, as always, to all our intrepid fellow developers and authors, who helped us to get our bearings in early versions of Flash CS5.

Contents at a Glance

Contents

Contents

Contents

Contents

Contents

Contents

Contents

Contents

Contents

Part I

An Introduction to Flash Web Production

If you're new to Flash or to multimedia production, this section gets you started on the right foot. If you are a veteran Flash user, this section gives you some perspective on the evolution of Flash and the workflow options available in Adobe Flash CS5.

Chapter 1 provides a comprehensive overview of the strengths and weaknesses of the Flash format and some background on where Flash came from and how it has evolved. Chapter 2 explores the various ways that Flash movies interact with other Web formats and introduces some of the issues that need to be considered when planning for specific audiences. Chapter 3 has expanded coverage of strategies for multimedia project planning, including descriptions of how to create flowcharts, site maps, and functional specification documents.

Understanding the Adobe Flash CS5 Blueprint

IN THIS CHAPTER

Exploring the uses of Flash CS5

Identifying Flash file types

Introducing the structure of Flash documents

S ince its humble beginnings as FutureSplash in 1997, the Flash authoring tool and the Flash platform have matured into a powerful tool for deploying a wide range of media content. With every new version released, the possibilities have increased for imaginative and dynamic content creation — for the Web and beyond. After Adobe acquired Macromedia in 2005, Adobe has expanded Flash capabilities in several Creative Suite products, as well as development tools such as Adobe Flex Builder. The Adobe user interface is consistent across powerhouse applications such as Adobe Photoshop, Adobe Flash, and Adobe Illustrator.

In this chapter, I introduce Flash CS5 and explore the many possibilities available for your productions. I also discuss how Flash compares to or enhances other programs that you may be familiar with.

Flash content can be viewed in a few different ways. The most common method is from within a Web browser, either as an asset within an HTML page or as a Web site completely comprised of a master Flash movie using several smaller Flash movies as loaded SWF assets. The Flash Player is also available as a stand-alone application (known as a *projector*), which can be used to view movies without needing a Web browser or the plug-in. This method is commonly used for deployment of Flash movies on CD-ROMs, floppy disks, or other offline media formats. With Adobe AIR, Flash content can be installed into computers as native desktop applications. Finally, with Flash CS5, content made in Flash can be published as iPhone and iPod touch applications, and released in Apple's App Store.

Cross-Reference
You can learn more about projectors and stand-alones in Chapter 22, "Using the Flash Player and Projector." ∎

The Key Is Integration

Flash has seen significant development over its 12 years in both capability and design. Consistently with each new release, designers and developers push the technology into new territory. In its current iteration, Flash CS5 enables you to create content that's compatible with Adobe Flash Player 10, one of the largest updates to the Flash Player. There are two sides of the integration coin: designing the user interface and high-end programming with ActionScript 3.0. Flash CS5 continues to satisfy both designers and programmers — all the new authortime visual effects in Flash CS5 and Flash Player 10 are fully programmable with ActionScript, the programming language of Flash.

Flash CS5 Professional, also referred to simply as Flash CS5, adds several enhancements to previous editions:

- **Adobe document import and export:** Because Adobe oversees the development of Photoshop, Illustrator, and Flash, it's much easier to coordinate file format interoperability between the applications. You have more options than ever to faithfully bring Photoshop, Illustrator, and After Effects content into Flash documents. Many of the CS5 tools can now export XFL (XML-based FLA) files and FXG (an XML-based image format) files that enable a smooth workflow from tools such as Illustrator and After Effects into Flash.

- **Improved animation and drawing features:** Adding realistic physics is now easier using the new Spring feature with IK animations. The Spring feature adds automatic "follow through" to IK animations for a more lifelike effect.

- **Improved text:** If you have ever wanted text that rendered from right to left, like many Asian languages, you now have that feature in Flash with the new Text Layout Framework (TLF). This feature adds support for new languages, multicolumn text, and right-to-left text. Flash CS5 also comes with a larger and more intuitive font embedding menu.

- **Code snippets:** Since the introduction of ActionScript 3.0, Flash programming has had a steep learning curve, especially for those who are entirely new to programming. In Flash CS5, there are many built-in snippets of code that you can apply to objects you create to add complex interactivity without having to write a line of code.

- **Video features:** In previous versions of Flash, adding cue points to video was something that could only be done either before the video was encoded or by using ActionScript. In Flash CS5, you can add cue points quickly and easily through the Properties panel. Flash CS5 also allows you to preview video in the Flash environment, without having to test your movie in the Flash Player.

Tip

If you're targeting a Flash Player 6 audience, you might want to consider targeting Flash Player 10 as well. Why? Flash Player 6 is capable of running Express Install scripts, which enable a Flash movie to automatically update the installed version of the Flash Player. Also, users with Flash Player 7 or later can receive automatic player updates. By default, Flash Player 7 checks Adobe's site every 30 days for new player updates. This process occurs silently in the background and doesn't require the user to upgrade his or her player installation manually. Theoretically, then, within 30 days of the release of any new Flash Player, including Flash Player 10, most browsers that had Flash Player 7, 8, or 9 will then have Flash Player 10. ■

For a complete list of features in Flash CS5, open the new browser-based help system by choosing Help ⇨ Flash Help, and then selecting Using Flash ⇨ Using Flash CS5 Professional ⇨ Resources ⇨ What's New ⇨ New Features.

Adobe also released new versions of Dreamweaver and Fireworks, as part of the CS5 Web Suite software bundle. The user interfaces for Flash, Dreamweaver, and Fireworks are very similar, each touting a Property inspector, dockable panel sets, and specialized tools to integrate the products with one another.

Although the broad array of Flash work created by Web designers and developers already speaks for itself, the sleek interface and the powerful new features of Flash CS5 surely inspire more challenging, functional, entertaining, informative, bizarre, humorous, beautiful, and fascinating experiments and innovations.

There are more ways to use Flash than there are adjectives to describe them, but here are just a few examples:

- Forms for collecting user information and dynamically loading custom content based on this interaction
- Real-time interaction with multiple users on a forum or support site, including live audio/video feeds of connected parties
- Complex online games with rich graphics and interaction, including multiplayer games
- A video portfolio using Flash Video capabilities and dynamic loading of content
- Animated ID spots and loading screens with built-in download detection
- A practical Web utility, such as a mortgage calculator or a search tool
- Robust chat rooms based on XML and server-socket technology
- An audio interface dynamically pulling in requested songs, using native Flash Player support for MP3 loading
- Interactive conceptual art experimentations involving several users, 3-D, or recording and playback of user interaction
- Shopping and e-commerce solutions built entirely by using Flash and server-side technology
- Interfaces for kiosks at museums, banks, and shopping centers
- Alternative content or movie attributes based on system capability testing (if a device or desktop doesn't support audio streaming, then a text equivalent of the audio transcript is presented to the user)
- Projectors used for creating slide show presentations in the style of PowerPoint, either on CD-ROM or an alternative storage device
- Broadcast-quality cartoons, advertising, or titling
- Optimized animations for the Web, and for mobile devices such as cellphones or PDAs

- An interface that addresses accessibility issues by modifying certain elements when a screen reader is active
- Flash movies specifically exported for use in digital video projects requiring special effects and compositing
- AIR applications built for the desktop that utilize data from popular social networking Web sites like Facebook and Twitter
- Casual, fun, addictive games for the iPhone

This list is obviously far from complete and is ever expanding with each new release of the program. As you can probably tell from this list, if you can imagine a use for Flash, it can probably be accomplished.

The topography of Flash CS5

Before you attempt to construct interactive projects in Flash, you should be familiar with the structure of the authoring environment. Even if you already know a previous version of Flash, learning this is advisable. That's because with the release of Flash CS5, Adobe has reorganized existing features to the interface and has either moved or improved other features and functionalities. So, to get a firm footing in the new interface, I strongly suggest that you work your way through this book — from the beginning.

Cross-Reference
Chapter 4, "Interface Fundamentals," introduces the updated Flash CS5 interface and gives you tips for customizing your workspace and optimizing your workflow. ■

Moreover, you need to proactively plan your interactive projects before you attempt to author them in Flash. An ounce of preplanning goes a long way during the production process. Don't fool yourself — the better your plan looks on paper, the better it performs when it comes to the final execution.

Cross-Reference
I detail the foundation for planning interactive Flash projects in Chapter 3, "Planning Flash Projects," and you will find these concepts reiterated and expanded in chapters that discuss specific project workflows. Chapter 19, "Making Your First Flash CS5 Project," is a great place to start applying these planning strategies. ■

I consolidated the overview of interactive planning in the early chapters of the book. In later chapters, I included step-by-step descriptions of real-world projects that allow you to see how all the theory and planning suggestions apply to the development of specific projects.

There are two primary files that you create during Flash development: Flash document files (.fla) and Flash movie files (.swf). I discuss both of these formats next.

File types in Flash CS5

Flash document files (.fla) are architected to provide an efficient authoring environment for projects of all sizes. Within this environment, content can be organized into scenes, and the ordering of scenes can be rearranged throughout the production cycle. Layers provide easy separation of graphics within each scene, and, as Guide or Mask layers, they can also aid drawing or even provide special effects. The Timeline shows keyframes, motion and shape tweens, labels, and comments. The Library (which can be shared amongst movies at authortime or at runtime) stores all the symbols in your project, such as graphics, fonts, animated elements, sounds or video, and components.

Flash documents

Throughout this book, you will see us refer to Flash documents (or Flash files), which are the .fla files created by Flash CS5 when you choose File ⇨ New and choose one of the Flash File options from the General category tab. Unlike some graphics applications, such as Adobe Illustrator, the file icon or file extension for Flash documents does not reflect the version of the authoring tool. For example, all previous versions of Flash and now CS5 save Flash documents as .fla files. You cannot open later version documents in previous versions of the authoring tool. You do not use Flash documents with the Flash Player, nor do you need to upload these files to your Web server. Always keep a version (and a backup!) of your Flash document.

Tip

Flash CS5 allows you to resave your Flash CS5 document file (.fla) as a Flash CS4 document file. Choose File ⇨ Save As and select Flash CS3 Document in the Save as type menu. If you save the document in this manner, you can open the Flash document file in the Flash CS4 authoring application. If the Flash CS5 document used features unavailable in Flash CS4, you receive a warning as you save the document in the Flash CS4 format. ■

In Flash CS5, you have the option to create six different types of Flash files: ActionScript 3.0, ActionScript 2.0, Adobe AIR 2, iPhone, Flash Lite 4, or Adobe Device Central. If you are targeting Flash Player 8 or earlier, you should always choose ActionScript 2.0. If you are targeting Flash Player 9 or later, and you want to use the advanced coding style of ActionScript 3.0, you should choose ActionScript 3.0. You can change your target version of ActionScript and the Flash Player at any time by clicking the Flash tab in the File ⇨ Publish Settings dialog box. If you want to deploy a desktop application, choose Adobe AIR 2. AIR applications require ActionScript 3.0. If you want to deploy content to mobile devices, use the Adobe Device Central option. This option automatically launches Device Central CS5, prompting you to choose a device profile to target with your Flash content.

New Feature

With the new iPhone file template, creating an iPhone application is now possible with Flash CS5. For more information about creating iPhone applications using Flash, see Chapter 22. ■

Note

Choosing the FLA File types ActionScript 3.0 and ActionScript 2.0 targets Flash Player 10 by default in the new document's publish settings. Be sure to change the targeted Flash Player version in the Flash tab of the Publish Settings dialog box (File⇨Publish Settings) to create Flash content targeted to the appropriate Flash Player version for your project. ■

Cross-Reference

Adobe Device Central CS5 is discussed in more detail in Chapter 20, "Publishing Flash Movies." ■

Figure 1.1 shows how Flash documents are composed of individual scenes that contain keyframes to describe changes on the Stage. What you can't see in this figure is the efficiency of sharing libraries among several Flash documents, loading other external assets (image, sound, video, or other Flash files) into a parent, or "master," Flash movie by using ActionScript, or creating interactive elements with scripting methods.

Flash movies

When you publish or test a Flash document, Flash CS5 creates a Flash movie file with the .swf file extension. This file format is an optimized version of the Flash document, retaining only the elements from the project file that are actually used. Flash movies are uploaded to your Web server, where they are usually integrated into HTML documents for other Web users to view. You can protect your finished Flash movies from being easily imported or edited in the authoring environment by other users.

Caution

The Protect from import option in the Publish Settings dialog box does not prevent third-party utilities from stripping artwork, symbols, sounds, and ActionScript code from your Flash movies. For more information, read Chapter 20, "Publishing Flash Movies." ■

Much of the information contained originally within a Flash document file (.fla) is discarded in the attempt to make the smallest file possible when exporting a Flash movie file (.swf). When your movie is exported, all original elements remain, but layers are essentially flattened and run on one timeline, in the order that was established in the Flash document. Practically all information originally in the file will be optimized somehow, and any unused Library elements are not exported with the Flash movie. Library assets are loaded into and stored in the first frame they are used in. For optimization, reused assets are saved to the file only once and are referenced throughout the movie from this one area. Bitmap images and sounds can be compressed with a variety of quality settings as well.

Tip

Flash Player 6 and later movies can be optimized with a specialized Compress Movie option that is available in the Flash tab of the Publish Settings dialog box (File⇨Publish Settings). When you apply this option, you see drastic file-size savings with movies that use a significant amount of ActionScript code. By default, Flash Player 10 movies automatically have this compression feature enabled. ■

FIGURE 1.1

Elements of a Flash document (.fla) in the authoring environment

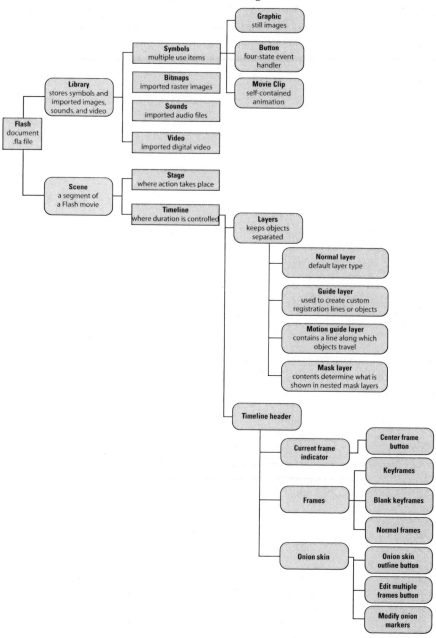

See Figure 1.2 for a graphic explanation of the characteristics of the Flash movie file (.swf) format.

Cross-Reference

I discuss Flash Player detection in detail in Chapter 21, "Integrating Flash Content with Web Pages." ■

There are several other ways in which Flash movies, or their parts, can be played back or displayed. Since Flash 4, the Publish feature has offered provisions for the export of movies or sections of movies to either the QuickTime digital video format, the QuickTime Flash layer vector format, or the Animated GIF format. Parts of movies can also be exported as a series of individual bitmaps or as vector files. Single frames can also be exported to these formats.

FIGURE 1.2

Overview of the Flash movie (.swf) format

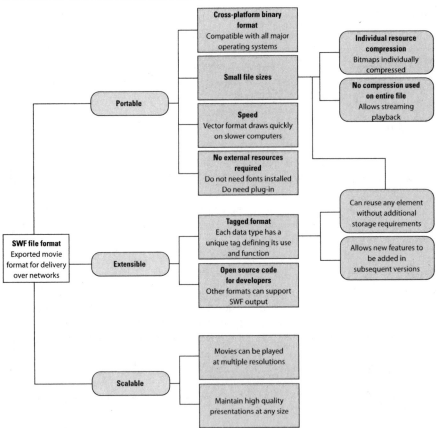

Using Flash Player Terminology

The difference between the naming conventions of the Flash Player plug-in and the Flash authoring software is potentially confusing. Adobe refers to its latest release of the player as Flash Player 10, tagging the version number at the end of the name rather than following the naming convention of some of its predecessors (that is, "Flash 5 Player"). One probable reason the Flash Player is numbered, rather than dubbed "CS" like the authoring software, is because a standard sequential number is required for plug-in detection.

When you publish Flash content to a Web site, don't be tempted to instruct visitors to download and install the "Flash CS5 Player." In versions past, you might have seen sites that required the "Flash MX Player." This terminology is confusing and misleading because there is no "Flash CS5 Player" for users to download. Always refer to the version number of the Flash Player, not the authoring tool.

Flash ActionScript files

ActionScript is the programming language used within Flash CS5 documents to create interactive functionality within the movie. You can store ActionScript code in external text files with the .as file extension. You can open .as files directly in Flash CS5 or your preferred code editing application, such as Adobe Flex Builder. ActionScript files can be compiled into a Flash movie by using the #include directive or the import keyword.

Flash video files

The Flash Video file format (.flv file extension) and AVC/H.264 video files (.f4v file extension) are used for any video content played within the Flash Player. This file extension is used by any tool that creates Flash Video content, such as Adobe Media Encoder, Sorenson Squeeze, or On2 Flix. You cannot open .flv files in the Flash CS5 authoring tool, but you can import them into a Flash document file (.fla) or you can load them at runtime into Flash Player 7 or later movies. Flash Video files can also be uploaded to an Adobe Flash Media Server application and streamed in real time to Flash Player 6 or later movies.

Flash Component files

The Flash Component file format (.swc file extension) is used for compiled clips included with Flash CS5 or that you purchase from third-party vendors or download from Adobe Exchange (www.adobe.com/exchange). You can't directly open a .swc file in the Flash CS5 authoring environment, but you can copy .swc files to your local settings for Flash CS5 so that the components show up in the Components panel. On Windows, you can copy .swc files to the following location. Note that ⊃ denotes a continuation of the directory path:

```
C:\Documents and Settings\[Your User Name]\Local Settings\Application ⊃
Data\Adobe\Flash 8\en\Configuration\Components
```

On the Mac, you can copy to this location:

```
[Startup disk]\Users\[Your User Name]\Library\Application Support\ ⊃
Adobe\Flash CS5\en\Configuration\Components
```

These locations are only used to store additional components; the default components for Flash CS5 are stored in the Flash CS5 application folder.

Note

The Flash Project file format (.flp file extension) is no longer used in Flash CS5. If you have FLP files from previous versions of Flash, you need to build a new project in the updated Project panel in Flash CS5 and link to your old project's files. For more information, read Chapter 3, "Planning Flash Projects." ■

The Many Worlds of Flash CS5

Flash is a hybrid application that is like no other application. On the immediate surface, it may seem (to some) to be a simple hybrid between a Web-oriented bitmap handler and a vector-drawing program, such as Adobe Illustrator. But although Flash is indeed such a hybrid, it's also capable of much, much more. It's also an interactive multimedia-authoring program and a sophisticated animation program suitable for creating a range of animations — from simple Web ornaments to broadcast-quality cartoons. As if that weren't enough, it's also the host of a powerful and adaptable scripting language.

Over the past decade, ActionScript has evolved from a limited drag-and-drop method of enabling animation to a full-fledged object-oriented programming language very similar to JavaScript. Flash ActionScript can work in conjunction with XML (eXtensible Markup Language), HTML, and many other applications and parts of the Web. Flash content can be integrated with server-side technologies, including but not limited to Web services, remoting services (AMF, or Action Message Format), and Adobe Flash Media Server. The Flash Player offers built-in support for dynamically loading images, MP3s, video, and other data. Flash can work seamlessly with just about any Web application service, including Adobe ColdFusion, PHP, Microsoft .NET services, and XML socket servers, to deliver streamlined dynamic interactive experiences.

So, what's this evolving hybrid we call Flash really capable of? That's a question that remains to be answered by content creators such as you. In fact, I'm hoping that you will master this application and show me a thing or two. That's why I've written this book: to put the tool in your hands and get you started on the road to your own innovations.

Because Flash is a hybrid application capable of just about anything, a good place to start working with this powerhouse is to inquire, "What are the components of this hybrid? And if they were separated out, how might their capabilities be described?" Those are the questions that I answer in this chapter.

Bitmap handler

In truth, Flash has limited capabilities as an image-editing program. It is more accurate to describe this part of the Flash application as a bitmap *handler*. Bitmap images are composed of dots on a grid of individual pixels. The location (and color) of each dot must be stored in memory, which makes this a memory-intensive format and leads to larger file sizes. Another characteristic of bitmap images is that they cannot be scaled without compromising quality (clarity and sharpness). The adverse effects of scaling an image up are more pronounced than when scaling down. Because of these two drawbacks — file sizes and scaling limitations — overuse or overdependence of bitmap images may reduce the speed at which your Web site loads into a user's browser. However, for photographic-quality images, bitmap formats are indispensable and often produce better image quality and lower file sizes than vector images of equivalent complexity.

Vector-based drawing program

The heart of the Flash application is a vector-based drawing program, with capabilities similar to Adobe Illustrator. A vector-based drawing program doesn't rely upon individual pixels to compose an image. Instead, it draws shapes by defining points that are described by coordinates. Lines that connect these points are called paths, and vectors at each point describe the curvature of the path. Because this scheme is mathematical, there are two distinct advantages: Vector content is significantly more compact, and it's thoroughly scalable without image degradation. These advantages are especially significant for Web use.

Vector-based animator

The vector animation component of the Flash application is unlike any other program that preceded it. Although Flash is capable of handling bitmaps, its native file format is vector-based. So, unlike many other animation and media programs, Flash relies on the slim and trim vector format for transmission of your final work. Instead of storing megabytes of pixel information for each frame, Flash stores compact vector descriptions of each frame. Whereas a bitmap-based animation file format struggles to display each bitmap in rapid succession, the Flash Player quickly renders the vector descriptions as needed and with far less strain on either the bandwidth or the recipient's machine. This is a huge advantage when transmitting animations and other graphic content over the Web.

Video engine

The Flash Player plug-in can be considered one of the world's smallest video plug-ins. Flash Player 10 amazingly includes several primary video codecs for rendering video files: Sorenson Spark (Flash Player 6 or later), On2 VP6-E (Flash Player 8 or later), On2 VP6-S (Flash Player 9 Update 3 or later), and AVC/H.264 (Flash Player 9 Update 3 and later). Each generation of video codec increases the compression and image quality possibilities for your video content. You can import source video files directly into Flash CS5 document files (.fla), or create separate video files (.flv, .f4v, .mp4) that load into your Flash movies. Users do not need to have Apple QuickTime, Real Network's RealPlayer, or Microsoft Windows Media Player installed in order to view video in a Flash movie. The Flash Player provides a seamless solution.

Cross-Reference
To learn more about this exciting aspect of Flash authoring, refer to Chapter 16, "Displaying Video." I also discuss the new Adobe Media Encoder CS5, an application designed to create the high-quality video content. ■

Audio player

Since Flash Player 6, Flash movie files (.swf) have had the capability to load MP3 files during runtime. You can also import other audio file formats into a Flash document file (.fla) during authortime. Sounds can be attached to keyframes or buttons, for background tracks or sound effects. A sound file's bytes can be distributed evenly across a timeline so that the .swf file can be progressively downloaded into the Flash Player, enabling a movie to start playing before the entire sound file has been downloaded.

Note

A runtime file is one that loads when the Flash Player is running in its host environment, such as a Web browser or the test movie window of Flash CS5. An authortime file is one that is imported into your Flash document while you're using Flash CS5. ■

Multimedia authoring program

If the heart of Flash is a vector-based drawing program, then the body of Flash is a multimedia-authoring program (or authoring *environment*). Flash document files (.fla) can contain multiple media assets, including sound, still graphics, animation, and video. Moreover, Flash is a powerful tool for creating truly interactive content because it enables you to add ActionScript commands to dynamically control movie file (.swf) playback. Whether you are designing simple menu systems or customized and intuitive experimental interfaces, Flash content can be authored to recognize and respond to user input.

Animation sequencer

Most multimedia-authoring programs have a component for sequencing content as animation, and Flash is no exception. But in Flash, the animation sequencer is the core of the authortime application. The Timeline window controls the display of all content — static or animated — within your Flash project. Within the Timeline window, there are two areas that enable you to organize content in visual space and in linear time.

Layers and layer folders enable you to keep track of content that has been placed into your Flash document. The visibility of each layer can be controlled independently, making it easier to isolate specific elements as you are authoring. Layers are viewed from front to back within each frame of the Timeline — items on upper layers overlay other items on lower layers. Any number of items can be placed on a single layer, but you have less control over the stacking order within a layer. Within the same layer, ungrouped vector lines and shapes will always be on the bottom level, whereas bitmaps, text, grouped items, and symbol instances will be on the upper level.

Tip

Flash CS5 documents can use Layer folders. This is invaluable for organizing projects that involve many separate elements. ■

Cross-Reference

For a detailed tour of the Flash CS5 environment, refer to Chapter 4, "Interface Fundamentals." I discuss the process of making artwork and managing groups and symbols in Chapter 5, "Drawing in Flash," and in Chapter 6, "Symbols, Instances, and the Library," respectively. ■

The structure that creates the illusion of movement in a Flash movie is a series of frames. Each frame represents a still moment in time. By controlling how the playhead moves through these frames, you can control the speed, duration, and order of an animated sequence.

By changing the content in your layers on each frame, you can manually create frame-by-frame animation. However, one of the things that makes Flash such a popular animation machine is its ability to auto-interpolate or *tween* animation. By defining the content on a beginning and an end keyframe and applying a motion tween or a shape tween, you can quickly create or modify animated shape transformations and the movement of elements on the Stage.

Cross-Reference

I discuss the many ways of creating Flash animation in Part III: "Creating Animation and Effects." ■

Within one Flash document, you can also set up a series of separate scenes; each scene is a continuation of the same Main Timeline, but scenes can be named and reordered at any time. Scenes play through from first to last without interruption unless Flash's interactive commands ("actions") dictate otherwise.

Cross-Reference

I introduce the steps for using ActionScript for simple control of movie playback in Part V: "Adding Basic Interactivity to Flash Movies." ■

Programming and database front end

The past few versions of Flash brought a vast expansion of the possibilities for integrating Flash interfaces with server-side technology and dynamic loading of content by using XML and server technologies such as Adobe ColdFusion, PHP, Microsoft .NET, JSP, Flash Remoting, and Adobe Flash Media Server. These improvements largely came out of the development and maturity of ActionScript as a viable programming language. Flash has developed into an alternative front end for large databases, which means it can serve as an online store, MP3 player, or multiuser game and chat room — an amazing feat for an "animation program"!

With Flash CS5 there are virtually infinite possibilities at your fingertips. Using the components that ship with Flash CS5, you can tap advanced data structures and display them in a Flash movie. You can load JPEGs, GIFs, PNGs, MP3s, and Flash Video files into Flash at runtime (or "on-the-fly"), without having to use a special server technology. You can use a wide range of data formats, from XML to Web Services (SOAP) to Flash Remoting.

There are many other enhancements to the programming environment and functionality of Flash that experienced users will appreciate and new users will come to value. ActionScript 3.0 continues the evolution of Flash's scripting language to a mature format, more closely adhering to ECMAScript 4. These changes support ActionScript's move toward acceptance as a standard, object-oriented programming (OOP) language on its own.

Tip
If you consider yourself a computer programmer (especially one who learned how to program in another programming language), you will likely want to try out Adobe Flash Builder. Flash Builder is the premiere authoring tool for enterprise-level Web applications running on the Flash platform. ■

Desktop application authoring program

You can now create your Flash content as an Adobe AIR package for deployment as a desktop application. What is AIR? AIR stands for *Adobe Integrated Runtime*, and it's a framework that enables your Flash content to run as an installed application, just like any other application on your desktop such as Microsoft Word! After a user has downloaded the AIR installer from Adobe's Web site (around 15MB), the user can install AIR applications from any Web site. AIR applications can utilize Flash content (SWF, and all of its supported runtime formats such as MP3, JPEG, PNG, and so on), HTML content (AIR has its own Web rendering engine), and PDF files.

iPhone application development program

Flash CS5 can be used to create iPhone applications. Flash iPhone applications are created entirely in Flash using ActionScript 3.0 to program the interactivity. Using code provided by Adobe, you can use ActionScript 3.0 to access data from the iPhone's accelerometer, touch screen, and GPS, and that information can be used in creating iPhone applications, including games.

Summary

- Flash CS5 combines many of the key tools for multimedia authoring into one nimble program. The integration it facilitates with other programs and languages promotes better Web content and more advanced applications.

- Flash content is not only found on the Web. For example, it is also used for CD/DVD-ROM authoring, broadcast graphics, offline interfaces, and business presentations.

- Flash CS5 is a multifaceted application that can create a wide range of interactive products for the ever-growing variety of Web-enabled devices that surfers use to access the Internet.

- Careful planning of Flash development will undoubtedly save you time and effort in the long run.

Exploring Web Technologies

O ver the years, many technologies have been developed to work in conjunction with Adobe Flash. Understanding the process of integrating these technologies will no doubt enable you to create more interactive and complex productions. If you're new to Flash, or you're looking for new ways to enhance or broaden the vision or scope of your Flash productions, you'll benefit from reading this chapter. It explores the placement of Flash within an ever-growing toolset for universal and "standards-based" Web development in use today.

Contextualizing Flash in the Internet Evolution

If you follow the development of "bleeding-edge" technology, you may have noticed how often software is created, updated, and made obsolete. At times, this cycle seems to happen almost on a daily basis. But exactly how many practical — and affordable — options exist for Web development? How can production teams develop consistent frameworks with a variety of server technologies to efficiently build Flash presentations and applications? In this section, I discuss how Flash CS5 continues to push the direction and limits of the Internet.

High expectations for Web experiences

Despite the devastation to Web production brought about by the "dotbomb" era (that is, the economic recession that occurred after many dotcom companies went out of business around the year 2000), the Internet economy has rebounded tremendously. People visiting your Web sites or using your

Web-based applications expect to experience engaging interfaces with amazing graphics and sound. Clients who hire you expect that you can produce this type of material. Clients may also believe that everyone will be able to visit the site and download material instantaneously (regardless of connection speed limitations), and that every visitor will have the same experience. Before you consider whether Flash is the best tool to meet your clients' goals, let's step back for a moment and consider Flash's history.

With every release of a new version of the Flash Player, Web developers have access to bigger and better capabilities. I've seen a vast evolution from the early days in 1997 of mere vector animations, which were vastly smaller in file size compared to standard GIF animations. In 1998, Flash Player 3 made a marked improvement by introducing more control over these animations. At that time, Web sites with small games started to arrive on the development scene. That was also the year when Macromedia Generator was introduced, enabling dynamic graphics and data for Flash movies. Many companies were apprehensive about investing in Flash development because Flash was relatively new, although it was gaining ground as an accepted form of Web delivery.

In 1999, when Flash Player 4 was introduced, this attitude changed a great deal. The new version was much more powerful and could accomplish many of the tasks that Generator provided in the past. Database interaction and dynamic content were suddenly possible in real time. However, Flash 4 was still a difficult application for developers to use; the programming interface for ActionScript code was limited by drag-and-drop functionality (which was avoidable only by using third-party software). This problem no longer existed in the 2000 release of Flash 5. Flash Player 5 could load XML data at runtime, and ActionScript "grew up" to come a bit closer to an object-oriented programming (OOP) language that strongly resembled JavaScript.

In 2002, Web designers and developers were handed the sixth version of Flash, dubbed "MX." Flash MX marked Macromedia's success at integrating all of their software products into a universal framework, where ColdFusion, Dreamweaver, Fireworks, Director, and FreeHand could all be used together to produce a new breed of Web experiences, including Rich Internet Applications. With the new software and player, XML data was processed remarkably faster, movies were made accessible to those with physical challenges, and Macromedia Generator was no longer necessary to incorporate dynamic graphics. Flash Player 6 could load JPEG and MP3 files at runtime. Developers could create reusable components that greatly decreased development time. Also, Flash Player 6 introduced support for video playback. Flash movies also became more browser friendly with named anchors that enabled specific sections of Flash movies to be bookmarked. ActionScript continued its development into more of a "real" programming language, as more objects and event handling were exposed in application programming interfaces (APIs). Perhaps most important, Flash Player 6 could integrate with new data transfer methods made available by Flash Remoting MX, which enabled serialized data to move more efficiently from application servers (such as ColdFusion MX) to Flash movies. Flash Communication Server MX 1.0 and 1.5, released shortly after Flash MX, enabled Flash movies to synchronize live data among several connected users simultaneously — developers could create live chat rooms, multiplayer games, and shared whiteboards, just to name a few applications. Flash Communication Server also added the capability to stream live or prerecorded audio/video streams to Flash Player 6.

Note

Flash Communication Server is now split into two different products: Adobe Flash Media Server and Adobe Flash Media Interactive Server. ∎

Flash Player 7 was overwhelmingly optimized for speed. Everything from video playback to text rendering to ActionScript performance was vastly improved over Flash Player 6. This feature alone encouraged business clients and Web surfers alike to adopt the new player version; everyone loves faster performance. Of course, there was a whole lot more to Flash Player 7. It enabled you to customize the contextual menu (that is, the right-click menu) that Flash movies running in the player display, and, by default, HTML hyperlinks within Flash text supported Open in New Window and Copy Link options in the contextual menu. On the Windows platform, mouse wheel scrolling was now supported for internal Flash elements. Small text sizes could be rendered more cleanly (or crisply). JPEG or SWF content could be loaded and displayed inline with Flash text. Style sheets and CSS files added new formatting options to Flash text, enabling you to share styles from DHTML documents with your Flash content. Video lovers were enticed by the capability to load Flash Video files (.flv) directly into Flash movies, without the use of Flash Communication Server MX. Printing control was far superior in Flash Player 7 and ActionScript with the `PrintJob` API. Flash MX's UI components had been completely revamped and released as V2 components, and Flash MX Pro 2004 Pro could use Data and Streaming Media components.

A seismic shift for the Flash platform occurred with the release of Flash Player 8. This player further improved text rendering capabilities with the new FlashType engine. Now you could pull off 8-point type without resorting to a limited range of pixel-based fonts. The new filter and blend modes revolutionized the visual expressiveness of Flash user interfaces and animated content. The amazing On2 VP6 video codec pushed more and more Windows Media, QuickTime, and RealOne media producers over to Flash Video. Sites like ABC.com and MTV.com migrated nearly all of their Web video offerings over to Flash Video. The expanded image file support for runtime loading in ActionScript left no excuses for building your own image management utilities in Flash — with Flash Player 8 you could load PNG, JPEG, progressive JPEG, and GIF images into the Flash movie.

When Flash Player 9 was released in 2006, Adobe, fresh after the acquisition of Macromedia, built Adobe Flex Builder 2, which opened the Flash platform to many programmers who didn't want to learn a designer-centric tool like Flash. Flash Player 9 offered a brand-new ActionScript Virtual Machine, or AVM, to process more complex ActionScript code. This new code base was dubbed ActionScript 3.0. Flash Player 9 had two AVMs, one for earlier ActionScript (1.0 and 2.0) and one for the brand-new ActionScript language (3.0). Shortly after Flex Builder 2 was released, Adobe's teams developed consistent user interfaces (UIs) for the flagship products. Adobe also continued Macromedia's commitment to pushing the Web to a new definition of excellence by offering Flash developers a wide range of tools to build incredibly powerful applications. Both Flex Builder 2 and Flash CS3 could use the strength of ActionScript 3.0 to build high-end Web applications. Flash Player 9 also enabled Flash content to go full screen and be viewed out of the browser window. Want to make that Flash Video clip go full screen? No problem! Flash Player 9 Update 3 extended video support by adding the popular AVC/H.264 video codec as well as its companion AAC audio codec for incredible video and audio quality that's compatible with other major video plug-ins such as Apple QuickTime Player. This update also provided cacheable runtime shared libraries for

Flex 3 projects, enabling fast loading and initialization of rich Internet applications (RIAs) built in Flex Builder 3.

Between Flash Player 9 and the release of Flash Player 10, Adobe released a new desktop platform based on Flash, HTML, and PDF technologies called Adobe AIR, or Adobe Integrated Runtime. This new platform enabled Flex developers to build Flash content that ran natively on the desktop computer, outside of a Web browser. AIR applications behave just like other installed applications, having access to system resources and local storage. You can do things like drag and drop files from the desktop to interactive elements within your AIR application!

Now, Adobe has created the tenth major release of the Flash Player: Flash Player 10. As discussed in Chapter 1, Flash Player 10 extends three-dimensional (3-D) support to all 2-D objects you can create with Flash drawing tools. Real-time streaming protocols for audio and video have been updated to improve quality of service during playback. Hardware acceleration available in newer computer and video card processors can be leveraged in Flash Player 10 to increase the speed at which graphics are composited on the screen, especially with full-screen video. Hydra, a scripting language for custom filter effects, has been added to Flash Player 10, enabling you to build your own filters that work not only in Flash movies but also in After Effects projects as well!

When Flash 5 was released, Flash was undoubtedly the key for Web branding, and it seemed as though every company wanted Flash content on its Web site. Flash has continued to enjoy this popularity, despite opponents calling the technology "unusable" or not compliant with Web standards. You could almost compare the introduction of Flash to that of the color television. It's difficult to return to largely static HTML pages after seeing the interactivity, animation, eye candy, and innovation that Flash sites offer to Web surfers — even those on slow connections or portable devices. Because of Adobe's efforts to keep the file size of the Flash Player smaller than most browser plug-ins, and the fact that it has been preinstalled on most systems for some time now, Flash remains a widely accessible and acceptable technology for Web deployment.

To Flash or not to Flash?

One of the crucial tasks of a Web designer or developer's job is to decide if Flash is the most appropriate tool to achieve the goals of a given project. Consider why you want — or need — to employ Flash in your work, because there are occasions when it may *not* be the best choice. It may not be wise to use this technology merely because it is "the thing to do" or is "cool." If you're pitching Flash projects to clients, it's a good idea to be prepared with reasons why Flash is the best tool to use to get the job done. Later in this chapter, I consider the benefits of other technologies, but for now consider what Flash can (and cannot) offer your projects.

An effective use of Flash

With the Flash CS5 authoring tool, you can create a wide range of presentation material or develop fully functional applications that run in a Web browser or on handheld devices:

- **Flash can generate very small file sizes while producing high-quality animation with optimal sound reproduction.** Even companies making world-renowned cartoons, such as Disney, use Flash for some of their work. Because of their small file sizes, Flash movies (such as cards or announcements) can even be sent via e-mail.

- **Nearly any multimedia file format can be integrated into Flash.** Vector images (such as EPS, FreeHand, Illustrator, and PDF files), bitmaps (GIF, PCT, TIFF, PNG, and JPEG), sound files (such as WAV, AIF, or MP3), and video (such as AVI and MOV) are all importable into your movies. Plug-in technology or third-party software is not required (although it does exist) to accomplish these imports. Nor is it required to play back your movies in Flash Player 10. Significant editing advantages sometimes exist when using imported files, such as symbol and layer formatting from FreeHand and Fireworks files. These features can be beneficial if you will be working with a client's raw resources.

- **Precise layouts with embedded fonts are possible with Flash.** Formatting is usually inconsistent when you use HTML to describe page layouts, and formatting can easily vary from one browser to the next. You can be confident your movies will be formatted and displayed consistently when viewed with the Flash Player.

Tip

Flash Player 8 and later add support for crisp-looking text at small point sizes. In previous versions of Flash, most embedded fonts did not display legibly at these sizes. You have precise control over how fonts render at small point sizes. ∎

- **Text, movies, images, and sound files can be displayed in your movie from a remote data source.** You can incorporate dynamic content into your movie as long as the data source (such as a database or XML file) can be accessed from your host Web server or application server. Flash Player 7 or later can consume Web services directly, allowing you to build B2B (business to business) applications that take advantage of public or private data sources, such as weather reports and stock information.

- **Just as you can receive information from a database in your movie, you can send data from your movie to the database.** Flash movies can accept user input and send the data to a server. Built-in components make it easier and faster than ever before to build interactive elements that do not require an advanced knowledge of ActionScript. Your forms have the potential to be much more engaging with animation or sound additions. You can also use this technology to track user progression throughout your site and send the information to a database.

- **With the proper server-side software, you can produce multiuser interactivity.** Since Flash Player 5, you have been able to use XML sockets for transmission of data between a socket server and one or more connected Flash movies. XML operates much faster when using Flash Player 6 and later. Also, with the release of Flash Communication Server MX (now Adobe Flash Media Interactive Server), developers now have a consistent API to create multiuser applications. Remote Shared Objects, one of the mechanisms employed by Adobe Flash Media Interactive Server, use an efficient and optimized binary protocol, Real-Time Messaging Protocol (RTMP), to broadcast data updates.

- **A wide range of external runtime assets can be loaded into a Flash movie.** You can create a master Flash movie and then load external files into it for each individual area of the interface or presentation. Using this method of asset management enables you to delegate tasks in a team production environment, where several designers and developers can work simultaneously. This workflow also enables you to create byte-optimized large Web sites and applications, in which assets are downloaded on an "as needed" basis while the user interacts with the Flash movie. External assets include all image formats supported by today's Web browsers, including standard and progressive JPEG files, GIF files, and PNG files. You can load MP3 and AAC audio files, as well as FLV or H.264-encoded video content. While image assets are always progressively downloaded, audio and video assets can be streamed in real time.

Note

A progressive download is any file type that can be used before the Flash Player actually receives the entire file. Progressive downloads are usually cached by the Web browser. You can stream MP3 files with the use of Adobe Flash Media Server or Adobe Flash Media Interactive Server. This server uses true streaming of all audio and video content, where nothing is cached by the Flash Player or the Web browser. ■

- **Creating components in Flash CS5 enables developers to form reusable template interfaces or assets for Flash movies.** The components that ship with Flash CS5 greatly reduce the development time of interfaces that require common UI elements such as text input areas and radio buttons. Components can be easily customized in the Properties panel, and many settings can be changed without the use of ActionScript.

Note

Many of the components that ship with Flash CS5 use the .swc file format in Flash documents. Components can be precompiled, which means that you cannot edit their internal elements or code unless you have access to the original source .fla file used to create them. ■

- **The Flash Player is available on many different platforms and devices, including Windows, Macintosh, Solaris, Linux, OS/2, SGI IRIX, Pocket PC, and many mobile devices.** Refer to www.adobe.com/shockwave/download/alternates for the latest version available for these and other alternative platforms. Just about any Web user can view Flash content by downloading and installing the latest version of the Flash Player.

- **Movies can be developed to run outside of the browser environment.** Projectors are Flash movies running from an embedded player, so you do not need a browser to view or use them. They can be burned onto DVDs or CD-ROMs, or saved to any other media-storage device. You can also use the new Adobe AIR framework to deploy Flash content as an installed application on the user's computer.

- **Like HTML pages, content from Flash movies can be sent to a printer.** The PrintJob API in Flash Player 7 or later ActionScript language offers you the capability to precisely control the layout of the printed page. The quality of the printed artwork and text from Flash movies is remarkable. You can send multiple pages to the printer at once and create content on-the-fly for the printed output.

These are only some of the things that Flash movies can do. Regardless of the intent of your production, verifying the use of this software is usually a good idea during preproduction. In the following subsection, I consider situations in which you may not want to use Flash to develop your content.

When not to use Flash

If you're enthusiastic about Flash and have used Flash for previous Web projects, you can easily develop a bias in favor of Flash. It may even be hard to consider that other options could be better for development. Knowing which technology is best for each solution will assist you in offering the best-quality products to your clients.

- **Flash movies play in a Web browser, using a plug-in.** Despite the near ubiquity of the Flash Player, there are still some users who may need to download it. If you're using Flash CS5 to create Flash Player 10 movies, many visitors trying to view your site may need to update their players. It is also important to keep in mind that some workplaces or institutions (such as schools) will not allow their workers or students to install applications that include plug-ins and ActiveX controls on the systems. Further, with the increase of mobile device Web browsing, people are becoming increasingly likely to visit your Web site on a smartphone or other Web-enabled device — many of which support only Flash Lite or no Flash Player at all (the iPhone, for example, cannot play browser-based Flash content).

- **The type and version of a Web browser can affect the functionality of a Flash movie.** Although internal ActionScript code should largely remain unaffected by browser brand and version, some scripting and interactivity with HTML documents (using JavaScript or VBScript) may be browser dependent.

Tip

Later releases of Flash Player 6 and all subsequent releases of the Flash Player now support the WMODE (Window Mode) parameter of Flash content across most browsers — previously, this parameter was supported only by Internet Explorer on Windows. If you've ever seen transparent-background Flash ads that whiz across the browser window, then you're already familiar with the use of the WMODE parameter. ■

- **Web browsers do not automatically redirect to alternative content if the Flash Player is not installed.** You, as a developer, are required to create detection mechanisms for the Flash Player.

- **3-D file formats cannot be directly imported or displayed in Flash movies.** To achieve 3-D-style effects, frame-by-frame animation or ActionScript is required. Adobe Director, however, has built-in features for importing, creating, and manipulating 3-D content.

Tip

You can use the Papervision 3-D framework to load and display 3-D objects in a Flash movie. For more information, visit the Papervision 3-D Web site at www.papervision3d.org. Also, in Chapter 16, "Displaying Video," you learn how a video of a 3D model can be used for 3D-like effects in a Flash Video. ■

- **Typical search engines (or spiders) have a difficult time indexing the content of Flash movies.** When you make Flash-based sites, you should create some alternative HTML content that can be indexed by search engines. If you simply place Flash movies in an otherwise empty HTML document, your Web site will not likely be indexed.

Tip

Flash CS5 can add XMP (eXtensible Metadata Platform) data to SWF files. Search engines can index this metadata to provide better placement of your Flash content within search results. Go to the Publish Settings dialog box (File ➪ Publish Settings), click the Flash tab, and then click the File Info button to add the extended metadata to your content. ■

- **Flash sites were never meant to completely replace text-based HTML sites.** For sites largely based on textual information with basic or simple graphics, there may be little point to using Flash. Selecting and printing text content from Flash movies is not always as intuitive as that of standard HTML sites. At this time, the Accessibility features of Flash Player 6 and later are supported only by Internet Explorer for Windows when used in conjunction with a select number of screen readers. A greater number of assistive technologies, however, support HTML pages.

Tip

You can add right-click menu support to HTML-styled text containing URL links. For example, this feature of Flash Player 7 and later movies enables a user to open a link in a new browser window. ■

- **In many circumstances, HTML is quicker, easier, and cheaper to develop than Flash content.** There are many established applications supporting HTML development, and clients can tap an ever-increasing designer and developer base for cheaper and competitive pricing.

Of course, there are always exceptions to any rule, and these suggestions should be considered as guidelines or cautions to be examined before you embark on any Flash development. In the following subsection, you examine other tools used to create multimedia content.

Alternative methods of multimedia authoring

Now let's focus on Flash's competition in the multimedia authoring arena. This section is not intended to give you a comprehensive background on these technologies. Rather, I seek simply to give you some context of Flash as it exists in the rest of the multimedia world.

Dynamic HTML

Dynamic HTML (DHTML) is a specialized set of markup tags that tap into an extended document object model (DOM) that version 4 browsers or later can use. Using `<layer>` or `<div>` tags, you can create animations and interactive effects with Web-authoring tools ranging from Notepad or TextEdit to Adobe Dreamweaver. You can actually combine Flash content with DHTML to create Flash layers on top of other HTML content. One problem with DHTML is that Mozilla-based browsers and Internet Explorer on Windows do not use it in the same way, but this problem is becoming more marginal as new versions of these browsers are released. Usually, you need to make sure that you have a specialized set of code (or minor modifications) for each browser type.

Tip

Flash Player 7 and later movies support the use of cascading style sheets (CSS) to share formatting specifications from DHTML pages with Flash text fields. ■

XML and XSL

XML stands for eXtensible Markup Language. XML looks like HTML, but it's really a language that can manage structured or related data, such as pricing information, contact information, or anything else that you would store in a database. XSL stands for eXtensible Stylesheet Language. XSL documents apply formatting rules to XML documents. Together, XML and XSL documents can create interactive data-driven Web sites. Although most browsers in use today can read and display XML and XSL documents, some older browsers do not support these formats. The Flash Player can be installed on just about every graphical Web browser available, regardless of the browser's version. As such, you can potentially reach more users with Flash content than you can with XML and XSL content. As you see later in this chapter, XML can also be used to supply data to Flash.

Adobe Director

Originally, Macromedia's flagship product, Director, was *the* multimedia powerhouse authoring solution. Since its inception in the 1980s, Director has had the benefit of many years to establish its mature interface and development environment. Director can integrate and control many media types, including video, audio, and entire Flash movies. Director also has an Xtra plug-in architecture, which enables third-party developers to expand or enhance Director's capabilities. For example, you can use an Xtra plug-in to tap hardware-specific input and output, such as a motion detector or pressure-sensitive plate connected to the computer's serial port. Director 8.5 and later have added true 3-D modeling support. You can create Shockwave games with textured models and lighting effects! However, there are two major drawbacks to Shockwave Director: It requires a larger download for the full player installation, and the player is available only for Windows and Macintosh platforms. Director remains a popular authoring tool for CD-ROM and DVD-ROM development.

Macromedia Authorware

Authorware, like Flash, was originally a technology developed by another company and then bought by Macromedia (and now Adobe) to add to its software lineup. Since the initial acquisition, Macromedia has significantly developed the features and capabilities of Authorware. It is an authoring application and a companion plug-in technology, with similar audio/video integration capabilities as Adobe Director. However, Authorware was developed with e-learning in mind. You can use it to structure training solutions and monitor student learning. I mention Authorware as a potential competitor to Flash because many Flash developers use Flash to create Web-training modules that interact with server-side databases.

Scalable Vector Graphics

The Scalable Vector Graphics (SVG) format is widely supported by some of the largest names in the industry, such as Microsoft and Adobe. This format has even been approved as a graphics standard for the Web by the World Wide Web Consortium (W3C), whose purpose is to form universal protocols regarding Web standards. SVG is much more than a graphics format; it is also an XML-based development language. Some Adobe tools, including Adobe Illustrator, can create files based on this technology. Adobe also creates the plug-in for using this file format on the Web, but the W3C is pushing for all browsers to provide built-in support for the format so that a third-party download is unnecessary. This may be necessary if SVG is ever to become a viable content format because Web surfers have been quite slow to adopt the SVG plug-in. For more information on this topic, you can refer to www.w3c.org/Graphics/SVG and www.adobe.com/svg.

Microsoft Silverlight

In 2007, Microsoft launched the first version of the Microsoft Silverlight plug-in, which closely matches the capabilities of the Flash Player plug-in. Silverlight 1.0 relies largely on a JavaScript-based scripting language to create interactive content with a tool such as Microsoft Expression Blend 2. Silverlight can play video content with the addition of the Windows Media Player plug-in for your Web browser. While Silverlight technology has yet to take hold with most Web sites, it is quickly gaining mind share with Web developers looking to add advanced data-driven capabilities to their online projects.

Microsoft PowerPoint

PowerPoint is usually considered a tool for making offline presentations to show in business meetings, conferences, and seminars. What is perhaps not as well known is how PowerPoint is sometimes used online for presenting such content. A PowerPoint viewer plug-in enables your browser to handle these files, and PowerPoint can export HTML versions of slide shows. Although PowerPoint enables anyone from a designer to a programmer to easily create slide-show presentations, Flash can be considered a more robust tool for creating dynamic, high-impact presentations.

Note

More and more designers who use Apple Mac OS X are choosing to create PowerPoint-like presentations in Apple Keynote, a product available in Apple's iWork bundle. ∎

SMIL, Real Systems RealPlayer, and Apple QuickTime

SMIL (Synchronized Multimedia Integration Language) also looks a lot like HTML markup tags. SMIL enables you to layer several media components in SMIL-compatible players such as the Real Networks RealPlayer and the Apple QuickTime Player. You probably have seen SMIL at work when you load RealPlayer and see the snazzy graphics that compose the welcome screen interface. With SMIL, you can layer interactive buttons and dynamic text on top of streaming video or audio content. You may not even think of SMIL as a competing technology, but rather a complementary one — Flash can be one of the multimedia tracks employed by SMIL! You can even use Flash as a track type in QuickTime, without the use of SMIL. When Flash 4 was released, Macromedia and Apple announced QuickTime Flash movies, which enabled you to create Flash interfaces that layer on top of audio-video content. The RealOne Player also plays "tuned" Flash files directly, without the use of SMIL. A tuned Flash file is weighted evenly from frame to frame to ensure synchronized playback. Note, however, that tuned files usually need to be strict linear animations without any interactive functionality.

Exploring Companion Technologies

Now that you have a better understanding of how Flash fits into the current World Wide Web, I can begin to discuss the technologies that contribute to Flash's well-being. In today's world of the Web developer, you not only need to know how to create your Flash movies but also how to implement Flash into existing environments, such as a Web browser or your business client's Web-ready (or not-so-Web-ready) application servers and related data sources.

HTML is here to stay

HTML is not going anywhere, regardless of the prolific nature of Flash on the Web. Using HTML to your advantage is very important because it is undeniably the best solution for certain forms of Web deployment. In addition, sites constructed entirely in Flash often require HTML to function properly. Here's how HTML works with Flash:

- **Displaying and formatting the movie on a Web page requires HTML.** It isn't always easy to hand-code HTML to work with ActiveX for Internet Explorer and the plug-in for Mozilla-compatible browsers at the same time.

- **Placing some content within a Flash movie is not possible, so you sometimes need to link it from your movie to an HTML page.** For example, some PDF files cannot be imported into a Flash CS5 document and will need to be linked from the Flash movie to be viewed separately with Adobe Reader. Or, you may need to access video files created for the RealOne Player or Windows Media Player. You can place links to these source files or link to an HTML document that embeds the source file.

Tip

If you want to integrate PDF documents with Flash movies, you might want to explore Macromedia FlashPaper. FlashPaper is a Flash movie file (.swf) that contains a document viewer and the document itself, enabling you to embed large print-ready documents on the Web or even within your own Flash movies. For more information on FlashPaper, see the FlashPaper section at www.flashsupport.com/links. ∎

- **If your end user is not willing or able to view your Flash content, HTML enables you to provide an alternative version of your Web site.** Despite the addition of accessibility options into Flash Player 6 and later, which enable screen-reader interaction, not all screen readers are currently able to access this feature. An HTML version of your content is sure to reach most of this potential audience.

Many people find learning, and perhaps even using, HTML to be painful and tedious. Accommodating the differences among browsers can sometimes be time consuming and dry work. However, knowing some HTML is highly recommended and well worth the effort. HTML should be understood by any Web professional. If you are uncomfortable with the code, using Macromedia Dreamweaver will help your transition into the HTML world.

Client-side scripting using JavaScript

ActionScript and JavaScript are similar beasts, especially since ActionScript developed into a full-blown language in ActionScript 2.0. By learning one language, you will be able to translate this knowledge with relative ease. Already knowing some JavaScript when entering the Flash realm definitely puts you at a strong advantage. However, JavaScript itself is frequently used in conjunction with Flash, as follows:

- With JavaScript, you can create customized browser popup windows that open from Flash movies. By "customized," I mean browser windows that don't have any scroll bars, button bars, or menu items across the top of the browser window.

- JavaScript can pass data into the Flash movie when the Web page containing the movie loads. Some browsers enable you to continually pass data back and forth between Flash and JavaScript. Also, you are able to dynamically pass variables from JavaScript right into the Flash movie.

- JavaScript can be used to detect the presence or absence of the Flash Player plug-in in the user's Web browser, with JavaScript libraries such as SWFObject. Likewise, you can use VBScript on Internet Explorer for Windows to detect the Flash Player ActiveX control. JavaScript (or VBScript) can redirect the Web browser to alternative content if the player is not installed.

- Flash movie properties such as width and height can be written on-the-fly by using JavaScript. You can also detect various system properties (which is also possible by using ActionScript) in JavaScript code and pass this information into Flash.

Tip

Flash Player 8 introduced the `ExternalInterface` API, which enables you to more easily pass parameters between a Flash movie and JavaScript. For more information on this functionality, read Chapter 21, "Integrating Flash Content with Web Pages." ■

The world of Web services

By using Flash CS5, you can tap an ever-expanding world of data transfer directly to your Flash movies. If you've stayed in the loop of Web technologies, you've likely heard of *Web services*, which is a generic term to describe a standardized approach to transfer data from one Web application to another. Web services use a format known as Web Services Description Language (WSDL), which uses a type of XML formatting called Simple Object Access Protocol (SOAP). It's not really important to know these acronyms as much as it is to understand what they do. WSDLs (pronounced "whiz-duhls") enable you to share complex data structures in a uniform, standardized manner.

As long as a technology such as the Flash Player or ColdFusion can interpret a Web service, it can utilize its data. And because all WSDLs use the same formatting, your Flash movie can easily access data from public services offered by various companies on the Web. You can also create your own Web services with application servers such as Adobe ColdFusion as well. Web services simply provide a gateway from which your Flash movie can access data over the Internet.

Web Resource

One popular Web service is the Amazon associates program. Just about anyone can become an Amazon.com associate. See `http://associates.amazon.com` **for more details about enrolling in Amazon's developer program for Web services. You don't have to use Amazon.com's Web Service, but it's a fun source of information to keep you engaged while you're learning how to use Web services with your Flash content. ∎**

Note

Don't forget Flash Remoting! Flash Player can send and receive data by using Flash Remoting gateways, which can be installed on a variety of application servers. Flash Remoting is built into Adobe ColdFusion and provides a faster and more efficient means of transferring data between a Flash movie and an application server than Web services can accomplish. ∎

Adobe server technologies

Nowadays, it's always helpful to have more than just client-side Flash development skills. With Adobe Flash Media Interactive Server, Flash Remoting, and Adobe LiveCycle Data Services, more and more business clients are looking for experienced Flash designers and developers to add real-time interactivity to their company's Web sites or Internet-aware applications. Applications created for Flash Media Interactive Server use server-side ActionScript (ASC files) to describe and control the interactivity between a Flash movie and the server's resources, including real-time streaming audio/video media and synchronized data updates between multiple Flash clients and the application.

Recognizing Project Potential

In this section, I provide an overview of the categories of Flash projects that you can produce. This is just a starting point to prime your creative juices and break through any self-imposed limiting perceptions that you may have about Flash media. The categories I have devised here are by no means industry-standard terms — they're broad, generalized groups into which most Flash development falls.

Linear presentations

In the early days of Internet growth, Flash shorts (cartoons) were the media buzz. These cartoons generally played from start to finish in a very linear fashion. Generally speaking, these movies load and then play — and count on catching the user's attention through the story and animation. These movies sometimes contain advanced ActionScript for animation, including randomized movement or content.

Note

Linear Flash presentations do not necessarily have to be displayed within a Web browser — or even online. Several film-production and advertising companies use Flash to create high-quality animation for use in broadcast TV and feature films. ■

Interactive presentations

Interactive presentations represent the next step up from linear presentations. They provide the user control over the way information is presented, the flow, or the experience altogether. Usually, Web sites of any construct will be considered an interactive presentation. If you have information or content in a section somewhere in a movie or Web site, then you probably have an interactive presentation. An interactive presentation enables end users to choose the content they see by enabling them to navigate throughout a site, bypassing some content while accessing other content. A Flash movie in this category may have all the content viewed stored in a container movie or across several Flash files linked to a main site.

Data-driven presentations

The data-driven presentations category of Flash development represents any movies that load external data (either dynamic or static) to deliver the presentation to the user. For example, a weather site that uses Flash may download dynamic Flash graphics of precipitation maps to display to the site's visitors. These graphics may be customized for each user of the site, depending on where he or she lives. *Data-driven* may even simply mean that text information within the Flash movie changes from time to time. Simply put, anytime information is separated from the actual Flash movie, you can say it is data-driven.

Data-driven applications (or Rich Internet Applications)

The data-driven applications category is somewhat loosely defined as those Flash movies that enable the user to accomplish some sort of task or enable a transaction from the Flash movie to use an external remote data source. For example, an online Flash ATM (that is, bank machine) could allow a bank customer to log in to the bank's secure server and transfer funds from one account to another or pay a bill. All these tasks would require a transaction from the Flash movie to the bank's server. Another example could be an online Flash shopping cart, in which visitors add products to their virtual carts and check out with their final order. Again, these tasks would require the Flash movie to send and receive data. The term Rich Internet Application, or RIA, was coined during the Macromedia MX product line launch and implies the use of integrated data and rich media within a graphical user interface (GUI), in or out of a Web browser. Typically, RIAs combine Flash movies with one or more server-side technology, such as Flash Remoting and Adobe Flash Media Interactive Server.

Summary

- Expectations of Web sites produced by Flash developers and designers grow with every new version of Flash. With an ever-increasing list of features and capabilities included with each version of the Flash Player, sites not facilitating new technology (such as new forms of interaction or media content) can easily become overlooked or considered uninteresting.

- Flash CS5 has many features that make it a vital piece of authoring software for Web sites and applications. Some of the main reasons to use it include small movie file sizes and the capability to integrate rich media content.

- There are several multimedia file formats available on the Web today. Although most users have many of the popular plug-ins installed, some users have restricted bandwidth and computer system environments. Flash has the capability to produce small movie files that can play identically across several platforms and devices.

- In order to develop advanced Flash projects, you should know the necessary HTML, JavaScript, and data-formatting standards (which now include Web services) that enable Flash to interact with other environments and data sources. These languages broaden the capabilities for interactivity and access to large amounts of data.

Planning Flash Projects

O ne of the most important steps — if not *the* most important step — to producing great Flash content is *knowing* what steps you'll have to take to move from the concept or idea of the Flash movie to the finished product. This chapter explores the basics of Flash production and how to use the Project panel in Flash CS5 to organize your files. Whether you're a freelance Web consultant (or designer) or a member of a large creative or programming department, knowing how to manage the Flash content production will save you plenty of headaches, time, and money.

Workflow Basics

No matter what the size or scope, every project in which you choose to participate should follow some type of planned workflow. Whether it's for print, film, video, or Web delivery (or all four!), you should establish a process to guide the production of your presentation.

Before you can explore the way in which Flash fits into a Web production workflow, I need to define a holistic approach to Web production in general. Figure 3.1 shows a typical example of the Web production process within an Internet production company.

Note

Web production processes have been generally derived from traditional software development processes. The methodologies for production discussed in this chapter all fit into a category known as the "waterfall model." In short, the waterfall model dictates that each phase of production is completed before the next phase is entered. One of the problems with the waterfall model is that the business client (usually) only sees the project working at the end of the production cycle.

In contrast, an "agile model" for production mandates a full production cycle on a smaller scale to be completed within one to four weeks, presenting a functional aspect of the project to the business client at the end of the iteration. It's beyond the scope of this book to discuss all the differences between a waterfall and agile approach, but you should make yourself familiar with these terms because they're becoming more widely used with Web production processes. ■

FIGURE 3.1

Two of the most common phases when generating Web content are preproduction and the actual production phase.

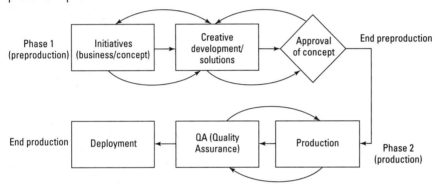

Note

The phases of production have been coined differently by various project managers and companies. Some interactive agencies refer to preproduction as an "architecture phase" or a "planning phase." Preproduction may also involve a "discovery phase," which is a span of time before the architecture phase wherein the requirements for a project are determined. ■

Phase I: Establishing the concept and goals

As a Web developer or member of a creative team, companies (or representatives for other departments) will approach you to help solve problems with projects. A problem may or may not be well defined by the parties coming to you. The goal of Phase I is to thoroughly define the problem, offer solutions for the problem, and approve one or more solutions for final production.

The next-to-last question points to a bigger picture, one in which the client may already have several emotive keywords that define their brand. Try to define the emotional heart and feeling of their message — get them to be descriptive. Don't leave the meeting with the words *edgy* or *sexy* as the only descriptive terms for the message.

Information Architects and User Experience

You may have already been bombarded with the idea of *information architecture*. Information architecture is the method by which sought data is represented and structured. Good information architecture is usually equivalent to intuitive user interface design — visitors to a well-organized Web site won't spend much time searching for what they want. More recently, the term "user experience design" is also bandied about, to refer to intuitive and user-centric interface design, organizing menus, buttons, navigation controls, and so on around the practical use of a product.

I mention information architecture because the steps in Phase I are similar to the steps that traditional architects take to build a comprehensive design and production strategy *before* they start to build any structure. Although this may seem obvious enough, the sad fact remains that many Internet sites (or projects) are planned as they're constructed. Indeed, we're told that production must move at Internet speed; thus, directives may be given without thorough research into other solutions for a given problem.

Tip

Never go into a meeting or a planning session without a white board or a big pad of paper. Documenting everyone's ideas and letting the group see the discussion in a visual format is always a good idea. If all participants are willing, it's often useful to record the meeting with a digital voice recorder or video camera so that it can be reviewed outside of the meeting. There are also products on the market that enable you to record every detail of a meeting, such as Adobe Acrobat Connect, which enables you to conduct live meetings, as well as record them, over the Internet. ∎

You can also start to ask the following technical questions at this point:

- What type of browser support do you want to have?
- Do you have an idea of a Web technology (Shockwave; Flash; Dynamic HyperText Markup Language, or DHTML; Scalable Vector Graphics, or SVG) that you want to use?
- Does the message need to be delivered in a Web browser? Can it be in a downloadable application such as a stand-alone player? A CD-ROM? A DVD?
- What type of computer processing speed should be supported? What other types of hardware concerns might exist (for example, hi-fi audio)?

Of course, many clients and company reps look to *you* for the technical answers. If this is the case, the most important questions are

- Who's your audience?
- Who do you *want* to be your audience?

Your audience determines, in many ways, what type of technology to choose for the presentation. If the client says that Ma and Pa from a country farm should be able to view the Web site with no hassle, you may need to consider using an older version of the Flash Player (such as Flash Player 8) or building a non-Flash presentation (such as HTML and CSS). If the client wants the text on the Web site well indexed by search engines, you may also need to consider building a non-Flash version of the content. However, if they say that their ideal audience is someone who has a 56K modem and likes to watch cartoons, then you're getting closer to a Flash-based presentation. If the client has any demographic information for their user base, ask for it upfront. Putting on a show for a crowd is difficult if you don't know who's *in* the crowd.

Determining the project's goals

The client or company reps come to you for a reason — they want to walk away with a completed and *successful* project. As you initially discuss the message and audience for the presentation, you also need to get a clear picture of what the client expects to get from you.

- Will you be producing just one piece of a larger production?
- Do they need you to host the Web site? Or do they already have a Web server and a staff to support it?
- Do they need you to maintain the Web site after handoff?
- Do they expect you to market the presentation? If not, what resources are in place to advertise the message?
- When does the client expect you to deliver proposals, concepts, and the finished piece? These important dates are often referred to as *milestones*. The payment schedule for a project is often linked to production milestones.
- Will they expect to receive copies of all the files you produce, including your source FLA files?
- What are the costs associated with developing a proposal? Will you do work on speculation of a potential project? Or will you be paid for your time to develop a concept pitch? (You should determine this *before* you walk into your initial meeting with the client.) Of course, if you're working with a production team in a company, you're already being paid a salary to provide a role within the company.

At this point, you'll want to plan the next meeting with your client or company reps. Give them a realistic timeframe for coming back to them with your ideas. This amount of time will vary from project to project and will depend on your level of expertise with the materials involved with the presentation.

Creative exploration: Producing a solution

After you leave the meeting, you'll go back to your design studio and start cranking out materials, right? Yes and no. Give yourself plenty of time to work with the client's materials (what you gathered from the initial meeting). If your client sells shoes, read up on the shoe business. See what the client's competitors are doing to promote their message — visit their Web sites, go to stores and compare the products, and read any consumer reports that you can find about your client's products or services. You should have a clear understanding of your client's market and a clear picture of how your client distinguishes their company or their product from their competitors'.

After you (and other members of your creative team) have completed a round of research, sit down and discuss the findings. Start defining the project in terms of mood, response, and time. Is this a serious message? Do you want the viewer to laugh? How quickly should this presentation happen? Sketch out any ideas you and any other member of the team may have. Create a chart that lists the emotional keywords for your presentation.

At a certain point, you need to start developing some visual material that articulates the message to the audience. Of course, your initial audience will be the client. You are preparing materials for them, not the consumer audience. I assume here that you are creating a Flash-based Web site for your client. For any interactive presentation, you need to prepare the following:

- An organizational flowchart for the site
- A process flowchart for the experience
- A functional specification for the interface
- A prototype or a series of comps

Tip

You can use tools such as Microsoft Visio (http://office.microsoft.com/) **or Omni Group's OmniGraffle for Mac** (www.omnigroup.com/applications/omnigraffle). **For more information on Visio 2007 Bible, published by Wiley, go to** www.flashsupport.com/books/visio. ■

An *organizational flowchart* is a simple document that describes the scope of a site or presentation. Other names for this type of chart are *site chart, site map, navigation flowchart,* and *layout flowchart.* It includes the major sections of the presentation. For example, if you're creating a Flash movie for a portfolio site, you might have a main menu and four content areas: About, Portfolio, Resumé, and Contact. In an organizational flowchart, this would look like Figure 3.2.

FIGURE 3.2

A sample organizational chart for a portfolio site

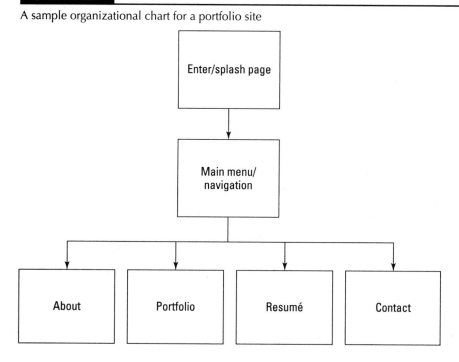

A *process flowchart* constructs the interactive experience of the presentation and shows the decision-making process involved for each area of the site. There are a few types of process charts. A basic process flowchart displays the decisions an end user will make. For example, what type of options does a user have on any given page of the site? Another type of flowchart shows the programming logic involved for the end-user process chart. For example, will certain conditions need to exist before a user can enter a certain area of the site? Does he or she have to pass a test, finish a section of a game, or enter a username and password? See Figure 3.3 for a preliminary flowchart for a section of my portfolio Web site. I discuss the actual symbols of the flowchart later in this chapter.

A *functional specification* (see Figure 3.4) is a document that breaks down the elements for each step in the organizational and/or process flowchart. This is by far the most important piece of documentation that you can create for yourself and your team.

FIGURE 3.3

The user watches an intro animation and is led through several short subsequent animations detailing each area of the portfolio. The user can then go to an area of his or her choice after this animation is complete.

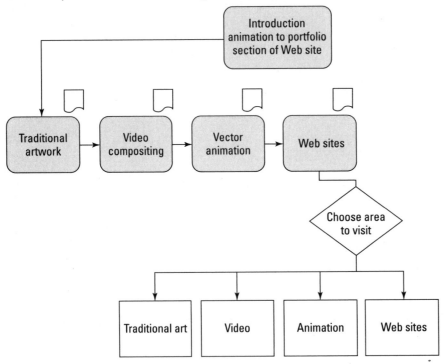

FIGURE 3.4

This functional spec displays the six components of a Flash-based navigation bar, which will appear on the main menu of my portfolio content site.

Project:	Flash interface v2.0		Section:	1 of 5 (Main Menu)
No.	**Type**	**Purpose**	**Content**	**Format**
1.A	Navigation bar	Provides easier access to site content.		A menu bar that is fixed at the top edge of the browser window.
1.A.1	Directory buttons	Provides a means of accessing any of the portfolio sections.	Names each content area. For example: audio, video, graphics, etc.	Horizontal menu list or ComboBox component (skinned).
1.A.2	Home button	Allows user to always get back to the opening page.	The text: "home"	Button component (skinned).
1.A.3	Search field	Provides a means of entering a specific word or phrase to search site contents.	A white text search field with the word "search".	Flash dynamic text field.
1.A.4	Sign up	Captures the users e-mail address for a site mailing list.	Text field(s) to enter name and e-mail address.	Button component generating a pop-up. Sign up using ColdFusion.
1.A.5	Back button	Allows the user to see the last page viewed without losing menu items.	The text "back".	Button component (skinned).
1.A.6	Logo or ID	Provides a means of personal branding.	A spider web, with text of the Web site name in Arial Narrow.	Graphics in Freehand and Flash.

Each page of a functional specification (functional spec, for short) lists all the assets used on a page (or Flash keyframe, Movie Clip) and indicates the following information for each asset:

- **Item ID:** This is part of the naming convention for your files and assets. It should be part of the filename, or Flash symbol and instance name. It should also be used in organizational and process flowcharts.

- **Type:** This part of the spec defines the name you're assigning to the asset, in more natural language, such as Home Button.

- **Purpose:** You should be able to clearly explain why this element is part of the presentation. If you can't, then you should consider omitting it from the project.

- **Format:** This column indicates what technology (or what component of the technology) will be utilized to accomplish the needs of the asset. In an all-Flash presentation, list the symbol type or timeline element (frames, scene, nested Movie Clips) necessary to accomplish the goals of the asset.

Note

Functional specs come in all shapes and sizes. Each company usually has their own template or approach to constructing a functional spec. The client should always approve the functional spec so that you and your client have an agreement about the scope of the project. ■

Finally, after you have a plan for your project, you'll want to start creating some graphics to provide an atmosphere for the client presentation. Gather placement graphics (company logos, typefaces, photographs) or appropriate "temporary" resources for purposes of illustration. Construct one composition, or *comp*, that represents each major section or theme of the site. In our portfolio content site example, you might create a comp for the main page and a comp for one of the portfolio work sections, such as Animation. Don't create a comp for each page of the portfolio section. You simply want to establish the feel for the content you will create for the client. I recommend that you use the tool(s) with which you feel most comfortable creating content. If you're better at using Illustrator or Photoshop to create layouts, then use that application. If you're comfortable with Flash for assembling content, then use it.

Caution

Do not use copyrighted material for final production use, unless you have secured the appropriate rights to use the material. However, while you're exploring creative concepts, use whatever materials you feel best illustrate your ideas. When you get approval for your concept, improve upon the materials that inspired you. ■

Then you want to determine the time and human resources required for the entire project or concept. What role will you play in the production? Will you need to hire outside contractors to work on the presentation (for example, character animators, programmers, and so on)? Make sure that you provide ample time to produce and thoroughly test the presentation. When you've determined the time and resources necessary, you'll determine the costs involved. If this is an internal project for your company, you won't be concerned about cost so much as the time involved — your company reps will want to know what it will cost the company to produce the piece. For large client projects, your client will probably expect a project rate — not an hourly or weekly rate. Outline a time schedule with milestone dates, at which point you'll present the client with updates on the progress of the project.

Exploring the details of the workflow process any further is beyond the scope of this book. However, there are many excellent resources for project planning. One of the best books available for learning the process of planning interactive presentations is Nicholas Iuppa's *Designing Interactive Digital Media* (Butterworth-Heinemann, 1998). I strongly recommend that you consult the *Graphic Artists Guild Handbook of Pricing & Ethical Guidelines* (Graphic Artists Guild, 2003) and the *AIGA Professional Practices in Graphic Design: American Institute of Graphic Arts* (Allworth Press, 1998), edited by Tad Crawford, for information on professional rates for design services.

Approving a final concept and budget

After you have prepared your design documents for the client, it's time to have another meeting with the client or company rep. Display your visual materials (color laser prints, inkjet mockups, and so on), and walk through the charts you've produced. In some situations, you may want to prepare more than one design concept. Always reinforce how the presentation addresses the client's message and audience.

When all is said and done, discuss the options that you've presented with the client. Gather feedback. Hopefully, the client prefers one concept (and its budget) and gives you the approval to proceed. It's important that you leave this meeting knowing one of two things:

- The client has signed off on the entire project or presentation.
- The client wants to see more exploration before committing to a final piece.

In either case, you shouldn't walk away not knowing how you'll proceed. If the client wants more time or more material before a commitment, negotiate the terms of your fees that are associated with further conceptual development.

Designing for Usability, by Scott Brown

As the author of this book mentions earlier in this chapter, the first step in developing a Flash site, or any other type of site, is to define the information architecture. In this tutorial, I show you how to define the goals and mission of the site.

Defining the goals and mission of the site

When you define the mission and goals for your project, you lay the foundation upon which to build it. To create a solid project foundation, you must begin by questioning everything, especially the company's business model. Start with these questions:

- What is the mission or purpose of the organization?
- Why does this organization want a Web site?
- Will the Web site support the mission of the organization?
- What are the short- and long-term goals of the Web site?
- Who is the intended audience?
- Why will people come to the site?
- Is the organization trying to sell a product?
- What is the product or products?
- Do I have a unique service?
- What makes the service different?
- Why will people come to the site for the first time?
- Will they ever come back?
- Why would they come back?

The list of questions can go on forever. After you've gathered a list of questions, you need to get the answers. Ask around the organization, ask your friends, ask strangers, ask anyone. After you've collected the answers, filter through them to create a list of goals based on the responses. From this list of goals, you must further define the answer to the question, "Who is the audience?"

Defining the audience

The audience can be defined as the potential users of the site and their intentions or tasks when they come to your site. Are they kids or adults? Are they Generation X, Y, or Z? Are they into rave music or country music?

So, who is your audience? It's not an easy question because there are so many possibilities. Start with a list of all the possible audiences that the organization would like to reach, and then rearrange the list in a ranking order of most important audience to least important audience. From the audience-ranking list, create a list of the possible goals and needs each audience has.

Creating character scenarios

With the list of possible goals, take the process one step farther by creating scenarios for the users. Think of it as writing a screenplay for your Web site. Create multiple characters who represent the majority of the visitors, giving them hobbies, likes, dislikes, and, most important, a task to complete on the site. The object of the scenario game is to get into the characters' heads to learn why and how they would use your site. Approaching the design from their viewpoints makes it easier for you to create a list of the needs and wants of the characters, a wish list, if you will.

After you write the scenarios, the next step in the process is to gather the team together and analyze the Web sites of the competition.

Note from the author: Character scenarios are often referred to as *use case scenarios.*

Analyzing the competition

Studying the competition gives you the chance to generate a list of the kinds of features they are offering and to determine whether your feature list, the one that you created from the scenarios, is missing anything. If your wish list lacks anything in comparison to your competition, now is a good time to expand the user's functionality requirements and to return to the scenarios to determine whether the competition's functionality matches your characters' needs. If it does, you should try to elaborate on the competition's functions and create new functions of your own — the classic case of outdoing your competition.

Reaching a consensus on what good design is

At this time in the process, have the team come together to develop a definition of what is "good site design." This step is most beneficial for any contract designer trying to gain an understanding of the client's design viewpoint. To create this "good design" definition, the team should observe a good number of sites and document everybody's likes and dislikes for each one. This way, everyone on the team will have a better understanding of what to strive for and what to avoid.

Structuring the content

Now you should have several documents to refer to — the project mission statement, the user functionality needs (wish list), and the organization's definition of good design. With these three documents in hand, the next step is to blend them into one master menu of content inventory. Think of each item on this list as a building block. You now have all the blocks needed to construct the site. The only problem is that these blocks are in a big pile and lack organization (structure). Naturally, the next step is to begin creating layouts of the site, providing structure. But before you can begin the page layout process, you need to educate yourself on some Web site usability issues.

Identifying factors of usability

Usability is a much-debated concept, but generally it means creating a site/project/interface that is functional and that your audience understands. A useable site aims to be a natural extension of a user's expectations and needs. A user-friendly site tries to mirror its structure to that of the user's experience and goals. Just to make the task at hand a little more complex, keep in mind that user expectations learned in other areas of life affect how the user will think your site works. So, how can you design a site to meet your user's expectations? Well, if you did your homework on your audience and wrote the character scenarios, you should have a pretty good idea of the target audience's expectations. Given that you know the general background of the user, you could include *metaphors* in the structure of the site. Using metaphors is a great way to help users draw upon knowledge they already have, thereby making the site easier to use. Matching the site structure to the user's experience minimizes the amount of time it takes for the user to learn how to operate or navigate the site. The shorter the learning curve for the site, the better. If you come to a site when you have a specific goal in mind, and it takes you ten minutes to figure out how to achieve your goal, would you call that a positive experience? Most likely not!

Your goal as the designer is to create an attractive site without distracting users from their goals. Forcing users to spend a noticeable amount of time trying to learn how to achieve their goals is very taxing on their patience, and it is a good way to create a negative experience. If you're trying to sell something, chances are you want customers to be happy, not annoyed. One way to make your customers' experience more enjoyable is to make it as easy as possible. So, how do you create a positive experience? Let's start with the most basic of user needs: the ability to navigate.

Users need to know at all times where they are in the site, where they have been, and where they can go. When developing a navigation system, be sure to keep the navigation visually consistent. Inconsistency in the navigation can confuse and frustrate the user. A great concept for a navigational aid is the use of a breadcrumb trail. The breadcrumb system is a visual way to show users the path they took to get to their current position in the site. This navigational convention is used on many resource sites and even in the Flash authoring environment itself — as you click to edit grouped shapes or symbols, the steps you take appear as text labels on the bar above the Stage. Beyond displaying the path of the user, this system gives the user the ability to backtrack to any page displayed in the path. However, remember that navigation is not the goal of the user, only an aid. The user is there to find or buy something; the user is there for the content. So, make the content the first read on all of your pages. Navigational elements are there to support the content, not eclipse it.

Of course, navigation isn't the only factor to consider when designing for usability. Other variables, such as the length of text on a page, can affect the usability of a site tremendously. It's a fact that reading text on a monitor is far more taxing on the eyes than reading text on paper. Therefore, people are less inclined to read large amounts of text on the Web. As designers, we must accommodate these changes in reading patterns. Keep these simple guidelines in mind when writing text for the Web. Try to make the text scannable, because readers skim Web content. Bold the important ideas or put key information in bulleted lists. But most of all, keep the text short.

In addition to the treatment of text, there are several other tips to help improve the usability of a site. The concept of redundant links is an excellent method to support users with different backgrounds and goals. With redundant links, a user has more than one way to get to the desired content. The user may have the option to click a text link, a graphic link, or even a text link that is worded differently. Each redundant link should be designed to accommodate a wide range of users. So, where on the page should all these usability elements go?

I can't tell you where you should place your navigation system or your redundant links. However, I can provide you with some information from eye-tracking studies that will help you make an educated decision. Yes, it is true that usability researchers are able to actually monitor and record what you're looking at when you're viewing a Web site. Researchers have found that when a Web page loads, our eyes are looking at the center of the page, and then move over to the left, and then sometimes to the right. Of course, these findings are dependent on the user's cultural background. Nevertheless, the scary finding is that the users rarely look to the right! This is most likely because most sites use the right side of the page as a place to add sidebar elements, items of lesser importance. This is also a good example of how a user's experience can affect his or her future experiences. So, how does Flash fit into Web site usability considerations?

Flash is a great design tool to create amazing interfaces. Flash gives the designer the freedom to create almost anything he or she desires. But the flexibility Flash gives to the designer is also the tool's greatest weakness from a usability perspective. Flash is great for creating animation; however, inexperienced Web designers can easily go overboard. Just because you can animate an object doesn't mean that you should. The eye is very sensitive to the smallest amount of animation or movement in its peripheral view, pulling the viewers' attention away from the site's main content. On the plus side, animation used as a transitional element is very beneficial for the user. Animated transitions enable the user to follow the navigation process and gain a better understanding of how the site might work.

Similar to the problem of animation abuse, Flash enables the designers to create their own graphical user interface (GUI) elements. This is great for the designers, but users are often left out in the cold with all this newfound freedom. This design freedom forces the user to learn, almost from scratch, how to operate a scroll bar or a navigation bar. If you recall, I mention earlier the importance of a short learning curve for the users. The extreme creative versions of standardized GUI elements might rank high on the "cool" scale, but they really throw a monkey wrench into the user's goal and expectations. GUI standards are developed to help create a consistent experience across all platforms, thereby eliminating any unpleasant surprises. Again, these usability problems can be avoided in Flash if you understand the issues at hand and are able to find solutions based on the set standards.

Other usability issues with Flash arise from the actual plug-in nature of Flash. Unfortunately, because Flash requires a plug-in to work in Web browsers, Flash movies do not communicate with the browser's Back button or History by default. In order to add this functionality, you can use external ActionScript and JavaScript libraries like SWFAddress, which can be found at www.asual.com/swfaddress/

Building mockups of the site

You are now ready to begin mocking up the site structure by using index cards, sticky notes, and other common office supplies. Creating these paper mockups saves the development team a large amount of time. The beauty of the paper mockups is that you can quickly create a navigational system and find the major flaws without spending long hours developing a beautiful rendering of a structure that may be flawed. There is nothing worse than spending months developing a product with a faulty structure only to discover the mistake just before launch!

Testing the site on real users

Testing the site is the most important step in creating a useable site. The key to testing the site is *not* to test it on people in the organization, but to test it on people in the target audience. Test the site on the real users. It's usually easier to test the site by using people who are familiar with the project. The problem with that practice is that the people are familiar with the project. You want to test fresh eyes and minds in order to get optimum feedback. For testing purposes, create a list of several tasks to complete on the site. The tasks should be pulled from the list of possible users' goals defined in the early steps of the project. As the test subjects navigate through your project, pay close attention to how long it takes them. How many times did they have to click to find what they were looking for? How many had to resort to using a search feature (or wished that they could)? What elements seemed to cause confusion or delay? What elements attracted or held the users' attention? After each test subject has completed a task, or tried, give him or her a post-task questionnaire with questions such as:

"How would you rate the quality of the content on this site?"

Unacceptable –3 –2 –1 0 1 2 3 Excellent

Also, leave some room for the test subject to elaborate on the questions. After the testing is finished, review your findings and determine what needs to be fixed. After the problems are fixed, test the site again, but on new users. Repeat the process until you have a product that meets the defined goals of the organization and the users. Keep asking yourself this question: Is the interface helping the users accomplish their goals? When all else fails, you can always depend on the greatest guideline of the century: Keep it simple. Oh, how true.

Phase II: Producing, testing, and staging the presentation

When your client or company executives have signed off on a presentation concept, it's time to rock and roll! You're ready to gather your materials, assemble the crew, and meet an insane production schedule. This section provides a brief overview of the steps you need to take to produce material that's ready to go live on your Web site.

Assembling assets

The first step is to gather (or start production of) the individual assets required for the Flash presentation. Depending on the resources you included in your functional spec and budget, you may need to hire a photographer, illustrator, animator, or music composer (or all four!) to start work on the production. Or, if you perform any of these roles, then you should start creating rough drafts for the elements within the production. At this stage, you can also gather high-quality images from the client for their logos, proprietary material, and so on.

Making the Flash architecture

Of course, I'm assuming that you're creating a Flash-based production. All the resources that you've gathered (or are working to create) in Phase 1 will be assembled into the Flash movie(s) for the production. For large presentations or sites, you'll likely make one master Flash movie that provides a skeleton architecture for the presentation, and use ActionScript to bring in material for the appropriate sections of the site.

Before you begin Flash movie production, you should determine two important factors: frame size and frame rate. You don't want to change either of these settings midway through your project. Any reductions in frame size will crop elements that weren't located near the top-left portion of the Stage — you'll need to recompose most of the elements on the Stage if you used the entire Stage. Any changes in your frame rate change the timing of any linear animation and/or sound synchronization that you've already produced.

Staging a local test environment

As soon as you start to author the Flash movies, you create a local version of the presentation (or entire site) on your computer, or a networked drive that everyone on your team can access. The file and folder structure (including the naming conventions) will be consistent with the structure of the files and folders on the Web server. As you build each component of the site, you should begin to test the presentation with the target browsers (and Flash Player plug-in versions) for your audience.

HTML page production

Even if you're creating an all-Flash Web site, you need a few basic HTML documents, including:

- **Plug-in detection with JavaScript** that directs visitors without the Flash Player plug-in to the Adobe site to download the plug-in.

Cross-Reference

For more info about detecting Flash using JavaScript, see Chapter 19. ■

- **HTML page(s) to display any non-Flash material** in the site within the browser.

You should construct basic HTML documents to hold the main Flash movie as you develop the Flash architecture of the site.

Staging a server test environment

Before you can make your Flash content public, you need to set up a Web server that is publicly accessible (preferably with login and password protection) so that you can test the site functionality over a non-LAN connection. This also enables your client to preview the site remotely. After quality assurance (QA) testing is complete (the next step that follows), you move the files from the staging server to the live Web server.

I've noticed problems with larger SWF files that weren't detected until I tested them from a staging server. Why? When you test your files locally, they're loaded instantly into the browser. When you test your files from a server — even over a fast DSL (digital subscriber line) or cable modem connection, you have to wait for the SWF files to load over slower network conditions. Especially with preloaders or loading sequences, timing glitches may be revealed during tests on the staging server that were not apparent when you tested locally.

Tip
You should use the Simulate Download feature of the Bandwidth Profiler in the Test Movie environment of Flash CS5 to estimate how your Flash movies will load over a real Internet connection. See Chapter 18, "Publishing Flash Movies," for more discussion of this feature. ■

Quality assurance testing

In larger corporate environments, you'll find a team of individuals whose sole responsibility is to thoroughly test the quality of a nearly finished production (or product). If you're responsible for QA, then you should have an intimate knowledge of the process chart for the site. That way, you know how the site should function. If a feature or function fails in the production, QA reports it to the creative and/or programming teams. QA teams test the production with the same hardware and conditions as the target audience, accounting for variations in:

- Computer type (Windows versus Mac)
- Computer speed (top-of-the-line processing speed versus minimal supported speeds, as determined by the target audience)
- Internet connection speeds (as determined by the target audience)
- Flash Player plug-in versions (and any other plug-ins required by the production)
- Browser application and version (as determined by the target audience)

Web Resource
It's worthwhile to use an online reporting tool to post bugs during QA. Many companies use the open source (freeware) tool called Mantis, a PHP/MySQL solution. You can find more information about Mantis at www.mantisbt.org/. Another popular bug reporting tool is Bugzilla (www.bugzilla.org). ■

After QA has finished rugged testing of the production, pending approval by the client (or company executives), the material is ready to go live on the site.

Maintenance and updates

After you've celebrated the finished production, your job isn't over yet. If you were contracted to build the site or presentation for a third party, you may be expected to maintain and address usability issues provided by follow-ups with the client and any support staff they might have. Be sure to account for periodic maintenance and updates for the project in your initial budget proposal. If you don't want to be responsible for updates, make sure that you advise your clients ahead of time to avoid any potential conflicts after the production has finished.

You should have a thorough staging and testing environment for any updates you make to an all-Flash site, especially if you're changing major assets or master architecture files. Repeat the same process of staging and testing with the QA team that you employed during original production.

Web Resource
You can find an online archived PDF version of Eric Jordan's tutorial, "Interface Design," on the book's Web site at www.flashsupport.com/archive. This tutorial was featured in Flash MX Bible (Wiley, 2002). ■

Using the Project Panel in Flash CS5

In this final section of the chapter, I show you how to use the Project panel in Flash CS5 by using some sample files provided on this book's CD-ROM. You jump right into the Project panel, so you may want to review some of the content in the Help pages of Flash CS5 before proceeding. The Using Flash ⇨ Using Flash CS5 Professional ⇨ Managing documents ⇨ Working with projects section in the Help pages (Help ⇨ Flash Help) contains useful information about the Project panel.

New Feature

The Project panel in Flash CS5 is completely different than the Project panel featured in the last three versions of the Flash authoring tool. The new Project panel is much easier to use than its predecessor, and you can set up project files with much less hassle. ■

Before you start using the Project panel, consider a scenario in which you would *want* to use the feature. The Project panel lets you access files related to a Flash production. You can include any file type you want in your project, and this is reflected in the Project panel. The panel essentially works as a modified file explorer, similar to Windows Explorer or the Finder (Mac), especially geared to Flash content. After you've created a Flash project, you can quickly open any document directly in Flash CS5 or another application. The project name is added as a new item in the drop-down menu at the top of the Project panel.

One important factor to keep in mind when you use the Project panel is that you should only open a local copy of the project's files on your computer. In this way, everyone working on the project has his or her own copy of the files. One member of the team can be editing, implementing, and testing changes while other members are doing the same with their copies. When a member is done editing a file, he or she can check the file back into the server.

Caution

Unless you're implementing a version control system with your project files, you need to make sure that two or more members of the team do not attempt to make edits to the same file simultaneously or make edits to a copy of a file. Version control systems can merge changes to the same document. For example, if two people edit the same ActionScript document (.as file), the version control system merges the changes into one file and even flags potential conflicts during the process. Also, it's important to note that version control software cannot merge changes in two Flash documents (.fla files) because such files are binary, not ASCII (or Unicode). Usually, version control systems can merge only text documents. ■

Here's a quick review of the procedures you follow:

1. **Establish a new project structure with files and folders on your local system.**
2. **Create a new project in Flash CS5.** The primary setting for a new project is the location of your Flash files, where you'll store your local copy of the project files.
3. **Edit panel and project preferences to suit the needs of your project (optional).**
4. **Open and edit a file in the project.**
5. **Publish an entire project.**

The headings that follow elaborate on these five steps, and include the step numbers for easy reference.

1. Establishing a project structure

Before you can start making or editing documents in Flash CS5 for a project, you need to define a folder structure that the Project panel can use. In this section, you learn how to define a site and establish a local mirror copy of your site's files on your machine.

1. **On your computer, choose a location that you can use to store all the files with a project.** For example, if you're on Windows, you can create a folder named `sites` at the root of your C drive. If you're on a Mac, you can create a folder named `sites` at the root of your startup drive, such as Macintosh HD.

2. **Inside of the `sites` folder, copy the `robertreinhardt.com` folder from the `ch03` folder located on this book's CD-ROM.** As shown in Figure 3.5, the `robert reinhardt.com` folder has two subfolders, `src` and `deploy`.

FIGURE 3.5

The layout of folders for a site named robertreinhardt.com

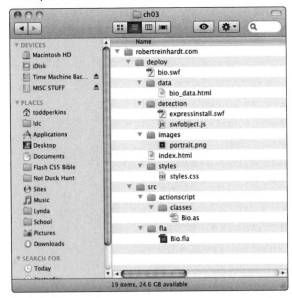

50

Tip

In Mac OS X, you can turn on Personal Web Sharing in the Sharing preferences (Apple menu ➪ System Preferences). When this service is started, Mac OS X automatically creates a `Sites` folder in your user folder on the startup disk. You can use this `Sites` folder to test content from a Web browser, using the path `http://localhost/~your_user_name`. **For example, if your username is joann, your local path to the** `Sites` **folder is** `http://localhost/~joann/`. ■

The `src` folder, short for *source*, will contain any source files, specifications, planning documents, raw assets (images, video, and sound), and so on. The `fla` folder inside of the `src` folder holds all Flash documents (.fla files) for the project.

The `deploy` folder, short for *deployment*, will contain any and all files that will be part of the final application, as a publicly accessible Web site or application. The `deploy` folder holds the files that will be uploaded to the public root folder of your Web server. These files are also called *runtime* files because they run in the Flash Player and Web browser from the live Web site. All the Flash movies (SWF files), runtime assets (JPEGs, MP3s, FLVs, and so on), and HTML documents will be kept here. The copy of `deploy` from the CD-ROM includes several subfolders to store external assets necessary for the Flash movie (SWF file) at runtime.

2. Creating the project in Flash CS5

After you create the file and folder structure, you're ready to create a new Flash project in Flash CS5.

1. **Open Flash Professional CS4.** Choose Window ➪ Other Panels ➪ Project (Shift+F8).

2. **In the top drop-down menu, select New Project (shown in Figure 3.6).**

FIGURE 3.6

The Project panel

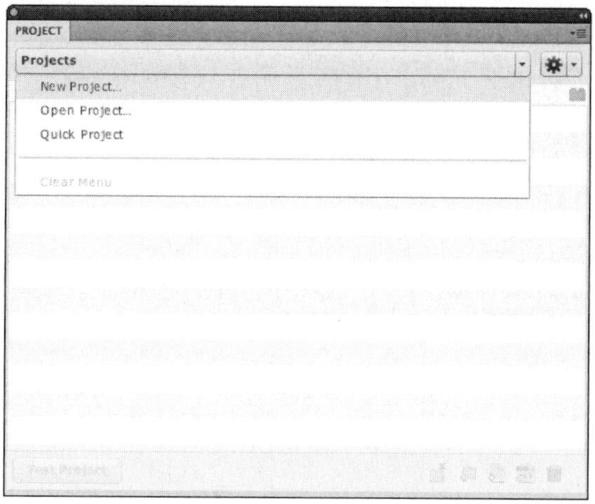

3. **In the Create New Project dialog box, type a name for your project in the Project name field, such as** robertreinhardt.com. Click the folder icon to the right of the Root folder field, and browse to the `robertreinhardt.com` folder on your computer. In the ActionScript Version menu, choose the version of ActionScript that you will use with your Flash project. For this example, ActionScript 3.0 (AS3) is used, so the ActionScript 3.0 option is selected. Review the example settings shown in Figure 3.7. Click the Create Project button to build a new project setting in Flash CS5.

FIGURE 3.7

The Create New Project dialog box

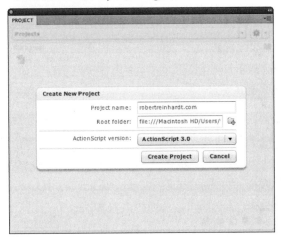

4. **After the project is created, you can expand the folder nodes to see the documents that reside in the project.** The Project panel automatically filters the file types shown in the folder nodes to include only those files commonly used in Flash production, such as .fla, .swf, and .as. When all the folder nodes are expanded (as shown in Figure 3.8), some files are not visible such as image, XML, HTML, and CSS files. In the next section, you learn how to modify preferences to add file extensions to the project's file filter.

It's highly likely that you'll have more than one Flash document (FLA file) in a project. As such, you should define the default document for the project. This file should be the master file, the one "most in charge" per se. This could be the Flash document that controls the loading of other runtime assets or the document that contains the most code. The published SWF file of the default document is the movie that is loaded into the Test Movie environment when you test a project. In the `src/fla` folder of the Project panel, right-click (or Control+click on the Mac) the `Bio.fla` document and choose Make Default Document in the context menu, as shown in Figure 3.9. The icon of the document should now include a gold star to indicate that it is the default document.

FIGURE 3.8

The structure of the site within the Project panel, with default file extensions visible

FIGURE 3.9

The Make Default Document option in the context menu for a FLA file

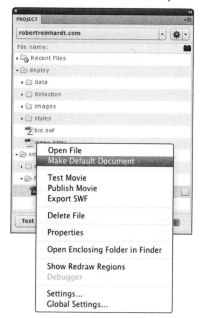

Tip

The check box to the right of a FLA file in the Project panel determines if the document is published when you click the Test Project button. All FLA files are unchecked by default. ∎

3. Changing project and panel preferences

After you have created a new project with existing files on your system, you can alter the Project panel's display of files and folders. In this section, you learn how to set up project properties and alter the panel preferences to show the additional runtime files (images, HTML, CSS, and so on) in the panel.

1. To create a shortcut to your ActionScript class files in the Project panel (and more important, to instruct the panel where to create new class files), click the options combo box at the top-right corner of the panel (marked with a gear icon), and choose Project Properties, as shown in Figure 3.10.

FIGURE 3.10

The options menu of the Project panel

2. In the Classes tab of the Project Properties dialog box, click the browse folder icon for the Save classes in field, as shown in Figure 3.11. Browse to the `classes` folder in the `src/actionscript` folder of the sample project files. Click OK to close the dialog box. The Project panel now displays the `classes` folder as a separate folder node (Figure 3.12). Note that a new folder was *not* created in the actual folder structure — you simply have a quicker way to find and access the class files for a project.

3. To change the file and folder filter preferences, choose Panel Preferences from the same options menu you used in Step 1. Click the Settings tab in the Panel Preferences dialog box, and enter the file extensions for the file types you want to see displayed in your Flash projects, as shown in Figure 3.13. For this example, you can enter the

following extensions: png, css, html, and js. Click OK when you've finished adding your preferred extensions. When you expand the folder nodes in the Project panel, you should now see all the files for the example project (Figure 3.14).

Tip

You may want to uncheck the Show hidden files option, which is enabled by default. Version control files, such as .svn and .git files, will be visible unless this option is unchecked. ■

FIGURE 3.11

The Classes tab of the Project Properties dialog box

FIGURE 3.12

The new classes node in the Project panel

FIGURE 3.13

The Settings tab of the Panel Preferences dialog box

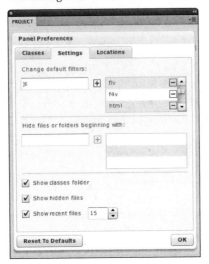

FIGURE 3.14

The updated file view in the Project panel

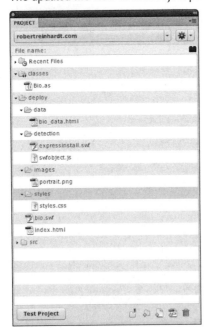

4. Opening and editing files in the project

After you create a project and set up your preferences, you can open and edit documents from the Project panel.

1. **Double-click the master document, `Bio.fla`, to edit it in the Flash authoring environment.**

2. **With `Bio.fla` open, take a look at how the `bio.swf` file (located in the `wwwroot` folder) is published.** Choose File ➪ Publish Settings. In the Formats tab, notice that a relative path is declared for the `bio.swf` file (see Figure 3.15) in the Flash field. The `../../deploy/` prefix tells Flash CS5 to publish this file two folders above the `fla` folder, inside of the `deploy` folder. Click Cancel to close the dialog box.

FIGURE 3.15

You can publish files with relative paths in the Formats tab.

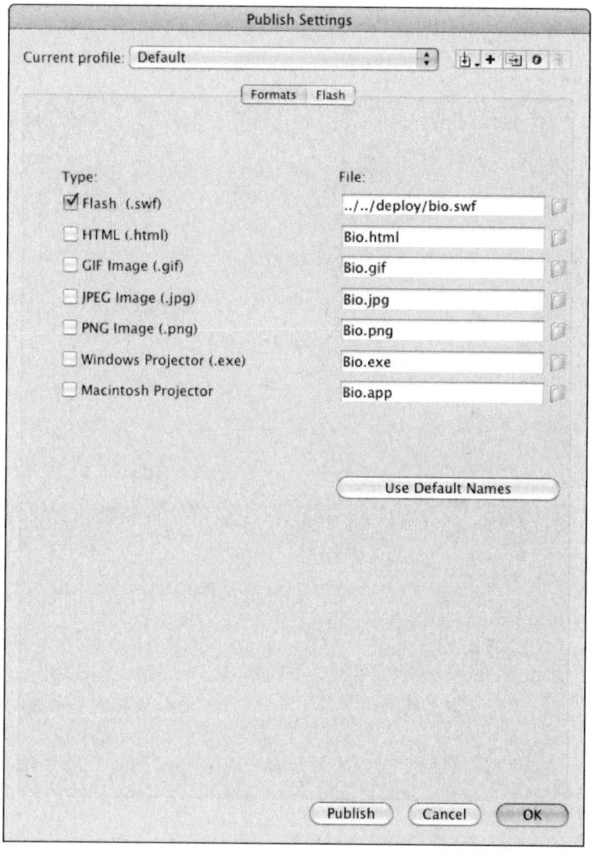

3. **You can also edit some text files, such as HTML and XML files, directly in the Flash CS5 authoring environment.** If you want to open a non-Flash-specific file in its associated application, you can right-click that file in the Project panel and choose Open File With Associated Application (Figure 3.16). If you have Adobe Dreamweaver associated with CSS files, you can right-click the `styles.css` file, choose this option, and edit the CSS file directly in Dreamweaver.

FIGURE 3.16

The contextual menu of a file in the Project panel

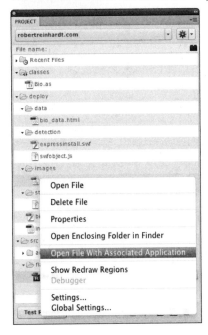

5. Publishing the entire project

In this final section, you learn how to test an entire project and view the master document's movie in the Test Movie environment.

1. **Click the Test Project button in the lower-left corner of the Project panel.** Flash CS5 publishes all the Flash documents (FLA files) set to publish in the project file. In our example, there's only one FLA file, `Bio.fla`. The newly published `bio.swf` file, located in the `deploy` folder, then opens in the Test Movie environment.

2. **When you finish testing the file, close the Test Movie window.** Remember, when you close and reopen Flash CS5, you can reopen all the project files for this example by choosing the site name in the Project panel's main drop-down menu.

On the CD-ROM
You can find the site files in the ch03 folder on this book's CD-ROM. ■

Summary

- Your clients rely on you to understand and guide the production process involved with Flash content creation.

- Careful planning helps you to create Flash solutions that best meet the goals of your project. The technical issues, such as usability, target audience, and delivery platform, should be balanced with the aesthetic aspects of experience design.

- To structure the development of Flash projects, many Web developers use a two-phase production model that involves six milestones: Business Initiative, Creative Solutions, Approval, Production, QA, and Delivery.

- During the production period, it is helpful to keep six key concepts in mind: asset assembly, a master Flash architecture, a local test environment, HTML page layout, a server staging environment, and proper QA testing. After production is finished, you also need to devise a strategy for systematic maintenance.

- You can use the Project panel in Flash CS5 to manage all the Flash documents for a site or application.

Part II

Mastering the Flash Environment

When you're ready to jump in and get started on the road to efficient and painless production, this section will give you all the information you need to feel comfortable in the Flash authoring environment. Chapter 4 introduces you to the updated Flash workspace and gives you tips for customizing the UI. You will learn where all your tools are stored and how to organize them to suit your workflow. Chapter 5 is where you'll find coverage of all the Flash drawing and selection tools, including an introduction to the new Spray Brush and Deco tools that enable you to create patterns with symbol instances. You'll also learn how to control snapping behavior and how to create and edit groups. In Chapter 6, you'll find out what makes Flash so much more powerful than simple vector graphics programs. Symbols and symbol instances are the basis for all optimized Flash projects, and the Library gives you all the options you need to keep your project assets organized.

Chapter 7 includes coverage of color issues specific to Web production and explains how to use the Swatches and Color panels to enhance your projects with custom colors, gradients, bitmap fills, and more. Chapter 8 guides you through the various options for creating and editing text in Flash, using the new Text Layout Framework. You will also learn how to control font display and how to create and use font symbols. Finally, in Chapter 9, you will be introduced to the more advanced tools for editing graphics and text in Flash, including the Free Transform and Gradient Transform tools.

Interface Fundamentals

This chapter gives you a tour of the Flash workspace and the various methods for organizing and navigating your documents. I define fundamental features of the authoring environment, but in some cases defer detailed explanation of functionality to later chapters. This chapter orients new users to the program and introduces experienced users to some of the new Flash CS5 features.

Getting Started

When you walk into a studio, the first thing you need to know is where to find your tools. Although you might have an idea of where to start looking based on experience, nothing improves your workflow more than being able to reach for something without hesitation. This kind of familiarity and comfort in a workspace is a prerequisite for the mastery of any craft.

Fortunately, many of the features of the Flash CS5 interface will look familiar to you if you've worked in other graphics applications. However, there are some unique features that you need to understand before you can tackle your Flash projects with the ease of an expert. WI begin by introducing the Flash interface and pointing out the tools available for managing and customizing your Flash "studio."

You'll soon notice that there is often more than one way to access an option. As I describe the steps for carrying out a task, I include shortcut keys or menu paths in parentheses. You should feel comfortable and ready to get to work in no time.

Welcome to Flash CS5

Flash CS5 presents the most polished and agile implementation, so far, of the flexible panel-based interface that has gradually evolved over the last few versions of Flash. Panels in Flash CS5 can now be resized more freely and docked or grouped easily with other panels or to the application window. Adobe has made a concerted effort with this release to streamline menus and smooth out workflow inconsistencies with various tools. Some small but significant modifications have also been made to the look and function of common tools, menus, and panels. I cover them as I discuss workflows for specific tasks throughout the book.

The changes in Flash CS5 are hinted at in the interface, but I give you a peek under the hood in this chapter. If you have been using Flash for a while, this version should speed up your workflow and boost your inspiration. If this is the first time you've tried Flash, you've picked a great time to start: Flash CS5 includes more ways to jump in and get started than ever before.

Start Page

The Start Page (shown in Figure 4.1) gives you quick access to tutorials and other help features and provides a handy way to choose the file you want to open or create.

Tip
Flash content for mobile phones and other devices is increasingly popular, and Adobe supports developers through Adobe Device Central with templates designed specifically for commonly used handheld devices in different markets. ■

By default, the Start Page should appear when you first launch Flash and any time you close all Document windows while the program is running. After you have opened or created a new file, the Start Page automatically closes to make room on your desktop. If you prefer not to use the Start Page, select the Don't show again check box at the bottom of the panel, or change the settings for On launch in General Flash Preferences (Edit ➪ Preferences or Flash ➪ Preferences). This leaves you with the more limited, but familiar, option of using the application File menu (or shortcut keys) to create and open files.

The links at the bottom of the Start Page connect you to online content available through the Adobe Web site. These links are worth investigating if you want to get a quick introduction to Flash and a peek at the vast range of online resources available.

Web Resource
If you want to introduce other friends or co-workers to the new features of Flash CS5, you can direct them to the information online at www.adobe.com/products/flash/features. **■**

One of the most useful links in the Start Page is to Flash Exchange (under the Extend title). If you are connected to the Internet this link connects you to the Adobe Exchange page, which includes a list of product-specific links. You can browse to the Flash Exchange for helpful tools and add-ons that Flash developers have made available through Adobe's site.

FIGURE 4.1

The Start Page provides quick access to file lists, templates, and resource links.

The first four options listed under the Create New title in the Start Page each target a different version of ActionScript — or rather they create a new Flash document with Publish settings auto-set to target a specific version of the Flash Player, using one of the various flavors of ActionScript:

- **ActionScript 3.0:** ActionScript 3.0 can only be used with Flash Player 9 or later and should be specified if you plan to use advanced code that requires AS 3.0 capabilities or if you want to access the new tools that rely on AS 3.0 and Flash Player 10.

- **ActionScript 2.0:** ActionScript 2.0 files created in Flash CS5 target Flash Player 10 by default, but these files can also be published to be backward-compatible with older versions of the Flash Player (as far back as Flash Player 6).

- **Adobe AIR 2:** Create Flash files that target the Adobe AIR runtime framework. Adobe AIR enables you to use your HTML/Ajax, Flex, or Flash development skills to build and deploy cross-platform, rich Internet applications to the desktop.

- **iPhone:** Create Flash files that can be published as an iPhone application. When published, Flash creates a native iPhone file (.app) that can be tested on an iPhone, iPod Touch, or other compatible device. These apps can also be sold via the App Store. In order to get Flash-iPhone apps on an iPhone, whether for testing or deployment, you will need to register as an iPhone Developer, which currently starts at $99 USD.

65

- **Flash Lite 4:** This option launches Adobe Device Central, which is a specialized authoring environment designed to support the development of Flash content for mobile devices. These files target the Flash Lite Player instead of the full Flash Player and are limited to a more simplified set of ActionScript (1.0 or 2.0, depending on the version of Flash Lite that is running on the target device).

Cross-Reference

To learn more about Adobe Device Central and authoring content for Flash Lite, refer to Chapter 18, "Publishing Flash Movies." ∎

The last several options in the Create New column of the Start Page enable you to launch a file for authoring or editing code in Flash without first creating a .fla:

- **ActionScript File:** Opens a file for authoring or editing ActionScript. File is saved with the .as extension.
- **Flash JavaScript File:** Opens a file for authoring or editing JavaScript for Flash. The file is saved with the .jsfl extension.
- **Flash Project:** Opens the new Flash Project panel to enable you to manage your Flash project files.
- **ActionScript 3.0 Class:** Opens a basic template file for an ActionScript 3.0 class. The file is saved with the .as extension.
- **ActionScript 3.0 Interface:** Opens a basic template for an ActionScript 3.0 interface. The file is saved with the .as extension.

If you select the Advertising option listed under Create from Template in the Start Page (or use the application menu to select File ➪ New), you will see a secondary (New Document or New from Template) dialog box that has two different views: General and Templates. If you want to access some of the Flash document styles from Flash 8 that are no longer listed in the main Start Page, simply choose the General view and you can see an extended list of possible file types.

Tip

The file Type list available in the General section of the New Document or New From Template dialog box is also a good way to browse the various file types because a preview and a description of each are available before you actually create and load a specific file. ∎

Help menu options

The Flash CS5 Help menu is a quick-access menu of guided entry points to a vast array of online resources. The Flash Exchange is an online resource created to support use and development of Flash extensions. It is a great place to look for new tools, components, and effects that you can download and add to your Flash toolkit. The Flash Support Center is Adobe's primary vehicle for the distribution of up-to-date information about Flash and Flash-related topics. It is a searchable area with current (and archived) articles on many Flash topics. You can also find links to downloads, documentation, forums, and many other invaluable Flash-related resources and updates.

Use Help ⇨ Manage Extensions to load the control panel for managing installed Adobe extensions for Flash as well as other applications in the Creative suite.

The Flash CS5 interface on Macintosh and Windows

Before discussing the various Flash menu items, panels, and miscellaneous dialog boxes that you can use to control and customize your workspace, I begin with a look at the interface with its array of toolbars and panels as they appear on Macintosh and Windows with the Essentials workspace loaded. Use the Workspace menu at the top of the Document window to choose Essentials or the application menu to select Window ⇨ Workspace ⇨ Essentials if you want to load or reload this workspace.

The Flash authoring environment has been polished into a flexible system of panels that can be resized from any edge and docked individually or easily arranged into tabbed groups that can be expanded or collapsed as needed. The implementation of panels is consistent across products in the CS5 suite for both Mac and Windows. Throughout the book, I discuss each panel in context with the tools and tasks where it is used. As you'll quickly find, there are many ways to arrange these panels for a customized workflow. Your preferred panel layouts for different tasks can be saved as custom workspace layouts and recalled from the Workspace menu. To give you an idea of how workspaces support different workflows, Adobe has included a menu of ready-made workspaces arranged to suit specific types of production.

Figure 4.2 shows how the Essentials workspace (Window ⇨ Workspace ⇨ Essentials) looks on the Mac.

Note

The Essentials workspace includes two tabbed panel groups that support commonly used features and reduce clutter: The Timeline and the new Motion Editor are in a tabbed group that sits below the Document window, and a new vertical Properties panel with contextual sections for Position and Size, Properties, and Filters is grouped with the Library panel. The expanded Library panel also includes a pull-down menu for loading library content from different documents without having to manage multiple floating panels. ■

In addition to the Essentials, Developer, Designer, and Debug workspace layouts, Flash CS5 ships with a Classic preset that loads several of the panels as a group collapsed to icon view and docked with the new vertical Properties panel, as shown in Figure 4.3.

New Feature

The Tools panel can now be resized horizontally or vertically, and it docks to any edge of the screen or with other panels. ■

Tip

To prevent docking while you are moving panels, press the Control key while dragging. ■

FIGURE 4.2

The Essentials workspace for Flash CS5 as it appears on Mac OS X

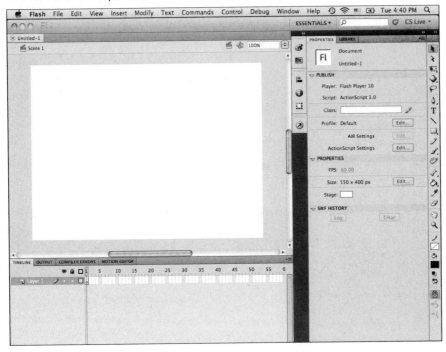

For clarity, I have capitalized terms that refer to specific Flash interface features such as Document window, Stage, Timeline, Tools panel, and Options area. You may see these words lowercase in other parts of the text, where they are used as general terms rather than as labels for specific parts of the Flash interface.

I describe the actual uses and options for most of these various interface elements in the context of where the elements are applied. To get started with Flash, I introduce the Properties panel, Tools panel, Document window, Scene panel, Timeline, and Controller, along with the related menu items. I discuss the remainder of the panels and windows, and how they are used, in chapters on drawing, animation, interactivity, and other specific production topics.

Note

The Main toolbar is an optional feature available only on the Windows version of Flash. This toolbar gives you quick access to commonly used tool and panel options, and it should not be confused with the Tools panel. The Controller and the Edit bar options found in the Window ➪ Toolbars menu have the same function on Windows and Mac versions. The Controller is used to control the position of the playhead in the Timeline, and the Edit bar (which docks to the top of the Document window) includes controls for navigating scenes, editing symbols, and changing view settings. ■

Cross-Reference

I cover the use of the History panel in Chapter 9, "Modifying Graphics." I describe the Project panel in Chapter 3, "Planning Flash Projects." ■

What to expect from the Properties panel

The Properties panel is a centralized place to access most common options for various authoring items. The Properties panel in Flash CS5 has a new vertical orientation, and as you activate tools or select items in the Document window, relevant properties load into organized, collapsible sections within the panel. You can select or modify most options directly in the Properties panel, but for some items, buttons appear that you can use to launch additional menus or dialog boxes.

Depending on what is currently selected, the Properties panel displays relevant attributes for a document, frame, symbol instance, component instance, shape, or text box. Popup menus and editable value fields make it quick and easy to make changes without hunting through panel sets or the application menu. As shown in Figure 4.3, when an element is selected that can have code attached to it, a gray arrow appears on the right edge of the Properties panel. Clicking this icon launches the Actions panel for editing code on individual frames or symbol instances.

Generally, you will only need to access other panels for a few specialized editing tasks. Figure 4.3 shows how the Properties panel changes to display options relevant to the currently selected item.

The top figure shows the Properties panel, as it appears when the PolyStar tool is active (selected in the Tools panel) — displaying Stroke and Fill colors and options, buttons for launching Settings dialog boxes for line styles, and tool Options. The bottom figure shows the Properties panel (with collapsed sections) as it appears when a Button symbol instance is selected on the Stage — displaying instance properties and options.

Notice the Filters section (collapsed) at the bottom of the Properties panel when a symbol instance is selected. I explain the application of filters in later chapters. For now, all you need to know is that you can use the Filters section of the Properties panel to add and sort live filter effects.

Because the Properties panel and the Tools panel provide access to all tool options (with the exception of some drawing and text attributes that are adjusted in the Preferences window), there are only four panels that you might need to open separately for additional options while drawing and editing graphics on the Stage. They are Color, for adding alpha, gradients, and custom colors; Align, for accurately arranging elements in relation to each other or to the Stage; Transform, for quickly making percentage-based scaling or rotation adjustments; and History, for tracking or changing your edits. You can optimize this simple setup even further by sorting panels into custom stacked or tabbed groups, as described in the next section.

FIGURE 4.3

The Properties panel, as it appears when the PolyStar tool is active (top), and when a Button symbol instance is selected (bottom)

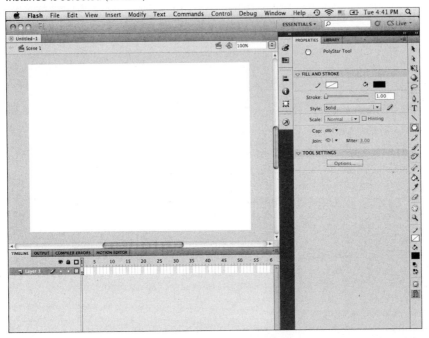

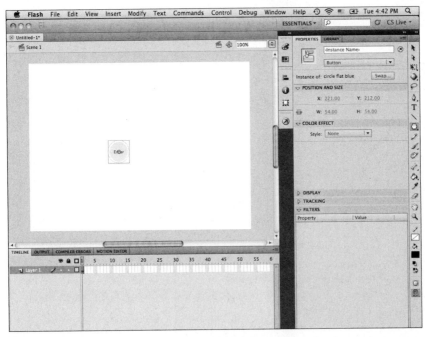

Managing Windows and Panels

Most interface elements have built-in display controls (see Figure 4.4 for the tabbed panel controls that you will see on both Mac and Windows versions), but you can also manage what appears in your workspace with the main application menu. Rather than go through a laundry list of all the application menu options, I note the various features that apply to individual windows and panels as I describe their uses.

Tip

Double-click the topmost (dark gray) bar to collapse the panel group to icon view (or use the Expand/Collapse arrow toggle). Double-click the panel tabs to collapse the panel to a narrow tabbed text view. ∎

FIGURE 4.4

The controls I note here on the tabbed Mac Color and Swatches panel group are consistent with the control icons you will see on other panels for both Mac and Windows.

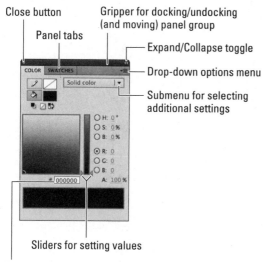

Close button

Gripper for docking/undocking
(and moving) panel group

Panel tabs

Expand/Collapse toggle

Drop-down options menu

Submenu for selecting
additional settings

Sliders for setting values

Text Field for displaying and entering values

Contextual menus

As in many other programs, you will find Flash contextual menus pop up in response to a right-click on a selected item in the Timeline, Library panel, or on the Stage. (Control+click for the Mac if you don't have a two-button mouse.) Contextual menus duplicate most functions and commands that are accessible either through the application menu or through the various panels and dialog boxes, which I discuss in this chapter. Because contextual menus show you only those options relevant to the element you have selected, they provide a handy authoring shortcut that can also help you get familiar with Flash.

Floating and docking panels

You can drag and drop individual panels to create vertical stacks or horizontal tabbed groups that maximize your workspace while keeping options handy. Figure 4.5 shows a tabbed panel group, a panel stack, and a free-floating panel.

Tabbed panel groups (left) are more space efficient than stacked (center) or individual floating panels (right).

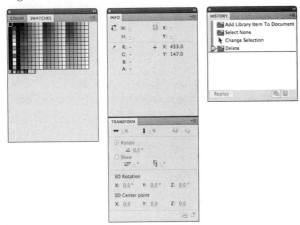

Grouping panels for tabbed access is more space-efficient than just docking panels to the sides of your workspace or stacking panels vertically, but you will probably still want to stack some panels or panel groups to keep your workspace orderly. To group, dock, or stack panels, follow these steps:

1. **Grab the panel (or panel group) by clicking on the top gray bar of the panel.**

Caution

Do not release the mouse until the panel is ready to dock! ∎

2. **Drag the panel until it overlaps another open panel or panel group or until it is close to a side or to the bottom of your screen.** When Flash recognizes the panel overlap, a blue docking highlight appears at the top, bottom, or side of the panel that you want to dock to or along the side of your screen. Dragging your panel on top of another panel adds it as a tabbed group, and dragging your panel toward the bottom or top of another panel stacks it vertically. Dragging a panel to the side or bottom of your screen makes it "stick" there, so you'll have fewer floating panels cluttering your work space.

3. **Release the mouse, and the panel should remain docked or stacked.**

Unstacking or undocking panels is easy: Just click the top gray area (or tab) and drag to pull any panel away from the other panels in a stack or group and make it free floating.

Focus: Making panels or windows active

Prior to Flash 4, only one area of the application required users to pay attention to focus — when they were selecting colors for either the stroke or fill — because it was easy to confuse the two. As the interface has grown to include more panels and windows that can be active at different times within the Flash environment, focus has become an important aspect of the program. What is focus? *Focus* is a term used to describe which part of the application is active, or has priority, at a given time. For example, all panels, such as the Actions panel, do not automatically "have focus" — this means that you have to click within the panel to begin working there. Similarly, to return to the Document window or Stage to edit an element, you must click there to return focus to that aspect of the application. The Properties panel can actually remind you what area or element is active because it displays the attributes of the currently active item. Otherwise, if a panel or dialog box doesn't seem to respond, just remember to *focus* on what you're doing.

Creating custom workspace layouts

Whether you have chosen a layout from the Window menu (Window⇨Workspace) or have just opened Flash with the default display, one of the first things you'll want to learn is how to customize the Flash environment to suit your workflow. Whether you're working on an 800-x-600 laptop screen, a 1024-x-768 dual-monitor setup, or a 1920-x-1200 LCD, panels give you the flexibility to create a layout that fits your screen real estate and production needs.

To save your current panel layout as a custom set that can be accessed from the Workspace menu the next time you open Flash, follow these simple steps:

1. **Open and arrange (by grouping or stacking) any panels that you want to include in your custom layout.**

2. **Go to Window⇨Workspace⇨New Workspace, or choose New Workspace from the Workspace drop-down menu at the top of the Document window.** A dialog box prompts you to name your layout.

3. **Enter a name that will help you remember why you made that panel set, such as** animation **or** scripting. Your custom layout now appears in the list of available workspaces in the drop-down menu (and in the application menu: Window⇨Workspace).

Deleting or renaming workspaces is easy. Choose Manage Workspaces from the drop-down menu or select Window⇨Workspace⇨Manage Workspaces from the application menu to open the dialog box for editing the list of saved layouts. As shown in Figure 4.6, you have the option of renaming or deleting any of the custom files that appear in the Workspace list.

Do you really love your custom layout? You can save workspace layouts just as you would project files in order to share them with other people or take them with you when you upgrade to a newer version of Flash (or move to another machine). When you want to add them to your current version of Flash, just place the files in the Workspace Layouts folder and they'll appear in the menu, ready for you to use. The only limitation is that workspace layout files cannot be shared between the Mac and Windows versions of Flash.

The dialog box for managing saved workspace layouts makes it easy to delete or rename your custom layouts.

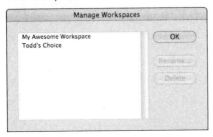

Workspace layouts are stored in a folder on your hard drive. After you find the Workspace folder, you can either add or delete any of these XML files and the Workspace menu in Flash will update to show only the files that you currently have saved there.

- The standard directory path on Windows is

  `C:\Documents and Settings\(username)\Local Settings\Application`
  `    Data\Adobe\Flash CS5\(language)\Configuration\Workspace`

- The standard directory path on Mac is

  `HD\Users: (username)\Library: Application Support\Adobe\Flash CS5\`
  `    (language)\Configuration\Workspace`

Keyboard shortcuts

Keyboard shortcuts enable you to work more quickly because you avoid the hassle of clicking through a menu to activate a feature with your mouse. This is a workflow trick that many people use even when working in text-editing applications. Instead of browsing to the Edit menu to find the Copy command, you can just press the key combination Ctrl+C/⌘+C. I have included the default keyboard shortcuts for most tools and features as they are introduced by listing them in parentheses after the tool or menu item name. When key options are different on Mac and Windows, I list both. Thus the convention for showing the keyboard shortcut for Copy in both Windows and Mac would be Ctrl+C or ⌘+C.

A default set of keyboard shortcuts is available without having to change any settings, and these shortcuts are listed after most commands in the various application menus. However, if you want to use different shortcut keys for certain tasks or add a new shortcut key for a custom panel group or tool, you can make changes to the default settings in the Keyboard Shortcuts dialog box shown in Figure 4.7 (Edit ⇨ Keyboard Shortcuts, or in OS X go to Flash ⇨ Keyboard Shortcuts).

Tip

By default, Flash CS5 uses the Adobe Standard set of built-in keyboard shortcuts, which is designed to be consistent on most applications in the Creative Suite. You can also select a built-in keyboard shortcut set from legacy versions of popular applications, including Flash 5, Illustrator 10, and Photoshop 6. Instead of manually changing a duplicate of the Adobe Standard set to match your favorite program, simply switch the Current Set using the menu list. ■

As shown in Figure 4.7, the Keyboard Shortcuts dialog box enables you to customize your Flash keyboard shortcuts to maintain consistency with other applications or to suit a personalized workflow. Not only can you choose keyboard shortcuts developed from other applications, but you can also save your modifications and custom settings. You can find the Keyboard Shortcuts dialog box in the application menu (Edit ⇨ Keyboard Shortcuts, or in OS X go to Flash ⇨ Keyboard Shortcuts). To create a new keyboard shortcut, you must first duplicate an existing set, from which you can then add or subtract existing shortcuts to form your custom set.

FIGURE 4.7

The Keyboard Shortcuts dialog box as displayed on Mac OS X. The appearance is slightly different on Windows, but the options available are the same.

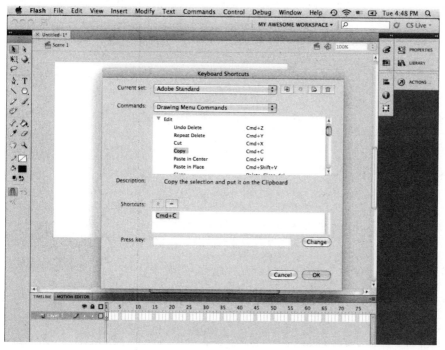

Tip

The Export Set as HTML button in the Keyboard Shortcuts dialog box (shown in Figure 4.8) is a fantastic way to create a formatted table of shortcut keys that you can post near your desk or share with other people. This option enables you to name the file and choose a location to save it. Drag the saved HTML file into a browser window to see a nicely formatted reference table that you can read on-screen or print out. ■

Note

Like workspace layout files, Keyboard Shortcut sets are stored on your hard drive. You can find them in the `Keyboard Shortcuts` folder in the same Configuration folder that I listed in the previous section for workspace layouts. You can navigate to this location on your hard drive and copy, back up, restore, delete, or otherwise manipulate any of these files from this folder. Keyboard shortcuts are transferable between machines, although I have had no success transferring them across platforms. ■

The Tools Panel

The vertical bar that appears docked on the left side of the interface in the Flash CS5 Essentials workspace is referred to as the Tools panel (see Figure 4.8). If you haven't just installed Flash, or if someone else has changed the defaults in Flash, you may not see the Tools panel on your screen. You can find it in the main Window menu (Window ➪ Tools) or open it with shortcut keys (Ctrl+F2/⌘+F2).

Controlling the Tools panel

The Tools panel can now be scaled and collapsed just like any other panel in Flash CS5. As you scale the panel, the tool icons reflow to fit in one long column or in a horizontal row or a combination of the two. It can also be hidden (and unhidden) along with other panels by choosing Window ➪ Hide Panels or by pressing the F4 key, or it can be opened and closed independently by choosing Window ➪ Tools (Ctrl+F2/⌘+F2).

Note

If you're using a Windows machine, don't confuse Tools with the menu item for Toolbars, which refers to a set of optional menus I describe in the section "The Flash CS5 interface on Macintosh and Windows" earlier in this chapter. ■

Tip

To drag the Tools panel to the edge of the program window, yet prevent it from docking, press the Ctrl key while dragging. ■

If you would rather not see the tooltips that appear when pointing to tool icons in the Tools panel, you can turn them off in your General Preferences. (In OS X, go to Flash ➪ Preferences ➪ General; in Windows, go to Edit ➪ Preferences ➪ General, and under Selection options, uncheck Show tooltips.)

FIGURE 4.8

The Mac Tools panel is shown here in long view with the keyboard shortcuts for each tool. Aside from system display characteristics and docking behavior, the Tools panel is identical on both Mac and Windows.

Reading the Tools panel

The Tools panel contains all 23 Flash tools, including 6 new Flash CS5 tools (see Figure 4.10 in the next section for tool icons and shortcut keys), as follows from left to right and top to bottom: Selection (arrow), Subselection, Free Transform (with Gradient Transform in the submenu), 3D Rotation (with 3D Translation in the submenu), Lasso, Pen (with Add, Delete, and Convert Anchor Points in the submenu), Text, Line, Rectangle (with other shape tools in the submenu), Pencil, Brush (with Spray Brush in submenu), Deco, Bone (with Bind in the submenu), Paint Bucket (with Ink Bottle in submenu), Eyedropper, and Eraser. The Flash View tools: The Hand and Zoom are below the drawing tools. Beneath the View tools is the Color area, with swatches for assigning Stroke color and Fill color, and buttons for Black and White and Swap Color (to reverse stroke and fill colors). The last section of the Tools panel is the Options area, where some of the available tool modifiers appear for any active tool.

Cross-Reference

I explain the application of individual tools and options in the Tools panel in the chapters related to specific production topics that make up the remainder of Part II, "Mastering the Flash Environment." ■

Using Tool options

Depending on the tool selected, the Options area may display some of the options, or properties, that control the functionality of that particular tool, whereas other controls may appear in the Properties panel or in a panel that launches separately. Of the options located in the Options area, some appear as submenus with multiple options, while others are simple buttons that toggle a property on or off. (For example, if the Lasso tool is selected, the Magic Wand option can be turned on or off by clicking a toggle button in the Options area.) If an option has more than two settings, these are generally available in a submenu.

Many of the options that appear within the Options area of the Tools panel can also be accessed from the Properties panel, from the application menu, or with keyboard shortcuts.

Customizing the Tools panel

Because the Tools panel is the most convenient place to store and access drawing tools, Adobe has provided a user-friendly interface that makes it possible to add, delete, or rearrange the tools (and icons) that appear in the Tools panel. Open the dialog box shown in Figure 4.9 by choosing Edit ➪ Customize Tools Panel (or Flash ➪ Customize Tools Panel on a Mac) from the application menu. A preview of the Tools panel (in short view) on the left side of the dialog box makes it easy to select any of the squares to add or delete the tools that are stored in each section of the panel. The interface is very flexible, making it possible to put all your tools in one square if you want to, or even add the same tool to multiple squares — unless you enjoy changing things just for the sake of changing them, the main reason to use this option is really to add new tools.

FIGURE 4.9

Use the Customize Tools Panel dialog box to add or rearrange the tools available in the Tools panel.

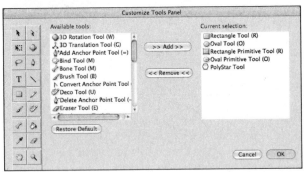

Any tool square that has more than one tool stored in it displays a small black arrow below the currently active tool to indicate that a drop-down menu is available. By default, the tool icons appear in the drop-down list in the order that they are added to the Current selection list in the Customize Tools Panel dialog box. The first tool added to the list shows up in its assigned square in the Tools panel unless one of the other tools in the same square is selected from the drop-down menu. The most recently selected tool in any square is visible until Flash is restarted or another tool is selected from the same square.

All assigned tool shortcut keys remain mapped to individual tools and can be used to activate a specific tool regardless of which square the tool is stored in. If all the tools are removed from a square, that space on the Tools panel is left blank. Thanks to the Restore Default button in the Customize Tools Panel dialog box, you can have fun moving, grouping, or even deleting tools from different tool squares with the knowledge that you can always go back to the original layout. To illustrate the steps for adding a new Flash tool and storing it in the Tools panel, I have included a brief tutorial on a custom Grid tool developed by Joey Lott.

Adding New Tools to Flash, by Joey Lott

Author's Note: Although it is beyond the scope of this book to describe the steps involved in actually scripting your own custom tools for Flash, I can tell you how to use custom tools that other developers have made. Joey Lott has generously agreed to let me include the code for one of his Flash tools on the CD-ROM. This brief tutorial is adapted from Joey's notes on how to install and use his "Grid" tool. I hope you will be able to follow these same steps to use other custom tools available from Adobe or from generous developers in the Flash community.

The first step to using a custom tool is to find the files that Flash needs to make the tool work in the authoring environment and the icon that will be visible in the Tools panel. Unless you happen to know some brainy coders, the best place to look for new custom tools is in the Flash Exchange area of Adobe's site (www.adobe.com/exchange).

The three files you will want to find and download are as follows:

- An XML file that describes the functionality of the tool and controls any "settings" that can be used to modify the final result

- A JavaScript-Flash file (.jsfl) that implements required methods for manipulating the Flash authoring tool based on parameters specified by the XML file

- A PNG file that will appear in the Tools panel as the icon for the custom tool

On the CD-ROM

I have included Grid.xml, Grid.jsfl, **and** Grid.png **on the CD-ROM in the CustomTool subfolder of the** ch04 **folder.** ■

You have to save these files in your Flash CS5 Tools folder so that the tool can be applied in the authoring environment.

- The standard directory path on Windows is

```
C:\Documents and Settings\(username)\Local Settings\Application
    Data\Adobe\Flash CS5\(language)\Configuration\Tools
```

- The standard directory path on Mac is

```
HD\Users:(username)\Library\Application Support\Adobe\Flash CS5\
    (language)\Configuration\Tools
```

After the three files for the Grid tool are saved to the Tools folder, the Grid tool is added to the list of available tools in the Customize Tools Panel dialog box.

The steps for adding the Grid tool icon to a square on the Tools panel are the same as those used to assign any tool to a specific location in the panel:

1. Open the Customize Tools Panel dialog box (Edit⇨Customize Tools Panel or Flash⇨Customize Tools Panel).

2. Select a location square on the Tools panel preview on the left side of the dialog box, select the Grid Tool from the list of Available tools, and click the Add button. (As shown in Figure 4.10, I chose to add the Grid Tool to the Line Tool square.)

3. Click OK to apply your changes and close the dialog box.

Now that the Grid tool icon has been added to the Tools panel, you will be able to select it from the square that you chose to store it in. As with the PolyStar tool, you will notice that when the Grid tool is active, an Options button appears in the Properties panel. Use this button to launch the Tool Settings dialog box (shown in Figure 4.11), where it is possible to control the number of rows and columns that you want to draw with the Grid tool.

After you choose settings for the grid and click OK to close the dialog box, you can draw a grid as easily as you would draw a rectangle with the Rectangle tool: Click the Stage and drag horizontally to create width and vertically to create height; the live preview lets you see how the grid looks before you release the mouse. You can select individual lines in the final vector grid, modify them with other drawing tools, group the lines, or convert them into a reusable symbol. This is a simple tool, but it creates perfect grids every time and saves you time and mouse miles, too!

Let's hope there will be many more useful and creative tools available that will open new possibilities for your Flash designs. You can continue to save other custom tool files to your Tools folder, and they will be added to the Available tools list in the Customize Tools Panel dialog box.

FIGURE 4.10

Any tool added to the Tools folder — by saving the relevant XML, JSFL, and PNG files there — appears in the Available tools list in the Customize Tools Panel dialog box.

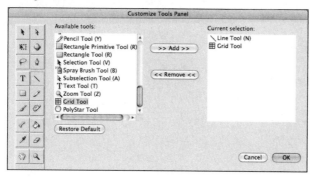

Caution

Obviously, it would be a big mistake to save a custom tool file to your Tools folder if it had the same name as an existing tool. Unless you want to overwrite existing Flash tools, make sure you're using unique names for any custom tools that you add. If you'd rather not change the name of a tool, simply add a unique number to the tool name to avoid overwriting other files with the same name. ■

FIGURE 4.11

After they have been added to the Tools panel, custom tools and options can be used as easily as other standard Flash tools.

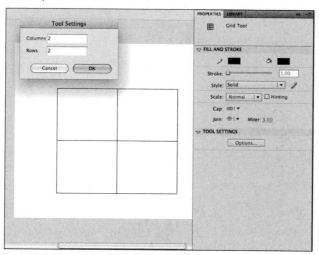

You can remove tool icons from the Tools panel at any time without actually deleting the files stored in the Tools folder, but if you decide you don't need a tool anymore, or if your Available tools list gets too cluttered, simply remove the relevant XML, JSFL, and PNG files from the Tools folder (save them somewhere else if you liked the tool, trash them if you didn't).

The Document Window

The Document window is the worktable of your Flash project. This window tells you what document (.fla) is currently active and shows you where you are working in the project. When you open or create a new Flash file, a new Document window appears on the screen. You can have multiple files open simultaneously — click to move from one Document window to another. You have the option of choosing a document type from the Start Page (discussed earlier in this chapter; shown in Figure 4.1) or from the New Document dialog box invoked by the New File command: File ➪ New (Ctrl+N/⌘+N).

Tip

If you prefer to bypass the New Document dialog box, you can create and open a basic Flash document in one step (by default this will be set to use ActionScript 3.0) by using the shortcut command Alt+Ctrl+N/ Option+⌘+N). ■

Figure 4.12 shows the New Document dialog box for Flash CS5. The dialog box includes a General tab for opening Flash documents and a Templates tab for opening Flash documents that match common Web ad sizes.

FIGURE 4.12

Use the New Document dialog box in Flash CS5 to create new documents or open template files.

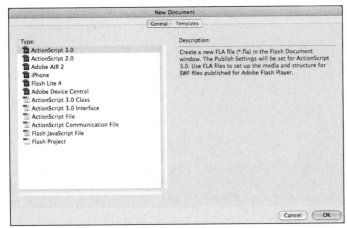

In addition to the basic Flash File (.fla) types targeting different versions of the Flash Player, the General tab includes several specialized file types which give developers more options for application development and script editing.

Controlling the Document window

Even when you choose to hide all panels (F4), the Document window remains visible; closing the window closes your Flash project. On Mac, the Document window is always free floating and can be moved anywhere on-screen by grabbing the top of the panel with your mouse or scaled by dragging any side of the panel. By default, on Windows, the Document window is maximized to fill the workspace and it cannot be scaled or moved independently, unless you first click the document Restore Down button (between the Minimize button and the Close button) in the top-right corner of the window (below the larger buttons that control the application). This "frees" the Document window from other panels in the program window so that you can move it around and scale it.

Flash CS5 optimizes screen real estate and makes it easier to work with multiple documents by automatically grouping open Document windows into the same tabbed format used for panels. As you create new documents or open existing documents during a session in Flash, they are added as sequential tabs along the top of the Document window. Click any tab to switch to a specific document, click and drag a tab to move it to a new position in the tab order, and click the small "x" icon to close a document.

Tip

If you need to see two tabbed Document windows side by side (to facilitate dragging items from one file to another or to compare two files), use the `Duplicate Window` command (Window ⇨ Duplicate Window) to make a clone of an original document. Any changes made in the cloned window also apply to the original file that is still available in the tabbed main Document window. Duplicate Document windows are indicated by a colon after the name followed by a number (a duplicate of `myFile` would be labeled `myFile:2`, then `myFile:3`, and so on), but these numbers do not affect the saved filename. To make things less confusing, you can close the tabbed version of the document and keep the free-floating clone as your working version. Take note of the shortcut keys for this command if you use it often: Alt+Ctrl+K/Option+⌘+K. ∎

The main reason you may want to alter the default placement of the Document window is to organize your panel layouts to suit a dual-monitor workstation. Although you can drastically change the size and location of the Document window, generally you will want it centered in your workspace and scaled to allow you to comfortably work with objects on the Stage. Figure 4.13 shows the Document window on Mac as it appears with default settings and with the Document Properties dialog box open.

New Feature

The Metadata fields that were in the Document Properties dialog box in Flash CS3 have been replaced with a new, more comprehensive metadata dialog box in Flash CS5. Available in Publish Settings — select the Flash category and then click the File Info button in the SWF Settings section. Title and description information entered in Publish Settings will be embedded in the published SWF file as metadata that will help search engines to find and catalog your Flash content. Unfortunately, this information is not automatically carried over to the HTML file published from Flash. ∎

FIGURE 4.13

The Document window as it appears with the Document Settings dialog box open

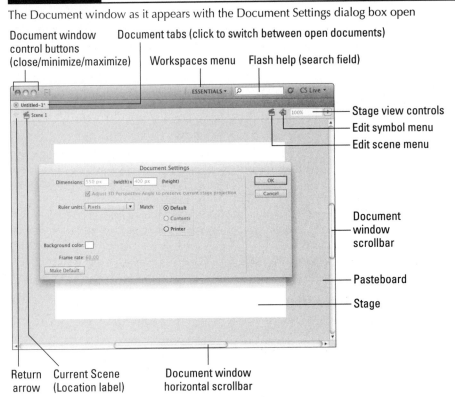

Document window control buttons (close/minimize/maximize)

Document tabs (click to switch between open documents)

Workspaces menu

Flash help (search field)

Stage view controls

Edit symbol menu

Edit scene menu

Document window scrollbar

Pasteboard

Stage

Return arrow

Current Scene (Location label)

Document window horizontal scrollbar

The default document settings of Flash automatically create new documents with a size of 550 x 400 pixels, a white background color, and a frame rate of 24. All these attributes are displayed in the Properties panel and can be changed at any time. Clicking the Edit button in the Properties section of the Properties panel launches the Document Properties dialog box, where you can enter a custom size or use the Match options to automatically create a document that fits your current printer page settings (Printer), include all the elements you have placed into your document (Contents), or restore the default size setting (Default).

Tip

If you want to change the default settings for all new documents, open the Document Properties panel by clicking the Edit button on the Properties panel or choosing Modify ➪ Document (Ctrl+J/⌘+J) from the application menu. After you have chosen the attributes you would like to assign to new documents, click the Make Default button at the bottom of the panel. ■

Reading the Document window

The white Stage area is the central part of the Document window that becomes the visible area or "screen" of a published Flash movie (.swf). As I noted earlier, you can change the color and size of this "background" at any time, but it is best to establish these settings before you begin creating other elements.

The light gray work area (also called the *Pasteboard*) that frames the Stage enables you to place elements into your project while keeping them out of the visible area. This feature is useful if you want to show only part of an element or animate it as it moves onto the Stage. A good example of the utility of the Pasteboard feature can be seen in some cartoons in which very large background artwork hangs off the Stage (or View area) until it's called upon or tweened through to create the effect of a camera pan. The Stage and the Pasteboard are always available in the Document window (unless you toggle the Pasteboard off in the View menu). The Essentials panel layout also includes the Timeline docked below the Pasteboard because this is generally the most convenient place to use it, along with the new Motion Editor.

Tip

You can strip the Timeline panel out of the Document window and leave it free floating, or you can redock it to the top or bottom of the Pasteboard. You can also dock the Timeline to either side of the Pasteboard, but this is usually an awkward view. ■

The narrow bar located above the Stage and Pasteboard is referred to as the Edit bar. This bar contains icons and a value box that help you navigate within a document.

Stage view control

Although the scale value box is at the end of the bar, I discuss it first because it can be useful even when you first begin putting artwork on the Stage. This value box, called the Stage View control, shows you the current scale of the Stage area and enables you to type new percentages or select a preset value from a submenu.

Note

The view percentages are based on the pixel dimensions of your project, as defined in Document properties, and your screen resolution. For example, if your project size is 500 x 400 pixels and your screen resolution is 1024 x 768, then the Stage area would occupy almost 50 percent of your screen if view scale was set to 100 percent (Ctrl+1/⌘+1). ■

The first three settings in the View submenu list are Fit in Window, Show Frame (Ctrl+2/ ⌘+2), and Show All (Ctrl+3/⌘+3); these settings automatically scale your Stage view to fit your current Document window size in various ways:

- Fit in Window scales the Stage view to fill the current Document window without cropping the visible area.

- Show Frame scales the Stage view to fill the current Document window with a narrow border of Pasteboard visible on all sides.

- Show All sets the Stage view to a scale that includes any elements you have placed on the Pasteboard outside the Stage. You can find these same view options from the application menu (View ➪ Magnification).

There are two additional tools available in the Tools panel (see Figure 4.9 earlier in the chapter), which also control your view of the Stage and Pasteboard within the Document window:

The Hand tool (H) allows you to move the Stage area within the Document window by "grabbing" it (clicking and dragging). Double-clicking the Hand icon in the Tools panel quickly gives you the same Stage view as choosing the menu item Show Frame.

Tip

To toggle the Hand tool on while using any other tool, without interrupting your selection, hold down the spacebar. ■

The Zoom tool, or magnifier (M), does just what the name implies: It adjusts the scale of your Stage view. The available magnification range is between 8 percent and 2,000 percent. However, you can apply this handy tool in a few ways. With the Zoom tool active, clicking consecutively on the Stage pulls in closer to artwork with the *Enlarge* option (Ctrl+[+]/⌘+[+]), or moves farther away with the *Reduce* option (Ctrl+[−]/⌘+[−] key). Each click adjusts the Stage view magnification by half. Pressing the Option or Alt key as you click toggles the Zoom tool between Enlarge and Reduce. Double-clicking the Zoom tool icon in the Tools panel always scales the Stage view to 100 percent (Ctrl+1/⌘+1). One last way of applying the Zoom tool while it is active in the Tools panel is to drag a selection box around the area that you want to fill the Document window. Flash scales the Stage view to the highest magnification (up to 2,000 percent), which fills the Document window with the selected area.

Edit options

Now back to the other icons on the Edit bar. The location label on the top-left edge of the window shows you the current scene and what part of the project you are editing. The sequence of labels that appear in this area is sometimes referred to as *breadcrumbs* because these labels show the steps, or the path, leading back to the Main Timeline from the location you're editing. When in Edit mode, you can use these sequential labels to step your way back to the Main Timeline of the current scene, or click the arrow in front of the labels to return to the Main Timeline of the first scene in your project. To the right is the Edit Scene icon, and at the far right is the Edit Symbols icon. Click these icons to access menus of scenes or symbols in the current document that can be opened and edited within the Document window.

Using scenes

The Scene panel (Shift+F2 or Window ➪ Other panels ➪ Scene) enables you to add, name, and sequence scenes. By default, when your Flash movie (.swf) is published, the scenes play in the order in which they are listed, as shown in Figure 4.14. Scenes can help to organize a Flash project into logical, manageable parts. However, with the increasingly robust power of ActionScript, there's been a trend among many developers to move away from scene-based architecture. Using individual Flash movies instead of scenes to organize sections of a project results in files that download more efficiently and that are easier to edit due to their modular organization. It's like the difference between one huge ball of all-purpose twine that's the size of a house and a large drawer filled with manageable spools, sorted neatly according to color and weight.

Dividing logical project parts into separate documents also facilitates efficiency in team environments, where developers can be working on different pieces of a project simultaneously. Scenes can still be useful for organizing certain types of projects, such as simple presentations without a lot of graphics, or for animators who prefer to organize a cartoon in one file before handing it off for integration into a larger site structure.

Adding named anchor keyframes is another useful option for linear Flash presentations. These enable Forward and Back buttons in a Web browser to jump from frame to frame or scene to scene to navigate a Flash movie.

FIGURE 4.14

The Scene panel showing document scenes in the order they will play back by default

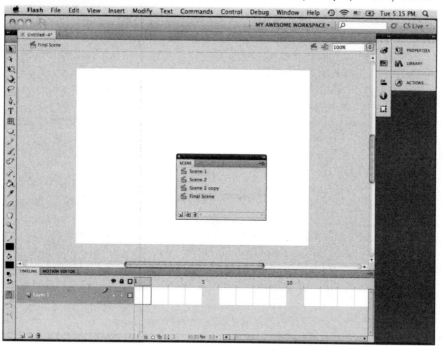

Tip

You turn the option of making the first keyframe in a new scene a named anchor keyframe on or off in the Timeline section of the General Preferences panel (Ctrl+U/⌘+U). ∎

Caution

Named anchors work well on Windows browsers but almost always fail on Mac browsers, so this is not a reliable option for Web navigation within a Flash movie if you expect some visitors to your site to be using Mac systems. ∎

To navigate and modify scenes from within the Document window:

- Click the Edit Scene button on the Edit bar and then choose the desired scene from the submenu.

- Navigate to a specific scene from the application menu with the View ➪ Go To command.

- To add a new scene, either use the Scene panel's Add button — indicated by the page icon — or, from the Insert menu, use Insert ➪ Scene. New scenes continue in the same auto-numbering sequence started with Scene 1. Thus, even if you delete Scene 2, the next added scene will be named Scene 3.

- Use the Duplicate button on the Scene panel to make a copy of a scene, including all content on the scene's Timeline.

- To delete a scene, use the Scene panel's Delete button — indicated by the trash can icon. (To bypass the alert asking if you want to delete the scene, use Ctrl+click/ ⌘+click.)

- To rename a scene, simply double-click the scene name within the Scene panel and type a new name. Using numbers in scene names does not affect playback order; the scenes play from the top to the bottom of the list.

- To rearrange scene order, simply click and drag a scene to alter its position in the Scene panel list. You can use actions to direct the movie to access scenes outside the default linear order. For more about actions, refer to Chapter 17, "Understanding Actions and Event Handlers."

Caution

Although scenes give you the visual impression of having a whole new timeline to work on, they are really continuations of the Main Timeline that begins in the first scene of your document. If you're using any actions to control your movie playback, it's important to avoid duplicate naming on frame labels or named anchors. Thus, even if it seems logical, it isn't a good idea to label the beginning of each new scene "intro" because you won't be able to differentiate these labels as easily for targeting with ActionScript. ∎

Using Document window menu options

There are several options available from the application menu that control display or editing in the Document window. These can be helpful when you're creating or placing elements on the Stage. All of these can be accessed from View on the application menu (notice the shortcut key combinations listed after most commands). The basic functions of these various commands are as follows:

- **Goto:** Leads to a submenu of scenes in the current movie, including four handy shortcuts to the First, Previous, Next, and Last scenes. This menu is also available from the Edit scene icon on the Edit bar in the Document window.

- **Zoom In:** Increases the scale of the Stage view by 50 percent.

- **Zoom Out:** Decreases the scale of the Stage view by 50 percent.

- **Magnification:** Leads to the same view options that are available in the Stage View Control on the top right of the Document window. Note that three of these options also have corresponding keyboard shortcuts.

- **Preview Mode:** Leads to a menu of various settings for rendering and displaying content in the authoring environment:

  - **Outlines:** Simplifies the view of elements on the Stage by showing all shapes as outlines and all lines as thin lines. This option is helpful when reshaping graphic elements. It also speeds up the display of complex scenes and can assist in getting the general timing and sense of a movie. It is a global equivalent of the outline options available in the Timeline window for layers and frames.

  - **Fast:** Turns off both anti-aliasing and dithering to speed up the display. The default is *off*, to create the most accurate screen image, and it is only recommended that you turn this option *on* if you need to reduce demand on your processor.

  - **Antialias:** Dithers the edges of shapes and lines so that they look smoother on-screen. It can also slow the display, but this is only an issue with older video cards. This is actually a toggle in opposition with the Fast command: Turn this On and Fast goes Off.

  - **Antialias Text:** As with Antialias, this is also a toggle in opposition to the Fast command. It smoothes the edges of text *only* and is most noticeable on large font sizes. You can have only one Antialias option on at a time, so you can make a choice between smoothing text or smoothing shapes, depending on what content you're working with.

  - **Full:** Use this option for the most "finished" or high-definition preview. If you are working on intensive animation, it may slow down rendering of the display in the authoring environment.

- **Pasteboard:** Makes the light gray area that surrounds the Stage available for use. When the Pasteboard is visible, your Stage area appears centered in the Document window when you apply Show Frame or Show All. If the Pasteboard has been turned off in the View menu, then the Stage aligns to the top left of the Document window.

Caution

Items that are selected and offstage when View ⇨ Pasteboard is toggled off can still be deleted, even if they are not visible. So it's best if you don't have anything selected when you choose to hide the Pasteboard. ■

- **Rulers:** Toggles the reference Rulers (which appear at the top and left edges of the work area) on or off — use Modify ⇨ Document (Ctrl+J/⌘+J) to change units of measurement. Rulers are a helpful reference for placing guides to align elements in a layout.

- **Grid:** Toggles visibility of the background Stage grid on or off. This grid does not export with the final Flash movie (.swf), but it does serve as an authoring reference. You can control the appearance of the Grid and the precision of grid snapping by adjusting the settings in the dialog box invoked with the Edit Grid command. When the Snap to grid option is active, it works even if the Grid is not visible. Edited Grid settings can be saved as the default by clicking the Save Default button, which enables you to have these settings as presets for all subsequent Flash movies.

Note

The default Grid size of 18 pixels is equal to 0.25 inch. Grid units can be changed by entering the appropriate abbreviation for other units of measurement (for example: 25 pt, 0.5", 0.5 in, 2 cm, and so on) in the Grid Spacing entry boxes. Although the specified units will be applied to the grid, they will be translated into the current unit of measurement for the Ruler. Thus, if the Ruler is set to pixels, and the Grid units are changed to 0.5 in, then, on reopening the Grid dialog box, the Grid units will be displayed as 36 pix (because pixels are allocated at 72 pix = 1"). Changing Ruler units via Modify ➪ Document also changes Grid units. ■

- **Guides:** When rulers are turned on, you can drag horizontal or vertical guides onto the Stage from respective rulers. These four commands control the parameters of these guides:

  - **Show Guides:** This is a simple toggle to either show or hide guides that you have dragged out from the rulers.

  - **Lock Guides:** This is a toggle that either locks or unlocks all current guides. This is useful to prevent guides from accidentally being moved after you have placed them.

  - **Edit Guides:** This command opens the Guides dialog box, where guide color and guide-specific snap accuracy can be adjusted. Also included are check boxes for the other three guide commands: Show Guides, Snap to Guides, and Lock Guides. This enables you to establish guide settings and then click the Save Default button to have these settings as presets for all subsequent Flash movies. To delete all guides from the Stage, press the Clear All button.

  - **Clear All:** The Clear All command gets rid of all visible guides in the current document. It does the same thing as the Clear All button in the Edit Guides dialog box.

- **Snapping:** Leads to a menu of various options for controlling snapping behavior in the authoring environment.

Note

When Snap to Pixels is turned on, a 1-pixel grid appears when the Stage view is magnified to 400 percent or higher. This grid is independent of the Show Grid command. ■

- **Hide Edges:** Hides selection patterns so that you can edit items without the visual noise of the selection pixel "highlight." This applies only to currently selected items and allows a clean view without having to lose your selection. Most useful for seeing colors or fine lines that may appear visually distorted by the selection pattern.

- **Show Shape Hints:** This toggles shape hints to make them visible or invisible. It does not disable shape hinting. Shape hints are used when tweening shapes.

Cross-Reference

For more about Shape tweens (or shape morphing) refer to Chapter 11, "Timeline Animation and the Motion Editor." ■

- **Show Tab Order:** This is a toggle to turn on or off numbers that will mark the tab order set in the Accessibility panel for elements in the authoring environment.

Working with Flash templates

The library of predefined Flash documents available in the Templates tab of the New Document dialog box (or in the Create from Template list of the Start Page) has been modified since Flash CS3. The templates now consist of only a series of Flash documents sized to match common Web ad aspect ratios. The more comprehensive list of templates available in Flash CS3 has not been carried over to CS5.

To work with a Flash template, open it as you would any other Flash document. You can then add your own content to the Stage or modify the Timeline and save the finished document with a new name.

You can also create your own reusable template from any Flash document by choosing File ➪ Save As Template. Before the template is saved, you are given options for naming and assigning a category and description, making it easy to manage a whole library of custom templates. The preview visible for each template is actually just the content on the first frame of the template document. In some cases, this does not provide much visual information for how the template might be used. If you use templates often or if you create your own templates, you may find it helpful to modify the default previews to make them more informative.

Tip

Although each template type has a different file structure and may contain different content, the preview for any template will include only the visible content in the Stage area on the first frame of the template file. Changing the content in the first frame of a template file also changes the preview for that template. ■

Tip

The standard directory path for the Templates folder on Windows is

```
C:\Program Files\Adobe\Flash CS5\(language)\Configuration\Templates
```

The standard directory path on Mac is

```
HD/Applications/Adobe Flash CS5/(language)/Configuration/Templates ■
```

Web Resource

If you are interested in creating custom template previews, visit www.flashsupport.com/archive **to find Bill Perry's tutorial and example files from Flash MX 2004 Bible (Wiley, 2004). ■**

The Timeline Window

The Timeline is like nothing you will find in your analog studio, unless you have a time machine that enables you to move forward and backward in time and up and down between dimensions. This may seem like a rather far-fetched analogy, but understanding the behavior and purpose of a timeline is often the most foreign new concept to grasp if you have not worked in other time-based applications (such as Macromedia Director). A clear understanding of timelines is critical to production in Flash. Even if you know how to use all of your other tools, not knowing the Timeline makes working in Flash like trying to work in a studio with no light.

Note

Flash MX Professional 2004 introduced an alternative to the Timeline authoring structure with form-based templates for application authoring. For more information on this feature, search Flash Help for "Slide screens and form screens." ■

The Timeline window is really composed of two parts: the Layer section, where content is "stacked" in-depth, and the Timeline/Frames section, where content is planned out in frames along the duration of your movie, like on a strip of motion picture film. In the Layer section, you can label or organize your "stacks" of frame rows. You can also lock or hide individual layers or just convert their display to colored outlines on the Stage while you are editing. In the Timeline section you can control where and for how long content is visible and how it changes over time to animate when the movie plays back. You can also add actions to control how the playhead moves through the Timeline, making it start and stop or jump to a specific frame.

Cross-Reference

You can find more on controlling the timeline for specific animation techniques in Chapter 10. Actions are introduced in Part V, "Adding Basic Interactivity to Flash Movies." ■

Controlling the Timeline window

On both Mac and Windows, the most common position for the Timeline in Flash CS5 is docked below the Document window. If you don't see the Timeline when you open Flash, go to Window ➪ Timeline (Ctrl+Alt+T/⌘+Option+T) to open it on-screen.

Tip

Double-clicking the Timeline tab expands or collapses it faster than using the application menu to open and close it completely. This feature also makes it easy to collapse the Timeline window so that it doesn't take up screen space, while still leaving it available to expand again when you need it. ■

You can always adjust the position, size, and shape of the Timeline to suit your workflow. You can dock the Timeline to any edge of the Document window, or group it with other panels. You can also move it anywhere as a floating window, even exile it to a second monitor — leaving the Document window all for the Stage and Pasteboard:

- Move the Timeline by clicking and dragging the title bar at the top of the window. If the Timeline is docked, click the Timeline name tab and drag to undock the Timeline and reposition it.

- If it's undocked, resize the Timeline by dragging any edge. If it's docked, drag the bar at the top of the Timeline that separates the layers from the Stage area, either up or down.

- To resize the layer area for name and icon controls (to accommodate longer layer names or to apportion more of the view to frames), click and drag the bar that separates the layer name and icon controls from the Timeline frame area.

Using the Timeline Controller toolbar

The Controller (Window ⇨ Toolbars ⇨ Controller) is a small bar of buttons that provides basic control of the playhead. Access to the Controller can be helpful if you need to pan back and forth along an extended section of the Timeline. You can keep it on-screen as a floating bar or dock it anywhere along the top or bottom of the Document window. Some developers prefer using the Controller to using shortcut keys for moving the playhead. Along with the commands available on the Controller bar, the application Control menu also lists some more advanced options, which I discuss in following chapters as they relate to animation and actions.

Caution

Playback speed within the document (.fla) is not as accurate as it is in the movie file (.swf), so the Controller is not intended as a replacement for the Test Movie command (Control ⇨ Test Movie or Ctrl+Enter/⌘+Return). ■

As you can see in Figure 4.15, the buttons on the Controller will be familiar to anyone who has used a remote control. The only special function to note is that the Play button toggles to start and stop; you don't have to use the Stop button.

Tip

Using shortcut keys is often the preferred way to move along the Timeline. On both Windows and Mac, pressing Enter/Return works as a toggle to start and stop the playhead. If you prefer to move along the Timeline frame by frame, pressing the period key (.) moves forward one frame and pressing the comma (,) moves back one frame. A more intuitive way to remember these keys is to look for the less than (<) and greater than (>) symbols and to think of them as arrows that move forward and backward. ■

Reading the Timeline

The Timeline graphically orders Flash content across two dimensions — time and depth — and provides you with some options for how this content is displayed on the Stage and within frames on the Timeline.

Visual display of time

The order of time is displayed by the sequence of frames arranged horizontally, from left to right, as they appear within the duration of your project. Thus, if your movie is set to 20 frames per second, frame 40 occurs at the 2-second point of your animation.

FIGURE 4.15

The Controller features familiar buttons that are used to control movement of the playhead

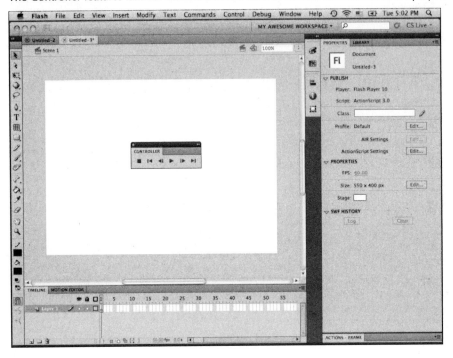

Note

Although they say that time and space are without limits, the Flash authoring environment supports about 32,000 frames, and the .swf format officially supports only around 16,000, which is actually so long that you might never find your way from one end of the Timeline to the other. Organizing your work with scenes and Movie clips, or even in multiple documents, should save you from ever having to use a Timeline even a tenth of this length. ■

Web Resource

For more details on the limits of Flash, refer to the Adobe Tech Note Index:

www.adobe.com/cfusion/knowledgebase/index.cfm?id=tn_14437 ■

You can insert, delete, copy, paste, and reorder frames as well as convert them to various specific frame types that control how elements animate. Current frame settings display in the Properties panel when a frame is selected, and you can also add/change a frame name or tween type here. The main controls for editing frames are found in the contextual menu (right-click on Windows or Control+click on Mac) or from the Timeline submenus under Edit, Insert, and Modify in the application menu.

Tip

As you work with frames, you'll find shortcut keys invaluable. These shortcut keys are listed in the application menu following most commands. ■

Visual display of depth

The Timeline layers enable you to separate content onto individual "transparent" work surfaces within the Document window. This enables you to animate or edit elements individually even if they occupy the same Timeline (or frame) space as other elements in the document. These layers are arranged vertically, holding content that stacks in the Document window from bottom to top. They enable you to organize content, actions, comments, labels, and sounds so that you can quickly find the parts of the project that you want to edit.

Tip

Layer folders are a huge help to organizing multilayered documents. With layers moved inside a folder, they can be opened up for editing or hidden away (collapsed) to reduce the number of layers you have to navigate. ■

You can insert, delete, move, or rename layers and folders, as well as adjust how content is displayed in the editing environment. Items placed on layers higher in the layer stack can visually obscure other items in layers beneath them, without otherwise affecting each other. With the layer control icons shown at the top of the layer stack, you can set layer visibility (the Eye icon), editability (the Lock icon), and the display mode (the Square icon) to regular or outline only. Note, however, that these settings are visible within the editing environment only and do not affect the appearance of the final movie (.swf).

Timeline window features

Figure 4.16 shows the Timeline window, as it appears when it is undocked or floating. The various controls of the window interface are labeled here, but I defer detailed explanations of some of these controls to the drawing and animation chapters where I show you how they are applied.

As shown in Figure 4.17, the principal features and controls of the Timeline are

Window features

- **Timeline (panel tab):** More than one Timeline can be opened and displayed in the Timeline panel at the same time. Individual Timeline tabs can be closed by clicking the "x" icon on the tabs, or the entire Timeline window can be minimized or closed by using the controls on the top-right corner of the Timeline panel.

- **Timeline header:** The Timeline header is the ruler that shows frame numbers and measures the time of the Timeline — each tick is one frame.

- **Playhead or Current frame indicator:** The red rectangle with a line extending down through all layers is the playhead. The playhead indicates the current frame. Drag it left or right along the Timeline to move from one area of the Timeline to another. Push it beyond the visible area to force-scroll the Timeline. You can also drag the playhead at a consistent rate for a preview of your animation; this is called *scrubbing* the Timeline.

FIGURE 4.16

The Timeline with callouts showing the principal features and control elements

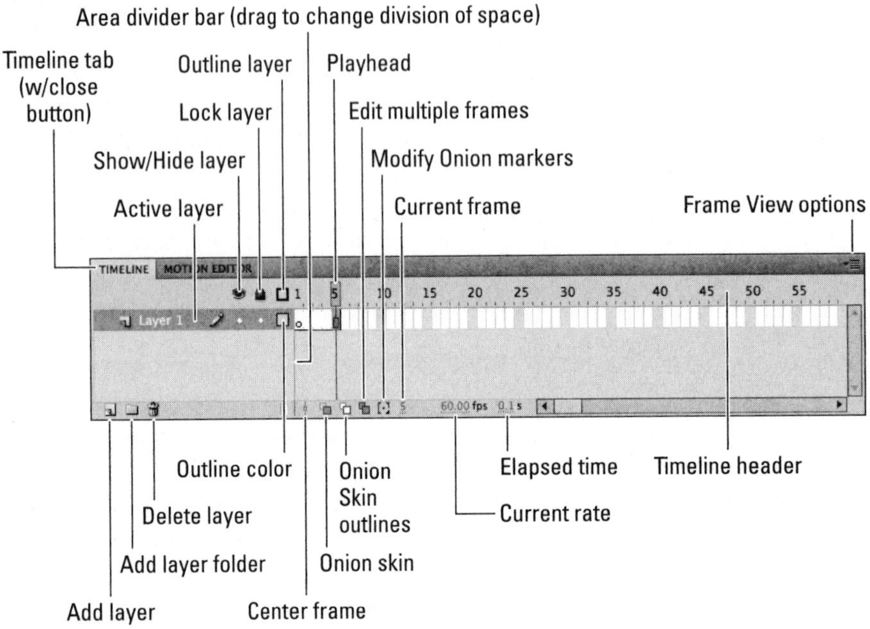

Tip

On Windows, if you have a mouse with a scroll wheel, you can scroll up and down through the layers; or by holding down the Shift key while you scroll, you can move the playhead forward and backward along the Timeline. If all of your layers (or layer folders) are already visible in the Timeline window, then the scroll wheel just scrolls you forward and backward along the Timeline without moving the playhead. ■

Layer controls

- **Active layer icon:** To make a layer active, either click the layer's name or select a frame or group of frames. The pencil icon appears, indicating that the layer is now active. That's in addition to this more obvious clue: The layer bar of the active layer is shaded darker than the inactive layer bars. Although you can select multiple layers or content on multiple layers, only one layer will be marked as active at a time. For more about frame selection and editing behaviors, see the section which follows this one.

- **Show/Hide layer toggle:** Click the dot beneath the eye icon to hide the contents of a layer from view on the Stage. When the layer is hidden, a red X appears over the dot. To return the layer to visibility, click the X. To hide or show all layers at once, simply click on the eye icon directly.

Caution

Hidden layers do export, and any content on the Stage within a hidden layer becomes visible upon export. Even if the content is offstage and not visible, it may add considerably to the file size when a Flash movie (.swf) is published, so you should save your document (.fla) and then delete these layers or convert them to guide layers before your final export. ■

- **Lock/Unlock layer toggle:** This toggle locks or unlocks the layer to either prevent or enable further editing. When the layer is locked, a padlock icon appears over the dot. To lock/unlock all layers at once, click directly on the lock icon.

- **Outline Layer toggle:** This toggles the colored layer outlines on or off. When on, the filled square icon changes into an outline, and all elements in that layer appear as colored outlines in the Document window. The outline color for the layer can be changed with the Outline Color control of the Layer Properties dialog box, which can be accessed by double-clicking the square Outline color icons in the layer stack or by choosing Modify ⇨ Timeline ⇨ Layer Properties from the application menu.

- **Frame View options:** This button, at the far-right end of the Timeline, accesses the Frame View options menu, which affords many options for the manner in which both the Timeline header and the frames are displayed.

- **Add layer:** Simply click this button to add a new layer above the currently active layer. By default, layers are given sequential numeric names. Double-click the layer name in the Layer bar to change the name. Click and drag any part of the Layer bar to move it to a new position in the stack, or drag it on top of a folder layer to place it inside the folder.

- **Add Layer folder:** This button enables you to create folders for storing groups of layers. New folders are automatically placed above the currently selected layer and labeled in the same number sequence as layers. They can be renamed or moved in the same way as other layers.

- **Delete layer:** This button deletes the currently active layer, regardless of whether it is locked. Flash always retains one layer in the Timeline, so if you have only one layer in your document, you can't delete it unless you add another layer to the Timeline.

Tip

Because using the Delete key on your keyboard does not remove an active layer or folder, but rather removes all the content from those frames, it can be helpful to get in the habit of right-clicking (Windows) or Control+clicking (Mac) a layer that you want to remove and choosing Delete from the contextual menu. You can always click the trash icon to dump a selected layer or folder, but this adds a few more mouse miles. ■

Frame controls

- **Center frame:** Click this button to shift the Timeline so that the current frame is centered in the visible area of the Timeline.

- **Onion skin:** This enables you to see several frames of animation simultaneously.

- **Onion Skin outlines:** This enables you to see the outlines of several frames of animation simultaneously.

- **Edit Multiple frames:** In general, onion skinning permits you to edit the current frame only. Click this button to make each frame between the onion skin markers editable.

- **Modify Onion markers:** Click this button to open the Modify Onion Markers popup. In addition to making manual adjustments, you can use the options to control the behavior and range of onion skinning.

Cross-Reference
Onion skinning is further described in Chapter 10, "Timeline Animation and the Motion Editor." ■

Timeline Status displays

- **Current frame:** This indicates the number of the current frame.

- **Current rate:** This indicates the frame rate of the movie, measured in frames, or frames per second (fps). The program default of 12 fps is usually a good starting point. Ideally, you should do some testing in the final playback environment before deciding on an optimal frame rate. You can double-click the Frame Rate Indicator to invoke the Document Properties dialog box (Modify ➪ Document or Ctrl+J/⌘+J) or set the frame rate directly in the Properties panel.

FIGURE 4.17

Flash Timeline conventions for naming and display of various frame and layer types

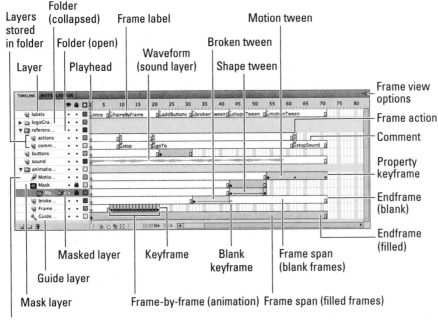

Note

The fps setting is not a constant or absolute; it really means "maximum frame rate." The actual frame rate is dependent upon a number of variables, including download speed, processor speed, and machine resources; these are variables over which you have no control. However, another factor, over which you do have control, is the intensity of the animation: Complex movement with multiple elements or many layers of transparency is more processor intensive than simple movement. Previewing real-world playback speed at different frame rates — on various machines — early on in your development process is very important. ■

- **Elapsed time:** This indicates the total movie time, measured in seconds (or tenths of a second), which will elapse from frame 1 to the current frame — provided that the movie is played back at the optimal speed.

Editing frames and layers

After you learn to recognize the visual conventions of the Timeline and how it displays different types of frames, you will be able to learn a lot about what is happening in an animation just by reading the Timeline. Figure 4.17 illustrates the Flash conventions for frame and layer display.

The Timeline features noted in Figure 4.18 are defined as follows:

- **Keyframe:** A keyframe is any frame in which the contents of the frame may differ from the contents of either the previous or subsequent frames. Filled (black) circles on the Timeline mark keyframes with content.

- **Blank keyframe:** A keyframe that does not contain any content has the same behavior as any keyframe, but it is marked by an empty (white) circle on the Timeline.

- **Property keyframe:** Property keyframes are unique to motion tween layers. They mark frames within a tween span where a property change is made. Property keyframes are auto-inserted when you make modifications to a target object in a motion tween. Property keyframes are represented by filled (black) diamonds on the Timeline.

- **Frame span:** Frame spans are the sections from a keyframe to an endframe (up to, but not including, the next keyframe to the right). Note that these spans can be selected by double-clicking, and dragged as a whole to a different location.

  - **Filled frame(s):** The intermediate frames in a span, following to the right of a keyframe (with content), are shaded gray.

  - **Empty frame(s):** The intermediate frames in a span, following to the right of a blank keyframe, are white. A black line also outlines the entire span.

  - **Endframe:** The final frame of a span, marked with a small white rectangle and a vertical line to the right of the rectangle.

- **Frame-by-Frame animation:** Frame-by-frame animation is animation composed entirely of keyframes. In a frame-by-frame animation, the content on every frame is changed manually (rather than tweened).

- **Tweened animation:** Tweened animation is movement or change in an element that Flash interpolates over a range of frames that extends from an initial keyframe. An arrow stretching across a colored frame span designates a shape tween or a classic motion tween. There are three types of tweens in Flash:

  - **Object-based motion tweens:** Motion tweens are indicated by a blue tint (without a black arrow) and can be applied only to symbols. Object-based motion tweens do not require an end keyframe.

  - **Classic motion tweens:** Motion tweens are indicated by a blue tint (with a black arrow) and can be applied only to symbols. Classic motion tweens require an end keyframe.

  - **Shape tweens:** Shape tweens are indicated by a green tint (with a black arrow) and can be applied only to primitive (nongrouped) shapes. Shape tweens require an end keyframe.

Note

A dashed line replaces the normal tween arrow for classic motion tweens and shape tweens if a tween is broken or missing an element required for the tween to render properly. The best fix for this is to remove the tween, check the contents of the beginning and ending keyframe to ensure that they are ready to tween, and then reapply the tween to the beginning keyframe. ■

Cross-Reference

For more coverage on making frame-by-frame animation and using tweens and motion presets refer to Chapter 10, "Timeline Animation and the Motion Editor." ■

- **Layer folder:** These folders are used to organize other layers, and they can be named and repositioned in the layer stack the same way as layers can. Layer folders do not have individual frame settings and thus show up in the Timeline display as a continuous gray bar. To expand (open) or collapse (close) folders, click the arrow toggle at the left of the folder name or use the contextual menu. Note that dragging a folder inside another folder creates subfolders.

- **Mask layer:** A mask layer is a layer that is used to selectively obscure the masked layers beneath it.

- **Guide layer:** A guide layer serves to hold content for reference only. Any elements on a guide layer are visible in the authoring environment but are not included with the final published SWF file.

Cross-Reference

For more about mask layers and guide layers, refer to Chapter 11, "Applying Filters, Blends, Guides, and Masks." ■

- **Frame Label:** Labels are used to give frames meaningful names, instead of using frame numbers. The advantage of this is that named keyframes can be moved without breaking ActionScript calls assigned to them. Upon export, labels are included as part of the .swf. Use the field in the Properties panel to add a label to a selected frame. Press Enter/Return after typing a frame label or comment to ensure that the label takes.

- **Comment:** Comments are special labels, preceded by a double-slash (*//*). Comments do not export, so you can be as descriptive as you need to be without adding to the .swf size. However, you won't be able to read long comments unless you leave a lot of space between keyframes. Add comments in the Properties panel the same way as you add labels; just be sure that your text is preceded by two forward-slash characters.

Note

The Properties panel includes a menu for selecting a frame text type. After you type into the Frame text field, you can select from three options in the Type menu: Name, Comment, or Anchor. Note: A frame "name" is generally referred to as a label. ∎

- **Waveform:** This squiggly blue line in the sound layer is the waveform of a placed sound. This visual reference for your sound makes it easier to synchronize animated elements to a soundtrack.
- **Frame actions:** The small *a*s in frames 10, 20, and 58 of the actions layer designate the presence of frame actions.

On the CD-ROM

If you want to see how the various layer and frame types look in the authoring environment and what happens when you publish the file, open `framesAndLayers.fla` (the Timeline shown in Figure 4.18) from the `ch04` folder on the CD-ROM. ∎

Frame specifics

The Timeline might look a bit chaotic or confusing at first, but there are a lot of cues to help you keep track of the content of your file. Empty keyframes are marked with an empty circle (white dot), the last frame of a span is marked with the empty bar icon, and keyframes with content are marked with a filled circle (black dot).

Flash MX 2004 introduced the option of using either Flash 4 or Flash 5 frame-selection behavior. In Flash 4, individual frames could be selected just by clicking them, even if they were part of a *span* (a series of frames following a keyframe). With Flash 5, span-based selection was introduced as the default behavior — all the frames in a span would be selected just by clicking one frame. Since Flash MX, the default has gone back to Flash 4 selection style, but double-clicking a frame selects a span. For the option of going back to the Flash 5 selection style, go to Edit ⇨ Preferences (or Flash ⇨ Preferences on OS X) and in the General section, under Timeline Options, select the Span-based selection check box.

Tip

Although double-clicking a frame in the default selection style selects a span of frames, if the span is moved, it automatically extends along the Timeline until it meets another keyframe. This can be helpful or annoying depending on what you are trying to accomplish. With Span-based selection behavior enabled, when you relocate a span, it does not auto-extend and the original span length is preserved. ∎

So that you can better understand the various frame-editing options available, I have listed them here with notes on the ways you can accomplish your intended result. Some of the methods differ, depending on whether you have enabled Span-based selection as described previously. For users of previous versions of Flash, this may take a little getting used to. For new users, deciding on a preference will be a matter of testing out both selection-style options. The default methods are listed here first, followed by the methods that differ when Span-based selection is turned on.

The default Flash CS5 selection methods are as follows:

- **Selecting frames:** The methods for selecting single frames and spans of frames have not changed since Flash 8.

  - **Frame spans:** To select a span of frames extending between two keyframes, double-click anywhere between the keyframes.

  - **Single frames:** To select a single frame within a span, or a keyframe outside of a span, simply click to select it.

Note

Motion tween layers behave differently than standard layers for shape tweens or classic motion tween spans. To select individual frames within a span on a motion tween layer, you must Ctrl+click/⌘+click. Single-clicking a frame anywhere in the span selects the whole span as a single object. ∎

  - **Multiple frames or spans:** To select multiple frames along the Timeline (within a span or independent of a span), click and drag in any direction until you have selected all the frames you want to include in the selection. You can also use Shift+click to add to a selection of frames.

Note

The difference between selecting a frame by dragging over it and moving a frame by selecting it and then dragging can be hard to differentiate. At first, you may find yourself moving frames that you only wanted to select. The trick is to be sure that you don't release the mouse after you click a frame before you drag to select other frames. Conversely, if your intention is to move a frame or a series of frames, you have to click and release the mouse to select them first and then click again and drag to move them. ∎

  - **Moving frames:** Select the frame(s) that need to be moved and then drag them to the new location.

  - **Extending the duration of a span on a normal layer:** There are two ways to change the duration of a span, which is the same result as inserting frames (F5) or removing frames (Shift+F5) after a keyframe. To change where a span begins, select the keyframe and then drag the keyframe to the position where you want the span to begin. To change where a span ends, Ctrl+click/⌘+click the endframe and drag it to where you want the span to end, or select a blank frame beyond the endframe where you want the span to end and insert a frame (F5). This automatically extends the span and moves the endframe to the frame you have selected.

- **Extending the duration of a span on a motion tween layer:** To extend the animation and shift the property keyframes, simply click and drag the end of the tween span. To extend the tween without moving the existing property keyframes, hold down the Shift key while dragging the end of the tween span.

Note

If you click and drag any frame or endframe in a standard layer without pressing the Ctrl key (or the ⌘ key on Mac), the frame is automatically converted into a keyframe as it is dragged to the new location. ∎

- **Copying frames:** Select the frame(s) that you want to copy. Choose Edit ⇨ Timeline ⇨ Copy Frames from the main menu and then Paste Frames into a new location, or press the Alt or Option key while clicking and dragging to copy selected frames to another location in the Timeline.

- **Pasting frames:** Select the frame where you want the copied or cut frames to be inserted (Flash automatically adds frames or layers below and to the right of the selected frame to accommodate the pasted content), and choose Edit ⇨ Timeline ⇨ Paste Frames from the menu.

Caution

Edit ⇨ Copy (Ctrl/⌘+C) is not the same as Edit ⇨ Timeline ⇨ Copy Frames (Alt+Ctrl+C/Option+⌘+C). Using Copy only "remembers" and copies the content from a single keyframe, whereas Copy Frames "remembers" and copies content from multiple keyframes and even from multiple layers. To insert this content correctly in a new location, you have to remember to use the corresponding Paste commands: Paste (Ctrl+V/⌘+V) or Paste Frames (Alt+Ctrl+V/Option+⌘+V). You may notice that the contextual menu offers only the plural options (Copy Frames or Paste Frames). This is because the plural command safely works to move content from a single frame or from multiple frames. The singular command is just a simpler shortcut key to use if you know that you want only the content from one keyframe. ∎

- **Inserting frames:** Select the point at which you want to insert a new frame, and select Insert Frame (F5) from the contextual menu or from the application menu (Insert ⇨ Frame). The visual "clue" that frames have been inserted is that the endframe of a span is moved to the right — this also pushes any following keyframes farther along the Timeline.

- **Inserting keyframes:** Select the point at which you want to insert a new keyframe, and select Insert Keyframe (F6) from the contextual menu or from the application menu (Insert ⇨ Timeline ⇨ Keyframe). Note that keyframes can be inserted within a span without extending the span (or pushing the endframe to the right). Thus, inserting a keyframe actually converts an existing frame into a keyframe. So, unlike frames, keyframes can be inserted without pushing other frames farther down the Timeline.

- **Inserting blank keyframes:** Select the point at which you want to insert a new blank keyframe, and select Insert Blank Keyframe (F7) from the contextual menu or from the application menu (Insert ⇨ Timeline ⇨ Blank Keyframe). Inserting a blank keyframe within a span clears all content along the Timeline until another keyframe is encountered.

Note

If you already have content in the current layer and you insert a keyframe, a new keyframe is created that duplicates the content of the endframe immediately prior. But if you insert a blank keyframe, the content of the prior endframe ceases and the blank keyframe will, as its name implies, be void of content. ■

On the CD-ROM

For a hands-on example of frame-based Timeline editing, refer to the file `frames_example.fla` in the ch04 folder of the CD-ROM that accompanies this book. ■

- **Removing frames (to shorten a span):** Select the frame(s) that you want to remove, and then choose Remove Frames (Shift+F5) from the contextual menu or from the application menu (Edit ⇨ Timeline ⇨ Remove Frames). This does not work for removing keyframes; instead, it removes a frame from the span to the right of the keyframe, causing all the following frames to move back toward frame 1.

- **Clearing a keyframe:** To remove a keyframe and its contents, select the keyframe and choose Clear Keyframe (Shift+F6) from the contextual menu or from the application menu (Modify ⇨ Timeline ⇨ Clear Keyframe). When a keyframe is cleared, the span of the previous keyframe is extended to fill all frames until the next keyframe on the Timeline. The same thing happens if you insert a keyframe in a span and then Undo it (Ctrl+Z/⌘+Z). Apply Undo (Edit ⇨ Undo) twice — the first Undo deselects the keyframe, and the second Undo clears it.

- **Cutting frames (leaves blank frames or keyframes):** To replace selected frames in a span with blank frames, while keeping content in the remainder of the span intact, select the frame(s) you want to "blank" and then choose Cut Frames (Alt+Ctrl+X on Windows or Option+⌘+X on Mac) from the contextual menu or from the application menu (Edit ⇨ Timeline ⇨ Cut Frames). This "pulls" the content out of only the selected frames, without interrupting content in surrounding frames or shifting any keyframes on the Timeline. The content that you cut can be pasted into another position on the Timeline (as described previously).

Caution

Selecting a frame or keyframe and pressing Delete removes the content from the entire span but does not remove the keyframe itself or change the length of the span. You can delete content from multiple layers this way, but it leaves all the empty frames and keyframes on the Timeline. ■

Tip

Flash MX 2004 introduced a command called Clear Frames (Alt+Delete/Option+Delete). This is a flexible command that eliminates the content on a selected frame, keyframe, or span of frames without changing the number of frames in a span. If you select a keyframe and apply Clear Frames, the keyframe clears and the content of the keyframe is removed. If you select a normal frame and apply Clear Frames, the selected frame is converted into a blank keyframe to eliminate the content in that frame while preserving the content in other frames within the same span. This command is also listed in the contextual menu and in the application menu under Edit ⇨ Timeline ⇨ Clear Frames. ■

- **Editing the contents of a keyframe:** Select the keyframe where you want to edit content. This moves the playhead to the selected frame so that its content is visible in the Document window, where it can be edited. Note that if you edit content on a keyframe or frame within a span, the changes apply to the current frame and the span it is part of.

Cross-Reference

I detail numerous techniques for editing content in later chapters of this book that address specific types of content. For the most relevant information, look for chapters that describe the types of content you are working with — vector art, bitmaps, sound, video, and so on. ■

The span-based selection methods are as follows:

- **Frame spans:** To select a span of frames extending between two keyframes, simply click anywhere between the keyframes.
- **Single frames within a span:** To select a single frame within a span on a normal layer, press the Ctrl key (on Windows) or the ⌘ key (on Mac) and click a frame. Keyframes or endframes can usually be selected with a simple click.
- **Single frames not within a span:** To select a single frame that is not part of a span, simply click to select it.
- **Multiple frames or spans:** To select multiple frames along the Timeline (within a span or independent of a span), Shift+click to add to a selection of the frames.

Figure 4.18 shows a Timeline that illustrates some editing points. The top layer shows the Original layer, with content starting on a keyframe on frame 1, followed by a span of 19 frames, putting the endframe on frame 20. This layer was copied into all three lower layers, with the result that the initial content of all four layers was the same. When a frame was inserted at frame 10 of the Insert frame layer, the content was extended, pushing the endframe of the span to frame 21. When a keyframe was inserted at frame 10 of the Insert keyframe layer, the content was maintained in the new keyframe, but the span was not extended, as indicated by the gray filled frames in the span from frame 10 to frame 20. When a blank keyframe was inserted at frame 10 of the Insert blank keyframe layer, the content was cleared following the new blank keyframe, as indicated by the white frames extending from frame 10 to frame 20.

Cross-Reference

For more information about how frames are used to author and control animation, refer to Chapter 10, "Timeline Animation and the Motion Editor." ■

FIGURE 4.18

Editing frames and keyframes on the Timeline

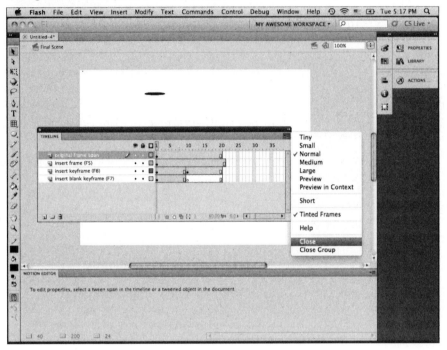

Layer specifics

Knowing how to work with layers makes all the difference between a well-ordered project and a chaotic mess of elements that you may never be able to sort out if you have to come back to edit later on. The necessity of a logical folder structure and consistent naming conventions is even more crucial in a team environment, where someone else may have to try to find her way around in your document. Like most good production habits, this may seem like extra work at first, but over time it pays off. As your projects get more complex and your archive of Flash documents grows, the few additional steps you take early on will be invaluable down the road.

Being organized doesn't mean you have to always put every layer into a folder, but rather that you just try to find the most efficient way of keeping track of where you've placed different elements. To make it easier to remember what content is on different layers, it's a good habit to give your layers meaningful names. It can also be helpful to use consistent abbreviations that help you to recognize what type of content is described by the name (such as "MC" for Movie Clip or "Anim" for animation). To edit a layer name, simply double-click the layer's name on the Layer bar and type into the text field.

Tip

With all Flash projects in my studio, I begin the layer structure by creating three layers titled "actions," "labels," and "functions" — these are always kept at the top of the layer stack. On projects that I want to document very carefully, I also add a "comments" layer where the type of action or function added on the other layers can be noted. Although these layers don't hold content that is visible on the Stage, they make it easy to quickly find any actions placed on the Timeline and to see labels and comments that give an indication of how the movie is structured. ∎

Cross-Reference

For detailed methods and suggestions on organizing Flash documents, see Chapter 3, "Planning Flash Projects" and Chapter 17, "Making Your First Flash CS5 Project". ∎

By default, new layers are stacked on top of the currently active layer. To rearrange layers, click in the area between the layer name and the layer toggle icons, and drag the layer bar to the desired position in the layer stack and release. To move layers into a folder, click and drag the layer bar onto any layer with a folder icon. To move a layer back out of a folder, drag it to a position above the folder name bar or below all the other layers contained in the folder.

The Layers contextual menu

Because many of the controls for layer options are built into the Timeline window, layer properties are one of the few attributes that are not displayed in the Properties panel (frame properties are visible when any layer is selected). The contextual menu (right-click on Windows or Control+click on Mac) provides convenient access to most of the commands you will need when editing layers, including commands otherwise found in the Layer Properties dialog box or in the application menu:

- **Show All:** Shows all layers. If some layers have had their visibility turned off, this makes them all visible.
- **Lock Others:** Unlocks the active layer and locks all other layers.
- **Hide Others:** Makes the currently active layer visible if it is not visible and hides all others.
- **Insert Layer:** Inserts a new layer above the currently active layer with an auto-numbered name that continues the number sequence of existing layers and folders.
- **Delete Layer:** Deletes the active layer and all content stored on that layer.
- **Guide:** Transforms the current layer into a guide layer — a reference layer that is visible only in the authoring environment (.fla).
- **Add Classic Motion Guide:** Inserts a new motion guide layer directly above the current layer and automatically converts the current layer into a guided layer.

Note

A guide layer differs from a motion guide layer. A motion guide layer is linked to a guided layer, which usually contains a (classic motion) tweened animation that follows a path drawn on the motion guide layer. A guide layer is not linked to a guided layer and is most often used for placing a bitmap design composition or other items used for design reference that should not be visible in the final movie (.swf). Neither guide layers nor motion guide layers export with the project when the file is tested or published. ∎

Note

Motion tween layers (created when an object-based motion tween is applied) contain motion guides, so a separate motion guide layer is no longer needed unless you are working with classic motion tweens. ■

- **Mask:** Transforms the current layer into a mask layer.

- **Show Masking:** Use this command on either the mask or the masked layer to activate the masking effect. Essentially, this command locks both layers simultaneously, which makes the masking effect visible.

- **Insert Folder:** Inserts a new folder above the currently active layer or folder with an auto-numbered name that continues the number sequence of existing layers and folders.

- **Delete Folder:** Deletes the currently active folder, along with all the layers stored in that folder.

- **Expand Folder:** Opens the current folder to make any layers stored inside visible in the layer stack and on the Timeline.

- **Collapse Folder:** Closes the current folder to hide any layers stored in the folder. The elements existing on these stored layers are still visible in the Document window and in the movie (.swf), but the keyframe rows do not show up along the Timeline.

- **Expand All Folders:** Opens all folders to show any stored layers visible in the layer stack and on the Timeline.

- **Collapse All Folders:** Closes all folders to hide any layers that have been placed in folders. The elements existing on these stored layers are still visible in the Document window and in the movie (.swf), but the keyframe rows do not show up along the Timeline.

- **Properties:** Invokes the Layer Properties dialog box for the currently active layer. The Layer Properties dialog box can also be invoked directly by double-clicking the "page" icon or the colored square icon on any layer and is always available in the application menu (Modify ➪ Timeline ➪ Layer Properties).

Cross-Reference

For more in-depth coverage of using layer types, refer to Chapter 12, "Applying Filters, Blends, Guides, and Masks." ■

Using Frame View options

The main place to find options for controlling the appearance of the Timeline within the window is in the submenu available from the Frame View options button.

As noted previously, the Frame View options menu is used to customize the size, color, and style of frames displayed within the Timeline. These features can prove very helpful when you're working with cartoon animation and want to see each frame previewed. Or, if you're working on an extremely long project with a huge Timeline, it can be helpful to tweak the size of the individual frames so that you can see more of the Timeline in the Timeline window.

When you use the Frame View option in conjunction with the Layer Height option of the Layer Properties dialog box, you can customize your Timeline display in several ways to better suit your particular project. Your options include:

- **Tiny, Small, Normal, Medium, Large:** These options afford a range of sizes for the width of individual frames. When working on extremely long animations, narrower frames facilitate some operations. Wider frames can make it easier to select individual frames and to read frame labels or comments.

- **Short:** This option makes the frames shorter in height, permitting more layers to be visible in the same amount of space. When working with many layers or folders, short layers help speed the process of scrolling through the stack.

- **Tinted Frames:** This option toggles tinted frames on or off. With Tinted Frames on, the tints are as follows:

  - **White:** Empty or unused frames (for any layer). This is the default. The white color of empty or unused frames is unaffected regardless of whether Tinted Frames is on or off.

  - **Gray:** There are two kinds of gray frames: (a) The evenly spaced gray stripes in the default (empty) Timeline are a quick visual reference that indicates every fifth frame, like the tick marks on a ruler. These stripes appear regardless of whether Tinted Frames are enabled. (b) The solid gray color with a black outline, which appears when Tinted Frames is enabled, indicates that a frame contains content, even if it isn't visible on the Stage.

  - **Blue:** Indicates a motion tween span.

  - **Green:** Indicates a shape tween span.

Note

Regardless of whether Tinted Frames is enabled, Flash displays tween arrows (and keyframe dots) across shape tween or classic motion tween spans. However, with Tinted Frames disabled, tweened spans are indicated by colored arrows, rather than colored fills, that show the type of tween. ∎

New Feature

Object-based motion tweens on motion tween layers are always indicated by a blue fill. Their appearance does not change when the Tinted Frames setting is toggled on or off. ∎

- **A red arrow:** Indicates a classic motion tween, when Tinted Frames are off.

- **A green arrow:** Indicates a shape tween, when Tinted Frames are off.

- **Preview:** As shown in Figure 4.19, the preview option displays tiny thumbnails that maximize the element in each frame. Thus, the scale of elements is not consistent from frame to frame.

- **Preview in Context:** As shown in Figure 4.19, when previewed in context, the same animation is seen with accurate scale from frame to frame (because elements are not maximized for each frame).

FIGURE 4.19

The Timeline displayed with the two preview options — Preview (left) and Preview in Context (right) — for the same frame-by-frame animation sequence

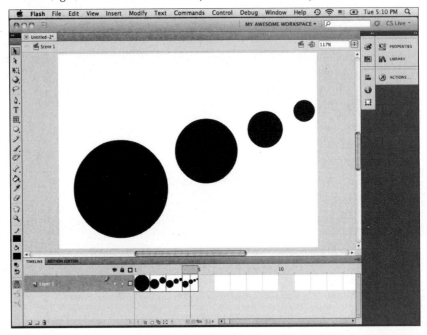

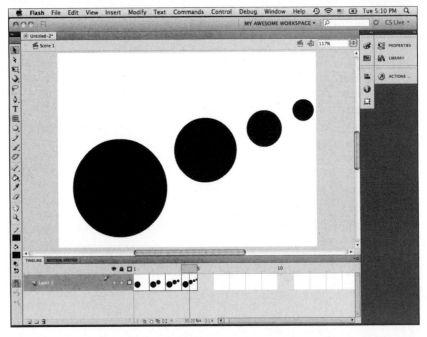

Note

The preview in frames option only shows content in keyframes. Thus, if you use this option to view a tweened animation, you see images displayed on the Timeline only for the first and last frames of the animation. ■

Printing

Although Flash is primarily a Web and animation program, it fully supports printed output. The functionality and specific dialog boxes vary slightly from the Mac to the PC, whereas other variations are subject to which printers and printer drivers are installed on your machine. The File ⇨ Page Setup dialog box is the most standard aspect of the program and the choices for paper size, margins, center positioning, and orientation are pretty intuitive.

The options available in the Layout area of the Page Setup dialog box on Windows or in the Print Margins dialog box on Mac (File ⇨ Print Margins) deserve a little more attention. The options here are

- **Print Margins** (Mac only): Note the Disable PostScript check box. When you're printing single large areas of color surrounded by complex borders, problems may occur on PostScript printers. If you encounter such problems, try using the Disable PostScript check box in the Mac Print Margins dialog box (Edit ⇨ Print Margins) or in the Windows Preferences dialog box (Edit ⇨ Preferences ⇨ General ⇨ Printing Options). Otherwise, divide the complex area into several simpler areas and use the Modify commands (Modify ⇨ Shape ⇨ Smooth/Straighten/Optimize) to reduce the complexity of these areas (which may, however, drastically alter your artwork — so save first!).

- **Frames:** Use this drop-down menu to choose to print either All Frames of the animation or the ecological default, which is to print the First Frame Only.

- **Layout:** There are three basic options:
  - **Actual Size:** This prints the frame at full size, subject to the accompanying Scale setting: At what scale do you want to print your frames? You enter a percentage.
  - **Fit on One Page:** This automatically reduces or enlarges the frame so that it fills the maximum printable area, without distortion.
  - **Storyboard:** This enables you to print several thumbnails per page in the following arrangements: Boxes, Grid, or Blank. There are accompanying settings for Frames Across, Frame Margin, and Label Frames. This is a great tool for circulating comps and promotional materials.

Tip

When printing Storyboard layouts, use File ⇨ Print Preview on Windows (or File ⇨ Print ⇨ Preview on Mac) to ensure optimal results. ■

The remaining options in the main menu differ on Mac and Windows machines, but the key tasks and locations are as follows:

- **Print:** Just print it! (The Mac option for Preview is found in the dialog box that opens from this command.)

- **Print Preview:** On Windows, use the Print Preview command to see an on-screen preview of how the printed output looks, based upon the options you've chosen in the Page Setup dialog box. On Mac, the Preview button is found in the Print dialog box (File ⇨ Print) and generates a PDF to give a preview of how the final page looks, based upon the options you've chosen in the Print Margins dialog box.

- **Send** (PC only): This command invokes the default e-mail client so that you can readily send the Flash file as an attachment.

It is important to note that the Document background color (or Stage color) is not included on printed output. If you want the background color to appear in your printed output, you must create a filled rectangle of the color that you want in the background and place it on a layer behind the other elements. The printer then recognizes this as artwork and includes it in the output.

Summary

- Flash CS5 offers some great new tools and workspace options in a flexible interface that is consistent cross-platform and with other applications in the Adobe Creative Suite.

- The new Motion tween layer type supports object-based motion tweens which are easier to create and edit than classic motion tweens. Motion tween layers can support a motion path with no need for a separate motion guide layer.

- The new Motion Editor enables you to work with individual tween curves for all the tweenable properties applied to a target object.

- The Start Page and robust Help features get you started quickly, whereas the options for saving custom workspace layouts and custom keyboard shortcut sets make it easy to optimize your workspace for specific production needs.

- The guided file setup workflow supported by Adobe Device Central gives developers a jump-start on Flash projects that target specific mobile environments.

- Tabbed panels, the new vertical Properties panel, and the new scalable Tools panel make it easy to optimize screen space and customize the editing environment to suit your monitor configuration and work style.

- Layer folders and frame-editing options make it easy to organize and navigate your document structure.

- Although Flash is mainly used to produce Web content, it fully supports printed output.

- If you need a quick reminder on any of the fundamental interface elements, this chapter will be your reference.

Drawing in Flash

This chapter introduces the primary tools for creating and manipulating vector graphics in Flash, as well as some features of the Flash environment that affect how elements behave. The primary drawing tools have self-explanatory names: the Line, Oval, Rectangle, PolyStar, Pencil, Brush, and Eraser. However, these tools have a variety of options and modifiers that make them more sophisticated than they may at first appear. In this chapter, you learn to apply the primary options of these tools to create shapes and line art.

The selection tools — Selection (arrow), Lasso, and Subselection — are found in the top section of the Tools panel, and these work as your "hands" within the drawing space of Flash, enabling you to select elements or grab and adjust specific parts of a shape or line.

The Pen is a powerful tool that draws lines by laying down editable points. You use both the Pen and Subselection tools to manipulate the points; you can also use them to select and edit all lines and shapes to manually optimize artwork.

Tip
Like the Pen tool in Illustrator, the Pen tool in Flash has a series of different modes that you can select from the same tool space in the Tools panel by clicking and holding the Pen tool icon. ■

The built-in shape-creation tools of Flash and the adjustable shape-recognition settings make it easy even for people who "can't draw a straight line" to create useable elements for Flash interfaces.

IN THIS CHAPTER

Using shape and drawing tools

Working with Drawing Objects and Shape Primitive tools

Setting Brush tool and Eraser tool modes

Creating optimized lines and curves

Choosing fill and stroke styles

Using selection tools and options

Controlling snapping behavior

Aligning, scaling, and rotating artwork

Knowing the Edit menu commands

Creating symbol patterns with the Spray Brush tool and the Deco tool

Tip

Tools for creating dynamically editable shapes based on an Oval Primitive or Rectangle Primitive can be selected from the same tool space as the basic Oval, Rectangle, and PolyStar tools. The shape primitives can be adjusted with controls in the Properties panel even after they are drawn to create a variety of useful polygons — including rounded or beveled rectangles and open circles or curves. ■

In addition to drawing, in this chapter you also learn to apply some of the terrific tools Flash provides to help you organize and align elements as you create layouts.

Cross-Reference

If you're comfortable using the core Flash drawing tools and design panels, you can skip to Chapter 9 for a deeper look into the options available for editing artwork, including the Free Transform tool, the Envelope modifier, new 3-D tools, and the Commands feature, which you can use to record and repeat authoring steps. ■

The primary drawing tools can be divided into two groups: geometric shapes and freehand lines and strokes. Line, Oval, Rectangle, and PolyStar fall into the first category; Pencil, Brush, and Eraser fall into the second.

Note

The default fill and stroke settings that Flash launches with are sufficient to get started with any of the drawing tools, but I introduce many more inspiring choices later in this chapter. ■

Tip

The Object Drawing option in the Tools panel provides a workaround to the standard overlap and merge behavior of raw graphics. If you prefer shapes or lines on the same layer to behave more like groups and not interfere with each other as you are drawing, you can enable the Object Drawing mode and work with any of the standard drawing and shape tools to create well-behaved, autonomous drawing objects. ■

There are two tools in Flash CS5 that enable you to create patterns by using symbols. If you have worked with Illustrator, the Deco tool and the Spray Brush tool workflow will be familiar: You select a symbol to use as your "ink" and then set the parameters for your "brush," and with a click on the Stage, Flash creates a cool pattern for you that consists of many instances of your base symbol(s). This can save you hours of time, and the symbol instances can still be selected and edited individually after they have been placed on the Stage as part of a pattern. These symbol-based drawing tools are discussed in more detail toward the end of this chapter.

Using Geometric Shape Tools

As shown in Figure 5.1, the prebuilt geometric shapes available for creating graphics in Flash are easy to access from the Tools panel. The basic Line, Oval, and Rectangle tools are straightforward but infinitely useful. The Oval Primitive and Rectangle Primitive tools make it easier to create more complex shapes without having to manually move points or merge multiple shapes. Instead, you can use settings in the Properties panel to control the corner radius of your rectangles or the inner radius and fill areas of your ovals. The PolyStar tool creates a wide variety of geometric shapes defined by a separate Tool Settings dialog box — available from the Options button in the Tool Settings section of the Properties panel. You can use custom stroke styles and the various fill options (described later in this chapter) with any of these shapes to create nearly any graphic you may need. Geometric shapes are more optimized than freehand drawings, and you can combine or modify them in multiple ways to create your graphics.

Note

The Rectangle Primitive and Oval Primitive tools are really not primitive at all — they create dynamic shapes that can be adjusted with controls on the Properties panel. However, if you choose to edit these shapes manually in the Document window, you are given an option to convert them to simple drawing objects. After shape primitives are converted to drawing objects, they can be edited directly in Edit mode but they no longer have the same options available in the Properties panel for modifying corner radius or fill angle settings. ■

FIGURE 5.1

The shape tools are all nested together in the Flash CS5 Tools panel.

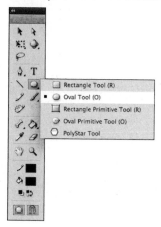

The Oval tool

Drawing with the Oval tool (O) creates a perfectly smooth oval. You draw ovals by clicking and then dragging diagonally from one "corner" of the oval to the other — dragging more vertically creates a taller oval, whereas dragging more horizontally creates a wider oval.

Tip

To constrain the shape to a perfect circle, hold down the Shift key before releasing the mouse. ■

The Oval tool has no unique options, but it can be filled with any of the fill colors available in the Swatches panel (described later in this chapter) as well as "outlined" with any of the stroke styles or colors. Figure 5.2 shows some of the huge variety of shapes you can create by using the Oval tool with different stroke and fill settings.

FIGURE 5.2

Shapes created with the Oval tool, using different stroke and fill settings

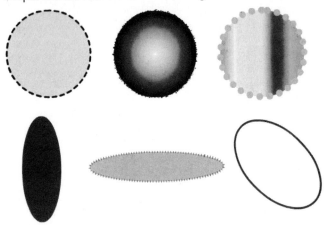

The Oval Primitive tool

If you need more complex shapes based on an oval, the Oval Primitive tool (available in the same drop-down Tools menu as the Oval tool) can save you a lot of time. With the Oval Primitive tool you can draw a basic oval and then modify angle and radius settings in the Properties panel (in the Oval Options section) to create donut or pie shapes, or open curves. Figure 5.3 includes just a few of the shapes that you can draw, along with the settings that were used to create them.

FIGURE 5.3

Shapes created with the Oval Primitive tool, using different angle and radius settings

 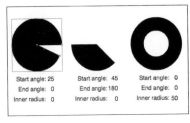

Don't overlook the Close path check box available in the Properties panel for oval primitives. By default, this check box is selected to create filled shapes, but if you prefer to create outlined shapes or curves, simply deselect the Close path check box. Figure 5.4 shows the same shapes as Figure 5.3, with the difference in effect created by deselecting the Close path check box.

FIGURE 5.4

Shapes created with the Oval Primitive tool, with the Close path check box deselected

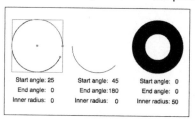

The Oval tool and Oval Primitive tool both have a "hidden" Settings dialog box that you can use to set the width and height of an oval before you draw it. To access this feature, select the Oval or Oval Primitive tool in the Tools panel (0), and then hold down the Alt (or Option) key as you click in the Document window where you want the shape to be drawn. The dialog box shown in Figure 5.5 pops up and you can set the width and height (in pixels). By default, the Draw from center check box is selected; if you prefer the shape to be drawn from the top-left corner (originating where you clicked), deselect the check box. After you have entered the settings and clicked OK, the shape is drawn for you to the correct dimensions.

FIGURE 5.5

The Oval Settings dialog box can be used to generate shapes with precise width and height settings, instead of estimating size as you draw them manually.

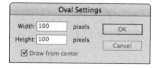

Tip

The Oval tool and the Oval Primitive tool have the same shortcut key (O), but you can toggle between the two by pressing the shortcut key again. ■

The Rectangle tool and Rectangle Primitive tool

The Rectangle tool (R) creates perfect rectangles, which means that all four sides are parallel, regardless of the length or width of the shape. Draw rectangles by clicking to place a starting corner and then dragging toward the opposite corner of your shape until you have the size and shape that you want.

Tip

To constrain the rectangle to a perfect square, hold down the Shift key before releasing the mouse. ■

Aside from choosing the stroke and fill to apply to a shape drawn with the Rectangle tool, there are also value boxes in the Properties panel under Rectangle Options for setting the radius for corners on the rectangle. The radius is set to 0 pt by default, to create rectangles with square or 90-degree corners. The range for radius settings is 100 pt to –100 pt, but unless the dimensions of the rectangle are equal to double the radius setting that you use, you will not see any additional effect by pushing the value farther. For example, the highest (or lowest) setting that would have a visible effect on a rectangle that was 30 x 30 pixels square would be 15 or –15. Choosing a more moderate radius setting creates rounded rectangles or squares with softened corners, and choosing negative values creates rectangles with indented corners (see Figure 5.6). By default, all rectangle corners are locked to have the same value, but if you want to create more interesting polygons you can click the lock icon in the Properties panel to "unlock" the corner values and enter different radius settings for each corner.

Caution

You'll want to choose the radius setting before you create a shape with the basic Rectangle tool because the radius cannot be reapplied or easily modified after the shape is drawn. ■

Tip

Like the Oval tool, the Rectangle tool and Rectangle Primitive tool also have a Settings dialog box that you can use to set the width, height, and corner radius to have Flash draw the shape for you. To access this feature, select the Rectangle tool in the Tools panel (R), and then hold down the Alt (or Option) key as you click in the Document window where you want the shape to be drawn. ■

Radius settings for rectangles made with the basic Rectangle tool cannot be adjusted after they are drawn, but shapes drawn with the Rectangle Primitive tool can be modified, using the options in the Properties panel, as long as they are not converted to drawing objects or broken apart into basic shapes.

Caution

The Corner Radius values do not reset automatically, so if you change the radius settings, you have to use the Reset button to return to drawing standard rectangles. Any radius setting entered in the Rectangle Settings dialog box accessed by Alt (or Option)+clicking in the Document window while the Rectangle tool is selected in the Tools panel is also transferred to the radius settings in the Properties panel. ■

FIGURE 5.6

Rectangles drawn with different radius settings create different degrees of roundness or inversion on the corners. Radius settings for rectangle primitives remain editable after they are drawn, and settings for basic rectangles "stick" and are not editable (from the Properties panel) after the shape is created.

Join and Miter settings

As shown in Figure 5.7, the Join menu includes three settings — Miter, Round, and Bevel — that you can apply to create three different join styles on any of your drawings or shapes with intersecting lines.

FIGURE 5.7

The three join styles available in the Join drop-down menu in the Properties panel create corners or angles with different types of line intersection.

When you select the Miter join style, you can further adjust the angle of the join by entering a setting between 1 and 60 in the Miter field. This field is a hot text value in Flash CS5, which means it can also be modified by clicking and dragging left or right to update the Miter angle. As shown in Figure 5.8, the visual difference between these different Miter angles is very subtle, and for most graphics you will probably be happy with the default setting of 3.

The sharpness of Miter joins can be adjusted by entering a setting between 1 and 60 in the Miter field.

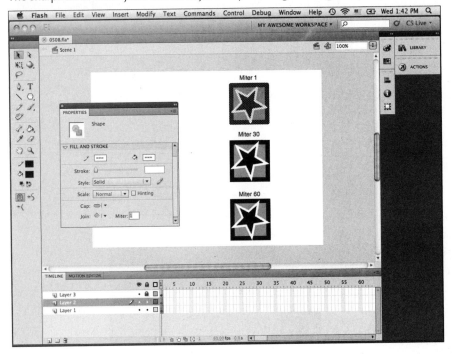

The PolyStar tool

The PolyStar tool is so named because it is a multipurpose tool that can make a whole variety of different polygons and stars. If you're using the default Tools set in Flash, you'll find the PolyStar tool at the bottom of the shape tools submenu in the Tools panel. There is no shortcut key for the PolyStar tool.

When the PolyStar tool is active, an Options button appears in the Properties panel to open a Tool Settings dialog box that enables you to control the type of shape you want to draw. The composite in Figure 5.9 includes the Properties panel as it appears when the PolyStar tool is active, as well as the Tool Settings dialog box with the two shape styles available: polygon or star. You can set the number of sides for either shape by entering a value between 3 and 32 in the Number of Sides field. As shown at the top of Figure 5.9, a standard five-sided star is as easy to create as a triangle — that is, a polygon with three sides.

FIGURE 5.9

A composite figure showing the Options button in the Properties panel (left) that launches the Tool Settings dialog box, used to create different shape styles (right)

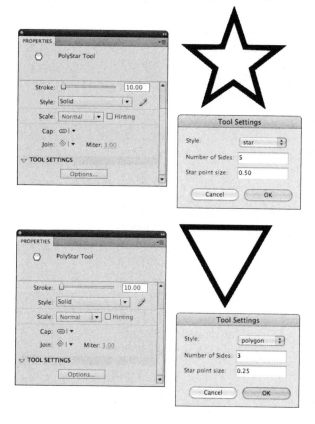

Note

If you are a little confused by the inconsistent workflow for accessing settings dialog boxes for the different drawing tools, don't worry, I was too! Hopefully, these glitches will be smoothed out in future releases of Flash. For now, I just have to live with the fact that there isn't an Options button in the Properties panel for launching the Settings dialog box for the Oval or Rectangle tool, and the Settings dialog box for the PolyStar tool doesn't show up when you Alt (or Option)+click in the Document window. ■

The fields in the Tool Settings dialog box look the same whether you select polygon or star in the Style menu, but Star point size does not affect polygon shapes. If you are drawing a star, enter any number between 0 and 1 to control the depth of the star points. This might not look like much of a range, but you can enter decimal numbers, so you actually have 99 possible settings! As shown in Figure 5.10, numbers closer to 0 create sharper stars and numbers closer to 1 create blockier shapes.

FIGURE 5.10

Star point size decimal settings between 0 and 1 create various star shapes.

Star point size: 0.00   Star point size: 0.50   Star point size: 1.00

The Line tool

Drawing with the Line tool (N) enables you to create a perfectly straight line that extends from a starting point to an endpoint, simply by clicking a start position and dragging to the end position before releasing the mouse. Just select the Line tool in the Tools panel and start drawing in the Document window. You can select various line styles and stroke heights from the Properties panel, as well as set the color with the popup Swatches panel accessible from the Stroke color chip on either the Properties panel or the Tools panel. I describe the various options for line styles and colors later in this chapter. Snapping settings and guides can be used to help control where a line is placed and how precisely it connects to other lines. The Line tool conforms to the snapping settings I describe later in this chapter.

Tip
To restrict the line to 45-degree-angle increments, hold down the Shift key as you drag out the line. ■

Figure 5.11 shows how a line previews as you drag and how it appears when the mouse is released and the current line style and stroke height settings are applied.

With the Cap option menu in the Properties panel, you can quickly switch a stroke from a rounded end to a square end to a flat or no cap end. Figure 5.12 illustrates how these cap styles render on a 10 pt line.

FIGURE 5.11

Line tool preview (top) and the final line (bottom), displayed when the mouse button is released and line style is rendered

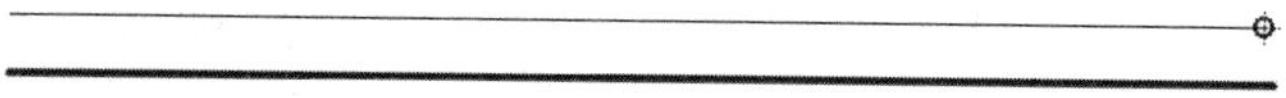

FIGURE 5.12

A 10 pt line rendered with different cap styles. These styles can be applied to any line using the Cap style menu in the Properties panel: None (top), Round (center), Square (bottom).

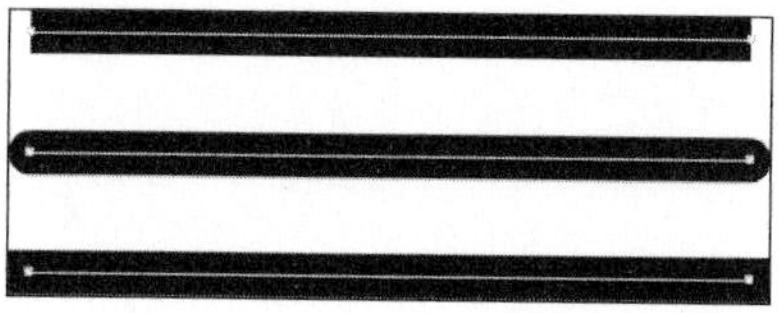

Using Drawing Tools

The tools for drawing freehand lines and strokes in Flash come with options for applying different combinations of line processing and shape recognition. So, what does that mean exactly? These are general terms for a class of options that you can set to assist accurate drawing and manipulation of basic shapes. These options can be applied dynamically as you draw with the Pencil or Brush tool, or applied cumulatively to an item selected with the Selection tool to clean up a shape or line that you've already drawn. These are some of the Flash assistants that can help even a drafting-challenged designer create sharp-looking graphics with ease.

Note
The biggest challenge when drawing in Flash is finding a happy medium between the degree of line variation and complexity required to get the graphic look you want, and the optimization and file size that you need to keep your artwork Web friendly. ■

The Pencil tool

You use the Pencil tool to draw lines and shapes. At first glance, it operates much like a real pencil. You can use the Pencil tool with different line styles as you draw a freeform shape. But a deeper examination reveals that, unlike a real pencil, you can set the Flash Pencil tool to straighten lines and smooth curves as you draw. You can also set it to recognize or correct basic geometric shapes. For example, a crude lumpy oval can be automatically recognized and processed into a true, or *perfect*, oval. You can further modify these shapes and lines after you've drawn them by using the Selection and Subselect tools.

When the Pencil tool is active, one option besides the Object Drawing toggle appears at the bottom of the Tools panel. This is actually a button for the Pencil Mode popup menu, which sets the Pencil tool's current drawing mode. The three modes, or drawing styles, for the Pencil are Straighten, Smooth, and Ink. These settings control the way that line processing occurs as you draw.

Figure 5.13 shows the same freehand drawing done with the different Pencil modes. The drawing on the left was done with the Straighten mode, the drawing in the middle was done with Smooth mode, and the drawing on the right was done with Ink mode. As you can see, each mode is more effective for certain types of lines and shapes.

FIGURE 5.13

Similar sketches made by using the three different Pencil modes to show how line processing affects various shapes: Straighten (left), Smooth (center), and Ink (right)

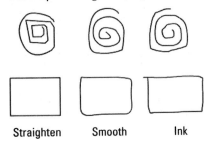

Straighten   Smooth   Ink

To create a pleasing finished result, you'll most likely use different Pencil modes when working on individual elements of your drawing. Here are some notes on the characteristics of the three Pencil drawing modes that you can select in the Tools panel:

- **Straighten:** Drawing with the Straighten option processes your drawings while taking into account both line and shape recognition. This means that nearly straight lines are straightened, and wobbly curves are smoothed. Approximate geometric shapes, such as ovals, rectangles, and triangles, are recognized and automatically adjusted.

- **Smooth:** Drawing with the Smooth option reduces the zeal with which Flash automatically processes your drawings. With the Smooth option, line straightening and shape recognition are not applied, but curved lines are smoothed. Additionally, a line that ends near another line is joined automatically, if the Connect Lines tolerance is set to Can be Distant.

- **Ink:** Drawing with the Ink option turns off all line processing. Lines remain as you've drawn them. Your lines are *not* smoothed, straightened, or joined. There will always be a slight difference between the line preview and the final, rendered line, but this setting is as close to raw sketching as you can get in the Flash drawing environment.

Adjusting Drawing Settings

You may adjust the degree to which shape recognition processes your Pencil drawings with the Drawing settings found in Edit ⇨ Preferences ⇨ Drawing (or Flash ⇨ Preferences ⇨ Drawing). By default, all the Drawing settings are Normal. You can adjust each option to make it more specific or more general. The optimal setting combinations depend on the style of drawing that you're trying to achieve, but in general, you really only need to adjust the default Normal settings for these controls if you find that you aren't getting the look you want by using the Straighten, Smooth, or Ink modes with the Pencil tool.

You can also choose to further simplify lines and shapes that you have drawn with the Pencil in Ink mode by using the Selection tool to select what you've drawn and then using either the Smooth or Straighten command by clicking the Smooth or Straighten button at the bottom of the Tools panel. Or, for maximum control, manually edit extraneous points with either the Pen or the Subselect tool (as I describe in the Pen and Subselect sections later in this chapter). Here are the various Drawing settings and options available in Preferences:

- **Connect Lines:** The Connect Lines setting adjusts how close lines or points have to be to each other before Flash automatically connects them into a continuous line or shape. This setting also controls how close to horizontal or vertical a line has to be for Flash to set it at an exact angle. The options are Must be Close, Normal, and Can be Distant. This setting also controls how close elements need to be to snap together when Snap to Objects is turned on.

- **Smooth Curves:** Smooth Curves simplifies the number of points used to draw a curve when the Pencil is in Straighten or Smooth mode. Smoother curves are easier to reshape and are more optimized, whereas rougher curves more closely resemble the original lines drawn. The options are Off, Rough, Normal, and Smooth.

- **Recognize Lines:** The Recognize Lines setting controls how precise a line has to be for Flash to recognize it as a straight line and automatically align it. The options are Off, Strict, Normal, and Tolerant.

- **Recognize Shapes:** The Recognize Shapes setting controls how accurately you have to draw basic geometric shapes and 90-degree or 180-degree arcs for Flash to recognize and correct them. The options are Off, Strict, Normal, and Tolerant.

- **Click Accuracy:** Click Accuracy determines how close to an element the cursor has to be for Flash to recognize it. The settings are Strict, Normal, and Tolerant.

These drawing settings do not modify the Straighten and Smooth options for the Selection tool, which reduce point complexity (or smooth angles) based on the settings you enter in the respective dialog boxes before you apply the command to a shape or line that has already been drawn.

The Brush tool

You use the Brush tool to create smooth or tapered marks and to fill enclosed areas. Unlike the Pencil tool, which creates marks with a single row of anchor points, the Brush tool actually creates marks by using filled shapes. The fills can be solid colors, gradients, or fills derived from bitmaps. Because the Brush paints only with a fill, the Stroke color chip does not apply to the marks drawn with the brush. The Brush tool is especially well suited for artwork created using a drawing tablet. A number of settings and options are available when the Brush tool is active, giving you precise control over the type of marks that it makes.

The Brush mode menu

The Brush tool includes options for controlling exactly where the fill is applied. The Brush mode option menu reveals five painting modes that are amazingly useful for a wide range of effects when applying the Brush tool: Paint Normal, Paint Fills, Paint Behind, Paint Selection, and Paint Inside, as shown in Figure 5.14.

FIGURE 5.14

The Brush tool and options (left); the Brush mode settings menu (right)

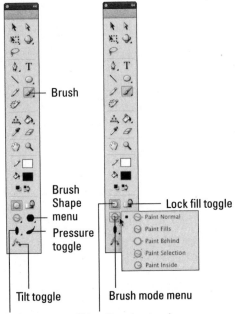

Brush

Brush Shape menu

Pressure toggle

Lock fill toggle

Tilt toggle   Brush mode menu

Brush size menu   Object Drawing toggle

Note

The Pressure toggle and the Tilt toggle are visible in the Options area only if you have a drawing tablet installed on your system. ■

Web Resource

To learn more about tablets and read some fun tutorials, visit www.wacom.com. ■

Figure 5.15 depicts the various ways in which the Brush modes interact with drawn and painted elements. The base image is a solid white rectangle drawn with a black outline. The boat outline is drawn with the Pencil tool in dark gray on top of the rectangle:

- A: **Paint Normal mode:** Applies brush strokes over the top of any lines or fills.

- B: **Paint Fills mode:** Applies brush strokes to replace any fills, but leaves lines untouched.

- C: **Paint Behind mode:** Applies brush strokes only to blank areas and leaves all fills, lines, or other items untouched. In Figure 5.15 (C), the only areas the brush mark covers are those in the background, outside the frame of the picture. Effectively, the brush has gone behind the entire shape. If the stroke had originated within the frame, it would have covered the white fill and gone behind the drawn gray lines and the black outline.

- D: **Paint Selection mode:** Applies brush strokes only to selected fills. In Figure 5.15 (D), a selection was made by Shift+clicking both the white fill inside the boat and inside the sail. The same gray brush marks drawn on the previous figure are now visible only inside the selected fills.

- E: **Paint Inside mode:** Applies brush strokes only to the singular fill area where the brush stroke was first initiated. As the name implies, Paint Inside never paints over lines. If you initiate painting from an empty area, the brush strokes won't affect any existing fills or lines, which approximates the same effect as the Paint Behind setting.

Caution

Painting with the background color (such as white) is not the same as erasing. Although painting with a background color may appear to accomplish something similar to erasing, you are, in fact, creating a filled item that can be selected, moved, edited, deleted, and erased. Even if you can't see it, it adds to your file size. Only erasing erases! ■

Brush size and shape options

Although similar to Stroke height and style, the Brush size and Brush shape settings are unique to the Brush tool.

Cross-Reference

The Lock Fill option is common to both the Brush tool and the Paint Bucket tool. For coverage of using the Lock Fill option with the Brush tool and the Paint Bucket tool, refer to Chapter 9, "Modifying Graphics." ■

In Flash, the size of applied brush marks is always related to the Zoom setting. Therefore, using the same brush diameter creates different-sized brush marks, depending on what Zoom setting you work with in the Document window (see Figure 5.16). You can paint over your whole stage in one stroke, even with a small brush diameter, if your Zoom is at a low setting such as 8 percent; or you can use a large brush diameter to make detailed lines if your Zoom is at a high setting such as 1,500 percent.

FIGURE 5.15

The result of painting with the Brush tool varies depending on the Brush mode. Paint Normal (A), Paint Fills (B), Paint Behind (C), Paint Selection (D), Paint Inside (E).

FIGURE 5.16

Marks made by using the same brush size applied with the Document View at different percentages of Zoom

The Brush Shape option is a drop-down menu with nine possible brush shapes that are based on the circle, ellipse, square, rectangle, and line shapes. (Refer to Figure 5.14.) The oval, rectangle, and line shapes are available in various angles. You can combine these stock brush shapes with the range of brush sizes available in the Brush Size menu to generate a wide variety of brush tips. When using shapes other than circles, note that the diameter sizes chosen in the Brush Size menu apply to the broadest area of any brush shape.

Additional Brush options for drawing tablets

If you use a pressure-sensitive tablet for drawing, two extra options appear in the Tools panel when the Brush tool is active. (The Pressure and Tilt toggles are shown at the bottom of the Tools panel in Figure 5.14.) The Pressure toggle enables you to use pen pressure on a tablet to vary the thickness of brush marks as you draw. Working on a tablet with this option, you can create organic-looking strokes that taper or vary in width as you change the amount of pressure applied to the tablet surface.

Tip

To achieve pressure-sensitive eraser marks, use the eraser on the tablet pen while the Brush tool is active rather than the Eraser tool in the Tools panel. ■

Figure 5.17 shows a series of tapered marks created with a pressure-sensitive tablet, using a single Brush size and a consistent Zoom setting.

FIGURE 5.17

Drawing with the Brush tool on a pressure-sensitive tablet (with the Pressure option turned on in the Tools panel) creates tapered, calligraphic marks.

If you're drawing on a tablet that supports this feature, activating the Tilt toggle enables you to control the thickness and direction of strokes with the movement of your wrist. The degree of tilt is determined by the angle between the top of your stylus (or pen) and the top edge of the drawing tablet. This is a very subtle control that you'll most likely notice if you're using a large, tapered (or "flat") brush style — and if you spend hours drawing on a tablet! I didn't include a figure to illustrate this feature because it is hard to tell from finished artwork how it affects your drawings, but experienced artists will appreciate the "feel" that this option adds to the drawing environment.

Note

Support for the Tilt feature varies on different drawing tablets. If you have a Wacom tablet, you can get current drivers and feature documentation from www.wacom.com. It is beyond the scope of this book to describe different types and features of drawing tablets, but the drawing options available in Flash have been tested on a wide range of tablets, so the chances are good that they will work for you. ■

The Eraser tool

The Eraser tool (E) is used in concert with the shape and drawing tools to obtain final, useable art. As the name implies, the Eraser tool is primarily used for rubbing out mistakes. When the Eraser tool is active, three options appear on the Tools panel, as shown in Figure 5.18. Eraser mode and Eraser Shape are both drop-down menus with multiple options. For Eraser Shape, you can select rectangular or oval erasers in various sizes. Eraser modes are similar to the Brush modes I described previously.

You use the Eraser tool's one unique option, the Faucet toggle, to clear enclosed areas of fill. Using the Faucet is the equivalent of selecting a line or a fill and then deleting it, but the Faucet accomplishes this in one easy step. Select the Eraser tool, choose the Faucet option, and then click any line or fill to instantly erase it. Clicking any part of a selection with the Faucet deletes all elements in the selection.

The interaction of Eraser modes and artwork is consistent with the Brush modes available for the Brush tool. The only difference is that instead of adding a mark to a specified part of a drawing, the Eraser removes marks in a specified part of a drawing. Aside from Erase Normal, Erase Fills, Erase Selected Fills, and Erase Inside, which you will recognize from the previous descriptions of Brush modes, there is also an Erase Lines mode that enables you to remove any lines without disrupting fills.

Note

The Eraser tool erases only lines and fills that are in the current frame of the scene. It won't erase groups, symbols, or text. When you need to erase a part of a group, you have two options: Select the group and choose Edit ⇨ Edit Selected from the application menu (or double-click the group), or select the group and choose Modify ⇨ Ungroup from the application menu (Ctrl+Shift+G or ⌘+Shift+G). ■

FIGURE 5.18

The Eraser tool has three basic options: Eraser mode, Eraser shape, and Faucet.

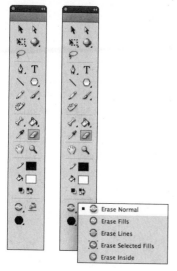

Tip

Drawing Objects have some of the same characteristics as grouped shapes, but they can be treated like raw shapes when you're using the Eraser tool — no need to break them apart. ■

The only alternative to using the Eraser tool to remove graphic elements or areas of drawings is to select them with the Selection, Subselect, or Lasso tool, and then delete them by pressing Delete (or Backspace).

Tip

To quickly erase everything in the current keyframe (even from multiple layers), double-click the Eraser tool in the Tools panel. Don't double-click on the Stage with the Eraser selected; just double-click the Eraser button on the Tools panel. And — poof! — everything in the keyframe is gone. ■

Creating Precise Lines and Bezier Curves with the Pen Tool

You use the Pen tool (P) to draw precision paths that define straight lines and smooth curves. These paths define adjustable line segments, which may be straight or curved — the angle and length of straight segments is completely adjustable, as is the slope and length of curved segments. To draw a series of straight-line segments with the Pen tool, simply move the cursor and click successively: Each subsequent click defines the endpoint of the line. To draw curved line segments with the Pen tool, simply click and drag: the length and direction of the drag determines the depth and shape of the current segment. Both straight- and curved-line segments can be modified and edited by adjusting their anchor points and tangent handles. In addition, any lines or shapes that have been created by other Flash drawing tools can also be displayed as paths (points on lines) and edited with either the Pen tool or the Subselect tool (described in the section "Putting Selection Tools to Work").

Tip

If you're working on a background color that is too similar to your Layer Outline Color, the points on your line will be difficult to see and adjust. Remember that you can always change the Layer Outline Color to contrast with the background. ∎

Creating shapes with the Pen tool takes a little practice, but it produces the most controlled optimization of artwork. Because no points are auto-created, every line and curve is defined only with the points that you place. This saves having to delete points from an overly complex path that may result from drawing with the Pencil or the Brush tool. To make drawing a little less mysterious, there is a submenu for the Pen tool that makes it easier to access some of its secondary capabilities. As shown in Figure 5.19, you can change the Pen tool from its default behavior of placing points (for drawing lines) to add, delete, or convert anchor points on a line that you've already drawn.

The Preferences for the Pen tool are located in the Pen tool section of the Drawing Preferences dialog box. (Choose Edit ➪ Preferences ➪ Drawing or on OS X, Flash ➪ Preferences ➪ Drawing.) There are three optional settings to control preview, point display, and cursor style:

- **Show pen preview:** When you select this option, Flash displays a preview of the next line segment, as you move the pointer, before you click to make the next endpoint and complete the line.

- **Show solid points:** Select this option to invert the default display behavior for points along a selected line. The default is to show selected points as solid (filled circles) and unselected points as hollow (empty squares). When turned on, this option shows selected points as hollow (empty circles) and unselected anchor points as solid (filled squares).

- **Show precise cursors:** This option toggles the Pen tool cursor between the default Pen tool icon and a precision crosshair cursor. This can make selecting points much easier and is recommended if you're doing detailed adjustments on a line.

FIGURE 5.19

The submenu for the Pen tool in the Tools panel makes it easy to change modes as you create or modify lines and curves.

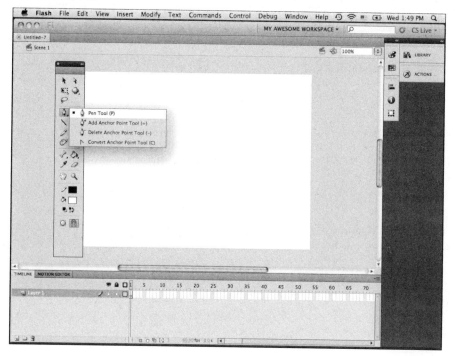

Tip

You can also use a keyboard shortcut to toggle between the two Pen cursor displays: Caps Lock toggles between the precise crosshair icon and the Pen icon when the Pen tool is active. ■

As you work with the Pen tool, you will notice that it displays a number of different icons to the lower right of the cursor. These Pen *states* tell you at any given time what action the Pen can perform on a line.

The Pen states and actions are as follows:

- The Pen displays a small (x) when it's over an empty area of the Stage and ready to place the first point in a line. Click to place the first point in a new line.

- When the Pen hovers over an endpoint that can be connected to close a path, it displays a small link icon (a square with a line through it). Click this point to close the path.

- When the Pen hovers over an endpoint that will not connect to close a path, it displays a slash (/). Click this point to select it as a starting point for a continuation of the path or as the first point for closing a path.

- When the Pen hovers over a curve point, it displays a carat (^) to indicate that clicking that point turns it into a corner point.

- When the Pen hovers over a corner point, it displays a minus (–) sign to indicate that clicking this corner point deletes it.

- When the Pen is over a path (a line between two points), it displays a plus (+) sign to indicate that clicking there adds a point to the path.

- With the Ctrl (or ⌘) key pressed, the Pen behaves like the Subselection tool, so it switches to the hollow arrow icon with a filled black box over lines, or a hollow white box over points.

- When adjusting a path with either the Pen tool or the Subselection tool, the default for selected points is a filled circle, whereas unselected points appear as hollow squares. Note that unselected points display a single tangent handle, bound toward the selected point, which displays two tangent handles.

Tip

Dragging with the Subselection tool around the area of a line that you want to adjust by using points and tangent handles makes these controls visible (as shown in Figure 5.20), so you don't have to try and find them by trolling around with your cursor and watching the Pen state icon. ∎

Figure 5.20 shows a line made with only straight-line segments and corner points, a line made with both straight segments and corner points and curved segments with curve points, and a line made of only curved segments and curve points. You can see that curved segments are controlled by tangent handles extended from the curve points, while straight segments just have corner points without tangent handles.

Now that you've toured the various Pen tool icons, Pen states, and line types, it's time to start drawing and see how these actually apply as you work. To draw and adjust a straight-line segment with the Pen tool, follow these steps:

1. **With the Pen tool active in the Tools panel, click to place the first point of your line on the Stage (wherever you want the line to start).**

2. **Choose the next position for a point and continue to click to create subsequent points and define individual line segments.**

   Each subsequent click creates a corner point on the line that determines the length of individual line segments.

Note

Each click is a point along a continuous line. To end one line and begin a new line, double-click to place the final point in a line. This "breaks" the line so that the next click places a starting point for a new line rather than a continuation of the same line. A line should be ended or completed — by double-clicking or by closing your shape — before using the editing keys described in Step 3. ∎

FIGURE 5.20

Lines made with the Pen tool can consist of straight segments and corner points (top), both straight segments with corner points and curved segments with curve points (middle), or only curved segments with curve points (bottom).

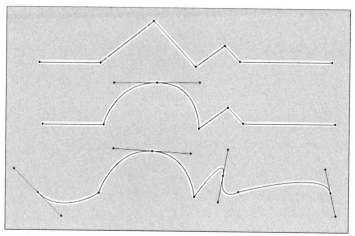

3. **To adjust straight segments, either switch to the Subselection tool in the Tools panel or press the Ctrl (or ⌘) key to temporarily toggle from the Pen tool to the Subselection tool, and then click a point to select it.** Continue pressing the Ctrl (⌘) key as you drag and move the point to change the angle or length of the segment.

Tip

When you're creating straight lines with the Pen tool, press the Shift key to constrain lines to either 45-degree or 90-degree angles. ■

To draw and adjust a curved line segment with the Pen tool, follow these steps:

1. **Click to create the first anchor point.**

2. **Move to the position on the Stage for the next anchor point, click to place it, and without releasing the mouse, drag the Pen tool in the direction you want the curve to go.**

3. **When the preview of the line matches the curve that you want in the final line, release the mouse and move to click and place the next point in the segment.** Repeat this process to create subsequent curve points for curved segments, or simply click elsewhere without dragging to place a point and make the subsequent segment a straight line with a corner point.

4. **As when adjusting straight segments, switch or toggle to the Subselection tool and then click a point to select it.** Then drag and move the point to change the angle or length of the segment, or, after selecting a curve point with the Subselect tool, click and drag the tangent handles of the point to adjust the depth and shape of the curve.

Although both corner points and curve points may be adjusted, they behave differently:

- Corner points and endpoints can be moved with the Subselection tool but they do not display tangent handles.

- Because a curve point defines a curve, moving the tangent handle of a curve point modifies the curves on both sides of the point.

- To convert a corner point into a curve point, simply select the point with the Subselection tool, and while pressing Alt (Option), drag the point slightly. A curve point with two tangent handles appears, replacing the original corner point.

- To adjust one tangent handle of a curve point independent of the other handle, hold down Alt (Option) while dragging the tangent handle that you want to move.

- To convert a curve point into a corner point, select the Convert Anchor point tool from the Pen submenu in the Tools panel and click any curve point once.

- Endpoints cannot be converted into curve points unless the line is continued or joined with another line. To join two endpoints, simply click one endpoint with the Pen tool and then move to the point you want to connect it with and click again. A new line segment is created that joins the two points.

- You can also use the arrow keys, located on your keyboard, to nudge selected corner and curve points into position. Press Shift to augment the arrow keys and to make them nudge 10 pixels with each click.

Note

You can also reshape any lines or shapes created with the Pen, Pencil, Brush, Line, Oval, Rectangle, or PolyStar tools later in this chapter. ■

Web Resource

If you are finding it difficult to make sense of all the different Pen modes and options for editing Bezier curves, you might find it helpful to refer to Adobe's online help. You will find detailed descriptions of each element involved in working with Bezier drawing tools in the section for Using Flash CS5 Professional ➪ Creating and Editing Artwork ➪ Drawing ➪ Drawing with the Pen tool. ■

Using Fill and Stroke Controls

Now that you know where to find and use the drawing tools, you can get more creative with color and line styles. In the following sections, I introduce you to the controls for setting the fill and stroke applied to artwork drawn in Flash.

Tip

When the Pen, Pencil, or Line tool is activated in the Tools panel, you will notice a new Hinting check box in the Properties panel. When selected, this option constrains all points to whole pixel values to ensure that the lines or strokes are not blurry (which is sometimes the case if control points land in between whole pixel values). ∎

Choosing colors

The stroke and fill colors that are applied with any of the drawing tools are determined by the current settings of the color chips located in the Flash Tools panel and in the Properties panel. You can set the fill and stroke colors before you draw something, or select an element on the Stage and adjust it by choosing a new color from the stroke or fill swatches. The Oval, Rectangle, PolyStar, Brush, and Paint Bucket tools all use the current fill settings — you can select colors before you draw a new shape or select an existing shape and modify it by changing the fill and stroke colors.

The color chips in the Tools panel display the most recently selected colors and are always visible regardless of what tool you're using. The Properties panel shows the color chip of the currently active item and displays the chips only if they can be applied with the tool you have active or to the item you have selected. Thus, if you select the Line tool, both Stroke and Fill color chips are visible on the Tools panel, but the Properties panel displays only a Stroke color chip (the Fill color chip displays a strikethrough icon). Although these chips indicate the current color, they're really also buttons: click any color chip to select a new color from the popup Swatches menu. The Swatches menu is shown in Figure 5.21 as it pops up from the Tools panel or from the Properties panel.

The popup swatches display the same color options as the main Swatches panel shown in Figure 5.22. Use shortcut keys (Ctrl+F9 or ⌘+F9) or select Window ➪ Swatches from the application menu to launch the Swatches panel. The Swatches popup includes an Alpha value box as well as a Hexadecimal color value box, another iteration of the No Color button (when it applies), and a button that launches the Color Picker. The Swatches menu opened with the Fill color chip includes the same solid colors available for Stroke, as well as a range of gradient fill styles along the bottom of the panel.

Cross-Reference

I discuss the custom palette options available in the Swatches panel in detail, along with the Mixer panel and other colorful issues, in Chapter 7, "Applying Color." ■

The current Swatches popup is opened by clicking the Stroke or Fill color chip in the Tools panel (left), or by clicking a color chip on the Properties panel (top right).

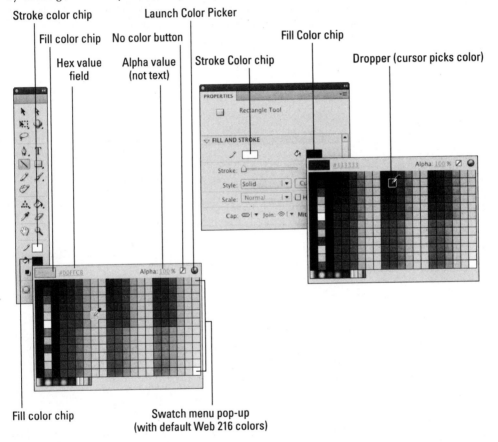

Stroke color chip

Fill color chip

Hex value field

Alpha value (not text)

No color button

Launch Color Picker

Stroke Color chip

Fill Color chip

Dropper (cursor picks color)

Fill color chip

Swatch menu pop-up (with default Web 216 colors)

FIGURE 5.22

Grouping the Swatches panel with the Color panel enables tabbed access to either panel.

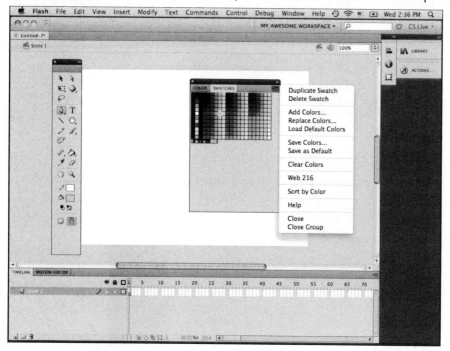

Choosing line styles

In Flash, for all tools that draw or display a line or outline, you control the thickness of the line — or stroke — either by dragging the Stroke Height slider or by entering a value in the Stroke Height numeric entry box. Both of these controls are available in the Properties panel, as shown in Figure 5.23. The stroke options are visible only when they can be applied — if a drawing tool that creates lines is active in the Tools panel or if you have selected an element with a stroke.

Note

Generally, in Flash, lines that are independent or not attached to any fill are referred to as lines, whereas lines or outlines on a filled shape are referred to as strokes. You use the same tools to create and edit lines and strokes. ■

Changes to stroke color and style apply to lines or curves drawn with the Pen, Line, Pencil, Oval, Rectangle, and PolyStar tools. For shapes, the changes apply only to the outline, not to the fill. As with fill color settings, you can select a stroke color and style before you create any artwork (as long as the tool you're going to use is active in the Tools panel), or you can select a line in the Document window with the Selection tool and change its appearance with the settings in the Properties panel.

FIGURE 5.23

The Properties panel gives you all the controls you need to select the stroke height, color, and style, as well as an option to control how strokes scale in the Flash Player and a new Hinting option to constrain points to whole pixel values.

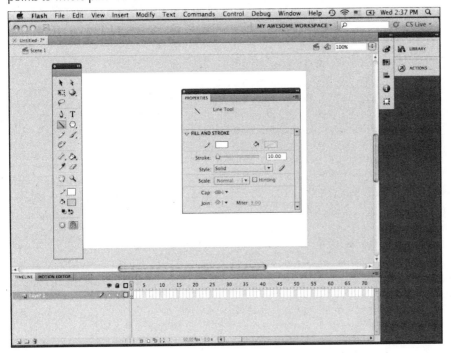

Tip

You can set stroke heights up to 200. In our experience, any stroke with a height setting of more than about 25 becomes rather unwieldy. If you need a mark that big, instead of a giant stroke, you are probably better off using one of the shape tools to create a filled area. ∎

Note

Depending upon the level of zoom, the height difference of some lines may not be visible on-screen, even though zooming in closer enables you to see that the stroke height is correct. Lines set to a height of 1 pixel or lower appear to be the same thickness unless the Stage view is zoomed to 200 percent or closer. However, all line heights still print correctly on a high-resolution printer and are visible in your final Flash movie (.swf) to anyone who zooms in close enough. ■

The Stroke Style drop-down menu (see Figure 5.24) offers the choice of Hairline or six standard, variable-width strokes. Hairline strokes always have the same 1-pixel thickness, even if the mark or shape that they outline is scaled larger after the stroke is applied. You can select and combine the other six line styles with any stroke height. If these styles do not deliver the line look you need, the Custom button (to the right of the Style menu) opens a Stroke Style dialog box (see Figure 5.24), which you can use to generate custom line styles by selecting from a range of properties for each preset line. Basic properties include stroke Thickness and Sharp corners. Other settings vary depending on what style of stroke you choose.

Tip

The Scale menu for strokes in the Properties panel enables you to control how lines scale when symbols are scaled in the authoring environment or the Flash movie is scaled in the Flash Player. ■

Note

Points are the default unit of measurement for determining the spacing and thickness of line segments in the Stroke Style dialog box. ■

To closely examine a custom line before you begin drawing with it, select the Zoom 4x check box beneath the preview area of the Line Style dialog box. Note the Sharp corners check box, which toggles this Line Style feature on or off — select the check box to turn Sharp corners on.

FIGURE 5.24

The Stroke Style dialog box is opened with the Custom button on the Properties panel. The properties that appear vary depending on the style of line you select for adjustment.

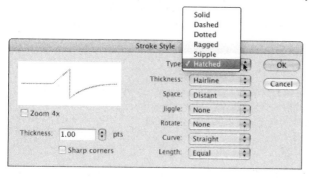

Tip

Although there is no way to save custom line styles within the Stroke Style dialog box, you can create a separate document (.fla) and save samples of your favorite lines there. This eases your workflow if you want to reuse custom line styles extensively. You can apply these styles quite easily to other lines by opening the document and using the Eyedropper tool in conjunction with the Ink Bottle tool. For more information, see the sections on the Eyedropper and the Ink Bottle tools in Chapter 9, "Modifying Graphics." ■

Of course, the best way to get an idea of the variety of possible strokes is to experiment with settings and sizes for each style, but there are a few things to keep in mind as you work with stroke styles in Flash:

- The Hairline line style provides a consistent line thickness that doesn't visually vary at different zoom levels. This is the best line style to choose if you're creating artwork that you want to scale without losing the original line width. Regardless of whether an object with this stroke is enlarged or reduced in size, the Hairline stroke always displays as 1 point wide (as shown in Figure 5.25).

FIGURE 5.25

Hairline strokes always display at 1 point, even if they are scaled in the authoring environment or in the Player.

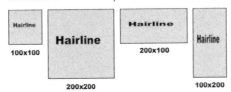

- The Solid line style draws a smooth, unbroken line. The customization variables for this style are limited to Thickness and Sharp corners. These two variables can also be adjusted on all line styles. The Solid line style is the optimal style for Web viewing because it requires fewer points to describe it and is consequently less file intensive. The smaller file sizes theoretically translate into faster download times when the artwork is transmitted over the Web. This really only becomes an issue if you're making extensive use of complex line styles.
- The Hatched line style thickness settings are different from the point size thickness settings that are available for all lines. The default thickness setting (measured in points) defines the thickness or height of the overall hatched line, whereas the hatch thickness setting defines the width of the individual vertical strokes that create the density of the hatched line texture.

Controlling stroke Scale behavior

The Scale option is available only for solid lines, but it is very helpful for ensuring the consistency of scaled UI elements with outlines such as buttons. The various scaling behaviors you can set by using the Scale menu work only if you convert the raw stroke into a symbol. To make this easier to understand, here are the steps for applying the Scale option:

1. **Select a Solid line style.**
2. **Set the stroke height to any height between 0.1 and 200.**
3. **Select the Scale behavior that works best for the specific element:**
   - **None:** This produces a stroke that does not scale. A Solid stroke with Scale set to None has the same consistency as a Hairline but you are able to use any stroke height — instead of being restricted to the 1-point height for Hairline strokes. Figure 5.26 shows how a sample graphic with a 3-point stroke and a Scale setting of None appears when transformed with different amounts of scaling.

FIGURE 5.26

Strokes with Scale set to None always appear with the original stroke height.

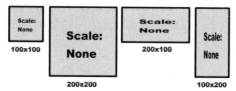

   - **Horizontal:** This produces a stroke that scales to match the horizontal transformation of an item. Vertical transformations have no effect on the scale of the stroke. Figure 5.27 shows how a sample graphic with a 3-point stroke and a Scale setting of Horizontal appears when transformed with different amounts of scaling.

FIGURE 5.27

Strokes with Scale set to Horizontal scale only in proportion to horizontal transformations.

- **Vertical:** This produces a stroke that scales to match the vertical transformation of an item. Horizontal transformations have no effect on the scale of the stroke. Figure 5.28 shows how a sample graphic with a 3-point stroke and a Scale setting of Vertical appears when transformed with different amounts of scaling.

FIGURE 5.28

Strokes with Scale set to Vertical scale only in proportion to vertical transformations.

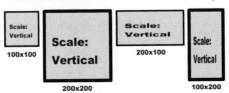

- **Normal:** This produces a stroke that scales proportionally when it is scaled in any direction. This is generally the best setting to use if you want lines to maintain the same relative size as other scaled elements. However, if you want lines to have a fixed size no matter how big or small other elements are scaled, it is best to use the None setting. Figure 5.29 shows how a sample graphic with a 3-point stroke and a Scale setting of Normal appears when transformed with different amounts of scaling.

FIGURE 5.29

Strokes with Scale set to Normal scale in proportion with the greatest transformation in any direction.

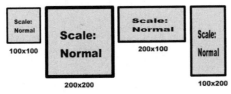

4. Convert the graphic that contains the stroke into a symbol (Movie clip, Graphic, or Button).

5. Scale instances of the symbol in the authoring environment or in the Player and you will notice how the stroke scaling is constrained based on the Scale setting that you applied to the original stroke (in Step 3).

If you have ever tried to reuse a graphic that needed to be scaled while maintaining a specific size ratio to other elements — either relative or fixed — you will appreciate the level of control the Scale menu affords. The most common use for this option is constraining the scale behavior of a custom button that has to be adjusted to fit text of varying lengths. Generally, you want the stroke on the button to remain consistent while the button is stretched to accommodate the text. If you apply the Vertical Scale behavior, you will have a button with a stroke that stays the same no matter how long you stretch it horizontally to fit your text. But if you decide the buttons need to be a bit bigger overall, you can apply a vertical transformation and the stroke grows proportionally. What more could I ask for?

Optimizing Drawings

Aside from making a drawing more geometric, the main advantage of simplifying a shape or line is that it reduces the number of points that Flash has to remember and, thus, reduces the final file size. This is especially important for projects such as cartoons or animations that include a large number of hand-drawn shapes.

The most powerful tool for optimizing artwork precisely is found in the Optimize Curves dialog box opened by choosing Modify ⇨ Shape ⇨ Optimize. This feature gives you the option to control the level of optimization from 0 to 100. The new Preview check box enables you to see how different levels of optimization affect your artwork before deciding on a final setting and applying the command. If you select the Show totals message check box, you will see a dialog box appear to inform you how many points have been removed and what percentage reduction has been achieved after the optimization has been applied to your graphic each time you apply the modification.

Figure 5.30 shows a sketch drawn with the Brush tool with default smoothing before and after Optimize Curves was applied. The reduction in points appears in the dialog box. For illustration purposes, I made a drastic adjustment by applying Optimization strength at 100. For practical purposes, you should find a balance between optimization and drawing complexity by testing a range of settings.

Tip

You can apply the Optimize Curves command to the same artwork multiple times to achieve maximum reduction of points, but keep an eye on the totals message because when your artwork reaches a threshold of smoothing, continuing to apply the command starts to add points. If you see a negative value in the percentage of reduction, use the Undo command to step back to the artwork with the fewest points. ∎

FIGURE 5.30

Before (ltop) and after (bottom) Optimize Curves is used to reduce the complexity of a drawing made with the Brush tool with default smoothing. The reduction in points translates directly into a smaller file size.

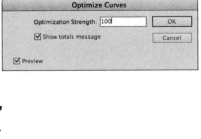

Putting Selection Tools to Work

Selection tools enable you to choose items that you want to edit in the Document window, as well as move or reshape specific elements. The three main selection tools — Selection, Subselection, and Lasso — provide different selection styles you can use for different editing tasks. The Subselection tool is used primarily as a companion to the Pen tool.

Tip
When you are busy with another tool, you can temporarily toggle to the Selection tool by pressing Ctrl (or ⌘). ■

The Selection tool

The Selection (arrow) tool (V) is used most commonly to select and move items — or multiple items — on the Stage. It is also used to reshape lines and shapes, in a way that is familiar to users who have worked in other vector graphics applications. The Selection tool's neighbor, which is differentiated with a white, rather than a black, arrowhead, is the Subselect tool (A). The Subselect tool is most useful for moving and editing anchor points created with the Pen tool and adjusting tangents on Bezier curves.

You can use the Selection tool to reshape a line or shape by pulling on the line (or shape) itself, or on its endpoints, curves, or corners. You can also use the Selection tool to select, move, and edit other Flash graphic elements, including groups, symbols, buttons, and text. When you click a raw stroke or fill, a mesh pattern appears to indicate that it has been selected. If the item you click is a symbol, a group, or a drawing object, a thin, colored line (called a *highlight*) indicates the selection status. You may set the highlight color in the General Preferences dialog box found under Edit ➪ Preferences (or in OS X, under Flash ➪ Preferences).

Tip

To temporarily turn off the selection mesh while editing an element, use View ➪ Hide Edges (Ctrl+H or ⌘+Shift+E). To toggle it back on, enter the same keyboard shortcut again. Even if you have toggled the selection off on one element, it is visible on the next element that you select. ■

Figure 5.31 shows a shape, a drawing object, a shape primitive, a group, and a Graphic symbol as they look when unselected (top) and as they appear when selected with the Selection tool. The first oval (a primitive shape) displays a mesh pattern when selected (left). The second oval (drawn with the Object Drawing option turned on), the third oval (drawn with the Oval Primitive tool), and the fourth oval (with the stroke and fill combined in a group) all display a thin, rectangular border when selected — the subtle differences being the color of the selection outline and the small, filled dot that designates the center point of the oval primitive. The final oval (which was converted into a Graphic symbol) displays a thin, rectangular border with a small crosshair icon in the top-left corner and a white transformation point in the center when selected (right). You can move groups and symbols but not edit them directly on the Stage with the Selection tool unless you go into Edit mode.

Note

Drawing objects show a similar selection highlight as grouped shapes but are actually a hybrid graphic style, which shares selected characteristics with raw shapes, grouped shapes, and Graphic symbols. Like raw shapes, you can modify drawing objects directly on the Stage with the Selection tool and any of the tools related to fills and strokes. Like grouped shapes, drawing objects do not erase or merge with other shapes if they overlap on the same layer (unless special commands are applied). ■

Tip

Shape primitives have similar behavior to grouped shapes, but they have special editing options in the Properties panel that make them easy to modify. However, in order to edit a shape primitive with any of the selection tools, it must be converted into a drawing object or broken apart into a basic shape. The dynamic edit options in the Properties panel will no longer be available. ■

Cross-Reference

I explain the various ways of using grouped shapes in graphics in Chapter 9, "Modifying Graphics," and I discuss using and editing symbols in Chapter 6, "Symbols, Instances, and the Library." ■

In addition to clicking a line or shape to select it, you can select one or more items by dragging a marquee around them when the Selection tool is active. This operation is called *drag-select*. You can add additional items to a current selection by pressing Shift and clicking the items in sequence. When you drag-select to make a selection, previously selected items are deselected and excluded from the selection. In order to include previously selected items, press Shift as you drag-select. When a group is selected and you drag to move it on the Stage, holding down Shift constrains the movement range of the elements to 45 degrees. This is helpful if you need to move an element up or down while keeping it on the same axis or baseline.

FIGURE 5.31

Top row shows items unselected; bottom row shows Selection tool highlights (L-R) for a shape, a drawing object, a shape primitive, a group, and a Graphic symbol

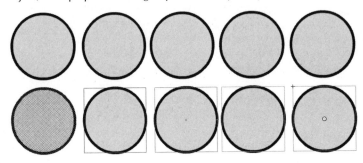

Deselect one or more items by using any of the following methods:

- Pressing Esc
- Choosing Edit ➪ Deselect All
- Using the keyboard shortcut Ctrl+Shift+A (or ⌘+Shift+A)
- Clicking anywhere outside all the selected items

You can also use the Selection tool for duplicating items. Simply select an item (or line segment) with the Selection tool and press Alt (Option) while dragging the item to a new location. The original item remains in place, and a new item is deposited at the end of your drag stroke.

Caution

Selecting a line with the Selection tool and then holding down Alt (Option) while dragging it to a new location duplicates it. Holding down Alt (Option) before dragging a line segment (that has not been selected) with the Selection tool adds a new corner point. ■

Moving multiple elements with the Selection tool

Text boxes, drawing objects, and groups are selected as single elements and move as a single unit. After you create text in a text box (I discuss text features in Chapter 8, "Working with Text"), Flash treats the text as one block, or group, meaning that all the individual letters move together when the box is selected. Similarly, a group of graphic elements — such as lines, outlines, fills, or shapes — can be grouped and moved or manipulated as a single element. However, when you move an item that is not grouped, only the selected part is moved. This situation can be tricky when you have ungrouped fills and outlines because selecting one without the other could unintentionally break up your shape. To group elements, select them all and apply the Modify ⇨ Group command (Ctrl+G or ⌘+G). If necessary, you can ungroup them later by using Modify ⇨ Ungroup (Ctrl+Shift+G or ⌘+Shift+G). I discuss grouping further in Chapter 9, "Modifying Graphics."

Tip

Double-clicking the fill of a shape that has an outline stroke and a fill selects both. You can also use this strategy on lines with multiple sections. Double-clicking one section selects all the connected parts of a line, rather than just the closest segment. ■

The Drawing Object mode and the Shape Primitive tools make it easier to keep strokes and fills together. Drawing objects and shape primitives behave like grouped shapes: When you click anywhere on the shape, the stroke and fill are both selected so they move together. If you have drawn basic shapes with the Object Drawing toggle turned off, you can use the Modify ⇨ Group command (Ctrl+G or ⌘+G) to group the lines and fills or use the Modify ⇨ Combine Objects ⇨ Union command to convert the raw lines and fills into a drawing object.

Modifying Selection preferences

In most cases, the default behavior for selection tools will support your workflow, but there are two preferences that you can modify to adjust selection behavior:

- **Turn off Shift select:** Prior to Flash 4, additional elements were added to a selection simply by clicking them. To use this older selection style, go to Edit (or on Mac Flash) ⇨ Preferences, and under General ⇨ Selection Options, clear the Shift select check box.

- **Turn on Contact-sensitive selection:** The standard selection behavior in Flash requires that a lasso or selection marquee completely enclose a group, drawing object, or symbol in order to select it. If you prefer to have these items included in a selection when the marquee touches any visible part, go to Edit➪Preferences and under General➪Selection options, select the Contact-sensitive selection and Lasso tools check box. Figure 5.32 illustrates the different selection results that you get when a marquee partially encloses a group, drawing object, or symbol when Contact-sensitive selection is left off (top) and when it is turned on (below).

FIGURE 5.32

To change the default nonselection result of partial selections in Flash (top), you can turn on Contact-sensitive selection behavior to select even partially enclosed items (below).

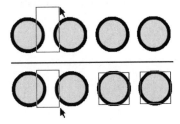

Using Selection tool arrow states to adjust or move drawings

In addition to the actions accomplished by selecting a line (or line section) and clicking an option, three arrow states — Move Selected Element, Reshape Curve or Line, and Reshape Endpoint or Corner — enable you to reshape and move parts of your drawings. It works like this: As you move the Selection tool over the Flash Stage, the arrow cursor changes state to indicate what tasks it can perform in context with various items (the line or fill) closest to the Selection tool's current position.

Tip

When reshaping brush strokes or other filled items with the Selection tool, make sure that you don't select both the stroke and fill before trying to reshape the outline. If you do, you'll be able to move only the entire brush stroke — you won't be able to reshape it. ■

Figure 5.33 shows a series of (magnified) images that demonstrate the various arrow states as they appear and are applied. On the left, the original shape is shown with the arrow states displayed as the cursor is moved over the center of the shape, over a corner (B), and over a line (C). The center image shows the preview as the Move Corner arrow is used to extend the corner of the square and the Reshape Curve arrow is used to stretch the curve. The final image on the right shows the resulting changes to the original square.

Figure 5.34 shows the various Selection tool arrow states used to modify a line. The lower images show the arrow state cursors, the center images show the preview as the mouse is dragged, and the top images show the resulting changes to the line when the mouse is released. You will notice that lines have to be selected in order to be moved without changing their shape with the Selection tool. If the line is not selected, the arrow displays only Move Corner or Reshape Curve states. If you want to add an angle to a line rather than add a curve, switch from Reshape Curve to Add Corner Point by holding down Alt (or Option) before clicking and dragging a line segment.

FIGURE 5.33

Selection tool arrow states used to reshape and reposition an element: Move Selected Item arrow, Reshape Corner arrow (B), and Reshape Curve arrow (C)

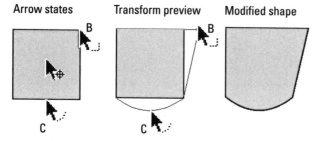

Arrow states   Transform preview   Modified shape

Caution

The icon visible next to the Selection tool arrow does not update when you switch from Reshape Curve to Add Corner Point by holding down Alt (or Option), but the behavior changes. After you click and move the line, the icon updates to match the behavior. ∎

FIGURE 5.34

Using Selection tool arrow states to reshape and reposition a line (L-R: Move Selected Item, Reshape Corner, Reshape Curve)

Tip
Some brush strokes are easier to reshape if you view them as outlines (as described in Chapter 4). ∎

Knowing your Selection tool options

Figure 5.35 shows the three options that appear at the bottom section of the Tools panel when the Selection tool is active: Magnet (or snap to objects), Smooth, and Straighten. Because the various snap controls can be confusing at first, I compare the Magnet tool with the other snap settings available in Flash, later in this chapter.

FIGURE 5.35

The Selection tool options available on the Tools panel

The Smooth and Straighten options available with the Selection tool (when a raw shape or drawing object is selected) are best used to clean up drawings by smoothing irregular curves or straightening crooked lines. Smoothing or Straightening reduces the number of bumps and variations (or points of transition) in a complex shape or line by reducing the number of points. The simplest curve or line is described by only one point at each end.

To simplify a shape or line, click the Selection tool and select the item you just sketched. Then click the Straighten or Smooth button in the Tools panel to get incremental adjustment. If you want more control over the way these commands are applied to your artwork, use Modify➪ Shape➪Advanced Straighten or Modify➪Shape➪Advanced Smooth to open the new Advanced

Straighten or Smooth dialog boxes. For hard-edged items such as a polygon, continue to click the Straighten button in the Tools panel or adjust the Straighten strength in the Advanced Straighten dialog box (with Preview turned on) until your rough sketch reaches the level of angularity that you like. For smooth-edged items that approximate an oval or an arc, continue to click the Smooth button in the Tools panel or adjust the Smoothing strength and the target angle range in the Advanced Smooth dialog box until your rough sketch has the amount of desired roundness.

Tip

The controls in the Advanced Smooth dialog box can be a little confusing, but if you look at your drawing and consider if there are any angles that you do want to preserve and then use the angle menus to set a value range that excludes the angle you do want to keep (and not smooth), then it makes a little more sense. For example, if you have a 90-degree angle in your artwork (a clean corner) and you don't want that rounded off but you do want wider curves to be smoothed and narrower curves to be smoothed, you would set the first angle setting to Smooth angles below 89 degrees and the second setting to Smooth angles above 91 degrees. This would leave your 90-degree angle unsmoothed while applying smoothing to all the other angles in your drawing. If you have a hard time telling the difference between one result and another, don't be dismayed: This is a very subtle adjustment. ■

As shown in Figure 5.36, the simplified shape usually needs some further adjustment to get the result that you want after some of the points have been removed. The tools used for adjusting individual curves and points are the Pen tool and the Subselect tool.

You can apply the Smooth and Straighten options with the Selection tool to any selected shape or line to reduce the number of points and modify the form. The specific effect that these options have on your graphics is dependent on the Drawing settings that were used to create the original lines and the level of straightening or smoothing that you choose. By minimizing complexity in freehand drawings or shapes, Smooth and Straighten gradually reduce an erratic graphic into the most simplified form that can be described with the fewest points possible, while making curved lines straighter (when you apply Straighten) or sharp angles more rounded (when you apply Smooth).

Note

In the example shown in Figure 5.36, I achieved maximum smoothing on all angles in the drawing by using only the Smooth angle above setting in the Smooth dialog box. With this set to 0 and the Smooth angle below check box deselected, you are allowing the smoothing algorithm to be applied to all angles in the drawing (from 0 degrees to 180 degrees). The same effect could be achieved by setting the Smooth angle below value to 180 and deselecting the Smooth angle above check box. ■

Although these assistants nudge a sketch or line style in the direction that you want, they don't add information; so don't be surprised if your drawing doesn't really look "better" or it takes a few tries to get the right balance between rough drawing and shape recognition.

Lines drawn with the Pencil tool (top left) can be selected with the Selection tool and simplified with the Advanced Smooth (center) or Advanced Straighten (right) options. A geometric shape (bottom) can be smoothed to have more curved lines (center) or straightened to have more angular lines (right).

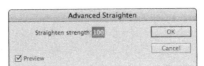

The Lasso tool

The Lasso (L) is a flexible tool, somewhat resembling the selection equivalent of the Pen tool crossed with the Pencil tool. You use the Lasso primarily to make freeform selections and to group-select odd or irregular-shaped areas of your drawing. After areas are selected, they can be moved, scaled, rotated, or reshaped as a single unit. You can also use the Lasso tool to split shapes or select portions of a line or a shape. As shown in Figure 5.37, it has three options in the Tools panel: the Polygon mode button, the Magic Wand, and the Magic Wand properties.

The Lasso tool works best if you drag a loop around the area you want to select. (Hence, the tool name Lasso!) But if you slip or if you don't end the loop near where you started, Flash closes the loop with a straight line between your starting point and the endpoint. Because you can use the Lasso tool to define an area of any shape — limited only by your ability to draw and use the multiple selection capabilities of Flash — the Lasso tool gives you more control over selections than the Selection tool.

Tip
To add to a previously selected area, hold down Shift before initiating additional selections. ■

FIGURE 5.37

The Lasso tool and options

Polygon mode

Polygon mode affords greater precision when making straight-edged selections, or in mixed mode, selections that combine freeform areas with straight edges. To describe a simple polygon selection, with the Lasso tool active, click the Polygon mode button to toggle on Polygon selection mode. In Polygon mode, you create selection points with a mouse-click, causing a straight selection line to extend between mouse-clicks. To complete the selection, double-click.

Mixed mode usage, which includes Polygon functionality, is available when the Lasso tool is in Freeform mode. To work in Freeform mode, the Polygon option must be in the off position. While drawing with the Freeform Lasso, press Alt (Option) to temporarily invoke Polygon mode. (Polygon mode continues only as long as Alt (Option) is pressed.) As long as Alt (Option) is pressed, a straight selection line extends between mouse clicks. To return to Freeform mode, simply release the Alt (or Option) key. Release the mouse to close the selection.

Note

Sometimes aberrant selections — selections that seem inside out, or that have a weird, unwanted straight line bisecting the intended selection — result from Lasso selections. That's usually because the point of origination of a Lasso selection is the point to which the Lasso snaps when the selection is closed. It takes a little practice to learn how to plan the point of origin so that the desired selection is obtained when the selection is closed. ■

The Magic Wand option and Magic Wand properties

The Magic Wand option of the Lasso tool is used to select ranges of a similar color in a bitmap that has been broken apart. After you select areas of the bitmap, you can change their fill color or delete them. Breaking apart a bitmap means that Flash subsequently sees the bitmap image as a collection of individual areas of color. (This is not the same as tracing a bitmap, which reduces the vast number of colors in a continuous-tone bitmap to areas of solid color.) After an image is broken apart, you can select individual areas of the image with any of the selection tools, including the Magic Wand option of the Lasso tool.

The Magic Wand option has two modifiable settings: Threshold and Smoothing. To set them, click the Magic Wand settings button to launch the Magic Wand Settings dialog box (shown in Figure 5.38) while the Lasso tool is active.

FIGURE 5.38

Use the Magic Wand Settings dialog box to adjust the selection range and level of smoothing.

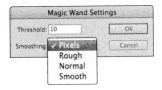

The Threshold setting defines the breadth of adjacent color values that the Magic Wand option includes in a selection. Values for the Threshold setting range from 0 to 200: the higher the setting, the broader the selection of adjacent colors. Conversely, a smaller number results in the Magic Wand making a narrower selection of adjacent colors. A value of zero results in a selection of contiguous pixels that are all the same color as the target pixel.

The Smoothing setting of the Magic Wand option determines to what degree the edge of the selection should be smoothed. This is similar to anti-aliasing. (Anti-aliasing dithers the edges of shapes and lines so that they look smoother on-screen.) The options are Smooth, Pixels, Rough, and Normal.

The Subselection tool

The Subselection (arrow) tool (A) is the companion for the Pen and is found in the Tools panel to the right of the Selection tool. The Subselection tool has two purposes:

- To either move or edit individual anchor points and tangents on lines and outlines
- To move individual objects

When you position the Subselection tool over a line or point, the hollow arrow cursor displays one of two states:

- When over a line, it displays a small, filled square next to it, indicating that the whole selected shape or line can be moved.

- When over a point, it displays a small, hollow square, indicating that the point will be moved to change the shape of the line.

Tip

If you use the Subselection tool to drag a selection rectangle around two items, you'll find that clicking and dragging from any line of an item enables you to move only that item, but clicking any point on an item enables you to move all items in the selection. ■

Figure 5.39 shows the use of the Subselection tool to move a path (A), to move a single point (B), to select a tangent handle (C), and to modify a curve by adjusting its tangent handle (D). Note that a preview is shown before releasing the handle.

FIGURE 5.39

Using the Subselection tool to modify lines and curves

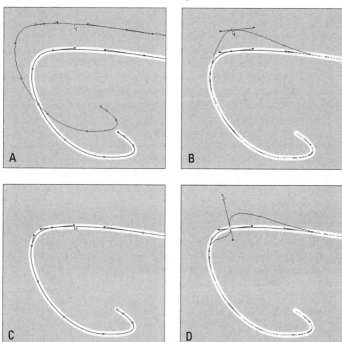

The Subselection tool is most useful for modifying and adjusting paths. To display anchor points on a line or shape outline created with the Pencil, Brush, Line, Oval, or Rectangle tools, simply click the line or shape outline with the Subselection tool. This reveals the points that define the line or shape. Click any point to cause its tangent handles to appear. If you have a shape that is all fill, without any stroke, you'll need to position the cursor precisely at the edge of the shape in order to select or move it with the Subselection tool.

To convert a corner point into a curve point, follow these steps:

1. **Click to select the point with the Subselection tool.**

2. **While pressing Alt (Option), click and drag the point.** A curve point with tangent handles appears, replacing the original corner point.

Note

By holding down Ctrl (or ⌘), the Pen tool can be used to mimic the function of the Subselection tool for moving lines or points but not for converting a curve point into a corner point. ■

An important use of the Pen tool/Subselection tool combo is editing lines for optimal file size. The simpler your shapes, the smaller your file size and the faster your movie downloads. Most often, this involves deleting extraneous points. There are a few ways to delete points:

- Select the line or outline with the Subselection tool, which causes the individual points to appear as hollow circles along the line. Select the point that you want to remove. Press Delete.

- Select a line or outline with the Pen tool, and then position the cursor over the point that you want to remove. The cursor updates and displays a small inverted v (^) to the lower right, which is the Corner Point cursor. Click the point with the Corner Point cursor, and continue to hover over the point. After clicking with the Corner Point cursor, the cursor updates and displays a small minus sign (–) to the lower right, which is the Delete Point cursor. Click the point with the Delete Point cursor to delete it.

- When deleting more than one point from a closed shape, such as an oval or polygon, use the Subselection tool to drag and select any number of points. Press Delete to eliminate the selected points. The path heals itself, closing the shape with a smooth arc or line.

Tip

If you use the Subselection tool to select a path and then Shift+select several points on it, those points can be moved in unison by dragging or by tapping the arrow keys. ■

Tip

The submenu available in the Tools panel for the Pen tool makes it easier to set the Pen mode to remove or convert points without having to keep such a close eye on the contextual cues. Simply choose the Pen mode that you want to work within the Tools panel, click the line you want to edit to make the points visible, and begin adding, subtracting, or converting points, depending on the setting you've chosen. ■

Designing and Aligning Elements

After you've drawn some lines or shapes, you'll want to organize them in your layout. Flash provides some useful tools to help with moving or modifying elements that are familiar if you've worked in other graphics programs. Aside from using the Flash grid and manually placed guides with various snap settings to control your layout, you can quickly access the Align panel or the Info panel to dynamically change the placement of elements on the Stage. The Transform panel is the most accurate way to modify the size, aspect ratio, rotation, and even the vertical or horizontal "slant" of an element.

The precise alignment possible with panels and snapping controls is especially helpful if you're working with detailed artwork or multiple shapes that need to be arranged in exact relation to each other.

Simplifying snapping settings

There are five independent snapping settings in Flash. Snapping is a feature that gives you guidance when moving elements on the Stage and helps to align elements accurately in relation to each other, to the drawing grid, to guides, or to whole pixel axis points. The five different snapping controls can be turned on and off in the View ⇨ Snapping submenu or in the Edit Snapping dialog box (shown in Figure 5.40), launched by choosing View ⇨ Snapping ⇨ Edit Snapping (Ctrl+/ or ⌘+/).

FIGURE 5.40

You can control Snapping settings in the Edit Snapping dialog box by using the Basic view, which shows only the top five check boxes, or the Advanced view, which expands the dialog box to include more Snap align settings, as shown here.

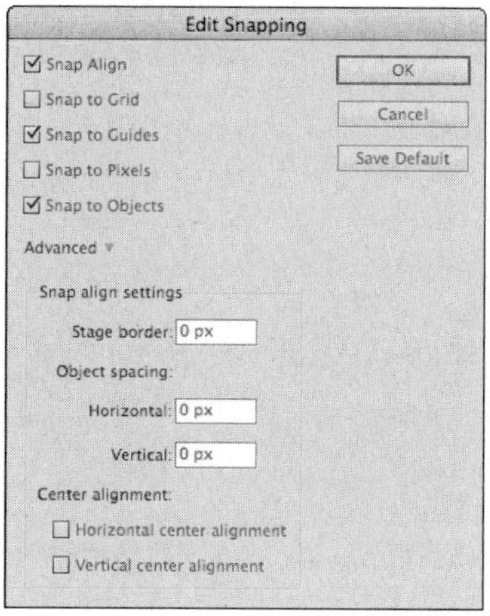

You can tell that an item is snapping by the appearance of dotted guide lines, as shown in the Snap Align example (see Figure 5.41), or by the appearance of a small circle beside the Selection tool arrow cursor, as shown in the Snap to Object and Snap to Grid examples (see Figure 5.42 and Figure 5.43). For best control of snapping position, click and drag from the center point or from an outside edge of an element.

The five main snapping modes are adjusted and applied as follows.

Snap Align

This feature gives you relative visual alignment guides as you move elements on the Stage. You'll either love or hate this option because it's the most "interactive" of all the snapping settings. The controls for Snap Align are in the Advanced settings of the Edit Snapping dialog box (shown in Figure 5.40). By default, Snap Align is set to display visual guides to alert you when an element is within 0 pixels of the movie border (aka the Stage edge), or within 0 pixels of another element in your layout.

As you move an element around on the Stage, you see dotted lines (see Figure 5.41) that alert you when the edge of the element is exactly 0 pixels from the edge of the Stage, or 0 pixels from the next closest fixed element. The dotted guide lets you know when the edges of the two elements are touching (or perfectly aligned), either vertically or horizontally. Modify the Movie border settings to change the alert or alignment distance between elements and the edge of the Stage. Modify the Horizontal or Vertical Snap tolerance settings to change the alert distance between elements. If you also want to see guides when elements are aligned to the center point of other elements, select the Horizontal or Vertical Center alignment check boxes.

Tip

If you change the Horizontal or Vertical Snap Align settings to show a dotted line when an item is a specific distance from another item (such as 10 pixels — this was the default setting in Flash MX 2004), you still see the dotted line show up when the items are touching or within 0 pixels of each other. The fixed-distance Snap Align cue can be very helpful if you are trying to arrange items but you need them to be more than 0 pixels apart. ∎

Snap to Objects

The Snap to Objects setting is a toggle that causes items being drawn or moved on-screen to snap to or align with other items on the Stage. Click the magnet icon in the Tools panel to turn snapping on or off (Shift+Ctrl+/ or Shift+⌘+/), or choose View ➪ Snapping ➪ Snap to Objects (a check mark appears next to the command if it's on). To control the tolerance of the magnet or the "stickiness" of the snap, use the Connect Lines setting found in Edit ➪ Preferences ➪ Drawing (or in OS X, Flash ➪ Preferences ➪ Drawing). By default, the Connect Lines tolerance is set at Normal. To make the magnet stronger, change the tolerance to Can be distant; to make it less strong, use Must be close. The Connect Lines control helps you to connect lines cleanly when drawing shapes or outlines.

FIGURE 5.41

Snap Align guides give visual feedback for various alignment settings.

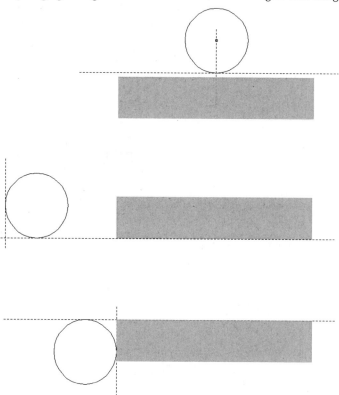

As shown in Figure 5.42, object snapping is indicated by the "o" icon near the center point as an item is moved from its original position (left). When the item is dragged close enough to another item to snap to it, the "o" icon gets slightly larger, which indicates to you to release the mouse (right). This same visual cue works if you drag an item by a corner point rather than from a center point. Ovals can be aligned to the center point or to any point along their outer edge.

FIGURE 5.42

Snap to Objects indicated by a change in the size of the center point (or corner point) "o" icon as an item is moved to overlap with another item

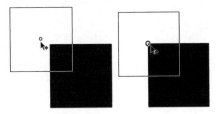

Snap to Grid

Snap to Grid (Ctrl+Shift+' [apostrophe] or ⌘+Shift+' [apostrophe]) is an option available under View➪Snapping➪Snap to Grid, which helps to align elements to guides or to the background grid. If Snap to Grid is turned on, elements show the snap icon by the Arrow cursor when you drag them close to a line in your grid, whether the grid is visible or not.

To control the tolerance of this snapping feature, use the settings found under View➪Grid➪Edit Grid (Ctrl+Alt+G or ⌘+Option+G). The Grid Settings dialog box also includes check boxes for Snap to Grid and View Grid — these just give you another way to turn these tools on or off. Adjust the default horizontal and vertical spacing of the grid lines by entering new pixel values in the text fields. The first three settings in the Snap Accuracy menu are the same as those for Snap to Object, but there is an additional setting, Always Snap, which constrains elements to the grid no matter where you drag them. Figure 5.43 shows the default 18-pixel gray grid as it appears when it's made visible (View➪Grid➪Show Grid) with the Stage view zoom at 200 percent.

FIGURE 5.43

The snap icon as it appears when an element is dragged onto a grid line with Snap to Grid turned on (snapping works regardless of whether the grid is visible or not)

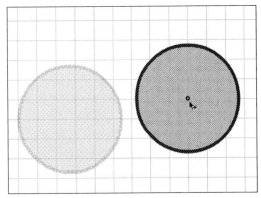

Snap to Guides

As I described in the previous chapter, guides are vertical or horizontal visual alignment tools that can be dragged onto the pasteboard or Stage *when rulers are visible*: Choose View ⇨ Rulers (Ctrl+Alt+Shift+R or ⌘+Option+Shift+R). If Snap to Grid is turned on when you drag guides out, they are constrained to the grid; otherwise, you can place guides anywhere. After guides are set, they are visible even if you turn rulers off; to toggle guide visibility use View ⇨ Guides ⇨ Show Guides (Ctrl+; [semicolon] or ⌘+; [semicolon]). As shown in Figure 5.44, Snap to Guides enables you to align an element to a guide, even if it is not aligned with the grid.

The snap icon as it appears when an element is dragged onto a guide with Snap to Guides turned on

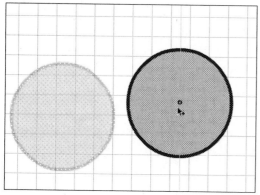

Note

Snap to Guides is independent of Snap to Grid, but guides can be placed only outside the grid when Snap to Grid is turned off. ∎

Tip

Rulers have to be visible to drag a guide onto the Stage, but after guides are placed, rulers can be turned off and guides will still be visible. ∎

Snap to Pixels

Snap to Pixels is the only "global" setting that causes all elements to align with a 1-pixel grid that is visible only when the View scale is set to 400 percent or greater. This setting does not necessarily help you to align elements with each other, but it does help to keep elements from being placed "between pixels" by constraining movement of elements on the X and Y axes to whole pixels, rather than allowing decimals. There is no shortcut key for turning Snap to Pixels on, but you can always toggle it on and off from the View menu by checking or unchecking View ⇨ Snapping ⇨ Snap to Pixel. Figure 5.45 shows how the pixel grid appears when the View scale is at 400 percent. Items are constrained to whole pixel axis points if they are dragged from the center or from an outside edge.

FIGURE 5.45

The pixel grid visible when View scale is at 400 percent or higher with Snap to Pixels turned on

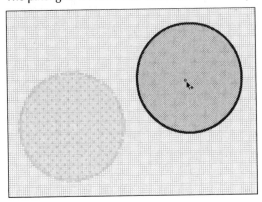

Caution

If an item is positioned between pixels — for example if the X, Y position is 125.5, 200.5 — the Snap to Pixel feature does not correct the position to a whole pixel value. Snap to Pixels constrains only the movement of items to whole pixel values. Thus, the item example given here could be dragged to a new location only by moving in whole pixel values; so it might end up at a new location such as 130.5, 225.5. If you want to keep items aligned to whole pixel values, use the input fields in the Properties panel to manually enter a starting location with whole pixel X, Y values, and then use the Snap to Pixel option to keep items aligned with the 1-pixel grid. ■

Tip

When you are working with an oval or other nonsquare polygon, you will notice that the X, Y values in the Properties panel may still show decimal pixel values even when Snap to Pixels is turned on. If you use the Info panel to change the shape's registration point from the default top-left setting to the center (click the center square in the Registration grid), you will have more success positioning and tracking the shape with whole pixel values. ■

Design panels

When you are drawing in Flash, the design panels — Align, Info, and Transform — can be your best friends. Use the Align panel to align, *regularize* (match the sizes of), or distribute several items on Stage, either relative to each other or to the Stage area. Use the Info panel to modify the coordinates, dimensions, and transformation points for items on the Stage. Use the Transform panel to scale, rotate, and skew an item.

Tip

You can also access width and height and x, y location values directly in the Position and Size section of the new vertical Properties panel. ■

The Align panel (Ctrl+K or ⌘+K), the Info panel (Ctrl+I or ⌘+I), and the Transform panel (Ctrl+T or ⌘+T) are available individually from the Windows menu, or they can be grouped into a tabbed panel that launches when you select any of the individual panels from the Window menu. Having these panels in a floating tabbed group is handy, but if you find that you use one more than the others, you might want to dock your favorite panels with the Properties panel for quick access.

The Align panel

The Align panel (Ctrl+K or ⌘+K), shown in Figure 5.46, is one of many features for which you'll be grateful every time you use it. It enables you, with pixel-perfect precision, to align or distribute items relative to each other or to the Stage.

FIGURE 5.46

Use the Align panel to both size and arrange items with ease.

The Align panel has five controls. The icons on the buttons show visually how selected items can be arranged:

- **To stage:** On the far right, you will notice a To stage button. When this button is selected, all adjustments are made in relation to the full Stage. To stage is actually a toggle you can turn on or off at any time — it retains the last chosen state even if the panel is closed and reopened.

- **Align:** There are six buttons in this first control. The first group of three buttons is for horizontal alignment, and the second group of three is for vertical alignment. These buttons align two or more items (or one or more items with the Stage) horizontally (top, middle, bottom) or vertically (left, middle, right).

- **Distribute:** This control also has six buttons: three for horizontal distribution and three for vertical distribution. These buttons are most useful when you have three or more items that you want to space evenly (such as a row of menu items). These buttons distribute items equally, again vertically or horizontally. The different options enable you to distribute from edge to edge, or from item centers.

- **Match size:** This control enables you to force two or more items of different sizes to become equal in size, and match items horizontally, vertically, or both.

- **Space:** This option enables you to space items evenly, again, vertically or horizontally. You may wonder how this differs from Distribute. Both are similar in concept, and if your items are all the same size, these options have the same effect. The difference becomes more apparent when the items are of different sizes:

  - Distribute evenly distributes the items according to a common reference (top, center, or bottom). For example, if one item is larger than the others, it may be separated from the other items by less space, but the distance between its top edge and the next item's top edge will be consistent with all the selected items.

  - Space ensures that the spacing between items is the same; for example, each item might have exactly 36 pixels between it and the next.

To align an item to the exact center of the Stage, do the following:

1. **Click to select the item you want to center.**

2. **Click the To stage toggle in the Align panel.**

3. **Click the Align horizontal center button.**

4. **Click the Align vertical center button.**

The Info panel

Use the Info panel (Ctrl+I or ⌘+I), shown in Figure 5.47, to give precise coordinates and dimensions to your items. Type the values in the fields provided, and by default, your item is transformed relative to its top-left corner. The only limitation to this panel is that your selected item must be a drawing object, a group, a shape primitive, or a symbol — anything but a raw shape. For raw shapes, the values in the Info panel are read-only. The universal workaround is to use the Size and Position settings in the new vertical Properties panel.

Caution

The registration point set in the Registration/Transformation point grid is actually a global setting that "sticks" even after you close the panel and change tools. After you change the registration point from top left to center, any new shapes or symbols that you create automatically have a center registration point. In most cases, it is best to stick with the default top-left registration point because this is the standard for items that are loaded or positioned with ActionScript. Changing the registration point on one item back to top left does not have any effect on other items that were created with a center registration point. ■

The Info panel has these controls:

- **Width:** Use this numeric entry field to alter the width of a selected item.

- **Height:** Use this numeric entry field to alter the height of a selected item.

Tip

Units for both Width and Height are measured in the units (pixels, inches, points, and so on) set in the Ruler Units option of the Document Properties dialog box found under Modify ➪ Document (Ctrl+J or ⌘+J). Note, however, that upon changing the unit of measurement, the item must be deselected and then reselected in order for these readouts to refresh and appear in the current units. ■

FIGURE 5.47

Use the Info panel options to change the location and appearance of an item.

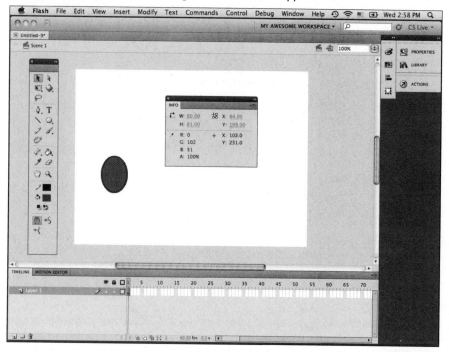

- **Registration grid:** The Registration grid is located just to the left of the numeric entry fields that are used for adjusting the X and Y location of any selected item. This grid consists of four small squares. Together, these squares represent the top corner of an invisible bounding box that encloses the selected item. Every shape created in Flash, even circles, resides within an imaginary rectangular bounding box that includes the extremities of the shape. The Registration grid enables you to toggle the selected item's registration point from the upper-left corner to the center of its bounding box. The T icon on the top-left square represents registration relative to the top-left corner of the item, and the O icon on the bottom-right square represents registration relative to the center of the item.

Note

The X (horizontal) and Y (vertical) coordinates are measured from the upper-left corner of the Flash Stage, which is the origin with coordinates 0,0. ■

- **X:** Use this numeric entry field to either read the X coordinate of the item or to reposition the item numerically, relative to the center point on the X (or horizontal) axis.

- **Y:** Use this numeric entry field to either read the Y coordinate of the item or to reposition the item numerically, relative to the center point on the Y (or vertical) axis.

- **RGBA:** This sector of the Info panel gives the Red, Green, Blue, and Alpha values for graphic items and groups at the point immediately beneath the cursor. Values for symbols, the background, or interface elements do not register.

- **+ X: / + Y:** This sector of the Info panel gives the X and Y coordinates for the point immediately beneath the cursor — including offstage or pasteboard values. A negative X value is to the left of the Stage, whereas a negative Y is located above the Stage.

To scale or reposition an item, select the item and then open the Info panel with shortcut keys or by choosing Window ⇨ Info:

- Choose to scale or reposition the item relative to either the center or the upper-left corner. (The icon toggles from the T icon on the top left to the O icon on the lower right to indicate the current setting.)

- To scale the item numerically, enter new values in the Width and Height fields, and then click elsewhere or press Enter to apply the change.

- To reposition the item numerically, enter new values in the X and Y fields (located in the *upper* half of the panel), and then either press Enter or click outside the panel to apply the change.

The Transform panel

The Transform panel (Ctrl+T or ⌘+T) gives you precise control over scaling, rotating, and skewing an item. With this panel, instead of making adjustments "by eye" — that may be imprecise — you enter numeric values in the appropriate fields and apply them directly to the selected item. As shown in Figure 5.48, the value fields in the Transform panel make it easy to modify the size and position of an element. However, after transformations are applied to an ungrouped basic shape or line, these numbers reset when the shape is deselected.

Tip

If you're using the Properties panel to resize an item by pixel values, don't overlook the constrain option. When an item is selected on the Stage, a small lock icon appears beside the Width and Height fields. Click the lock to preserve the aspect ratio of an element as you enter a new value for width or height. ■

FIGURE 5.48

Use the Transform panel to scale, rotate, and skew items.

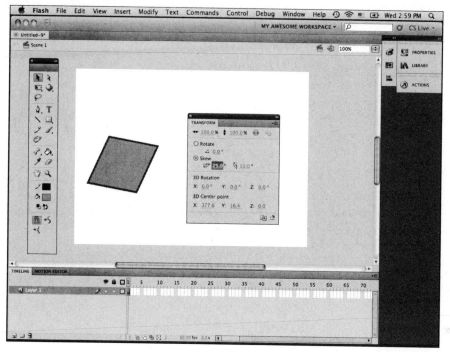

Some other powerful transform options are available from the Tools panel and from the Transform submenu of the Modify menu. I explain these more-complex editing tools in Chapter 9. "Modifying Graphics." However, the best place to start with transform options is the Transform panel, and these options are applied as follows:

- **Scale:** Use this to size the selected item by percentage. Enter a new number in the Scale field and press Enter. The shape scales to the specified percentage of its original size. To constrain the shape to its current proportions, click the Constrain check box. After a line or shape is deselected, the values in the Transform panel reset. The quickest way to get back to the original settings is to immediately use Edit ➪ Undo (Ctrl+Z or ⌘+Z) until it is reset. You can also get back to the original size mathematically by applying a new percentage that compensates for the changes you made before deselecting the item.

Tip

When you are using the Transform panel with groups, drawing objects, shape primitives, and symbol instances, you can reference or reset the original settings, even after the item has been deselected. I explain making and using symbols in Chapter 6, "Symbols, Instances, and the Library." ■

- **Rotate:** Click the radio button and then specify a rotation for the selected item by entering a number in the Rotate field. Press Return or Enter to apply the change to the selected item. The item rotates clockwise around its center point. To rotate an item counterclockwise, enter a negative number in the Rotate field.

- **Skew:** Items can be *skewed* (slanted in the horizontal or vertical direction) by selecting the Skew radio button, and then entering values for the horizontal and vertical angles. Pressing Return or Enter skews the item to the values entered.

- **Duplicate Selection and Transform:** Press this button and Flash makes a copy of the selected item (including shapes and lines) with all transform settings that have been applied to it. The duplicate is pasted in the same location as the original; select it with the Selection tool and move it to a new position to separate it from the original. Your original is left unchanged.

- **Remove Transform:** This button, at the bottom-right corner of the panel, removes all transformation settings for a selected object. You can always use the Remove Transform (or "Reset") button for instances, groups, or type blocks to get back to 100 percent scale with no rotation or skew. However, after a shape or line is deselected, this button does not work. For shapes, this is really more like an "Undo All" button.

Cross-Reference

I discuss the 3-D rotation and 3-D center point options as they relate to working with 3-D symbols in Flash in Chapter 9, "Modifying Graphics." ∎

The Edit Menu

I discuss many of the commands in the Edit menu in Chapter 4, but some of these commands can be helpful for creating or modifying graphics and are worth mentioning again here:

- **Undo:** When you make a mistake, before you do anything else, apply this command to get back to where you started. The default number for combined Undos that Flash remembers is 100; the maximum number is 300. Because Undo "memory" occupies system memory, you can set this level much lower if you find you don't rely on it. This setting is controlled in the General tab of the Flash Preferences dialog box.

Note

It is possible to switch the Undo behavior from Document-level (the default behavior) to Object-level (legacy Flash-style). Document-level Undo stores a combined history stack for all items in the current document, while Object-level Undo stores individual history stacks for each item stored in the library. The benefit of using Document-level Undo (the default setting for Flash CS5) is that more commands or editing steps can be undone. For a complete list of steps that cannot be undone if you opt to use Object-style Undo (including most Create and Delete commands in the Library panel), refer to the section on Using the Undo, Redo, and Repeat menu commands in the Using Flash booklet in the Help panel. The Undo behavior and the number of undo steps that you want to buffer are controlled in the General section of the Preferences dialog box: File ⇨ Preferences or Flash ⇨ Preferences. ∎

Note

Undo does not transcend focus: You cannot Undo work on the Stage from the ActionScript panel: You must first return focus to the Stage to exercise Undo. ■

- **Redo:** The anti-Undo, this redoes what you just undid.
- **Repeat:** If you have not just used Undo, you will see this as an option that enables you to "double" whatever edit you may have made, or to apply it to another item.

Cross-Reference

The History panel provides a flexible, nonlinear option for backtracking or repeating steps as you create and edit graphics. You can also use the History panel in conjunction with the Commands menu to track and save authoring steps that you can archive and reuse. I discuss these features in Chapter 9, "Modifying Graphics." ■

- **Cut:** This removes any selected item(s) from the Document window and places it on the Clipboard.
- **Copy:** This copies any selected item(s) and places it on the Clipboard, without removing it from the Document window.
- **Paste in Center:** Disabled if nothing has been copied or cut, this command pastes items from the Clipboard into the currently active frame on the currently active layer. You can also paste text into panel value fields.

Note

The Paste in Center command places items in the center of the currently visible area in the Document window, not in the center of the Stage. Double-click the Hand icon in the Tools panel to center the Stage in the Document window before using Paste in Center if you want the pasted item to be placed in the center of the Stage. ■

- **Paste in Place:** This is like Paste, except that it pastes the object precisely in the same area of the Stage (or Work area) from which it was copied (but it can be on a new layer or keyframe).
- **Clear:** This removes a selected item(s) from the Stage *without* copying it to the Clipboard.
- **Duplicate:** This command duplicates a selected item or items, without burdening the Clipboard. The duplicated item appears adjacent to the original.
- **Select All:** This selects all items in the Document window in the currently active keyframe of the project.
- **Deselect All:** This deselects all currently selected items.
- **Find and Replace:** This command launches a powerful option that enables you to specify elements in a current Flash document or scene and modify them with settings you choose in the Find and Replace dialog box. For more detailed information on using the Find and Replace command, refer to Chapter 9, "Modifying Graphics."
- **Find Next:** This is a shortcut that searches through a Flash document or scene and finds the next item that matches the criteria set in the Find and Replace dialog box.

- **Timeline:** This submenu provides access to the most common commands used to modify frames in the timeline: Cut Frames, Copy Frames, Paste Frames, Clear Frames, Remove Frames, and Select All Frames. These commands are also available in the contextual menu on any frame in the timeline. This submenu also includes the commands for converting timeline animation into reusable script-based motion elements that can be copied, pasted, or saved to share or use in other Flash files.

- **Edit Symbols:** Select an instance of a symbol and choose this command to modify the content of the symbol in Edit mode, an edit space that is independent from the Stage. For more about symbols and editing symbols, refer to Chapter 6, "Symbols, Instances, and the Library."

- **Edit Selected:** This command is enabled only if a group or symbol is selected on the Stage. It makes a selected group or symbol available in Edit mode. This same kind of edit space is invoked for symbols by choosing Edit Symbol.

- **Edit in Place:** This command opens a selected group or symbol in a separate tab of the Document window (shown in the location label area of the Document window) and enables you to edit this group or symbol while still seeing the other elements on the Stage, dimmed in the background for reference.

Tip

Double-clicking a group or symbol on the Stage with the Selection tool has the same result as choosing the Edit in Place command. ∎

- **Edit All:** From Edit mode, Edit All is used to go back to editing the main Flash scene. You can also do this by clicking the Scene location label of the Document window.

Creating Patterns with Symbols Using the Spray Brush Tool and the Deco Tool

Although the Deco tool and the Spray Brush tool are stored in the Tools panel along with all the other drawing and selection tools, I discuss them here in their own section because they are fundamentally different than the tools covered so far in this chapter. Instead of helping you to make lines or shapes manually, these tools auto-create patterns based on settings that you enter before you use them. And instead of using a fill or stroke color to create patterns, these tools use symbols (either the default symbol or a Movie clip or Graphic symbol that you create and then select from the library). The Spray Brush tool is great at making random patterns with variations in size, rotation, and distribution of symbol instances that make up the "spray." The Deco tool gives you powerful WYSIWYG tools for imposing order and geometric precision to the layout of multiple symbol instances, and the power to grow your own (easy to animate) vine patterns with just a click of your mouse.

These tools may require a little more work upfront (with setup and/or custom symbol creation), but they have the power to save you hours of time: Instead of tediously placing and positioning individual elements on the Stage to create a complex pattern or fill effect, you can simply click your mouse and Flash distributes instances of your selected symbol across the Stage, arranged exactly as you have specified. Magic! These tools are so fun and easy to use that I expect to see complex geometric patterns and funky random fills in many more Flash movies.

Cross-Reference

For information on how to create your own symbols, skip ahead to Chapter 6, "Symbols, Instances, and the Library". ■

Applying random "ink" with the Spray Brush tool

The Spray Brush tool shares space in the Tools panel with the old-fashioned Brush tool. To toggle between the two, click and hold the Tool space until the popup shows both tools, and then select the one you want to work with. The icon for the Spray Brush gives you a good clue for how this tool works: like a can of spray paint. When you select the Spray Brush, you won't see options in the Tools panel as you do for the standard Brush tool, but instead you see controls in the Properties panel for selecting the symbol you want to work with and setting the size and angle of the Brush (which for this tool is actually the spray area covered when you click without moving your cursor). Figure 5.49 includes the Tools panel with the Spray Brush selected and the Properties panel with the Symbol and Brush settings used to create the pattern of dots shown on the far left. The special beauty of the Spray Brush tool is that the distribution of dots is somewhat random. If you have ever tried to create a "random" pattern by placing individual elements on the Stage, you will truly appreciate how much time and effort this tool can save.

You can use the Spray Brush without creating any custom symbols by simply leaving the Symbol setting for Spray on no symbol (the Default shape check box will be selected). With this workflow you can choose a color for your spray, and you can choose the area that the "ink" (or small dot/particles) scatter in with each click, but you can't alter the shape or size of the particles in the spray. The maximum settings allowed for width and height of the Brush area match the size of your current Stage size, but you can spray as large an area as you want by holding down the mouse and dragging to spray. Each time you click and release the mouse with the Spray Brush, you create a group of symbol instances. These groups can be selected and edited individually after they have been sprayed onto the Stage.

Tip

To make editing easier, you might consider using the Select All (⌘+A) command and then ungrouping the spray groups so that you can handle the particles individually without having to click-in to a group to edit in place. ■

FIGURE 5.49

With the default settings in the Properties panel, the Spray Brush creates a random pattern of dots as you click and drag on the Stage.

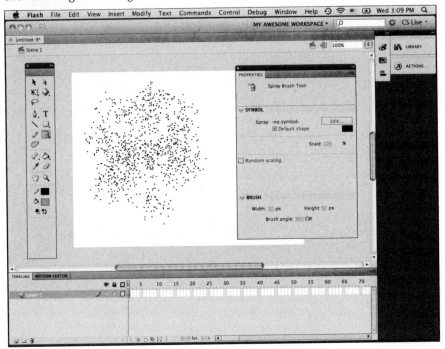

As shown in Figure 5.50, the Spray Brush gets a lot more interesting when you have some symbols in your library to work with.

To specify a custom symbol spray pattern, do the following:

1. **Select the Spray Brush tool in the Tools panel.**

2. **Click the Edit button in the Symbol section of the Properties panel.** The Swap symbol dialog box appears, which shows a list of all the symbols in your current library. Select the symbol you want to use as your spray particle.

3. **Choose scale settings for the symbol.** In most cases, you get a more interesting result if you set the scale to less than 100 percent. You can use really large particles, but the Spray Brush is designed to work best with smaller particles (less than 100 pixels in width or height).

FIGURE 5.50

Select a custom symbol as the spray, and then adjust the settings to create patterns by using multiple instances of your symbol with each click of the Spray Brush.

4. **Use the random settings to make the spray more interesting and organic:**

    - Random scaling adjusts the size of the particles so that there are varying sizes in each spray. The specific sizing is random and unpredictable, but the particles can vary from 1 x 1 pixel to the size set by your scale setting in Step 3.

    - Rotate symbol adjusts the alignment of the spray so that your symbol instance is not always in its original position. It varies from 0 to 360 degree rotation, but the rotation of particles in each group is consistent.

    - Random rotation adjusts the alignment of the particles in each spray so that your symbol instance is in varying positions within each group. This option creates a nice random texture if you are working with an irregularly shaped particle.

5. **Set the size of the spray area by using the Brush width and height settings.** Choose a value between 0 and the width or height of your current document. Experiment with this setting to get the result you like best, but I found that an area equal to half the current document size worked well for controlling the brush while not restricting the distribution of symbols too much.

6. **Set rotation for the spray area (if you like), using the Brush angle setting.** Choose a value between 0 and 360. This setting has a visible result only if you have unequal values for the width and height of your spray area (set in Step 5). Using a rotation of 90 has the same final result as swapping your Brush width and height settings.

7. **Click and drag to spray a symbol pattern onto the Stage.** Move the mouse to cover more area, or keep the mouse in one area to create a layered effect with a buildup of spray (or stacked symbol instances).

Symbol instances are sprayed and grouped each time you click the mouse. As shown in Figure 5.51, you may end up with a lot of groups if you click and spray multiple times.

FIGURE 5.51

Use Select all to see the symbol instance groups that make up a layered pattern created by the Spray Brush applied with multiple mouse clicks.

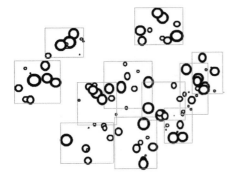

Creating order and pattern with the Deco tool

The Deco tool (U) is more like 13 tools in one. It's represented by one icon in the Tools panel, but as shown in Figure 5.52, when you select it, you see a drop-down menu in the Property inspector that enables you to choose from 13 different drawing effects:

New Feature

Out of the 13 mini-tools inside the Deco tool, only 3 existed in Flash CS4 — Vine Fill, Grid Fill, and Symmetry Brush. The new Deco tools in Flash CS5 create stylized artwork and animations for you automatically. ■

FIGURE 5.52

The Deco tool in the Tools panel has 13 different drawing effect options in the Property inspector that produce distinctly different results, 3 of which are shown here: (far left, top to bottom) Vine Fill, Building Brush, Flower Brush. They all work by auto-arranging symbol instances or pre-built shapes on the Stage, but each has its own settings and controls for modifying the layout.

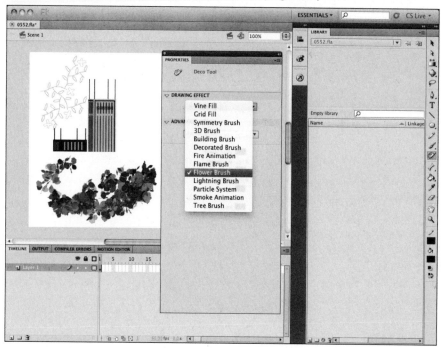

- **Vine Fill:** Auto-draws a vine pattern with leaf and flower symbols arranged on simple stems. The pattern originates where you click your mouse but continues to grow until it fills the shape that you have selected to place it in or you stop the effect (by hitting Esc or selecting another tool in the Tools panel). You can use the default symbols to create the vine (a simple leaf shape and a basic flower), assigning each a color if you want, or you can select your own symbol from the library for one or both of the leaf and flower elements.

- **Grid Fill:** Arranges symbol instances in rows and columns based on the spacing and scale you set in the Property inspector (Advanced Options). The pattern originates where you click your mouse and continues tiling outward until it fills a shape or you stop the effect. You can tile the default symbol (a black square) or choose any Movie clip or Graphic symbol in your library.

- **Symmetry Brush:** Provides control handles that enable you to direct the placement of multiple symbol instances in geometric patterns:
  - Reflect Across Line
  - Reflect Across Point
  - Rotate Around Point
  - Grid Translation
- **3D Brush**: Gives a simulated 3-D drawing effect to symbols or using the default square shape. As you use the Deco tool in 3D Brush mode, objects drawn toward the top of the screen are smaller than those drawn toward the bottom of the screen, simulating a vanishing point.
- **Building Brush:** Draws one of four different buildings or a random building as you click and drag your mouse upward, creating the top of the building where you release your mouse button.
- **Decorated Brush:** Allows you to use 1 of 20 predefined shapes to draw along a path.
- **Fire Animation:** Automatically creates an animation of a fire burning. The colors of the fire can be controlled through the Properties panel, along with whether the animation should end with the fire burning out.
- **Flame Brush:** Creates stylized flames as you drag your mouse, which gets darker the longer the mouse button is held down. In the Properties panel, you can set size and color of the flames.
- **Flower Brush:** Draws one of four different types of flowers. The colors of the flowers can be controlled through the Properties panel, along with choosing whether flower clusters are connected with stems.
- **Lightning Brush:** Creates bolts of lightning, which can be animated, colored, sized, and simplified in the Properties panel.
- **Particle System:** Builds an animation of a particle system, which supports the default square shape, or any of up to two symbols you define. The particle system gives control over speed, direction, and size of the particles in the animation.
- **Smoke Animation:** Creates animated smoke. The Properties panel allows you to define the size, speed, duration, and color of the smoke in the animation. In addition, like the fire animation effect, you can choose whether to let Flash create the end of the animation for you.
- **Tree Brush:** Automatically creates 1 of 20 tree or vine patterns as you drag your mouse. Through the Properties panel, you can choose a design and control colors of the trees you create.

Growing patterns with the Vine Fill drawing effect

The Vine fill creates a simple pattern with the default symbols (as shown in Figure 5.52), but you can use it as a base for much more detailed designs. Keep in mind that the symbols you choose for the Leaf and Flower don't actually have to be leaves or flowers — they can be any symbol you choose. In Advanced Options you can choose a color and angle for the vine stem and also set a scale for the overall pattern and a length for the vine segments. As with any symbol instance, you have the option of editing your leaf and flower symbols after they have been drawn as part of the vine pattern. Figure 5.53 compares a Vine fill drawn with custom leaf and flower symbols with the same vine after the leaf and flower symbols have been edited.

You'll notice that the Vine fill "grows" in a kind of organic way after you click to start the fill. You can capture this fill pattern as frame-by-frame animation by selecting the Animate Pattern check box at the bottom of the Property inspector Advanced Options for the Deco tool Vine Fill drawing effect. The Frame step setting controls how often a new frame is added as the pattern grows: The range from 1 to 100 represents the percentage of the total pattern that is included in each frame. A setting of 100 puts only one keyframe on the timeline with the finished pattern in it, showing 100 percent of the drawing in just one step. A setting of 1 adds as many keyframes as there are elements in your vine pattern, showing the drawing in incremental steps with a keyframe for each step. For most purposes, a setting somewhere in the middle works just fine.

FIGURE 5.53

A Vine fill created with custom leaf and flower symbols (left) can be edited after it is drawn to have a very different look (right).

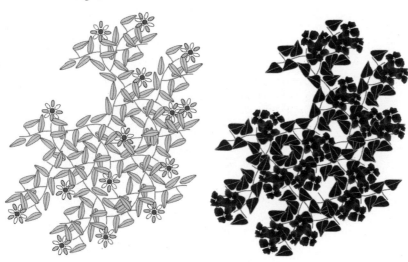

Caution

The Vine fill works best if the symbols you choose for the leaf and flower nodes are small in size: generally under 25 pixels in any direction. If the symbols are too large, the vine has no room for both leaves and flowers unless you make the segments really long — which makes the pattern look less like a vine and more like a series of long lines. If you are working with large symbols, you can either edit the graphics to scale them down or you can set the Pattern scale to a lower value to make the symbol instances small enough to fill the vine with a decent density of leaves and flowers. ■

Tip

If you like the look of larger leaves and flowers, it works better to create the fill pattern with small graphics and then edit the source symbols to scale the graphics larger; the symbol instances for the leaves and flowers update but the vine pattern is not disrupted. This was the workflow for the vines shown in Figure 5.53. ■

Tiling patterns with the Grid Fill drawing effect

The Grid Fill does just as its name implies: it fills an area with a grid-based pattern of symbol instances. The default graphic is a black square (as shown in Figure 5.52), but you can specify any Movie clip or Graphic symbol in your library. As shown in Figure 5.54, the options for Grid Fill (available after you activate the Deco tool in the Tools panel and select Grid Fill from the drop-down menu in the Property inspector) enable you to choose a Fill symbol and set the horizontal and vertical spacing and scale for the symbol instances. The pattern starts wherever you click your mouse on the Stage, and it continues to tile outward until you stop the effect (by hitting Esc or choosing another tool in the Tools panel) or until it hits the inside edges of whatever shape you have chosen to fill. The tile is symmetrical in all directions, so you might find that there are empty spaces left in a filled graphic because the fill hit an area that it could not tile evenly. Figure 5.54 shows just three examples of tiled fills created with the Deco tool and the Grid Fill drawing effect.

As with all the Deco tool artwork, the symbol instances for Grid fills are grouped each time you click to start a fill, and the source symbols and symbol instances can be edited after the fill pattern is created.

Creating reflected patterns with the Symmetry Brush drawing effect

The Symmetry Brush has four different modes, and each mode has a different guide that appears on the Stage, enabling you to control the placement of symbol instances in a geometric pattern. Although the guides are unique for each mode, the principle is the same — use the guide to set up placement of symbol instances, and then click to place them on the Stage while the drawing effect builds a reflected pattern each time you click. Figure 5.55 shows the guides and the pattern created by each with the default graphic (a black square).

FIGURE 5.54

Grid Fill creates a tiled pattern of symbol instances with the spacing and scale you choose. Here are just a few options: You can make the default shape small and dense (top), use a bitmap in a Graphic symbol as a fill for another shape (middle), or even apply the effect more than once to get layered geometric patterns (bottom).

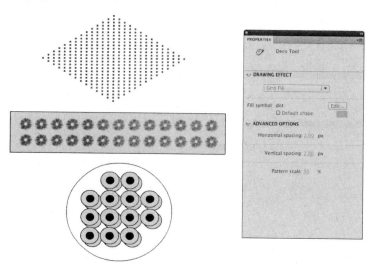

FIGURE 5.55

The four Symmetry Brush modes enable you to use draggable guides to dynamically control the placement and spacing of symbol instances: Reflect Across Line (A), Reflect Across Point (B), Rotate Around Point (C), and Grid Translation (D).

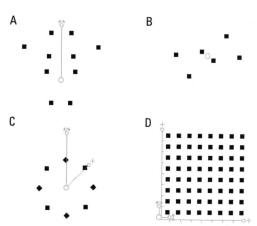

These guides are tricky to describe and are best explored in a tactile way, but here is some explanation for each one:

- **Reflect Across Line:** Click and drag the guide center point to position the guide in the area of the Stage where you want the pattern to originate. Click and drag the direction point — marked with a double arrow — anywhere within a 360-degree arc to orient the line that creates the reflection axis. Click on either side of the line to place symbol instances and expect to see an exact reflection on the other side of the line, mirroring placement on the Stage and distance from the axis.

- **Reflect Across Point:** Click and drag the guide center point to position the guide in the area of the Stage where you want the pattern to originate. Click on any side of the center point to place symbol instances and expect to see an exact reflection on the other side of the point, mirroring placement on the Stage and distance from the axis.

- **Rotate Around Point (aka the clock-face effect):** Click and drag the guide center point to position the guide in the area of the Stage where you want the pattern to originate. Click and drag the direction point — marked with a double arrow — to anywhere within a 360-degree arc to orient the starting position for the first symbol instance in the circular pattern. Click and drag the spacing point — marked with an x — to anywhere within a 180-degree arc to set the angle of reflection.

    Click anywhere around the two lines and expect to see reflections oriented around the center point and repeated as many times as there is room for in the reflection area. If you drag the spacing point closer to the direction point, you increase the reflection area and more symbol instances fill the space. If you drag the spacing point farther away from the direction point, you decrease the reflection area and fewer symbol instances fill the space.

Note

If the spacing point is 180 degrees from the direction point (forming a straight line), you see only one reflection for each symbol instance you place, but the effect is different than the Reflect Across Line pattern because the reflected instances are at the opposite end of the axis line rather than directly across. ∎

- **Grid Translation:** Click and drag the guide center point to position the guide in the area of the Stage where you want the pattern to originate. Click and drag the spacing points — marked with plus signs (+) — to set the endpoints for the fill pattern on the x and y axis. Click and drag the position guides — marked with double arrows — to adjust the rotation angle for the grid. One pointer changes the rotation of individual symbol instances in relation to each other, creating a skew effect, and the other pointer changes the rotation of the whole group of symbol instances in relation to the center point. Click to place a symbol instance in the grid area and expect to see a grid fill the space between the two spacing points.

One quick way to get a feel for the varied powers of these different Symmetry Brush modes is to create a pattern in one mode and then change the mode in the Property inspector without modifying the artwork on the Stage. This enables you to see how different the patterns made by each guide can be even with the same source symbol instances and placement.

Summary

- The geometric shapes available from the Tools panel are a quick, accurate way of creating basic elements that you can customize with various fill and stroke styles.

- The Primitive Shape tools for creating dynamic ovals and rectangles make it much easier to draw and modify shapes without having to start from scratch or make permanent manual changes to the original shape to create rounded rectangles, open circles, and other useful graphics.

- Settings dialog boxes for the Oval tool and the Rectangle tool make it possible for you to set the width and height of these shapes *before* they are drawn.

- The Pencil, Brush, and Pen tools enable you to draw freeform or Bezier lines that you can edit by using the Pen submenu, Selection tool arrow options, or the Subselection tool.

- The Object Drawing option can be turned on while creating graphics with any of the drawing or shape tools. Drawing objects are hybrid graphics that share selective characteristics with shapes, grouped shapes, and Graphic symbols.

- Enhanced Smoothing controls, a Tilt toggle, and a Pressure toggle give artists who use tablets lots of options to customize the Flash drawing environment.

- The Scale control in the Properties panel gives you more precise control over strokes that will be scaled in the authoring environment (as symbol instances) or in the Flash Player (as final published content).

- Optimizing artwork manually by editing points with the Subselection tool, or automatically by using the Optimize Curves option, can greatly reduce file size by simplifying lines and curves.

- The Smooth and Straighten modifiers in the Tools panel are now augmented by dialog boxes that give you more control over the level of optimization — and in the case of Smoothing, the exact angles that you want to target. To access these more advanced smoothing controls, select Modify ➪ Shape ➪ Advanced Smooth or Advanced Straighten from the application menu.

- By adjusting and applying the various snapping modifiers, you can control how "auto" alignment behavior affects elements as you work. The Edit Snapping dialog box enables you to set or modify snapping behaviors quickly.

- You have the option of using Document-level Undo or going back to the legacy-style Undo (Object-level). There are advantages to using Document-level Undo (which is the default), but the legacy option has been maintained in response to users who wanted to go back to the Undo style that they were familiar with from older versions of Flash.

- New pattern tools enable you to use symbol instances as the basis for geometric or random fill patterns. The Spray Brush works like a spray can to scatter symbol instances as particles on the Stage. The Deco tool offers a range of different modes and guides for creating more organized patterns based on reflection and grids, plus a fun Vine Fill mode that lets you design your own organic fill with leaf and flower nodes.

Symbols, Instances, and the Library

S ymbols are the key to file size efficiency and interactive power in Flash. A *symbol* is a reusable element that resides in the current movie's document Library, which you access with Window ⇨ Library (⌘/Ctrl+L). After you convert an item in your Flash movie into a symbol, each time you use that item on your Main Timeline or within a Movie Clip Timeline, you're working with an *instance* of the original symbol. Unlike using individual graphic elements, you can use many instances of a symbol, with little or no addition to the file size.

Using symbols helps reduce the file size of your finished movie because Flash needs to save the symbol only once. Each time a given symbol is used in the project, Flash refers to its original profile. To support the variations of an instance, Flash needs to save information about the *differences* only — such as size, position, proportions, and color effects. If a separate graphic was used for each change, Flash would have to store a complete profile of all the information about that graphic — not just the changes, but also all of the points that specify what the original graphic looks like.

Furthermore, symbols can save you a lot of time and trouble, particularly when it comes to editing your movie. That's because changes made to a symbol are reflected in each instance of that symbol throughout the movie. Let's say that your logo changes halfway through production. Without symbols, you would have to find and change each copy of the logo. However, if you've used symbol instances, you need only edit the original symbol — the instances are automatically updated throughout the movie.

Tip

The pattern drawing tools in Flash CS5 — Spray Brush and Deco — are an excellent use of symbols. Using multiple instances of a symbol to create a pattern enables you to quickly change the look of even complex patterns by editing the original symbol. ■

In this chapter, you learn to create and edit basic symbol types stored in your Document Library. You also learn to use symbol instances, both within the Main Timeline and within other symbols, and to modify individual instances of a symbol.

Understanding the Document Library

The Library (⌘/Ctrl+L) is the storehouse for reusable elements, known as *symbols,* which can then be placed as symbol *instances* within a Flash movie. Imported sounds and bitmaps are automatically placed in the Library. Upon creation, Graphic symbols, Button symbols, and Movie Clip symbols are also stored in the Library. It's a good practice to convert main items within a Flash document into symbols and to then develop your project from instances derived from these original symbols.

The main document Library panel, shown in Figure 6.1, is used to access stored assets for any files that are currently available in the tabbed Document window. Each file has its own unique Library list that displays all symbol assets used in the file as well as any assets that were imported or added to the Library to be saved with the file.

Tip

The Flash Library panel includes a drop-down menu that provides quick access to the Library list of any project files (.fla) loaded into the Document window. Changing the view within the main Library panel is faster and more space efficient than opening and managing multiple Library panels. ■

Tip

All Library panels can be scaled vertically and horizontally by clicking and dragging the sides or the bottom of the panel. Panels can be docked to any other Library panel or to the Properties panel or the Document window — wherever you find it most convenient to keep your source symbols handy. ■

FIGURE 6.1

The main document Library panel provides access to assets for open .fla files (top left). Common Libraries (bottom) and other saved .fla files (top right) can be opened as External Libraries and used as asset source files.

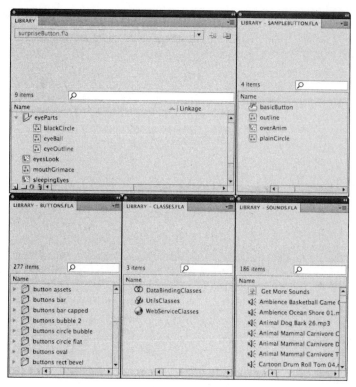

Working with Common Libraries and External Libraries

External Libraries are panels that open separately from the main Library panel to provide access to stored assets for files that are not currently open in the Document window. You can open any saved Flash file as an External Library by choosing File ➪ Import ➪ Open External Library and browsing to the file that you want to load. All the stored symbols from your selected file will be visible in a floating External Library panel, but the document will not be visible in the Document window, and you cannot edit the symbols in the External Library unless you copy them to the main Library panel or to the Stage of a file that is open in the Document window.

Flash ships with three External Libraries called Common Libraries. These panels hold ready-made elements that you can drag into any document Library (or onto the Stage or Pasteboard in an open Document Window) to use in your own projects. Common Libraries behave exactly like any other

External Library. Choose Window ⇨ Common Libraries to open the submenu of Common Libraries that ship with Flash. The Buttons Library contains a selection of pre-built Flash elements that you can reuse in any Flash project. The Classes Library contains compiled scripts that are used with the AS2 components that also ship with Flash. The Learning Interactions found in CS3 are no longer included as a Common Library, but the new CS5 Sound Library is an amazing resource with over 180 optimized sound files ready to drag and drop into your Flash movies. Many of the sounds are also built to loop seamlessly, so you can create background sounds without bloating your file size.

Tip

Preview sounds by selecting them in the Library list and then clicking the play button in the preview window. ■

You can open and use the Common Library panels and any other External Library panels as free-floating panels (as shown in Figure 6.1) or you can stack or group them for tabbed access (as shown in Figure 6.2). After you copy assets to one of the document asset lists in the main Library panel (or into any of your project files in the Document window), you can close the External Library and work with the copied symbols without changing the original symbol source.

FIGURE 6.2

You can organize Common Libraries and External Libraries into panel stacks (left) or tabbed groups (right).

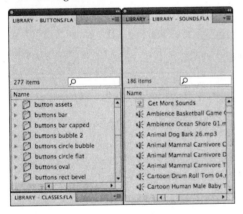

A helpful feature in all Flash CS5 Library panels is a new search field (as shown in Figures 6.1 and 6.2). You will find it right above the asset list marked by a small binocular icon. You can type the name of a specific element or just the first letter of the elements you want to find and sort in the asset list; as you type, Flash shows you all elements that match the information you are entering. For example if you type in **b**, you might see "flowerButton," "symbol2," "BeamScan," and so on — anything with the letter *b* in the name. If you typed the full word **bu** you would see only "flower-Button" in the asset list. This feature can save a lot of time if you are sorting through a complex file with many elements stored in the Library. The search even looks in folders and shows you any matching items.

Tip

To add your own buttons, symbols, or even complete libraries for specific projects, first save them in a Flash document (.fla) with a descriptive name; then place that Flash file in the Libraries folder within the Configuration folder for Flash CS5 on your hard drive. ■

The source files for the External Libraries that show up in the Common Libraries menu are stored in the Libraries folder of the Configuration folder for Flash CS5.

- The standard directory path on Windows is:

    `C:\Program Files\Adobe\FlashCS5\ (language) \Configuration\Libraries`

- The standard directory path to the application config folder on Mac is:

    `HD\Applications\Adobe Flash CS5\(language)\Configuration\Libraries`

Working with multiple Document Libraries

The Flash Library panel, shown in Figure 6.3, includes a drop-down project menu that lists all currently open files. This is a great space saver that makes it much easier to switch between different document Libraries without having to manage separate floating panels. By default, the Library panel switches views as you tab from one document to another in the Document window, but changing the Library view does not change the Document view — in other words, the Library panel is connected to the Document panel but not the other way around. This makes it easy to access a different Library while maintaining the view of your current file in the Document window.

If you want to keep a Library asset list for one project visible in the Library panel while tabbing to a different project file in the Document window, you can use the handy Pin toggle in the Library panel. Click the tack or pushpin icon to pin or "stick" the current asset list so it won't change when you tab to a new project in the Document window. Don't forget to click the Pin toggle again to turn it off when you want to unstick the Library asset list.

There are times when you may want to see the contents of more than one Library at a time — to compare files or to drag items from one Library to another. Click the New Library Panel button to create a duplicate floating Library panel at any time. You can then use the drop-down menu to switch the project view in one of the Library panels to compare items or to drag the contents of one Library to another. Like External Libraries or other floating panels, Document Library panels can be grouped (for tabbed access), stacked, or floated as individual panels.

You can access elements stored in the Library of any other Flash document (without opening the actual .fla file in the Document window) by choosing File ➪ Import ➪ Open External Library from the application menu and browsing to a .fla file. The Library opens next to the Document window of your current project as a floating panel that can be handled exactly like any of the Common Libraries. External Libraries (Library panels for files that are not open in the Document window) do not show up in the drop-down menu of the main Document Library panel, but they can be grouped or stacked with the main Document Library if you need to keep them handy without eating up screen space.

FIGURE 6.3

The Flash document Library panel includes a project menu, Pin toggle, and New Library button. As shown, you can use the New Library Panel button to launch a clone panel (right) for the current project view in the main Document Library (left).

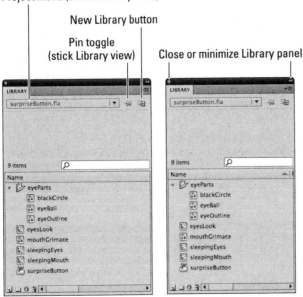

Project menu (select Library view)

New Library button

Pin toggle
(stick Library view)

Close or minimize Library panel

You can copy assets from an External or Common Library to a current Document Library by dragging items from the source Library onto the current document Stage, or directly into the Library panel. This also works if you have two documents open, and you want to move assets between the two Libraries. It is also then possible to drag or copy and paste elements directly from one document Stage onto another or drag an item from a source document Stage into a current document's Library.

Note

Open documents are loaded into the tabbed Document window. If you want to view more than one Document Stage at a time, use the Window⇨Duplicate Window command to create a clone of one of the tabbed documents. You can then use the tabbed UI in the main Document window to switch views to any other open document while keeping a view of the cloned document in the duplicate Document window. ■

The shared Library feature makes it possible to link assets between project files (.fla) during production by using *authortime* sharing, or to link multiple published movie files (.swf) on the server with *runtime* sharing. Shared libraries create a more optimized workflow than saving individual copies of assets in multiple documents. You can learn more about linking symbols in your project filesin "Using Authortime Shared Libraries" later in this chapter.

Reading the Library panel

Every Flash document has its own Library panel, which is used to store and organize symbols, sounds, bitmaps, and other assets such as video files. As shown in Figure 6.4, the item highlighted — or selected — in the Sort window is previewed in the Preview window. Each item in the Library has an icon to the left of the name to indicate the asset type. Click any heading to sort the window by Name, Kind (type), Use Count, or Linkage (all headings shown in Figure 6.1).

FIGURE 6.4

The Document Library (scaled to a narrow view)

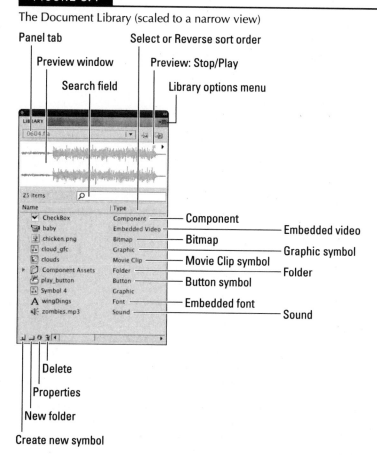

If the item selected in the Library is a Button symbol, a Movie Clip, or a sound file with more than one frame on its timeline, a controller appears in the upper-right corner of the Preview window. This Preview Stop/Play controller pops up to facilitate previewing these items. It's equivalent to the Play command in the options menu. As shown in Figure 6.5, the library options popup menu lists a number of features, functions, and controls for organizing and working with items in the Library.

FIGURE 6.5

The Library panel and the options popup menu

The following commands, found in the Library options menu, enable you to add or modify content stored in your document Library:

- **New Symbol:** Choose this command to launch the Create New Symbol dialog box where you can name and choose properties for a symbol, and then click OK to open Edit mode and place or create graphics on the symbol timeline. When a new symbol is created, it is stored at the root of the Library Sort window. You can drag it inside of any existing Library folders.

- **New Folder:** Items in the Library can be organized in folders. The New Folder command simply creates a new folder within the Sort window. New folders are "untitled" by default; double-click the folder text to type a custom folder name. This menu command is equivalent to the New Folder button at the bottom of the Library panel.

- **New Font:** Use this command to open the Font Symbol Properties dialog box, which is the first step in creating a font symbol for use within a Shared Library.

- **New Video:** Creates a new empty `Video` object in the Library.

- **Rename:** Use the Rename command to rename the currently selected item in the Sort window. Double-click any item title in the list to achieve the same thing.

- **Delete; Duplicate:** Select Duplicate to create a copy of an item and Delete to delete an item in the Sort window.

- **Move to:** Use the Move to option to open the Move to dialog box. You can move the currently selected element to an existing folder in your Library list or create a new folder (which will appear in your main Library list) to move it to.

Note

You can also move Library items to folders by dragging them onto any folder icon. ■

- **Edit:** Choose Edit to access the selected symbol in Edit mode.

Tip

Double-clicking a symbol on the Stage takes you into Edit in Place mode, a variant of Edit mode that enables you to see other elements on the Stage dimmed in the background for layout reference as you modify the symbol. ■

- **Edit with:** Provided that you have appropriate external applications installed, most imported assets (such as sounds, bitmaps, and vectors) have this command available to jump to the external editing environment of your choice.

- **Properties:** This command opens the related Properties dialog box for the particular symbol type — Sound, Bitmap, Symbol, Component, or Video Properties. The Properties dialog box is a central control that enables you to rename an element, access Edit mode, or access the Linkages dialog box from one location. This is also where you can define or edit the Source for any element.

- **Play (or Stop, if currently playing):** If the selected asset has a timeline or is otherwise playable (such as a sound), click this to preview the asset in the Library Preview window. If the asset is currently playing, this option is updated to Stop — in which case, click to stop playing.

- **Update:** Use this option if you've edited items subsequent to importing them into Flash. Items update without the bother of re-importing. You can also use this option to swap in a new element of the same kind to replace an item already used in your project.

- **Properties:** Use this command to open the Properties dialog box for the currently selected item (Symbol Properties, Sound Properties, Bitmap Properties, Font Symbol Properties, Video Properties, or [Component] Linkage Properties).

- **Component Definition:** This library option opens the Component Definition dialog box, which you use to assign parameters to Movie Clips to create your own components or modify parameters for compiled components. (Components are Movie Clips with customizable behavior that can be reused in projects.)

Tip

You can also use the Component Inspector panel to set component parameters. ■

- **Shared Library Properties:** Use this command to open the Shared Properties dialog box, which is another aspect of runtime Shared Libraries.

- **Select Unused Items:** Select Unused Items to find any items stored in the Library that have not been used in the current project.

Tip

Unused items are not included in your published movie file (.swf), but they add weight to your project file (.fla). The Select Unused Items command is a handy way to find these files so you can delete them to stream-line your project file. Use Save and Compact or Save As to save your .fla file minus the extra weight of the unused items that you have deleted from the Library. ■

- **Expand Folder/Collapse Folder:** Use this command to toggle the currently selected folder in the asset window open or closed.

- **Expand All Folders/Collapse All Folders:** Use this command to toggle all folders and subfolders in the asset window open or closed.

- **Help:** Launches a Web browser to access Adobe help with info on Managing Assets in Flash or the local Flash help documents (if you are not connected to the Internet).

Selecting New Symbol, Duplicate, or Properties from the options menu while you have a symbol (Graphic symbol, Button symbol or Movie Clip) selected in the Library list launches the Symbol Properties dialog box, as shown in Figure 6.6. Use this dialog box to change the symbol's name and/or behavior (as a symbol type — Graphic, Button, or Movie Clip).

Note

If you choose the Properties option with other asset types selected, such as sound, video, or bitmaps, the Properties dialog box relevant to each item type launches rather than the Symbol Properties dialog box. ■

FIGURE 6.6

The Symbol Properties dialog box. Note the button for Advanced options — this expands the dialog box to include Linkage and Source information for the selected element.

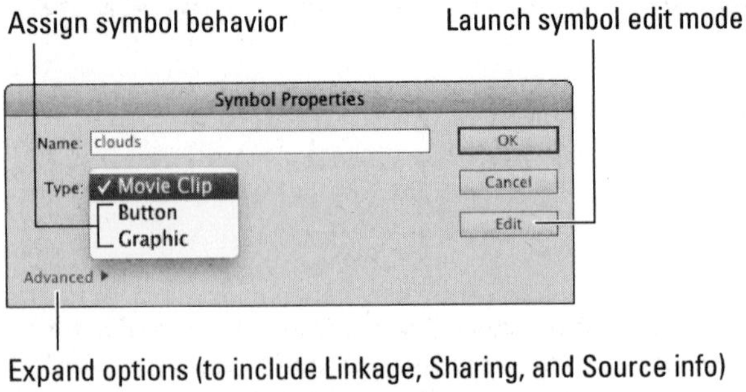

Assign symbol behavior   Launch symbol edit mode

Expand options (to include Linkage, Sharing, and Source info)

Organizing Library panels

When your movies start to become complex, you'll find that the Library gets crowded, and it can be hard to find symbols. When this happens, you'll appreciate the capability to create and name folders for your symbols. You can organize your Library folders however you like, but here are a few suggestions for greater productivity:

- Create a separate folder for each scene.

- Create folders for symbol types, such as buttons, sounds, or bitmap imports.

- Store all symbols or graphics that relate to a specific element (such as a logo or an animated element) together in one folder.

Tip

The Search field included in all the CS5 Library panels is a wonderful tool for finding and organizing assets and should save beleaguered developers a bit of time and frustration. ■

When you build complex layered structures in your movie — a Movie Clip symbol on the first frame of a Button symbol, with a text symbol on the layer above it, and a sound on the layer above that — the Library doesn't visually track this hierarchy. But you can indicate this: Just put all the associated symbols in a folder with a name that describes the final element. You can also nest folders within other folders. Working with folders in the Library is almost exactly the same as working with folders in the Layers area of the Timeline window, as follows:

- To create a folder, click the folder icon at the bottom-left corner of the Library.

- To move a file or folder into another folder, simply drag it over the target folder icon.

- To move a folder that's been nested within another folder back to the top level of the Library, drag the folder until it is just above the Library list and over the word Name and release.

Note

Putting symbols in different folders does not affect the links between them and their instances (as opposed to the way moving a graphic file into a new folder breaks an existing link on a Web page). Flash tracks and updates all references to Library items whenever you rename or move them into separate folders (within the same Library). ■

The Movie Explorer is a great way of getting a visual overview of the nested relationship of symbols, Movie Clips, and other items within your document. Refer to the end of this chapter for more on the Movie Explorer.

Caution

If you change the Undo behavior in your Flash Preferences from Document-level to Object-level, you'll lose the option to undo some authoring steps. For example, any item that is deleted from the Library is gone forever, including all instances throughout the current document (.fla). If you decide that you shouldn't have deleted an item, the only cure is to close the file without saving any changes. When you reopen the file, the Library should be intact as it was the last time the file was saved. ■

Resolving Conflicts between Library Assets

Importing or copying an asset into your current project Library occasionally opens a Resolve Library Conflict alert box asking if you want to Replace Existing Items and Instances. This alert box appears when you are trying to add a new asset to your Library with the same name as an asset already present in your current document. If you choose not to replace the existing item, the newly added items have the word *copy* added to their filenames. For example, if you have an item named *photo* in your current Library and attempt to add another item to the Library with the same name, the new item is given the name *photo copy* in the Library. To rename the added item, simply double-click the item name in the Library list and type a new name.

If you choose to replace the existing item in your Library, all instances are replaced with the content of the newly added item. If you choose to cancel the import or copy operation, the selected items are not added to your current document and the existing items stored in the Library are preserved.

Tip
Flash offers an option to Import to Library that is especially useful when you want to bring in a series of items. Instead of having all the items dumped onto the Stage in your Document window, you can load them directly into the project Library. Select File ➪ Import ➪ Import to Library. ■

Defining Content Types

Understanding the behavior of various media types and learning to streamline asset management unlocks the true potential of Flash for combining compelling content with small file sizes. The basic structures for storing, reusing, and modifying content within a Flash project are not complicated, but the reason for using various symbol types does deserve explanation.

Raw data

When you create graphics directly in Flash, using the shape tools, text tool, or any of the other drawing tools, you produce raw data or *primitive shapes*. You can copy and paste these elements into any keyframe on the timeline, but they do not appear in the project Library. Each time the element appears, Flash has to read and render all the points, curves, and color information from scratch because the information is not stored in the Library. Even if the shape looks exactly the same on keyframe 10 as it did on keyframe 1, Flash has to do all the work to re-create the shape every time it appears. This quickly bloats the size of the .swf file. Also, because each element is completely independent, if you decide to make any changes, you have to find and edit each appearance of an element manually. This is a daunting task if your project involves animation or nested symbols.

Tip

The Find and Replace feature (Option/Alt+F) makes it easier to accomplish mundane editing tasks on multiple items within your Flash project file. I introduce the myriad uses for Find and Replace in Chapter 9, "Modifying Graphics." ∎

Tip

If you want to convert a raw graphic into a drawing object after it has been created, select the graphic on the Stage and apply the Modify ➪ Combine Objects ➪ Union command from the main menu. The raw graphic then behaves exactly like any other drawing object. To revert a drawing object to a raw graphic, use the Modify ➪ Break Apart command. ∎

Drawing objects and shape primitives

You create drawing objects by turning the Object Drawing option toggle on in the Tools panel while using any of the drawing or shape tools. (This option is on by default, so if you haven't touched the toggle in the Tools panel, you will find yourself creating drawing objects when you use any of the drawing tools to make graphics.) Drawing objects have some of the characteristics of raw shapes and groups. They can be modified directly on the Stage (without having to click in to Edit mode) but they are self-contained and do not merge with or cut into other graphics on the same layer — unless you apply one of the Combine Objects commands. They can't be motion-tweened and they are not stored in the Library unless they are converted into one of the symbol types. The hybrid characteristics of drawing objects suit some workflows very well, but some graphic artists prefer to work in normal or Non-Object Drawing mode. Drawing objects can be combined seamlessly with raw graphics and symbols, and turning the Object Drawing option on or off does not have any effect on graphics you have already created.

The Oval Primitive and Rectangle Primitive tools provide another way of making basic shapes with the advantage of using controls in the Properties panel that can be changed or reset even after the shapes are drawn. Like drawing objects, shape primitives do not merge with or erase other shapes, but they are not stored in the Library.

Caution

Shapes or lines made with the Drawing Object toggle turned on and shapes made with the Oval and Rectangle Primitive tools have some special behaviors in the authoring environment, but like basic shapes and groups, drawing objects and shape primitives are not stored in the Library unless they are converted into symbols. Symbols are the only method of storing artwork that reduces the file size impact of graphics that occur on more than one frame of a Flash movie. ∎

Groups

One step toward making raw data more manageable is to use groups. By grouping a filled shape with its outline stroke, for example, it becomes easier to select both parts of the shape to move around in your layout. If you added a text element that you also wanted to keep aligned with your artwork, you could add this to the group as well. Groups can be inclusive or cumulative so that you can select multiple elements and create one group (⌘/Ctrl+G) that can be accessed on the same edit level by double-clicking the whole group once. If you add another element (even another group) to the first group, you will find that you have to click in to a deeper level to edit individual elements. In this way, groups can grow more and more complicated, which is helpful if you're trying to keep multiple elements in order.

The important thing to remember about groups, however, is that they are *not* symbols. Although groups have a similar selection highlight to symbols, you will notice that they don't have a cross-hair icon in the center, and that the group information won't appear in your project Library. No matter how careful you are about reusing the same raw data and grouping elements to keep them organized, when it comes to publishing your movie (.swf) or trying to update any single element, you will be no better off than if you had just placed raw elements wildly into your project. Flash still treats each shape and line as a unique element, and the file size grows exponentially each time you add another keyframe containing any of your raw data, even if it is grouped. The best way to use groups in your project is for managing symbols, or to organize elements that you plan to keep together and convert into one symbol.

Caution

Using groups helps organize raw shapes or other elements in your FLA files, but it does not help to optimize the final SWF file. Using a lot of groups in your project file can actually add weight to the final published .swf. ■

Native symbols

Imported sound, video, bitmap, or font symbols are stored automatically in the Library to define *instances* of the asset when it is used in the project. In addition, three basic *container* symbol types can be created in the Flash authoring environment: Movie Clip symbols, Graphic symbols, and Button symbols, which all have timelines that can hold images, sounds, text, or even other symbols. Although it is possible to make the behavior of a symbol instance different from the behavior of the original symbol, it is generally best to decide how you plan to use a certain element and then assign it the symbol type that is appropriate to both its content and expected use in the project.

Tip

Dragging a primitive shape or group into the Library panel from the Stage automatically opens the Convert to Symbol dialog box so that you can name and assign a symbol type to the element before it is added to your Library. ■

To make a decision on what type of symbol to use, it helps to have a clear understanding of the benefits and limitations of each of the symbol types available in Flash. Each symbol type has specific features that are suited to particular kinds of content. Each symbol type is marked with a unique icon in the Library, but what all symbols have in common is that they can be reused within a project as symbol instances, all defined by the original symbol. A Flash project Library may contain any or all of the symbol types in the following sections, all created directly in Flash.

Graphic symbols

Graphic symbols are used mainly for static images that are reused in a project. Flash ignores any sounds or actions inside a Graphic symbol. Graphic symbols do not play independently of the Main Timeline and thus require an allocated frame on the Main Timeline for each frame that you want to be visible within the symbol. If you want a Graphic symbol to loop or repeat as the Main Timeline moves along, you have to include another whole series of frames on the Main Timeline to match the length of the Graphic symbol timeline for each loop.

A drop-down Options menu in the Properties panel enables you to control Graphic symbol playback. Select a Graphic symbol instance in your document and open the Looping section of the Properties panel to access the three settings in the Options menu:

- **Loop:** This is the default setting for Graphic symbols. If the Graphic symbol extends along a timeline beyond its original length, the symbol restarts from the beginning. Graphic symbol looping does not play independently of the Main Timeline like Movie Clip looping — you still have to match the number of frames on the Main Timeline with the number of frames that you want to play in the Graphic symbol timeline.

- **Play Once:** This setting eliminates looping by allowing the Graphic symbol timeline to play, and then holding on its last frame if it extends along a timeline beyond its original length.

- **Single Frame:** This setting holds the Graphic symbol on one frame so that it behaves like a static graphic. You can select a specific frame within the Graphic symbol timeline to display as the static graphic. The appearance of the Graphic symbol is the same regardless of how far it extends along a timeline.

Movie Clip symbols

Movie Clips are actually movies within a movie. They're good for animations that run independently of the movie's Main Timeline. They can contain actions, other symbols, and sounds. You can also place Movie Clips inside of other symbols, and they are indispensable for creating interactive interface elements such as animated buttons.

Movie Clips can continue to play even if the Main Timeline is stopped. Thus, they need only one frame on the Main Timeline to play back any number of frames on their own timeline. By default, Movie Clips are set to loop. So, as long as there is an instance of the Movie Clip visible on the Main Timeline, it can loop or play back the content on its own timeline as many times as you want it to, without needing a matching number of frames on the Main Timeline. Movie Clip playback can be controlled with ActionScript from any timeline or even from an external code (.as) file.

Button symbols

Button symbols are used for creating interactive buttons. Button symbols have a timeline limited to four frames, which are referred to as *states*. These states are related directly to user interaction and are labeled Up, Over, Down, and Hit. Each of these button states can be defined with graphics, symbols, and sounds. After you create a Button symbol, you can assign independent actions to various instances in the main movie or inside other Movie Clips. As with Movie Clips, Button symbols require only one frame on any other timeline to be able to play back the three visible states (frames) of their own timeline.

Components

Components are prebuilt Movie Clips for interactive Flash elements that can be reused and customized. Each component has its own unique set of ActionScript methods that enable you to set options at runtime.

Imported media elements

A Flash project Library also stores certain types of imported assets to define instances of the asset when instances are used in the movie. You can place these imported assets into native Flash symbol structures by converting a bitmap into a Graphic symbol or placing a sound inside a Button symbol, for example.

Bitmaps

Bitmaps are handled like symbols: The original image is stored in the Library and any time the image is used in the project it is actually a copy, or an *instance,* of the original. To use a bitmap asset, drag an instance out of the Library and onto the Stage. You manage Export settings for individual bitmaps from within the Library by choosing Properties from either the contextual menu or the Library options menu. However, you cannot apply color or alpha effects or any Flash filters to the bitmap instance unless you convert it into a native Flash symbol type (Graphic, Button, or Movie Clip).

Vector graphics

Vector graphics, upon import from other applications, arrive on the Flash Stage as a group, and unlike bitmaps may be edited or manipulated just like a normal group drawn in Flash. These elements are not stored in the Library until they have been converted to a native symbol type.

Caution

In previous versions of Flash, vector graphics consisting of drawing objects or shape primitives could be motion-tweened without being converted into symbols, but the new tweening workflow in Flash CS5 requires symbols for motion tweening. If you try to apply a motion tween to an element that is not already a symbol, you will be prompted by a dialog box to convert it or cancel the tween. Although drawing objects and shape primitives have benefits in the authoring environment, they do not get stored in the Library and have the same impact on file size as other raw vector graphics. ■

Sounds

The Library also handles sounds like symbols. However, they can be assigned different playback behavior after they are placed on a timeline. Flash can import (and export) sounds in a range of sound formats. Upon import, these sound files reside in the Library. To use a sound, drag an instance of the sound out of the Library and onto the Stage. You manage export settings for sound files within the Library by choosing Properties from either the contextual menu or the Library options menu. You can define playback behavior and effects with the Properties panel after placing a sound on a timeline.

Graphic Symbols versus Movie Clip Symbols

Graphic symbols are a quick and tidy way of placing static information into a timeline, whereas Movie Clip symbols animate independently on their own timeline. Graphic symbols should be used to hold single frames of raw data, or multiple frames when it is important to preview your work while designing it, as with linear animation. You must use Movie Clips when ActionScript is involved, or when an animation must run regardless of what is happening around it. However, using one type of symbol instead of the other may not always involve clear-cut choices, because, often, either works. Consequently, to use symbols effectively, it's important to know the pluses, minuses, and absolutes of both Graphic symbols and Movie Clips. Here are some tips to keep in mind:

- Instance properties of Graphic symbols (height, color, rotation, and so on) are frozen at design time, whereas Movie Clips can have their instance properties set on-the-fly with ActionScript. This makes Movie Clips essential for programmed content such as games.

- Scrubbing the Main Timeline (previewing while working) is not possible with Movie Clips, although it is possible with Graphic symbols. This makes Graphic symbols essential for animating cartoons. Eyes open, eyes closed — it's that big of a difference.

- Movie Clips can't (easily) be exported to video or other linear mediums. This is only significant if you plan to convert your .swf files to another time-based format.

- A Graphic symbol's instance properties are controlled (modified) at design time, with the options available in the Properties panel. One advantage is that this is simple and sure because you have an instant preview of what's happening. In addition, this information is embedded right in that particular instance of the Graphic symbol — meaning that, if it is either moved or copied, all this information comes with it.

- You can control a Movie Clip's instance properties at design time or set them with ActionScript. One advantage is that the actions do not need to be directly linked to the Movie Clip, which has the concurrent disadvantage that you must take care when moving Movie Clips that have visual qualities defined with ActionScript.

- Graphic symbols that are animated (have more than one frame), and are nested with other animated Graphic symbols, may have problems with synchronization. For example, if you have a pair of eyes that blink at the end of a 10-frame Graphic symbol, and you put the Graphic symbol containing those eyes within a 5-frame Graphic symbol of a head, the eyes will never blink. The head Graphic symbol will run from frame 1 to frame 5, and then return to frame 1, only displaying the first 5 frames of the eyes Graphic symbol. Or, if you nest the eyes Graphic symbol into a 15-frame head Graphic symbol, they will blink on frame 10, and then every 15 frames. That's 10 frames, and then blink, and then they loop back to frame 1; however, when reaching frame 5 this time, the movie they are in loops back to frame 1 (it's a 15-frame movie), and, thus, resets the eyes to frame 1.

- Movie Clips do not have the problem/feature described in the preceding bullet point. They offer consistent, independent timeline playback.

Authors' note: This comparison was contributed by Robin and Sandy Debreuil for the *Flash 5 Bible* (Wiley, 2001), and I still like how they articulate the important distinction between Graphic symbols and Movie Clip symbols.

Cross-Reference

Importing and using sounds effectively is a critical topic I cover in Chapter 14, "Adding Sound." ■

Video assets

Video assets, as with font symbols, can be embedded or linked. Embedded video assets, like bitmaps, can have color, alpha, and filter effects applied if they are first converted to a native Flash symbol type.

Cross-Reference

Flash supports alpha channels in video files. This opens up a whole range of exciting options for integrating video with other Flash content. For comprehensive coverage of working with video in Flash CS5, refer to Chapter 14, "Displaying Video." ■

Font symbols

Font symbols are symbols created from font files to make them available for use in dynamic text fields. Font symbols can also be defined as shared fonts to make them available to multiple movie files (.swf) without the file size burden of embedding the font into each file individually.

Editing Symbols

Because every instance of a symbol is linked to the original, *any* edit applied to that original is applied to every instance. There are several ways to edit a symbol, which I cover in the following sections.

Modifying a symbol in Edit mode

Edit mode opens the Stage and timeline of the selected symbol in the Document window, replacing the view of the current keyframe in the Main Timeline with a view of the first keyframe in the symbol's timeline. To open a symbol in Edit mode, do one of the following:

- Select an instance on the Stage and choose Edit ⇨ Edit Symbols, or Edit Selected from the application menu.

- Select an instance on the Stage and right-click (Command/Ctrl+click), and then choose Edit from the contextual menu.

- Select an instance on the Stage and use the shortcut key (⌘/Ctrl+E).

- Double-click a symbol in the Document Library. (Double-clicking bitmaps, sound, video, and other nonnative symbol types launches the Properties dialog box instead of opening Edit mode.)

Editing a symbol in a new window

This method is useful if you're working on two monitors and want to quickly open a new window to edit in while keeping a view of the Main Timeline open and available. On Mac, these two windows are always separate, but you can click either window to switch back and forth. On Windows, you can switch between these windows by choosing from the Window menu.

To edit a symbol in a new window, select an instance on the Stage and right-click (⌘/Ctrl+click), and then select Edit In New Window from the contextual menu.

Editing a symbol in place

The advantage of Edit in Place is that, instead of opening the symbol in a separate edit space, you can edit your symbol in context with the surrounding movie. Other elements present on the current keyframe are visible but dimmed slightly and protected from any edits you make on the selected symbol. To edit a symbol in place, do one of the following:

- Select an instance on the Stage and choose Edit ⇨ Edit in Place from the application menu.
- Select an instance on the Stage and right-click (⌘/Ctrl+click), and then select Edit in Place from the contextual menu.
- Double-click the instance on the Stage.

Editing symbols from the Library

You might not have an instance of your symbol available to select for editing in the Document window, but you can still edit it. Just edit it from the Library. Open your movie's Library with Window ⇨ Library from the application menu (⌘/Ctrl+L). Select the symbol in the Library that you want to edit and do one of the following:

- Double-click the symbol's icon (not its name) in the Library list.
- Right-click (⌘/Ctrl+click) and then select Edit from the contextual popup menu.
- If you have opened the Symbol Properties dialog box (see Figure 6.6), you can move to Edit mode by clicking the Edit button.

Returning to the Main Timeline or scene

After you edit your symbol, you'll want to go back to the scene in the Main Timeline to make sure that your changes work properly. Just do one of the following:

- Choose Edit ⇨ Edit Movie from the application menu or use the shortcut keys — ⌘/Ctrl+E.
- Double-click in any empty area of the Edit Stage.

- Click the Return arrow at the left edge of the Edit bar to step back through any nested timelines until you reach the Main Timeline.

- Select the scene name in the left corner above the Stage view in the Document window, as shown in Figure 6.7.

FIGURE 6.7

The location label in the Document window Edit bar is used to identify the current edit space and to return to the Main Timeline of the current scene.

Return arrow steps back through nested elements to return to Main Timeline

Return to Main Timeline (Scene 1)

Return to Button ("basicButton") Timeline

Return to Movie Clip ("overAnim") Timeline

Currently editing Graphic symbol ("outline") Timeline

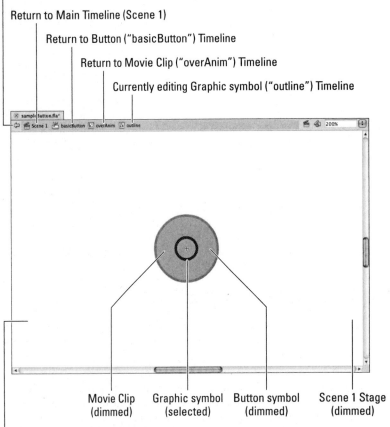

Movie Clip   Graphic symbol   Button symbol   Scene 1 Stage
(dimmed)   (selected)   (dimmed)   (dimmed)

Symbol edit space for graphic symbol seen in Edit in Place mode

Staying Oriented in Edit Space

Graphics editing in Flash occurs in one of two places: in the Main Timeline and on the Stage; or within a symbol, which has its own edit space and timeline. But how do you know when you are on the Scene Stage or when you are in Edit mode? Here's one clue: At the top of the Document window is the Edit bar. If you're working on the Scene Stage, you'll see a single tab with the name of the scene. Unless you name your scenes, this tab should simply say Scene 1 (or Scene 2). However, in Edit mode, a second tab appears to the right of the scene name: This tab displays the name and icon of the current group or symbol (Movie Clip, Graphic symbol, or Button symbol). If you're editing a nested symbol, more tabs may appear. In this manner, you have convenient access to the hierarchy of your assets, no matter how deeply they are nested.

Edit mode is much like working on the regular Stage. You can draw with any of the drawing tools, add text, place symbols, import graphics and sound, and use ActionScript. When you're done working with a symbol, you have an encapsulated element, whether it is a static Graphic, a Movie Clip, or a Button. You can place this element as many times as needed on your Stage or within other symbols. Each time you place it, the symbol's entire contents and timeline (if it is a Button or a Movie Clip) are placed as well, identical to the original symbol stored in the Library. Remember that even if you access Edit mode from an instance on the Stage, all changes that you make propagate to every other instance derived from the original symbol in the Library. The only color changes that you can make to one instance at a time without affecting the other instances of the same symbol are those you apply by using the Color menu on the Properties panel, or by applying filters and blend modes to instances as I explain later

The Stage (if it is not zoomed to fill the screen) is surrounded by a gray area. This is the work area or pasteboard, and it indicates the visible edges of the final movie as defined in the Document properties. The dimensions of any symbol, however, are not limited to the size of the Stage. If you make your symbols too large, when you place them on the Stage, portions that fall outside of the Stage are not visible in the final movie (.swf), but they still export and add to the file size. Remember that it is always possible to scale a symbol instance to make it smaller than the original symbol if necessary.

Modifying Instance Properties

Every instance of a symbol has graphic variables that you can modify. These properties apply only to the specific instance, not to the original symbol. Display properties such as brightness, tint, and alpha (transparency) can all be modified without creating a new symbol. An instance can also be scaled, rotated, and skewed. Filters and blend modes enable a range of cool visual effects that you can apply to symbol instances. With the Type menu in the Properties panel, you can also change the symbol type behavior of an instance without changing the original symbol. As I previously discuss, any changes you make to the original symbol in Edit mode are updated in each instance. This still holds true even if some of the instances also have properties that are modified individually.

Note

Scaling, rotating, and skewing in 2-D space is kinda fun but the 3-D tools in Flash CS5 enable you to move or rotate a symbol in 3-D space. Use the 3D Rotation or 3D Translation tools to modify symbol instances along the x, y, or z axis to create the illusion of depth on your Flash Stage. 3-D tools are discussed in more detail in Chapter 9, "Modifying Graphics". ∎

Applying basic color effects to symbol instances

Each instance of a symbol can have a variety of color effects applied to it. The basic effects are changes of brightness, tint, and *alpha* (transparency). Tint and alpha changes can also be combined for special effects. To apply color effects to a symbol instance by using the Properties panel:

1. **Select the instance in the Document window that you want to modify.**

2. **Select one of the options from the Style drop-down menu in the Color Effect section of the Properties panel.** Figure 6.8 shows the basic color effect options that can be applied to any symbol type.

FIGURE 6.8

The color effect Style menu has basic options to choose from (left). After a color effect is selected, the settings for that effect are available in the Properties panel (right).

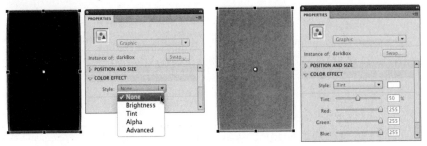

The options available from the color effect Style menu are as follows:

*   **None:** No effect is applied.
*   **Brightness:** Adjusts the relative brightness or darkness of the instance. It ranges from 100 percent (white) to –100 percent (black); the default setting is 0 percent (no visible change to instance appearance). Use the slider to change the value or just type a numeric value into the entry field.
*   **Tint:** Enables you to shift the color of an instance. Either select a hue with the color picker or enter the RGB values directly, and then select the percentage of saturation (Tint Amount) by using the slider or by entering the percentage in the entry field. This number ranges from 0 percent (no saturation) to 100 percent (completely saturated).

- **Alpha:** Enables you to modify the transparency of an instance. Select a percentage by using the slider or by entering a number directly. The Alpha percentage (or visibility setting) ranges from 0 percent (completely transparent) to 100 percent (no transparency).

- **Advanced:** When you select the Advanced option from the Style menu, numeric values appear in two columns that enable you to adjust both the tint and alpha settings of an instance. The controls on the left reduce the tint and alpha values by a specified percentage, whereas the controls on the right either reduce or increase the tint and alpha values by a constant value. The current values are multiplied by the numbers on the left and then added to the values on the right.

Cross-Reference

The Advanced option includes a range with negative alpha values. Potential uses for this capability, together with more information about using color effects and other methods of transforming symbol instances, are detailed in Chapter 9. ■

Changing the symbol type of an instance

You don't need to limit yourself to the native behavior of a symbol. For example, there may be times when you want a Movie Clip to have the behavior of a Graphic symbol so that you can preview animation by scrubbing the Timeline. You don't have to go through the extra effort of creating a new symbol — just use the following steps to change the type of the instance as needed:

1. **Select the instance in the Document window you want to modify.**

2. **From the symbol Type drop-down list at the top of the Properties panel, select the desired behavior.** As shown in Figure 6.9, you can assign Graphic, Button, or Movie Clip behavior.

FIGURE 6.9

You can change the behavior of any selected symbol instance with the drop-down symbol Type menu in the Properties panel.

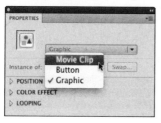

Cross-Reference

The more-complex uses of symbol instances are covered in Part V, "Adding Basic Interactivity to Flash Movies." ■

Swapping symbols

You may need to replace an instance of one symbol with an instance of another symbol stored in your project Library. Luckily, you don't have to go through and re-create your entire animation to do this — just use the Swap Symbol feature, illustrated in Figure 6.10. This feature only switches the instance of the symbol for an instance of another symbol; all other modifications previously applied to the instance remain the same. Here's how to swap symbols:

1. **Select the instance that you want to replace.**

2. **Click the Swap symbol button in the Properties panel, choose Modify ⇨ Symbol ⇨ Swap Symbol from the application menu, or right-click (⌘/Ctrl+click) and choose Swap Symbol from the contextual menu.**

3. **Select the symbol that you want to put into the place of your current instance from the list of available symbols in your project Library.**

4. **Click OK to swap the symbols.**

FIGURE 6.10

Use the Swap Symbol dialog box to choose a replacement for a symbol instance without losing any transformations that have already been applied.

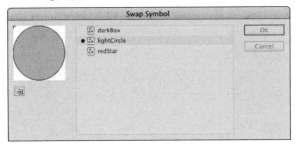

Building Nested Symbol Structures

Understanding the various symbol types individually is the first step, but the next step is integrating these building blocks to create organized, optimized Flash projects that are extensible, easy to edit, and fast to build. Although I cover the workflow for different types of Flash projects in other parts of this book, I can synthesize the overview of different symbol types by walking through the steps of creating a Button symbol with some nested animation and Graphic symbols.

To demonstrate building an animated Flash movie from various symbol types, I made a Button symbol called basicButton that uses some raw shapes, some Graphic symbols, and some Movie Clips, all nested inside a Button symbol timeline.

On the CD-ROM

The starting source file (`sampleButton.fla`) for this series of demonstrations is on the CD-ROM that accompanies this book in the ch06 folder. ■

Converting a raw shape into a Graphic symbol

The best way to begin creating any graphic element is to first consider the final shape that you need and to try to find the most basic primitive shapes that you can use to build that element. Keep in mind that instances can be scaled, skewed, and adjusted with color effects. Instead of drawing three circles to make a snowman, you would make just one circle and convert that into a symbol so that you could build your snowman from scaled instances of just one symbol stored in the Library. A resourceful animator I know built a Christmas tree by reusing instances of a symbol he had made for a dog's tail in the same animation — a wagging tail and a tree all built from just one Graphic symbol stored in the Library! Raw graphics can be converted into Graphic symbols after they have been drawn, or you can first create a new Graphic symbol and then draw the raw shapes directly inside the Graphic symbol in Edit mode — either way, the end result is a contained visual element that is stored in the Library to define any instances that you need to place in your movie.

To build the simple graphics used in `basicButton`, you can begin by converting a raw shape into a Graphic symbol:

1. **Select the Oval tool and set the fill color to green and the stroke color to black with a stroke height of 3.**

2. **Click on the Stage and hold down the Shift key while dragging out the shape to create a perfect circle.** Double-click the fill with the Selection tool to select both the stroke and the fill, and then use the Properties panel to set the width to 75 and the height to 75. (If the Constrain check box is selected in the Properties panel, you only need to enter **75** in one of the value fields and the circle will scale evenly.)

Tip

An alternative workflow supported in Flash for creating an oval (after completing Step 1) is to Option/Alt+click in the Document window to open the Oval Settings dialog box. Enter 75 for the width and height of the circle and click OK. Flash renders a circle in the Document window, centered on the point you clicked. ■

Note

If you open the Library panel — Window ⇨ Library (⌘/Ctrl+L) — you will notice that the shape you've drawn is not visible in the asset list because raw data is not stored in the Library. ■

3. **While the stroke and the fill are both still selected, press F8 or choose Modify ⇨ Convert to Symbol from the application menu.**

4. **In the Convert to Symbol dialog box, choose Graphic for the symbol type and give the symbol the name** plainCircle. Click OK. You should now see the plainCircle symbol with the Graphic symbol icon next to it in the Library panel.

Tip

You always have the choice of creating artwork on the Main Timeline and then converting it into a symbol or first inserting a new symbol and then creating artwork in the symbol drawing space. Either workflow achieves the same end result. In the plainCircle example, start by selecting Insert ➪ New Symbol (⌘/Ctrl+F8). Enter the settings noted in Step 4, and then complete Steps 1 and 2 to draw the circle on the Graphic symbol timeline rather than on the Main Timeline. When you go back to the Main Timeline, you won't see an instance of plain-Circle on the Stage, but the Graphic symbol should now be in the Library, and you can drag an instance into the Document window whenever you need it. ■

You can now reuse instances of this Graphic symbol in your document in as many places as you need it just by dragging an instance onto the Stage from the Library panel.

Note

For the basicButton example, you will need an instance of plainCircle inside of a new Button symbol rather than on the main Stage, so you can delete any instances of plainCircle from the Main Timeline before continuing with additional steps. ■

Using Graphic symbols in a button

Button symbols are similar to Movie Clips that have a special timeline structure linked to mouse states. For a button to take you to a new point on the Main Timeline or to load any other elements, ActionScript must be added to the button instance.

Cross-Reference

I discuss adding actions to buttons for more advanced interactivity in Chapter 15, "Understanding Actions and Event Handlers." ■

In this example, the button simply works as a structure for an animation that reacts to the mouse. Begin by inserting a new Button symbol:

1. **Click the New Symbol button in the Library panel or choose Insert ➪ New Symbol from the application menu or use the shortcut keys (⌘/Ctrl+F8).**

2. **In the Create New Symbol dialog box, choose Button as the symbol type, and for this example give the symbol the name** basicButton. Click OK. This Button symbol is now stored in the Library and automatically opens in Edit mode in the Document window, so you can add some content to the button.

   You will notice that the Button Timeline shows four keyframes with labels that define the button state by mouse behavior: Up, Over, Down, and Hit. These various keyframes can have multiple layers and contain any visual element or sound that you want. The button states function as follows:

   • **Up:** Any elements placed in the Up keyframe are associated with the button as it appears on the Stage when the button is present but not activated by any mouse interaction.

   • **Over:** Any elements placed in the Over keyframe are associated with the button when the mouse rolls over it on the Stage, but as soon as the mouse rolls off the button it reverts to its Up state.

- **Down:** Any elements placed in the Down keyframe are associated with the button only when the mouse is over it and clicked and held down. As soon as the mouse is released, the button reverts to its Over state.

- **Hit:** The Hit keyframe is actually never visible on Stage, but this instead defines the area of the button that is "sensitive" to the mouse. Whatever shape is present on this frame is considered part of the button's *hit area*. It is important to note that it is better not to have holes or gaps in the hit area unless it is intended. For example, if you have text as a button, it is best to use a solid rectangle that matches the width and height of the total text area. Using the actual text would result in an irregular button hit area — whenever the mouse rolls into the space between letters, the button would revert to its Up state and could not be clicked.

Tip

If you ever need an "invisible" button in your project, you can create one by adding artwork to the Hit keyframe only of a Button symbol. The button is visible in the authoring environment as a bright blue preview shape (defined by the graphics in the Hit state), but when the .swf file is published, the only indication that a button is on the Stage is the change in the mouse cursor when it enters the Hit area. You can add ActionScript to an invisible button to trigger events in your animation or to control the behavior of other elements in your movie. I discuss invisible buttons in more detail in Chapter 15, "Understanding Actions and Event Handlers." ■

For this example, you create animation to be placed into the various visible states, but the main shape of the button will always be consistent, so you can begin by creating a layer to define the main shape of the button.

3. Rename Layer 1 of the Button symbol timeline as buttonOutline and insert two frames (F5) after the first keyframe to create a span of three frames (visible for Up, Over, and Down).

4. With the playhead set on the first keyframe, drag an instance of plainCircle onto the button Stage and make sure that it is now visible in the Up, Over, and Down states of the button, but not on the Hit state.

5. Center the instance on the button Stage by using the Align panel (⌘/Ctrl+K).

6. Select the instance of plainCircle and copy it to the Clipboard (⌘/Ctrl+C).

7. Create a new layer and name it hitArea.

8. Insert a blank keyframe (F7) on frame 4 (Hit). To paste the copy of plainCircle into the center of the blank Hit keyframe, use Paste in Place (⌘/Ctrl+Shift+V). If you have done a straightforward paste instead, make sure that the instance of plainCircle is centered to the button Stage.

The timeline of your Button symbol should now look like Figure 6.11.

9. Return to the Main Timeline by clicking the Scene 1 label in the Edit bar or by double-clicking an empty area of the Stage.

10. If you don't see an instance of your basicButton on the Stage of the Main Timeline, drag an instance out of the Library and place it on the first frame of the Main Timeline.

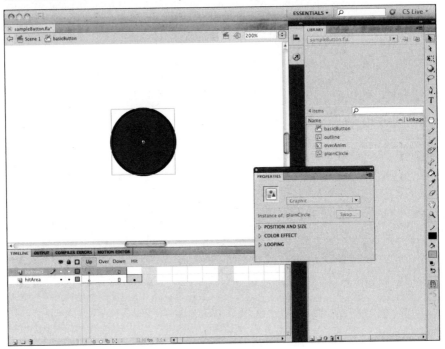

FIGURE 6.11

The Edit mode view of the basic Button symbol timeline, with Up, Over, Down, and Hit states defined with instances of the plainCircle Graphic symbol

Animating Graphic symbols in a Movie Clip

After you have created some Graphic symbols to define your basicButton, you can now start building some animation to add to it. You can build animation by placing artwork in keyframes on the Main Timeline, but this limits how you can use the animation and can make it difficult to add more elements to your project without disturbing the keyframe structure of the animation. If you need animated elements that can be reused, and quickly moved to different parts of the Main Timeline or placed into a Button symbol timeline, it is best to begin by creating a Movie Clip.

1. Click the New Symbol button in the Library panel or choose Insert ➪ New Symbol from the application menu, or use shortcut keys (⌘/Control+F8).

2. In the Symbol Properties dialog box, choose Movie Clip as the symbol type and give this symbol the name overAnim.

3. Create a new circle on the first frame of the Movie Clip Timeline with a black stroke (with a height of 3) and no fill. Select the outline with the Selection tool and use the Properties panel to set its width and height to 25. Then use the Align panel to center it on the Stage.

4. **Convert this raw shape into a Graphic symbol (Modify ⇨ Convert to symbol or F8) with the name** outline.

5. **Insert nine frames (F5) on the Movie Clip Timeline so that you have a span of frames from frame 1 to frame 10 with the outline Graphic symbol visible.**

6. **Select the instance of outline on the Stage in frame 1 and right-click/Ctrl+click and select Create Motion Tween from the contextual menu.** (Or use the Application menu to select Insert ⇨ Motion tween.)

7. **Now select the instance of the outline in frame 10 and use the Properties panel to change the width and height of the outline to 50 pixels high and 50 pixels wide.** The graphic should stay centered on the Stage, but you can use the Align panel to make sure.

   You should now be able to drag the playhead from frame 1 to frame 10 in the timeline and see an animation of the outline growing in size. Figure 6.12 shows the view of the outline instance on frame 10 with a tween from frame 1 to frame 10.

FIGURE 6.12

The symbol timeline of the Movie Clip "overAnim" showing a motion tween of the Graphic symbol "outline," from frame 1 to frame 10

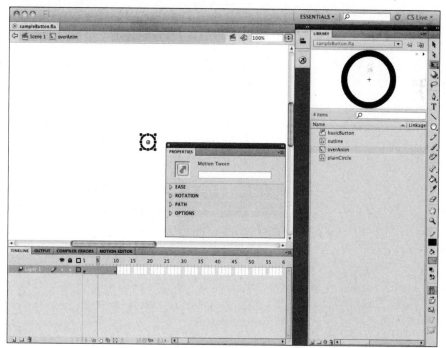

Adding a Movie Clip to a Button symbol

The final step in our example is to add the overAnim Movie Clip to the basicButton symbol. This is the secret to animated Button symbol: By nesting multiframe Movie Clip animations into the single frames assigned to the Up, Over, and Down states of the Button symbol timeline, you can create different animated "reactions" as the mouse rolls over or clicks the button.

1. **To go back inside your button and add animation in Edit mode, double-click the instance of basicButton on the Stage or the symbol in the Library.**

2. **Create a new layer in the Button symbol timeline and name it** outlineAnim. Make sure that this new layer is above the original buttonOutline layer.

3. **On the outlineAnim layer, insert a new keyframe (F6) on frame 2 (Over).**

4. **Drag an instance of overAnim from the Library onto the button Stage in the keyframe you just created, and use the Align panel to center it.**

5. **To ensure that the animation is visible only on the Over state of the button, make sure that the content on the overAnim layer occupies only one frame on the Button symbol timeline.** If the overAnim symbol extends into frame 3, either insert a blank keyframe (F7) or remove a frame (Shift+F5) to keep it contained on frame 2.

   Your Button symbol timeline should now look like Figure 6.13.

You can test your Button symbol with this animation added to see how it is working by pressing ⌘+Return/Ctrl+Enter on the keyboard to view the movie (.swf) in the Test Movie environment. Now when you roll over the green button with your mouse, you should see the outline circles animate. Remember that you still have only one keyframe on your Main Timeline, so this demonstrates how both a Button symbol and a Movie Clip symbol play back their own timelines even if they are placed into a single frame on another timeline. You still need to add some animation for the Down state of the basicButton, so close the Test Movie (.swf) window to go back to the Button symbol timeline in the Document window.

FIGURE 6.13

The timeline of the Button symbol basicButton with the Movie Clip overAnim placed on the Over keyframe of the outlineAnim layer

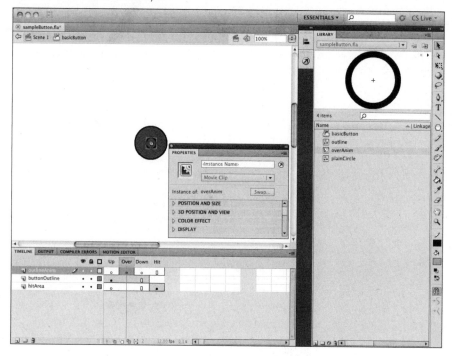

Modifying a MovieClip instance

Instead of creating an entirely new animation to display on the Over state of our basicButton, you can reuse the overAnim Movie Clip and change its appearance by adding a color effect to the instance.

1. Double-click the basicButton symbol instance to enter Edit mode.

2. Add a new layer to the Button symbol timeline and name it outlineAnimTint.

3. Insert a blank keyframe on frame 3 (Down).

4. Drag an instance of the overAnim Movie Clip from the Library, or just copy the Over frame on the outlineAnim layer and paste it into the blank keyframe you just created.

5. Select the instance of the overAnim Movie Clip that you placed on the Down keyframe and, in the Color Effect section of the Properties panel, choose Tint from the Style menu.

6. Choose white as the tint color from the Swatches that pop up from the color chip, and then enter a tint value of 100 percent by using the slider or by typing into the value box.

   Your Button symbol timeline should now look like Figure 6.14.

FIGURE 6.14

The basicButton Timeline with an instance of the overAnim Movie Clip placed on the Down keyframe and modified with a color tint

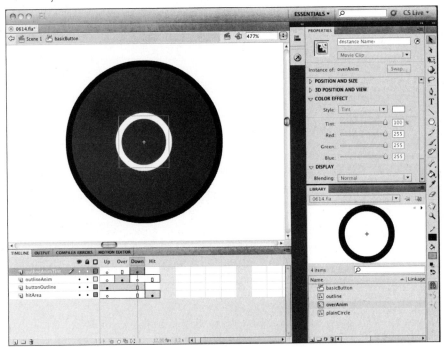

Test your animated button again (Ctrl+Enter/⌘+Return) and you will see that the animation now appears when you click the button. But instead of the original black that appears on the Over state, the animation for the Down (click) state is white. The three visible states of your button should now resemble Figure 6.15.

The finished animated button as it appears in the Up, Over, and Down states

Up state   Over state   Down state

You have seen how symbols are created, nested, and modified, and you are probably realizing that this basic animated Button symbol is only the beginning.

On the CD-ROM

If you want to deconstruct another layered symbol structure, I have included a silly, but slightly more complex, animated button on this book's CD-ROM. You will find the source file, `surpriseButton.fla`, in the `ch06` folder. Figure 6.16 shows the three visible button states and diagrams the basic symbol nesting. ∎

As your symbol structures get more layered and complex, it can be helpful to have some guidance when you are trying to navigate to a specific item in your project or just trying to remember exactly how you organized things as you were building. Although careful use of layer names, frame labels, and symbol names is indispensable, the Movie Explorer (introduced later in this chapter) is a great assistant for finding your way through the structure of any Flash document.

FIGURE 6.16

The animation as it appears in the three visible button states, Up, Over, and Down, with a diagram of the basic nested elements visible in each state

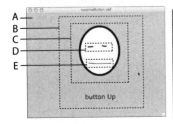

A — | | | | | | | Main Timeline: frame 1
B — | | | | ⓧ | surprise (Button): frame 1 "Up"
C — eyeOutline (Graphic Symbol instance 2)
D — | D | sleepingEyes (Movie Clip): frame 2
E — | E | sleepingMouth (Movie Clip): frame 2

button Up

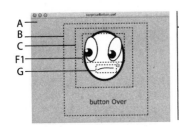

A — | | | | | | | Main Timeline: frame 1
B — | | ⓧ | surprise (Button): frame 2 "Over"
C — eyeOutline (Graphic Symbol instance 2)
F1 — | | | | F1 | | | | eyesLook (Movie Clip instance 1): frame 4
G — mouthGrimace (shape)

button Over

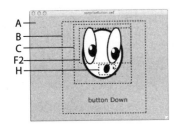

A — | | | | | | | Main Timeline: frame 1
B — | | B | ⓧ | surprise (Button): frame 3 "Down"
C — eyeOutline (Graphic Symbol instance 2)
F2 — | | | | | | | | F2 | eyesLook (Movie Clip instance 2):
                                            frame 8
H — mouthSurprise (shape)

button Down

Note: ⓧ = Hit frame of Button symbol

9-Slice Scaling for Movie Clip Backgrounds

Have you ever tried to resize the same background graphic to fit different content and found that the aspect ratio or corner angles were no longer consistent? This can be frustrating, and the work-arounds in older versions of Flash — creating unique graphics for each use or manually splitting up scalable and nonscalable areas of a background or border — were time consuming and some-times ineffective. The good news is that Flash includes a feature designed to solve this problem. The 9-slice, or Scale 9, option helps you selectively define the scaleable area of a Movie Clip to make it easier to transform and reuse.

To truly appreciate this feature you have to try it. Here's how:

1. **Create a new symbol in your Flash document (Insert ➪ New Symbol).**
2. **Enter a name for your symbol and select Movie Clip as the symbol type.**
3. **Select the check box to Enable guides for 9-slice scaling (shown in Figure 6.17).**

FIGURE 6.17

Enable guides for 9-slice scaling is an option in Advanced symbol properties.

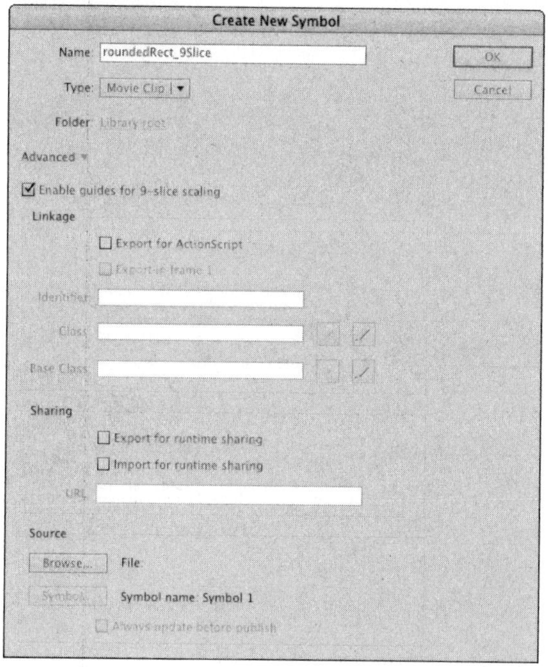

Tip

Expand the Symbol Properties dialog box by clicking the Advanced button if you don't see the check box for 9-slice scaling. ■

4. **Click OK and enter the edit space for the new symbol; you'll notice a grid of dotted guidelines on the Stage.** These four guides are used to split shapes into nine different regions (or slices) to control how the graphic is interpolated if the MovieClip instance is scaled.

Don't worry about the guides just yet. Create your artwork on the Stage with any of the shape or drawing tools.

Note

The most common use for Scale 9 is to preserve the corners on rounded rectangles used as button icons. For our example, wl created a rounded rectangle by setting Fill and Stroke in the Properties panel, activating the Rectangle Primitive tool in the Tools panel, and then holding down Option (or Alt) and clicking on the Stage to open the Rectangle Settings dialog box. This makes quick work of creating a button icon — simply enter a width, height, and corner radius and click OK. The rectangle is drawn on the Stage for you. ∎

5. **Make sure that your graphic is positioned in the center of the Stage.** Select all elements and use the center horizontal and center vertical buttons in the Align panel with the To stage toggle turned on.

6. **When you have your graphic sized and aligned as you want it, click and drag the guides to position them so that the curved areas of your graphic are not distorted when the scaled instance is rendered.** This is difficult to describe with text, but Figure 6.18 shows a centered rectangle with guides positioned to protect the rounded corners of the rectangle while allowing the center area of the graphic to be stretched when the symbol instance is scaled.

FIGURE 6.18

You can drag the four slice guides to isolate the outside edges of a graphic that should be protected when the center area is stretched to scale.

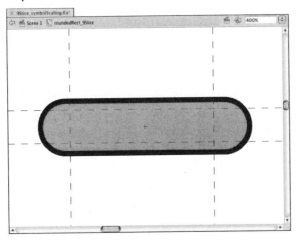

7. **To test the results of 9-slice scaling on your symbol, return to the Main Timeline and drag an instance of your symbol onto the Stage.** Use the Transform tools or the Transform panel to change the size or aspect ratio of the symbol instance. I scaled the rounded rectangle symbol instance in our example horizontally to 150 percent.

Note

A symbol with 9-slice scaling enabled appears with the dotted grids in the preview pane of the Library panel. The grids are not visible when the symbol is placed on the Stage. ■

Tip

The effect of 9-slice scaling is visible in the authoring environment, so you don't have to test your movie to see the results of using this feature on a scaled Movie Clip. ■

The difference between 9-slice scaling and normal scaling is visible in the .fla and in the published .swf. As shown in Figure 6.19, the symbol without 9-slice scaling (left) is distorted when it's scaled larger, and the symbol with 9-slice scaling enabled (right) scales gracefully and preserves the original shape of the rounded corners.

On the CD-ROM

The example file shown in this section is also saved on the CD-ROM. Open 9Slice_symbolScaling.fla or .swf from the ch06 folder. ■

How does this magic happen? If the final symbol is scaled horizontally, the three center sections (from left to right) stretch while the corners and the top and bottom edges are constrained. If the final symbol is scaled vertically, the three sections (from top to bottom) stretch while the corners and the left and right edges are constrained. If the symbol is scaled in both directions, the t-shaped center section stretches to fit, while the corners remain protected. It might take a few tries to get the hang of using 9-slice scaling, but it saves you a lot of time if you need to design consistent scalable graphics.

FIGURE 6.19

The symbol with 9-slice scaling enabled is rendered consistently in the .swf without any distortion. The rounded corners at the original size (top right) match the rounded corners at the scaled size (lower right).

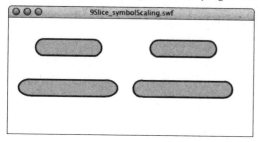

You can enable 9-slice scaling when you create a new symbol, or you can enable it in the Symbol Properties dialog box for existing Movie Clip symbols — select the symbol in the Library list and choose Properties from the contextual menu or the panel Options menu.

Tip

If you create a Movie Clip with artwork first and then enable 9-slice scaling by accessing the Symbol Properties dialog box from the Library, the slice guides automatically align to the outside edges of your artwork. You may still need to adjust the guides to get the exact result that you want, but the starting point will be much closer than if you enable the 9-slice scaling guides before you create the artwork. ■

Using the Movie Explorer

The Movie Explorer panel is a powerful tool for deciphering movies and finding items within them. You can open it from the application menu by choosing Window ➪ Movie Explorer (Option/Alt+F3).

Note

The Find and Replace command is a much more efficient choice if your goal is to dig up specific elements such as fonts or colors that you want to replace in your project file. I discuss the many uses of the Find and Replace feature in Chapter 9, "Modifying Graphics." I include coverage of the Movie Explorer here because it is still the best tool for discovering the structure of a file. ■

The Movie Explorer is an especially useful tool for getting an overview and for analyzing the structure of a Flash movie. This means that you can see every element in its relationship to all other elements, and you can see this all in one place. However, it's also useful for troubleshooting a movie, for finding occurrences of a particular font, and for locating places where you refer to a certain variable name in any script throughout a movie. As an editing tool, you can use it as a shortcut to edit any symbol, for changing the properties of an instance, or even for doing multiple selections and then changing the attributes of the selected items. Furthermore, the Find function is an incredible time-saver when working on complex project files.

Figure 6.20 shows the Movie Explorer as well as the Movie Explorer Settings dialog box, which you can open by clicking the Customize Which Items to Show button in the Movie Explorer (Customize is the far right icon in the row of filter buttons).

FIGURE 6.20

The Movie Explorer displaying the file structure for the button example created in the previous section

Filtering buttons

As shown in Figure 6.20, there are several icon buttons across the top of the Movie Explorer panel. These are called filter buttons, and they have icons representative of their function. Click any button to toggle the display of those elements in your file. Note, however, that the Movie Explorer's display becomes more crowded as you select more buttons, and that it performs more slowly because it has to sift more data. From left to right, the buttons filter the display of the following kinds of content:

- Text
- Button symbols, Movie Clips, and Graphic symbols (placed instances)
- ActionScript
- Video, sounds, and bitmaps (placed instances)
- Frames and layers
- The Movie Explorer Settings dialog box

Also note the Find field. It enables you to search through all items that currently appear in the Movie Explorer to find specific elements by typing in the name of the symbol, instance, font name, ActionScript string, or frame number.

The display list

Below the icons is a window with the display list. Much like Windows Explorer, or the Mac Finder, the Movie Explorer displays items hierarchically, either by individual scene or for all scenes. These listings are expandable, so if you have selected the Text button, an arrow (or on Windows, a plus [+] sign) appears beside the name of any scene that includes text. Clicking the arrow (or plus sign) displays all the selected items included in that scene. This type of visual data display is also referred to as a "tree structure." Clicking a plus sign (or arrow) expands a "branch" of the tree. At the bottom of the display list, a status bar displays the full path for the currently selected item.

In Figure 6.21, the Text filter button has been selected. As shown, clicking the arrow sign beside the Text icon in the display list shows the complete text, including basic font information.

FIGURE 6.21

The Movie Explorer for the surpriseButton example included on the CD-ROM, with the Text filter button chosen to view text and font information inside the file

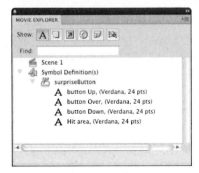

The Movie Explorer Options menu

The Options menu is accessed by clicking the options triangle in the upper-right corner of the Movie Explorer panel. These commands enable you to control how much detail is shown in the display list and also to perform edits or revisions after you've found the specific items that you want to modify:

- **Go to Location:** For a selected item, this transports you to the relevant layer, scene, or frame.

- **Go to Symbol Definition:** This jumps to the symbol definition for the symbol that's selected in the Movie Elements area. (For this to work, both Show Movie Elements and Show Symbol Definitions must be toggled on.)

- **Select Symbol Instances:** This jumps to the scene containing instances of the symbol selected in the Symbol Definitions area. (For this to work, both Show Movie Elements and Show Symbol Definitions must be toggled on.)

- **Show in Library:** If the Library window is not open, this opens the Library and highlights the selected item. Otherwise, it simply highlights the item in the Library.

- **Rename:** This enables you to easily rename selected items.

- **Edit in Place:** Use this to edit the selected symbol in context on the Stage.

- **Edit in New Window:** Use this to edit the selected symbol in Edit mode in a separate window from the main Document window.

- **Show Movie Elements:** One of two broad categories for how filtered items are viewed in the display list, Show Movie Elements displays all elements in the movie, organized by scene.

- **Show Symbol Definitions:** This is the other category of the display List, which shows all the items that are related to each symbol. Both Show Movie Elements and Show Symbol Definitions may be displayed simultaneously.

- **Show All Scenes:** This toggles the display of Show Movie Elements between selected scenes and all scenes.

- **Copy All Text to Clipboard:** Use this command to copy text to the Clipboard. Text may then be pasted into a word processor or into another editing application.

Cross-Reference
I discuss text-related features in more detail in Chapter 8, "Working with Text." ■

Caution
Unfortunately, getting text back into Flash is not as easy as copying it to the Clipboard. If you copy a large amount of text to another application, you have to manually update individual text blocks in your Flash document to integrate any changes that were made to the text outside of Flash. ■

- **Cut:** Use this command to cut selected text.

- **Copy:** Use this command to copy selected text.

- **Paste:** Use this command to paste text that has been copied from Flash or another application.

- **Clear:** Use this command to clear selected text.

- **Expand Branch:** This expands the hierarchical tree at the selected location; it's the menu equivalent of clicking the tiny plus (+) sign or right-facing arrow.

- **Collapse Branch:** This collapses the hierarchical tree at the selected location; it's the menu equivalent of clicking the tiny minus (–) sign or down-facing arrow.

- **Collapse Others:** This collapses the hierarchical tree everywhere except at the selected location.

- **Print:** The Movie Explorer prints out, with all the content expanded, displaying all types of content selected.

You can also access the commands found in the Movie Explorer options menu via the contextual menu.

The contextual menu

Select an item in the Movie Explorer and right-click (/⌘/Ctrl+click) to open the contextual menu related to that particular item. Nonapplicable commands are grayed out.

Figure 6.22 shows the contextual menu of the Movie Explorer. Among the most useful commands is the Goto Location option at the top. When you can't find an item (because it's on a masked layer or is invisible), this command can be a lifesaver.

FIGURE 6.22

The Movie Explorer's contextual menu

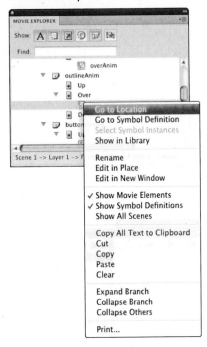

When you are planning or looking for ways to improve a project, the Movie Explorer can provide an excellent map to the structure and function of what you've already accomplished. Whenever it's relevant, print out the Movie Explorer; this can function as project documentation for finished work, providing a reference of all scripting and Movie Clip placement. As such, it can make returning to a project months later much easier. It can also facilitate collaboration among developers, whether they share the same studio or need to communicate long distance. Finally, for all the reasons I listed in this chapter, you can also use the Movie Explorer as a tool for both learning and teaching.

Now that you have a handle on working with symbols in one project file, let's go to the next step and see how you can work with symbols in multiple Flash files.

Using Authortime Shared Libraries

Flash gives you two options for working with shared assets: authortime and runtime shared Libraries. Authortime sharing enables a development team to maintain consistency during production on multiple versions of a file or on various project files that use the same symbols by using a centralized internal source .fla file for fonts or other assets. Runtime sharing reduces file sizes and makes it easier to dynamically update content in projects that involve multiple .swfs without having to republish all the files. In runtime sharing, a Library of assets is created and published as a source movie (.swf) that is uploaded to the server to be shared with multiple linked movies (.swfs). Source assets in shared libraries can include any element that is normally created in a Flash movie, as well as assets such as bitmaps, fonts, sounds, or video that are imported and usually embedded in individual project files (.fla).

Runtime sharing involves URLs and linkage info, but authortime sharing is relatively simple and can be accomplished without even publishing any .swf files. You can update or replace a symbol in your current project (.fla) with any other symbol accessible on your local network. Any transformations or effects applied to instances of the symbol in your project file are preserved, but the contents of the symbol stored in the project Library are replaced with the contents of the new (or modified) source symbol that you choose to link to.

Note

For clarity, I will refer to the currently open .fla file as a project file, and the .fla that contains symbols that you want to link to as the source file. In real-world production, you can give the files any name you want. However, adding a special identifier such as "Library" or "Source" to the .fla filenames that you plan to use for sharing can help you (and your team) minimize confusion. ∎

On the CD-ROM

I have included two sample files with some basic symbols that you can use to try out the symbol-linking feature. Both `shapeProject.fla` and `shapeSource.fla` are in the `ch06` folder on this book's CD-ROM. ∎

To link a symbol from one project Library to another, you need a source file and a project file. Open the project file and follow these steps:

1. In the current project (or `shapeProject.fla`) Library panel, select the symbol (Graphic symbol, Button, or Movie Clip) that you want to link to a source symbol.

2. Choose Properties from the contextual menu or from the Library options menu, and under Source in the Symbol Properties dialog box, click the Browse button to find the .fla file that contains the symbol you want to use as a source. After you find the .fla that will be your source, select it in the file list and click Open (as shown in Figure 6.23).

   The Select Source Symbol dialog box (shown in Figure 6.24) opens automatically to enable you to choose the specific symbol in the source library that you want to link to the symbol in your current project file.

Tip

You can also click the Advanced button in the Create New Symbol dialog box to access Source options and set linkage when you first create a symbol in your project. ∎

3. Select a symbol in the source Library file list and click OK to close the Select Source Symbol dialog box.

FIGURE 6.23

Browsing for a source file in the Symbol Properties dialog box

FIGURE 6.24

The Select Source Symbol dialog box, where you specify a linked symbol

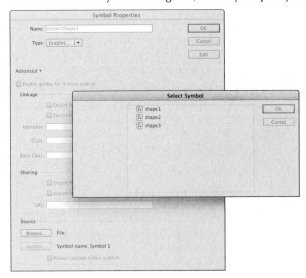

Before you close the Symbol Properties dialog box, notice that the path to the source file is now listed and that you can select a check box for Always update before publishing (as shown in Figure 6.25). Select this check box if you want Flash to check for changes in the source file and automatically update all linked symbols each time you publish a .swf from the project file.

FIGURE 6.25

The source path shown in the Symbol Properties dialog box with the Always update before publishing check box selected

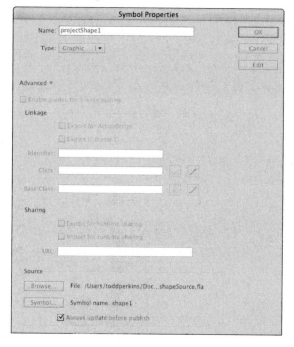

4. **Click OK to close the Symbol Properties dialog box.** The symbol name in your project Library remains the same, but the content of the symbol in all instances used in your project file should now contain the updated content that will match the content of the symbol you chose in the source file.

5. **Save your project file to preserve the linkage information for your symbol.**

Should any changes be made to the content of the symbol in the source .fla, you can either publish a .swf from the project file to see Flash automatically check for changes and update all linked symbols (with the Always update before publishing check box selected in the Symbol Properties dialog box), or you can use the Update command to manually get the most recent version of the symbol into your project file before you publish a .swf. To see how this works, follow these steps:

1. **Open the source .fla and make some changes to the symbol (using Edit mode) that you originally linked to and then save and close the file.** You can change the appearance of the symbol, but don't change the symbol name.

2. **Open a project file that contains the symbol you want to update, and either ensure that the Always update before publishing check box is selected in Symbol Properties before publishing an .swf to force Flash to check for changes to the source symbol and automatically update your project Library, or go to Step 3.**

3. **Select the symbol in the Library and use the options menu or the contextual menu to select the Update command.**

4. **In the Update Library Items dialog box (shown in Figure 6.26), select the symbol that you edited in the source Library and click Update.** You now see the content of the symbol in your project Library updated to reflect the changes made in the source file.

Use the Update Library Items dialog box to manually update the content of symbols in your project file.

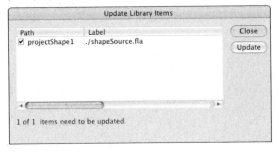

It probably seems like more hassle than it's worth to keep content current in one or two files, but you will find it very helpful should you need to update symbols in multiple project files consistently.

Summary

- You can organize the Library with folders and symbols and rearrange assets without breaking their linkage to instances deployed within the project.

- The Flash Library panel streamlines the controls for working with multiple documents. Instead of having to manage a separate Library panel for each open document, you can view different Library lists within a single panel.

- The Flash CS5 Library can be docked and scaled like any other panel. The new search field at the top of the panel makes it easier to find items in complex project files.

- Symbols are the building blocks of Flash. They save you time, reduce your file size, and add flexibility to your movies. When you use ActionScript to control symbol behavior or display, symbols are considered as objects within an object-oriented authoring environment.

- Flash handles imported sounds, bitmaps, and video assets as symbols. They reside in the Library, and instances of these assets are deployed within a Flash project.

- In addition to imported assets, there are three other kinds of symbols that can be created within Flash: Graphic symbols, Movie Clips, and Button symbols.

- Movie Clip symbols and Button symbols have timelines that play independently from the Main Timeline. Although Graphic symbols also have their own timelines, they are still tied to the Main Timeline and require a frame for every frame of their own timeline that is visible.

- Using symbol instances within a project is as easy as dragging an asset or symbol from the Library and onto the Stage, although it's usually best to have a new layer ready and to have the appropriate keyframe selected.

- You can edit symbols a number of ways. Any edits to a symbol in Edit mode are reflected by all instances of that symbol throughout the project.

- 9-slice scaling solves the problem of distorted graphics due to inconsistent scaling on multiple symbol instances. You can reuse and resize a rounded rectangle or pill button without worrying about mismatched stroke widths and stretched corners.

- The Properties panel offers a central control for modifying individual symbol instances. You can modify the color and transparency of instances of a symbol via the Color Effect controls. Furthermore, you can reassign symbol types by using the Type drop-down menu and can even replace specific instances with other symbol instances by using the Swap symbol button.

- The Movie Explorer is a powerful tool for navigating movies and finding specific items within them.

- Shared Libraries streamline your workflow if a project involves multiple files that use assets that may need to be updated. Shared libraries are also useful for keeping files current and consistent in a team production environment.

Applying Color

Before I get into the specifics of applying color with Flash, I want to discuss some of the fundamental theory behind working with color that's destined to appear on the Web. Limited color displays are not as common as they were in the early days of Web graphics, but it is useful to have a basic understanding of the various contexts and limitations of digital color. This chapter introduces some resources that may be helpful to you for Flash work and as references for color issues that may come up in other productions. Whether you're designing corporate graphics or creating a photo album to share online, consistent and accurate color is a key factor in the quality of your projects. I explore the options available in Flash for choosing and modifying your color palette by using the Color panel and discuss how colors can be accessed from the Tools panel. I also show you how to work with the Properties panel menus, Swatches panel, and Color panel to select, change, mix, and apply solid colors, gradients, and even bitmap fills.

Cross-Ref

I cover filters and blend modes in Chapter 11, "Applying Filters, Blends, Guides, and Masks." You can use these features to modify the color and appearance of symbols, but they do not replace the basic color tools (described in this chapter) used to modify text, shapes, and Graphic symbols. ∎

Introducing Color Basics

Computer monitors display color by using a method called *RGB color*. A monitor screen is a tightly packed array of pixels arranged in a grid, where each pixel has an address. For example, a pixel that's located 16 rows down from the top and 70 columns over from the left might have an address of 70,16.

The computer uses these addresses to send a specific color to each pixel. Because each pixel is composed of a single red, green, and blue dot, the colors that the monitor displays can be "mixed" at each pixel by varying the individual intensities of the red, green, and blue color dots. Each individual dot can vary in intensity over a range of 256 values, starting with 0 (which is *off*) to a maximum value of 255 (which is *on*). Thus, if red is *half-on* (a value of 127), while green is *off* (a value of 0), and blue is fully *on* (a value of 255), the pixel appears reddish blue or purple.

The preceding paragraph describes unlimited, full color, which is sometimes referred to as *24-bit color*. Most computers now use 24-bit color to deliver cleanly rendered graphics without a hitch. In the early days of Web graphics, computer systems were incapable of displaying full color; these limited color displays were either 8-bit or 16-bit. Although a full discussion of bit depth is beyond the scope of this book, it is important to note several points:

- Using 24-bit color is required to accurately reproduce photographic images and smooth color transitions in gradients.

- Because 8-bit and 16-bit systems are color challenged, they can display only a limited number of colors, and they must dither-down anything that exceeds their *gamut,* which is their expanse of possible colors. *Dithering* means that, in order to approximate colors that are missing from the palette, the closest colors available are placed in proximity to each other to fool the eye into seeing a blended intermediate color. This can result in unwanted pixel patterns.

- Some image formats, such as GIF, use a color palette that limits them to 256 colors. This is called *indexed color.* Indexed color is ideally suited for reproducing vector graphics that have solid fills and strokes but often creates noticeable *banding* (uneven color) when applied to photographic images.

- Bitmap (or photographic) images do not accurately translate an indexed color palette, so matching color between GIF images and JPEG images can be unpredictable, because the JPEG expands the original indexed palette of a GIF file to include colors that may not be within the Web-safe color palette.

- Calibration of your monitor is essential for accurate color work. For more information, check out the Datacolor learning page at `http://spyder.datacolor.com/learn_whyandwhen.php`.

Discussing Web-safe color issues

By default, the Swatches panel (Ctrl+F9 or ⌘+F9) loads with Web 216 colors, and if the swatches are modified, this swatch palette can always be reloaded from the Options menu at the upper right of the panel. Web 216 restricts the color palette to Web-safe colors. However, *intermediate colors* (meaning any process or effect that generates new colors from two Web-safe colors) — such as gradients, color tweens, filters, transparent overlays, and alpha transitions — are not constrained to Web-safe colors.

Note

The Mac and Windows platforms handle their color palettes differently, so browsers don't always have the same colors available to them across platforms. For designers, these differences led to inconsistent, unreliable color — unless they were careful to choose colors from the Web-safe palette. The Web-safe palette is a selection of 216 colors that's consistent on both the Mac and Windows platforms for Firefox (Mozilla), Internet Explorer (PC only), and Safari and Chrome (WebKit). The Web-safe palette contains only 216 of 256 possible indexed colors, because 40 colors can vary between Mac and Windows displays. ∎

When there are more than 16 million possible colors, why would you settle for a mere 216? Consider your audience. Choose a color strategy that enables the majority of your viewers to see your designs as you intend them to appear. Web-safe color is not a concern for most people these days, but there may be a few exceptions. For example, if you're designing an e-commerce site for a very broad audience on a mix of platforms with the potential for some users to be on very old monitors, then you might consider limiting your work to the Web-safe palette. On the other hand, if you're designing an interface for a stock photography firm whose clients are most likely using newer computers, then color limitations are probably not an issue. In either case, keep in mind that no one will see the exact same colors that you see. The variables of hardware, calibration, ambient light, and environmental influences are unavoidable. If you do settle for 216 colors, remember that the value of color in Web design (or any design or art for that matter) has to do with color perception and design issues, and numbers have little to do with that.

Using hexadecimal values

Any RGB color can be described in hexadecimal (hex) notation. This notation is called *hexadecimal* because it describes color in base-16 values, rather than in base-10 values like standard RGB color. This color value notation is used because it describes colors in an efficient manner that HTML and scripting languages can digest. Hex notation is limited to defining *flat color,* which is a continuous area of undifferentiated color. In HTML, hexadecimal notation is used to specify colored text, lines, backgrounds, image borders, frame cells, and frame borders.

A hexadecimal color number has six places. It allocates two places for each of the three color channels: R, G, and B. So in the hexadecimal example 00FFCC, 00 signifies the red channel, FF signifies the green channel, and CC signifies the blue channel. The corresponding values between hexadecimal and customary integer values are as follows:

16 integer values:	0 1 2 3 4 5 6 7 8 9 10 11 12 13 14 15
16 hex values:	0 1 2 3 4 5 6 7 8 9 A B C D E F

The Web-safe values in hexadecimal notation are limited to those colors that can be described by using combinations of the pairs 00, 33, 66, 99, and FF. White is described by the combination FFFFFF, or all colors *on* 100 percent. At the other end of the spectrum, black is described by the combination 000000, all colors on 0 percent, or *off.* A medium gray would be described by the combination 666666, or all colors on 40 percent.

Using color effectively

According to some designers, the issue of color on the Web has been seriously confused by the misperception that people can set numbers to give them Web-safe colors, and that, if they do this, they will have *good* color. When designers get caught up in the excitement of layered patterns and multicolored text, they sometimes overlook the fact that the end result isn't very legible or "easy on the eyes." A little restraint can go a long way toward making your designs both appealing and legible. Although I all want to be creative and unique, certain color rules can actually be more liberating than restricting.

Although unconventional design choices can add an element of surprise, a touch of humor, or just a visual punch that helps your layout stand out from the rest, it is vital that you don't compromise your end goal. When you get noticed, you want to deliver your message successfully — whether that message is "Buy this product" or just "Hey, this is a cool site." If you start to carefully deconstruct the layouts that grab your attention, you will probably find that there are consistencies to the choices that were made in the design, regardless of the content. You'll begin to notice that even the most bizarre or cutting-edge designs share certain features that make them eye catching and memorable.

Much of the underlying strategy in a design may be transparent, or not *consciously* perceived by the viewer. But don't make the mistake of thinking that individual preference is completely unpredictable. The secret to successful design is leveraging the unconscious visual language that your audience is physically and culturally conditioned to respond to. Individual viewers may have specific preferences for certain colors or styles, but they all recognize and understand many of the same visual conventions.

Although learning to apply all these conventions and to integrate them into your own design style can take years of study and practice, there are some fundamental "truths" that will serve you well, no matter how long you've been designing:

- **Color is relative:** Humans perceive color relative to the context of other colors in which the color is set. Most art schools offer at least one course about color. They often start with color experiments that are conducted with pieces of colored paper. An early assignment is to make three colors look like more than three colors — by placing small scraps of the same color on larger pieces of different colors. Students are always amazed to learn how much a person's perception of a single color is influenced when it's placed on different-colored backgrounds. Figure 7.1 shows how the same shade of gray can appear lighter or darker depending on the background color. The lesson is that color is *not* an absolute — it never was before computers, and it never will be to the human eye.

- **Contrast is king:** Only one thing is more important than color: contrast. *Contrast* is the relative difference in lightness or darkness of items in a composition. Here's a good test: Take a colorful design that you admire and reduce it to grayscale. Does it still work? Contrast is a major factor in good color composition. Figure 7.2 shows different amounts of contrast created by relative differences in value.

FIGURE 7.1

The same gray circle displayed on different background values appears to be darker or lighter by comparison.

FIGURE 7.2

Varying levels of color contrast determine legibility and emphasis.

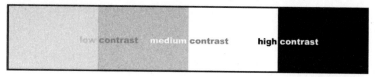

To ensure a strong design, it can be helpful to work on your initial layouts in grayscale. When you have contrast working for you, you can start to add color with the confidence that the design will not be visually *muddy* — or hard to read — because of poor contrast. Often, the same color scheme can be a disaster or a huge success, all depending on the contrast you create in the design. The concept of contrast also applies to other characteristics of your design — size, texture, even mood. Try to use contrast wherever you want to create emphasis or add drama. But remember: If you make everything huge and flashing red, or extra-small and pale gray, you will no longer have any contrast. The strength of contrast is in variety. Figure 7.3 shows how contrast can be achieved by varying the size and style of your text — even if the font stays the same. Create even more contrast by mixing fonts with different visual character: A sans-serif with thick strokes contrasts nicely with a script font with calligraphy-style strokes.

FIGURE 7.3

Variety in the size and shape of elements also adds visual contrast.

low **MEDIUM** **HIGH**
contrast contrast c o n t r a s t

- **Less is more:** Don't be afraid of empty space; the impact of individual elements is often dependent on having a little room to breathe. One element in a striking color is much more effective than a whole page filled with competing colors.

- **Start at the beginning:** Visual hierarchy is the best secret weapon in any designer's arsenal. Although you may not be sure what the most important element is in your design, if you don't give readers a place to start, chances are you'll lose their attention. By deciding on the order of importance for elements in your design and then using contrast, size, and color to guide readers through your layout, you'll create motivation for them to actually stick around long enough to absorb your message. Think of your content as the elements of a good story: In order to make the narrative compelling, you have to have a catchy intro, a juicy middle, and a rewarding ending or payoff. You might argue that you want to let readers make their own choice about where to start (like starting at the back of a novel), but if you don't create a visual structure, readers won't feel empowered to make any choices. Presented with a big muddle of uncertain order, they will most likely move on to a design where they can find the beginning, middle, and end at a glance, before deciding what they want to read first. Figure 7.4 shows a layout with poorly defined visual hierarchy compared to an example with stronger contrast and clearer hierarchy. The page with the more clearly defined hierarchy gives the reader more clues about the order of importance of each element on the page. Of course, these examples don't even use color, but as I mention earlier, it can be best to plan the structure of your layout before adding color to support it.

FIGURE 7.4

Adding contrast to a weak design (left) makes for a stronger visual hierarchy (right) and orients readers in your layout.

Weak contrast = muddy visual hierarchy   Strong contrast = clear visual hierarchy

Here's the bottom line: Color can help a good design look *great,* and when used with strategy, it can help engage the viewer and sell your message. But no amount of color can save a poorly planned design, so consider the underlying structure, contrast, and visual hierarchy of your layout before adding color.

Innumerable books on color theory and many different software solutions that can provide inspiration and take the guesswork out of choosing color schemes are out there. These are just three sources that can help you create harmonious color families for your designs:

- **Kuler from Adobe Labs:** This color-focused site offers ready-made themes submitted by designers, a color forum, and a Flash-based Web tool that you can use to create your own color themes. Themes are available for download if you are signed in to the Adobe site and can be used with any of your Adobe CS applications. Explore themes or contribute your own at http://kuler.adobe.com.

Tip

You can access the Kuler application directly from Flash by selecting Window ⇨ Extensions ⇨ Kuler. This makes it easier to quickly search for themes or create your own while working in Flash. The best part is an option to load themes into the Flash Swatches panel with just one click! ■

- **Color Schemer:** A handy utility that generates a palette of harmonious colors for any key color that you want to start with. The full version of the software is available in a Windows version and an OS X version. The online version is helpful regardless of what platform you use. Try it out at www.colorschemer.com/online.html.

  You can generate lists of RGB or hexadecimal colors from the Web-safe palette and choose to darken or lighten all colors in the palette until you find the exact color set you like. Color Schemer also offers a basic color tutorial that will help you understand how to generate harmonious palettes. You can find it at www.colorschemer.com/tutorial.html.

- *Pantone Guide to Communicating with Color*: A wonderful reference book by color guru Leatrice Eiseman (published by North Light Books in 2000). This colorful book includes a wealth of information about the science and psychology of color, as well as a guide to a whole range of color families, grouped according to mood. Get inspired to add meaningful color to your projects.

Tip

The Pantone system for specifying ink color is the industry standard for communication between designers and printers. Pantone swatch books are indispensable and well worth the investment if you do any print work. Visit www.pantone.com to learn more. Pantone has also developed systems to help designers and retailers who need to specify and display color consistently in a digital environment. Visit www.therightcolor.com to learn more if you are developing online catalogs or other projects that require precise color matching. Pantone also offers swatch books with both CMYK and hex color values printed on them to make color matching between screen graphics and printed graphics easier. If you are a designer who "thinks in Pantone," you might find it worthwhile to invest in Pantone's Colorist software. Available for Windows and for Mac, Colorist makes Pantone swatches available from programs that do not have built-in Pantone color libraries (including Flash and Fireworks). ■

Working in the Swatches Panel

The Swatches panel (Ctrl+F9 or ⌘+F9) is the most commonly used source for selecting colors as you work in Flash. Although the controls for loading or modifying specific palettes are available only on the main Swatches panel, both the Tools panel and the Properties panel give you quick pop-up menus to access whatever colors are currently loaded. If the main Swatches panel isn't visible, you can always find it in the application menu under Window⇨Swatches. Figure 7.5 shows the Fill Swatches for the default Web 216 colors as they appear in the popup menu in the Tools panel (A), on the main Swatches panel (B), and in the Properties panel popup (C). The Swatches panel is shown with the Options menu that is invoked by clicking the top-right corner of the panel.

Tip

For a quick way to change the transparency of a selected color, go to the Swatches popup menu and try out the handy Alpha field. You can also adjust Alpha levels on fill colors by using the Color panel. ∎

Tools that create fields of color, or fills, include the Brush, the Paint Bucket, and the various Shape tools. Each of these tools is accompanied by the Fill color button, which appears in the Tools panel and in the Properties panel. Although the Fill Swatches popup menu is similar to the Stroke popup menu, it has one significant difference: It includes another row of swatches at the bottom, which are gradient swatches — click one to fill with a prebuilt gradient style.

Tools that create lines, or strokes, include the Line, Pencil, Ink Bottle, Pen, and — because they create outlines around fills — any of the Shape tools. These tools rely on the Stroke color button, which appears in both the Tools panel and the Properties panel.

For all drawing tools, basic color selection is accomplished by clicking either the Stroke or Fill color buttons and then choosing a color from the Swatches popup. This popup displays the same swatch set that is currently loaded in the Swatches panel. It also includes a hexadecimal color-entry box — which facilitates keyboard entry, as well as cut-and-paste of hex values. Depending upon the tool you select, the Swatch menu available from the Tools panel may display a No Color button above the solid swatches as well as a button that launches the Color Picker.

Tip

You can remove a fill or stroke from a selected shape or Drawing Object by using the None (or No Color) button in any of the Swatches menus. If the line or stroke shows the selection grid, you can also use Edit⇨Clear or press the Backspace (Delete) key to remove a line or stroke. Shapes can be selected directly; Drawing Objects must be in Edit mode. ∎

Tip

If you decide after you invoke the Swatches popup that you don't want to change your selected color after all, hit the Escape key or make sure that your mouse is over the original color swatch when you click to close the popup. ∎

The color chips appearing on the Tools panel always display the most recently selected Stroke and Fill colors, and the Properties panel displays the color chips relevant to the active tool or the currently selected item.

FIGURE 7.5

The default color palette as it appears in the Tools panel popup (A), the Swatches panel (B), and the Properties panel popup (C)

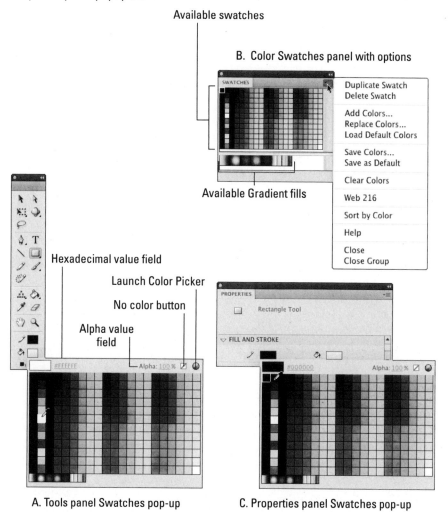

Available swatches

B. Color Swatches panel with options

Duplicate Swatch
Delete Swatch

Add Colors...
Replace Colors...
Load Default Colors

Save Colors...
Save as Default

Clear Colors

Web 216

Sort by Color

Help

Close
Close Group

Available Gradient fills

Hexadecimal value field

Launch Color Picker

No color button

Alpha value field

A. Tools panel Swatches pop-up

C. Properties panel Swatches pop-up

Note

Drawing Objects behave like grouped shapes, but the fill and stroke colors applied to Drawing Objects can be modified without opening them in Edit mode. When a Drawing Object is selected (by single-clicking) with the Selection tool, the selection grid isn't visible (as it would be on a raw shape), but you can apply a new fill or stroke color by using any of the Swatches menus. To open a Drawing Object in Edit mode, double-click with the Selection tool. ■

If the color you want is not available in the current Swatches menu, you may opt to invoke the Color Picker by clicking the Color Picker button. Alternatively, you may also open the Color panel to create a new color and add it to the currently loaded selection of swatches. The Swatches panel enables you to load, add, delete, and modify various color sets for individual documents. Whatever changes are made to the Swatches panel are saved with the document (.fla) that is currently active.

Tip

With any of the Swatch popups active, your cursor icon turns into an Eyedropper. If you roll over colors outside of the swatches area while continuing to hold down the mouse, you will notice that you can "sample" colors from anywhere on your desktop. When you find a color you like, release your mouse and the color loads into Flash as your currently selected color. Don't forget to add the color to the Swatches panel if you want to save it in the color library of your current file. I describe the steps for adding and saving swatches later in this chapter. ■

Swatches panel options

Think of the Swatches panel (see Figure 7.6) as a paint box or a way to organize your existing swatches and to manipulate the display of colors that are available in the other panels. Use the Swatches panel to save color sets, import color sets, and reorder or change selected colors. The options menu of the Swatches panel provides the controls used to sort or modify individual swatches as well as various color sets:

- **Duplicate Swatch:** Use this to duplicate a selected swatch. It can be useful when you want to make a range of related color swatches by duplicating and then editing a series of swatches with the Color panel.

Tip

You can duplicate a selected swatch with just two clicks. First, select a swatch with the Selection tool or use the Dropper tool to pick a color from any item on the Stage. As you move the cursor into the space below the current solid swatches set (above the gradient swatches), the cursor icon changes from a dropper into a paint bucket. Just click, and a new swatch is added to the color set. Changed your mind? Hold down Ctrl or ⌘ and click the added swatch with the scissors that replace your mouse cursor, and the swatch disappears. ■

- **Delete Swatch:** Botched a swatch? Select and delete it here.

- **Add Colors:** Opens the Import Color Swatch menu, which is a simple dialog box used to locate, select, and import color sets. Add Colors retains the current color set and appends the imported color set at the bottom of the panel.

Caution

Be careful about creating huge color sets! In some cases, the Swatch color popups may extend beyond the visible screen and you'll have to use the Swatches panel to scroll to choose colors that are hidden off-screen. This can happen if you add colors from a complex GIF image to the default Web 216 set. ■

- **Replace Colors:** Also opens the Import Color Swatch menu. However, Replace Colors replaces the current color set when it loads the selected color set. With the exception of the gradient swatches, if the current set has not been saved, it will be lost.

- **Load Default Colors:** Clears the current color set and replaces it with the default Web 216 swatch palette. Again, if the current set has not been saved, it will be lost. Flash allows you to change the specification for your default color palette if you prefer not to use Web 216. (See Save as Default, below in this list.)

- **Save Colors:** Opens the Export Color Swatch menu, which is used to name and save color sets to a specific location on your hard drive. Color sets may be saved in either the Flash Color Set (.clr) or Color Table (.act) format, which can be used with Fireworks and Photoshop. Gradients can only be imported and exported from Flash by using the .clr format.

- **Save as Default:** Saves the current swatch set as the default set to be loaded in the Swatches panel for all new Flash documents.

- **Clear Colors:** Removes all colors currently loaded in the Swatches panel, leaving only the black-and-white swatches and a grayscale gradient.

- **Web 216:** Loads the Web-safe palette. This option makes it safe to mess with the swatches in Flash because no matter what you do, you can always just reload this original default color set.

Tip

You can override the default Web 216 color set by switching the Color panel to either the RGB or HSB (hue, saturation, brightness) color spaces. You can then mix your own fresh colors, add them to the Swatches panel, and save that palette as the default. Another alternative is to locate the Photoshop Color Tables on your hard drive (or download a specialty color table from the Web) and replace the default set with a broader gamut. ■

- **Sort by Color:** This organizes the swatches by hue instead of by mathematical number and can visually be a more logical way to find colors in your current set. Note, however, that after you apply this sort, you have no way to toggle back to your original swatch order (other than reloading the default Web 216 swatch set). So it is best to save any custom palette first before sorting so that you have the option of going back to the other display if you prefer it. Figure 7.6 shows the Web 216 palette as it appears by default sorted numerically (left) and as it appears sorted by color (right).

FIGURE 7.6

The Web 216 palette as it appears by default sorted by number (left), and how it appears after being sorted by hue with the Sort by Color option (right)

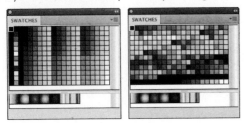

Importing custom palettes

The option of loading custom swatches is helpful if you're developing a Flash project that you want to match with a predefined palette — whether this is out of necessity or just for inspiration. For example, you can match your Flash elements to a corporate logo or to the range of hues in a photo that you love. In addition to loading the colors in a specific GIF file, Flash allows you to load RGB color palettes from other graphics applications that have been saved as Color Tables (in the .act or .clr format).

Loading a custom color theme from the Kuler panel

Flash CS5 includes a panel to access Kuler, a fun color tool from Adobe that organizes color into a series of five selected swatches called a *theme*. This Web-based extension includes a ratings system and live comments on themes created and uploaded by a growing community of Kuler users. You can browse themes to use as is or modify, or create your own theme from scratch by using an interactive color wheel and a menu of color modes. Figure 7.7 shows the browse mode (left) and the create mode (right) of the simplified Kuler application included with Flash CS5 (Window ⇨ Extensions ⇨ Kuler).

After you've chosen or created a theme (series of swatches) in Kuler, you can use the handy one-click Add to Swatches button at the bottom of the Kuler panel (see Figure 7.7) to automatically add the swatches in your selected theme to the main Flash Swatches panel. If you create a Kuler account, you can also use the online MyKuler page to save and sort your favorite themes.

Tip

If you would prefer to have only the swatches that you are moving from Kuler show up in the Swatches panel, use the Clear Colors command in the Swatches panel Options menu before you add the theme from the Kuler panel. By default, a black swatch and a white swatch remain in the Swatches panel even after you apply the Clear Colors command, but otherwise, you will have a clean slate for your Kuler theme swatches. ■

Five colors may be all you need to create a perfect design, but if you need more, don't hesitate to add a few more themes to your Swatches panel or modify the colors in the Color panel to create additional variations.

FIGURE 7.7

The Kuler panel in Flash CS5 can be used to browse color themes made by other people (left) or to create your own custom theme with Adobe's user-friendly color tool (right).

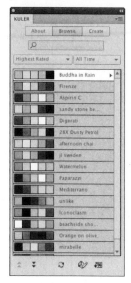
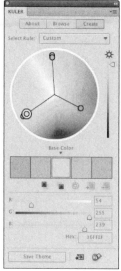

Tip

Don't forget to upload the themes you are especially proud of to the Kuler site to share with other people too. Choose a descriptive name and check back to see what people have to say about your color savvy! ■

Loading a custom GIF color palette

To simplify your Flash Swatches to match the colors in a company logo or other GIF image, follow these steps:

1. Choose Replace Colors from the Swatches panel options menu, and in the Import Color Swatch dialog box, specify a GIF file to define the imported color set.

2. After Flash loads the colors from the GIF image into the Swatches panel, save the document (.fla) to keep these colors as the loaded set.

3. To organize the loaded color set in the Swatches panel by hue, choose the Sort by Color option. You can always add or delete swatches from this new set.

4. If you want to use your custom color set in other files, use the Save Colors command in the Swatches panel options menu to save a Color Table (.act) or Flash Color Set (.clr).

A sample source GIF image and the resulting imported Swatches palette are shown in Figure 7.8.

FIGURE 7.8

The simple logo GIF (left) that I specified as the source for the Replace Colors command. The resulting colors loaded in the Swatches panel (right) match the colors in the logo.

Tip

The color settings defined in the original authoring environment (such as Adobe Illustrator or Photoshop) for saved GIF files affect the colors available for loading to the Flash Swatches panel. For the widest range of colors, use 256 colors and an adaptive palette. To get only the exact colors used in a graphic, manually restrict the number of colors that can be included by typing a number that matches the number of colors in the original graphic. For example, if a logo that you plan to use as a source file for your swatches is red, blue, yellow, black, and white, restrict the GIF to five colors when you export it from the original authoring application. ■

Creating and loading a custom color table

If you want to save a color palette that matches the hues in a photograph that is not already in GIF format, you can also generate a color table in Photoshop.

To create a color table in Photoshop (or Illustrator), follow these steps:

1. **Open a source bitmap image (.jpeg, .tif, .psd, or .png).**
2. **Use the Save for Web and Devices command to access the settings that allow you to choose the file type and color space that you want to export.** To create a color table, set the file type to GIF, choose Adaptive (or Restrictive if you want your swatches to be Web safe) color, and set the number of colors you want to include in the color table. Although you can include anywhere from 2 to 256 colors in your color table, you will not likely need more than 16. Preview the swatches in the Color Table (on the right side of the Save for Web dialog box).

Note

Although Photoshop includes a menu option for creating a color table (Image ➪ Mode ➪ Color Table), this option is available only if the source image is first converted to Indexed color. Also, the Color Table dialog box offers only limited control of the swatches that are exported, so I prefer to use the Save for Web workflow. ■

3. **When you have a set of swatches that you are happy with, choose Save Color Table from the Color Palette menu** (accessed from the icon in the top-right corner of the Color Table preview). The settings used for the sample file are shown in Figure 7.9.

4. **Give the color table a name that you will remember (such as** tulip_field**) and save the ACT file to a folder where you can find it again**. Creating a Custom Palettes folder on your system, where you can store and organize any of the color tables or source GIFs that you may want to use again, is a good idea.

5. **Open a Flash document (.fla), and from the Swatches panel options menu choose Add Colors if you want new colors added to the currently loaded set (or Replace Colors if you want to use only your new colors).**

6. **From the Import Color Swatch dialog box, browse to your color table (.act) file and select it.** Flash loads the new colors into the Swatches panel, and you can then sort and save this set with your document.

FIGURE 7.9

Use the Save for Web command and the Color Table settings in Adobe Photoshop to create a custom color palette from a photograph.

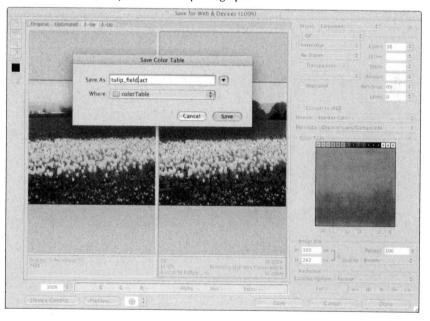

The sample source bitmap image and the resulting color table loaded into the Swatches panel are shown in Figure 7.10.

FIGURE 7.10

A photo (in GIF format) used to generate a color table (.act), and the resulting color set loaded into the Flash Swatches panel

 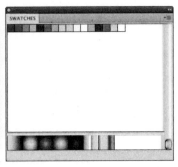

On the CD-ROM

In the previous example, I created a color table from an image of a tulip field. You can find the source bitmap (`tulip_bitmap.tif`) and the color table (`tulip_field.act`) files, along with a Flash document (`tulip Colors_loaded.fla`) that has a GIF imported and the color palette loaded, in the `colorTable` folder in the `ch07` folder on the CD-ROM. ■

Using the Color Panel

Think of the Color panel as the "boss" of the Swatches panel. The Swatches panel handles the color inventory and serves up the available colors, but the Color panel has the power to modify those colors and add variations to the current set. The Color style menu available on the Color panel allows you to choose the type of color pattern that you want to work with — including solid colors, linear and radial gradients, and bitmap fills.

Tip

Gradient styles can be used with strokes as well as with fills. This option has potential for creating custom line styles for borders and other decorative lines. ■

As shown in Figure 7.11 and Figure 7.12, the Color panel enables you to create new colors, with settings in any of three color spaces — RGB, HSB, or hex — using either manually entered values or the "rainbow" color picker field. All colors are handled with four channels, which are RGBA (red, green, blue, alpha); these values can be individually adjusted by using the Color value fields and slider controls. The Tint slider control enables you to dynamically shift your current color darker or lighter. A Fill or Stroke color selected in any of the Swatch menus appears in the Color panel where it can be modified.

FIGURE 7.11

The Flash Color panel

Black and white color button
(resets to black stroke, white fill)

No color button (clears stroke or fill)

Swap color button (reverses stroke and fill color)

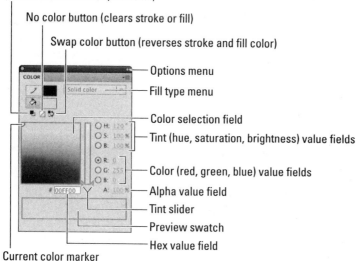

— Options menu
— Fill type menu
— Color selection field
— Tint (hue, saturation, brightness) value fields
— Color (red, green, blue) value fields
— Alpha value field
— Tint slider
— Preview swatch
— Hex value field

Current color marker

As shown in Figure 7.12, colors modified in the Color panel can be added to the palette loaded in the Swatches panel — just select Add Swatch from the Color panel options menu and the color is added below the colors currently loaded in the Swatches panel.

FIGURE 7.12

Colors modified in the Color panel can be added to the Swatches panel.

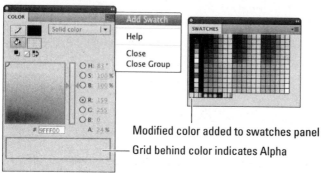

Modified color added to swatches panel
Grid behind color indicates Alpha

Any color swatch selected in the Swatches panel is loaded into the Color panel as a starting point only — modifications made in the Color panel do not change the original color in the Swatches panel. The new color or gradient that you create by using the controls in the Color panel (shown in Figure 7.13) are added as a new swatch only when you select Add Swatch from the options menu. You can always edit your custom color by selecting the new (saved) swatch, but the modified version is treated as a new color and also has to be added to the Swatches panel separately.

Tip

Unlike swatches selected from the Swatches panel, a fill or stroke selected in the Document window can be edited "live" in the Color panel. You can see the changes you make applied to the original fill or stroke if it remains selected. ■

Caution

The colors you create and add to the Swatches panel are saved with the document (.fla) as long as you do not reload the default set or overwrite the loaded swatch set. If you want to save your custom mixed colors, remember to save the Flash color set (.clr) to a folder by using the Save Colors command in the Swatches panel before you reload the default Web 216 color set or Replace Colors with a new palette. ■

FIGURE 7.13

The Color panel preview swatch splits to compare colors as you use the Color Picker or the Tint slider to make adjustments.

Current color marker

Current color   Last chosen color

When you select a color from the Swatches popup palette, the cursor converts to a Dropper tool that enables you to sample color from anywhere in the interface just by clicking the color you want to pick up. You can pluck colors from icons in the Flash application, from any element that you have in the Document window, and even from elements on your desktop or in other application windows that are currently open.

Tip

The same Dropper feature is available from any of the Swatches popups, but the colors you select this way are not stored in the Swatches panel unless you use the Color panel's Add Swatch option. ■

Note

The mouse cursor does not always display as a Dropper but if you have a popup Swatches palette active, you will notice that the color chip at the top of the palette will update to match the color that your cursor is over and if you click to select it, the color loads into the currently active color chip (fill or stroke). ■

Adjusting fill and stroke transparency

The Alpha control in the Color panel (and in the Swatches popups) is used to adjust the transparency of stroke and fill colors, either to modify a selected graphic (shape or Drawing Object) or to create a new color that can be added to the Swatches panel.

There are two ways to change the alpha value for a selected color: Either drag the Alpha slider until the preview display looks right, or enter a numeric value directly in the Alpha value box. Numeric entry is useful when you already know what level of transparency is required, and the slider is useful for tweaking the transparency by eye to get it just right — as indicated in either the stroke or fill color chip or the color preview in the Color panel. In Figure 7.14, a stroke color and a fill color have both been adjusted to 50 percent alpha and then added to the Swatches panel. While the Alpha slider is being dragged to a new setting, the preview displays the original 75 percent alpha value (at the bottom) as well as the current 50 percent alpha value (at the top). The rectangle below the panels shows the 50 percent alpha stroke and fill applied to a shape. The Flash grid has been turned on (View ⇨ Grid ⇨ Show Grid) so that the alpha is easier to see — on a flat white background, the color just looks lighter rather than transparent.

Caution

Alpha transparency results in more of a performance hit than a color tint, especially if there are a lot of overlapping animated transparencies. If you can achieve the effect that you want by using a tint instead (fading to a solid color), then save the alpha effect for graphics that you need to layer on top of other elements or textured backgrounds. ■

Cross-Reference

You can apply blend modes to symbols to create different types of layered effects. I describe this feature in Chapter 9, "Modifying Graphics." ■

FIGURE 7.14

New levels of alpha can be applied to fills and strokes, and the modified swatches can be added to the Swatches panel for reuse.

Most recently set stroke color

Most recently set fill color

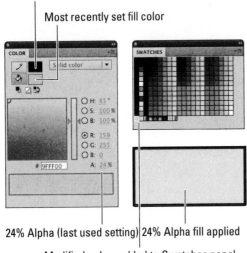

24% Alpha (last used setting) | 24% Alpha fill applied

Modified colors added to Swatches panel

Working with gradient fills

Gradients are composed by blending two or more colors together in bands across a plane (*a linear gradient*) or from the center to the edge of an object in concentric circles (*a radial gradient*). You can modify these two basic styles of gradient fill to create virtually unlimited variations.

Figure 7.15 shows the gradient-editing controls in the Color panel, with the preview display for a linear gradient on the top, and for a radial gradient on the bottom. When working with linear gradients, the position of the color pointers on the Edit bar correspond to control points on the blend from left to right. When used in conjunction with radial gradients, the Gradient Edit bar corresponds to the *radius*, or a slice from the center out to the edge, of the circular gradient. Color pointers at the left end of the Gradient Edit bar represent the center — or inside — of the radial gradient, and color pointers at the right end represent the outside border. The active color pointer is identified by a black fill in the pointer, and unselected color pointers have a white fill in the pointer.

FIGURE 7.15

The Color panel displaying edit controls and preview for a linear gradient (on the top) and for a radial gradient (on the bottom)

Current hex value for selected color pointer

Fill type menu

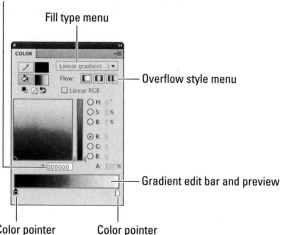

Overflow style menu

Gradient edit bar and preview

Color pointer (left for Linear gradients, center for Radial gradients)

Color pointer (right for Linear gradients, edge for Radial gradients)

The main Swatches panel and any of the fill Swatches popups display the prebuilt linear and radial gradients that are included in the default palette. To edit an existing gradient swatch, just select it from any of the fill Swatches popups or select it from the main Swatches panel, and it loads into the Color panel where the relevant controls appear automatically. The other option is to start by choosing a gradient style from the central fill Type menu on the Color panel to load a basic linear or radial gradient. After you create a custom gradient in a document, your settings appear when you go back to the Color panel menu. To start with an unmodified default gradient, just select one from the fill Swatches palette. Figure 7.16 shows the two methods of selecting a gradient style to work with.

FIGURE 7.16

You can select default gradient styles (and saved custom gradients) from any of the fill Swatches popups, or set one of the basic grayscale gradient styles with the fill Type menu in the Color panel.

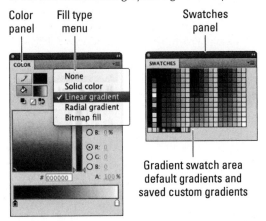

Color panel   Fill type menu

Swatches panel

Gradient swatch area
default gradients and
saved custom gradients

Controlling gradient fill colors

The colors in a gradient and the distribution of blending are adjusted by sliding the color pointers along the Gradient Edit bar in the Color panel. These pointers are the access points to the key colors that define the gradient. After you click a pointer to make it active, you can assign the color that will be blended in its range, either by double-clicking to invoke the Swatches popups or by picking a color in the color selection field. You can also use the value fields and the color slider controls to modify an assigned color in a gradient the same way as any solid color. Although you may never need more than two or three points to create your gradients, Flash CS5 supports up to 15 control points in a single gradient.

Caution

When you are editing a gradient fill, selecting a solid color swatch from the Swatches panel does not have the same effect as selecting a solid color swatch from the Swatches popup for each color pointer in the Color panel. Clicking a solid color swatch in the Swatches panel replaces your entire gradient in the Color panel with a solid fill style. Clicking a swatch from a Swatches popup on one of the gradient color pointers replaces only the color on the currently selected pointer — leaving the rest of your gradient intact. ■

You can adjust the pattern of the blend by clicking and dragging any of the color pointers to slide them to new positions along the Gradient Edit bar. You can add additional color pointers to the gradient range by clicking anywhere along the Gradient Edit bar. These additional pointers create new control points in the gradient that can be dragged to new positions or assigned new colors to define the gradient pattern. To remove color pointers, simply drag them downward away from the Gradient Edit bar; they detach and disappear, taking their assigned color and control point with them. Figure 7.17 shows a basic radial gradient modified with the addition of a new control point and changes to the control point colors. To save a custom gradient to your Swatches panel, choose Add Swatch from the Color panel options menu.

By selecting an element on the Stage, you can also apply or modify an existing gradient fill or stroke by using the Color panel. When an item is selected in the Document window, you see the current fill and stroke displayed in the Color panel. Any changes you make in the Color panel while the item is selected updates on the item dynamically. Remember to select Add Swatch from the options menu if you want to store the new gradient in the Swatches panel.

Note

The current fill (and/or stroke) of an item selected in the Document window is automatically loaded in the Color panel. ■

FIGURE 7.17

A two-point radial gradient from white to black (on the left), modified by setting the left pointer to gray and adding a central color pointer set to white (on the right)

Two-point radial gradient   Three-point radial gradient

Tip

To make it easier to see how a gradient looks in a selected shape, you can toggle off the display of the selection mesh by using Shift+Ctrl+E (Shift+⌘+E). ■

If you need some new ideas for gradient styles, Illustrator or Fireworks would be a great addition to your toolkit. Flash supports the import of Fireworks PNG files, and most filters and gradient styles added in Fireworks are preserved and editable when the file is imported to Flash. Fireworks ships with a huge library of ready-made gradient styles, including simple but handy Rectangle and Contour styles and fancier ones such as Satin, Starburst, and Ripple. Some of these gradient styles are too complex for the Flash authoring environment to support, but you can import them as bitmaps and jump out to Fireworks to edit them if you need to. You can add Fireworks or Illustrator gradient styles that Flash supports to your Swatches panel and reuse or modify them. Now those same old shaded buttons you have to keep making might just be more fun!

Using alpha settings with gradients

As I mention previously, all the normal Color sliders and value fields apply to control points on a gradient. You may have noticed already that this means you can add alpha to the blend range of any gradient. To create a soft transition between a bitmap or a patterned background and a solid color, you can create a gradient from a 0 percent alpha to a 100 percent alpha of the same solid color. To demonstrate just one application of this feature, I will walk through the steps of adding the appearance of a vignette (or softened edge) to a photograph imported into Flash:

1. **Import a bitmap into Flash and place it on the Stage; then lock the bitmap layer.**

2. **Create a new layer above the bitmap layer and name it** gradient **(see Figure 7.18).**

FIGURE 7.18

An imported bitmap placed on the Stage with a new layer above it for the gradient

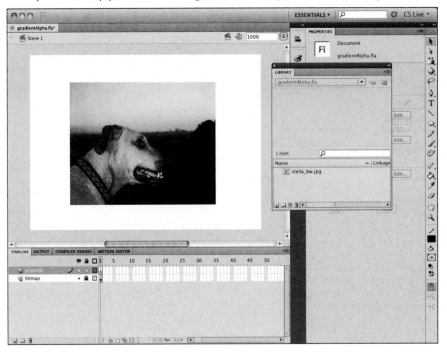

3. **Open the Color panel and set the fill Type to radial, or select the default grayscale radial gradient from the fill Swatches panel.** Leave the Overflow menu on the default (Extend) setting.

Cross-Reference

The Overflow style menu for gradient and bitmap fills in the Color panel provides more control over fill rendering. Three Overflow settings determine how the edges of a gradient or bitmap image are rendered if they need to extend beyond the bounding box of the original applied fill. I include more detailed coverage of these settings in Chapter 9. ■

4. Select the Rectangle tool and use the Properties panel to set the stroke color to black, with a stroke height of 2.

5. Select the gradient layer and then use the Rectangle tool to drag out a rectangle on the Stage that is the same size as the photograph on the layer below (see Figure 7.19).

FIGURE 7.19

Finished rectangle with a radial gradient fill and a black stroke of 2. The rectangle is dragged out to match the size of the photograph on the layer below.

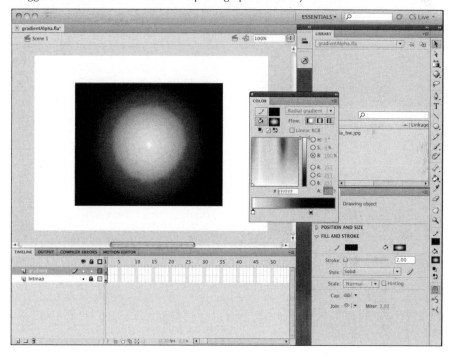

6. Select the fill of the rectangle and then select the left (white) color pointer on the Gradient Edit bar and assign it a color of black (see Figure 7.20). Set the Alpha value on the left color pointer to 0 percent.

FIGURE 7.20

Both color pointers are assigned a color of black for the selected gradient fill, and the left pointer is assigned Alpha 0 percent.

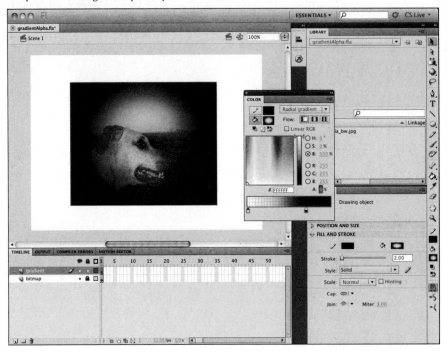

7. Press Shift+Ctrl+E (Shift+⌘+E) to hide the selection mesh and adjust the position of the color pointers by sliding them along the Gradient Edit bar, until you like the way the blend looks on top of the photo (see Figure 7.21).

Tip

If you applied the Drawing Object option when you drew the original gradient rectangle, you won't have to worry about turning off the selection mesh. The thin, blue outline that shows up on a selected Drawing Object doesn't interfere with the live gradient preview like the dotted mesh that appears on a selected raw shape does. ∎

Cross-Reference

Select any gradient item (fill or stroke) with the Gradient Transform tool (nested in the Tools panel with the Free Transform tool) and you see the edit handles that you can use to modify the center point, scale, and rotation of your gradient within the selected item. I describe the Gradient Transform tool in more detail in Chapter 9, "Modifying Graphics." ∎

FIGURE 7.21

You can preview the final gradient as you move the color pointer to adjust the edges of the alpha blend.

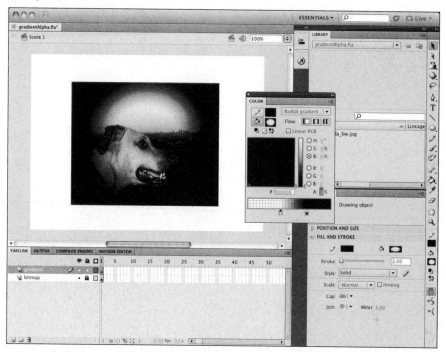

Tip

As you read through the steps in this example, you might have wondered why I assigned the same color to both color pointers; because one of the pointers is set to an alpha value of 0 percent, perhaps it doesn't matter which color is used? The answer is that you can create a "fade" effect with a radial gradient made from two different colors, but the blend is not clean unless you use only one color. Although the endpoint of the gradient assigned an alpha value of 0 percent is "clear," the interstitial bands of the gradient are tinted by whatever color you have assigned to the color pointer before changing the alpha value. ■

Selecting bitmap fills

Another handy feature available in the Color panel is the Bitmap fill option. This option enables you to choose any bitmap, in the Library or elsewhere on your system, to use as a fill for shapes drawn in Flash. When the image loads into a selected shape, it tiles to fill the shape.

To apply a bitmap fill directly to an existing shape, perform the following steps:

1. **Select the fill of a shape (or select a Drawing Object) with the Selection tool.**

2. **Open the Color panel and choose Bitmap from the fill Type menu.**

3. **If you have bitmaps stored in your current document Library, they will be available from the Bitmap Preview area of the Color panel.** Simply click the thumbnail of the bitmap that you want to apply and it automatically fills the selected shape.

4. **If you do not have any bitmaps available in the current document, selecting Bitmap from the fill Type menu in the Color panel launches the Import to Library dialog box, where you can browse your system and specify a bitmap to be imported and applied as a fill.**

Figure 7.22 shows a selected shape with a bitmap fill applied from the available thumbnails in the Color panel Preview area.

FIGURE 7.22

A bitmap fill applied to a selected shape. The bitmap is chosen from images stored in the Library, which appear as thumbnails in the Color panel Preview area.

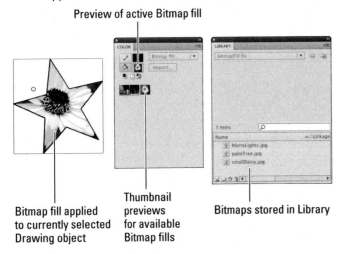

Preview of active Bitmap fill

Bitmap fill applied to currently selected Drawing object

Thumbnail previews for available Bitmap fills

Bitmaps stored in Library

Cross-Reference

The appearance of a Bitmap fill varies depending on how it is loaded (or assigned) to a specific item. I cover the various ways of loading Bitmap fills and the results you can expect in more detail in Chapter 9, "Modifying Graphics." ∎

Working with Droppers, Paint Buckets, and Ink Bottles

So far in this chapter, I've introduced the various ways of controlling your palette and setting stroke and fill colors on items selected with the Selection tool. There is one other set of tools used for applying colors and fills that makes modifying existing artwork even easier. You have already seen the Dropper tool in action when you select a color from the Swatches popups — the mouse pointer automatically converts to a dropper and allows you to pick up a color from any visible element to be loaded into the active fill or stroke color chip.

This same tool can be summoned at any time by clicking the Eyedropper tool (I) icon in the Tools panel. Notice that when the Eyedropper tool is used to pick up a fill color or bitmap, it immediately converts into the Paint Bucket tool (K) if you roll outside the area of the item you've sampled. The Paint Bucket enables you to dump the selected fill into any other shape just by clicking inside its fill area. If you have a fill or stroke selected when you invoke the Eyedropper tool, any other fill or stroke (color or style) that you pick up with the Dropper tool is applied instantly to the selected item.

When you sample a stroke with the Eyedropper tool, it converts into an Ink Bottle tool (S), which you can use to apply the stroke to any other item. If the item already has a stroke, it will be modified, and if the item did not previously have a stroke, the Ink Bottle tool adds one.

Summary

- The science of color on the computer is far from accurate. Many variables are involved in the presentation of color over the Web.

- Web-safe color does not ensure "good color" — many strategies go into applying color skillfully, but contrast can be the defining factor that makes or breaks your design.

- Although Flash doesn't directly support color scheme plug-ins, colors can be loaded into the Swatches panel from source GIF files or custom color table (.act) files, or they can be sampled with the Dropper tool to load them into the active color chip.

- Adobe's online color theme tool, Kuler, is now built into Flash in a handy panel that includes a one-click button for loading themes into the Swatches panel.

- The Swatches popup available from any of the color previews or color pointers in the Color panel gives immediate, intuitive access to the currently loaded swatches and all custom colors that have been added to the main Swatches panel. It also permits direct insertion of hexadecimal values.

- The Color panel is used to create and modify gradients and select bitmaps to be used as fills, in addition to adjusting the alpha and tint of new or existing colors. Custom colors added to the current swatches are available in any of the Swatches popups.

- Flash supports 15-point gradients and many editable gradients imported from Fireworks, Illustrator, or Photoshop.

- The Eyedropper, Paint Bucket, and Ink Bottle tools work together to select and apply fill and stroke colors. I discuss the options for these tools, along with the Gradient Transform and Free Transform tools, in Chapter 9, "Modifying Graphics."

- Advanced color capabilities of Flash include color tweening, blend modes, scriptable color, and negative alpha. I discuss these topics in more detail in subsequent chapters.

Working with Text

For designers who love fonts, Flash is a dream come true. Even if you never plan to animate anything, you may want to use Flash simply to see your fonts displayed how you want them, wherever and whenever you need them on the Web. Of course, there are a few exceptions to this unequivocal freedom, but Flash has options that give you text styles to meet nearly any project criteria.

Because Flash is a vector program, it enables you to integrate most fonts within the movie without any fuss. For standard text content, this means that fonts don't have to be rendered into bitmap elements — the SWF files that Flash publishes (or exports) include all the necessary information for the font to appear properly on every browser as long as the Flash Player is installed.

New Feature

Flash CS5 uses a new engine called the Text Layout Framework, or TLF, to render text in Flash Player 10. TLF adds full support for bidirectional text, flow of text through multiple text fields, and improved control over the appearance of text. Throughout this chapter, you learn how to use TLF text in your Flash movies. ■

In this chapter, I introduce the various text types available in Flash and explain how and why they are used. This chapter also covers some basic font management issues and offers strategies for handling fonts in your project files (.fla) as well as in your published movies (.swf).

Flash includes some nifty options for handling vertical and right-to-left-reading text. I show you these options, along with the other character and paragraph controls and the live filters available in the Properties panel. In this chapter I also touch on some features for optimizing text and working with international character sets in Flash.

Considering Typography

Typography is the formal term for the design and use of text. Although Flash has the capability to deliver finely designed typography to your audience, this is no guarantee that Flash solves all type design challenges. Unfortunately, no matter how well Flash renders text, it can't disguise bad design or make up for a designer's lack of knowledge about working with type. As with color, sound, animation, or any other specialized area of production, the amount you can learn about typography is really only limited by your interest.

Although many people can get by without ever studying typography formally, they are missing the chance to leverage one of the most powerful and complex tools of graphic design. Computers have changed the way that final designs are created, but they have not changed the fundamental principles and uses of typography. The best part about studying typography is that your knowledge will be equally useful no matter what medium or digital tool you are working with.

Because type is such an important and long-standing aspect of design, there are innumerable resources available to guide and inspire you. Just wander through the graphic design section of any bookstore or do a search online for *typography,* and you will find something that can introduce you to the basics or help develop the skills you already have.

This chapter includes some common typography terms that are familiar to most people who have designed with text. Although a more detailed explanation of the source and meaning of these terms is beyond the scope of this book, you can follow visually how things like *tracking* and *leading* apply to text in Flash.

Text Field Types in Flash

Flash allows you to include text in your projects in a variety of ways. Often one Flash project will contain several different text types, each suited to a specific kind of content. I describe the steps for creating text boxes and editing type later in this chapter, but begin here with an overview of the three main Text Layout Framework text types used in Flash:

- **Read-only:** As its name implies, this text is neither selectable nor editable at runtime.

- **Selectable:** Selectable text can be selected with a mouse cursor and can be copied and pasted. It is not editable.

- **Editable:** Commonly used for forms and other interactive text fields, editable text can be selected and changed by a user at runtime.

Caution

TLF text requires you to publish your SWF file using Flash Player 10 and ActionScript 3.0. If you must target an earlier version of the Flash Player, or an earlier version of ActionScript, you must use the Classic Text engine. In addition, when a SWF that utilizes TLF text is published, Flash creates an extra SWF file that needs to be included in the same folder as your main SWF when you deploy your project to the Web or elsewhere. ■

Cross-Reference

Flash CS5 also supports the legacy text engine by the name of Classic Text. Since the Text Layout Framework is the preferred method for using text in Flash, use of the Classic Text engine is not covered in this book. For more information about classic text, see Adobe Flash CS4 Professional Bible (Wiley, 2009). ■

On the CD-ROM

You will find examples of text field styles in the `textSamples.fla` file in the `ch08` folder on the CD-ROM. ■

The Text tool (see Figure 8.1) is used to create text boxes and to enter and modify type. When you first create a text box in Flash, the default text type is Read Only, but you can assign it a different text type in the Properties panel at any time. Subsequent text boxes are automatically assigned the type style you have selected most recently. This makes it quicker to create a series of text boxes of the same type, but it means you should double-check the settings if you need text boxes of different types.

Cross-Reference

Text boxes can be animated, just like any other objects in Flash. Animation is discussed in Part III: "Creating Animation and Effects." ■

FIGURE 8.1

The Properties panel includes all the text controls organized into a series of drop-down sections. These controls are available when the Text tool is active or a text box is selected on the Stage.

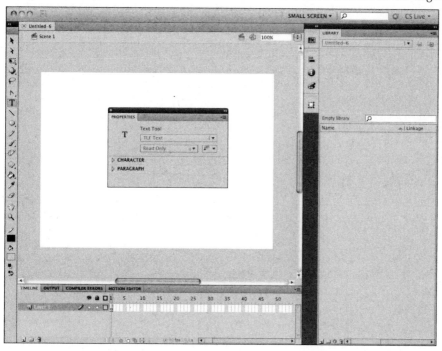

Tip

The various options for anti-aliasing in Flash should enable you to find a setting that renders smooth, legible text, even at small point sizes. If it turns out that you still prefer aliased text, simply choose the Bitmap text (no anti-alias) setting from the drop-down menu to preserve the original pixel font outlines. ■

Tip

The Advanced Character section of the Properties panel exposes the Link entry field, which is only available for Read Only and Selectable text fields. This helpful feature allows you to select sections of Read Only or Selectable text and enter a URL to create a text link to a Web page or to an e-mail address in your Flash movie without any additional coding. ■

By default, TLF text boxes are horizontal, and they can be either *expanding* boxes, which allow you to keep typing along one line as it extends to fit the type, or *fixed-width* boxes, which constrain your text box to a set width and auto-wrap the text to fit. When you select a text field, you can tell the difference between an expanding and a fixed-width field, because fixed-width fields have white squares at the top-left and bottom-right corners. When you click on a selected expandable text field, you see a white circle at the bottom right of the text field. Figure 8.2 shows the respective icons for expanding, or *label,* text and for fixed-width, or *block,* horizontal text.

FIGURE 8.2

The handle icons for expanding (left) and fixed-width (right) horizontal text boxes

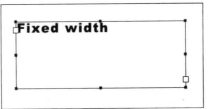

Tip

All text boxes and text fields in Flash have handles that make it possible to resize the text area just by clicking once with the Selection tool and then dragging one of the handles. Scaling the text area does not change the size of the type as it does in some other applications. ■

TLF text boxes in Flash include the option for left-to-right-reading or right-to-left-reading vertical text boxes. Have you ever wanted a line of text characters to stack vertically, but found it tedious to use a hard return between each letter? Thanks to vertical text, you can easily switch your type alignment from horizontal to vertical, with characters that are either stacked or rotated. These options are configurable in the Break drop-down menu in the Advanced Character section of the Properties panel. This eliminates the headache of trying to read sideways while editing type — with a simple menu choice you can switch from vertical to horizontal and back again with no hard returns or freehand rotations required. Figure 8.3 illustrates how the vertical text and rotate text options change the orientation of static text.

FIGURE 8.3

A vertical TLF text box

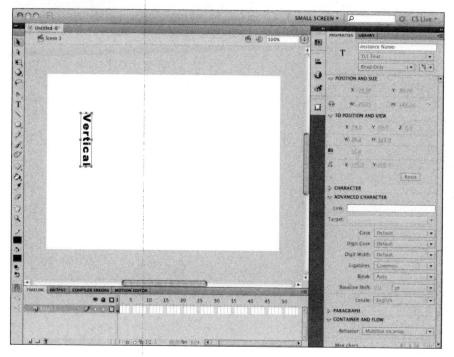

Aside from giving designers authoring in English more options for cool layouts, this feature makes Flash much friendlier for designers authoring in language sets that require vertical or right-to-left character flow. You can modify the alignment of vertical text to anchor it to the top, center, or bottom of the text box.

New Feature

With TLF text in Flash CS5, languages other than English see far superior support than in previous versions of Flash. By using the Locale drop-down in the Advanced Character section in the Properties panel, you can set the language for a text field, and Flash automatically supports the correct text orientation. For example, Arabic text automatically writes from right-to-left, without you having to make any other adjustments in Flash. ■

Although the default orientation for text in Flash is horizontal and left to right, you can easily modify existing text boxes by using the Orientation menu options in the Paragraph section of the Properties panel. These settings are "sticky" so that new text boxes have the same orientation unless you choose another option from the menu. The default settings can also be modified in the Vertical text settings in the Text category of the Flash Preferences dialog box, as shown in Figure 8.4 (File ➪ Preferences or, in OS X, Flash ➪ Preferences). To make all new static text boxes automatically orient vertically, select the Default text orientation check box. To change the default text flow, select the Right to left text flow check box. You also have the option of disabling kerning on vertical text by selecting the No kerning check box.

FIGURE 8.4

Changing the default Vertical text settings in the Flash Preferences dialog box

Tip

You can control the size of the new font previews in your Font menu by choosing a setting from the last drop-down menu in the Text category of Flash Preferences (see Figure 8.4). If you prefer to keep things simple and just browse font names without previews, deselect the check box for Show font preview and you revert to a Flash CS3–style Font menu. ∎

Editable text fields

Think of an editable text field as an empty window with a name attached to it. When text or data is sent to the Flash movie (.swf), it is sent to a specific named text instance, which ensures that it appears in the proper window or editable text field. TLF text fields can display information supplied from a database, read from a server-side application, or loaded from another Flash movie (or another part of the same Flash movie).

Tip

Whenever animating an editable text field that is not using device fonts, I recommend embedding the font used in that text field. This step ensures the text in the field renders properly in the Flash Player. ∎

Tip

If you change the size of an expanding text field by dragging one of the selection handles, the field automatically converts into a fixed-width text field. To change a fixed-width text field into an expanding text field, double-click the square fixed-width handle icon. ■

The Text Tool and the Properties Panel

Although Flash is neither a design program, like Illustrator, nor a traditional page-layout program, like InDesign, its text-handling capabilities are robust and easy to use. Although you can create nearly any style of text directly in Flash, you can also import text created in other applications as vector artwork. With compatible applications such as Illustrator and Photoshop, you can even preserve your type in editable text boxes when it is imported to Flash.

Working with the Text tool

The Text tool, shown in Figure 8.5, delivers a broad range of control for generating, positioning, and modifying text. Although the Text tool is located in the Flash Tools panel, when the tool is active, the controls for working with text are in the Properties panel.

FIGURE 8.5

The Text tool is used to create text boxes and text fields in Flash.

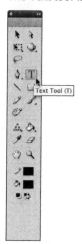

Creating TLF text boxes

To create text in your current Flash document, click the Text tool in the Tools panel (or press T on your keyboard) to activate it. You may choose to create new text in your Document window with either of two methods:

- **Label text:** To enter text on one extending line, click the Document Stage and begin typing. To control the width of a line of label text, you can either enter hard returns with the Enter or Return key as you type or you can convert the label text into block text by dragging any of the handles to a specific width or height — the round label text icon changes to a square block text icon to indicate that the box is now constrained.

Tip

If your text continues beyond the viewable area of the Document window, you can add some line breaks, click and drag to move the label text box, or choose View ⇨ Pasteboard and use the scroll controls on the Document window to shift your view of the text as needed. ■

- **Block text:** To define the area that will constrain your type by auto-wrapping as you enter more characters, click the Document Stage and drag the text area to the size that you want. You can change the size of your block text at any time by dragging the handles that appear when the text area is selected or in Edit mode. Refer to Figure 8.2 (right image) for an example of the square box text icon.

Tip

Convert a text block into label text by double-clicking the square corner icon (visible in Edit mode), which changes to a round icon to indicate that the box is now extending instead of constrained. ■

Note

You can use the blue handles that appear when you select a text box with the Selection tool to change the size of your text boxes or text fields without double-clicking or using the Text tool to enter Edit mode. However, the icons that indicate whether a text box is extending (label text) or constrained (block text) are visible only in Edit mode. ■

One characteristic of the Flash Text tool that might surprise you is that label text fields that do not contain any text are cleared from the Stage. As long as a text box contains even one character, or is defined as a fixed-size block, it remains on the Stage until you delete or move it manually. Adobe Illustrator has adopted this same behavior because it eliminates the hassle of a project cluttered by empty invisible text boxes. Editable text fields *will* remain visible even if you have not entered any text characters at authortime.

Modifying or deleting text

Flash handles text as a group, which allows you to use the Text tool to edit the individual letters or words inside a text area at any time by clicking the text box and then typing or drag-selecting specific characters. To select the whole block or group of text, you can click once anywhere on the text with the Selection tool.

To delete individual characters, click and drag to select them with the Text tool or use the Backspace key (the Delete key on a Mac). To delete a whole group of text, select it with the Selection tool and then use the Backspace key (or Delete key).

Tip

Double-clicking a text block with the Selection tool invokes Edit mode and activates the Text tool — this enables you to modify the individual characters or change the text box style, without having to switch to the Text tool first. Holding down the Shift key as you use the arrow keys to move left or right in a text field selects the text as the cursor moves across it. ■

You can use most common text-editing/word-processing commands in Flash. Cut, Copy, and Paste move selected text within Flash and also between Flash and other applications that handle type. Flash provides a built-in Check Spelling command and a handy Search and Replace command.

The Check Spelling settings are quite sophisticated, and you can customize them by using the Spelling Setup dialog box available from the application menu (Text ➪ Spelling Setup) or launched with the Setup button in the Check Spelling dialog box. As shown in Figure 8.6, these options enable you to work with language-specific features and control what areas of your Flash document to include when Check Spelling is applied.

FIGURE 8.6

The Spelling Setup dialog box gives you a range of settings to control how the Check Spelling command is applied to your documents.

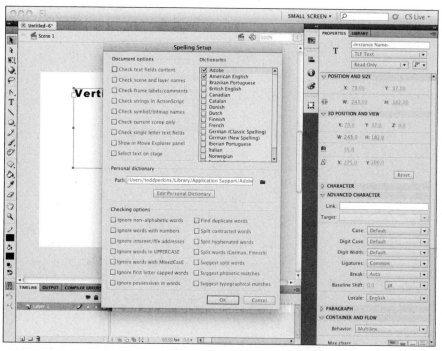

After you choose your settings, you can choose Text ⇨ Check Spelling from the application menu, and Flash opens the Check Spelling dialog box (shown in Figure 8.7). You can then go through various text elements in your Flash document and modify or replace errors (with the help of suggestions), as you would in any other program with a spell-check feature.

FIGURE 8.7

Check spelling with ease in Flash

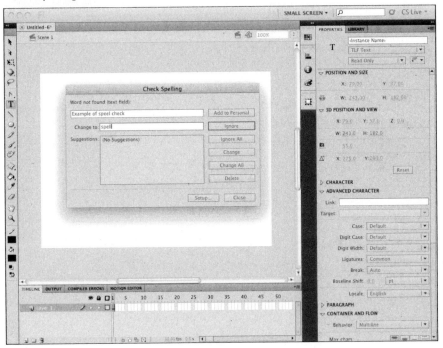

The Movie Explorer panel makes it easy to find and modify text if you are working with a complex document. To access this feature if it is not already open, use the application menu (Window ⇨ Movie Explorer) or the Alt+F3/Option+F3 shortcut keys to invoke the Movie Explorer panel, and modify text in any of the following ways:

- **To see all the text used in your current document:** Set the Movie Explorer to Show Text with the option button at the top of the panel. The contents of each text box is listed along with the font and point size that is used.

- **To search for a specific item:** Enter the font name, instance name, frame number, or ActionScript string in the Find field of the Movie Explorer panel.

- **To edit the contents of individual text boxes:** Double-click any listing in the Movie Explorer panel, and type in the field as you would if you were editing a filename in any other list.

- **To specify a new font or font size:** Select any text item listing that you want to change in the Movie Explorer and then simply change the font settings in the Properties panel. Use Shift+select to select multiple items in the Movie Explorer if you want to apply a change to more than one text box at a time.

- **To copy text:** Use the Copy command in the Movie Explorer options menu to copy a currently selected line of text to the Clipboard, or to copy all the text in your current document to the Clipboard without having to select items individually in the Movie Explorer, use the Copy All Text to the Clipboard command in the Movie Explorer options menu.

Setting text attributes in the Properties panel

The Text tool does not include options in the Tools panel because the extensive text controls are centrally located in the Properties panel. You create all Flash text in text blocks or boxes with the same Text tool, but when you create text, you can assign it specific appearance settings and behavior with the Properties panel.

Although you can always access font selection, size, and style menus from the application menu (Text ⇨ Font, Text ⇨ Size, and Text ⇨ Style), the options for controlling text are not visible in the Properties panel unless the Text tool is active or you select a text box with the Selection tool. The options available in the Properties panel vary slightly, depending on the kind of text you select.

Text options

When working with TLF text, you can modify the following text attributes in the Properties panel. As shown in Figure 8.8, these settings are organized into named sections of the Properties panel:

- **Text field instance name:** This identifier allows the Flash Player to put your dynamic data in the correct field.

- **Text Engine**
  - **TLF Text:** The preferred type of text when working in Flash CS5. TLF text uses Flash Player 10 and ActionScript 3.0 to render the highest quality text in the Flash Player.
  - **Classic Text:** Flash's legacy text engine. Use Classic Text when targeting Flash Player versions earlier that Flash Player 10, or ActionScript versions earlier than 3.0.

- **Text Type**
  - **(TLF Text options):** TLF text gives three options — Read Only, Selectable, and Editable. Set this behavior first to invoke the relevant options in the Properties panel.
  - **(Classic Text options):** The text type drop-down at the top of the panel enables you to specify Static Text, Input Text, or Dynamic Text for your text box type.

- **POSITION AND SIZE** (This section appears in the Properties panel only if you select a text box in the Document window.)
  - **X and Y:** Values are auto-filled relative to the top-left corner when you place a text box on the Stage, but you can use these fields to change the position at any time. It can be especially helpful if you want to ensure that your text box is aligned precisely in a specific location or to a whole pixel value position.

- **W**(idth) and **H**(eight): These values are auto-filled when you create a text box in the Document window.

- **3D Position and View** (This section appears in the Properties panel only if you select a text box in the Document window.)

  - **X, Y, and Z:** Values are auto-filled relative to the top-left corner when you place a text box on the Stage, and control the 3-D position of the text field. X and Y values control the horizontal and vertical positions of the text field, respectively, while the Z position controls its depth.

  - **W**(idth) and **H**(eight): These values are auto-filled when you create a text box in the Document window and are governed by the values set in the POSITION AND SIZE section.

  - **(Camera):** Controls the position of the simulated 3-D camera. Changing this setting applies to all objects in the Flash project.

  - **(Vanishing Point):** Controls the vanishing point for simulated 3-D depth. Changing the vanishing point applies to all objects within the Flash project.

FIGURE 8.8

The main options available for TLF text in the (expanded) Properties panel

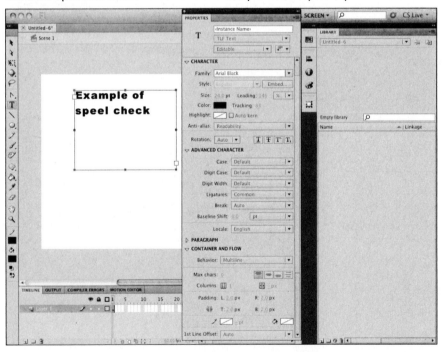

- CHARACTER
  - **Family:** When the Text tool is active, this field displays the name of the current font. Click the arrow button to open a scrolling menu of available fonts. Choose a font from this scrolling menu to set the font for the next text element that you create. Or, to change the font of existing text in the Document window, first select individual characters with the Text tool or the whole group with the Selection tool, and then choose a different font from the scrolling menu. When you select a font from the Properties panel menu, you'll see a preview of the highlighted font in the style or typeface that will appear.

  - **Style:** If the font you have chosen in the Family menu (above) includes designed styles and you have them installed, they show up in this menu. For example, if you have selected *Verdana* in the Family menu, you might see *Bold Italic* show up in the Style menu. If designed styles are not available, then you can apply faux Bold and/or faux Italic style to the text by using this menu.

Note

Many computer programs (including Flash) that handle type permit you to approximate a bold and/or italic version of a font, even if this style is not available in the original installed font; this has led to some confusion about font styles. If a font was originally designed to include a bold or italic version, it will be available in the Style menu after you have chosen the font family. With many fonts, the faux Bold or faux Italic style may appear very similarly to the designed Bold or Italic style, but with well-designed fonts, the shapes and proportions of individual characters are designed separately for each style. Theoretically, the original designed letter shapes for each style should look better than a normal letter shape thickened with an outline to create a faux Bold style, or slanted to create a faux Italic style. Type designers will sleep better at night if you use the faux style options only as a last resort. ■

  - **Embedding:** When preparing a file for export, you can control how much font information is included with the SWF. The Font Embedding dialog box from the Font Embedding button in the Properties panel is explained in the next section.

  - **Size:** When the Text tool is active, it displays the current font size in the Size entry field. You can change the font size by holding your mouse down over the text area and sliding it left or right to decrease or increase the value, respectively, or by clicking and typing a specific point size number in the field.

  - **Tracking:** You use this value field to change the space between individual letters. The default setting of 0 applies the built-in tracking and kerning of the font; any setting between +1 and +1000 adds space between characters; any setting between −1 and −60 decreases space between characters (extreme settings cause the letters to overlap or reflect).

  - **Leading:** This value field changes the space between lines. A higher value creates more space, while smaller values create less space. Values can be set based on points (pt) or percentages relative to the default setting (%) using the Leading drop-down menu.

Tip

With a section of text selected, you can use the arrow keys (along with Ctrl/cmd or Shift modifier keys) to increase or decrease spacing between characters. The higher the Zoom setting, the smaller the spacing increments will be. ■

- **Type Color chip:** Click this button to open the Swatches popup menu, which in addition to offering current and temporary swatches also enables you to acquire a color from anywhere within the interface by sampling with the dropper arrow.

- **Highlight Color chip:** This button opens the Swatches popup menu to allow you to select a color to apply to the background of the text, as if it were highlighted.

- **Auto kern check box:** If the font includes built-in kerning information, which evens out the spaces between letter forms, select this to activate automatic kerning. On vertical text, this setting can be overridden by the Vertical text settings in the Flash Preferences dialog box (refer to Figure 8.4). When No Kerning is selected in Preferences, the Auto kern check box in the Properties panel applies only to horizontal text.

- **Anti-alias option menu:** Use this menu to select the level of anti-aliasing (or smoothing) to apply when the Flash Player renders your type. If you do not want to include font outlines in your file, select Use device fonts to render text by using a font that is available on each user's computer.

- **Rotation option menu:** Use this menu to control the rotation of characters in a text box. Text can be set to have no rotation, 270 degree rotation, or to automatically choose rotation based on the current language set in the Locale menu in the ADVANCED CHARACTER section.

- **Underline/Strikethrough:** Use these buttons to add lines beneath or through text.

- **Superscript/Subscript:** These two toggle buttons modify the baseline alignment of your text. Superscript shifts horizontal text above the baseline and vertical text to the right of the baseline. Subscript sets horizontal text below the baseline and vertical text to the left of the baseline. Note: If you set a text field to be selectable or dynamic, you cannot use the Superscript or Subscript toggles.

- **ADVANCED CHARACTER**
  - **Link entry:** This option is available only for horizontal read-only or selectable text fields. By selecting a text box or an individual word in the Document window and then entering a URL in this Link entry field, you can add a hyperlink to selected text. The text link is identified in the authoring environment with a dotted underline — the underline is not visible in the published SWF file, though you can change the formatting of your link text to include an underline if you prefer. The mouse pointer also changes in the Flash Player to indicate a link when it is positioned over the text.

Tip

Though link text is somewhat limited in the Flash authoring environment, it is possible to add more features to your links, including rollover states, using ActionScript. Another option is to leave spaces in your text and use a button symbol for your link. ■

- **Target menu:** This menu is accessible after you enter a URL in the Link field, and it allows you to select a destination for the loaded URL. The options should be familiar to anyone who has worked with HTML page structures. For more information, refer to the description of the navigateToURL() action in Chapter 15.

- **Case:** This menu controls casing of text. Text can be set to display as Uppercase, Lowercase, or to Small Caps. The Default option does not modify the casing of the text field.

- **Digit Case:** Controls presentation of numbers. In some fonts, digits are not all aligned to the baseline of the text, and some numbers are significantly below the baseline. To keep numbers aligned, use the Lining setting, and to keep the original style of the font, use the Old Style setting.

- **Digit Width:** Controls space between numbers. The Proportional setting spaces digits depending on the width of each digit, and the Tabular setting gives each digit an equal amount of space.

- **Ligatures:** Specifies control over how ligatures are rendered. The options (in order from no ligatures to most extreme ligatures) are Minimum, Common, Uncommon, and Exotic.

- **Break:** Set the intervals at which line breaks are created. The Auto setting creates line breaks using word wrap, so full words are not broken between lines. The All setting creates a new line for each character in the text box. The Any setting creates line breaks when the text reaches the end of the text field's width, even if it breaks a word in multiple parts. The No Break option does not automatically add line breaks.

- **Baseline Shift:** Allows you to adjust the baseline of the text, moving it up (positive values) or down (negative values). The baseline shift can be set using points (pt), percentages (%), or to the superscript or subscript level.

- **Locale:** Sets the character locale for the language you are using.

- **PARAGRAPH**

  - **Align:** These four buttons modify the alignment of text for Left, Center, Right, or Justified. The four justification settings control the last line of text — whether it's aligned to the start of a line, the center, the end, or fully justified. When you're editing, the alignment you choose affects only those paragraph(s) you've selected. When entering text, use these options to predetermine the alignment before text entry, and all subsequent text will be aligned accordingly. On vertical text, these buttons modify alignment to Top, Middle, Bottom, Start Justification, Center Justification, End Justification, or Full Justification.

  - **Margins:** Set the values for left and right text margins. On vertical text, these values modify top and bottom margins, respectively.

  - **Indent:** Set the values for indenting.

  - **Spacing:** Set the values for line spacing. On vertical text these values modify the top margin and column spacing, respectively (which makes the indent setting redundant with the left or top margin setting on vertical text).

- **Text Justify:** Control appearance of justified text. The space in the text can be added in between letters (Letter spacing) or with words (Word spacing).
- **CONTAINER AND FLOW**
  - **Behavior:** Control how the text box handles multiple lines. The Single line mode uses one line only, the Multiline no wrap mode only creates new lines with a hard return, and the Multiline mode wraps words to form multiple lines automatically.
  - **Max chars:** Specify the maximum number of characters for the text field. This option is only available for Editable text fields.
  - **(Vertical alignment):** Control vertical alignment of the text within the text box. Options include align to top, center, bottom, or justify spacing between lines.
  - **Columns:** Divides the text field into columns.
  - **(Column gutter width):** Control amount of pixels of space between columns.
  - **Padding:** Set the values for padding the space between the text inside the block and the edge of the block. Padding can be linked, using the Lock padding button, so there is equal space on all four sides of the text.
  - **Border/Background colors:** Set the border and background colors for the text block.
  - **1st Line Offset:** Adjust the position of the starting point of the text, moving it based on a point value (pt), the current Line Height value, or based on the highest point of an ascending character (Ascent). The Auto mode uses the last used setting.
- **COLOR EFFECT:** Allows control over color settings, such as Alpha, Tint, and Brightness.
- **DISPLAY:** This area controls the blend mode of the text field and whether the text field should be cached as a bitmap object.

Cross-Reference

Blend modes are discussed in more detail in Chapter 11. ■

- **FILTERS:** This area of the Properties panel can be used to apply and manage live filters that enable you to add visual effects to your text.

Cross-Reference

Filters are described later in this chapter and in more detail in Chapter 11. ■

Font Embedding

By default, Flash embeds the characters you enter in TLF text field so that they appear properly on any computer. Things get a little more complicated when you begin to use ActionScript to control the text in those text fields because there is the possibility for content to be added *after* the file is published. Instead of just auto-embedding every possible character, Flash enables you to control your file size by choosing the characters that are available at runtime. The Font Embedding dialog box (shown in Figure 8.9) is there to help you define the most relevant character set to embed with your specific text field.

New Feature

The updated Flash CS5 Font Embedding menu gives streamlined access to embedding fonts and creating font symbols by combining the content of multiple menus in a single, user-friendly interface. ■

You can embed an entire font, a certain part of a font (uppercase letters, lowercase letters, or just numbers, for example), or you can enter a more selective range of characters by typing them directly into the field at the bottom of the dialog box (under "Also include these characters:"). The Auto Fill button automatically loads all the unique glyphs or characters in the currently selected text box into the Include field to be embedded with the final SWF. The counter for total number of glyphs (at the bottom of the dialog box) updates based on your settings, to show the estimated total number of unique glyphs that are embedded with the final exported file.

Note

The Font Embedding options include international language sets and specialized sets such as music symbols. These glyph sets can be very large, but this is a useful feature if you are creating dynamic text fields that need to display specialized characters or alternative glyphs. ■

FIGURE 8.9

The new Flash CS5 Font Embedding dialog box for specifying embedded font information to be exported with your final SWF

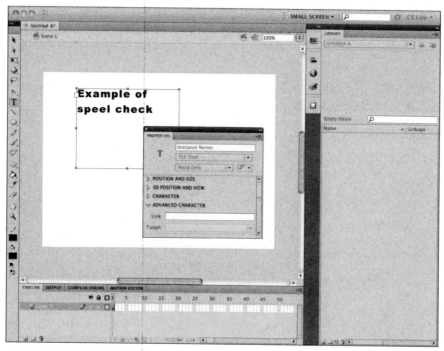

Application menu commands

Some of the text settings in the Properties panel are also available from the application Text menu:

- Under Text ⇨ Font, you can select from the same available fonts listed in the Properties panel's Family menu, but the list is slightly larger so it is easier to read.

- Under Text ⇨ Size, you can select a specific font point size from a list, instead of using the Font size slider in the Properties panel.

- Under Text ⇨ Style, the commands include:
    - **Bold:** Ctrl+Shift+B/⌘+Shift+B
    - **Italic:** Ctrl+Shift+I/⌘+Shift+I
    - **Faux Bold** (for fonts that don't have a built-in bold style)
    - **Faux Italic** (for fonts that don't have a built-in italic style)
    - **Subscript**
    - **Superscript**

- Under Text ⇨ Align, the commands include:
    - **Align Left:** Ctrl+Shift+L/⌘+Shift+L
    - **Align Center:** Ctrl+Shift+C/⌘+Shift+C
    - **Align Right:** Ctrl+Shift+R/⌘+Shift+R
    - **Justify:** Ctrl+Shift+J/⌘+Shift+J

- Under Text ⇨ Letter Spacing, you will find a list of options that offers an alternative way to adjust the space between characters. If you have the Properties panel open as you apply these commands manually, you see the letter spacing or tracking value field update. Manual tracking has the advantage that you can apply it either to selected (highlighted) text characters or to the pair of text characters on either side of the cursor:
    - **Increase:** To increase text character spacing by one-half pixel, press Ctrl+Alt+→/ ⌘+Option+→. To increase text character spacing by two pixels, press Shift+Ctrl+Alt+→/Shift+⌘+Option+→.
    - **Decrease:** To decrease text character spacing by one-half pixel, press Ctrl+Alt+←/ ⌘+Option+←. To decrease text character spacing by two pixels, press Shift+Ctrl+Alt+←/Shift+⌘+Option+←.
    - **Reset:** To reset text character spacing to normal, press Ctrl+Alt+↑ /⌘+Option+↑.

- **Check Spelling:** Opens the Check Spelling dialog box (shown in Figure 8.7).
- **Spelling Setup:** Opens the Spelling Setup dialog box (shown in Figure 8.6).

Controlling flow between multiple text fields

Flash CS5 allows you to display one section of text through multiple flowing text fields. The connected text fields can even be on different layers. There are two different ways to set up flow between multiple fields.

One way to create flow between text fields is to begin with a text field that has more text than it has space to display. This is recognizable by a red box at the bottom right of the text field that is selected, as shown in Figure 8.10. To continue this text in a new text field, click the red box, and then click in an empty area on the stage to create a new text field, which is shown as linked to the original text field (Figure 8.11). This step can be repeated to continue flow into as many text fields as necessary.

Another way to create flow between multiple text fields is to connect one overflowing text field to a preexisting empty text field. To do this, click the bottom-right red square in the overflowing text field, and then click on the empty text field to establish the connection. Before clicking on the text field, your cursor should turn into a link icon, showing that clicking will create a link to that text field.

To break connection between linked text fields, double-click the top-left blue triangle icon of a linked text field, as shown in Figure 8.12.

FIGURE 8.10

A text field containing overflow text shows a red box at the bottom right.

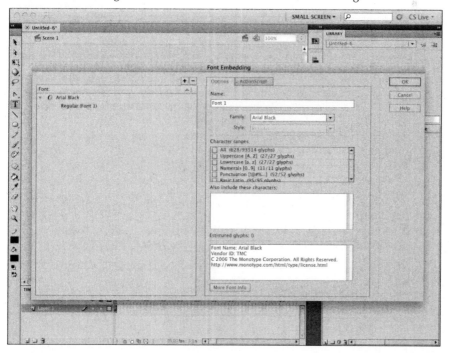

FIGURE 8.11

TLF text fields show flow with a triangle icon and a line connecting the first text field's bottom-right corner to the next text field's bottom-left corner.

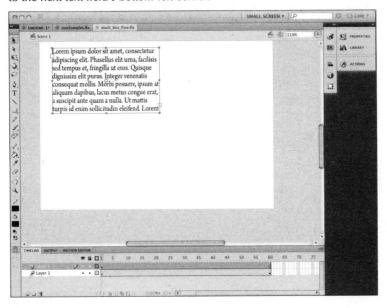

FIGURE 8.12

Disconnect linked text fields by double-clicking the blue triangle link icon at the top left of a linked text field.

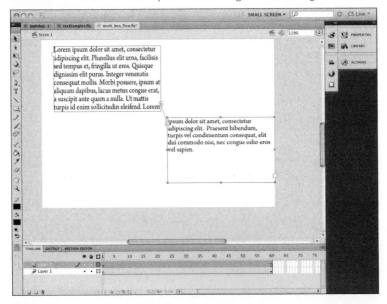

Font Export and Display

By default, Flash embeds all fonts used in TLF text boxes in order to deliver WYSIWYG (what-you-see-is-what-you-get) display in the published movie (.swf). As long as font outlines are available for the text you use in your Flash document (.fla), the published movie (.swf) appears consistently, regardless of what fonts the user has installed on his or her machine.

In order to edit a Flash project (.fla), you need to have the original fonts available, unless you are willing to view the document with a substitute font in the authoring environment. If you select a text box that appears with a substitute font, you should still see the name of the original font listed in the Properties panel, although it will be marked by parentheses. As long as the font formatting is not modified, Flash preserves all the original font information so that when the document (.fla) is opened again on a machine that has the original font, any edits that were made by using the default font are rendered correctly. Although you can make text edits while working with a default font, you need to have the original font installed in order to publish the final movie (.swf) with the design intact.

Smoothing text with anti-alias settings

The consistent text display of embedded fonts is what endears Flash to type-obsessed designers, but a small price must be paid: Every embedded font adds to the final file size, and anti-aliasing (smoothing) can sometimes make fonts too blurry. The good news is that for most projects, the additional weight is not an issue, and the anti-aliasing controls in Flash make it easy to customize the level of anti-aliasing as needed. If file size is a critical issue, you may choose to use device fonts or a runtime shared library. If you prefer the look of bitmap (aliased) fonts, that setting is still available in the Font rendering menu (see Figure 8.13).

Figure 8.14 compares aliased with anti-aliased text in two published SWFs: one with Anti-alias for readability applied (left) and one with Anti-alias for animation applied (right).

On the CD-ROM

For a truer (on-screen) comparison between these different text options, refer to the files in the textSmoothing folder inside the ch08 folder on the CD-ROM. ∎

The Anti-alias for readability setting does an amazing job of rendering smooth, legible type, even at small sizes. This setting has only two drawbacks: It contributes to larger file sizes and it can only be rendered with Flash Player 8 or later. The Anti-alias for animation setting smoothes text almost as well as the Anti-alias for readability setting, but it ignores kerning information in order to create slightly smaller files and to render animated text more quickly. This is the only anti-aliasing option that renders on older versions of the Flash Player.

FIGURE 8.13

The Font rendering menu makes it easy to choose a setting that suits your design style and file size requirements.

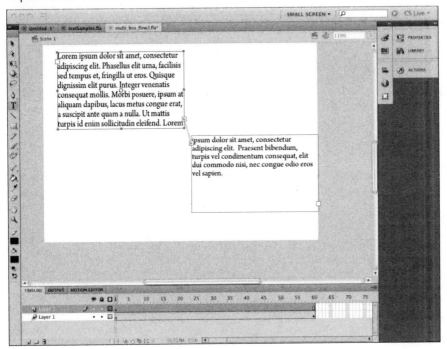

Note

Anti-aliasing TLF text requires you to embed the font so it will render properly in the Flash Player. ■

Note

If you are working on OS X, you may not notice much difference between aliased and anti-aliased text because the system applies automatic smoothing on any screen text, even on application menu lists. Although this feature cannot be turned off completely, the text smoothing controls in your System preferences panel (in the Appearance category) allow you to specify between the lowest setting (only smoothes text larger than 12 points) and the highest setting (only smoothes text larger than 4 point). The default setting smoothes any text larger than 8 points. ■

FIGURE 8.14

The two default settings for anti-aliasing in Flash (readability and animation) render more smoothly than Bitmap (aliased) text.

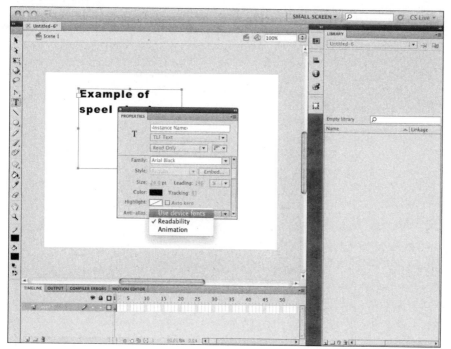

Understanding device fonts

Device fonts are three basic font style designators identified by a preceding underscore in your font menu. These fonts will be familiar to anyone who has worked with HTML text. Although they are not as exciting as some custom fonts, entire design styles are based on these "generic" fonts — think minimal and unpretentious. You will find the three device font designations, _sans, _serif, and _typewriter, in either the Properties panel font menu or in the application menu under Text ⇨ Font. These device font labels tell the Flash Player to use any equivalent font available on a viewer's system. The formatting that you have applied to the text in your Flash document (.fla), such as bold or italic style and point size, is preserved and applied to the font the Flash Player selects from the viewer's system to render the text in your movie (.swf).

To give you an idea of how device fonts relate to installed fonts, _sans usually becomes Arial or Helvetica, _serif usually becomes Times or Times New Roman, and _typewriter becomes Courier. Because these settings utilize the default fonts on the user's machine, Flash doesn't have to include their outlines in the exported SWF, and the final movie file size is reduced.

Device fonts are always available and always take little time to render, but they cannot be rotated or skewed and occasionally they vary slightly in their metrics from player to player and across platforms. Another important difference between standard embedded fonts and device fonts is that Flash anti-aliases or smoothes embedded fonts, while device fonts remain unsmoothed or aliased.

Working with the Use Device Fonts setting

You will notice that even if you have not used one of the device fonts from your font menu, you can still select the Use Device Fonts setting in the Anti-alias menu. This is a terrific "compromise" option if you strive for more specific control over the Flash Player's font choices but still want to take advantage of the file size savings device fonts offer. When the Use Device Fonts setting is applied, the font is not embedded — only the Font name, Font family/style (serif/sans serif/mono-space), and other information are added to specify the font, which adds no more than 10 or 15 bytes to the final SWF file. This information is used so that the Flash Player on the user's system knows if the font is installed or not. If the original font is available, it appears exactly as you designed it. If the original font is not present, then the Flash Player still knows whether the substitute font should be serif or sans serif.

The Use Device Fonts option also works as a toggle to turn off anti-aliasing. This means that even if the user has all the fonts used in your Flash movie installed, Use Device Fonts changes how the type appears:

- **When Use Device Fonts is selected**: No anti-aliasing or smoothing is applied to the device font, whether it is available on your system or not.
- **When Use Device Fonts is *not* selected**: The font outline is embedded and all characters are smoothed (even if the font is available). Smoothed text can sometimes be too blurry at small point sizes.

To accurately preview the Use Device Fonts setting on your machine, if you have a font manager (as most Web designers do), you need to make sure that you're careful about your font activation settings. Make sure that activation is turned *off* for the fonts that you want to test so that the Flash player does not find them when it renders the movie (.swf) — this enables you to see what might happen to your design when your system auto-substitutes other fonts.

For best results with this specific Use Device Fonts option, I suggest that you limit your font selection to those fonts that most of your audience is likely to have (all those common fonts that come installed with their machines), or those that translate into one of the default device fonts without wreaking havoc on your design. It is better to be conservative and design your layout with Times, Arial, and Courier than to go wild with custom fonts that will most likely be substituted very differently when the movie is viewed on someone else's machine. Otherwise, for unusual fonts, I suggest that you either embed the full font outline information (and apply one of the anti-alias settings) or, for limited areas of text (such as headlines), that you use the Bitmap text option to generate a custom aliased outline or break the text apart to manually create vector shapes, as I describe later in this chapter.

Troubleshooting font display

Although Flash does an amazing job of displaying fonts consistently and cleanly, even on different platforms, the success of your font export depends entirely on the quality and completeness of the font information available when the Flash document is created (.fla). Because Flash can access font information on your system while you are working in the authoring environment, many of the font display problems that can come up during production are visible only when the Flash movie (.swf) is published.

To display fonts in the published movie (.swf), the Flash Player relies on the font information embedded in the movie, or on the fonts installed on the user's system. If there are discrepancies between the information available to the Flash Player and the font information that was available to the Flash authoring application when the document was created, you will run into font display problems.

When you encounter problems with fonts (as you almost always do at some point), a good guide to font management is indispensable. I can't describe everything that can go wrong when working with fonts here, and solutions often vary depending on how you are storing and managing your fonts. Ideally, you should find resources that are specific to the platform and programs you are using.

TrueType, Type 1 PostScript, OpenType, and bitmap fonts (Mac only) can all be used in Flash. Although Flash exports the system information about the fonts that are used, a damaged or incomplete font may still appear correctly in the authoring environment (.fla). However, the exported movie (.swf) will appear incorrectly on other systems if the end user doesn't have the font installed. This is due to the fact that Flash can display the font within the editor by using the screen font; it does not recognize that particular font's outline and can't export information needed to display the text in the SWF. You can avoid font display problems by using the universal device fonts (_sans, _serif, or _typewriter fonts).

Controlling font substitution

If Flash cannot find font information on your machine to match what is specified in a file (.fla) when you open it in the authoring environment, you are notified by the Font Mapping dialog box (shown in Figure 8.15) and prompted to select fonts installed on your system to substitute for display.

Note
If you publish or export a document without viewing any of the scenes containing missing fonts, the dialog box appears only when Flash attempts to publish or export the SWF. ■

The first time that a scene with missing font information appears in the authoring environment, you are prompted by the Font Mapping dialog box to choose one of the following options:

- **Choose Substitute fonts:** The Font Mapping dialog box enables you to specify individual substitutions from the fonts available on your system for each missing font. The Missing Fonts column in the dialog box lists all fonts specified in the document that Flash can't find on your system. To choose a substitute font for a missing font, select the font name in the Missing Fonts list and then use the Substitute font menus at the bottom of the dialog box to specify a font family and style. Click OK to apply the settings and close the dialog box.

- **Apply System Default:** This button substitutes missing fonts with the Flash system default font. You can always change the Font Mapping default settings in the Text category of Flash preferences when you have the document open (Edit ➪ Preferences ➪ Text, or on OS X, Flash ➪ Preferences ➪ Text).

FIGURE 8.15

The Font Mapping dialog box is used to view missing fonts and to modify mapping of substitute fonts.

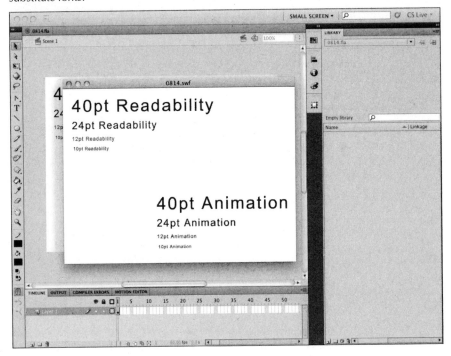

Even though the text appears in a substitute font, Flash includes the name of the missing font in the Properties panel font menu (see Figure 8.16). Flash preserves the original font specification when the file is saved so that the text appears correctly when the document (.fla) is opened on a system with the missing fonts installed. You can even apply the missing font to new text by selecting it from the font menu in the Properties panel.

Because appearance attributes such as size, leading, and kerning may render differently with a substitute font, you may have to adjust any modifications you make while viewing text in a substitute font when the document is opened on a machine with the original font available.

FIGURE 8.16

The missing font name appears in the font menu, even when text appears in a substitute font in the authoring environment.

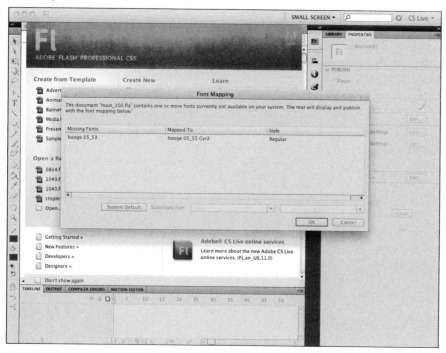

To view all the missing fonts in the currently active document or to reselect font mappings, choose Edit ⇨ Font Mapping (or in OS X, Flash ⇨ Font Mapping) from the application menu and repeat the same steps described previously to choose new substitute fonts. To view all the font mapping settings saved on your system or to delete font mappings, close all Flash documents before opening the Font Mapping dialog box or making changes to the listed mapping.

Font Symbols and Shared Font Libraries

Using font symbols and shared libraries in your Flash authoring workflow offers several benefits that can make it worth the little time it takes to set them up. Although you can nest a static text box inside any other symbol type if you want to reuse a specific text element in your movie, this does not change how the text is published in the Flash document. Using instances of a symbol to place repeated text elements, such as logos or taglines, offers the same benefits as converting artwork into symbols — you can make changes to the symbol stored in the library and the change is propagated to every instance in your document, and you can also modify the appearance of individual instances without changing the original symbol.

The difference between text nested in another symbol type and a real font symbol is that font symbols can actually be used to store the display information for an entire font. When placed into a runtime shared library, font symbols can be used to link text in one movie to the font display information in a source movie; this allows you to use custom fonts without having to embed the font information in every Flash movie (.swf) individually. This workflow is especially effective on projects that involve multiple .swf files using the same custom fonts. The bonus is that if your client suddenly decides that they prefer "Leonardo script" to "Chickenscratch bold" (or whatever font switcheroo they might come up with), you can make the change in your source font symbol without even opening any of the other files (as long as the new font is given the same name and it still fits in your layouts).

This all sounds great so far, right? Now for the reality check: Because you are storing font information in a separate file from your layouts, there is one more factor that you have to manage. The source font library (.swf) can be in the same directory as your other movie (.swf) files, or it can be stored on a completely different server. It is very important to decide on the storage location of your source font files (.fla and .swf) before you begin linking text in your other Flash documents (.fla) to shared font symbols because the URL that defines the relative or absolute path is stored in each .fla file, and your font links will be broken if you later change the source movie's location.

Note
Runtime shared assets do not need to be available on your local network when you are editing .fla documents that rely on linked assets, but the shared asset .swf must be available at your specified URL in order for the published movies (.swf) to display the linked assets at runtime. ■

As you can imagine, having your font links fail is a major disaster; therefore, many developers believe that relying on an external font source isn't worth the risk. On the other hand, there is always an element of uncertainty with Web delivery, so it might not be fair to eliminate what is otherwise an excellent way to optimize font management in your Flash layouts. As with any Web production, just be sure to test early and often as you develop a Flash project that uses shared fonts.

You can use shared libraries to store other symbol types, but it is best to organize different kinds of assets in separate FLA files. For now, I focus on making font symbols and creating a source file for a shared font library.

Creating a font symbol

Font symbols can be integrated in your workflow in two ways. If you plan to use font symbols within a Flash document (.fla) simply as a way to make edits faster in that one document, and you don't mind exporting the font information with every SWF, you can create a font symbol directly in the main library of your current document and rely on authortime sharing to update instances of the font. However, if you want to save file size by linking to the font symbol information for runtime sharing, you should open a new Flash document before creating your font symbols. In either case, the initial steps for creating a Flash font symbol are the same:

1. **Open the Library panel where you want to store the font symbol.**
2. **From the library options panel, choose New Font (see Figure 8.17).**

FIGURE 8.17

Choosing to insert a new font symbol from the Library panel options menu

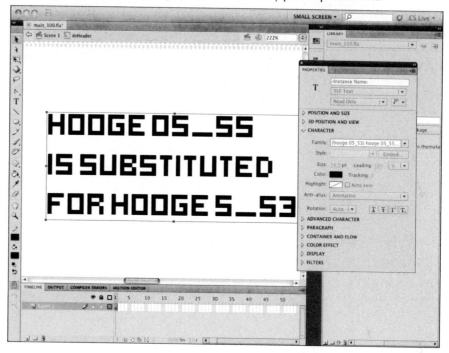

3. **In the Font Embedding dialog box that appears, enter a name for your font symbol and select the font you want to embed in the file (see Figure 8.18).** The name that you enter shouldn't be the same as the original font name but rather should indicate how the font is being used in your project. For example, if you are using an Impact font for your titles, instead of naming the font symbol "Impact" you could name it "titleFont" or some other name that informs you (and the rest of your team) how the font is being used.

4. **If you also want the option to use faux Bold or Italic style on text linked to your font symbol, select the Style check boxes for Bold and/or Italic to include these characters with the embedded font.** Select the Bitmap text check box to create aliased outlines of your font symbol. If you choose to render an aliased outline of a font, you also need to enter the font size that you want to use by typing it in the Size field. This increases the size of your source movie only — the additional size is not passed on to other SWF files that link to the font symbol for runtime sharing.

Selecting a font to store in the new font symbol and giving it a reference name

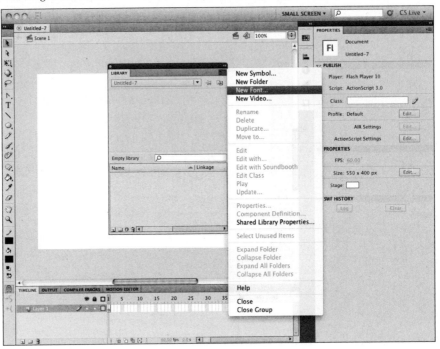

Caution

If you create a font symbol without the Bold or Italic options selected in the Font Embedding dialog box, and then try to apply the options in the Properties panel to create faux Bold or Italic style on text that is linked to the symbol, you will encounter one of two problems. If the text you are modifying is in a static text box, then the applied styles will appear, but the additional font information for the modified characters will be exported with your published file, thus increasing the size of the .swf. If the text you are modifying is in a dynamic or input text field, the text will not display in the published SWF file because the Flash Player will not find the font information needed to render the bold or italic type on-the-fly. These same rules apply to aliased outlines rendered at a specific font size. ■

5. Now when you browse the font menu available in the Properties panel or from the application menu (Text⇨Font) you will see your new font listed with the other fonts installed on your system. Font symbols are also differentiated from regular fonts in the menu with an asterisk (*) following the name it has been given (see Figure 8.19).

The next step required to use the font symbol in your project depends on how you choose to integrate font symbols into your workflow. As I mention earlier in this chapter, using symbols for authortime asset sharing can make propagating changes throughout a document easier, but any assets used in your document will still be embedded in each movie (.swf) that you publish. Creating a separate library for storing symbols and linking these as runtime shared assets in multiple movies takes a little more work, but it gives you the benefit of both streamlined updates and smaller file sizes. The most appropriate workflow depends on the scope and content of your particular project and on how willing you are to manage the risks involved with using runtime shared assets.

Font symbol names are followed by an asterisk in the Properties panel's font family menu (or in the application Text menu). Font symbols are also added to the Library list.

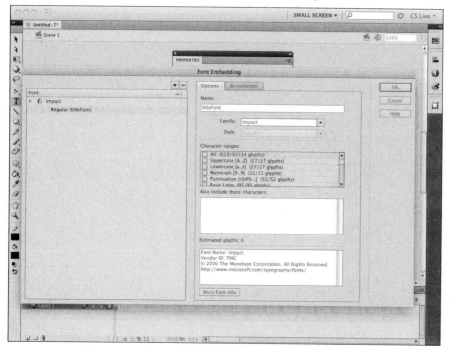

Updating font symbols at authortime

If you intend to use a font symbol as an authortime shared asset only, you can simply leave it in your current library so that the font is available in the font menu whenever you want to use it in your project. You can modify any of the text boxes that use your font symbol in the same way as any other text. There is no limit on the number of colors or sizes that you can use or on what you can type into each text box.

The main reason that this is a more flexible workflow than simply nesting text inside other symbols for reuse is that you can actually change the *content* used in individual text boxes that reference a font symbol, whereas you can only modify the *appearance* of text that is nested in a symbol instance.

The process for updating instances of a font symbol used within one Flash document (.fla) is much the same as updating any other symbol type or imported asset stored in the library:

1. **Open the current document library and select the font symbol that you want to modify.**

2. **Choose Properties from the library options menu or from the contextual menu.**

3. **In the Font Embedding dialog box, simply select a new font from the font menu, but don't change the font name that you had previously chosen.** (Now it makes sense why naming your font symbol with the same name shown in the font menu isn't a good idea, right?)

   You will find that all text that was in your old font is updated to the new font that you have chosen, while maintaining all other formatting and style attributes.

Tip

If you don't see your text boxes update to the new font immediately after you change it in the Font Embedding dialog box, you may need to click one of the text boxes with the Selection tool — this usually prompts Flash to refresh the display. ■

Using font symbols in runtime shared libraries

In order to make your font symbol available for use in other Flash movies without having to embed the font information in each file, you need to create links from individual *destination* files to your *source* file or shared library. This workflow optimizes file sizes by eliminating the storage of redundant font information between linked movies. As with HTML files, you have to specify a path in order for the Flash Player to locate font information in one movie (.swf) for text display in another. Because the font information is retrieved from an SWF file by the Flash Player and supplied to another SWF for text display, it is referred to as *runtime* asset sharing.

If you have already followed the steps to create a font symbol in an otherwise empty Flash document (.fla), the next part of the process is to enter an identifier and a location (path) that will "lead" the Flash Player to your shared library. As I mentioned previously, you need to know where the published source movie (.swf) will be stored before you can create font links to other documents. The location (or path) can be relative or absolute.

Tip

To keep your linkage intact while preserving source file version numbers as you develop your project, you might want to use the Publish Settings dialog box to give your published source SWF a generic name (such as `titleFontSource.swf`) while using a more specific naming convention for your source FLA files (such as `titleFontSource101.fla`). This eliminates the hassle of going back to your destination movies and changing the linkage information if you decide you need to move to a new version name to keep track of modifications to your source file (.fla). ■

To help clarify how runtime shared fonts are stored and accessed, I walk through the three possible scenarios for font symbol use and show you how each appears in the authoring environment (.fla) and in the published movie (.swf).

On the CD-ROM

The Flash files illustrated in this section are included in the ch8 folder on the CD-ROM. You will find both the fontSource files (shared library file) and the fontLink files (destination document) in the fontSymbols_ complete folder with final linkage properties. As long as the files are kept together in the same storage location, the font linkage should remain intact. If you want to use unfinished files to complete the steps in this section, open the files in the fontSymbols_start folder. I have also included a fontEmbed example file with the same text entered on the Stage but with embedded font information (including uppercase, lowercase, and punctuation for Impact) rather than linked font information to demonstrate the difference in file size. ■

The first file you will be working with is a source document, or the Flash document that contains the font symbols that you want to use as runtime shared assets.

Caution

If you are using the files from the CD-ROM to follow this example, you may need to modify the font symbol in fontSource.fla to match a font that you have on your system (instead of "Impact") before you can use Test Movie to publish the SWF file (Step 5). ■

1. **Open your source document and select your font symbol in the library.** If you are looking at the files on the CD-ROM, open fontSource.fla from the fontSymbol_ start folder and select the font symbol called NewFont in the library.

2. **Choose Properties from the library options menu or from the contextual menu.** Check the boxes to identify character ranges to embed.

3. **From the Font Embedding dialog box (see Figure 8.20), access Linkage properties by clicking the ActionScript Tab**.

4. **Choose TLF for the outline format, and select the Export for runtime sharing check box.** Notice that Export in frame 1 is automatically selected as well — leave that check box selected for now.

5. **In the Class field, change the original font symbol name (in our example NewFont) to something that helps you to remember what this font symbol is used for in your project (such as titleFont).** This Class name appears after the font symbol name in the library.

Caution

Don't close the Font Embedding dialog box until you have completed the next step. ■

6. **In the URL field (at the bottom of the dialog box), enter the path to the storage location for the source movie (.swf) that you will publish after you have finished choosing settings in the source document (.fla).** The link can be relative or absolute depending on how you will be storing your project .swfs:

   • If you are planning to keep the source movie (.swf) in the same folder as your individual destination movies (.swf), all you need to enter in the URL field is the name of your source .swf file — in our example, fontSource.swf.

   • If the source .swf file will be stored in a different folder or even on a separate server than the destination (linked) .swf files, you must enter an absolute path (Web address) in the URL field to specify the exact storage location of your source .swf file, such as http://yourserver.com/projectdirectory/sourceName.swf.

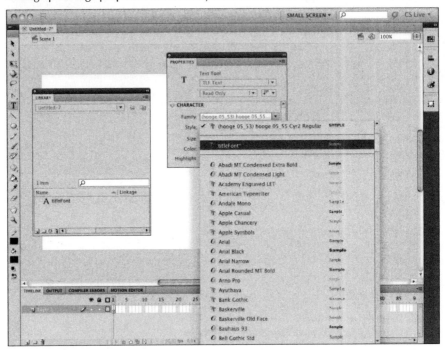

FIGURE 8.20

Setting up Linkage properties for a font symbol in the Flash source document (.fla)

7. **Save your source .fla file to the final storage location by using File ⇨ Save (Ctrl+S/⌘+S) and test your source .swf by using Control ⇨ Test Movie (Ctrl+Enter/⌘+Return).** Although nothing appears in the published .swf, if you turn on the Bandwidth Profiler (from the application menu: View ⇨ Bandwidth Profiler, or with shortcut keys [Ctrl+B/⌘+B]), you see the size of the font information for all the embedded characters included in your font symbol. Our sample font symbol source file was 17K (see Figure 8.21).

You have successfully created and saved a runtime shared asset. Now you can create another Flash document that references the font information stored in `fontSource.swf` so that you can use your custom font without having to embed the font information:

1. **Create a new Flash document or open the `fontLink.fla` file from the CD-ROM, and make sure that you have the Library panel for the current document open.**

2. **Link another document to the font information in your shared library in one of two ways:**

   • If you have already created a document that uses font symbols as described in the section on authortime sharing and decide to link to a runtime shared asset instead, you can enter the identifier and the URL of the shared library movie (.swf) in the Linkage properties for any font symbol in your library. Enter the identifier and the URL exactly as they appear in your font source file, but use Import for runtime sharing instead of

Export for runtime sharing (as shown in Figure 8.21). You should now find that all instances of the font symbol in your current document are updated with the font information stored in the shared asset movie (.swf) — as long as it is available on your server when you publish the movie for your current document.

Note

To enter linkage information manually, you need to have a font symbol in the document Library selected so that you can access the Font Embedding dialog box from the options menu or from the contextual menu. ■

- If you are authoring a document (.fla) that does not yet contain any font symbols and you want to link to your runtime shared asset, you can simply drag the font symbol from the source library into the current document library. With your destination document and Library panel open, choose File ➪ Open or File ➪ Import ➪ Open External Library and navigate to the Flash document (.fla) for your shared asset. You can then drag your source font symbol from the shared asset library and drop it into your destination document library. If you access Properties for the font symbol that you dragged into your library, you will see that Flash automatically inserts the identifier and URL for the shared asset. You can now use the font in your new document, and it is linked to the font information stored in the runtime shared asset movie (.swf).

FIGURE 8.21

The published source movie (.swf) with embedded font information for the font symbol to be used in other destination movies as a runtime shared asset

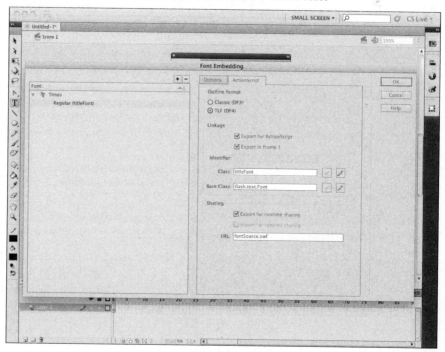

3. **When a font symbol in your library has the identifier and URL entered in its Linkage properties, you can use the linked font in your document by selecting it from your font menu and using the Text tool as you normally would.** When you publish your movie (.swf), you will notice that your file size is much smaller than it would be with embedded font information. For an example of this, compare the file size listed in the Bandwidth Profiler shown in Figure 8.22 (linked = 143 B) with Figure 8.23 (embedded = 4754 B).

FIGURE 8.22

Linkage settings for a font symbol in a destination movie refer to the font information stored in the runtime shared library.

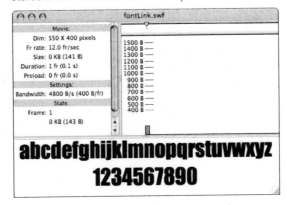

4. **If you decide that you want to disable runtime sharing for a font symbol in a destination document, you can clear the Import for runtime sharing check box in the Properties dialog box.** The font information for the characters used in your file are now embedded with the SWF file, so the file size is larger, but the Flash Player no longer requires access to the shared asset.

Caution

Text rendered with advanced anti-alias settings (Anti-alias for readability or Custom anti-aliasing) must be embedded. For text using linked font information, use the Anti-alias for animation setting. ■

FIGURE 8.23

The published SWF file from a document using linked font information from a runtime shared asset

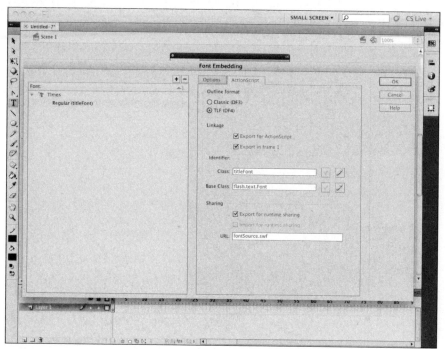

FIGURE 8.24

The published SWF file from a document using embedded font information

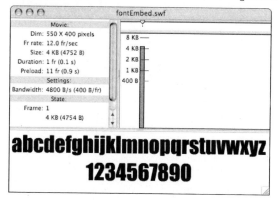

Modifying Text

In addition to all the text-handling capabilities I discuss earlier in this chapter, there are some fun ways that you can modify the appearance of text to create custom effects. Static text fields can be scaled, skewed, or flipped, and the color or alpha can be changed while keeping the text editable. In early versions of Flash, if you wanted to create a drop shadow or special fill effect, it was necessary to break the text apart to create individual shapes. Luckily, live filters were introduced with Flash 8 that could be applied to text or graphics to create special effects that can easily be added, combined, or removed while preserving the original, editable object.

New Feature

In Flash CS5, filters are now available in the Properties panel. ∎

On the CD-ROM

I have included the Flash files for the modified text shown in this section on the CD-ROM. If you want to look at these in the Flash authoring environment, you can open the file `modifyText_manual.fla` or `modify Text_filters.fla` in the `ch8` folder. ∎

Editing text manually

Figure 8.25 illustrates some of the ways that text can be modified without using filters. Any of these styles of manually modified text are compatible with older versions of the Flash Player.

Tip

If you plan to animate individual text characters, you can quickly move each letter onto its own layer by first applying the Break apart command (Ctrl+B/⌘+B) to a text box and then using the Distribute to Layers command (Shift+Ctrl+D/Shift+⌘+D). ∎

FIGURE 8.25

Text boxes can be modified with Free Transform options (top). To create individual characters, apply Break apart once (middle), and apply it again to create graphic text (bottom). Graphic text can be modified like any other shape in Flash.

Custom text information adds to your file size, so it is best to reserve these treatments for special text such as titles or graphics. If you are working with longer sections of text (such as an article or a story), it is better to use common fonts or device fonts to help keep your files smaller and to make the text easier to read.

Tip

With long sections of text, you may need to add scrolling, and this is much easier to do if you use dynamic text or live filters. If you use modified static text or graphic text, you can still add scrolling behavior by creating animation and controls manually, but this is more time consuming and requires your final SWF to have more information embedded in it. ■

Scaling text

By selecting a text box with the Free Transform tool, you can scale your text by dragging the transform handles, but this is not recommended as a way to increase the size of text unless it has been broken into vector shapes. Flash has to interpolate the normal font outlines to scale text this way, which can result in jagged edges when the movie is published. When sizing text, it is much better to simply modify the font size setting (by selecting or entering a new point size) to ensure a clean outline when the text is exported.

Sampling and sharing text attributes

If you want to use the same font attributes on a variety of text boxes, it is often best to modify one text box so that it has all the qualities you want — including color, size, font, style, and line or character spacing. You then have two options for transferring these attributes to other text boxes by using the Eyedropper tool:

- **To modify existing text boxes:** You can select other text boxes with the Selection tool and then activate the Eyedropper tool in the Tools panel and click your modified text to sample its attributes and transfer them to all the other selected text boxes simultaneously. This is much more efficient and consistent than trying to remember what settings you used and changing them manually on different text boxes.

- **To set attributes for new text boxes:** You can load the visual attributes of any manually modified text into the Properties panel by activating the Eyedropper tool and clicking the text to acquire its appearance. The Text tool is automatically activated after text is sampled, so you can immediately begin creating new text with the settings now loaded in the Properties panel.

Converting text into vector shapes

The Break apart command (Ctrl+B/⌘+B) is used to reduce symbols to grouped shapes, and it can also be used to modify static text. Applying Break apart once to a text box breaks a line of text into individual characters; applying the command again converts the characters into *graphic text* (vector lines and fills). Individual text characters can be grouped or changed to symbols. To make it easier to use individual characters in tweened animation, you can apply the Distribute to Layers command (Modify ⇨ Timeline ⇨ Distribute to Layers) to automatically place each character on its own layer.

Graphic text can be modified by using any of the drawing tools, reshaped with the Selection and Subselect tools, or distorted with any of the Free Transform options. You can also select special fills, such as bitmaps or gradients, to create patterned text, or use the Eraser tool to delete pieces of the letter shapes (see Figure 8.26).

Using the Eraser tool to delete parts of a graphic letter shape

However, after text characters have been converted to lines and fills, they can no longer be edited as text. Even if you regroup the text characters and/or convert the text into a symbol, you can no longer apply font, tracking, or paragraph options. To streamline your workflow, consider how you can combine graphic text with normal text for some effects — instead of converting all text into graphic shapes.

There are a few tips and guidelines to remember when converting text to shapes in Flash:

- To convert text characters to component lines and fills, you must first select or highlight the text characters that you want to convert, and then choose Modify ➪ Break apart from the application menu. To undo, choose Edit ➪ Undo (Ctrl+Z/⌘+Z) from the application menu.

- Rotation and Break apart can be applied only to fonts with available outline information, such as TrueType fonts.

- On Macs, PostScript fonts can be broken apart only if a type manager is installed that handles PostScript fonts.

- Breaking apart a text field that has filters applied to it removes the filters before the text is converted into shapes.

As you experiment with graphic text, you may want to refer to some of the other chapters that cover working with shapes.

Moving beyond the box with live filter effects

Flash filters open up the possibilities of creative text treatments even if you aren't all that "creative." With one handy little section at the bottom of the Properties panel (Filters), you can modify your text without breaking it apart. Filters can even be applied to dynamic text because the filters are rendered at runtime; they're "live." Filters are easy to add and combine, and you can edit the content of your text field at any time without breaking the effect. Figure 8.27 shows just a few simple examples of how you can modify text fields by using Flash filters.

FIGURE 8.27

A few of the effects that can be added to text by using filters while preserving the editability of the text field

Filters can be found in the Properties panel in the Filters section. To apply filters to a text field, select the text field, and then use the controls in the Properties panel to add or adjust filters (see Figure 8.28). Filters can be combined and layered to create a wide range of visual effects.

Cross-Reference

You can animate filters by creating a tween span and then using the Motion Editor to adjust these settings over time. There is also a new library of motion presets built into Flash CS5 (Window ⇨ Motion Presets), which can be applied to text fields or to graphics to create animated effects and transitions. But animation involves getting to know the Motion Editor, and I will save that discussion for Part III, "Creating Animation and Effects." ■

FIGURE 8.28

Adding and combining filters in text fields is easy with the Filter controls in the Properties panel.

Summary

- Flash CS5 makes working with text easier and more precise than ever by utilizing Text Layout Framework text. This allows you to have far superior control over your text than in previous versions of Flash.

- Flash offers robust and well-organized text-editing controls, but you can make the most of these tools only if you are familiar with, at least, the basic principles of typography.

- Studying the history of type in visual communications is one of the most practical and inspiring things you can do to improve your design skills.

- The option for converting any font into an aliased outline that can be embedded with the final movie (.swf) overrides the default smoothing or anti-aliasing that can make some text look slightly blurry.

- Complete font information must be available on your system in order for Flash to render and export the text properly to the final movie (.swf). If you need to open a Flash file (.fla) that includes fonts not available on your system, you can choose temporary substitute fonts without damaging the original font information stored in the file.

- Creating font symbols and storing them in shared libraries for either authortime updates or runtime linkage can help you manage large projects by centralizing font sources and making updates faster and easier.

- Linkage properties for font symbols are accessed via the Advanced button in the Font Embedding dialog box.

- You can add visual interest to your text with filters while still keeping options open for editing the content of the text field. Because filters are rendered dynamically, they can be applied to TLF text even if the content changes at runtime.

Modifying Graphics

After becoming familiar with the Flash authoring environment and learning to use the Drawing tools, you are now ready to move on to the fun part: messing with the basic shapes and text elements you have made to achieve custom results.

In this chapter, you revisit some of the core tools to show you new ways to apply them. I also introduce some specialized tools that exist only to transform your artwork. Following a look at how the Eyedropper, Paint Bucket, and Ink Bottle work together to modify strokes and fills, I show you how to use the Gradient Transform tool to create custom fills.

The Modify Shape submenu offers some special commands you can apply to alter lines and fills, whereas the Modify Transform submenu includes various options for skewing, stretching, rotating, flipping, and rotating shapes.

Before explaining the Flash stacking order and how to create compound shapes, I introduce the powerful Free Transform tool and the Envelope modifier that enables you to warp and distort multiple shapes simultaneously. Other features worth exploring include the stepped Break apart command on text and the indispensable Distribute to Layers command — these two features combined make animating text infinitely easier than it was in early versions of Flash.

Cross-Reference
For coverage of advanced color effects and filters, refer to Chapter 11, "Applying Filters, Blends, Guides, and Masks." ■

Last but not least, I cover the Find and Replace command and the History panel. I introduce the options for these flexible features and demonstrate some ways you can use them to modify your graphics, without even using any tools!

As I introduce various techniques and tools, I show you how to apply them for modifying artwork and adding the illusion of depth and texture to your 2-D graphics.

Sampling and Switching Fills and Strokes

You can always use the Selection tool to select a stroke or fill so that you can modify it by using any of the Swatches popups or the Stroke Style menu on the Properties panel. But, what do you do if you want to add a stroke or fill to a shape that was drawn without one or the other? The answer to this dilemma is found in a trio of tools that work nimbly together to provide one of the most unique graphics-editing solutions found in Flash. You use the Eyedropper tool to acquire fill and stroke styles or colors, and use the Paint Bucket and Ink Bottle tools to transfer these characteristics to other shapes.

Note
These tools only apply changes directly to shapes, shape primitives, or drawing objects, so to modify an element that has been grouped or converted into a symbol, you must first access the element in Edit mode. ■

The Eyedropper tool

As I introduced in Chapter 7, "Applying Color," the dropper icon that appears when you use the Selection tool to select colors from any of the popup Swatches menus is similar to the Eyedropper tool available in the Tools panel. However, when pulled out of the Tools panel directly, the Eyedropper tool (I) has slightly different behavior. Although you cannot use the Eyedropper tool to sample colors from elements outside the Document window, you can use it to sample line and fill styles or to simultaneously change the stroke and the fill color chips to the same sampled color.

Cross-Reference
For more information about this feat, refer to Chapter 7, "Applying Color." ■

Note
When used to acquire colors, the Swatches panel Eyedropper tool is limited to picking colors from swatches within the panel. However, the droppers that you access from the Swatches popup menus in the Color panel or Tools panel can acquire colors from other visible areas, such as the system background, items on the desktop, or items open in other applications. The functionality of this feature is not totally consistent, so here are some tips to making it work:

When picking colors by using the dropper from the Color panel swatches popup, press and hold the mouse as you roll over color chips in the popup or colors anywhere on your desktop and release the mouse only when you are hovering over the color that you want to sample. The preview in the swatches popup changes as you roll over different colors, and the color chip changes when you release the mouse to load the color that you have selected.

If you are using the dropper from the Tools panel color chip swatches popup, the behavior is a bit different: Click once on the color chip to open the swatches popup, and then move the dropper to roll over any color in the popup or on your desktop and click again to pick the color and load it into the current color chip. The droppers available from the swatches popups for any of the color chips in the Properties panel work the same way as the droppers in the Tools panel swatches popup, but they are limited to picking colors from within the Flash application (or the currently loaded swatches). ∎

The Eyedropper tool doesn't have any options in the Tools panel because they are all built in. As you hover over an item, the Eyedropper tool displays a small icon to indicate whether it is over a line or a fill that can be sampled by clicking. When a line is sampled, the Eyedropper tool automatically converts to the Ink Bottle tool, and when a fill is sampled, the Eyedropper tool converts to the Paint Bucket tool.

The composite image shown in Figure 9.1 shows the icons that appear when you use the Eyedropper tool to sample a fill (A) and apply it to another shape with the Paint Bucket tool (B), and sample a stroke (C) and apply it to another shape with the Ink Bottle tool (D).

FIGURE 9.1

The Eyedropper tool used to sample a fill and apply it with the Paint Bucket tool (A, B) and to sample a stroke and apply it with the Ink Bottle tool (C, D)

A: Sampling a fill with the Eyedropper tool

B: Applying a fill with the Paint Bucket tool

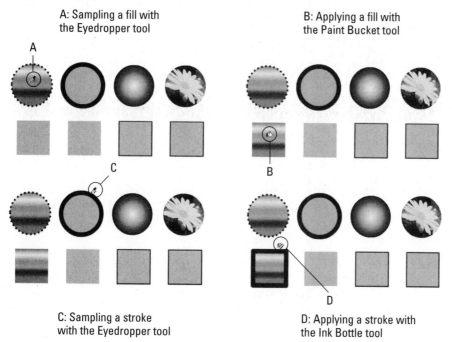

C: Sampling a stroke with the Eyedropper tool

D: Applying a stroke with the Ink Bottle tool

Any items already selected when the Eyedropper tool samples a stroke or fill immediately acquire the applicable stroke or fill style. This is the quickest way to transfer the fill or line styles of one element to a whole group of elements. Figure 9.2 shows the Eyedropper tool used to sample a fill with one (A) or more (B) elements already selected.

FIGURE 9.2

The Eyedropper tool also instantly converts selected elements to the sampled fill or stroke style.

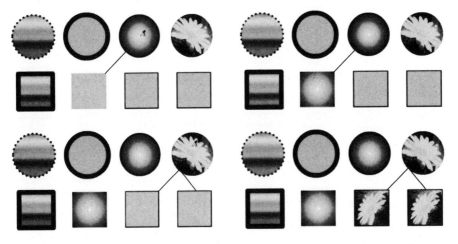

A: One item selected while fill is sampled with Eyedropper

Result: One item converted to new fill style

B: Two items selected while fill is sampled with Eyedropper

Result: Two items converted to new fill style

Tip

When you press and hold the Shift key while clicking a line or stroke color with the Eyedropper tool, the Fill and the Stroke color chips both convert simultaneously to the newly selected color so that it can be applied with any of the other drawing tools. ■

The Ink Bottle tool

You use the Ink Bottle tool (S) — refer to Figure 9.1 (D) — to change the color, style, and thickness of existing outlines. It is most often used in conjunction with the Eyedropper tool. When the Ink Bottle tool is in use, pay attention to the following three options:

- The current Stroke Color option on the Tools panel or the Properties panel
- The Stroke weight (or thickness) setting in the Properties panel
- The Stroke Style setting in the Properties panel

The Ink Bottle applies the current stroke color and line style, either sampled with the Eyedropper tool or chosen from the popup in the Tools panel or the controls in the Properties panel.

Caution

When you click to sample a line with the Ink Bottle tool, all other currently selected lines are changed simultaneously. ∎

The Ink Bottle tool is especially useful for applying custom line styles to multiple lines. You can build a collection of custom line styles either off Stage or in a special custom line palette saved as a single-frame Flash movie. You can then acquire these line styles whenever you want to reuse them.

Tip

You can add Flash files with graphics libraries that you plan to reuse to the application's Libraries folder so that they can be easily accessed from the Window ⇨ Common Libraries menu. ∎

Note

Depending on the level of zoom, some lines may not appear accurately on the screen — though they print correctly on a high-resolution printer. You may adjust Stroke weight in the Fill and Stroke section of the Properties panel. ∎

The Paint Bucket tool

You use the Paint Bucket tool to fill enclosed areas with color, gradients, or bitmap fills. Although the Paint Bucket tool is a more robust tool than the Ink Bottle tool, and it can be used independently, it's most often used in conjunction with the Eyedropper tool. As discussed earlier in this chapter, when the Eyedropper tool picks up a fill, it first acquires the attributes of that fill and then automatically changes itself to the Paint Bucket tool. When the Paint Bucket tool is active, shown in Figure 9.3, two options are available from the Tools panel: Lock Fill and Gap size. The Gap size drop-down menu offers four settings to control how Flash handles gaps or open spaces in lines when filling with the Paint Bucket tool.

FIGURE 9.3

The Paint Bucket tool and Gap size options

When you use the Eyedropper tool to acquire a bitmap fill, the Eyedropper tool is automatically swapped for the Paint Bucket tool and a thumbnail of the bitmap image appears in place of the fill color chip. This procedure also automatically engages the Paint Bucket Lock Fill option.

Note
The scale of the bitmap fill is consistent, no matter how it is selected and applied. As described later in this chapter, you can use the Gradient Transform tool to modify the scale of a bitmap fill as needed. ■

Caution
Using the Paint Bucket to fill with white (or the background color) is not the same as erasing. Painting with white (or the background color) may appear to accomplish something similar to erasing. However, you are, in fact, creating a filled item that can be selected, moved, deleted, or reshaped. Only erasing erases! ■

Another helpful behavior of the Paint Bucket tool is that the exact location where you click to apply the Paint Bucket tool defines the highlight point for the fill. This has no visible effect when filling with solid colors or bitmap fills, but when filling with gradients it affects how the fill is rendered within the boundaries of the shape. Figure 9.4 illustrates how the highlight of a gradient fill varies based on where it was "dumped" with the Paint Bucket.

Tip
You can also adjust the highlight and the center point of the rendered gradient with the Gradient Transform tool after a shape is filled. ■

FIGURE 9.4
The highlight location of gradient fills can be defined by the position of the Paint Bucket tool when the fill is applied to a shape.

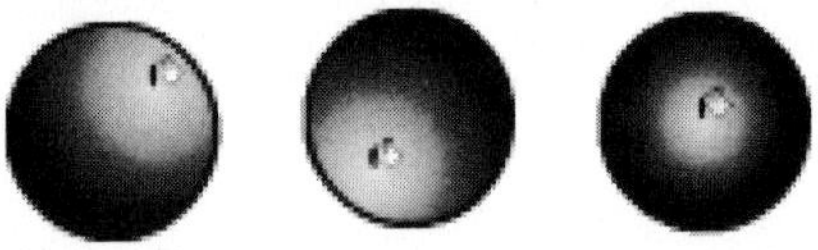

As with the Ink Bottle tool, the Paint Bucket tool can be especially useful for applying custom fill styles to multiple items. You can build a collection of custom fill styles either off-screen (on the Pasteboard) or in a special, saved, custom-fills-palette, single-frame Flash movie. You can then acquire these fills whenever necessary.

Caution
If you click with the Paint Bucket tool on one of several selected fills, all the selected fills simultaneously change to the new fill. ■

Using the Paint Bucket Gap size option

As shown in Figure 9.3, the Gap size option drop-down offers four settings that control how the Paint Bucket treats gaps when filling. These settings are Don't Close Gaps, Close Small Gaps, Close Medium Gaps, and Close Large Gaps. These tolerance settings enable Flash to fill an outline if the endpoints of the outline aren't completely joined, leaving an open shape. If the gaps are too large, you may have to close them manually with another drawing tool. Figure 9.5 illustrates how the Gap size option settings affect the Paint Bucket fill behavior.

Tip

The level of zoom changes the apparent size of gaps. Although the actual size of gaps is unaffected by zoom, the Paint Bucket's interpretation of the gap is dependent upon the current Zoom setting. When zoomed in very close, the Paint Bucket tool finds it harder to close gaps; when zoomed out, the Paint Bucket tool finds it easier to close gaps. ∎

FIGURE 9.5

Paint Bucket fill applied with various Gap size settings: (A) original oval outline with decreasing gap sizes, left to right, with no fill; (B) gray fill applied with Don't Close Gaps; (C) gray fill applied with Close Small Gaps; (D) gray fill applied with Close Medium Gaps; (E) gray fill applied with Close Large Gaps

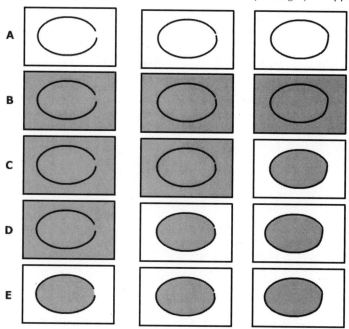

Using the Paint Bucket Lock Fill option

The Paint Bucket's Lock Fill option is the same as the Brush Lock Fill option — it controls how Flash handles areas filled with gradient color or bitmaps. When this button is turned on, all areas (or shapes) painted with the same gradient or bitmap appear to be part of a single, continuous, filled shape. The Lock Fill option locks the angle, size, and point of origin of the current fill to remain constant throughout any number of selected shapes. Modifications made to the fill in one of the shapes are applied to the other shapes filled by using the same Lock Fill option.

Cross-Reference

Working with gradient colors is discussed in Chapter 7, "Applying Color." ■

To demonstrate the distinction between fills applied with or without the Lock Fill option, I created five shapes and filled them with a bitmap with Lock Fill off. As shown in Figure 9.6, on the left, the image was rendered individually from one shape to the next. On the right, those same shapes were filled with the same bitmap, but with Lock Fill on. Note how the image is now continuous from one shape to the next. Bitmap fills are automatically tiled to fill a shape, so the bitmap fill on the right was also scaled with the Gradient Transform tool to make it easier to see the continuation of the image between the various shapes.

FIGURE 9.6

Fill applied with Lock Fill turned off (left), compared with fill applied with Lock Fill turned on and then scaled by using the Gradient Transform tool (right)

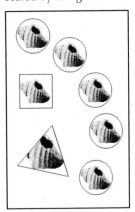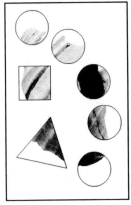

Note

When you use the Eyedropper tool to pick up a fill or gradient from the scene, the Lock Fill button is automatically toggled on. ■

Caution

If the shapes you are filling with the Paint Bucket tool were created with the Object Drawing option turned on or drawn with one of the Shape Primitive tools, you can use the Lock Fill option to get a fill that continues from one shape to the next, but when you try to adjust the fill with the Gradient Transform tool, you will find that the fills are transformed individually instead of as a group. The workaround for this glitch is to use raw shapes when you apply a locked fill that you plan to transform. If you started with drawing objects or shape primitives, use the Break Apart command before you try to use the Gradient Transform tool to adjust a continuous fill on multiple shapes. ■

Transforming Gradients and Bitmap Fills

You can find the Gradient Transform tool (F) in a drop-down within the same tile on the toolbar as the Free Transform tool (Q). Gradient Transform is used only to modify bitmap or gradient fills and does not apply to simple color fills. The Gradient Transform tool does many of the same things the Free Transform tool does, but it modifies only the *fill* of a shape without changing the stroke or outline appearance at all. This type of adjustment is a lot like shifting, rotating, or scaling a larger piece of material behind a frame so that a different portion is visible.

The Gradient Transform tool has only one option in the Tools panel, but, as with the Eyedropper tool, it does apply differently depending on the type of fill selected. To use the Gradient Transform tool, select it in the Tools panel, and then simply click an existing gradient or bitmap fill. A set of three or four adjustment handles appears, depending on the type of fill. The following three transformations can be performed on a gradient or bitmap fill: adjusting the fill's center point, rotating the fill, and scaling the fill. The extra set of adjustment handles appearing on bitmap fills enables them to be skewed. The Magnet option in the Tools panel toggles on Snapping behavior, making it easier to constrain transformations to even adjustment increments. Figure 9.7 illustrates the various adjustment handles on three types of fills.

FIGURE 9.7

The Gradient Transform tool applied to a radial gradient (A), a linear gradient (B), a tiled bitmap fill (C), and a scaled bitmap fill (D). Each handle type has an icon to indicate its function.

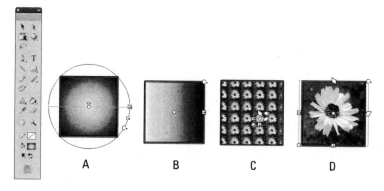

The position of these handles may shift if a fill (or bitmap fill) has been variously copied, rotated, or pasted in any number of ways. The fundamental rules are as follows:

- The round center handle moves the center point.
- The extra center pointer on radial gradients moves the highlight.
- The round corner handle with the short arrow rotates.
- The square edge handles scale either vertically or horizontally.
- The round corner handle with a long arrow scales symmetrically.
- The diamond-shaped edge handles on bitmap fills skew either vertically or horizontally.

Tip

To see all the handles when transforming a large element or working with an item close to the edge of the Stage, choose View ⇨ Pasteboard from the application menu or use the shortcut keys Shift+Ctrl+W/Shift+⌘+W. ■

Adjusting the center point with the Gradient Transform tool

If the fill is not aligned in the shape as you would like it to be, you can easily move the center point to adjust how the shape outline frames the fill. To adjust the center point, follow these steps:

1. **Deselect the fill if it has been previously selected.**
2. **Choose the Gradient Transform tool from the Tools panel.**
3. **Click the fill.**
4. **Bring the cursor to the small circular handle at the center of the fill until it changes to a four-arrow cursor, pointing left, right, up, and down, like a compass, indicating that this handle can now be used to move the center point in any direction.**
5. **Drag the center circular handle in any direction you want to move the center of the fill.**

Figure 9.8 shows a radial gradient (left) repositioned with the Gradient Transform tool (right).

Adjusting the center point of a gradient fill with the Gradient Transform tool

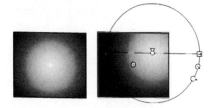

The Gradient Transform option enables you to adjust the highlight of a radial gradient without moving the center point of the fill. As shown in Figure 9.9, you can drag the extra pointer above the center point circle to move the highlight of the gradient along the horizontal axis. If you want to move the highlight along a vertical axis, use the rotate handle to change the orientation of the fill.

The Gradient Transform handle enables you to adjust the highlight of a radial gradient without moving the center point of the fill.

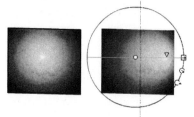

Tip

The Paint Bucket tool is also a handy way to set the highlight point of a gradient fill. Select the gradient that you want to apply, and then click inside the shape where you want the highlight to be. You can keep clicking in different areas of the shape with the Paint Bucket to move the highlight around until you like it. ■

Rotating a fill with the Gradient Transform tool

To rotate a gradient or bitmap fill, find the small circular handle that's at the corner of the fill. (In a radial gradient, choose the lower circular handle.) This circular handle is used for rotating a fill around the center point. Simply click the circular handle with the Rotate cursor and drag clockwise or counterclockwise to rotate the fill. Figure 9.10 shows a bitmap fill (left) as it appears when rotated clockwise (right).

Tip

Activate the Snap to Objects toggle in the Tools panel if you want to use snapping behaviors to help guide rotating or scaling of a fill. (Turn behaviors on or off in the application menu under View ➪ Snapping.) ■

Rotating a bitmap fill with the Gradient Transform tool

Adjusting scale with the Gradient Transform tool

To resize a bitmap fill symmetrically (to maintain the aspect ratio), find the round corner handle with an arrow icon, which is usually located at the lower-left corner of the fill. On rollover, the diagonal arrow icon appears, indicating the direction(s) in which the handle resizes the fill. Click and drag to scale the fill symmetrically. On radial gradients, you use the round-corner handle with the longer arrow icon to scale with the gradient aspect ratio constrained. Linear gradients have only one handle for scaling, and this handle always scales in the direction of the gradient banding.

To resize a fill asymmetrically, find a small square handle on either a vertical or a horizontal edge, depending on whether you want to affect the width or height of the fill. On rollover, arrows appear perpendicular to the edge of the shape, indicating the direction in which this handle resizes the fill. Click and drag a handle to reshape the fill.

Figure 9.11 shows the three fill types with their respective scale options. Linear gradient fills (left) can be scaled only in the direction of the gradient banding, but they can be rotated to scale vertically (lower) rather than horizontally (upper). Radial gradient fills (center) can be expanded symmetrically (upper) with the circular handle, or asymmetrically (lower) with the square handle. As with linear gradients, they can be rotated to scale vertically rather than horizontally. Bitmap fills (right) can be scaled by the corner handle to maintain the aspect ratio (upper), or dragged from any side handle to scale asymmetrically (lower).

Caution

Adjusting bitmap fills with the Gradient Transform tool can be tricky business. On tiled fills, the transform handles are often so small and bunched together that they are difficult to see. On full-size bitmaps, the handles are sometimes outside the Stage, and it can be hard to find the handle that you need. It can also be unpredictable where the handles appear when you select a bitmap fill with the Gradient Transform tool — often they are outside the shape where the fill is visible. Our advice is to use this workflow only when you have no other choice. In general, it is a much better idea to decide on the size for a bitmap and create a Web-ready image that you can use without scaling before you import it to Flash. ∎

Note

The right column of Figure 9.11 is a good example of how changes applied to one tile in a bitmap fill are passed to all the other tiles within the shape. ∎

Setting gradient fill overflow styles

As you work with scaled gradient fills, you will quickly notice that your shape is always filled from edge to edge but that the fill area may not appear quite how you'd like it to. In early versions of Flash, you were stuck with the solid color fill around the edges when a gradient was scaled smaller inside of a shape. This default behavior is now part of the Overflow menu in the Color panel that gives you some other options for how a gradient renders when it is scaled down. As shown in Figure 9.12, there are three different overflow styles:

- **Extend**: Extends the colors on the outside edge of the gradient to create a solid fill beyond the edge of the rendered gradient
- **Reflect**: Alternates flipped (reflected) versions of the original gradient until the shape is filled from edge to edge
- **Repeat**: Renders the color pattern of the original gradient repeatedly until the shape is filled from edge to edge

FIGURE 9.11

Scaling fills symmetrically (top) and asymmetrically (bottom)

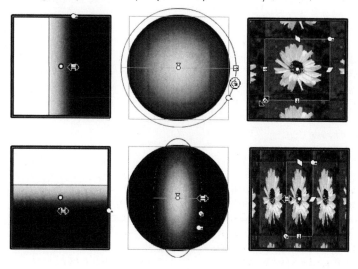

FIGURE 9.12

Different overflow styles applied to a linear gradient (top right) and a radial gradient (bottom right) using the Overflow menu in the Color panel (left). Overflow styles applied to the fills from left to right: Extend, Reflect, Repeat

Skewing a bitmap fill with the Gradient Transform tool

To skew a bitmap fill horizontally, click the diamond-shaped handle at the top of the image; arrows appear, parallel to the edge of the fill, indicating the directions in which this handle skews the fill. Drag to skew the image in either direction. Figure 9.13 shows a bitmap skewed horizontally (left) and vertically (right). Note that the skew procedure is still active after it has been applied, meaning that the skew may be further modified — this behavior is common to all functions of the Gradient Transform tool.

FIGURE 9.13

Skewing a bitmap fill with the Gradient Transform tool

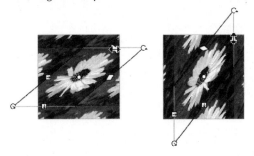

Note

Gradient fills cannot be skewed; they can be scaled only on the horizontal or vertical axis. ■

Tip

If you get carried away with the Gradient Transform tool and you want to get back to the original fill position and size, double-click the center icon of the shape to reset all transformations. ■

Gradient Transform Used for Lighting Effects

You apply the Gradient Transform tool most often to get a patterned fill or a gradient aligned and sized within its outline shape. A simple way of adding more depth to shapes is to modify gradient fills so that they appear to reflect light from one consistent source. You can choose to emulate a soft light for a more even illumination, or to emulate a hard, focused light that emphasizes dramatic shadows. As you create a composition on the Stage, you can use the Gradient Transform tool to modify individual elements so that they appear to share a common light source. Figure 9.14 illustrates how a default radial gradient (left) can be modified to emulate a soft (center) or hard (right) illumination.

FIGURE 9.14

Applying Gradient Transform to create different illumination effects

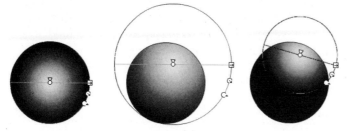

To show how these lighting effects can be applied to create the illusion of 3-D, I created a little scene by using only radial fills that were modified with the Gradient Transform tool. Figure 9.15 shows the radial gradients as they appeared when I drew them with the default settings (left) and how the scene appeared after I modified the gradients with Gradient Transform and some basic shape scaling as I describe later in this chapter.

On the CD-ROM

If you want to deconstruct this example, I have included the file on the CD-ROM with both the unmodified and the final transformed shapes. You will find the file named SphereLighting.fla in the ch09 folder of the CD-ROM. ■

FIGURE 9.15

The Fill Transform tool used to modify default radial gradient fills (left) to create the illusion of 3-D lighting effects (right)

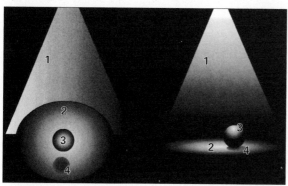

Applying Modify Shape Menu Commands

Three specialized commands found in the application menu (under Modify ➪ Shape) provide modification options that you cannot achieve with any other tools in Flash.

Cross-Reference

I discuss the Selection tool, Subselection tool, and the Smooth, Straighten, and Optimize commands (also found in the Modify Shape menu), in Chapter 5, "Drawing in Flash." ■

Convert Lines to Fills

Lines to Fills does exactly what its name implies: It converts lines defined by single points into shapes defined by an outline of editable points. To apply the Lines to Fills command, simply select any lines that you want to convert before choosing Modify ➪ Shape ➪ Convert Lines to Fills. After a line has been converted in this way, you can edit it like any other filled shape, including adding bitmap or gradient fills or applying the Selection or Subselection tools to adjust the corners and curves of the outlined shape.

Tip

You can render strokes and lines by using gradients without converting them into fills. ■

Creating scalable artwork

The Lines to Fills command is especially important because it provides the one solution for maintaining line-to-fill ratios when scaling raw graphics that would require lines to appear at smaller than 1 point size. Fills do not have the same display limitation as lines, and they maintain visual consistency as they are scaled larger or smaller. In Figure 9.16, the image on the left was drawn with the Pencil tool to make lines around the eyes and on the whiskers of the cat cartoon. When it was scaled, the lines were not visually consistent with the fills. The image on the right was modified by using the Lines to Fills command before scaling it down to 25 percent size. In this case, the ratio between the outlines around the eyes and the whiskers was consistent with the other filled shapes in the cartoon.

Tip

If you convert your raw graphic into a symbol before you scale it, the ratio of lines to fills also stays consistent. ■

Cross-Reference

The stroke scale settings in the Properties panel are discussed in Chapter 5, "Drawing in Flash." These settings are helpful for maintaining a specific stroke weight on graphics that will be scaled horizontally or vertically, but they do not solve the display issue discussed here (and shown in Figure 9.16), when scaled lines need to appear at less than 1 point. ■

FIGURE 9.16

Use the Lines to Fills command to ensure consistency when scaling raw graphics.

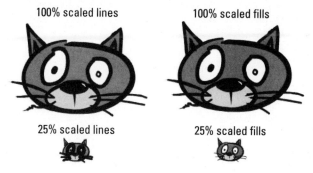

100% scaled lines   100% scaled fills

25% scaled lines   25% scaled fills

Note

Remember that in Flash, the smallest line size that can be displayed is 1 point. Lines with a height of less than 1 point all appear to be the same size on-screen when viewed at 100 percent scale. The difference in size is visible only when the view is scaled larger (zoomed in). However, the lines print correctly on a high-resolution printer and are visible in the published .swf if the content is zoomed. ■

Expand Fill

The Expand Fill command has two options you can use to size fills up or down evenly on all sides of a shape. To apply the command, select the fill(s) that you want to modify, and then choose Modify ⇨ Shape ⇨ Expand Fill. The Expand Fills dialog box appears, where you can choose to expand or inset (shrink) the fill by a specific pixel value. Keep in mind that this command applies differently than a normal scale modification. The fill expands or shrinks from all sides evenly, so an extreme modification can cause a shape to bloat to the extent that unfilled areas are obscured, or conversely it can cause a shape to shrink to the point that some of the areas are no longer visible. When applied moderately, the Expand Fill command can be very helpful for adjusting multiple filled shapes consistently, without scaling lines in the same area of the artwork.

Caution

You cannot apply the Expand Fill command to drawing objects with strokes unless you first break them apart or open them in Edit mode so that you can select the fill without also selecting the stroke. ■

Figure 9.17 includes a rectangle, a cartoon cat, and a sketch of some grapes. The original shapes are shown on the left, the expanded fills in the center, and the inset fills on the right. As you can see, expanding fills often obscures the strokes surrounding a shape, whereas choosing to inset a fill leaves space between the fill and any surrounding stroke.

FIGURE 9.17

Modifying an original shape (A) with the Expand Fill command, using the Expand option (B) or the Inset option (C), respectively, bloats or shrinks a fill by a specified pixel amount.

Note

Each of the fills in the graphics shown in Figure 9.17 was added by clicking or Shift+clicking (rather than dragging out a selection marquee) to avoid including any strokes in the final selection that were modified with the Expand Fill command. ■

You can also use the Expand Fill command to create custom text forms. Figure 9.18 shows how the original text shape (left) can be modified by using either the Expand or Inset option. To create bloated balloon-like text (center), or shrunken, eroded text (right), you first have to apply the Modify⇨Break Apart command (Ctrl+B/⌘+B) twice to reduce the text to simple filled shapes. By selecting all the letter shapes before applying the Expand Fill command, you can modify the whole word at the same time.

FIGURE 9.18

Text broken apart into letter shapes (A) can be expanded (B) or inset (C) to create custom text effects.

Expand **Expand** Expand
A   B   C

Soften Fill Edges

The Soften Fill Edges command was the closest thing to a static blur available before Flash 8. Fortunately, Flash 8 and newer versions support a much more sophisticated Blur filter that renders smoother softened edges and enables you to change the color of the item even after the blur is applied. The only advantages that the Soften Fill Edges command has over the Blur filter are that you can use it to modify raw shapes or drawing objects and choose whether to render it inside or outside the item's original fill boundary. This command, as with the Expand Fill command, can be applied only to fills and gives you the option to expand or inset the shape by a specific number of pixels.

Caution

Flash enables you to select a line and choose the Soften Edges command from the Modify ➪ Shape menu. After you apply the command, however, the line just disappears from the Stage — surprise! If you make this mistake, you can recover your line by immediately choosing Edit ➪ Undo (Ctrl+Z/⌘+Z). ■

The blurry effect of Soften Fill Edges is created by a series of banded fills around the original fill that decrease in opacity toward the outermost band. You can control the number and width of these bands by entering values in the Soften Fill Edges dialog box (shown in Figure 9.19) to create a variety of effects, from a very subtle blurred effect to a dramatic stepped appearance around the edges of the fill.

FIGURE 9.19

The Soften Fill Edges dialog box with settings for controlling the edge effect

The Soften Fill Edges dialog box controls the following features of the fill modification:

- **Distance:** Defines the number of pixels the original shape expands or shrinks
- **Number of steps:** Sets the number of bands that appear around the outside edge of the fill
- **Expand or Inset:** Controls whether the bands are added to the outside edge of the fill (expand) or stacked on the inside edge of the shape (inset)

Figure 9.20 shows how the original fill (left) appears after Soften Fill Edges is applied with the Expand option (center), or with the Inset option (right).

FIGURE 9.20

Applying Soften Fill Edges with the Expand option and with the Inset option

The width of the individual bands equals the total number of pixels set in Distance divided by the Number of steps. When the edge of the shape is magnified, the individual bands can clearly be seen. Figure 9.21 compares a series of eight bands, each 1 pixel wide, created by using a Distance setting of 8 and a Number of steps setting of 8, compared with the smooth softened edge that results from applying a Blur filter with an X and Y setting of 8.

A magnified view of the banded edge of a fill created by applying Soften Fill Edges (left) compared to the smooth softened edge created by applying the Flash Blur filter (right)

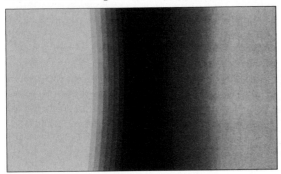

As with the Expand Fill command, Soften Fill Edges can create interesting text effects when applied to broken-apart letter shapes. Figure 9.22 shows an effect created by combining the original white text with a "shadow" made by applying the Soften Fill Edges command to a broken-apart copy of the text that was filled with dark gray.

Tip

You can achieve an effect similar to the shadow shown in Figure 9.22 by applying the Glow filter to an editable text field and selecting the knockout option. I cover the various Flash filters in Chapter 12, "Applying Filters, Blends, Guides, and Masks." ■

A glow effect created by layering the original text over a copy that was broken apart, filled with dark gray, and modified by using Soften Fill Edges

Free Transform Commands and Options

The commands you have seen so far in this chapter are generally used for localized modification of lines or fills. In this section, I introduce some commands that are applied to create more dramatic change of whole items or even groups of items.

You can apply the basic transform commands to any element in the Flash authoring environment, but it is important to know that any transformations applied to symbols, groups, drawing objects, or text blocks are saved in the Info panel even if they are deselected and then reselected later. This enables you to easily revert these items to their original appearance. The transform settings for primitive shapes, on the other hand, are reset to the default values in the Info panel as soon as they are deselected. This means that while a primitive shape is actively being modified, you can revert to the original appearance, but as soon as you apply a change and deselect the shape, its modified appearance will be considered original the next time you select it. As shown in Figure 9.23, there are various ways to access the transform commands available in Flash.

FIGURE 9.23

The various ways to access transform commands in Flash — the Transform panel (lower left), the Modify Transform submenu (center), and the Free Transform tool (right)

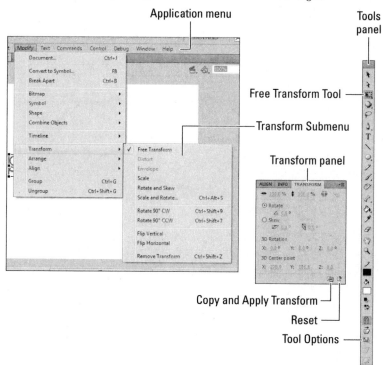

The Transform panel

The Transform panel (Ctrl+T/⌘+T) includes value fields for horizontal and vertical scale percentages, degrees of rotation, and degrees of vertical and horizontal skew. You can use these fields for visual reference or as a way to enter precise transform values. The Transform panel also includes two important buttons:

- The Copy and Apply Transform button is used to duplicate the selected item with all transformations included. When you select this button, you may not notice that anything has happened to your selected item — this is because Flash places the duplicate exactly on top of the original. To see both the original and the duplicate, drag the duplicate to a new position in the Document window.

- The Reset button reverts a transformed symbol, group, or text field to its original appearance and returns all values in the Transform panel to the default settings. You can also achieve this by choosing Modify ➪ Transform ➪ Remove Transform. If you want to remove only the most recently applied modification, use Edit ➪ Undo (Ctrl+Z /⌘+Z).

The Modify Transform menu

The commands found in the application menu under Modify ➪ Transform enable you to choose specific combinations of transform options as well as a couple of "shortcuts" for commonly needed modifications. Special note should be taken of the two commands that are unique to the application menu:

- **Rotate 90 degrees CW or Rotate 90 degrees CCW:** Used to rotate any selected items by a half-turn in the chosen direction (clockwise or counterclockwise) around the central axis point of the selection.

Tip

You can also use shortcut keys to rotate any selected item in 90-degree increments. To rotate an item 90 degrees clockwise, use Shift+Ctrl+9/Shift+⌘+9. To rotate an item 90 degrees counterclockwise, use Shift+Ctrl+7/Shift+⌘+7. ■

- **Flip Vertical or Flip Horizontal:** Used to place the item in a mirrored position either on the vertical axis (calendar flip) or the horizontal axis (book flip).

The Free Transform tool

The Free Transform tool (Q), available directly from the Tools panel, enables you to apply transform commands dynamically with various arrow icons. These icons appear as you position the pointer over the control points or handles of the selected item. You can also invoke various transform states from the contextual menu. Although the position of these arrow icons can vary with the position of the pointer, they provide a consistent indication of what transformation will be applied from the closest available handle. To finish any transformation, simply deselect the item by clicking outside of the current selection area.

- **Move arrow:** This familiar arrow indicates that all currently selected items can be dragged together to a new location in the Document window.

- **Axis point or transformation point:** By default, this circle marks the center of shapes as the axis for most transformations or animation. By dragging the point to a different location, you can define a new axis or transformation point for modifications applied to the item. To return the axis point to its default location, double-click the axis point icon.

- **Skew arrow:** This arrow is generally available on any side of an item between transformation points. By clicking and dragging the outline, you can skew the shape in either direction indicated by the arrows.

- **Rotate arrow:** This arrow is generally available near any corner of an item. By clicking and dragging, you can rotate the item clockwise or counterclockwise around the transform axis. Note that if you position the arrow directly over the closest corner handle, the Rotate arrow is usually replaced with the Scale Corner arrow. To rotate around the opposite corner point without moving the axis point, press the Alt (Option) key while dragging. To constrain rotation to 45-degree increments, press Shift while dragging.

- **Scale Side arrow:** This arrow is available from any handle on the side of an item. Clicking and dragging scales the item larger or smaller, in one direction only, relative to the transform axis.

- **Scale Corner arrow:** This arrow appears only on the corner handles of an item and is used to evenly scale the item larger or smaller, in all directions from the transform axis. To constrain the aspect ratio of the shape, press Shift while dragging.

Transforming shapes, symbols, text, and groups

Figure 9.24 shows how a symbol (or drawing object) and a shape appear differently after they have been modified, deselected, and then reselected with the Free Transform tool. The symbol (left) displays transform handles that are aligned with the originally modified item, and the values of the transformation settings are preserved in the Transform panel. The shape (right), however, displays transform handles aligned to default values unrelated to the original modifications, and the values in the Transform panel are reset to their defaults.

FIGURE 9.24

The Free Transform handles and Transform panel settings that appear for a symbol or drawing object (left) and for a simple shape (right) that have been reselected after an initial modification

Free Transform limit options

The first two options in the Tools panel for the Free Transform tool (shown in Figure 9.23) are toggles to limit the modifications that can be applied to a selected item. It can sometimes be easier to use the Free Transform tool with more specific behavior. When the Rotate and Skew button or the Scale button is toggled on, all other modifications are excluded.

The Rotate and Skew toggle protects the selected item from being scaled accidentally while you're rotating or skewing it. This Tools panel option is equivalent to choosing Modify ➪ Transform ➪ Rotate and Skew from the application menu.

The Scale toggle protects the selected item from all other transformations while it is being sized larger or smaller. This Tools panel option is equivalent to choosing Modify ➪ Transform ➪ Scale from the application menu.

Free Transform special shape options

The last two options in the Tools panel for the Free Transform tool — Distort and Envelope — are not available for symbols, groups, or text fields. However, when you're transforming drawing objects or primitive shapes, you can use these two options to create complex modifications not easily achieved with other Flash tools.

Note
Remember that you can access the raw shapes in a group or symbol by entering Edit mode. You can also convert text fields into shapes by applying the Break Apart command (twice). ■

Distort works by widening or narrowing the sides of the item, or stretching out the corners. This transform option does not bend or warp the shape; it allows sides of the shape to be scaled individually. To apply Distort, first select a shape with the Free Transform tool in the Tools panel, and turn on the Distort toggle in the Options area of the Tools panel. You can then click and drag handles on the sides or corners of the item to stretch or compress individual sides. This is equivalent to selecting a shape with the Selection tool and choosing Modify ➪ Transform ➪ Distort from the application menu or selecting Distort from the contextual menu.

Tip
You can also apply the Distort option to a shape that has been selected with the Free Transform tool by pressing Control (⌘) while dragging a side or corner handle. To taper a shape or move two adjoining corner points an equal distance simultaneously, press Shift while dragging any corner handle with the Free Transform tool. ■

Figure 9.25 shows an original shape being modified with the Distort option (left), and the final shape with distort handles, as they appear when the shape is reselected (right).

The Envelope option enables you to work with control points and handles much the same way you would when editing lines or shapes with the Subselection tool. The powerful difference is that the Envelope can wrap around the outside of multiple items so that the control points and handles curve, scale, stretch, or warp all the lines and shapes contained within the Envelope selection.

FIGURE 9.25

Free Transform applied to a shape, using the Distort option

To apply the Envelope, first select a shape or multiple shapes with the Free Transform tool and then toggle on the Envelope option in the Tools panel. The Envelope offers a series of control points and tangent handles. The square points are used to scale and skew the shape(s), whereas the round points are actually handles used to control the curve and warp of the shape(s). You can also access the Envelope option by selecting the shapes you want to transform and choosing Modify ⇨ Transform ⇨ Envelope from the application menu, or by selecting Envelope from the contextual menu.

Figure 9.26 shows an original shape being modified with the Envelope option (left), and the final shape with Envelope handles, as they appear when the shape is reselected (right).

FIGURE 9.26

Free Transform applied to a shape, using the Envelope option

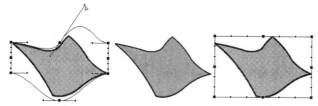

Manipulating Symbols in 3D Space

You can create faux-3D effects by skewing and scaling graphics with the Free Transform tool (as described in the previous section); however, this task has been made a whole lot easier by the new 3D tools available in Flash CS5. Instead of using your math and geometry skills to approximate perspective, you can simply click and drag intuitive handles and Flash applies distortion to your graphics to give them the appearance of existing in 3D space.

The 3D Rotation tool and the 3D Translation tool are both found in the Tools panel just below the Free Transform tool. Settings for these tools can be accessed in the Transform panel when the 3D tools are active or a 3D symbol is selected in your Document window. If you haven't worked with 3D tools before, the various options can be a little disorienting at first, but with a little trial and error you will soon get your bearings.

Note

To use the 3D tools in Flash, the Publish settings of your FLA file must be set to Flash Player 10 and ActionScript 3.0. All elements must be converted into Movie Clip instances to apply 3D Rotation or Translation. ∎

To help you get started, I have included definitions for some of the terms you will come across when working with Flash symbols in 3D space:

- **x-axis:** Sets the position of the symbol in relation to the Stage, tracked from left to right. Rotating (transforming) a symbol around the x-axis is like flipping a Rolodex. Moving (translating) an object along the x-axis makes it appear closer to the left or right side of the Stage.

- **y-axis:** Sets the position of the symbol in relation to the Stage, tracked from top to bottom. Rotating a symbol around the y-axis is like turning a revolving door. Moving an object along the y-axis makes it appear closer to the top or bottom of the Stage.

- **z-axis:** Sets the position of the symbol in relation to the depth of the space. This is the third axis that was added to Flash CS5 to support transformation and rotation of symbols for (faux) 3D. Rotating an object around the z-axis is like spinning a bicycle tire or moving the hands of a clock, although the center point can be adjusted so it is not always in the middle of the symbol. Moving an object along the z-axis makes it appear larger (closer) or smaller (farther away).

- **3D Translation:** Changing the location of a symbol in 3D space is called a translation. The 3D Translation tool provides handles for moving a symbol along the x, y, and z-axis individually.

- **3D Transformation:** Rotating an object in 3D space is called a transformation. The 3D Rotation tool provides handles for rotating a symbol along the x, y, and z-axis individually or along the x and y-axis at the same time — for "free rotation."

- **3D Center point:** By default, the 3D center point is usually the center point of the symbol, but by moving the 3D center point you can change the way 3D transformations (rotations) affect the symbol, in the same way that changing the center point for scaling or rotating an object in 2D space modifies the outcome of any changes.

- **Global 3D space:** This is the default setting for the 3D tools and means that any changes to location or rotation of a symbol are made in relation to the main Stage drawing area.

- **Local 3D space:** This is an alternative setting for the 3D tools (a toggle button at the bottom of the Tools panel appears when 3D tools are active), and it restricts changes to location or rotation of nested symbols to the drawing space of the container symbol.

Cross-Reference

3D rotations and translations can be animated to create cool effects, but I defer discussion of tweened 3D to Chapter 10, "Timeline Animation and the Motion Editor." ∎

Controlling the camera view: Perspective and vanishing point

There is only one camera view in the authoring environment for your Flash movie. The camera view consists of a perspective angle and a vanishing point: These global settings are available in the 3D Position and View section of the Properties panel when a symbol with 3-D translation or rotation is selected on the Stage. Changing the settings affects all 3-D symbols in your Flash movie but does not affect other elements.

Note

If you are controlling 3D Movie Clips with ActionScript rather than using the 3D tools in the authoring environment, you can create multiple vanishing points and unique camera views for each Movie Clip. ■

The perspective angle sets the viewing "lens" for all of your 3D elements. The range of settings for perspective angle is from 1 degree to 180 degrees. The default perspective angle is 55 degrees to approximate a standard camera lens view. Think of the perspective angle setting as the zoom factor of your viewing lens. Smaller numbers move the view farther away and make 3D transformations less dramatic — they flatten the view. Larger numbers move the view closer and make 3D transformations more extreme — they emphasize any changes in the angle or rotation of an element. Figure 9.27 shows the same 3D Movie Clip (a rectangle with a 45-degree y-axis rotation), viewed with three different perspective angle settings.

FIGURE 9.27

Increasing the perspective angle setting "zooms" the view closer, making 3D transformations look more extreme. The same Movie Clip viewed with three different perspective angle settings (from L-R): 10 degrees, 50 degrees (the default setting), 120 degrees.

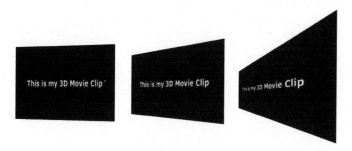

Another way to understand this feature is to compare it to our normal perception of objects in real space. If you are looking at a sculpture from a distance of 30 feet and you walk 10 steps to the left or right, your view does not change very much — you still see more or less the same side of the sculpture. However, if you are standing closer to a sculpture, say, 3 feet away, and you walk the same 10 steps to the right or left, your view changes dramatically.

Tip
If you change the Stage size of your Flash document, the perspective angle changes automatically to preserve the appearance of existing 3-D symbols. You can turn this behavior off in the Document Properties dialog box. ■

The Vanishing point setting determines the endpoint of the z-axis and controls the direction that 3-D symbols travel if they are moved along their z-axis. Imagine it as an invisible anchor point in deep space that has a magnetic pull that makes all of your 3-D translations extend in its direction. In real space, the vanishing point is that place in your field of vision where parallel lines seem to come together. If you were looking down a road on a perfectly flat plain, it would be the spot where the road appeared narrower and narrower until finally it ended in a dot on the horizon — that dot is the location of the vanishing point.

By default, the vanishing point is set in the center of the Stage, but you can modify the setting at any time to a different x, y location — on or off the Stage. To view or set the vanishing point in the Properties panel, a 3-D symbol must be selected on the Stage. Figure 9.28 illustrates the result of a 45-degree x-axis rotation with vanishing points in different locations. Figure 9.29 illustrates how the vanishing point affects the direction that a 3-D symbol travels as it moves along the z-axis.

FIGURE 9.28
The location of the vanishing point determines the endpoint for the z-axis and the direction that objects recede into space. The same Movie Clip with a 3-D rotation viewed with three different vanishing point locations (from L-R): top-left corner of the Stage, center of the Stage (the default setting), and bottom right corner of the Stage.

Transforming symbols with the 3D Rotation tool

The 3D Rotation tool enables you to spin objects around the x, y, or z-axis and creates the illusion of depth by skewing and scaling your graphics based on the degree of rotation and the vanishing point and perspective angle settings. Figure 9.30 shows a simple rectangle with a drop shadow added (top) and the result of a 45-degree rotation applied along the x, y, and z-axis, respectively.

FIGURE 9.29

The location of the vanishing point determines the direction that 3-D objects travel when they move along the z-axis. The original symbol (top left) looks smaller but remains centered when a 200-pixel translation along the z-axis is applied with the vanishing point in the middle of the Stage (top right). The same translation along the z-axis has a different result when the vanishing point is located in the top-left corner of the Stage (bottom left) or in the bottom-right corner of the Stage (bottom right).

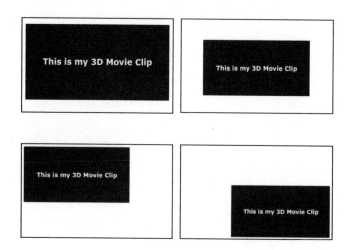

To apply the 3D Rotation tool (W), activate it in the Tools panel, then select a symbol on the Stage. When you select a symbol with the 3D Rotation tool, a target overlay (shown in Figure 9.30) appears, guiding you in moving the symbol in 3-D space. The red vertical crosshair enables x-axis rotation, the green horizontal crosshair enables y-axis rotation, the inner blue circle enables z-axis transformation, and the outer orange circle enables free transformation (around the x- and z-axis at the same time). To rotate an object, click and drag from the guide that represents the axis you want to use — dragging clockwise adds a positive transformation, and dragging counterclockwise adds a negative transformation. An object can be rotated around any axis from 0 degrees to 360 degrees in a positive or negative direction. When you release the mouse, you will notice that the 3D Position in the Properties panel updates, and if you have the Transform panel open (Window ⇨ Transform), you can see the exact degree of rotation in the 3D Position and View section of the panel.

Note

If you rotate an object more than 180 degrees, Flash automatically updates the values in the Transform panel to the smallest equivalent value. For example, applying a positive transformation to rotate an object 190 degrees around the x-axis has the same end result as applying a negative transformation to rotate it –170 degrees, so after you release the mouse and apply the transformation, Flash updates the value in the x-axis field of the Transform panel to be –170 degrees rather than 190 degrees. ■

FIGURE 9.30

The same degree of rotation (here 45 degrees) has different visual results when applied to the three different axes of a 3-D Movie Clip (x, y, z). You can rotate an object around just one axis or you can combine two (or even all three) to position a symbol exactly where you want it in the faux 3-D space of the Flash Stage.

Original Rectangle
(symbol)
with
drop shadow

Transform panel
(showing
3D
rotation)

3D rotation on x axis

Result:
rectangle
with 45 degree
y rotation

3D rotation on y axis

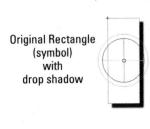

3D rotation on z axis

3D rotation on z axis

Result: rectangle with 45 degree z rotaion

The final result of 3-D rotation is affected by the location of the 3-D center point. The 3-D center point is indicated by the white dot at the center of the 3-D target overlay when the 3D Rotation tool is active and a 3-D symbol is selected. The default location for the 3-D center point is at the center of the selected symbol. Click and drag to reposition the center point (or transformation center point) to another location on your current symbol or even outside of the symbol. Moving the 3-D center point away from the center of the symbol increases the arc of any 3-D rotations — this can be helpful for specific effects but it can also make it more likely that your symbol will move dramatically and end up outside the viewable Stage area. Double-click the 3-D center point dot to reset it to the center of the symbol. If you prefer to set rotation values in the Transform panel, select the symbol you want to modify and use the hot text fields for x-, y-, and z-axis in the 3D Rotation section of the panel. You can also modify the location of the 3-D center point by using the hot text fields for x-, y-, and z-axis in the 3D Center point section of the Transform panel. Figure 9.31 shows the difference in result when the same rectangle is rotated around the y-axis with three different 3-D center point locations.

FIGURE 9.31

The 3-D center point determines the origin point for 3-D transformations. Here you can see how a y-axis rotation applies differently when the 3-D center point is located in the center of the symbol (A), compared to the top-left corner of the symbol (B) or the bottom-right corner (C).

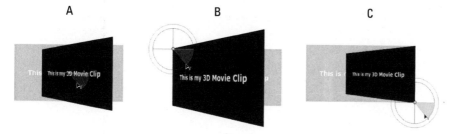

Tip

The Remove Transform button at the bottom-right corner of the Transform panel returns your symbol to its unmodified state with just one click. The Duplicate Selection and Transform button beside the Remove Transform button makes an exact copy of your current selection — but be warned that you won't notice until you move the copy because it will be stacked on top of your original. ∎

Symbols can be rotated in global space (relative to the main Stage drawing area), or if they are nested Movie Clips, they can be rotated in local space (relative to the container Movie Clip's drawing area). The toggle for global or local rotation is at the bottom of the Tools panel when the 3D Rotation tool is selected — the default setting is for global rotation.

Tip

You can temporarily toggle the 3D Rotation tool from global mode to local mode while dragging to move a symbol along any axis by pressing the D key. ■

To rotate multiple objects simultaneously, activate the 3D Rotation tool (W) in the Tools panel, and then select multiple symbols on the Stage (Shift+click or drag a selection field around multiple items). The Rotation guides/target will be centered on the most recently selected item. All the selected symbols rotate around the 3-D center point, which appears in the center of the guide. To change the position of the 3-D center point, you can do any of the following while you have a selection active on the Stage:

- Drag the center point to a new location.
- Shift+double-click any of the current symbols to move the center point to that symbol.
- Double-click the 3-D center point to auto-position it at the center of the current group of selected symbols.
- Change the values for the x, y, z location of the 3-D center point in the Transform panel.

Moving symbols with the 3D Translation tool

The 3D Translation tool enables you to move objects forward and backward in space along the z-axis, left and right in space along the x-axis, and/or up and down in space along the y-axis. For nested Movie Clips, 3D Translations can be global (relative to the main Stage) or local (relative to the parent Movie Clip's drawing area). To apply the 3D Translation tool (G), activate it in the Tools panel, then select a Movie Clip on the Stage. As shown in Figure 9.32, the 3D Translation tool consists of two arrow guides for moving along the x- and y-axis and a center blue dot for moving along the z-axis. Click the head of the red horizontal arrow and drag your object left or right along the x-axis. Click the head of the green vertical arrow and drag your object up or down along the y-axis. Click the blue dot and drag your object forward or back along the z-axis. To reposition the guides for the 3D Translation tool, press and hold Alt/Option and then click and drag the blue dot to a new location. Double-clicking the center blue dot auto-positions the guides back at the center of your symbol.

Changes to the location of your 3-D symbol updates the x, y, and z values in the Position and View section of the Properties panel. These values are also hot text fields, so you can position your 3-D symbol by changing the values directly in the Properties panel. Moving an object along the z-axis changes its apparent size relative to the Stage. The apparent width and height also appear in the 3D Position and View section of the Properties panel, but these are read-only values, unlike the original width and height values in the Position and Size section of the Properties panel, which are editable hot text fields. You can also move multiple items simultaneously with the 3D Translation tool; Refer to the instructions for the 3D Rotation tool in the previous section.

FIGURE 9.32

The 3D Translation tool provides controls for moving symbols along the x-, y-, and z-axis.

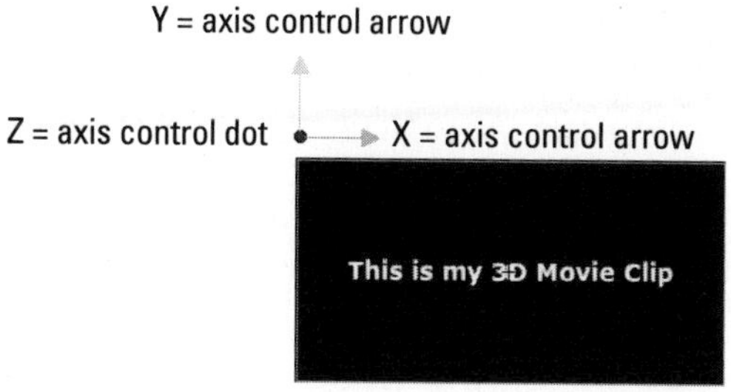

Y = axis control arrow

Z = axis control dot   •——→ X = axis control arrow

This is my 3D Movie Clip

Modifying Item Types

In previous chapters, I have focused on the features of the timeline and how your Flash projects are ordered in time from left to right. Now you are going to look at the arrangement of items from the front to the back of the Stage, or the stacking order of elements in Flash. In this section, I explain how multiple items can be moved together, and how the Union, Break apart, and Trace bitmap commands are applied to change item types.

Stacking order

Within a single layer, Flash stacks items of the same type in the same order they are placed or created, with the most recent item on top, subject to the *kind* of item. The rules that control the stacking order of various kinds of items are simple:

- Within a layer, ungrouped raw shapes or lines are always at the *bottom* level, with the most recently drawn shape or line at the top of that layer's stack. Furthermore, unless you take precautions, drawn items either compound with, or cut into, the drawing beneath them.

- Groups, drawing objects, and symbols (including bitmaps) stack above lines and shapes in the *overlay* level. To change the stacking order of several items, it's often advisable to group them first, as I describe in the next section of this chapter.

To change the stacking order within a layer, first select the item that you want to move. Then, do one of the following:

- **To move the item to the top of the stacking order,** choose Modify ⇨ Arrange ⇨ Bring to Front (Alt+Shift+↑/Option+Shift+↑).

- **To move an item to the bottom of the stacking order,** choose Modify ⇨ Arrange ⇨ Send to Back (Alt+Shift+↓/Option+Shift+↓).

- **To move the item up one position in the stacking order,** choose Modify ⇨ Arrange ⇨ Bring Forward (Ctrl+↑/⌘+↑).

- **To move the item down one position in the stacking order,** choose Modify ⇨ Arrange ⇨ Send Backward (Ctrl+↓/⌘+↓).

Remember the stacking-order rules: You won't be able to bring an ungrouped drawing above a group or symbol. If you need that drawing on top, group it and then move it, or place it on a separate layer.

Cross-Reference
I detail the Align panel (Ctrl+K/⌘+K) used to distribute items in a layout in relation to each other or to the Stage in Chapter 5, "Drawing in Flash." ∎

To stack an item in a lower layer above an item in a higher layer, you simply change the order of the layer among the other layers: First, activate the layer, and then drag the Layer bar to the desired position in the layer stack of the timeline.

Tip
Regardless of the number of layers in a Flash project (.fla), neither the file size nor the performance of the final .swf file is adversely affected because Flash flattens layers upon export. ∎

Grouping

As discussed in Chapter 5, grouping shapes or lines makes them easier to handle. Instead of manipulating a single item, group several items to work with them as a single unit. Grouping also prevents shapes from being merged with or cropped by other shapes. In addition, it's easier to control the stacking order of groups than it is to control ungrouped drawings. Here's how to create groups:

1. **Use Shift+click to select multiple items or drag a selection box around everything that you want to group.** This can include any combination of items: shapes, lines, and symbols — even other groups.

2. **Choose Modify ⇨ Group (Ctrl+G/⌘+G).** The selected elements are now grouped.

3. **To ungroup everything, select the group and then use Modify ⇨ Ungroup (Ctrl+Shift+G/⌘+Shift+G).** Ungrouping only separates grouped items; it does not break apart bitmaps, symbol instances, or text as the Break apart command does.

Caution
Be careful when ungrouping. Your newly ungrouped drawings may alter or eliminate drawings below in the same layer. ∎

To edit a group:

1. **Select the group and then choose Edit ⇨ Edit Selected, or double-click the group.** Everything on the Stage — except for items in the group — is dimmed, indicating that only the group is editable.

2. **Make changes in the same way you would edit individual primitive shapes or symbols.** If there are other groups or symbols included in a larger group, you'll have to click in deeper to edit those items. You can keep double-clicking on compound groups to

gradually move inside to the deepest level or primitive shape available for editing. You can use the location labels to move back out level by level (or double-click an empty area of the Stage), or go to Step 3 to return to the Main Timeline.

3. **To stop editing the group, choose Edit ⇨ Edit All, or use the location labels to return to the main scene.** Other items on Stage return to normal color.

Applying Break apart

The Modify ⇨ Break apart command (Ctrl+B/⌘+B) is rather like an Undo command for groups, drawing objects, and symbols as well as a deconstruction tool for text and bitmaps. To use Break apart, simply select an item and then apply the command. Occasionally you must apply the Break apart command more than once to reduce a compound group to its core shapes. When applied to a symbol instance, Break apart reduces the instance to raw shapes that no longer are linked to the original symbol stored in the library.

Breaking apart text

Text reduced to shapes by using Break apart can be filled with gradients and bitmaps and also modified with the shape Transform options. I show specific examples of using the Break apart command in Chapter 8, "Working with Text," and in Chapter 15, "Importing Artwork." Figure 9.33 illustrates how text is broken apart in two stages so that the original block (left) is first separated into individual letters (center), and then when broken apart a second time, it is reduced to shapes (right).

FIGURE 9.33

A text field (left) broken apart once (center) and then once again (right)

Caution

Breaking apart complex symbols or large text blocks can add to the file size of your final movie. ■

Creating Metallic Type

To demonstrate how text characters can be modified after they've been converted to shapes, I have applied some gradient fills to create the illusion of shiny metal letters. The file for this effect is titled `metalType.fla` and is included in the `ch09` folder of the CD-ROM. Start with a document that has a dark gray background.

1. First type a word or words on the Stage to create a text block. This effect works best if applied to a bold, sans serif font at a fairly large point size. I used Verdana bold set at 50 pt.

2. Select the text block and apply the Break apart command (Ctrl+B/⌘+B) once to break the text block into individual letters, and then a second time to convert the letters into shapes.

3. With the letter shapes still selected, load a default grayscale linear gradient into the Color panel and then adjust it so the gradient is dark at each end with a highlight in the center. Set the left and far right Color pointers to black (#000000) and then add a new Color pointer in the center of the Edit bar and set it to white (#FFFFFF), as shown in Figure 9.34.

FIGURE 9.34

Text shapes selected and filled with a custom linear gradient created in the Mixer panel

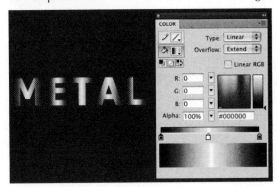

4. Use the Gradient Transform tool to rotate the gradient fill clockwise to a 45-degree angle in each letter shape. You may also scale each fill slightly or adjust individual center points to align the highlight on each letter, as shown in Figure 9.35.

FIGURE 9.35

Linear gradients aligned in each letter shape with the Gradient Transform tool

5. To create a more three-dimensional look, make a copy of all the letter shapes in a new layer below the current layer. Use the Copy (Ctrl+C/⌘+C) and Paste (Ctrl+V/⌘+V) commands. Turn the visibility of the original layer off (click the Eye icon) for now so you can see only the copied letter shapes.

6. Select all the copied letter shapes, and using the Color panel, reverse the gradient fill colors. Set the center Color pointer to black and both end Color pointers to white, as shown in Figure 9.36.

FIGURE 9.36

Copied letter shapes on a new layer with reversed gradient fill applied

7. Use the Modify ➪ Shape ➪ Expand Fill command to expand the fill in all the selected letters by 2 pixels.

8. If you turn the visibility of both layers back on, you should see that you now have two opposing gradient fills, and the copied letter shapes are slightly larger than the original letter shapes. Figure 9.37 compares the letters with the original gradient and the letters with the modified gradient.

FIGURE 9.37

Original letter shapes with gradient fill (top) and copied letter shapes with reversed and expanded gradient fill (bottom)

9. Lock the original layer, and then select all the copied letter shapes on the lower layer and drag them behind the original letter shapes so that they're aligned just slightly above and to the right of the original shapes. This creates the illusion of a metallic beveled edge on the original letter shapes, as shown in Figure 9.38.

FIGURE 9.38

Copied letter shapes aligned behind the original letter shapes to create the illusion of a beveled metallic edge

Breaking apart bitmaps

When applied to bitmaps placed in the Document window, Break apart enables you to select the bitmap image with the Eyedropper tool to apply as a fill to other shapes. This is not the same as tracing a bitmap, which reduces the vast number of colors in a bitmap to areas of solid color and converts it to vector format, as described in the section that follows. Figure 9.39 shows an imported bitmap placed on the Stage and sampled with the Eyedropper tool to create a colored fill in the rectangle below (left) compared to the same bitmap broken apart and sampled with the Eyedropper tool to create an image fill in the rectangle below (right).

FIGURE 9.39

A bitmap and the fill that results from sampling it with the Eyedropper tool when it is intact (left) and when it has been broken apart (right)

It isn't necessary to break apart bitmaps to use as fills because they can be specified with the Mixer panel, as described in Chapter 7. But breaking apart bitmaps enables you to selectively edit them and modify the visible area of the bitmap with the shape Transform options.

Caution

Although you can apply the Distort and Envelope modifiers of the Free Transform tool to a bitmap after it has been broken apart, they may not give you the result you expect. Instead of distorting or warping the actual bitmap image, you'll find that these modifiers reveal how Flash "sees" bitmap fills. The visible area of the bitmap is not really treated as a shape but rather as a mask, or shaped window, that enables a certain part of the bitmap to be visible. You can distort or warp the viewable area, but the bitmap itself is not modified, as it is when you apply the Rotate or Skew modifiers. ■

Figure 9.40 illustrates a bitmap that has been broken apart (left) so that colored areas in the background of the image can be selected with the Magic Wand option of the Lasso tool (center) and then deleted to leave the flower floating on the white Stage (right). You can clean up any stray areas of unwanted color by using the Lasso tool or the Eraser tool.

FIGURE 9.40

A bitmap broken apart and selectively deleted, using the Magic Wand option of the Lasso tool

About the Magic Wand option

You use the Magic Wand option of the Lasso tool (shown at the bottom of the Tools panel in Figure 9.40) to select ranges of a similar color in either a bitmap fill or a bitmap that's been broken apart. After you select areas of the bitmap, you can change their fill color or delete them, without affecting the Bitmap Swatch in the Color panel. You can adjust what pixels the Magic Wand picks up by modifying the Threshold and Smoothing settings in the dialog box opened by clicking the Magic Wand settings button in the Options area of the Tools panel.

Magic Wand Threshold setting

The Threshold setting defines the breadth of adjacent color values that the Magic Wand includes in a selection. Values for the Threshold setting range from 0 to 200 — the higher the setting, the broader the selection of adjacent colors. Conversely, a smaller number results in the Magic Wand making a narrower selection of adjacent colors.

A value of zero results in a selection of contiguous pixels that are all the same color as the target pixel. With a value of 20, clicking a red target pixel with a value of 55 selects all contiguous pixels in a range of values extending from red 35 to red 75. (If you're comparing selection behavior with Photoshop, you'll notice a slight difference because in Photoshop a Tolerance setting of 20 selects all contiguous pixels in a tighter range of values extending from red 45 to red 65.)

Magic Wand Smoothing setting

The Smoothing setting of the Magic Wand option determines to what degree the edge of the selection should be smoothed. This is similar to anti-aliasing. (Anti-aliasing dithers the edges of shapes and lines so that they look smoother on-screen.) The options are Pixels, Rough, Normal, and Smooth. Assuming that the Threshold setting remains constant, the Smoothing settings differ as follows:

- **Pixels:** Clings to the rectangular edges of each pixel bordering similar colors.
- **Rough:** With this setting, the edges of the selection are even more angular than with Pixels.
- **Normal:** Results in a selection that's somewhere between Rough and Smooth.
- **Smooth:** Delivers a selection with more rounded edges.

Tracing bitmaps

You use the Trace bitmap command to convert an imported image from a bitmap to a native Flash vector graphic with discrete, editable areas of color. This unlinks the image from the original symbol in the library (and also from the Bitmap Swatch in the Color panel). You can create interesting bitmap-based art with this command. However, if your intention is to preserve the look of the original bitmap with maximum fidelity, you must work with the settings — and you will most likely find that the original bitmap is actually smaller in file size than the traced vector image. Figure 9.41 includes a selected bitmap image on the left and the final vector image that resulted from the settings shown in the Trace Bitmap dialog box on the right.

FIGURE 9.41

Select a bitmap (left) and choose settings in the Trace Bitmap dialog box to define the final vector image (right).

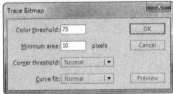

Tip

The Trace Bitmap dialog box includes a handy Preview button that enables you to test settings before you apply them. The preview is rendered more quickly than the final trace conversion, and using this option saves you from having to use the Undo command and then reopen the Trace Bitmap dialog box each time you want to try a different setting. ■

To trace a bitmap, follow these steps:

1. **Use the Selection tool to select the bitmap that you want to trace.** It can be in Edit mode or directly on the Stage.

2. **Choose Modify ⇨ Bitmap ⇨ Trace Bitmap to open the Trace Bitmap dialog box and set the options according to your needs:**

   - **Color threshold:** This option controls the number of colors in your traced bitmap. It limits the number of colors by averaging the colors based on the criteria chosen in Color threshold and Minimum area. Color threshold compares RGB color values of adjacent pixels to the value entered. If the difference is lower than the value entered, adjacent pixels are considered the same color. By making this computation for each pixel within the bitmap, Flash averages the colors. A lower Color threshold delivers more colors in the final vector graphic derived from the traced bitmap. The range is between 0 and 500, with a default setting of 100.

   - **Minimum area:** This value is the radius, measured in pixels, which Color threshold uses to describe adjacent pixels when comparing pixels to determine what color to assign to the center pixel. The range is between 1 and 1,000, with the default setting being 8.

   - **Curve fit:** This value determines how smoothly outlines are drawn. Select Very Tight if the shapes in the bitmap are complex and angular. If the curves are smooth, select Very Smooth.

   - **Corner threshold:** This setting determines how sharp edges are handled; choose Many Corners to retain edges and Few Corners to smooth the edges.

3. **Click OK.** Flash traces the bitmap, and the original pixel information is converted to vector shapes. If the bitmap is complex, this may take a while. Depending on the settings you have chosen, the final look of the traced graphic can vary between being very close to the original or very abstracted.

Tip

If your objective is for your traced bitmap to closely resemble the original bitmap, set a low Color threshold and a low Minimum area. You'll also want to set the Curve fit to Pixels and the Corner threshold to Many Corners. Be aware that using these settings may drastically slow the tracing process for complex bitmaps and result in larger file sizes. If animated, such bitmaps may also retard the frame rate dramatically. ■

As shown in Figure 9.42, the traced bitmap can vary in how closely it resembles the original bitmap. The image in the center was traced with lower settings to achieve a more detailed image: Color threshold of 25, Minimum area of 2 pixels, Curve fit of Pixels, and Corner threshold of Many Corners. The image on the right was traced with higher settings to create a more abstract graphic image: Color threshold of 300, Minimum area of 25 pixels, Curve fit of Very Smooth, and Corner threshold of Few Corners.

FIGURE 9.42

Bitmap images can be traced to create different styles of vector graphics by using low settings (center) or high settings (right).

Caution

If you drag a bitmap from the Library panel onto the Stage and then attempt to acquire the bitmap fill by first tracing the bitmap and then clicking with the Eyedropper tool, be careful of how selection affects the results. If the traced bitmap is still selected, clicking with the Eyedropper tool acquires the nearest color and replaces the entire traced bitmap with a solid fill of the acquired color. If the traced bitmap is not selected, the Eyedropper tool simply acquires the nearest solid color and loads it into the fill color chip. ■

Working with Drawing Objects and Combine Object Commands

Drawing objects were introduced with Flash 8 to make the drawing environment a little more user friendly. In older versions of Flash, you had to take special care to avoid unexpected results when shapes overlapped on the same layer (as described in the section on working with compound shapes). There are times when compound shapes can be helpful, but most people will find it easier to work with drawing objects. If you turn the Object Drawing toggle on (in the Options area of the Tools panel) at any time, it remains on until you turn it back off. This makes it easy to draw in the mode that suits you best without having to remember to turn the toggle on or off all the time.

Tip

If you draw a shape with the Object Drawing toggle turned off and decide that you would prefer to work with a drawing object rather than a raw shape, simply select the shape and use the Modify ⇨ Combine Objects ⇨ Union command to convert the shape into a drawing object. Conversely, drawing objects can be reverted to raw shapes by using the Modify ⇨ Ungroup or the Modify ⇨ Break Apart command. ■

In the simplest terms, drawing objects are containers for raw shapes. They cannot hold animation (like symbols can) or even other drawing objects. If you try to add a drawing object to the Stage when you have another drawing object open in Edit mode, you see a warning dialog box when you return to the Main Timeline. As shown in Figure 9.43, Flash automatically converts the original drawing object into a group so that the new drawing object can be nested inside it.

Drawing objects cannot contain animation, symbols, or other drawing objects — they are intended as holders for raw shapes only.

If you have worked in Flash before, you may be wondering why you would even bother to use a drawing object instead of just using a simple group to manage raw shapes. Like groups, drawing objects do not show up in the document library and they cannot have filters applied to them. However, unlike groups, you can modify drawing objects without having to open them in Edit mode, and you can animate them by using Classic motion tweens without first converting them into symbols. Another key reason to use drawing objects is to take advantage of the Combine Objects commands (as shown in Figure 9.44). These commands will be familiar to anyone who has used the Pathfinder panel in Illustrator:

- **Union:** Merges the selected objects into one combined object.
- **Intersect:** Deletes everything except the area of the topmost object where it overlaps the lower objects.
- **Punch:** Deletes the topmost object and punches out the area where it overlaps other objects.
- **Crop:** Deletes everything except the areas of the lower objects where the upper object overlaps.

Two drawing objects (far left) combined, using various Combine Objects commands to get different final results (from left to right): Union, Intersect, Punch, Crop

There are only a few other things to keep in mind when working with drawing objects:

- You can modify drawing objects with the Selection and Transformation tools in the same way as raw shapes, but you cannot select the fill and stroke inside a drawing object individually unless you open it in Edit mode.

- You can change the appearance of the fill and stroke separately just by selecting the object and using any of the swatches menus, but if you try to apply the Expand Fill command to a drawing object that contains a stroke, you see the stroke disappear unless you have ungrouped or broken apart (into raw shapes) the drawing object or opened it in Edit mode.

- The selection highlight for drawing objects and groups selected on the Stage look exactly alike, but you can tell what type of item you are working with by checking the item description in the Properties panel. Groups and drawing objects share some characteristics, but they are *not* the same thing.

- The Lock Fill option doesn't work with drawing objects in the same way that it works with other filled shapes. Although you can use the Lock Fill command to create a fill that visually continues from one object to another, you will find when you try to apply the Gradient Transform tool that you have to adjust the fills individually for each object.

Cross-Reference

As described in Chapter 5, you also have the option of creating shape primitives by using the Oval Primitive and Rectangle Primitive tools. Shape primitives have many of the same advantages as drawing objects, but they can be modified by using settings in the Properties panel — including handy controls for rounded corners and precise curves. ■

Caution

If you try to open a shape primitive in Edit mode, you see a warning dialog box with the option of converting the shape primitive into a drawing object (if you say OK, you lose access to the special settings in the Properties panel). ■

Working with Compound Shapes

If you have been drawing and modifying artwork in Flash with the Object Drawing option turned off, you've probably noticed that Flash has a unique way of handling lines and fills that reside on the same layer of your document. Items of the same color merge, whereas items of a different color replace or cut out other items where they overlap. Flash treats lines or strokes as separate items than fills, so these can be selected and moved or modified independently of each other, even if they are the same color. Figure 9.45 shows how Flash allows lines and fills to be selected individually, even if they are the same color.

Tip

By double-clicking an element, you can select all the related segments. This works for selecting the stroke and fill of a shape or for selecting connected sections of a segmented line (such as the four sides of a rectangle). ■

FIGURE 9.45

A gray oval fill with a gray stroke may not appear to have a discrete outline, but Flash allows these two elements to be selected separately.

Both lines and fills are divided into segments at points of intersection. Figure 9.46 shows a fill split into two independent shapes by drawing a line on top of it (top) or modified by merging with a fill of the same color and being cut out by a fill of a different color (bottom).

FIGURE 9.46

A fill split by an overlapping line drawn on the same layer (top). Two fills of the same color merge into a compound shape when they intersect on the same layer (bottom).

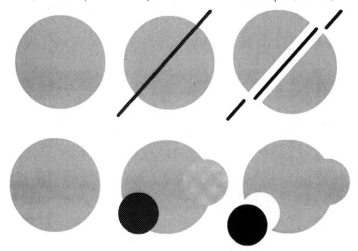

These behaviors can be destructive or helpful to your artwork, depending on how you manage individual elements. The key point to remember is that primitive shapes cannot be overlapped on the same layer while deselected without affecting each other. If items are grouped or converted into drawing objects or symbols, they remain independent and are not compounded or deleted by intersection with other items. Items on layers are also autonomous and do not merge with or erase items that exist on other layers.

You can move lines or fills over other primitive shapes without affecting them, as long as they remain selected. As soon as they are deselected, they intersect or merge with adjacent primitive shapes on the same layer. Figure 9.47 illustrates the process of moving a selected shape over and then off of another shape while keeping the two shapes independent (top), and the result if the shape is deselected while it is overlapping another shape, before being reselected and moved, to create a compound shape (bottom).

A shape moved across another shape while being continuously selected (top) compared to a shape that is deselected while on top of another shape, and then reselected and moved (bottom)

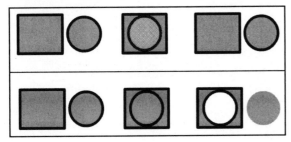

Editing with Find and Replace

Although you can use the Movie Explorer to search for some elements in a project file so that they can be modified, it doesn't automate updates in the same speedy way that the Find and Replace panel, shown in Figure 9.48, does.

Note

Find and Replace is opened from the Edit window rather than from the Window menu, but it does open a real panel and not just a dialog box. Although the Find and Replace panel takes up a lot of room on your desktop, you could dock it with other panels for quick access if you prefer that to using the menu or shortcut keys. ■

If you have used the Find and Replace feature in any other application (even in a basic text-editing program), you will be familiar with the main buttons in the Find and Replace panel (Find Next, Find All, Replace, and Replace All). Open the Find and Replace panel by choosing Edit ➪ Find and Replace in the application menu (Ctrl+F/⌘+F).

FIGURE 9.48

The Find and Replace panel makes revisions so easy, they're almost fun.

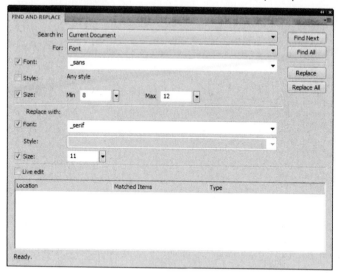

The real benefits of using this panel become clearer when you look at the items you can select to search for; these include:

- **Text:** Search for words, partial words, or whole paragraphs in text fields, frames, layers, parameters, strings, or in ActionScript in your current project or current scene.

- **Font:** Search for fonts by name, style, and even size, within your current project or scene.

- **Color:** Pick a color from the popup swatches (or enter a hexadecimal value in the field) to search for fills, strokes, or text where a specific color is used in the current project or scene.

- **Symbol/Sound/Video/Bitmap:** Use the handy drop-down list that lists all symbols (or sounds, or video, or bitmaps) used in your current project to pick a symbol to search for and a symbol to use as a replacement.

As you select each item in the For: drop-down list, options relevant to that item become available in the panel. These options give you very precise control over the type of edits that you want to make. Now that replacing a color or font, or even a specific word in your entire project file, is as easy as making a few quick selections in the Find and Replace panel, those dreaded last-minute revisions might almost seem fun.

Caution

Although any effects or transformations that you have applied to a symbol instance (and any formatting you have applied to text) should be preserved if you change it by using the Find and Replace panel, you have to verify that the newly inserted content appears as you expect it to. If a font is much larger, it might not fit into your layout, or if a replacement bitmap is much larger or smaller than the original, you may have to make some manual adjustments to get everything polished. These are the same kinds of adjustments you would expect to make if you used the Swap symbol feature. ■

Using the History Panel

The History panel found in the Other Panels list (Ctrl+F10/⌘+F10) enables you to escape the linear limitations of Undo/Redo. As you work in your project file, the History panel records your editing steps in a sequential list (see Figure 9.49). The History panel stores steps taken in the active project file during the current editing session only. It does not store steps from the last time you had a project file open or from other files edited during the same session. You *can* save and move steps from one file or session to another, but it requires you to use some of the special features of the History panel, described later in this section.

The History panel lists steps taken as a file is authored or edited.

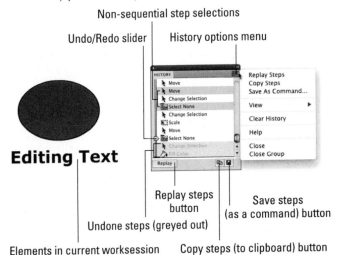

Non-sequential step selections

Undo/Redo slider | History options menu

Editing Text

Replay steps button

Save steps (as a command) button

Undone steps (greyed out)

Copy steps (to clipboard) button

Elements in current worksession

Note

Flash gives you the option of using Document-level Undo (which creates one History/Undo stack for all the items in a current session) or the legacy-style Object-level Undo (which creates a unique History/Undo stack for key editing areas of the Flash authoring environment: Stage, Movie Clip timelines, and the ActionScript panel). The default is set to Document-level Undo, but if you find it helpful to be able to step back through Movie Clip edits individually, you can change this setting in the General section of Flash Preferences. To access the object-level Undo stack, you must open a Movie Clip (not an instance) in Edit mode. ■

Caution

Making changes to your Undo style or number of saved steps in Flash Preferences clears the History panel, deleting all the Undo steps for your current session. ■

You can use the History panel as a reminder of the steps taken to create a special graphic effect, or you can use it as a nonlinear authoring control. Should you need to get back to a specific step in your authoring session, you can use Undo (Ctrl+Z/⌘+Z) over and over and over, or you can simply open the History panel and drag the edit pointer on the left side of the panel upward to go back in time until you reach the point at which you want to jump back into authoring. As long as you don't make any edits at an earlier point in the History list, you can easily scroll forward again if you need to redo your steps — without wearing out the Ctrl+Y/⌘+Y keys! However, if you undo a step (or a series of steps) and then make changes to your project file, you can no longer redo the steps in the History panel. This is where the History panel does behave a little like a time machine — as long as you don't change anything, you can jump backward and forward in time, but as soon as you change something, you lose the option of going "back to the future."

Tip

Click to the left of a step in the History panel to jump to that point without scrolling. All steps listed after the point that you click will be undone and grayed out until you scroll forward again (or click to the left of an item closer to the bottom of the list). ■

The options menu and the buttons along the bottom of the History panel are the keys to the more advanced editing tasks that you can accomplish when you take your steps a step farther. (Refer to Figure 9.49 for callouts on the location of History panel controls.)

Replay Steps

The Replay Steps control repeat or reapply a series of sequential or nonsequential steps in your current History list:

1. **Select sequential items by dragging or by Shift+clicking the text labels in the list.** Select nonsequential items by Ctrl+clicking/⌘+clicking.

2. **With a step (or series of steps) selected, you can apply the step(s) to a new item —** by selecting the item with the Selection tool and clicking the Replay button or choosing Replay Steps from the options menu.

All currently selected steps are applied (in order) to the item, and a new step labeled "Replay Steps" is listed in the History panel. You can use the Replay Steps item in the History list to apply the same steps again without having to select the original steps individually.

Copy Steps

This command enables you to move steps from one document to another. Here's how it works:

1. **Select steps from your History panel list (as described in the previous section).**
2. **Choose Copy Steps from the options menu.**
3. **In the Flash document where you want to reuse the steps, select an item to which you want to apply the steps.**
4. **Choose Edit ➪ Paste in Center (Ctrl+V/⌘+V).**

The editing steps copied from your original file are applied to the item in your current file and a new item is added to the History panel, labeled Paste Steps.

Clear History

This is a helpful command to use if you want to start from a clean slate before performing a series of editing steps that you plan to save. Clear History deletes all the listings in the History panel of your current document. You can't undo this choice, but you will see a Warning dialog box that gives you the chance to change your mind before it's too late. (Closing a Flash document also clears the History list.) The number of steps listed in the History panel can be limited by the *Undo levels* set in the General Flash Preferences dialog box. The default setting is 100, but it can be set as high as 300 or as low as 2. Every item recorded in the History panel eats up some memory and disk space, so choose the lowest setting that suits your authoring style.

History View

You should leave this setting on Default unless you plan to use the History panel as a tool for helping you write new JavaScript commands. This is a very exciting potential use of the History panel, but it is beyond the scope of this book. If you are familiar with JavaScript, you can try different View settings to get more information that helps you deconstruct the steps in an editing workflow.

Save As Command

If you're not quite ready to start writing your own JavaScript from scratch, this is a terrific shortcut that makes it easy to save and reuse custom editing workflows:

1. **Select the step(s) from the History panel that you want to save and reuse.**
2. **Choose Save As Command from the options menu (or click the small disk icon at the bottom right of the History panel).**

3. **In the Save as Command dialog box, give the command a meaningful name.** You might call the steps used to create a fancy custom-type treatment "Headline style."

   By the magic of Flash, your custom command now appears in the Command menu list.

4. **You can apply your specific editing steps in any document by selecting an item and choosing Commands ⇨ Headline style (or whatever commands you have created and named).**

The options at the top of the application Command menu give you some controls for managing your custom commands and for using commands from other sources. The Get More Commands menu item loads a link to the online Flash Exchange, where you can find new commands contributed by other Flash developers (look for JavaScript Flash or .jsfl files). If you download a custom command script, you can use the Run Command menu option to browse to the .jsfl file and apply it to an item in your current project. The possibilities are wide open.

Summary

- After you've mastered the basic drawing tools in Flash, there are innumerable methods for modifying artwork to create custom effects.

- You can use the Eyedropper, Ink Bottle, and Paint Bucket tools together to select and apply fill and stroke styles to multiple items or to swap styles between items.

- You can use the Gradient Transform tool to modify gradient fills and bitmap fills for precise alignment and appearance inside individual shapes.

- The new 3-D tools (3D Rotation and 3D Translation) make it easier to simulate 3-D space by providing intuitive controls for rotating and shifting Movie Clip symbols along the x-, y-, and z-axis (available only in Flash CS5 targeting Flash Player 10 or later).

- The Perspective angle and Vanishing point settings (available in the Properties panel when a 3-D symbol is selected) control the view or camera lens for your entire Flash movie (but only have an effect on 3-D symbols).

- Drawing objects share some characteristics with raw shapes, groups, and symbols, but they have a unique role in Flash authoring.

- Shape primitives must be converted into drawing objects if you want to open them in Edit mode, but this workflow removes access to the settings available in the Properties panel that make it easy to modify Oval or Rectangle primitives.

- Drawing objects and shape primitives, like groups and symbols, do not interact when they overlap on the same layer. If you want to merge or crop drawing objects, the Combine Objects commands provide some options that will be familiar to people who have used pathfinder options in other vector drawing programs.

- The Free Transform tool has two powerful options that you can apply to shapes or drawing objects only, as well as two options that restrict the Free Transform behavior to make it easier to achieve specific tasks.

- Flash organizes artwork with specific parameters, and you can use the Modify ⇨ Arrange commands to help define the stacking order when you're working with similar items on the same layer.

- You can use the Break Apart command to convert bitmaps and text so you can edit them like shapes to create special effects.

- You use the Trace bitmap command to convert imported bitmaps into vector graphics with varying degrees of detail.

Part III

Creating Animation and Effects

Now that you're comfortable with the Flash tools and making static graphic symbols and groups, it's time to move on to creating animated elements and dynamic effects. Chapter 10 gives you all the information you need to start working with time-based content. Learn to create frame-by-frame and tweened animation and how to use Movie Clips to control display of content on multiple timelines. Meet the Motion Editor and learn how to use it to edit property keyframes and custom easing curves. Chapter 11 is dedicated to introducing the creative possibilities of the filters and blend modes available in Flash CS5, as well as coverage of how to create mask and guide layers when you need them. You will also get an introduction to the amazing IK tools in Flash CS5 that bring the power of inverse kinematics to the Flash authoring environment.

Timeline Animation and the Motion Editor

I n this chapter, I discuss the basic methods and tools used to create animations in the Flash authoring environment. Animation is the process of creating the illusion of movement or change over time. Animation can be the movement of an item from one place to another, or it can be a change of color over a period of time. The change can also be a *morph*, or transformation, from one shape to another. Any change of either position or appearance that occurs over time is animation. In Flash, changing the contents of successive frames (over a period of time) creates animation. This can include any or all of the changes I have mentioned, in any combination.

Note

Animation is possible without extending Flash content beyond one frame, but this requires you to apply transformations to graphics by using ActionScript commands and/or mathematical equations that are executed by code rather than triggered by the Flash timeline. I suggest you use ActionScript 3.0 Bible (Wiley, 2008) as a companion to this book when you are ready to go to the next level with your Flash projects. ∎

Basic Methods of Flash Animation

Flash supports three basic methods of animation:

- **Frame-by-frame animation** is achieved by manually changing the individual contents of each of any number of successive keyframes.

- **Keyframe-based tweened animation** is achieved by defining the contents of the start and endpoints of an animation (with keyframes) and allowing Flash to interpolate the contents of the frames in between. Flash CS5 has two kinds of keyframe-based tweening:

- Shape tweening
- Classic (motion) tweening
- **Object-based motion tweening** is an amazing evolution of keyframe-based (or Classic) motion tweening. In Flash CS5, you can now apply a tween to a target object on the Stage, and by simply moving or transforming the object, property keyframes (and a motion path, if needed) are auto-created to track and animate the changes. The many benefits of the tween method and the Motion Editor are explained in more detail later in this chapter.

Advanced Flash developers tend to animate almost exclusively by controlling Movie clips with ActionScript. Although this might seem intimidating to illustrators or animators who are more comfortable using analog tools, this programmatic approach to creating motion (and even artwork) dynamically makes sense. After all, computer animation is the art of orchestrating items according to various properties over time — and in the digital realm. numbers describe all properties, even color.

Note
The Motion Presets panel enables users to create or import, save, reuse, and share custom tween patterns. These XML-based tween files work more seamlessly than Timeline Effects ever did. ■

Flash components, the Motion Presets panel, and the Copy Motion as ActionScript 3.0 command make it easier than ever for beginning programmers to integrate ActionScripted elements into Flash projects. But, before you jump into scripted animation, it helps to know how to animate in the Flash authoring environment by using layers, frames, and symbols.

Frame-by-Frame Animation

The most basic form of animation is frame-by-frame animation. Because frame-by-frame animation employs unique drawings in each frame, it's ideal for complex animations that require subtle changes — for example, facial expressions. However, frame-by-frame animation also has its drawbacks. It can be very tedious and time consuming to draw unique art for each frame of the animation. Moreover, all those unique drawings contribute to a large file size. In Flash, a frame with unique art is called a *keyframe*. As shown in Figure 10.1, frame-by-frame animation requires a unique drawing for every movement or change, which makes nearly every frame a keyframe.

The example shown in Figure 10.1 (`keyframe.swf`) was created by inserting a series of blank keyframes (F7) and then working backward from the artwork in the final frame to paste the text and erase letters in (reverse) sequential keyframes. In the final effect, the text appears letter by letter until the whole word is written out in keyframe 10. This process of modifying your original artwork in each frame to create a sequence is one use of frame-by-frame animation. Another approach is to create completely unique artwork in each blank keyframe (F7).

FIGURE 10.1

When you use keyframes to gradually add to the artwork, the text appears to be written out letter by letter in the final animation.

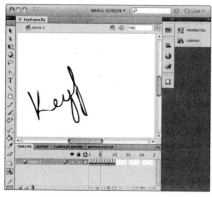 

As shown in Figure 10.2, the changes in the lines from frame to frame can add a lot more motion to the final animation. If you are a skilled illustrator, you will be able to keep enough consistency from keyframe to keyframe that the animation will seem to be the same shape or figure moving to a new position. If you are an aspiring illustrator, you may end up with a lot more variation among your drawings! As long as you are not trying to get a very precise sequence, this variation can actually be a lot of fun to watch — every line dances and moves in your final animation. Keep in mind that you are not restricted to just one series of frames; you can keep adding elements with their own keyframe sequences on separate layers.

On the CD-ROM

The source files for the examples in this section are included on the CD-ROM — they're in the `Keyframe` **folder of the** `ch10` **folder.** ■

The images shown in Figure 10.2 are from the file `faceFramebyFrame.fla`. This sequence of drawings was originally done on top of a short video clip of a real person. If you're learning to draw motion, video can be a good starting point — place it in a guide layer so it won't add to the file size of your final movie. If you work in a loose style, the roughness of the individual traced drawings can add more life to the final animation.

A loosely sketched sequence can be paced by adding more "repeater" frames between the unique keyframe images.

Adding keyframes

To add a keyframe to the Timeline, select the frame that you want to convert into a keyframe and then do one of the following:

- Convert a frame into a keyframe:
  - Right-click (or Control+click on Mac) the frame and select Insert Keyframe from the contextual menu.
  - Choose Insert ➪ Timeline ➪ Keyframe from the application menu.
  - Press F6 on the keyboard.
- Convert a frame into a *blank* keyframe:
  - Right-click (or Control+click on Mac) the frame and select Insert Blank Keyframe from the contextual menu.
  - Choose Insert ➪ Timeline ➪ Blank Keyframe from the application menu.
  - Press F7 on the keyboard.

Note

If you select a frame in a span, the selected frame converts to a keyframe without adding to the length of the span. If you insert a keyframe at the end of a span, the keyframe adds to the length of the sequence. If you convert a frame in a span to a blank keyframe, all content clears from the keyframe and the following frames of the span. ∎

Tip

If you need to make a sequence of keyframes, but you would rather not have to press F6 or F7 repeatedly to create individual keyframes, you can select a range of frames and use the Modify ➪ Timeline ➪ Convert to Keyframes (F6) or Modify ➪ Timeline ➪ Convert to Blank Keyframes (F7) command to quickly convert all selected frames to keyframes or blank keyframes. ∎

Creating frame-by-frame animation

The basic steps for creating a frame-by-frame animation are as follows:

1. **Select the frame in which you want your frame-by-frame animation to begin.** If it's not already a keyframe, use Insert ➪ Timeline ➪ Keyframe (F6) to convert it.

2. **Either draw or import the first image for your sequence into this keyframe.** Wherever possible, use symbols and flip, rotate, or otherwise manipulate them for reuse to economize on file size.

3. **Select the next frame and either carry the artwork from the previous keyframe forward for modification by adding a keyframe (F6), or, if you want to create a completely new image from scratch or place a different imported image, make the next keyframe a blank keyframe (F7).**

4. **Continue to add keyframes and change the contents of each keyframe until you complete the animation.**

5. **Play back your animation by returning to the first keyframe and then selecting Control ➪ Play from the application menu (Enter or Return key).** Or, preview the animation in the test movie environment by choosing Control ➪ Test Movie (Ctrl+Enter/ ⌘+Return).

Modifying Multiframe Sequences

To control the pacing of your animation, you can add more frames (F5) between the keyframes (creating a *span*) or add more keyframed (F6) images to the sequence to extend its length. Adding more frames between keyframes "holds" or pauses the animation until the playhead hits the next keyframe with changed content. In the example shown in Figure 10.2, the face holds on some frames while the butterfly continues to move in keyframed drawings on its own layer. To speed up (or shorten) animation, you can remove frames (Shift+F5) or keyframes (Shift+F6) to shorten the sequence. You can make changes in the length of a span by selecting a frame in the span that you want to modify and using the application menu commands (or shortcut keys), or you can simply drag the endframe of the span to change its position on the Timeline.

Tip

If you drag the endframe of a span to a new position, Flash automatically inserts a new keyframe to mark the new position. If you want to change the length of a span without adding more keyframes, hold down the Ctrl/⌘ key while clicking and dragging the endframe to a new position. ■

Inserting more frames does work to slow down an animated sequence, but generally if you insert more than two frames between keyframes the movement is interrupted and the animation starts to look too choppy. Try adding more keyframes to the sequence with very subtle change to the content in each keyframe if you want to create a slower, smoother animation.

Frame Rate and Animation Timing

An underlying factor that affects the playback of all animation is the project frame rate. The frame rate appears in the Document Properties dialog box (Modify⇨Document) or in the Properties panel if you click in the Document window of an open file without selecting any items on the Stage. The allowable frame rate range is between 0.01 and 120 frames per second (fps) — the default setting in Flash CS5 is 24 fps. The most commonly used range is somewhere between 12 fps (for most Web sites and for low-bandwidth animation) and 24 fps (for faster animation and complex effects intended for broadcast).

It might seem like a good idea to push the frame rate higher to get smoother-looking animation, but the reality of Web delivery is that you can't be sure that your audience will have the bandwidth or the processor speed to play back the animation as you intended. There is nothing worse than seeing your gorgeous animation stuttering and dropping frames. In most cases, 12 fps provides all the momentum you need to drive your animation and effects — you can create quick cuts, smooth fades, or anything in between just by adjusting your artwork and pacing your frames appropriately.

Although you can always change the frame rate after you've authored a file, it makes sense to decide on a final frame rate *before* you start designing and testing complex animation sequences. Re-timing animation by inserting or removing frames and changing the duration of tweens is always an option, but it is painful to go back and try to match the original pacing of a file that was created by using a different frame rate.

Note

The default frame rate in Flash CS5 is 24 fps. This reflects the fact that most people viewing Flash Player 10 content have enough processor speed and bandwidth to handle smooth playback of high-fidelity animation. ■

By default, Flash loops the content on your timeline, so if you want a sequence to be repeated, you don't need to draw it over and over again. If you notice that your animation disappears before it loops to play again, check to make sure that there are no extra empty frames at the end of the sequence, or that the endframe of one of your sequences is not farther down the Timeline than the endframe of the element that disappears. Although you won't see anything on the Stage in these frames, Flash still plays those frames if they exist on the Timeline. Obviously, blank frames can be used in an animation whenever you want to empty the Stage — either as a pause between sequences or to create the illusion that your artwork has disappeared.

To illustrate how blank frames play back in an animation, we've created a silly example with a face and a rectangle that persist in every frame and some text that exists only on some frames (see Figure 10.3).

FIGURE 10.3

You can insert blank keyframes to clear artwork from the Stage. Remember that the playhead continues along the Timeline if there are frames on any one of the layers, even if the artwork on other layers is no longer present.

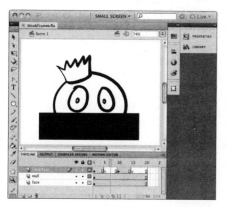

Onion skinning

Traditional animators worked on layers of transparent cels using a light table. This made it possible for them to create consistent drawings and to plan the pacing of movement in a sequence of cels. As you move from keyframe to keyframe in Flash, you might feel that you are working blind because you can see the artwork only on the current frame. If you are creating artwork for a sequence of related keyframes, it is crucial to have some visual indication or "map" of the changes from frame to frame. Fortunately, Flash has an effective digital version of the traditional light table — this handy feature is called *onion skinning*. In Flash, onion skinning enables you to see several frames of your artwork displayed at one time. The onion skin markers on the timeline determine the number of frames that are visible. You can turn onion skinning on or off whenever you need to by using the toggle buttons at the bottom of the Timeline window. As shown in Figure 10.4, there are actually two options for onion skinning: Onion Skin or Onion Skin Outlines.

Tip

Layers that are locked will not be onion skinned, even if there is artwork on multiple frames within the onion skin markers — this is helpful if you need to keep the view from getting too cluttered with multiple overlays. Generally, onion skinning works best if all layers are locked except the layer that you plan to edit. ■

The current frame (indicated by the position of the playhead) is displayed at 100 percent opacity, while the other frames in the sequence are displayed at a slightly reduced opacity or as outlines, depending on the Onion Skin button you have selected.

Tip

If you don't like the color of the outlines that appear when you turn on Onion Skin Outlines, you can change the setting for Outline color in the Layer Properties dialog box. (Double-click the layer icon or choose Properties from the contextual menu.) ■

The number of frames that are included in the onion skin display can be controlled either by choosing a setting from the Modify Onion Markers menu (shown in Figure 10.5) or by selecting the round marker handles with the Selection tool and sliding them to a new position on the Timeline. The number of frames that you select from the Modify menu is shown before and after the current frame — so in our example with Onion 2 selected, the onion markers actually span five frames (the current frame, plus two frames on each side).

Editing multiple frames

One of the drawbacks of manually creating unique artwork on every frame is that changes can be very time consuming. If you decide to change the color or size of an element or perhaps edit out a feature of your artwork, repeating this edit on every frame of a sequence is tedious and labor intensive.

Tip

The Find and Replace panel (Edit ⇨ Find and Replace) makes it easier to replace colors and text in a Flash document, but erasing or moving an element that appears in a multiframe sequence can still be time consuming. ■

FIGURE 10.4

Onion Skin shows grayed out or ghosted artwork on multiple frames, and Onion Skin Outlines shows colored outlines of the artwork on multiple frames. It's hard to see the "color" here, but notice that the lines are thinner with Onion Skin Outlines (right).

FIGURE 10.5

You can control the number of frames visible when onion skinning is turned on with the Modify Onion Markers menu or by dragging the onion skin markers to a new position on the Timeline.

Fortunately, Flash provides a Timeline option that can make repeated edits on multiple frames much more efficient. Edit Multiple Frames enables you to see and select items on multiple frames for simultaneous modification. As shown in Figure 10.6, the Edit Multiple Frames option is turned on with the toggle button below the Timeline. When this feature is active, you can use any of the selection methods (Selection tool, Lasso, application menu, or shortcut keys) to select the parts of your artwork that you want to move, modify, or delete. This feature is especially helpful for edits that need to be consistent from frame to frame, such as moving all of your artwork to a new position in your layout.

Tip

Using the Lock feature to protect layers that you don't want to edit makes it much easier to select and edit multiple elements on specific layers. Using the Lasso tool or the Selection tool to drag-select items on the Stage includes only items on unlocked layers in your selection. The Select All command (Edit⇨Select All) makes quick work of ensuring that all unlocked elements within the Edit handles are selected before you apply a change. ■

FIGURE 10.6

With Edit Multiple Frames toggled on, you can select elements on individual keyframes in a sequence (left) to be modified simultaneously (right).

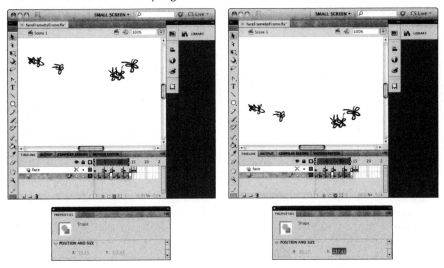

The frames visible and available for selection are marked by a gray span on the timeline with start and end handles. You can adjust the number of frames included in the span with the Selection tool by clicking and dragging the round handles on the timeline to a new position.

Using Tweens for Animation

Tweening is one of the most powerful capabilities of Flash. Whether you are creating character animation or motion graphics, or even the most basic button effect, you will find tweening indispensable. After you have planned your animation and created the initial artwork, you can use Flash tweening to generate the transitional images between one keyframe and another. This is the tool that makes it possible for artists to quickly generate smooth, precise animation — without spending half their lives manually filling in unique graphics on every frame. Instead, you can establish a beginning point and an endpoint, and make drawings, or key art, only for each of those points. Then you let Flash interpolate and render, or *tween,* the changes between the keyframes. Tweening can be used to render changes in size, shape, color, position, and rotation.

Tweening also minimizes file size because you don't have to include unique information on each frame in the animation. Because you define the contents of the frames at the beginning and endpoint (keyframes), Flash has to save only those graphics, plus the values needed to make the *changes* on the frames in between. Basically, Flash has to store only the difference between the beginning frame and the endframe so that the images on the frames in between can be calculated and rendered.

The other significant benefit of using tweens to generate an animated sequence is that if you want to make a change, you only need to modify the beginning or endpoint and Flash instantly updates the images in between.

Three kinds of tweens can be created in Flash — shape tweens, motion tweens, and Classic (motion) tweens — each applied for specific purposes. The type of tween that you want to apply is selected from the frame or object contextual menu or from the application Insert menu. Tween types are represented on the Timeline by a colored fill. Motion tweens are represented by a blue fill without an arrow, and shape tweens and classic tweens are represented by a fill with a continuous arrow on the span between the start keyframe and the end keyframe of the animation — a green fill for shape tweens and purple fill for classic tweens.

Note

There is one other type of tween layer that Flash auto-creates to hold IK armatures: Pose layers are marked by a small running figure, and like motion tween layers, they save changes made to the contents of the layer in property keyframes to enable animation. Pose layers cannot be inserted or created manually, they are only added to your layer stack when you use the Bone tool to link symbol instances or create an armature inside of a shape. This workflow is described later in this chapter. ∎

Note

If a shape tween or classic tween is incomplete, either because the wrong tween type has been applied or because information on one of the defining keyframes is missing, the continuous arrow is replaced with a dashed line. ∎

Cross-Reference

Because the new object-based motion tween model introduced with Flash CS5 is the preferred workflow, I do not discuss classic tweening in detail in this edition of the book. For more information on classic tweening, refer to the archived "Timeline Animation" chapter from Flash CS3 Professional Bible (Wiley, 2007) on www.flashsupport.com/archive or search the Flash Help files for "classic tween." ■

Shape tweening

Shape tweening is useful for morphing basic shapes — for example, turning a square into a circle, or animating the drawing of a line by tweening from a dot to a finished line. Flash can shape tween only raw *shapes* or drawing objects, so don't even try to shape tween a group, symbol, or editable text — it won't work. You can tween multiple shapes on one layer, but for the sake of organization and animation control, it's best to put each shape on its own layer. This enables you to adjust the speed and length of shape tweens individually and also makes it much easier to figure out what's going on if you need to edit the file later.

Tip

The Object Drawing (J) toggle in the options area of the Tools panel makes your production process more streamlined if you are drawing items to animate. Drawing objects are a more flexible art type, but they can still be shape tweened like raw shapes. You can make objects with any of the normal drawing tools as long as you select the Object Drawing toggle. If you want to convert a raw shape into an object after it is drawn, select the shape, and then choose Modify ➪ Combine Objects ➪ Union from the application menu. ■

On the CD-ROM

The smileTween.fla example file is located on the CD-ROM in the shapeTween subfolder of the ch11 folder. ■

Figure 10.7 shows an animated "smile" created by interpolating the graphics between a dot and a curved stroke with a shape tween. Flash nimbly handles this simple transition, rendering a gradually extending line on the frames between the dot of the pursed mouth and the final curve of the smile.

Here are the steps for creating a shape tween:

1. **Select the frame in which you want to start the animation.** If it's not already a keyframe, convert it to one (F6).

2. **Draw your starting image on the Stage (see Figure 10.8).** Always remember that shape tweening works only with *shapes* or drawing objects — not groups, symbols, or editable text. To shape tween these items, you first need to break them into shapes (Modify ➪ Break Apart). It also helps to keep your animated graphics on a separate layer from the rest of your artwork.

FIGURE 10.7

After a dot is drawn on keyframe 1 and an arc is drawn on keyframe 5, a shape tween is applied to render the shapes on the frames in the span between, creating an animation.

FIGURE 10.8

The contents of the first keyframe in your span define the starting point for the shape tween.

3. Insert a keyframe (F6) on the Timeline where you want the animation to end, and modify the artwork to define the endpoint of the animation (see Figure 10.9). If you want to create the artwork in the final frame from scratch, insert a blank keyframe (F7) instead of a keyframe that includes the artwork from the first keyframe.

The contents of the final keyframe after your span define the ending point for the shape tween.

4. **Select the keyframe at the beginning of the span that you want to interpolate with a shape tween.** Remember that results are easiest to control and modify if you tween only one shape per layer.

5. **Choose Shape Tween from the application Insert menu or choose Create Shape Tween from the contextual menu (opened by right-clicking or Control+clicking the keyframe where you want to start the animation).** The span between the start keyframe and the end keyframe of your animation appears with a green fill and an arrow to indicate that a shape tween has been applied, as shown in Figure 10.10.

When the applied tween is selected in the Timeline, the Properties panel updates to present two options in the Tweening section (shown in Figure 10.11):

FIGURE 10.10

On the first keyframe, specify Shape as the tween type with the contextual menu (or choose Create Shape Tween from the application Insert menu).

FIGURE 10.11

Easing values and animation Blend style can be selected in the Tweening section of the Properties panel.

- Set the Ease value if you want to vary the rate or speed of the animation. This is useful if you want to create the effect of acceleration or deceleration. If you want your animation to start slowly and progressively speed up, push the value down (by clicking and dragging left) to add an Ease In. This causes "in" to display adjacent to the slider and updates the value field with a negative number (between –1 and –100). For an animation that starts fast and progressively slows, push the value up (by clicking and dragging right) to add an Ease Out. The word "out" appears and a positive number (between 1 and 100) displays in the value field. If you want the rate of your animation to stay constant, leave the value in the middle (0). You can also click (and release) the hot text value field to type any number between –100 and 100 directly into the field.

Note

I added an Ease In (–100) to the `smileTween` sample file to make the animation look a little more realistic. ∎

- Select a Blend type from the drop-down menu. Distributive blending creates smoother interpolated shapes, whereas Angular blending creates interpolated shapes that preserve corners and straight lines. If your endpoints contain shapes with corners and lines, select Angular blending. Otherwise, use the default Distributive blending.

6. Preview the animation by choosing Control ⇨ Play (Enter) from the application menu, or use Control ⇨ Test Movie (Ctrl+Enter/⌘+Return) to publish a SWF.

Tip

If the overall speed of the tween seems too fast or too slow, you can extend or reduce the length of the span. The fastest way to increase the span on all visible layers is to move the playhead to the center of the span, make sure that none of the frames are selected on any of the layers and that the layers are all unlocked, and then use the F5 key to add more frames. I added five frames to the overall span of the `smileTween` sample to slow the animation down. ∎

Note

If you delete the artwork on the start or the end keyframes, you will notice that the arrow icon on the Timeline is replaced with a dashed line. This indicates that the tween is broken or incomplete. To restore the tween, it is usually best to select the first keyframe and choose Remove Tween from the application Insert menu (or from the frame contextual menu). Then check your timeline and your artwork to make sure that you have shapes on both a beginning and an end keyframe for Flash to interpolate. When you think all the elements are in place, select the first keyframe and reapply the shape tween by using the Insert menu (or the contextual menu). ∎

Adding shape hints

Because Flash calculates the simplest way to interpolate from one shape to another, you occasionally get unexpected results if the shapes are complex or extremely different from one another. Shape tweening becomes less reliable the more points there are to be calculated between the defined keyframes. In the example, I have added a keyframe at the end of the span with the eyes of the character changed from circles to stars. I want the animation to be a smooth transition from the rough circle to the star shape in each eye. As shown in Figure 10.12, a basic shape tween results in some odd in-between shapes.

FIGURE 10.12

When a shape tween is added to create an animation from one keyframe to another, the transition artwork that Flash generates may not look how you expect it to.

One way of making the in-between artwork more precise is to insert keyframes in the middle of the shape tween so that you can manually adjust the shapes that Flash has generated. Another option that enables you to control a tween without modifying any artwork is to add *shape hints* for Flash to follow when rendering the in-between shapes. Shape hints enable you to specify points on a starting shape that should match with specified points on the final shape. This helps Flash to "understand" how the shapes are related and how the transitional images should be rendered. Compare Figure 10.12 with Figure 10.13 to see the improvement that shape hints can make in the precision of in-between shapes.

On the CD-ROM

To compare the difference made by adding shape hints to the animation, open `eyeTween.fla` **(or .swf) and** `eyeTweenHints.fla` **(or .swf) from the** `shapeHints` **subfolder in the** `ch11` **folder on the CD-ROM.** ∎

FIGURE 10.13

Placing shapes on individual layers and adding shape hints to control the way that Flash renders in-between shapes improves the precision of shape tweens.

Caution

When you are copying and pasting a span of frames into a new timeline — such as from the Main Timeline to a Movie clip timeline — Flash disconnects the shape hints from the shape. When pasting is confined to a single timeline, hints stay as you placed them. ■

Shape hints can be added only to artwork on keyframes that define the beginning and ending points of a shape tween. To add shape hints to the artwork in a shape tween, follow these steps after you have created a basic shape tween:

1. **Select a shape on the starting keyframe and choose Modify ➪ Shape ➪ Add Shape Hint from the application menu (Shift+Ctrl+H/Shift+⌘+H).** Flash places a small red circle, labeled with a letter *a*, onto the Stage — this is your first shape hint. Additional hints can be added, and they will also be identified alphabetically.

2. **To specify a point on your starting shape, use the Selection tool to select and move the first hint (a) — position it on an area of the shape (for example, a corner or a curve) that you want to match up with an area on the final shape, as shown in Figure 10.14.**

FIGURE 10.14

Shape hints positioned on a shape in the starting keyframe for a shape tween

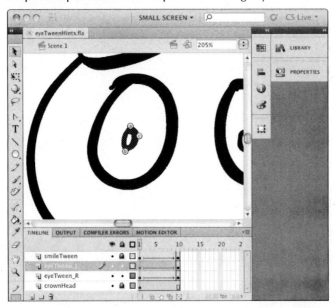

When you move the playhead to the final keyframe of your shape tween, you will see a lettered hint that matches the one that was placed on the starting keyframe.

3. **Position this hint with the Selection tool so that it marks the area of the final shape that should match up with the area specified on the starting shape.** Flash recognizes the hint only if it attaches correctly to the artwork. You will know that your hints are positioned properly when their fill color changes from red to green on the final keyframe (see Figure 10.15) and from red to yellow on the starting keyframe.

4. **Preview the new in-between shapes by** *scrubbing* **the Timeline (dragging the play-head with the Selection tool to review frames in the tweened sequence).**

FIGURE 10.15

Shape hints aligned to points on a shape in the ending keyframe of the tween

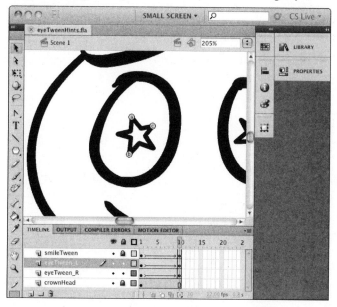

5. **Continue to add or reposition hints until Flash renders the in-between shapes correctly.**

6. **To remove an individual hint, drag it off the Stage with the Selection tool.** To remove all hints from an active keyframe, choose Modify ⇨ Shape ⇨ Remove All Hints from the application menu. A shortcut is to right-click (Control+click on Mac) any of the hints to open the contextual menu, shown in Figure 10.16, for these and other options as you are working.

Tip

If the shape hints are not visible after you have placed them, make sure that the Show All Hints option in the contextual menu is toggled on, or use the application menu to choose View ⇨ Show Shape Hints (Alt+Ctrl+H/Option+ ⌘+H). This option is available only if the layer and keyframe that contain the hints are currently active. ∎

FIGURE 10.16

The contextual menu offers some options for working with shape hints.

Motion tweening

Motion tweening is useful for animating Movie clips, Graphic symbols, and editable text; however, it cannot be used to animate groups, drawing objects, or raw shapes (unless these are first converted into Movie clip or Graphic symbols). As the name suggests, motion tweening is applied to move an item (or target object) from one place to another, but it's capable of much more. Motion tweening can also be used to animate the scale, skew, rotation, color, or transparency of a symbol. Flash filters and the new 3-D properties available in Flash CS5 can also be animated with motion tweens, as described later in this chapter.

Note
Motion tweening can only be applied to one target object per layer — use multiple layers to motion tween multiple targets in the same span of the Timeline. ■

Like a shape tween, a motion tween is more efficient than frame-by-frame animation because it doesn't require unique content for each frame of animation. Yet it is *not* appropriate for all effects — sometimes you'll need to use either frame-by-frame animation or shape tweening to create the kind of in-betweens you want in a sequence.

On the CD-ROM
Create your own file from scratch, or open `motionTween_start.fla` from the `motionTween` subfolder of the `ch11` folder on the CD-ROM. To view the final animation, open `motionTween_final.fla` (or .swf) from the same location. ■

Object-Based Tweens versus Classic Tweens

The workflow used to create motion tweens in versions of Flash older than CS4 required the same keyframe setup as shape tweens, and the resulting tween on a normal layer could easily be disrupted by accidentally adding new artwork or deleting content on one of the keyframes. These keyframe-based motion tweens are now referred to as classic tweens. There are special cases when classic tweens are required, but for most workflows the new motion tween model gets the job done more easily and effectively.

Here are the limitations you may encounter with the newer motion tween model that could prompt you to use classic tweening as a workaround:

- Drawing tools cannot be used on a tween layer.
- Frame scripts are not allowed in a motion tween span.
- Object scripts for a tween target cannot be changed in a motion tween span.
- Eases apply for the duration of a tween span. To achieve easing on specific frames within a tween span, custom ease curves are required.
- Motion tweens can animate only one color effect per tween span.
- You cannot swap symbols or set a specific frame of a graphic symbol to appear in a property keyframe within a tween span.

Here is a summary list of the benefits of the new motion tween model that will hopefully convince even those who don't like change to leave classic tweening in the past:

- Motion tweens require only an initial keyframe. All subsequent property keyframes required to track changes made to the target object are auto-created as you make edits to the target object on the motion tween layer.
- Target objects that change position during a tween span automatically have an editable motion path assigned to them. This Bezier motion path can be easily modified or moved without having to relink the object to the path.
- Motion tweens are required to animate 3-D objects. Classic tweens cannot be applied.
- Motion tweens consider text a tweenable object type.
- Motion tween spans are treated as a single object on the timeline and can be resized, moved, or extended without the hassle of selecting multiple keyframes.
- A target object can be swapped out or deleted and replaced with another tweenable object without losing any of the tween properties. The properties are applied to any new target object pasted into the tween layer without disrupting the animation.

The new tweening method uses a property keyframe concept that is slightly different than the traditional keyframes used in classic tweens. Property keyframes are represented on the Timeline by black diamond-shaped markers rather than the filled circle marker associated with a standard keyframe. Keyframes are used to place an element on the Stage whereas property keyframes are used to modify or move an element within an object-based tween span. Keyframes can be added manually to the Timeline on any layer type, but property keyframes are auto-added to tween layers only when you make a change to a selected element in a tween span either on the Stage or by using the Properties panel or Motion Editor. Multiple property keyframes can be stored within a single frame or keyframe on the Timeline, and you can view them independently in the Motion Editor or by modifying the View Keyframes setting in the tween layer contextual menu.

Here's how to create a motion tween:

1. **Select the frame in which you want to start your animation.** If it's not already a key-frame, make it one by choosing Insert ⇨ Timeline ⇨ Keyframe (F6).

2. **Draw or import the image that you want to tween.** Remember that you can motion tween only symbols and text (editable text blocks).

   • If you already have the element as a symbol in your current Library, you can just drag an instance from the Library onto the Stage. Place each symbol that you want to animate on a separate layer, as shown in Figure 10.17.

   • If you are using a raw shape, group, drawing object, or bitmap, you have the option of converting it into a named Movie clip or Graphic symbol before applying the tween or applying the tween and saying "yes" to the dialog box prompt, allowing Flash to convert the target object into an auto-named Movie clip for you.

FIGURE 10.17

The artwork on the first keyframe of the span you want to motion tween should be a symbol or a text box on its own layer, unless you want to let Flash do the dirty work for you and worry about renaming the symbols it adds to your Library later.

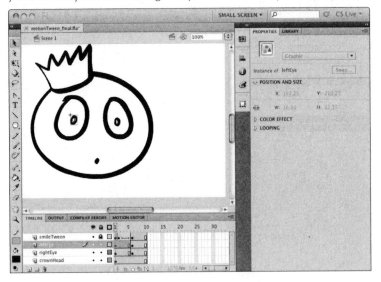

3. **Apply a motion tween.** There are two ways to do this:

   • Select the target object on the Stage and apply the Insert ⇨ Motion tween command from the application menu, or right-click (Control+click on Mac) and select Create Motion Tween from the contextual menu.

   • Select any frame following the initial keyframe containing the target object and apply a motion tween by using either the contextual menu or the application menu.

The tween span appears in the Timeline as a blue fill. If the tween has a target object, the initial keyframe is a black (filled) dot; if the tween does not have a target object the initial keyframe is a white (empty) dot.

4. **Scrub the Timeline to any frame within the tween span where you want to modify the target object.**

5. **Select the target object and edit it as you would any symbol in your Flash movie — using tools in the Tools panel or settings in the Properties panel.** Remember that you can move tweened elements, as well as scale, skew, rotate, or add filters to them. In our example, I wanted the character to glance up and to the side, so I scrubbed to the last frame in the tween span and moved the eye symbol to the final position I wanted the tween to land on and scaled it up to 125 percent (as shown in Figure 10.18). Finally, to give the animation a little more character, I modified the straight motion path by clicking and dragging with the Selection tool to create a slight curve.

6. **After you have a tweened animation working for the first eye and a motion tween span set up for the second eye, select the first eye and use the Copy Motion and Paste Motion commands in the contextual menu to apply the same scale and motion path properties to the second eye tween.**

FIGURE 10.18

Modify the features of the symbol that you want to interpolate with a motion tween at any point in the tween span — Flash auto-inserts property keyframes to keep track of the changes.

Read This Before Using Create Motion Tween

If you have not converted your artwork into a symbol before using the Create Motion Tween command, Flash automatically converts any item in the selected keyframe into a Movie clip symbol with the generic name of Symbol followed by a number (Symbol1, Symbol2). Although this might seem like a handy shortcut, it actually creates a mess that you will need to clean up later.

Because the symbols are auto-created and named, you do not have the same control over how your Library is organized and how your artwork is optimized. It is much better to analyze the most efficient way to convert your artwork into symbols and to reuse those symbols as much as possible than to allow Flash to make generic symbols that may be redundant. As with all elements in your Flash project, it is also much more useful to assign meaningful names to your symbols that will help you navigate the project when you need to make edits.

Manually creating and naming your own symbols before assigning a tween to specific keyframes or target objects helps avoid redundant or confusing items being added to your document (.fla) Library. The warning dialog box for motion tweens always reminds you if you haven't converted the target object into a symbol — instead of choosing OK and letting Flash do the work for you, choose Cancel and convert your target object into a named symbol before reapplying the tween.

Modifying motion tween properties

In addition to the changes that you can make to an animated target object on the Stage by using the Selection tool and the Transform panel, there are some specialized options available in the Properties panel when you select a motion tween span (blue shaded frames on a tween layer). These settings can be used to add finesse to an animation after you have your basic motion tween working:

- **Ease:** As described previously in the Shape tweening section, Ease settings control the interpolation pattern of a tween. A default setting of 0 interpolates the changes in the motion tween at a consistent rate from beginning to end. Increasing the Ease value (within a range of 1 to 100) makes the change start more quickly and then gradually slow down — creating an *ease out*. Decreasing the Ease value (within a range of –1 to –100) makes the change start more slowly and gradually speed up — creating an *ease in*. Easing in works well to build anticipation, and easing out works well to make items settle more naturally at the end of a motion.

Tip

As you try different Ease values, you may realize that you want your tween to ease in and ease out, but still move quickly in the middle. Luckily, the Motion Editor enables custom easing control by using a visual curve to map the rate of interpolation in a tween. Using curves to adjust easing anywhere along a tween rather than applying a fixed value on the initial keyframe opens up a whole range of creative possibilities and makes the process a lot more fun. The Motion Editor is discussed later in this chapter. ■

- **Rotation:** You can rotate tweened items with this option. You can set the number of rotations or the degree of rotation. One rotation is equal to 360 degrees — Flash automatically calculates the number of whole rotations when you enter a rotation of more than 360 in the degree field. If you want your target object to do only a partial rotation, enter a value less than 360 degrees. Select a rotation direction from the drop-down menu: None rotates your item in the direction that requires the least amount of motion, while Clockwise and Counterclockwise rotate your item in the indicated direction. In both cases, the rotation is completed as many times as you specify in the Rotate value field or as many times as Flash calculates from the value you enter in the degree field. If you type 0 in the Rotate field, or select None from the drop-down menu, no rotation occurs (other than rotation that has been applied to the symbol with the Transform panel). As shown in Figure 10.19, I applied an Ease out value of 100 to the sample file from the previous section, motionTween, to make the eye motion look more natural.

Note

The 3D Rotation and 3D Translation tools can be applied to a Movie clip in a tween span to convert it into a 3-D symbol. Settings for 3-D symbols can then be modified on the Stage or in the Properties panel. ∎

Caution

Alpha effects and intensive filters in motion tweens slow most fps (frames per second) settings. The only way to make sure that the fps is honored, no matter how intensive the animation might be, is to use a stream sync sound that loops over the course of any critical fps playback. For more on the relationship between streaming sounds and fps rate, see Chapter 12. ∎

FIGURE 10.19

Basic options for motion tweens are available in the Properties panel when a tween span is selected in the Timeline.

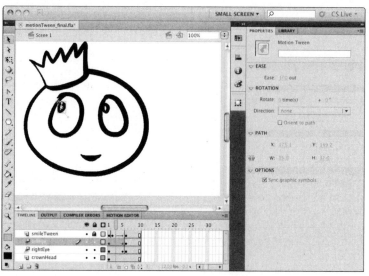

- **Orient to path:** When your item follows a path (or motion guide), turning this selection on forces the item to orient its movement to that path. I describe this feature in more detail in the section later in this chapter on editing motion paths.

- **Sync Graphic symbols:** When this setting is activated on a tween, you can replace the symbol in the first keyframe and it automatically updates in the remaining frames and in any other synchronized keyframes that follow. This setting is also important if your animation is contained within a Graphic symbol. Flash recalculates the number of frames in a tween on a Graphic symbol's Timeline so that it matches the number of frames available on the Main Timeline. Sync ensures that your animation loops properly when the animated symbol is placed in the Main Timeline, even if the frame sequence in the Graphic symbol is not an even multiple of the number of frames assigned to the symbol in the Main Timeline.

Tip

You can tell if a tweened sequence is synchronized by observing that the vertical lines separating the keyframes from the span are not visible when this setting is applied. ∎

Working with motion tween spans and layers

When you apply a motion tween to a target object, the tween span is rendered on a special tween layer — you'll notice that the standard layer icon changes from a simple page to something that looks like a square in motion. If the target object is the only element on the original layer when you apply a motion tween, the layer *converts* from a standard layer into a tween layer. However, if there are other elements on the original layer, the target object moves to a new auto-inserted tween layer *created* by Flash. In either case, the tween span occupies the same number of frames in the tween layer as the target object occupied on the original layer. The exception to this rule occurs when the target object occupies only one frame in the original layer, in which case Flash adds enough frames to the tween span to create one second of animation. That is, if the frame rate of your Flash movie is 24 fps, the default length for auto-created tween spans will be 24 frames.

Other elements can be motion tweened on the same span of the Timeline, as long as they are on separate layers (see Figure 10.20). You can interpolate different features on each tween and also apply any control settings (property keyframes or keyframes) that you want — Flash reads and renders the motion on each tween layer independently.

FIGURE 10.20

Multiple items can be animated simultaneously by creating tweens on individual layers.

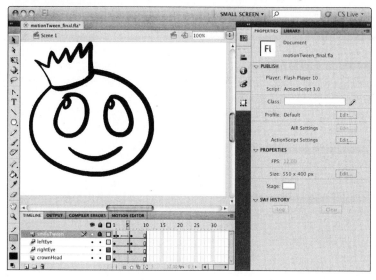

Tween layers restrict some authoring options to protect the tween span:

- **Adding graphics:** You cannot add additional elements to a tween layer with the drawing tools or the Text tool. If you attempt these actions, a dialog box reminds you that tween layers do not support drawing.

- **Adding symbols:** If you paste a symbol or drag a symbol from the Library onto the Stage while a tween layer (with a target object) is active, a dialog box gives you the option of replacing the original target object with the new symbol you are trying to place. Choose OK only if you want to swap the symbols for the duration of the tween.

- **Pasting graphics:** If you try to paste a raw shape (including shape primitives or drawing objects) onto the Stage while a tween layer is active, Flash tries to interpret the shape as a motion path. If the shape is anything but a simple stroke with a beginning and endpoint, a dialog box reminds you that the shape is not a valid motion path and cannot be pasted into a tween layer.

- **Adding keyframes:** You can add keyframes (F6) and empty keyframes (F7) to a tween layer but only before or after a tween span. Using the Insert Keyframe command from the application menu or the F6 shortcut on a frame within a tween span (the blue shaded frames on a tween layer) actually inserts a *property* keyframe (marked by a black diamond), locking all properties for the target object to their current value on that frame. This is not a recommended workflow unless you have a special reason for locking all properties on that frame. It's best to rely on Flash to create individual property keyframes as needed when you modify the target object or use the tween layer contextual menu to

385

specify the property you want to keyframe (Insert Keyframe ➪ Position, Scale, Skew, and so on). Using the Insert ➪ Timeline ➪ Blank Keyframe command from the application menu or the F7 shortcut within a tween span has no result.

As you work with content on tween layers, there are some special workflows that will help you manipulate motion tween spans:

- **Extending animation:** A motion tween span can be as short as one frame. Dragging the end of a tween span to the right extends the animation farther along the Timeline, shifting all the property keyframes as needed to keep the flow of the animation consistent. The longer a tween span is, the longer the animation takes to complete, so any motion or change in properties will be slower. Conversely, dragging the end of a tween span to the left shortens the duration of a tween and makes any changes happen more quickly. Keep in mind that the speed of the overall animation is also constrained by the frame rate setting for your Flash movie.

- **Extending a tween span:** Holding down the Shift key as you drag the end of a tween span lengthens the tween span without moving any of the property keyframes. This means that the pacing for changes in position or property that you have already established in your animation do not change, but the final state of the target object is visible on the Stage as long as the blue tween span is extended along the Timeline. You can, of course, make additional changes to the target object at any point in the tween, regardless of which method you use to extend the span.

- **Moving a tween span:** You can move a tween span by selecting it as a single object and dragging it to a new location on the Timeline — either on the same layer or on a different layer. If you drag a tween span onto a normal layer, it converts into a tween layer. Any existing content in the frames where you place the tween span is cleared and replaced with the animation in the tween span.

- **Replacing a target object:** As described earlier, you can drag or paste a new symbol into a tween layer and Flash gives you the option of replacing the current target object. You can also select the current target object and use the Swap Symbol command to choose a new target object from your Library. You can even delete the original target object and then drag or paste a symbol into the tween layer to automatically become the new target object without any fear of "breaking" the tween — another benefit of the new motion tween model over the old classic motion tween.

- **Viewing property keyframes:** As you make changes to a target object in a motion tween span, you will see diamond-shaped markers added to the timeline to mark each property keyframe. If you want to control which property keyframes are visible in the span, use the tween layer contextual menu (right-click or Control+click on Mac) to access the View Keyframes submenu. By default, all properties are set to visible. Click any property in the list to toggle it off or back on or use the global settings of All or None.

Editing motion paths

One of the most elegant aspects of the object-based motion tween model is that motion paths are auto-created on the same layer as the target object. Points along the path correspond to frames in the tween span, and the position or shape of the path can be changed at any point in the tween.

Note

This workflow is miles ahead of the classic tween model in previous versions of Flash that required a separate layer for a manually created motion guide and necessitated careful alignment and snapping to keep the tweened object attached to the path. ■

To create and edit a motion path in a motion tween span, follow these steps:

1. **After setting up a motion tween (as described in the previous section), scrub the Timeline to any frame in the tween span (besides the starting keyframe).** If you want the motion to happen over the duration of the tween span, scrub to the final frame in the span. In our example, I moved the playhead to frame 20 and then selected the target object. Select the target object on the Stage and move it to a new X, Y location — use the Selection tool to click and drag or enter new X and/or Y values in the Position and Size section of the Properties panel.

   As shown in Figure 10.21, after you move a target object, a blue line appears, marking the shortest distance between the original location of the target object and the new location of the target object. The dots along this motion path represent the individual frames in the span between the original keyframe and the frame where you moved the target object. The frame where you moved the target object to a new location becomes a position property keyframe.

FIGURE 10.21

The initial keyframe in the motion tween sets the starting position for the target object (left); moving the target object to a new position in any other frame of the tween span creates a motion path and inserts a position property keyframe (right).

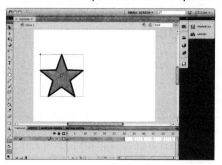
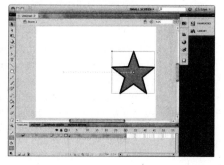

Caution

If you move the target object at a frame in the middle of the span and then decide you want to move it again in a frame farther along the span (or farther back), just keep in mind that any frames where you move the target object become position property keyframes. These are visible in the Timeline and on the motion path as diamond-shaped markers. If you prefer to enable Flash to interpolate the motion evenly from beginning to end within a tween span, remove any interstitial position property keyframes and work with the motion guide or the easing curves to create the motion pattern you want between the initial keyframe and the final frame in the tween span. If you leave in a series of random position property keyframes, you may find that your animated motion lags or speeds up unexpectedly in different sections of the motion path. ∎

2. **Scrub the timeline to preview the motion as the object follows the path.** If you are happy with the motion, you're finished! If you like to change the route that the target object takes, the motion path can be modified with the Selection tool or the Subselection tool. In our example, I clicked and dragged the motion path to add a large curve for the target object to follow. As shown in Figure 10.22, this new path is longer but there is still the same number of frame markers (round dots) along the path — equal to the number of frames between the first keyframe and the final position property keyframe in the tween span.

FIGURE 10.22

The motion path can be modified with the Selection tool (left) to change the route that the target object takes between keyframes within the tween span (right).

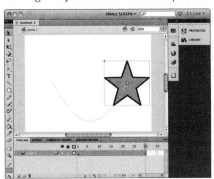 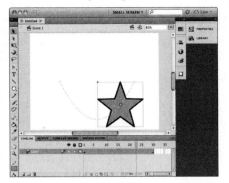

Cross-Reference

You might notice that the motion path is actually a Bezier path, and you can use the Subselection tool and the Pen tool to modify control points and handles to adjust the curves and angles in the motion path just as you would any other stroke. The white squares that mark position property keyframe changes along the motion guide when the line is selected with the Pen or Subselection tool are cubic Bezier anchor points; these can be used for controlling the shape of the line. The smaller round dots along the line mark all the "normal" frames in the span and cannot be used as control points for changing the shape of the line unless you convert a frame into a property keyframe (by manually changing the position of the target object on that frame). Refer to Chapter 5 if you need information about working with Bezier controls. ∎

3. **If you want to move the whole path (and the target object) to a different location on the Stage, click (and release) to select the path and then click and drag it to a new location.** This is different than clicking (and not releasing) the mouse to drag the path in order to change its shape.

You can delete the path at any time and the position property keyframes are deleted along with the motion path. You can also copy and paste the path if you want to reuse it or have multiple items follow the same path on different tween layers.

Adding control to animation along a motion path

Even after you have succeeded in modifying a motion path in a tween span, you may find that the movement of the animated element is not exactly as you would like. Fortunately, you can modify how a target object follows a motion path in a few different ways.

Using Orient to path

The first control to consider is found in the Properties panel when the first keyframe of your motion tween is selected. The Orient to path check box (shown in Figure 10.23) creates property keyframes on every frame of the tween to track changes in rotation (z-axis), helping the target object stay oriented as it follows a curved path and keeping it headed along the path. When Orient to path is not active, an animated item maintains the same orientation throughout the tween, with no relation to the curves or loops in the path.

FIGURE 10.23

By default, a tweened item maintains the same orientation as it moves along a curved path (left). Selecting Orient to path keeps an animated item headed along the curves or loops in a motion path (right).

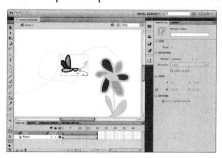

Registration and center point alignment

The second important factor that determines how an animated element moves along a motion path is where the registration point of the symbol is located. By default, the registration point is generally at the center of the symbol, but this may not be the point of the item that you want to snap to the path. To modify the alignment of a target object, you can modify the registration point of the symbol (see Figure 10.24).

To modify the registration point of a tweened symbol on a motion path, follow these steps:

1. **Select the symbol on the first keyframe of the tween.**

2. **Activate the Free Transform tool in the Toolbox, and drag the registration point (small white circle icon) to a new location.** You'll see the motion path move to snap-align to the new registration point on the target object. You may have to select the motion path and move it back into position in relation to the Stage or artwork on other layers, but the target object also moves and the new registration point remains locked to the path.

FIGURE 10.24

When Free Transform is active, you can modify the registration point that defines how a target object tracks along a motion path without changing the alignment of the artwork in relation to the symbol center point.

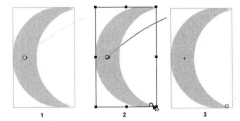

Working with motion presets

As many of us had to learn the hard way, animation is not as easy as it looks. Something as simple as a bounce or a dimensional zoom requires attention to timing and scale — and if the animation is going to have any dimension or character, physical properties of weight and density need to be conveyed as the object moves or reacts to other elements in the scene. Although experienced animators can create believable motion without breaking a sweat, this can be a tall order for even the most skilled graphic designer or programmer. In an attempt to make the learning curve a little less steep, Adobe has included a collection of starter animation presets. These ready-made object-based motion tweens can be previewed and applied from the Motion Presets panel (Window ➪ Motion Presets). Only one preset can be applied to a target object; applying a second preset replaces the first one.

To apply a Motion preset, follow these steps:

1. **Open the Motion Presets panel (shown in Figure 10.25).** Preview animation by selecting any presets listed in the Default Presets folder (or any other folder if you have loaded or saved custom presets of your own).

2. **Select a tweenable target object on the Stage (on its own layer) and click the Apply button in the Motion Presets panel.** If the object you have selected is not a Movie clip or a Graphic symbol or a text field, a dialog box reminds you that the object must be one of these element types before the motion preset can be applied.

The motion preset creates a tween by using your selected object as the target. You can scrub the Timeline to preview the result (or use the Test Movie command). The tween span, property keyframes, or motion path applied to your target object by the motion preset may not align as you expect with your Stage size or elements on other layers — that's why these are considered animation starter files.

Caution

If you apply a motion preset and then decide to remove it, using the Remove tween command removes the tween span from the Timeline, but property changes applied to the target object may still "stick." You can use the Properties panel to remove filters or color effects or other changes made to your target object by the motion preset, but this can be a little tricky to dig through. Another option is to use the Undo command rather than the Remove tween command to get rid of any changes the motion preset made. ■

FIGURE 10.25

The Motion Presets panel

You can modify the animation created by a motion preset in the same way you would modify any other motion tween. If you end up with a customized result that you want to save and use again, simply select the tween span or the target object and use the contextual menu to choose Save as Motion Preset. You can also click the page icon at the bottom of the Motion Presets panel to save your selected tween as a preset. Motion presets are stored as XML files in the following directory locations:

- **Windows:** HD\Documents and Settings\<user>\Local Settings\
  Application Data\Adobe\Flash CS5\<language>\Configuration\Motion
  Presets\
- **Mac:** HD/Users/<user>/Library/Application Support/Adobe/Flash
  CS5/<language>/Configuration/Motion Presets/

Motion preset XML files can also be exported or imported, using the Motion Presets panel.

Web Resource

For more detailed information about working with custom motion presets, including how to create a preview for a custom XML file, refer to Adobe Help: Using Flash CS5 Professional ⇨ Timelines and Animation ⇨ Motion tweens ⇨ Applying motion presets. ∎

Note

If you are working with classic tweens, the Copy Motion and Paste Motion commands can be a helpful shortcut for reusing animation patterns. These commands can be found in the contextual menu when a tween span is selected, or in the Application menu under Edit ⇨ Timeline. For more information about using the Copy Motion and Paste Motion commands with classic tweens, refer to the archived content from Flash CS3 Professional Bible (Wiley, 2007): "Chapter 11: Timeline Animation" at http://www.flashsupport.com/archive. ∎

Adjusting Easing and Tween Properties with the Motion Editor

Custom easing curves can be created and manipulated in Motion Editor panel. The panel is docked for tabbed access with the Timeline panel when you load the Essentials Workspace, or you can add it to any Workspace layout by choosing Window ⇨ Motion Editor. As shown in Figure 10.26, the Motion Editor panel enables you to see individual tween properties separated out into discrete layers. The values on each keyframe of a specific property can be viewed and modified by using numeric hot text controls and/or visual tweening curves that graph property changes (vertically) over time (horizontally, left to right).

This panel may be a little intimidating when you first open it, but keep in mind that you don't really *need* to use this panel unless you want to fine-tune the animation you've already created with other Flash tools. You can think of the Motion Editor as the engine room: If everything is going smoothly up on deck and you are happy with the way the animation is running, there's really no need to go down below and get your hands dirty. On the other hand, if you like to see how things work, the Motion Editor does a great job of laying out all the changes that happen in a tween span so that you can analyze it in frame-by-frame and property-by-property detail.

FIGURE 10.26

The Motion Editor panel displays the property values for property keyframes in a selected motion tween span. Individual values can be modified, using hot text controls or tweening curves.

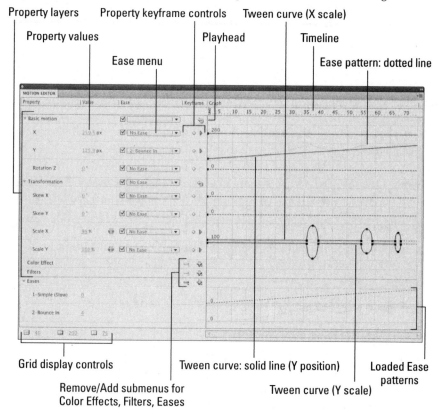

Property layers   Property keyframe controls   Tween curve (X scale)

Property values   Playhead   Timeline

Ease menu   Ease pattern: dotted line

Grid display controls   Tween curve: solid line (Y position)   Loaded Ease patterns

Remove/Add submenus for Color Effects, Filters, Eases   Tween curve (Y scale)

You can modify the individual curves of any of these properties should you want them to be rendered at a different pace to create a custom tween effect:

- **Basic motion:** This section groups together the X, Y, and Z (rotation) values for the target object. Because these properties are always related (a target object always has an X, Y, and Z value to locate it on the Stage), their property keyframes have to match up and they have some special editing rules that other properties don't have:

  - You can add or remove control points on the tween curves for these properties, but you cannot modify them with Bezier controls.

  - To toggle interstitial keyframes in a tween span for these properties from roving to non-roving, use the contextual menu or drag a roving keyframe to a vertical frame divider to make it non-roving.

- It is best to edit the basic motion of a target object by working directly with the motion path on the Stage. The Motion Editor can be helpful for moving property values to new frames in the tween span or for setting exact pixel values for the target location in some property keyframes.

Note

Roving keyframes enable Flash to render motion more smoothly by shifting keyframes as needed over the span of a tween. Non-roving keyframes lock specific X, Y, and Z values (or target object positions) to specific frames within a tween span. ■

- **Transformation:** This section groups together the Skew and Scale properties for both the x and y axis of the target object. Any differences in size or skew between the target object in the initial keyframe and the last property keyframe of a tween span can be interpolated at different rates.

- **Color Effect:** You can control any color changes from one property keyframe to the next in a tween by editing the tween curve. You can add color effects to a target symbol by using the submenu in the Motion Editor or by using the settings in the Properties panel.

- **Filters:** If filters have been applied to create changes in an item's appearance in the span of a tween, the pattern of change can be adjusted with custom easing. Filters can be added to a target symbol from the submenu in the Motion Editor or from the Properties panel.

Tip

To link X and Y value pairs so that they always match when changes are made to either property, click the Link X and Y Property Values button (to the left of the Ease menu) for either property. ■

In most cases, you only need to create custom tween curves for one or two properties to achieve a very polished final result. The possibilities can be a little overwhelming at first and the flexibility of custom easing curves might work against you: As you modify the curves in myriad ways, it can be difficult to keep track of which curves work best for specific effects. Fortunately, a few tricks can help as you experiment:

- Use the Properties panel controls first because these are a little less complicated. The settings you apply with the Properties panel are translated into curves that you can use as a starting point when you shift over to the Motion Editor.

- Copy and paste patterns from one property to another if you have created a tween curve that you like and you want another property to progress in the same pattern. Right-click (or ⌘+click on Mac) in the graph area of a tween pattern that you want to copy and choose Copy from the contextual menu. Select the graph area of a property layer that you want to change and use the contextual menu to choose Paste to instantly shift the curve to match your custom settings. This technique also works to copy custom easing patterns and to apply a custom easing pattern to a property tween curve.

- To reverse the direction of a property tween, select the graph area and choose Reverse Keyframes from the contextual menu.

- If an individual curve gets too complicated or you change your mind, just use the contextual menu in the graph area to choose Reset Property.

- Use the Reset Values button for the category to reset all the curves for a section of properties in the Motion Editor to non-tweened values.

Controlling property views in the Motion Editor

As in the Properties panel, you can control what property values are visible in the Motion Editor by expanding and collapsing sections of the panel with the property layer controls. When a property layer arrow is twirled down, the property name, value setting (for current position in the tween span), Ease setting (if any), and visual tween curve (plotted across the frames of the current tween span) are all visible. To facilitate editing in the tween curve area of the panel, you can click any expanded layer a second time to expand the layer view even farther. The number of frames visible in the tween curve area and the height of expanded and collapsed layers can be modified with the Grid display controls (bottom-left corner of Figure 10.26) to suit your screen size (or eyesight):

- **Graph size:** Sets the minimum height of the layers in the graph for collapsed layers. Can be set in a range between 20 pixels and 20 pixels less than the current setting for Expanded Graph size.

- **Expanded Graph size:** Sets the maximum height for expanded layers in the graph. Can be set in a range between 20 pixels more than the current (collapsed) Graph size and 500 pixels. I found 200 to be a good working size.

- **Viewable frames:** Zooms in and out of the current tween span to show a set number of frames in the curves area of the panel. The range is from 1 frame to the total number of frames in the currently selected tween span.

Caution

Patterns in your tween curves and eases can be hard to see in the Motion Editor if you are zoomed in too close to the tween span. It helps to zoom out and get oriented by pushing the number of viewable frames up to show your complete tween span before zooming in again, if needed, to focus on a more limited number of specific frames. The timeline only shows numbers every fifth frame, so it becomes more useful as a navigation aid when you look at ten or more frames at a time. ■

Editing tween curves and property key frames

The tween curves in the Motion Editor track changes in object properties over the life of your tween span. Most properties can be modified independently from frame to frame (changes can be locked in by using a property keyframe or they can be interpolated in a curve from one control point to the next). Tween curves can be edited in a similar way to strokes (or motion paths), using the Selection tool or the Pen tool:

- Drag control points left or right to set a property value at a specific frame in the tween span. Dragging a control point left sets the value sooner in the tween, and dragging it right sets it later in the tween.

Caution

Dragging a control point past other control points on the same property curve clears those points. ■

- Increase a property value by dragging a curve or control point toward the top of the grid. Decrease a property value by dragging a curve or control point toward the bottom of the grid.

- Add or Remove control points by moving the playhead to the frame you want to edit and using the Add or Remove Keyframe button in the Motion Editor (yellow diamond icon between next and last keyframe buttons).

Tip

You can also use the contextual menu to add or remove control points as well as using shortcut keys with the Selection tool: Ctrl+click/Option+click on an empty area of the curve to add a point, or on an existing point to remove it. ■

- Curves with smooth points can be adjusted with Bezier handles. To toggle a control point between corner and smooth modes, Alt+click/⌘+click the point. Tween curves pass through smooth points as rounded curves with incremental value changes, and corner points enable more abrupt changes in value with an angled transition.

Tip

To adjust a specific curve point, you can also use the contextual menu to choose Smooth Point, Smooth Right, Smooth Left, or Corner Point. ■

Eases and custom eases

Although tween curves and eases appear on the same grid, they are edited differently. Tween curves are generated when you make any changes to a tweened property, and they enable you to edit the curve directly to adjust the rate of change for a specific property at any time. Eases are preset interpolation patterns that enable you to control the percentage of change that happens in each section of a tween span; you can also think of this as the pattern of the change. Easing is applied only if you want the *rate of interpolation* for a specific property (or all tweened properties) to change over the span of a tween. If you want the interpolation to be spread evenly on all frames that come between one property keyframe and the next, you don't have to add any easing.

Eases are managed in the Eases section at the bottom of the Motion Editor and applied by using the Ease menu for each property layer (shown in Figure 10.26). As discussed in the Animation Strategies chapter of this book, animation relies heavily on physics and the laws of the natural world. For this reason, Adobe was able to anticipate some of the ease patterns that you might find most useful and include them in the Eases submenu (available when you click the plus icon (+) at the top of the Eases section of the Properties panel). Any eases that you add to the Eases section of the Motion Editor are available in the Ease menu for each property in the layers above. For Figure 10.26, I added just two of the ready-made eases that ship with Flash CS5 to the Eases section of the panel to give you an idea of how different these patterns can be. I also applied the Bounce pattern to the tween for the Y value of the Basic motion property so that you can see how the dotted ease pattern overlays the original tween curve.

It takes some practice to get the feel for using easing curves to control tweens, but I'm sure you can already see how many more options for different styles of motion you'll have if you use easing:

- **Diagonal lines continue in an even motion.** The more closely the percentage of change matches the progression in frames, the more even the transformation will be. (Try any of the Simple eases.)

- **Gradual curves can add smooth acceleration or deceleration.** A reverse curve that creates gradual slopes at the beginning and end as well as a steeper pitch in the middle creates an Ease In/Ease Out effect. (Try the Stop and Start ease or the Sine Wave ease.)

- **Bumps in a curve can add a stuttering motion.** For example, if an anchor point at the frame 10 marker is set at the 50% change line and you add an anchor point at the frame 15 marker that is set to pull the curve back down to the 25% tween line, you cause the tween to progress and then reverse and then progress again at a quicker rate to reach 100% transformation by the last frame of the tween. (Try the Bounce ease or Sawtooth Wave ease.)

- **Flat (horizontal) lines add pauses.** The frames continue, but the percentage of change is forced to plateau or hold at a specific point of transformation. (Try the Square Wave ease or Random ease.)

- **Vertical lines create quick jumps.** The percentage of change has to increase, but it doesn't have any frames to gradually make the change. (Try the Square Wave ease or the Random ease.)

Caution

You can add or delete eases at any time, but keep in mind that removing an ease from the Eases section of the Motion Editor also removes it from any property layer that you've applied it to. ∎

After you add an ease to a tween property, you can still edit the tween curve (either in the Motion Editor or by making changes to the target object on Stage or in the Timeline), and the ease curve responds, but it keeps its basic shape. Ease curves can be modified in the Eases section of the Motion Editor by changing the hot text values within the allowable range for each ease pattern: Patterns with one long curve enable you to push the pattern from one end of the tween to the other and flip the pattern by changing the value from negative to positive (making it an ease in or an ease out), while repeating patterns with discrete sections joined by corner points enable you to set the number of repeating sections in the pattern.

Tip

If you set easing for a tween span in the main Properties panel, the value of Ease In or Ease Out that you apply renders in the Motion Editor as a Simple(Slow) curve, and the value applies to all tweened properties. This is a good way to get an idea of how the visual curve relates to the standard easing values. ∎

If you need to go beyond the ease patterns that ship with Flash CS5, you can select the Custom option at the bottom of the Add Ease menu in the Motion Editor. This adds a Custom layer in the Eases section with an editable (solid rather than dotted) line loaded in the graph area. You can use the Selection or Pen tool to modify this line with Bezier handles or by adding additional curve or corner points. Custom patterns are available in the Ease menus for any of the property layers, and changes that you make to your patterns update on any layers that you've added them to.

Tip

You can add as many custom ease patterns to the Motion Editor as you need to — they will all have the same name, but they will also be numbered in the order that you added them so you can tell them apart. Custom eases are saved with your Flash project file but do not carry over from one file to the next (unless you do some copying and pasting from file to file or use motion presets to save your animation along with any custom eases). ■

As with anything else, it pays to start simple. Experiment with changing the ease curve of one property, and if you get something you like, copy it to a new custom ease layer before you move on with another modification. If a curve works great to create an interesting effect on one property, try applying it to something else. Before long, you will have a library of files with cool tween patterns that you can copy and paste from, instead of having to re-create a curve from scratch each time.

Animating 3-D properties

I describe the process for working with 3-D symbol properties in Chapter 9, but you can take this feature a step farther and animate the changes you make to 3-D position or rotation. If you have already created a 3-D symbol on the Stage by applying the 3D Rotation (W) or 3D Translation tool (G) to a Movie clip, you can use the 3-D symbol as a target object for a motion tween. Changes made to the target object on the Stage by using the 3-D settings or tools create property keyframes that are interpolated in the tween span and displayed in the Motion Editor along with other properties.

A great way to get started with 3-D animation is to try one of the motion presets that tween 3-D properties. After you apply a motion preset (as described earlier in this chapter), you can modify any of the settings or curves in the Motion Editor. I used the motion preset for 3D Rotation ("spiral-3D" from the Default Presets folder in the Motion Presets panel) as a starting point in our example file. This motion preset animates the target object around the z-axis, but the final result is that the object ends up looking backward in the end frame of the tween, as shown in Figure 10.27.

To create a more seamless looping animation, I used two different approaches:

- In the 3D_rotationRepeat.fla file, I made the animation look as though the graphic is rotating 180 degrees to face backward and then rotating the opposite direction to face forward again. I did this by inserting a control point on the Rotation Y tween curve, setting the value on the new property keyframe to 180 degrees, and then changing the value in the final property keyframe to 0 degrees. As shown in Figure 10.28, the resulting tween interpolates the rotation from 0 degrees to 180 degrees and then back from 180 degrees to 0 degrees. The animation is faster because the graphic rotates forward and then backward through the 180-degree arc within the same number of frames, but you can always extend the tween farther along the Main Timeline to give the animation more time.

FIGURE 10.27

The spiral-3D motion preset tweens the Rotation Y property for the target object from 0 degrees to 180 degrees over a span of 50 frames. In the final frame of the tween, our target object is backward. When the tween loops, the object "jumps" back to its proper orientation when the playhead returns to the initial keyframe in the tween.

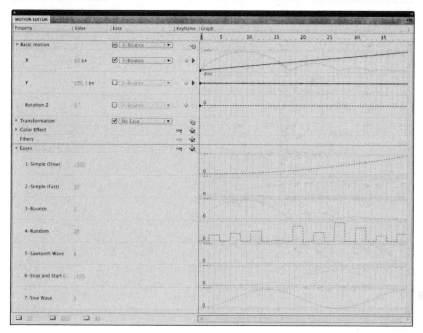

Tip

The same effect I created by modifying the curve for the Rotation Y property can be achieved on animation with multiple property changes, or even on frame-by-frame animation sequences by editing the Main Timeline. Copy the whole tween span and place the copy farther down the Timeline on the same layer to follow seamlessly after the first tween. A shortcut for creating a copy of a tween span is to hold down the Alt (Option) key while dragging the span to a new location, and then use the contextual menu to choose Reverse Keyframes on the copied span. Repeating and reversing a tween span is almost always a good way to get a seamless looping animation and to avoid a "blip" at the end of your sequence when the position in the final frame of a tween jumps back to the starting position at the beginning of the span. Having a tween run forward and then run backward before returning to the beginning of the span creates a seamless transition. ■

FIGURE 10.28

Creating a repeating pattern in a tween curve with matching values in the final property keyframe and the initial tween keyframe creates a smooth transition for looping animation.

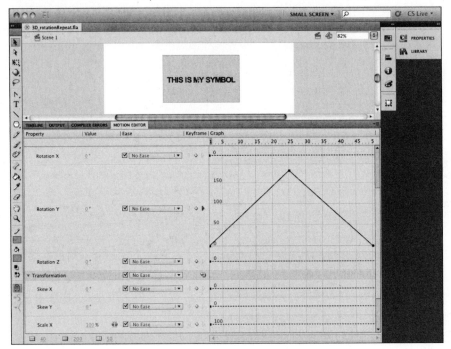

- In the 3D_rotationFlip.fla file, I inserted a property keyframe halfway through the tween (when the target object was approximately 90 degrees along the z-axis or "sideways" to the viewer) and applied a vertical flip to the graphic (Modify ⇨ Transform ⇨ Flip Vertical) so when the graphic finished the second half of the tween it would not appear backward. This is equivalent to setting the Scale X property for the graphic to –100. Because any changes made to a tweened target object on the Stage are interpolated in all the frames between property keyframes, the flip I applied was being eased in during the first half of the tween span and this interfered with the smooth rotation animation. Figure 10.29 shows the original tween curves after I applied the flip in frame 26 of the tween span.

FIGURE 10.29

Flipping the target object on the Stage resulted in a tweened curve interpolating the change in the Scale X property from 100 to –100 over the first half of the tween span.

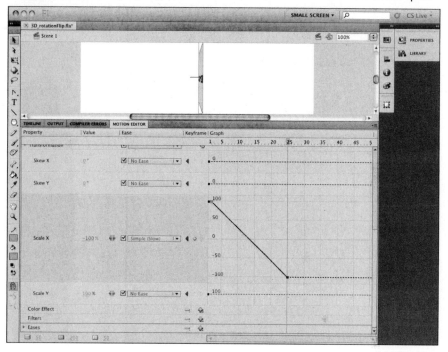

The solution is to force the flip to happen in just one frame instead of tweening it over all the frames in the first half of the span. This is accomplished by using two property keyframes side by side in the Timeline with an X-scale of 100 in the first keyframe (or no flip) and an X-scale of –100 in the second keyframe (or full flip). You can either make these changes directly to the target object on the Stage by using the Transform panel to modify the X-scale value on two frames somewhere around the center of the tween span, or you can open the Motion Editor and modify the tween curve for the Scale X property in the Transformation section of the panel. Insert a new control point just before the control point that flips the graphic, and then move the new control point up to keep the curve flat (no transformation) for the first half of the tween span, with a sharp drop from +100 to –100 over just one frame, as shown in Figure 10.30.

FIGURE 10.30

Inserting a new control point on the curve enables us to force the change in Scale X value to happen over just one frame instead of interpolating it over the first half of the tween span. Adding and shifting the control point on the curve is equivalent to adding a property keyframe and forcing the Scale X value to its original value in the frame just before the frame that changes it to –100.

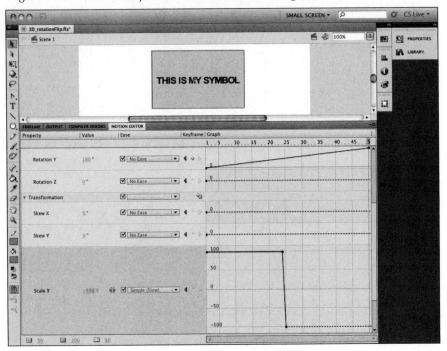

On the CD-ROM

To see the original animation created by applying the motion preset for 3D Rotation, open `3D_rotation Preset.fla` **from the** `3DTween` **subfolder in the** `ch10` **folder on the CD. Compare the original with the modified files,** `3D_rotationRepeat.fla` **and** `3D_rotationFlip.fla`, **found in the same folder.** ∎

Although describing these changes takes up a lot of page space, it really is just a couple of quick editing steps, and you can see how much time is saved by using motion presets and the Motion Editor rather than creating animation from scratch. The key to success when working with animation (2-D or 3-D) is to first understand the individual properties and how changes in their value modify the appearance of your target object. Testing property changes first by using a nonanimated target object enables you to plan the key positions in your animation. If you then work with the Motion Editor, you will have a better idea of which curves you need to modify and the values to enter on property keyframes to get the animated result you are hoping for. If you know where you want to start and how you want to end, Flash does a pretty great job of figuring out all the steps in between to render smooth animation.

Flash CS5 Interface With Essentials Workspace

Learn to customize your workspace in Chapter 4.

Flash CS5 Interface With Designer Workspace

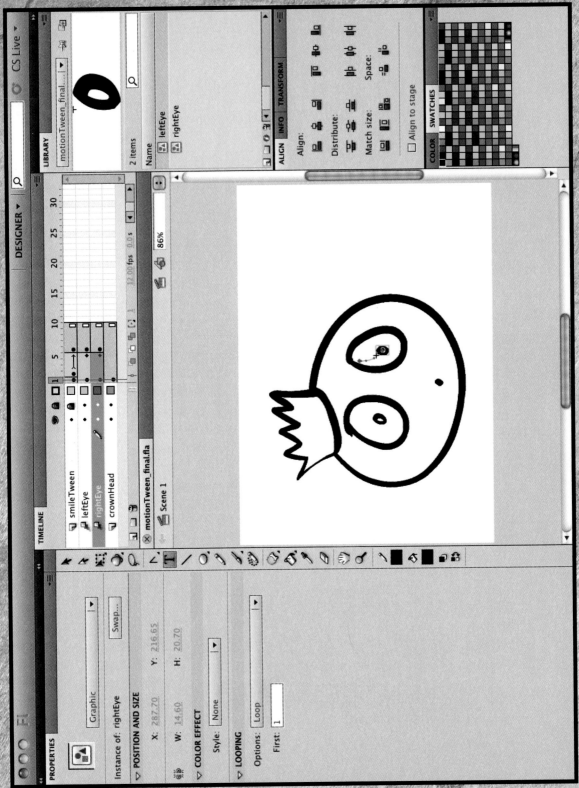

Learn to customize your workspace in Chapter 4.

Working with Color

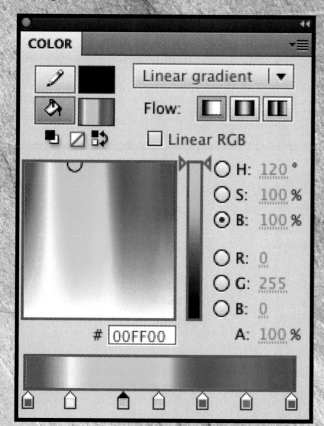

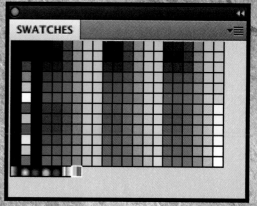

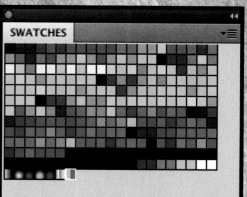

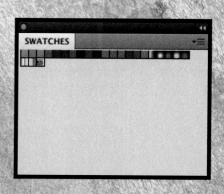

Get to know the Flash CS5 Color and Swatches panels in Chapter 7.

Use the Adjust Color filter to quickly modify graphics

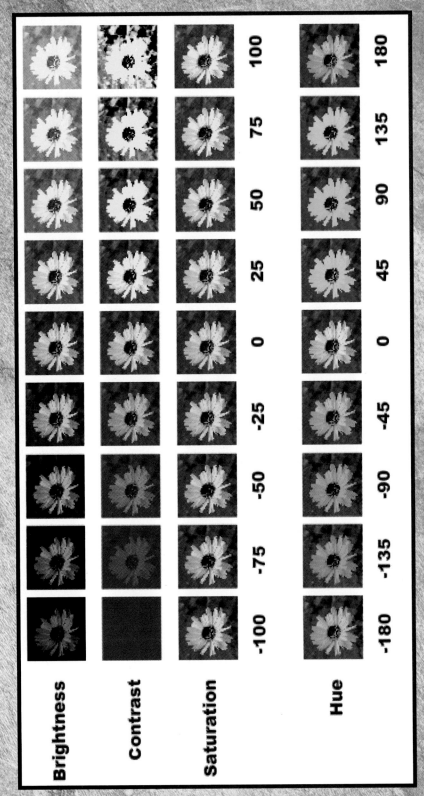

Learn to use the Flash filters in Chapter 11.

Use the Adjust Color filter to quickly modify graphics

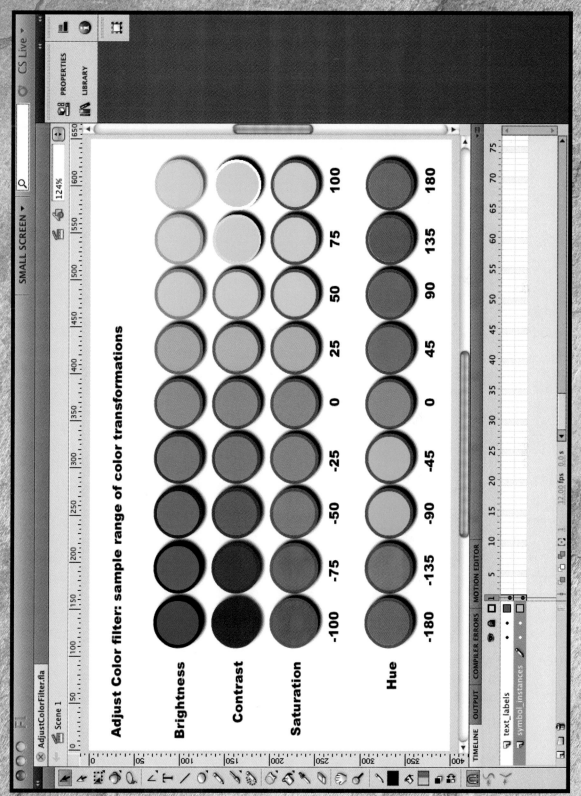

Learn to use the Flash filters in Chapter 11.

Use the blend modes for static and animated effects

Learn to use the Flash filters in Chapter 11.

Make better drop shadows and other dynamic effects

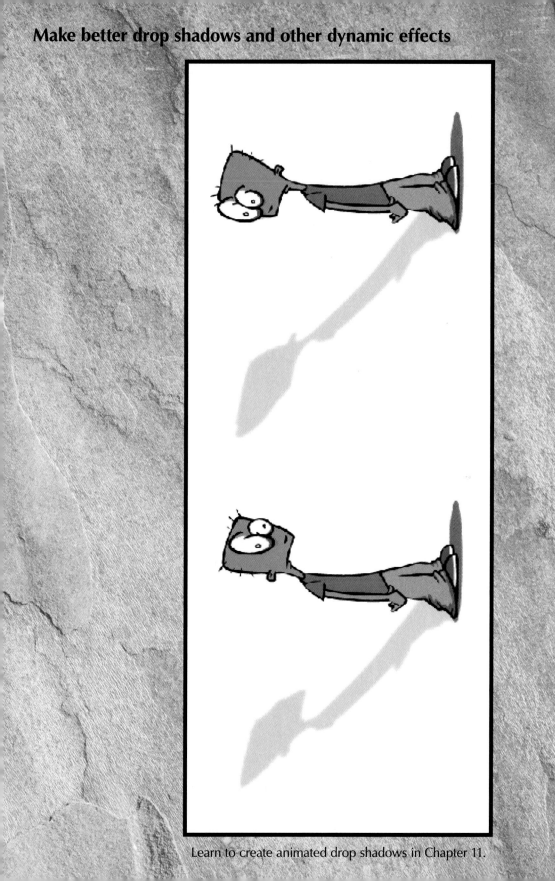

Learn to create animated drop shadows in Chapter 11.

Create artwork with Flash drawing and effects tools

Create and modify custom gradients for lighting effects in Chapter 9.

Use Flash tools to make instance-based patterns

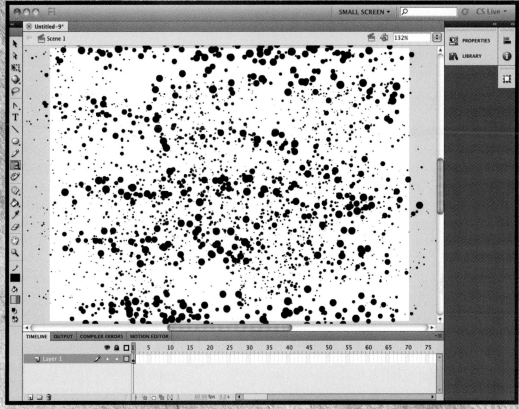

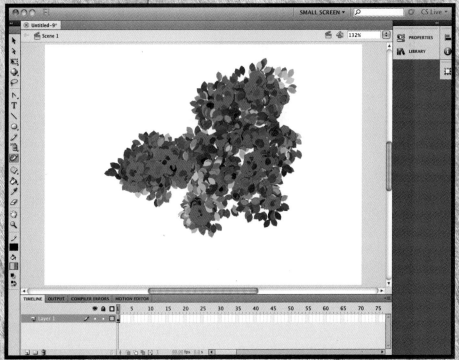

Discover the Spray Brush tool and the Deco tool in Chapter 5.

Expand your horizons with the 3D and IK tools

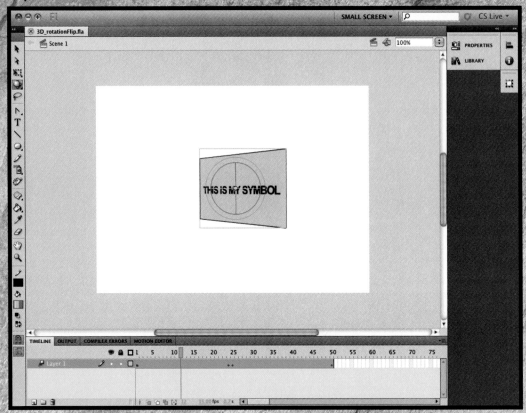

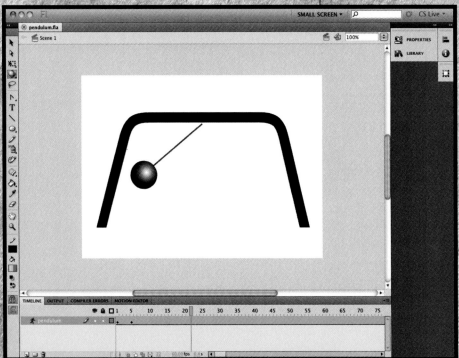

Learn to add the new Spring effect to IK animations in Chapter 10.

Build complete Flash CS5 projects

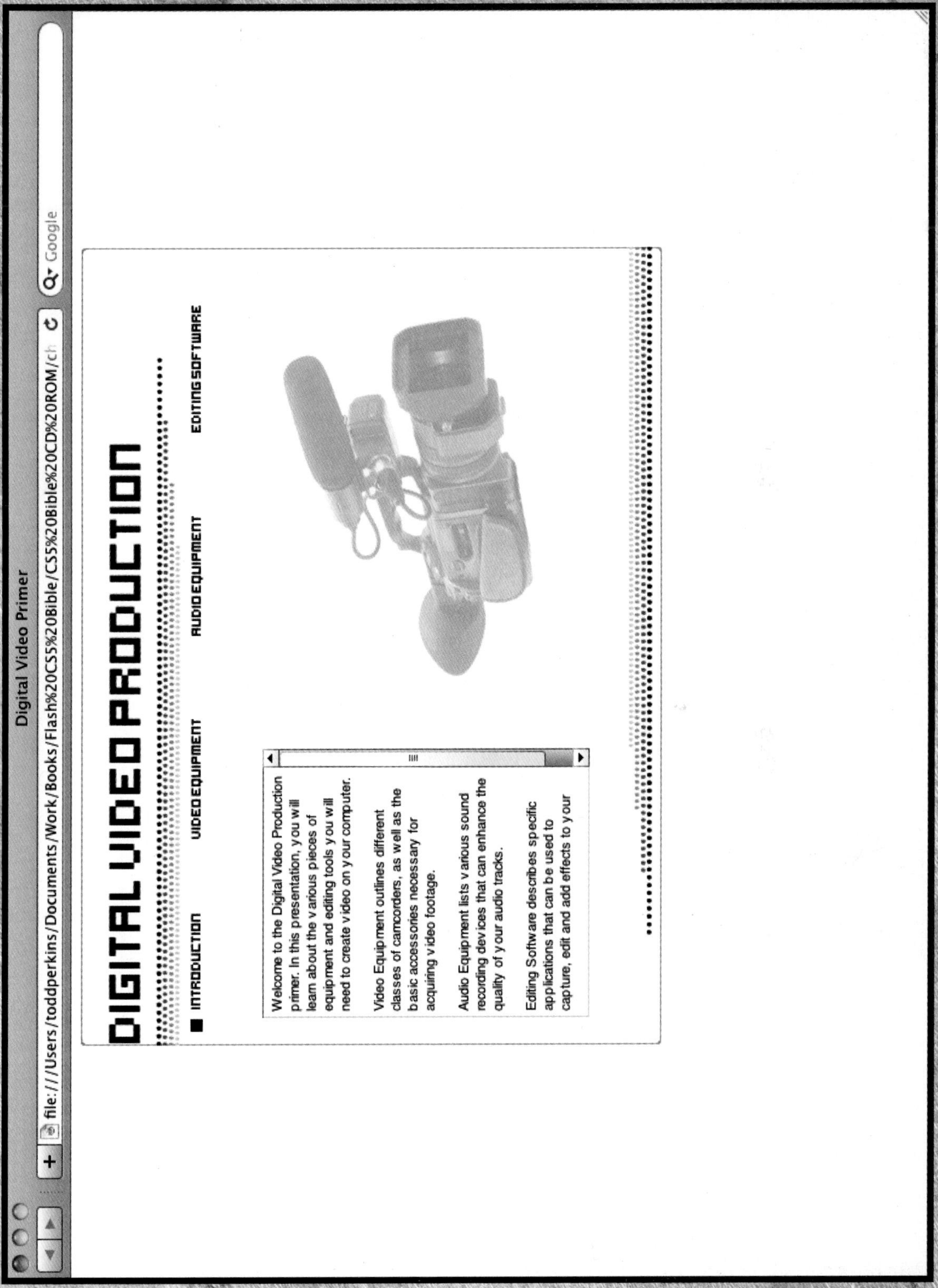

Concepts and examples apply to real-world workflow.

Harness the power of ActionScript to enhance creativity

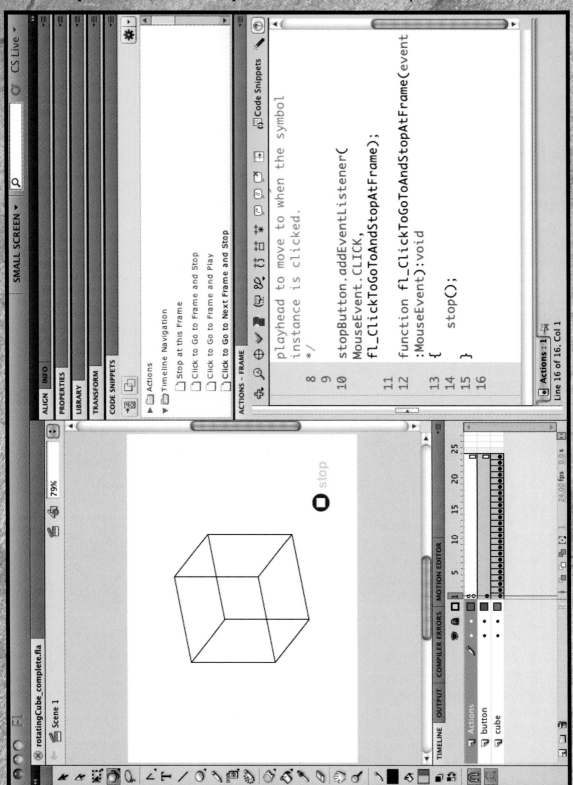

Let ActionScript take you to the next level of Flash interactivity.

Import and optimize artwork in Flash

For guidelines on importing artwork, see Chapter 13.

Learn about live previews and adding cue points to videos in Chapter 14.

Create Flash-based desktop applications using Adobe AIR 2.0

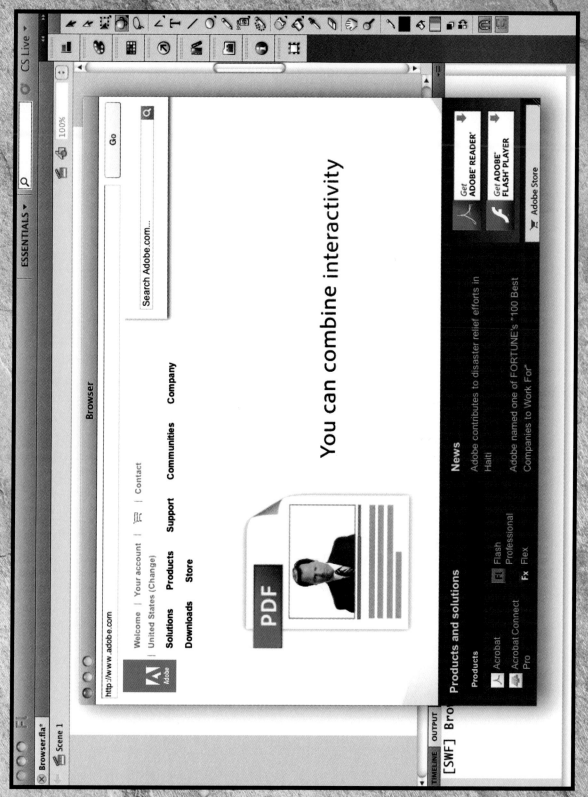

Utilize features unique to the AIR Flash Player in Chapter 21.

Experiment with iPhone and iPod touch development using Flash CS5.

Integrating Multiple Animation Sequences

So far in this chapter, I've looked at creating different types of animation on the Main Timeline. Adding multiple tweens to the Main Timeline can soon result in a jumble of colored spans and keyframes that might be hard to navigate when you need to make edits. Authoring all animation sequences on the Main Timeline also puts you at risk of unintentionally displacing multiple sequences as you make edits.

The best solution for keeping your project (.fla) files manageable as you continue to add animation is to move animation sequences off the Main Timeline and organize them instead on individual symbol timelines. This makes it much easier to move or reuse animation and also ensures that any edits you make to individual animation sequences do not disrupt sequences on other symbol timelines. Graphic symbols and Movie clip symbols can both be used to hold multiple layers of animation, but they have different uses.

As I discuss in Chapter 6, all symbols have their own timelines, so you could just as easily store an animation in a Graphic symbol as in a Movie clip. However, there are some important differences to keep in mind:

- A Graphic symbol timeline must still be tied to frames on the Main Timeline, while a Movie clip timeline plays back independently, regardless of how many frames it is assigned on the Main Timeline.

- The benefit of using a Graphic symbol to store an animated sequence is that it can be previewed frame by frame directly in the authoring environment, even if it is nested. You *can* preview animation on a Movie clip timeline in Edit mode, but you cannot see how the animation on the Movie clip timeline syncs with animation on other symbol timelines or with the Main Timeline until you publish the movie or use the Test Movie command.

- Another significant limitation of Graphic symbols is that they cannot be targeted with ActionScript. Movie clip symbols can be targeted with ActionScript to control the playback of each symbol instance independently, as opposed to having all animation tied to frame sequences on the same (main) timeline.

The extent to which you separate and nest animated elements depends on the complexity of the project and also on how you intend to reuse animation. In general, any elements that will always be linked together on playback can be stored in the same symbol. If you want to have the option of altering playback speed or placement of certain elements independently, then these should be stored in discrete symbols. For example, if you have an animated logo that may be used in a project separately from an animated title, then these two elements should be in individual symbols. On the other hand, if the logo always appears in the same way with the title, then these two elements can be stored in a single symbol (on separate layers, if necessary).

Tip

It is always possible to use the Properties panel to change the behavior (or symbol type) of a symbol instance on the Stage. If you are working with multiple Movie clips and you need to sync some parts of the animation, it can be helpful to temporarily assign a Movie clip instance Graphic symbol behavior so that you can see the animation on its timeline in the main authoring environment. Don't forget to switch the instance back to Movie Clip behavior before you publish your movie. ■

Moving tweens onto symbol timelines

Certainly, it is more efficient to plan your project structure before you begin adding animation so that you can nest animation in symbols as you create the project, but Flash is flexible enough to enable you to optimize the organization of your animation sequences even after you have strewn them around on the Main Timeline.

To illustrate how tweens are moved from the Main Timeline to symbol timelines, I will modify a file called `tweensTimeline.fla`, which includes layers with shape tweens, motion tweens, and classic motion tweens keyframed on the Main Timeline.

On the CD-ROM

I have included two files in the `Integrate` subfolder of the `ch11` folder on the CD-ROM for you to refer to: the original `tweensTimeline.fla` with tweens on the Main Timeline, and the modified `tweensNested.fla` with tweens moved onto symbol timelines. ■

To reorganize a file (.fla) that has animation built on the Main Timeline, follow these steps:

1. **Analyze the Main Timeline carefully to see how the various animated sequences need to relate to each other in the final SWF file.** Decide which frame spans and layers you need to keep tied together and which should be independent.

2. **Pay close attention to how the transitions between different animated sequences are handled on the Main Timeline.** If two different phases of a tween share a common keyframe (for example, if you have scaled an element in one tween and then rotated the same element in a span that continues from the final keyframe of the first tween), you must keep these tweens together or else insert an additional keyframe before you separate them in order to keep both tweens intact.

Tip

Object-based tween spans that follow each other on the same tween layer can simply be selected and dragged to move apart from each other; Flash automatically inserts a blank keyframe to hold the space between the two tween spans on the Timeline. ■

Tip

To be certain that linked sequential tweens can be separated without getting messed up, it can be helpful to add two manually inserted "divider keyframes" at the point that you want to split the tween: You can remove the tween from the first divider keyframe, leaving the second divider keyframe (F6) to maintain the beginning of the tween that follows. This ensures that there is no interpolation between the end keyframe of the first tween and the start keyframe of the second tween. ■

3. **Select the span or Shift+select the beginning and end keyframes of the sequence that you want to move off the Main Timeline.** Clicking the layer icon also selects all frames and tween spans on a layer.

4. **With all frames in the sequence selected, choose Copy Frames from the contextual menu (see Figure 10.31) or Edit ⇨ Timeline ⇨ Copy Frames from the application menu (Alt+Ctrl+C/Option+⌘+C).**

You can select frame spans on multiple layers to move at one time. Be sure to use Copy Frames rather than simply Copy to move all the frames to the Clipboard.

5. **Create a new symbol by choosing Insert ⇨ New Symbol from the application menu (Ctrl+F8/⌘+F8).** Set the symbol type to Movie Clip or Graphic and give it a name that will be useful for identifying the animation, as shown in Figure 10.32.

After you click OK to close the Create New Symbol dialog box, the symbol automatically opens in Edit mode — you will see the symbol timeline rather than the Main Timeline in the Timeline window.

FIGURE 10.32

In the Create New Symbol dialog box, select a symbol type and enter a meaningful name for your new symbol.

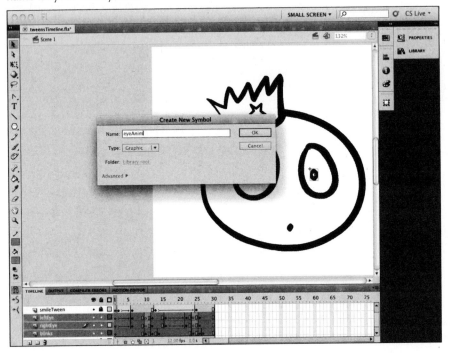

6. **Select the first frame of the symbol timeline and choose Paste Frames from the contextual menu, as shown in Figure 10.33.** Or choose Edit ➪ Timeline ➪ Paste Frames from the application menu (Alt+Ctrl+V/Option+⌘+V).

   Flash automatically inserts enough layers and frames to accommodate the content you paste into the symbol timeline (see Figure 10.34). Your animation sequence is now stored inside the symbol, and you can easily access it from the Library for reuse or editing.

Create as many new symbols as you need to hold all the individual animation sequences that you want to work within your project. When you are finished, you should have a set of easily identifiable named symbols in your Library containing animated elements that are now efficient to edit or reuse.

Note
You may notice that there are two consecutive motion tween spans on the tween layer for the starAnim sequence. Although these could have been integrated into one tween span by working with property keyframes and curves in the Motion Editor, I opted to leave them separate so that I could reuse the Movie clip that contained the animation of the star spinning without the animation of it falling. ■

FIGURE 10.33

Select the first frame in your new symbol timeline and use Paste Frames to insert the frames and layers from the Clipboard.

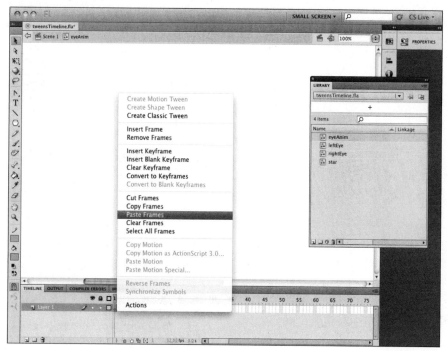

Organizing symbol instances on the Main Timeline

In the previous section I suggested *copying* your animation sequences from the Main Timeline to be pasted into individual symbol timelines — even though this results in redundant content. The rationale for leaving the original sequences on the Main Timeline rather than cutting them as you move content into separate symbols is that they provide a useful reference for where the symbol instances should be placed on the Stage and how they should be arranged on the Main Timeline. The simplest way to "rebuild" your animation, using the nested symbols you have created, is to insert a new layer for each symbol on the Main Timeline directly above the original sequence that was copied. As you drag each symbol instance onto the Stage, you can align the artwork with the original sequence on the Stage and also determine how many frames the symbol should occupy on the Main Timeline.

FIGURE 10.34

When you use Paste Frames to place the content from the Clipboard into your symbol, layers and keyframes are preserved.

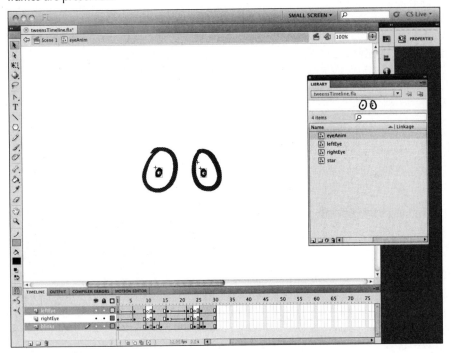

Using the example from the previous section, I show you how to replace the tweened sequences on the Main Timeline with nested symbol instances:

1. Insert a new layer on the Main Timeline directly above the original tweened sequence by selecting the original layer and using the New Layer button in the Timeline window or choosing Insert ➪ Timeline ➪ Layer from the application menu (or the contextual menu).

Caution

Check the labels above the Timeline to be sure that you are editing the Main Timeline (Scene 1) and not one of the named symbol timelines. If there are any names listed in the crumb menu to the right of Scene 1, click the back arrow or the Scene 1 label to return to the Main Timeline before you start placing symbol instances on the Stage. ■

2. Drag an instance of your nested animation symbol from the Library onto the Stage in the new layer and align it with the content on the other layers (see Figure 10.35).

Tip

Use the Lock Others command to protect content on your original layers while you drag and position the symbol instance on your new layer. Your keyboard arrow keys can be helpful for "nudging" an item into final alignment if dragging is not precise enough. ∎

FIGURE 10.35

The original animation layers can help you to sequence and visually align the new symbol instances as you rebuild your project.

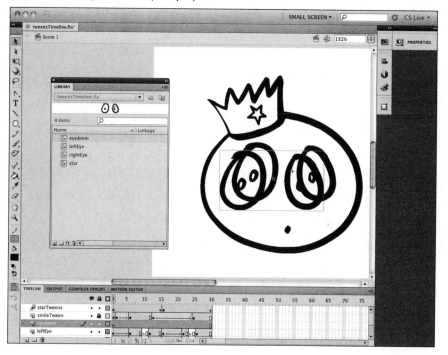

After you finish placing the new symbol instance in the Main Timeline, you can delete the layers containing the original tweened sequences (which are now redundant). You will quickly see how much cleaner and easier to modify the Timeline becomes when the tweened and frame-by-frame sequences are replaced with nested symbol instances, as shown in Figure 10.36.

FIGURE 10.36

The Main Timeline becomes easier to manage as you replace the tweened and frame-by-frame sequences with nested symbol instances.

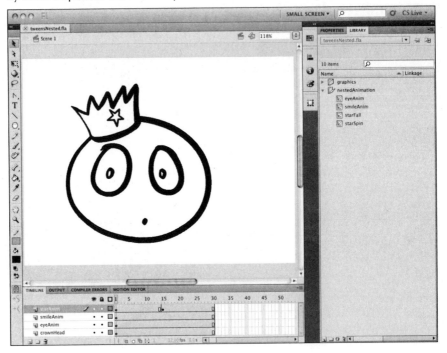

In the previous example, I moved the timeline animation sequences to Graphic symbol timelines to make it easier to preview the animation on the Main Timeline. However, in most production contexts, it is best to use Movie clip symbols to hold animation because instances of Movie clips can be targeted with ActionScript. Also, Movie clip timelines loop independently of the Main Timeline, so you can repeat an animation sequence as many times as you want, either by holding on a single frame of the Main Timeline or by extending the span of the Movie clip so that it remains visible as the Main Timeline continues to play. In the next section, I work with Movie clip symbol instances to demonstrate how to reuse animated symbols and how to add some variation to the instances.

Reusing and Modifying Tweened Symbol Instances

Cleaning up the Main Timeline is one good reason to move animation onto symbol timelines. An even better reason is to make it easier to reuse and modify instances of the animated symbols after you have them stored in your Flash Library.

In the our example file, I have placed multiple instances of a Movie clip on a layer in the Main Timeline to create some animated background elements (see Figure 10.37).

FIGURE 10.37

Movie clips make it easy to use multiple instances of an animated element.

As discussed in previous chapters, you can modify the appearance of symbol instances without having to edit the contents of the original symbol. This can be helpful when you are working with static elements, but it really becomes indispensable when you are working with animated elements. Imagine the time it would take to copy and paste a series of tweens or a frame-by-frame sequence on the Main Timeline and then to edit the artwork on each keyframe just to change the scale or the color of your animated element each time you want to use it. Now be very happy that the little extra time spent moving your animated sequences off the Main Timeline and into symbols makes it possible to drag and drop your animated elements and then to scale, rotate, or apply filters or color effects to get endless variations without ever having to edit the original keyframe artwork.

On the CD-ROM

I have included the original and the modified version of our example file so that you can see how the symbol instances were changed — compare tweensModify_start.fla and tweensModify_final.fla in the Modify subfolder in the ch11 folder of the CD-ROM. ∎

In our example (see Figure 10.38), I have modified the appearance of some of the animated stars by transforming instances of the original `starSpin` Movie clip.

FIGURE 10.38

By transforming symbol instances, you can add almost endless variation to the appearance of your animated sequences without having to modify any keyframe artwork.

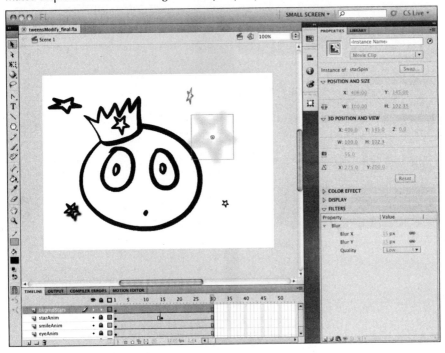

The beauty of symbols is that you always have the option of modifying the appearance of individual symbol instances or making global changes by modifying the artwork in your original symbol. If you decide that an element should be changed every place that it appears, editing the original symbol is much quicker than modifying all the symbol instances individually.

Tip

If you decide that you want to keep the static shape, but not the animation or the link to the original symbol in the Library for some of the symbol instances you have placed on the Main Timeline, you can use Modify ⇨ Break Apart (Ctrl+B/⌘+B) to "break" the link to the animated symbol. The original artwork (or static shape) remains on the Stage, but any changes made to the original symbol in the Library are not carried over to the now unlinked shape. ∎

You can use ActionScript to control the playback of each element independently of the Main Timeline. For example, instead of stopping everything on the Main Timeline, you can place a `stop()` action on the starSpin symbol timeline to hold the animation of the stars while the other elements continue to play (as shown in Figure 10.39, top). Any ActionScript placed directly on the symbol timeline applies to all instances of the symbol. If you are working with Movie clip symbols, you have the additional option of naming individual symbol instances and *targeting* them with ActionScript placed on a keyframe in the Main Timeline (as shown in Figure 10.39, bottom). This method enables you to stop the animation on some stars, while letting others continue to spin as the animation on the Main Timeline plays.

On the CD-ROM

To see the difference between adding ActionScript directly to a symbol timeline to stop all instances and targeting a specific named symbol instance with ActionScript on the Main Timeline, compare `stopSymbol.fla` **(or .swf) with** `stopInstance.fla` **(or .swf).** ■

FIGURE 10.39

ActionScript can be added to symbol timelines (left) or used to target symbol instances (right) to control the playback of animated elements, independent of the Main Timeline.

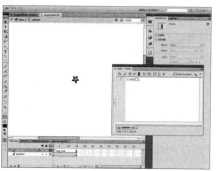

Cross-Reference

For more information about controlling symbol timelines and symbol instances with ActionScript, refer to Part V, "Adding Basic Interactivity to Flash Movies." ■

Creating IK Armatures with the Bone Tool and Bind Tool

Inverse Kinematics or IK is an animation technique that is familiar to anyone who has worked with more specialized character animation or modeling programs. Instead of animating the individual parts of an object as isolated elements, IK creates relationships or links between elements so that the movement of one element affects the movement of other related elements. The classic example of this is a hand moving while connected to a wrist, which is also connected to an elbow, and then to a shoulder. Each distinct part of the structure can initiate movement, but as one part moves, the other parts of the structure stay connected to it and move accordingly. This example is consistent with the behavior of IK bones in Flash because the bones do not bend, but the joints between the bones enable the shape to move in almost any direction, subject to the varying limitations in rotation and movement of each joint. For example, the shoulder joint can move quite freely in a circular motion but it can't easily change its position in space (unless the torso moves), while the elbow joint has a more limited range of rotation but a greater freedom of movement in space.

If you have spent time trying to animate characters or design elements in Flash with multiple parts that you wanted to move individually, while keeping them connected to each other, you will appreciate how much easier this type of animation is in Flash CS5. The Bone tool enables you to apply IK in two ways: You can link individual symbol instances so that they can move as a chain or rotate in relation to one another or you can create a skeleton inside of a shape that can be used to control the movement of the shape for realistic animation.

The Bone tool gets its name from the fact that the links that make up an IK armature are similar to the bones in a skeleton: They do not bend, but they rotate at joints and allow the symbol instances or shapes around them to bend and change size and position within a controllable range. Armatures can be linear or branched. You may want to experiment with linear structures to get a feel for the hierarchy of bones and the characteristics of joints before you move on to creating more complex branched structures.

Note

The IK tools are only available if your project file is targeting Flash Player 10 and using ActionScript 3.0. ∎

To create a linear IK armature linking a series of symbol instances, follow these steps:

1. **Place a series of symbol instances on the Stage**. You can use multiple instances of the same shape or a variety of different symbol instances. Our starting file with seven scaled instances of the same circle symbol is shown in Figure 10.40.

2. **Activate the Bone tool (X) and click on the symbol instance that you want to start your bone chain.**

Note

The initial symbol instance in the chain will have a fixed x, y position by default, while the connected instances can be moved on the Stage with the Selection tool. Think of the first symbol instance as the anchor point of your animation. If you wanted to have a blade of grass that could bend and move in the wind, you would start from the root of the grass and grow the chain upward instead of starting at the top of the grass and growing the chain down toward the root. ∎

3. **Hold down the mouse and drag to see a preview of the bone that will connect the first symbol instance to the next one in your chain.** Release the mouse when the end of the bone is connected to the next symbol in the chain. The endpoint of the bone automatically snaps to the center point of the symbol instance as you drag over it.

A series of symbol instances arranged on a single layer in Flash are ready to be connected by the Bone tool into an IK armature.

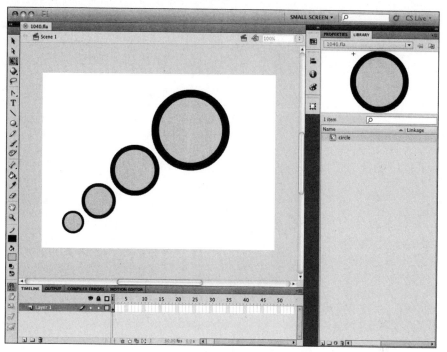

4. **Click the second symbol in the chain and drag a new bone to connect to the third symbol in the chain.** Continue clicking and adding sequential bones to create a series of joined symbol instances. Figure 10.41 shows our sample file with the first half of a bone chain created to connect the symbol instances into an IK armature.

Notice that each time you connect a symbol with a bone to add it to your bone chain or IK armature, Flash moves the symbol onto an auto-created pose layer (designated by a small running figure) in the Timeline. If you start with six symbol instances in a layer on the Stage and then connect them all with the Bone tool, you will see that the original layer is empty and all the symbols are on the pose layer when you are finished creating your bone chain. You can select symbol instances in the chain to access instance properties or select the individual bones in the armature to access IK controls in the Properties panel.

As you connect each symbol instance with a bone, the instance becomes part of your IK armature and is moved onto the auto-created pose layer.

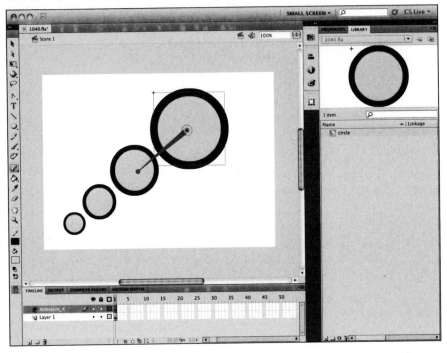

As shown in Figure 10.42, each bone has settings for the following properties:

- **Speed:** This setting is used to slow down the movement of bones to simulate weight. The default setting of 100 percent is equal to free motion or no weight. The lowest setting of 0 percent is equal to no motion or dead weight. In most cases, you will get a nice feeling of organic weight by using values in the middle of this range.

- **Joint Rotation:** By default this setting for movement around the bone joint is enabled and unconstrained. If you want to freeze a joint, deselect the Enable check box. If you want to limit the range of motion for the joint, select the Constrain check box and set a Minimum and/or a Maximum angle of rotation within the 360-degree range of the joint.

Tip

Positive and negative angles are calculated from the original position of the bone. A value range of –45 degrees to 45 degrees would allow the joint to move to both sides of its current position within a 90-degree arc. A value range of 0 to 90 degrees would also enable the joint to move in a 90-degree arc but only to one side (clockwise) from its current position. ■

FIGURE 10.42

You can select each bone in an IK armature to access controls in the Properties panel and fine-tune the behavior of your chain.

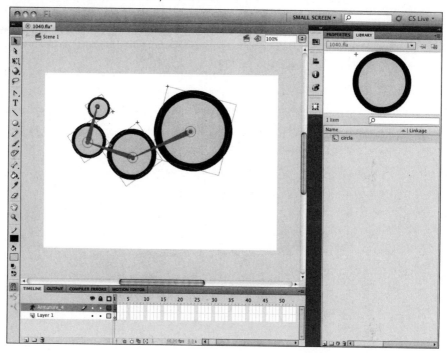

- **Joint X Translation and Joint Y Translation:** By default, these settings for movement of a joint within the chain are disabled. This keeps the length of bones in a chain fixed and makes it a little easier to get predictable motion as you click and drag an IK armature to create poses. If you want more freedom to move individual symbol instances or bones within a chain and you don't mind dealing with bones growing or shrinking within your armature, you may choose to enable free movement along the x and/or y axis by selecting the Enable check box for the respective property. Values are in pixels and are calculated relative to the original position of a bone on the Stage. To limit how far joints can move from their original location, you can set Minimum and/or Maximum values for either axis.

Tip

Although you can enable a joint to move within a range that takes it well outside the Stage area, you might find it easier to control your armature if you use conservative ranges for the X and Y Translation properties to keep the armature from drifting too far outside the Stage. ∎

The pose layer that Flash creates to hold your IK chain is a special layer type that, like a motion tween layer, will capture changes that you make on the Stage and save them in property keyframes.

Note

A pose layer can only contain one armature. If you are working with multiple armatures, you can animate each one on its own pose layer. ■

If you want to animate your IK armature, follow these steps:

1. **Extend the frame span by inserting additional frames on the pose layer.** Select the initial frame in the span and use the F5 key add one frame at a time or select the frame number that you want the span to extend to and then use the F5 key to auto-extend the span to that frame.

2. **Scrub the Timeline to a frame where you would like to add a new pose.**

3. **Use the Selection tool or the Properties panel to make changes to the position (or shape) of your armature.** As shown in Figure 10.43, a property keyframe has been added to the span of the pose layer to save the changes. If you scrub the Timeline, you see an animation of the symbol instances in your IK chain moving from the original position to the new position (or series of poses) that you created in the pose layer.

FIGURE 10.43

You can change the position of your IK chain in a series of property keyframes to create poses that are animated on the pose layer.

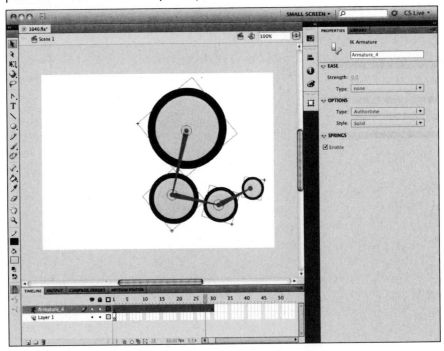

Selecting any frame in the span of the pose layer loads settings for the IK animation into the Properties panel. As shown in Figure 10.44, you can apply easing to the animation as well as choose whether the IK armature is animated at authortime (enabling you to create a series of poses and a set animation sequence) or at runtime (enabling the viewer to click and drag the armature to interact with it "live"). You can also change the bone display Style from the default setting of Solid to Wire or Line to find the view that suits you best.

Adding Spring to IK animations

Realistic physics can be automatically added to IK animations using the new Spring feature. To add Spring, first select a frame span for an IK animation, and then make sure the Enable Springs box is checked in the Properties panel (Figure 10.44). Spring can then be applied to individual bones through the SPRING section of the Properties panel once a bone is selected (Figure 10.45). The Strength value controls the power of the spring effect (higher values mean more extreme springs), and the Damping value controls the decrease of the spring effect over time. A damping value of 0 allows the spring to continue indefinitely, while a value of 100 slows the spring effect over the least amount of frames.

FIGURE 10.44

Enable Springs must be checked in the Properties panel when an animation is selected in the Timeline for an animation to allow Spring effects.

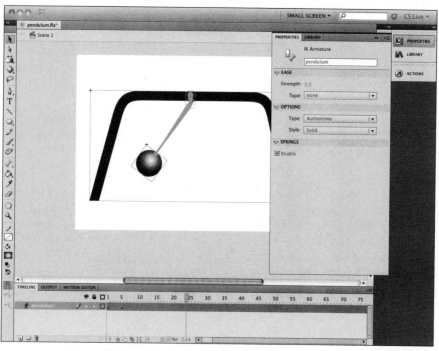

FIGURE 10.45

Control the spring effect using Strength and Damping in the Properties panel after a bone is selected.

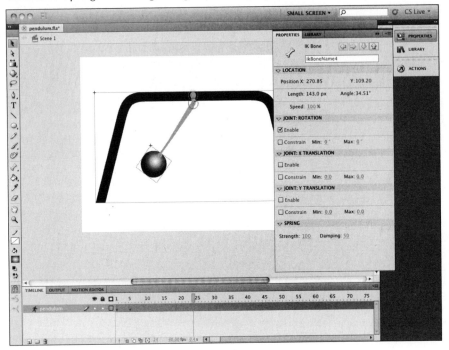

New Feature

In Flash CS5, more life can be added to IK animations using a new feature called Spring. Adding Spring to IK animations can make those animations more realistic by applying real-world physics. These physics extend the animations you create to automatically show additional movement. ■

One example of a spring in action is a pendulum animation. To best apply the spring effect, start the armature animation in the pose you want at the beginning, and after a few frames, define the end pose for the animation. Instead of applying the spring effect in between the start and end frames, Flash applies the effect over many (sometimes hundreds) of frames, so you will need to expand the about of frames by extending the number of frames in the Timeline in order to see the full animation. In the pendulum example in Figures 10.46 and 10.47 the pendulum is at the top of a swing on frame 1, the finished pose is on frame 5, and the Timeline is extended to 500 frames. With a spring strength of 100 and damping of 50, Flash creates the left swing animation, and the pendulum swings back and forth until it comes to a stop in the middle (Figure 10.48).

FIGURE 10.46

The pendulum posed to the top-right on frame 1

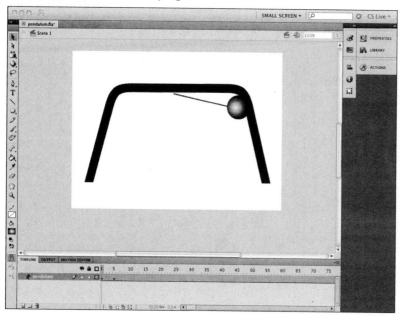

FIGURE 10.47

The pendulum posed to the desired end of the animation on frame 5

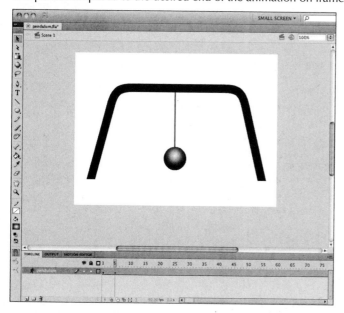

FIGURE 10.48

The animated pendulum showing spring in the Flash Player

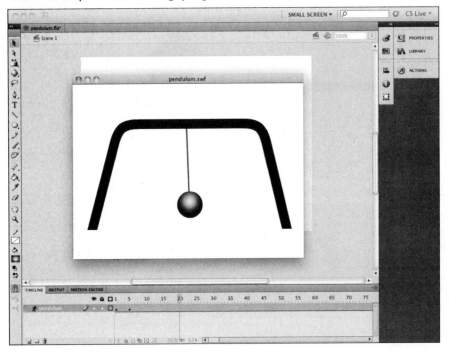

Animating shapes with IK

Up to this point, I have worked with bones using symbols, but bones can be added to shapes as well. However, the way that bones interact with symbol instances is quite different from the way they control the movement of a shape. To create an IK armature inside of a shape, follow these steps:

1. **Use the Brush tool or any of the shape drawing tools to create a filled shape that you want to add an IK skeleton or armature to.** IK works best if you make a simple, solid shape without a stroke. Our starting shape is shown in Figure 10.49.

2. **Select the Bone tool in the Tools panel.**

3. **Click inside the shape and drag to create the first bone in the armature.** In most cases, you will want to start at one end of the shape and continue clicking and dragging to set up a series of bones that progress to the other end of the shape. The shorter you make the bones, the more joints you can include in the armature and the more "flexible" the shape will be.

FIGURE 10.49

A simple filled shape drawn in merge or object drawing mode can be transformed into an articulated shape by adding an IK armature with the Bone tool.

As with bones added to symbol instances, bones added to a shape will be saved on a new pose layer that can be used to animate the articulated IK armature. A preview of our example shape (with bones added) being moved into a new pose is shown in Figure 10.50.

One challenge of animating shapes with IK bones is that the outline of the shape will sometimes distort or fracture as you move the skeleton. The companion tool for the Bone tool, called the Bind tool (Z), helps you control how the shape relates to the bones in your armature. The way these two tools work together is similar to how the Subselection tool works with the Pencil or Pen tool. After you have created an armature inside of a shape with the Bone tool, you can use the Bind tool to select a bone and see the related control points along the edges of the shape highlighted (with a yellow outline). You can also use the Bind tool to select individual points along the edge of the shape and see the related bone or bones highlighted (with a yellow outline). These two different views of the armature-shape relationship are shown in Figure 10.51.

FIGURE 10.50

Moving one bone in the armature drags the other bones along in a continuous chain that controls the motion and form of the articulated shape. Changes to the shape will be saved as property keyframes on the pose layer to create an animation of the motion.

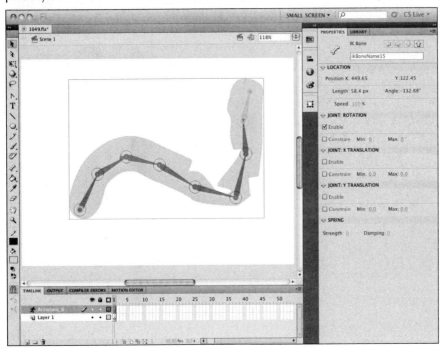

FIGURE 10.51

Bones can be selected with the Bind tool to show the points that are bound to them (left), or points can be selected with the Bind tool to show which bone(s) they are bound to (right).

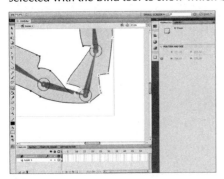
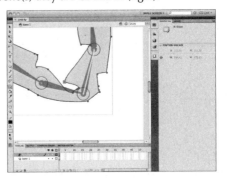

In this way, you can get a clearer idea of how the shape is tied or bound to the bones. More important, you can reassign points or bind them to different bones within the armature. To do this, simply click a point on the edge of the shape with the Bind tool and drag the yellow highlight to the bone that you want it to be tied to, or conversely, you can click a bone with the Bind tool and then drag highlights to specific points along the edge of the shape. Either way, you will be able to adjust the way that the shape reacts to changes in the position of the bones. Keep in mind that points can be bound to more than one bone. The Bind tool is most helpful for smoothing out distortion around joints that are very close together, where outline points may be connected to the wrong bone(s).

Although the IK tools (the Bone tool and the Bind tool) make the task of animating related shapes infinitely easier, they do not eliminate the learning curve for creating this type of animation. It takes a lot of experience to make the most of IK and to anticipate exactly how an armature should be designed and tuned to support different shapes and poses.

Web Resource

As you push your skills into new territory, it helps to find some animation role models who can lead you in defining your style and exploring the full potential of the tools. You can find some inspiring examples and some approachable tutorials online at `www.coldhardflash.com`, a site that features work from a range of independent Flash animators and Flash animation studios. ■

Runtime bitmap caching

We're all waiting for the day when intensive animation plays as smoothly on the Web as it does when output for offline viewing. That day is getting closer with every build of the Flash Player. Flash 8 introduced a feature to optimize playback of complex vector graphics in Movie clip or Button symbols by caching them as bitmaps, or *surfaces*, at runtime. The benefit of caching complex vectors as bitmaps is that the Flash Player does not have to tie up the CPU by constantly redrawing these background vectors as other elements are animating in front of them. Your animation will play back faster and smoother. You can apply this option with ActionScript or by selecting a Movie clip (or Button) instance in the Document window and selecting the check box in the Properties panel to Use runtime bitmap caching.

Runtime bitmap caching optimizes Web playback only for Flash movies with complex background images that are static or panned vertically or horizontally. The position, but not the content, of the cached symbol can change without requiring the Flash Player to redraw the vector information. Bitmap caching fails if the Movie clip (or Button symbol) is larger than 2880 pixels in any direction or if the Movie clip is rotated. You will not notice a significant improvement with bitmap caching on simple vector graphics. Before you publish your final Flash movie, it is always best to test with bitmap caching turned on and turned off to see which delivers the best performance for the specific graphics and animation in your file.

Bitmaps

As I mention previously, when you're designing with Flash for the Web, use raster (bitmap) images with a careful eye on their file size. But for broadcast output, there's no limit. Not only can you use as many images as you'd like (within system constraints), but also doing so makes a richer, far more attractive finished product. And, unlike the SWF format, when they're output as raster video, even animations built with a lot of bitmaps play at the proper frame rate. So move, animate, scale, and rotate them — even play sequences of them. The sky and RAM are the only limits.

Make Flash work for you

I could fill an entire book with illustrations of the various ways that you can move, edit, and recombine your animated timeline sequences, but the basic principles are always the same. Use symbols to keep your files optimized and your options open. Nest symbols to keep your project organized. Try to keep your Main Timeline uncluttered and easy to modify by putting frame-by-frame animation and tweens on symbol timelines. Use Movie clip symbols if you plan to target instances of the symbol with ActionScript. Let Flash do as much work for you as possible, but don't be afraid to manually tweak animated sequences by applying custom tween curves, inserting property keyframes, or modifying artwork. Use layers to keep elements organized and when you need to animate multiple items on the same span of the Timeline. Plan and design your animation in logical sections rather than in complex groups — you can add complexity by nesting multiple symbols. Avoid redundant work and keep your files small and easy to manage by reusing artwork and animation whenever possible.

Summary

- The Flash authoring environment includes several features that have been adapted from tools that are used for creating traditional animation. Onion skinning, keyframes, and tweens are the digital equivalents of layered transparent cels, key art, and manual in-betweens.

- There are three basic ways to create animation: frame-by-frame animation, two types of keyframed animation (shape and classic motion tweens), and a new object-based motion tween that uses property keyframes rather than standard keyframes. Most projects require a combination of all three types of animation.

- The new motion tween model is object based, which makes it possible to delete the target object without "breaking" the tween and transfer the animation properties easily to a new target object. Object-based tweens do not require keyframes but instead track changes made to the target object on auto-inserted property keyframes. Property keyframes can be modified (along with animation curves and easing curves), using the new Motion Editor panel.

- Tween spans for object-based motion tweens exist on tween layers (a new layer type) that limit editing options in order to protect the tween.

- You can use shape tweens only to interpolate raw shapes (including broken-apart text), and you can use motion tweens only to interpolate editable text or symbols.

- Tweens add less to file size than frame-by-frame animation because Flash calculates the difference between the keyframes instead of having to store unique artwork for every frame in a sequence. However, tweens can be very processor intensive if complex transitions or alpha layers need to be interpolated and rendered.

- You can modify the pace of tweened animation by extending or shortening the span of the tween and also by adjusting the Easing settings to create acceleration or deceleration in a sequence.

- The Motion Editor opens a whole range of possibilities for controlling the interpolation of properties in a tween. Properties can be set to progress along a single curve, or their individual curves can be modified to create more sophisticated tween effects.

- The Motion Presets panel gives you a list of ready-made animation patterns that can be applied to Movie clip symbols and modified by using the Motion Editor panel.

- Saving your own motion presets (or importing XML files for other custom motion presets) enables you to reuse animation patterns without having to use ActionScript or repeat tween steps for timeline animation that you want to use on more than one item.

- The Bone tool and Bind tool make it possible to create poseable chains of symbol instances or shapes with articulated skeletons. These articulated elements are referred to as armatures and enable you to leverage inverse kinematics (IK) to quickly animate related elements on auto-created pose layers.

Applying Filters, Blends, Guides, and Masks

This chapter introduces you to some of the key tools in the Flash authoring environment that support *expressiveness* — another term for creative options for designers. If you've worked with other graphics programs, you'll appreciate the creative potential of filters and the Blends menu built into the Properties panel. If you've never used a filter or heard of a blend mode, you'll be relieved to discover how easy it is to apply these features and amazed at how much they can do to enhance your projects.

I also explain how layers can do more than just hold the content of your Flash movie, and show you how to turn normal layers into guides or masks.

Applying Filters in Flash

Filters offer shortcuts for adding visual polish to your Flash designs. Instead of manually editing shapes to create drop shadows or adjusting gradient fills to create bevels, you can simply apply a live filter and use the built-in settings to adjust the final effect. Filters are rendered on-the-fly, and although they change the appearance of your symbol instances, they do not result in any additional symbols being generated and added to the library. In addition, filters do not interfere with the "editability" of your content — you can always modify the original text or symbol instance without "breaking" the filter effect. Filters can be layered in any order, and you can make modifications to the individual filter settings at any time. You can also add or control filters at runtime with ActionScript, but for now I'll focus on applying filters in the authoring environment — which doesn't require any code! Filters are rendered as you add or adjust them so you can always see just what you'll get when the final movie is published.

Adding and adjusting filters

As shown in Figure 11.1, filters are now in their own section of the CS5 vertical Properties panel. To apply a filter, follow these steps:

1. **Select an item on the Stage that is compatible with filters — a Movie clip instance, Button symbol instance, or text field.**

2. **Open the Properties panel, and scroll down or resize the panel until you can see the Filters section (click the arrow on the left to twirl the Filters live list open if it isn't open already).**

3. **Click the small Add Filter page icon (shown in Figure 11.2) on the far left side of the row of control buttons at the bottom of the Filters section.** This opens the Filters menu (shown in Figure 11.1).

After a filter is selected from the drop-down menu, it appears in the live list in the Filters panel and you see the filter effect (with default settings) applied to your selected item.

The Filters section of the Properties panel makes it easy to add live effects.

As shown in Figure 11.2, the settings for each applied filter are accessible in twirl-down sections of the live Filters list. You can keep all the twirl-down sections open so filter settings are visible (by scrolling or expanding the Properties panel), but it's easier to manage the list if you collapse the filter settings and only open them one at a time when you need to modify a setting. The settings vary for each filter, but after you become familiar with the options, you'll find it easy to adjust individual filters. To remove a filter at any time, simply select the name of the filter in the live list and click the trash can (–) icon at the bottom of the panel section.

New Feature

All blue numeric values for filter properties are hot text fields that can be adjusted by clicking and dragging or by double-clicking and then typing new values. ■

Tip

Applied filters can be temporarily toggled off (and back on) to preview different filter combinations by clicking the eye icon at the bottom of the panel section. ■

FIGURE 11.2

Individual settings for applied filters can be adjusted at any time by selecting a filter in the live list. Controls for filters have been improved in CS5, and they are easily accessible in the Properties panel.

Open live filter(twirled down)

Collapsed live filter(twirled up)

Filter properties

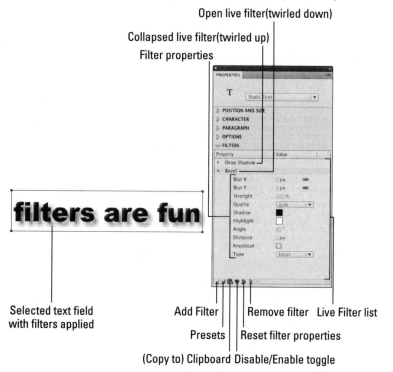

Selected text field
with filters applied

Add Filter   Remove filter   Live Filter list

Presets   Reset filter properties

(Copy to) Clipboard Disable/Enable toggle

Some filter effects have unique controls, but most are created with different combinations of a series of basic settings. The default filter settings are a good starting point, and in some cases they might even give you the result you want, although most likely you'll need to modify the settings to achieve a satisfactory final effect.

It would be an overwhelming task to document every combination of settings on every filter, but an overview of the main settings will provide you with enough guidance for experimentation:

- **Blur X, Blur Y:** Sets the distance that the edge of a shape extends horizontally (X) and vertically (Y) to create a graduated or softened edge for shadow, blur, bevel, and glow effects. This has the same effect as the distance setting in the Soften Fill Edges dialog box for shapes. The default blur distance is 5 and the range is from 0 to 100. By default, the lock icon is turned on to constrain the X and Y settings to the same value, creating a symmetrical, graduated effect. If you prefer to make the X and Y settings independent of each other, toggle the constrain option off by clicking the lock icon.

- **Strength:** Sets the opacity of the rendered effect. The default setting is 100. The range is from 0 to 1,000. However, for all practical purposes, the effective range for most filters is from 0 (invisible) to 100 (solid center area with normal falloff in graduated area). Increasing the strength of a filter beyond 100 percent adds opacity to the stepped (or softened) areas of the shape. The opacity is increased incrementally from the most solid area to the least solid area of the stepped edge.

Caution

At the maximum Strength setting of 1,000 percent, all the steps within the blur distance of a filter are rendered at 100 percent opacity, which usually counteracts the visual impact of the filter. The result is an expanded solid shape with a slightly jagged edge, rather than a nice-looking shadow or bevel. ■

- **Quality:** Sets the fidelity or smoothness of the rendered effect. This setting has a major impact on the performance of the published movie. By default, Quality is set to Low. As the quality is increased to Medium or High, gradients are rendered more smoothly and the steps in blurs are softened, but the performance of the final movie is reduced. Your Flash movies perform better if you can achieve the visual effect you need by making adjustments to the Color and/or Blur settings rather than increasing the Quality setting.

Tip

To make a Glow or Drop Shadow look less harsh, adjust the color to be a closer match to the background color rather than reduce strength or increase quality. Color settings have the least impact on the performance of the final movie. ■

- **Angle:** Sets the direction of offset to be applied with the Distance setting. If Distance is set to 0, changing the Angle (or degree of offset) has no visible effect. The default is a 45-degree angle and the range is 0 to 360 degrees. The higher the Distance setting, the more obvious the offset direction or angle will be.

- **Distance:** Sets the pixel value for the distance between the center point of the original item and the center point of the rendered filter (gradient). The default setting is 5 and the range is from –32 to 32 pixels. If the distance setting is 0, the rendered gradient and the original item are center aligned.

Caution

If the Distance setting is 0 and the Blur setting is less than 5, it can be hard to see a filter effect if it is rendered outside (or behind) the original item. ■

- **Color:** Click color chips to access currently loaded swatches and set colors used to render Drop Shadow or Glow effects. The default solid color for Drop Shadow is Black (#000000); the default solid color for Glow is Red (#FF0000). The solid color that is set with the color chip automatically fades from solid to transparent to create a soft glow or shadow effect. The Bevel filter requires both a Shadow and a Highlight color — by default, these are set to black (#000000) and white (#FFFFFF), respectively. The Gradient Bevel and Gradient Glow filters make it possible to add multiple colors to rendered gradient effects. Click the color anchors on the gradient strip to access currently loaded swatches and set control points in the gradient.

Note

The opacity of the center color anchor for gradient bevels and the left (outer) color anchor for gradient glows are fixed in position and set to 0 percent alpha. The color of these pointers can be changed, but the alpha level and anchor position can be changed only on the other anchors (or new anchors added to the gradient strip). ■

In addition to the adjustable settings, there are some check box options that expand the visual possibilities for filters:

- **Knockout:** Converts the original shape into a transparent area, while leaving the rendered effect visible in any area that was not cut out by the original shape.
- **Filter types:** For Blur and Drop Shadow filters, this is a check box to switch the rendered gradient from outside to inside the boundary of the original shape. For the multicolor gradient filters (Bevel, Gradient Glow, and Gradient Bevel), the options are listed in a drop-down menu that enables the filter to be set to render inside (Inner), outside (Outer), or inside *and* outside (Full) the boundaries of the original item.

Caution

The Bevel filter works best when left at the default Inside setting. Outside and Full bevels require some adjustment to create a realistic, dimensional result rather than a messy, doubled-up drop-shadow effect. ■

Tip

Inner Gradient Glow effects are easier to create with a custom gradient fill instead of applying the Gradient Glow filter with the Inner setting. A gradient fill is also less demanding at runtime than a Gradient Glow filter. ■

- **Hide object:** This option is the secret to creating sophisticated drop shadows (as I describe later in this chapter). When Hide object is enabled, the original object disappears, but the drop shadow is preserved.

Note

Although Hide object and Knockout both convert the original shape into a transparent area, they do not have exactly the same result. The Hide object option preserves the entire gradient area rendered by a filter effect, and the Knockout option creates a "cutout" effect when combined with filters that are not set to render inside the boundaries of the original shape. Although Hide object can be selected when the Knockout option is also selected, there is no visible difference to the rendered graphic. If you decide to use the Knockout option, it is best to uncheck the Hide object option to avoid rendering redundant filters at runtime. ■

The filter settings described thus far relate to the various gradient-based filters. You will notice that the Adjust Color filter settings are unique. The values available with the Adjust Color filter settings for adjusting various color qualities will be familiar to anyone who has worked in image-editing programs like Photoshop or Fireworks. Flash updates the selected item on the Stage as you make color adjustments, so it is easy to experiment with the filter settings. However, it is important to know when to apply the Adjust Color filter and when to use the color controls available from the Properties panel.

Cross-Reference

I discuss the differences between the Adjust Color filter and the Color Effect settings in the Properties panel later in this chapter. ■

Creating dimensional shadows

One limitation of the Drop Shadow filter is that it does not have a built-in skew setting. The workaround for creating a drop shadow with more depth illustrates how you can use the Hide object option and the Transform panel to enhance shadows created with the Drop Shadow filter. Here are the steps:

1. **Place a text field, Movie clip, or Button instance on the Stage.**

2. **Create a new layer below the original content layer. Click the Insert Layer icon in the Timeline (or choose Insert ⇨ Timeline ⇨ Layer from the application menu).** Drag the new layer to reorder it below the original layer in the layer stack.

3. **Copy the item from Step 1 to the new layer.** To do this, select the keyframe where the item exists and hold the Option key while dragging the keyframe content to the new layer, or select the item and use the copy command (Ctrl+C/⌘+C), and then activate the new layer and use the Paste in Place command (Shift+Ctrl+V/Shift+⌘+V).

4. **Lock the original content layer.**

5. **Select the duplicate item on the lower layer and use the Transform panel to apply a stretch and skew.** As shown in Figure 11.3, I set the vertical scale to 130 percent and the horizontal skew to –45 degrees.

6. **Open the Filters panel or activate the Filters tab in the Properties panel.**

7. **Click the plus symbol and select Drop Shadow from the Filters list.** In the Drop Shadow settings, select the Hide object check box. Otherwise, the default settings are a good place to start.

   As shown in Figure 11.4, the default settings can be modified to create a softer shadow. In our example, the shadow Color was changed to medium gray (#666666), the Strength was set to 50 percent, and the Quality was set to Medium.

On the CD-ROM

I've included the finished file shown in Figure 11.4 on the CD-ROM so you can see how the shadow animates along with the original character. `CharacterAnim_Shadow.fla` **and** `CharacterAnim_shadow.swf` **are both in the** `DropShadow` **subfolder of the** `ch11` **folder on the CD-ROM.** ■

Use the Transform panel to modify the duplicate symbol instance so it creates a more realistic offset shadow.

A Drop Shadow filter applied to the skewed symbol instance with the Hide object option enabled, and a few adjustments to the default settings, results in a more realistic, dimensional shadow.

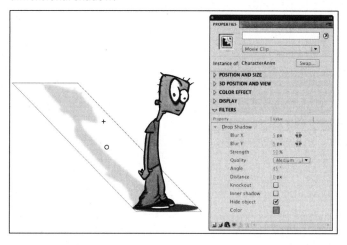

Combining filters and saving custom presets

Multiple filters added to one item are rendered in the order they appear in the live list, from top to bottom. Changing the order of filters by dragging a filter name up or down in the live list changes the final result of the combined effect, but the settings for each filter are preserved and editable.

If you have created a special combination of filters or found a custom filter setting that you want to reuse, the Presets option makes it easy to save and access your own list of filter effects.

To save a filter setting or filter combo to the Presets menu, follow these steps:

1. Select the item that has the filters and settings applied that you want to save.

Note
All filters in the live list for the selected item will be saved with the preset, including any filters that are toggled off. When the custom filter is applied from the Presets menu to another item, the settings will be identical. ∎

2. In the Filters section of the Properties panel, click the multi-page icon to open the filter Presets menu (as shown in Figure 11.5). From the Presets menu, select Save As.

FIGURE 11.5

The Presets menu in the Filters section of the Properties panel enables you to manage and apply any custom filter settings or filter combinations that you want to save for reuse.

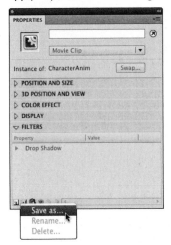

3. Type a name for your custom filter settings or filter combo (as shown in Figure 11.6) and click OK.

FIGURE 11.6

You can name and save custom settings for a specific filter or a combination of filters in the Presets menu for reuse.

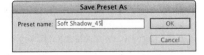

The named preset is added to the bottom of the Presets menu, along with any other saved Presets (in alphabetical order), shown in Figure 11.7, and can be applied to other items.

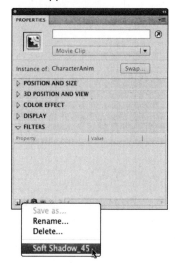

FIGURE 11.7

Saved filter presets appear alphabetically in the Presets menu — the presets are saved on an application level for reuse in any active document.

Caution

When a preset is applied to an item, any other filters that have been applied to that item are cleared and replaced with the filters (and settings) that were saved with the preset. To see the live filter list for the applied preset, you may have to deselect and then reselect the item to which it was applied — forcing the panel to update. ■

After a preset is applied to an item, the settings can be modified on that item without corrupting the saved preset. Unfortunately, the Presets list doesn't have a centralized edit option, but you can select the Rename or Delete option from the Preset menu to load your list of currently saved presets into dialog boxes that enable you to rename an item or remove an item from the list. If you want to share your filter presets with other people, all you have to do is provide them with the XML file that is saved for each preset in the Flash Configuration folder. The standard file paths for saved filter presets are as follows:

Windows:

```
C:\Documents and Settings\username\Local Settings\Application Data\
    Adobe\Flash CS5\language\Configuration\Filters\filtername.xml
```

Mac:

```
Macintosh HD/Users/username/Library/Application Support/Adobe/Flash
    CS5/language/Configuration/Filters/filtername.xml
```

After the XML files are copied into the same location on other people's computers, the presets appear in their Presets menu when they start Flash CS5. Filter swapping is an easy way to share creative resources and to keep effects consistent for projects that rely on filters for a specific look.

Although you may occasionally find it helpful to combine filters, it is best to try and achieve the result you want by first adjusting the settings of a single filter and/or modifying the symbol instance by using the Color Effect settings in the Properties panel or the Transform tools. As with any intensive effect rendered at runtime, multiple filters have a negative impact on the performance of the published Flash movie.

Animating filters with motion tweens

The Flash engineers have done a great deal of work to make it as easy as possible to combine filters with motion tweens for animated effects. The result is a very intuitive system that works behind the scenes to support tweens while preserving editable filter settings.

Note

Filters are not necessarily incompatible with shape tweens, but because filters can only be applied to symbols or text fields and shape tweens can only be applied to primitive shapes, filters and shape tweens never get a chance to work together. The only workaround for this rule is to create a shape tween inside of a Movie clip and then apply a filter to the Movie clip. In this case, the final visual result is a combination of a shape tween and a filter, but they remain on separate timelines. ■

You can apply a filter to an item and then tween it, or you can select an item that has been tweened and add a filter to enhance the motion — in most cases, you'll get exactly the animated effect you were hoping for. The only time you'll need to know what is going on behind the scenes is when you don't get the result you want on the first try.

Here are some notes that should help you troubleshoot if things go wrong when you try to combine filters and motion tweens:

- Filters "stick" to symbol instances, so if you insert a keyframe (with the same content as the initial keyframe) and set up a motion tween, the settings and the stacking order in the live list automatically match in the first keyframe and the last keyframe of the tween.

- If you add a filter to a symbol in one keyframe of a tween, Flash automatically adds a matching filter with all the settings adjusted to create "no effect" to the symbol in the other keyframe. This is also called a "dummy filter" because it has no visible effect on the symbol, but it is required to support the tween.

- If you remove a filter from a symbol in one keyframe of a tween, Flash automatically clears the matching filter from the other keyframe.

- If you apply different filters (or different combinations of filters) on two different keyframes and then apply a tween, Flash analyzes the symbol with the most filters and applies dummy filters to the symbol in the other keyframe to support the tween. The visual difference between the two symbols is interpolated in the span of the tween.

- You can modify filter settings to create a visual change from the first keyframe to the last keyframe in a motion tween. The differences are tweened evenly across the span unless you use the Motion Editor to adjust the interpolation.

- The knockout and type of gradient (such as inner, outer, or full) filter settings do not interpolate properly as part of a tween if they are set differently on the beginning and end keyframes. If the filter options in the first keyframe and the end keyframe of a tween are inconsistent and cannot be interpolated properly, Flash applies the options set in the first keyframe to the frames in the span of the tween.

Using the Motion Editor to control filter interpolation

By default, the interpolation of any differences in filter settings from the first keyframe to the last frame matches the interpolation of the motion tween — that is, the filters change at the same rate as any other characteristics of the item that have been modified to create animation in the tween. The default Simple (Slow) easing setting applies equally to all changes in the characteristics of an item. As described in Chapter 11, if you need more precise control over the interpolation of different aspects of a tween, you can use the Motion Editor to add easing for tweened characteristics including Motion, Transformation, Color Effect, and/or Filters. As shown in Figure 11.8, the Motion Editor enables you to create a unique interpolation curve for each of the various properties that can be animated in a tween. You can set a unique curve to apply to all properties, or set unique curves for selected properties, leaving the default curve for others.

To access easing settings for filter properties in a tween:

1. **Select a motion tween in the Timeline or select a tweened item on the Stage.**

2. **Click the Motion Editor tab (to the right of the Timeline tab in the Essentials CS5 workspace layout).**

3. **Scroll down until you see the filter properties that you want to modify or adjust in the tween.** Note that each property in an applied filter has its own easing setting. The options available for easing depend on the eases you have loaded into the Easing section of the Motion Editor. By default, Simple (Slow) is loaded and available as a setting for all properties.

4. **To add additional easing options, click the plus (+) icon in the Eases section of the Motion Editor.** Select a preset easing curve from the drop-down menu (shown in Figure 11.9), or add your own custom curve — if you can think of any that aren't already in the list!

Tip

If you want a larger view of a specific easing curve, double-click any row to expand it. Double-click again to return it to normal height. ■

FIGURE 11.8

The interpolation of filters in a tween can be controlled separately from the interpolation of other characteristics by adding and/or adjusting a custom easing curve.

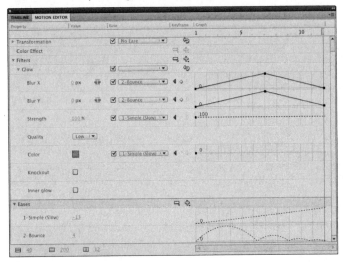

FIGURE 11.9

Add as many of the preset easing curves as you want in the Easing section of the Motion Editor, or create your own custom easing curve.

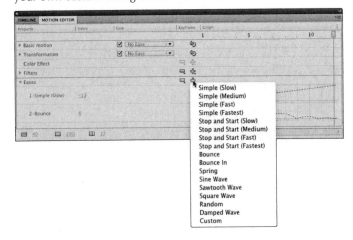

Controlling Color: Properties versus Filters

The Adjust Color filter loads a set of controls for making color adjustment to Movie clips, Button symbols, and text fields. The best way to explain these controls is to compare them to other Flash color settings. Some of these controls are unique and some replicate settings available in the Color panel (for raw shapes, shape primitives, and drawing objects) and/or in the Properties panel Color menu. These three different color control areas are shown in Figure 11.10, with an additional diagram (A1) to call out the features of the Color panel that overlap with slider settings for the Adjust Color filter.

The controls shown in Figure 11.10 enable various workflows for setting and adjusting color in the Flash authoring environment. In most cases, you start with the Color panel (or Swatches panel) to choose and/or modify fill and stroke colors for initial primitive shapes or drawing objects. After the raw graphics are converted into reusable symbols, the Color Effect settings available in the Properties panel and/or the Adjust Color filter can be applied to modify symbol instances without changing the original fill and stroke colors. The sliders and hot text values for adjusting color with either of these options are easy to use, and you will most likely achieve the result you want with just a little experimentation. However, there are important differences between the Color Effect properties and the Adjust Color filter settings, and the interaction of the different settings can become quite complex. To clarify the functions (and the advantages or limitations) of the various settings available with these two options, I have included a brief section for each.

Web Resource

If you want to learn more about various color models and the differences between HSV/HSB (hue, saturation, value; or hue, saturation, brightness) and HSL (hue, saturation, lightness) color spaces, a good place to start is Wikipedia: http://en.wikipedia.org/wiki/HSB_color_space. ■

FIGURE 11.10

The options for adjusting color in Flash include the Color panel (A), the Color Effect menu (B), and the Adjust Color filter (C) — which enable instance-level color transformations similar to the raw color edits supported in the Color panel.

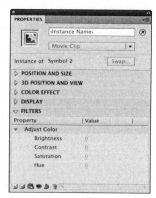

A   B   C

Adjust Color filter

Figure 11.11 shows a sample of the range of color transformations that can be achieved with the hot text controls that load into the Filters section of the Properties panel when you apply the Adjust Color filter to Movie clip instances, Button instances, or text fields.

Cross-Reference

The grayscale version of the sample color transformations shown in Figure 11.11 gives you a hint of what is possible with the Adjust Color filter, but the color version of this figure included in the color insert in this book is much more informative. ■

On the CD-ROM

I have included the source file with the various transformed Movie clip instances shown in Figure 11.11 on the CD-ROM. Open AdjustColorFilter.fla **from the** ColorEffectsvsFilters **folder in the** ch11 **folder on the CD-ROM to see the samples in the Flash authoring environment. To see these same transformations applied to a sample bitmap, open** AdjustColorFilter_bitmaps.fla **from the same location. ■**

FIGURE 11.11

The Adjust Color filter enables subtle color transformations of symbol instances and text fields.

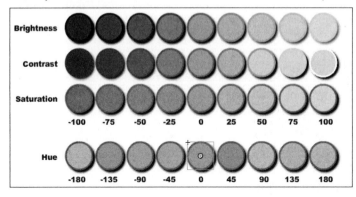

Finally, you can make subtle adjustments (on an instance level) to Movie clips, Button symbols, and text fields, without having to go back to the Color panel and change the stroke and fill colors of the original symbol. Unlike the Color Effect options in the Properties panel, the Adjust Color filter makes it easy to combine different types of color transformation without manually adjusting individual RGB values. By default, all settings are loaded as "neutral" — values are set to 0 so that no color transformation is visible on the selected item when the filter is first applied. Color transformations are applied for instant visual feedback as the values are adjusted. Filters apply on an instance level, and settings can be modified at any time by selecting an instance and choosing Adjust Color from the live filter list in the Properties panel. The following values can be applied individually or in combination to Movie clips, Button symbols, and text fields:

- **Brightness:** Alters the RGB values for the original color to make it appear lighter or darker without changing the hue. The range for filter Brightness is –100 to +100. The default or no change value is 0. The numeric value that appears in the Brightness field is added to the RGB values of the original color to create a new shade, within the minimum and maximum values of 0 and 255, respectively. For example, a red fill (255, 0, 0) set to +50 brightness transforms into light red (255, 50, 50). The same red fill (255, 0, 0) set to –50 brightness transforms into dark red (205, 0, 0). As shown in Figure 11.12, the results of changing Brightness with the Adjust Color filter are different than the results of changing Brightness with the Color Effect settings.

Note

Although the range for the Brightness filter and the Brightness Color Effect might seem the same at first glance, the significantly different results that these two options achieve are due to one being a relative (or percentage-based) setting and the other being an absolute (or decimal-based) setting. The Brightness filter is applied as an absolute numeric value, and the Color Effect Brightness property is applied as a relative percentage-based value. Regardless of the original color, setting Color Effect Brightness to 100% shifts the RGB values to white (255, 255, 255) and –100% Brightness shifts the RGB values to black (0,0,0). Any other Brightness setting is calculated as the percentage between these two extremes, and the RGB values are transformed accordingly. ∎

FIGURE 11.12

Numeric settings applied with the Adjust Color filter Brightness result in less extreme value changes than Percentage settings applied with the Color Effect Brightness.

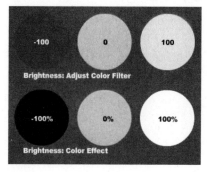

On the CD-ROM

I have included the source file for Figure 11.12 on the CD-ROM. The file is called Brightness_FiltersVsEffects.fla. ∎

- **Contrast:** At the minimum contrast setting of –100, all RGB values are forced to 64, 64, 64, making everything medium gray. The RGB values at the maximum contrast setting of 100 vary depending on the original colors, but they are forced closer to 0 or 255. The default or no change value is 0. The greater the numeric difference between RGB values, the greater the amount of contrast. In visual terms, light colors get lighter and dark colors get darker as contrast is *increased*, whereas all colors are brought closer to medium gray as contrast is *decreased*.

- **Saturation:** Saturation can also be thought of as the intensity or purity of color. At the minimum saturation setting of –100, the image is rendered in grayscale with no color intensity, similar to the hues found closer to the *bottom* of the color selection field in the Color panel. At the maximum saturation setting of 100, the colors are as intense or as close to pure color as possible, similar to the hues found closer to the *top* of the color selection field in the Color panel.

- **Hue:** The Hue slider has a different range than the other Adjust Color filter sliders. To span the full range of the 360-degree color wheel, the slider values are from –180 to 180. The default or no change value is 0. If you were looking at a real color wheel, reducing the hue value would be equivalent to moving counterclockwise around the wheel, and increasing the hue value would be equivalent to moving clockwise around the wheel. At either extreme (–180 or 180), the resulting color would be directly opposite the original color on the color wheel. The relationship of colors directly opposite on the color wheel is known as *complementary*.

Web Resource

There are many books and online resources dedicated to color theory, and there are many different versions of the color wheel. A good explanation and an illustration of an RGB color wheel can be found at `www. color-wheel-pro.com/color-theory-basics.html`. **Color Wheel Pro** is one of many software programs available to help designers create successful color schemes by using color wheel relationships as a guideline. ■

Caution

Flash Filters (including the Adjust Color settings) are compatible only with Flash Player 8 and later. If you plan to publish content for earlier versions of the Flash Player, you are limited to using the Color Effect settings in the Properties panel to make adjustments to the appearance of symbol instances, or using the Color panel to modify the original stroke and fill colors in primitive shapes. ■

Color properties

As I introduced in Chapter 6, "Symbols, Instances, and the Library," the Color Effect settings in the Properties panel provide some options for modifying the appearance of symbol instances without changing the original symbol stored in the library. After a Color Effect style is selected from the Color drop-down menu, the controls needed to apply the color adjustment appear in the Properties panel. By default, "neutral" settings (0 percent change) are loaded as a starting point. After the values for a property are modified, they are stored and loaded as the default when you select another instance. The Color Effect settings loaded in the Properties panel are simple and intuitive and enable you to make basic color adjustments by using familiar controls:

- **Brightness:** The Brightness Color property has the same range as the Brightness setting in the Adjust Color filter (–100 to 100); however, as described previously, the Brightness property creates more drastic color transformations because it is applied as a relative or percentage-based value. At the minimum Brightness setting (−100), all RGB values are forced to black (0,0,0), and at the maximum Brightness setting (100), all RGB values are forced to white (255,255,255).

- **Tint:** The color theory definition of a tint is a color produced by adding white to a pure color. The Tint property in Flash enables you to select any color (not just white) to "mix" with the original color. You can also select how much of the new color you want to mix with your original colors — from the lowest setting of 0 percent to the maximum setting of 100 percent. At the minimum setting, the original colors are unchanged. At the maximum setting, the new tint color completely replaces all the original colors. At the default setting of 50 percent, the rendered color values are an even mix of the original colors and the selected tint color.

- **Alpha:** This setting controls how opaque the selected instance will be. The values that control alpha are counterintuitive (as they are in the Color panel). At the minimum alpha level of 0 percent, the item is transparent. At the maximum alpha level of 100 percent, the item is fully opaque or "solid."

Using advanced color effects: Understanding relative and absolute color settings

The Advanced effect option shown in Figure 11.13 includes two columns of settings for Red, Green, and Blue color channels, plus the setting for Alpha. These settings are accessible when a symbol instance is selected on the Stage and the Advanced option is chosen from the Style drop-down menu in the Color Effect section of the Properties panel. Although these columns may seem redundant at first, they actually provide very different options for controlling the appearance of instance color. The important difference between these two types of controls is that the first column creates *relative* changes by applying percentage-based adjustments, and the second column creates *absolute* change by adding or subtracting integer values.

FIGURE 11.13

The default Advanced effect settings shown with the symbol instance testStar, with no effect applied

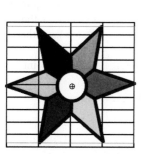
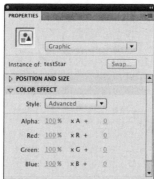

Tip

The most recent transformation that was applied to an item by using any of the other Color Effect styles is preserved if you decide to switch to the Advanced color effect style. The equivalent values are transferred to the RGB or Alpha values for the Advanced color effect. This is a helpful way to get started with more complex transformations instead of starting from scratch. For example, you could select a Tint setting and then switch to the Advanced color option to add an alpha setting that would be combined with the RGB values carried over from the original tint. ∎

Other than playing with these settings, the easiest way to understand what some of the possible combinations produce is to dig out your calculator and find a chart of RGB color swatches (with decimal values rather than hex values). By taking the RGB values in your original instance, multiplying them by the percentage entered in the relative value field, and adding the value shown in the absolute color field, you arrive at the new RGB value that appears in the symbol instance when the effect is applied. If this sounds confusing, read on.

On the CD-ROM

Because color examples are not very helpful illustrated in black and white, I have included the relevant graphics in a Flash file that you can open for reference. Compare the Advanced Color Effect (relative) layer with the Advanced Color Effect (absolute) layer in `colorEdits.fla` **in the** `ColorEffectsVsFilters` **folder in the** `ch11` **folder on the CD-ROM.** ∎

Relative color control

The first column of values adjusts the color of the instance relative to the percentages of color (or alpha) present in the original with a range of –100 percent to 100 percent. The default, or "no effect," setting is 100 percent. With these controls, 100 percent red does not change everything to pure red or 255 red, but rather it displays 100 percent of the current percentage of red in the existing colors. For example, yellow (255, 255, 0) cannot be made more orange by increasing the amount of red because 255×100 percent is still 255 — the maximum amount of red. However, if you reduce the percentage of green to 45 percent of the original value, the ratio of red is increased, making the visible color shift to orange (255, [255×45 percent], 0 or 255, 102, 0).

This process of reducing the amount of the opposite (or complementary) color to alter the ratio of colors is called *subtractive* color adjustment, and it can be helpful to remember some basic color theory to predict how it will alter the appearance of your symbol instance. Because the color value changes that you make are applied to all the colors in your symbol, the overall effect can be more complex than just shifting one color in your palette. You will find, for example, that *reducing* the percentage of red and green to 0 for the testStar symbol instance (see the `colorEdits.fla` file on the CD-ROM) causes the gray and white areas to shift to blue, whereas the red and green areas shift to black, and the originally black areas remain unaltered.

Because the maximum value for relative Alpha is also 100 percent, this control cannot be used to increase the alpha setting of an instance. For example, a symbol that has an alpha fill of 50 percent cannot be made to appear more solid because 100 percent of 50 percent is still only 50 percent alpha.

Absolute color control

The settings in the right column are referred to as *absolute* color controls because they add or subtract color in concrete amounts regardless of the color values in the symbol instance. The scale of absolute color is from –255 to 255, and the default or "no effect" setting is 0. When absolute color is applied to a symbol instance, it is possible to make more drastic global color changes than you can make with relative color adjustments.

The effect of absolute color value changes made with the Advanced color effect is similar to the effect of using the Tint color effect. What makes these controls more advanced is that not only can you add a tint by increasing the value of certain colors, but you can also add an *inverse* tint by using negative values. So, for example, you could add a red tint to all the colors present in the test-Star symbol instance, with the exception of white and pure red (which already contain 255 red), by entering a value of 255 Red, or you could add a yellow tint to all colors containing blue by entering a value of –255 Blue; this makes pure blue (0, 0, 255) turn to black (0, 0, 0), and white (255, 255, 255) turn to pure yellow (255, 255, 0).

On the CD-ROM

You can see the original `testStar` symbol instance and several modified examples, including those described in this section, in the Advanced Color Effect (absolute) layer of `colorEdit.fla` in the `ColorEffectsVs Filters` folder in the `ch11` folder on the CD-ROM. ■

Perhaps one of the most unique feats that absolute values can perform is to make a symbol instance that contains alpha fills or strokes appear less transparent. Because the alpha settings are absolute, it is possible to shift an item with an original alpha setting of less than 100 percent to any opacity level between invisible (–255) and completely solid (255).

If you've entered negative values in the relative alpha setting, you can even make an area with an alpha fill visible while solid areas are made invisible. Consider a shape that has an area of solid fill (100 percent or 255 alpha) and an area of transparent color (40 percent or 102 alpha). If this shape is converted into a symbol and then modified by using the Advanced color effect options, you could enter a relative alpha value of –100 percent and an absolute alpha value of 255. When these effect settings are applied, the solid fill in the symbol instance would be invisible with 0 percent alpha (255 × –100 percent + 255 = 0), whereas the originally transparent fill would be visible with 60 percent alpha (102 × –100 percent + 255 = 153). Compare the modified test-Star instance shown in Figure 11.14 with the original instance shown in Figure 11.13.

The confusion that these settings sometimes cause has created debate about whether negative alpha settings can really be applied. As long as you can remember that outside of the absolute settings for the Advanced color effect, 0 percent alpha is invisible, whereas with the Advanced color effect settings, a 0 alpha setting is equal to no effect, you will be able to prove as I just did, that negative alpha effects can be used to invert alpha values, similar to the way that negative color effects can be used to invert color values.

FIGURE 11.14

Using a combination of relative and absolute alpha values, the transparency levels in the original `testStar` instance can be inverted.

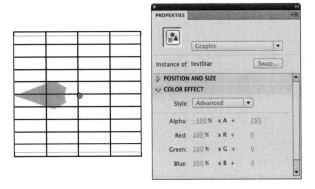

Layering Graphics with Blend Modes

If you use Photoshop or other image-editing applications, you may be familiar with using blend modes, although for many people this remains a somewhat mysterious tool. Blends are rendering tools that analyze the pixel values of overlapping images (the blend image and the underlying base images) to create a rendered image that is a mix of the two. The type of blend applied determines the formula used to generate the pixel values in the combined image. Blend modes can be applied to Movie clip and Button symbol instances in the authoring environment by using the Blending menu in the Properties panel (shown in Figure 11.15). The blend image interacts with any underlying images that it overlaps, even if they are not on the same layer.

Tip

The line breaks that separate the blend modes in the Blending menu may seem arbitrary, but they actually differentiate the blend modes into groups based on the type of effect they have on images. Keep this in mind while you read the descriptions of each blend mode in the next section; you will start to notice similarities in the modes that are grouped. ■

Understanding blend modes

Predicting the exact outcome of various blend modes is tricky because blends use different formulas on a pixel-by-pixel basis to mix the blended image with underlying images, and the result depends on the pixel values of both the underlying images (or *base color*) and the overlapping image (or *blend color*). The most common advice for working with blends is to experiment until you get a result that you like — I encourage you to do exactly that! However, it is helpful to have some idea of how each blend works and what visual problems they can solve. Compare Figure 11.16, which shows two source bitmaps (left and center), overlapped with blending set to Layer or Normal (right), to Figure 11.17, which shows the results of Flash blend modes applied to mix the images in various ways.

The Blending menu is available in the Display section of the Properties panel when you select a Movie clip or Button instance.

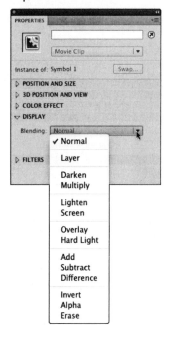

A base image (left) and a blend image (center) overlapped with blend mode set to Normal or Layer create a standard layered graphic with no mixing of pixel values (right).

Base image   **Blend image**   **Layer (or Normal)**

Note

You'll notice that I didn't include an image in Figure 11.17 to illustrate the Layer blend mode applied by itself. That is because the Layer blend mode has no effect, unless it is combined with a nested Erase or Alpha blend mode. ■

FIGURE 11.17

The 12 different effects that can be created by applying blending to layered images. The results vary depending on the images that are combined, but the formula used for each blend type is consistent. Unlike other blend modes, the Alpha and Erase blend modes require a nested structure with a Layer blend applied to the parent symbol instance.

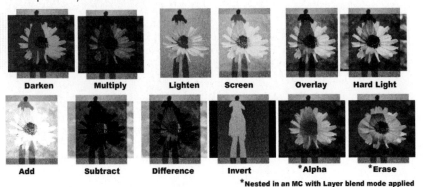

| Darken | Multiply | Lighten | Screen | Overlay | Hard Light |
| Add | Subtract | Difference | Invert | *Alpha | *Erase |

*Nested in an MC with Layer blend mode applied

The blend modes available in Flash include the following:

- **Normal:** The default blend mode for new symbol instances. No interpolation is applied and pixel values are left unchanged.

- **Layer:** Creates no visual effect on its own, but is required for Alpha and Erase blend modes to work.

- **Darken:** Compares the brightness of the pixels in the base image with the pixels in the blend image. Pixels in the base image that are lighter than the blend image are replaced with pixels from the blend image. Pixels in the base image that are darker than the blend image are left unchanged.

- **Multiply:** Multiplies the RGB values of the pixels in the base image with the pixels in the blend image. The resulting pixels are a darkened combination of both the base image and the blend image. Multiplying any color with black results in solid black; multiplying any color with white leaves the pixels unchanged.

- **Lighten:** Compares the brightness of the pixels in the base image with the pixels in the blend image. Pixels in the base image that are darker than the blend image are replaced with pixels from the blend image. Pixels in the base image that are lighter than the blend image are left unchanged. The blend image always disappears when it's layered over white.

- **Screen:** Analyzes the color values and multiplies the inverse of the blend and base colors. The resulting pixels are a lightened combination of both the base image and the blend image. Screening with black leaves the base image unchanged. Screening with white produces solid white. The blend image always disappears when it's layered over white.

- **Overlay:** Pixels are screened or multiplied depending, on the pixel values in the base image. If the base color is lighter than mid-gray, the image is lightened (screened), and if the base color is darker than mid-gray, the image is darkened (multiplied). The blend image overlays the base image while preserving the highlights and shadows of the base image. The resulting image is an even blend of the base image and the blend image, usually with increased contrast in both images. Overlaying black results in a shaded version of the base image. Overlaying white results in a bleached version of the base image. The blend image disappears when it's layered over any pure color (black, white, pure red, pure green, and so on).

- **Hard light:** Pixels are screened or multiplied, depending on the pixel values in the blend image. If the blend color is lighter than mid-gray, the image is lightened (screened). If the blend color is darker than mid-gray, the image is darkened (multiplied). The base image is mixed with the blend while preserving the highlights and shadows of the blend image. Overlaying pure black or pure white results in solid black or solid white, respectively.

- **Add:** Adds the color values of the blend image to the color values of the base image. The result is a bleached-out combination of the two images. Adding pure white results in a solid white image; adding pure black has no effect on the base image.

- **Subtract:** Subtracts the blend color value from the base color value. The result is a darkened combination of the two images. Subtracting pure white from any color results in a solid black image. Subtracting pure black has no effect on the base image.

- **Difference:** Analyzes the color values in the base and the blend and subtracts the brighter values from the darker values. The result is a reversal of color values. Black blended with any color has no effect. White blended with any color inverts the color. The resulting image looks like a film negative of the combined images.

- **Invert:** Inverts the base image in any areas overlapped by the blend image. The contents of the blend image have no bearing on the transformation of the base color values; the blend image acts merely as an "active area" for the inversion effect.

- **Alpha:** Alpha blend mode can be used to apply the contents of a nested Movie clip with alpha areas as a mask for an image in a parent Movie clip with Layer blend mode applied.

- **Erase:** Erase blend mode can be used to apply the contents of a nested Movie clip as an eraser to cut out an area of an image in a parent Movie clip with Layer blend mode applied.

Tip

Using a solid fill with Alpha set to 0 percent in an Alpha blend has the same effect as using a solid fill in an Erase blend. ■

Applying basic blends

That's a lot of visual calculation to try and imagine without actually using blends. The steps for applying the "basic blends" (all but Alpha and Erase) are straightforward:

1. **Select a Movie clip or Button symbol instance that you want to use as a blend image to layer with underlying base images.**

Tip

Images on layers above the layer with the blend symbol instance are not transformed by the blend mode. Don't forget that you can use the Modify ⇨ Arrange commands if you need to modify the stacking order of images on the same layer. ■

2. **Open the Display section in the Properties panel, and from the Blending menu, select a blend type.**

That's it! You can see how the blend image interacts with different base images by dragging it to overlap other images in your Flash authoring environment. Color effects and filters can be used in combination with blend modes to get different hybrid results. All these effect tools interact to transform graphics rendered in the authoring environment, but they remain editable and each can be adjusted independently on an instance level. You can apply multiple blend modes on the same layer, but only one blend mode to any single symbol instance. The only compound blend modes are Alpha and Erase, which must be applied on a symbol timeline and combined with a Layer blend mode on the parent symbol instance, as described in the next section.

Caution

The background color of your Flash movie interacts with blend modes too. This is helpful to remember if the blend image is larger than the base image and you start getting unexpected results in the overhang areas. Applying a Layer mask to the blend image so that it is trimmed to match the base image removes any unwanted overhang areas that are mixing with the background color. ■

Applying compound blend modes: Alpha and Erase

Alpha and Erase blends are a great complement to Flash's standard masking tools, which can be counterintuitive at times. If you want to create a cutout in a shape by using a traditional mask, you actually have to create a shape on a mask layer that covers all the areas *except* the area you want to cut out. If you have been working in Flash for a while, this workflow is probably second nature, but when it comes to more subtle mask effects, like gradients or irregular shapes, it can be a headache to have to reverse-engineer a mask graphic. With Alpha blends, what you see is what you get — or rather, what you *don't* see is what you *won't* get! The steps for creating a compound blend are as follows:

1. **Create a Movie clip with content that will function as the base image (or convert an existing graphic that you want to mask into a Movie clip).**

2. **Open the Movie clip in Edit mode to access the Movie clip timeline.** To do this, double-click an instance on the Stage or the symbol name in the Library list.

3. **Create a new layer on the Movie clip timeline above the existing content that will be the base image for the Alpha or Erase blend.** To protect the base image(s), you may want to lock all layers but the new layer.

Note

The base image or color can be any graphic type — shape primitive, drawing object, bitmap, or symbol instance — as long as it is nested inside of a Movie clip or Button symbol. The blend image has to be a Movie clip or Button symbol instance. ■

4. **In the new layer, create a graphic that will act as a mask.** Blend masks are the opposite of normal Flash layer masks in that the content in the Alpha or Erase blend symbol instance defines an area to make *invisible* in the base image rather than an area to make *visible*.

Caution

Any content in a symbol instance with an Erase blend mode applied defines the area to be punched out of (or erased from) the underlying base image. The content of a symbol instance with an Alpha blend mode applied has no effect unless it contains areas with transparency; the amount of information erased from the base images will match the level of Alpha transparency in the blend symbol instance. A symbol instance with content set to 0 percent Alpha and applied as an Alpha blend has the same effect as an Erase blend. ■

5. **Convert the content on the blend layer into a Movie clip or Button symbol.**

6. **Select the symbol instance and position it on the Stage (still on the base image Movie clip timeline) to overlap the base image so that it defines the area you want to Erase or Alpha out.** Next, use the Blending menu in the Properties panel to apply an Alpha or Erase blend mode. The content of the blend image disappears, but don't panic — continue to the next step to complete the compound blend.

7. **Return to the Main Timeline.** (Double-click an empty area of the Stage or use the Scene button at the top of the Document window.)

8. **Select the parent symbol instance (that contains your base image and the currently invisible blend image), and use the Blending menu to apply a Layer blend.** If you opened the base symbol from the Library in Step 2, make sure that you have an instance dragged onto the Stage on the Main Timeline so you can apply the Layer blend mode to the instance.

Voila! You should see the content of your blend image punched out (Erase blend) or rubbed out (Alpha blend) of the base image; either the background color of the Flash movie or any underlying images on the Stage will be visible through the empty areas created in the base image.

On the CD-ROM

Open `Erase_blend.fla` **from the** `Blending` **folder in the** `ch11` **folder on the CD-ROM if you want to analyze an example of the nested symbol structure required to render Erase and Alpha blend modes successfully.** ■

In addition to supporting a more intuitive workflow for creating masks and enabling Alpha-based masks, compound blends can be used to create animated transition effects. Continue to the next section if you want to try using an Alpha blend to create an animated color fade effect.

Creating an animated Alpha blend

The following example uses an animated Alpha blend to selectively fade out a black-and-white image to reveal a color image. The trick for this effect is to use two instances of the same color image, with the Adjust Color filter applied to make one instance a grayscale version. There are a lot of steps, but the final file structure is straightforward and the effect is pretty cool, so let's get started:

1. Open a new Flash document.

2. Import a color bitmap and convert it to a Movie clip (or place an existing Movie clip instance on the Stage, preferably one with bright colors).

3. Place two instances of the Movie clip on the Stage so that they are layered and aligned — select both instances and use the Vertical Center and Horizontal Center align commands.

4. Select the topmost Movie clip instance and use the Adjust Color filter (in the Filters section of the Properties panel) to set the Saturation of the image to −100. This drains the color out so that it looks grayscale.

5. With the grayscale Movie clip instance still selected, use the Blending menu (in the Display section of the Properties panel) to apply Layer blend mode. You won't see any visible change yet.

6. Double-click the grayscale Movie clip instance to access the Movie clip timeline in Edit mode.

7. Create a new layer at the top of the layer stack in the Movie clip timeline. Lock the other layer(s) with the bitmap or graphics you plan to use as a base image.

8. Select the Oval tool (O) in the Tools panel and set the Fill color to use a default radial gradient. Use the Color panel to apply 0 percent Alpha to the left color anchor. This should create a circular gradient fill that has a transparent center that fades out to black. Set the stroke color to None.

9. Click and drag on the Stage to create a circle that covers only a small area in the center of the original image. In our file, the circle image was 100 × 100 pixels.

10. Select the new circle and convert it into a Movie clip named `alpha circle`.

11. Use the Blending menu to apply an Alpha blend mode to the `alpha circle` Movie clip instance. The circle Movie clip disappears, but don't panic. As you can see by the filled keyframe on the layer, the content is still there and you can select it to see the selection outline for the invisible instance.

12. Double-click the `alpha circle` instance to access the Movie clip timeline and insert frames (F5) to extend the span of the circle graphic to frame 20. Convert frame 20 into a keyframe (F6).

13. Select the circle graphic in keyframe 20 and use the Transform panel or the Position and Size section of the Properties panel to increase the size of the circle so that it is larger than the bitmap base image. I scaled the circle up to 400 × 400 pixels.

14. Select keyframe 1 (still in the alpha circle timeline) and apply a shape tween. You should now be able to scrub the Movie clip timeline to see the small circle in frame 1 scaling up to the size of the larger circle in frame 20.

15. In order to see the Alpha blend applied as a mask, you have to return to the Main Timeline (click the Scene button). The grayscale bitmap image should now have an area in the center that is "erased" in a soft, gradient circle that allows some of the color image to show through.

16. The animated effect is visible only in the published SWF file or the Test Movie environment. Press Ctrl+Return/⌘+Return to test the file and preview the animation.

On the CD-ROM

To see the final result of our example file, open anim_Alpha_blend.swf from the Blending folder in the ch11 folder on the CD-ROM. To analyze the file structure, open anim_Alpha_blend.fla from the same location. ∎

You can always go back inside the nested symbols to modify the level of alpha in the blend image or change the style of fill from a radial gradient to a linear gradient or even a solid fill (with alpha set to less than 100 percent). The level of masking matches the level of alpha in the contents of the Alpha blend symbol instance. Alpha blends can be used to mask any type of image — even bitmaps or shape primitives. The only requirement is that the Alpha blend must be applied to a symbol instance and that symbol instance must be nested inside a Movie clip with a Layer blend applied. This is just one way of using a blend mode to create an interesting visual effect. There are many other possibilities, and when you understand the workflow for applying basic and compound blends, the rest is just a matter of experimentation!

Working with Special Layer Types: Guides and Masks

Besides storing and organizing the contents of your Flash project, layers offer some special features that help you create more advanced animation. Standard layers can be locked, hidden, or displayed as outlines, but they can also be converted into guide layers or mask layers. You can use each of these layer types to accomplish specific authoring tasks.

Flash gives you the flexibility to quickly change the behavior of layers at any time in the authoring environment so that you can take advantage of the special characteristics of each of these layer types as needed.

With the layer buttons at the lower-left corner of the Timeline window, you have the option of creating standard layers and folder layers. If you have already created a standard layer, you can convert it into a guide, mask, or folder layer by using the contextual menu (opened by right-clicking or Ctrl+clicking the layer bar) or by changing settings in the Layer Properties dialog box (opened by double-clicking the layer icon or by choosing Modify ⇨ Timeline ⇨ Layer Properties from the application menu).

Flash automatically converts layers if you drag them into specific positions in the stacking order with other layer types. Although this sounds a bit cryptic, it will make sense as you read about each layer type and how it affects other layers. Each layer type has a unique icon, as shown in Figure 11.18.

FIGURE 11.18

A unique icon in the layer stack identifies each of the layer types. You can quickly assign or change the behavior of a layer by using the contextual menu.

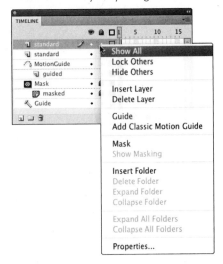

Note

Motion guide layers (shown in Figure 11.18) are now considered a "classic" feature because motion guides are created automatically on the same layer as your tweened item when you use the new tweening workflow in Flash CS5. This is a wonderful improvement to Flash, and in most cases motion guide layers are not missed. If you want to learn more about classic motion guides and how to apply them, refer to the archived content from Flash CS3 Professional Bible (Wiley, 2007): "Chapter 13: Applying Layer Types." You can find it online at www. flashsupport.com/archive. ∎

Using guide layers

Guide layers are the only layer types (aside from classic motion guide layers) that are not exported with your final Flash movie (.swf). Guide layers are used primarily when you need to use an element as a reference in the authoring environment (.fla), but you don't want it to be part of the finished movie (.swf). To convert an existing layer into a guide layer, you can use the contextual menu and select Guide. Alternatively, you can open the Layer Properties dialog box (shown in Figure 11.19) by double-clicking the layer icon (or choosing Modify ➪ Timeline ➪ Layer Properties from the application menu) and then selecting the Guide check box.

Tip

As you are developing a project, it can be helpful to "turn off" certain layers while you're testing content on other layers. For example, by temporarily turning a layer that contains a large background graphic into a guide layer, the movie (.swf) renders more quickly for preview in the Test Movie environment. Remember to turn all layers that you want exported back into normal layers before publishing your final movie (.swf), either by unchecking Guide in the contextual menu or by selecting the Normal check box in the Layer Properties dialog box. ∎

FIGURE 11.19

Use the Layer Properties dialog box to convert a standard layer into a guide layer, mask layer, or even a layer folder.

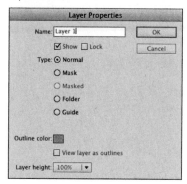

You can place bitmaps and video sequences in guide layers if you want to use them as references for drawings or animated sequences that are drawn in Flash; think of it as working with tracing paper to redraw images. The content on a guide layer adds to the file size of the Flash document (.fla), but it won't be included with or add to the file size of the exported movie (.swf). Guide layers are also useful when organizing layouts in Flash that require special alignment, such as a circular or diagonal arrangement of multiple elements.

To create a guide layer that serves as a reference for aligning a custom layout, follow these steps:

1. **Add a new layer to your Flash document (.fla) and make it a guide layer.** Use the contextual menu or the Layer properties dialog box to convert a standard layer into a guide layer.

2. **Place an imported image on the guide layer for reference, or use the Flash drawing tools to create any guide image needed (such as a circle or a freeform line).**

3. **Drag the guide layer below your art layers in the stacking order, or add a new layer above the guide layer if you need a fresh layer for arranging artwork.**

4. **Make sure that Snap to Objects is active by toggling on the Magnet option in the Tools panel or choosing View ⇨ Snapping ⇨ Snap to Objects in the application menu.**

Note

The guide layer workflow is especially helpful if you are trying to match a layout or design comp that might have been given to you in another format. Unfortunately, the Snap to Objects feature works only if the content of your guide layer is in a vector format. If you are working with a .pdf or a bitmap in the guide layer, the Snap to Objects feature won't be any help for aligning items on other layers with the content of the guide layer: In this case, you will find standard workspace guides (dragged onto the Stage with rulers toggled on in the View menu) more helpful. ∎

5. Use the Arrow tool to drag elements on the art layers into alignment with the reference on the guide layer (see Figure 11.20).

FIGURE 11.20

Use snapping to align the center point of elements on your art layers with a reference shape or line on your guide layer (in vector format).

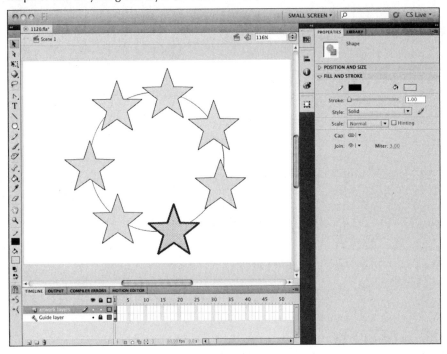

When you test your movie (Ctrl+Enter/⌘+Return), you won't see the content of the guide layer appear in the SWF (see Figure 11.21).

6. Add to or modify the reference content on the original guide layer or add additional guide layers if needed.

Adding masks

In the real world, a mask is used to selectively obscure items beneath it. In Flash, a mask layer is used to define the *visible* area of layers nested beneath it. Multiple layers can be nested as *masked* layers beneath a single mask layer. As with guide layers, the content on mask layers is not visible in the final SWF because it is intended only to modify how content in nested masked layers is rendered.

FIGURE 11.21

The content of the guide layer is not visible when the movie is published or viewed in the Test Movie environment.

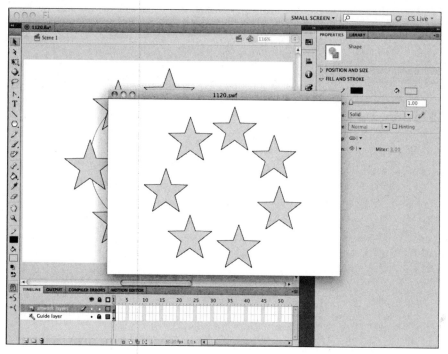

On the CD-ROM

The various examples discussed in this section can be found in the `MaskLayers` subfolder of the `ch11` folder. You may find it helpful to examine the structure of these files to understand the many ways that mask layers can be applied. ■

Almost any symbol or filled shape (excluding strokes) may be used to create a mask. However, Flash ignores bitmaps, gradients, transparency, colors, and line styles in a mask layer. Masks may be animated or static. The only other limitations are that you cannot apply a mask to content in another mask layer, and mask layers cannot be placed within Button symbol timelines.

Caution

Although groups, text boxes, and Movie clips or Graphic symbols can all be used to define a mask, only one such item is recognized on a single mask layer. You can use multiple primitive shapes to define a mask, but they override all other items existing on the same mask layer. ■

Masking with a filled shape

Here's how to create the simplest form of mask:

1. **Make sure that the content that will be visible through the mask is in place on its own layer, with visibility turned on.** This becomes the masked layer.

2. **Create a new layer stacked above the masked layer.** This becomes the mask layer.

3. **In the mask layer, create the "aperture" through which the contents of the masked layer are viewed.** This aperture can be any filled item, text, or placed instance of a symbol that includes a filled item. (Of course, lines can be used as masks if they are first converted to fills with the Modify ⇨ Shapes ⇨ Convert Lines to Fills command.)

4. **Position your mask content over the content on the masked layer (see Figure 11.22) so that it covers the area that you want to be visible through the mask.**

5. **Right-click (or Ctrl+click) the layer bar of the mask layer to open the contextual menu (see Figure 11.23), and choose Mask from the menu (or use the Layer Properties dialog box to change the layer behavior from Normal to Mask).**

   The layer icons change to indicate that the masked layer is now subordinate to the mask layer and both layers are automatically locked to activate the mask. The contents of the masked layer are now visible only through the filled portion(s) of the mask layer, as shown in Figure 11.24.

6. **To reposition, or otherwise modify, the mask layer, temporarily unlock it (see Figure 11.25).**

7. **To reactivate masking, lock the mask layer again (and confirm that the masked layer is also locked).** The contextual menu for mask layers and masked layers includes Show Masking. This handy command locks the mask layer and all nested masked layers for you.

Caution

When you first start working with mask layers, it is easy to forget to lock both the mask layer and the masked layer to make the mask effect visible. If you are ever having trouble editing or viewing your masked effect, just remember that when the layers are unlocked, the mask art is visible and editable, and when the layers are locked, the final masked effect is "turned on." ■

FIGURE 11.22

Position the content on the upper layer to cover the area that you want visible in the lower layer(s) when the mask is applied.

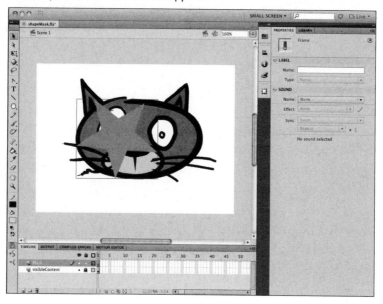

FIGURE 11.23

Convert the upper layer into a mask layer by selecting Mask from the contextual menu.

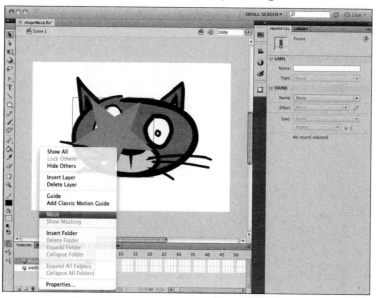

FIGURE 11.24

When the mask is active, the content on the mask layer is no longer visible, but it defines the visible area of the content on the masked layer underneath.

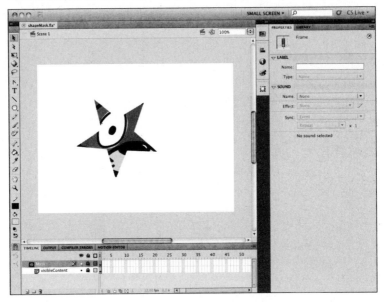

FIGURE 11.25

With the mask layer unlocked, the contents are visible and editable.

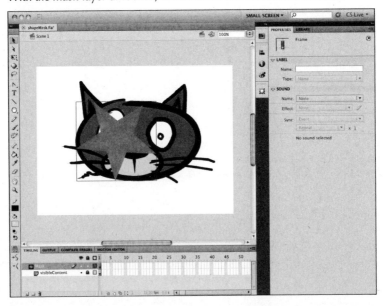

Masking with a group

Multiple filled shapes can also be grouped and used as a mask, as long as the mask layer doesn't also contain primitive ungrouped shapes. Grouped shapes on the same layer as ungrouped shapes are ignored when the mask is applied. If a mask is composed of multiple items, using a group makes it easier to position the mask, as shown in Figure 11.26.

FIGURE 11.26

Grouped filled shapes make it easier to position multipart masks.

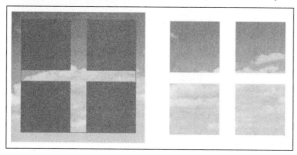

Masking with a symbol instance

As you are reminded in nearly every chapter of this book, working with symbols is working smart because doing so helps to reduce file size. Because symbols composed of filled shapes can be used as masks, there's no reason not to use a symbol from your Library to make a mask. (If you've already made a shape on your mask layer, go ahead and convert it into a symbol so that you can use it again without adding to the final file size.) Reusing symbol instances to define masks is especially logical if you are making multiple masks that all have the same basic shape. For example, if you need a rectangular or oval mask, you will often find a symbol in your Library that was created to define the active area of a button or some other basic element. It is smarter to modify an instance of an existing symbol so that it works as a mask rather than to add redundant elements that increase your file size.

Note

Although in theory you can use a Button symbol instance as mask artwork, note that a Button symbol instance placed into a mask layer no longer functions as a button. The result of this workflow is similar to selecting a Button symbol instance and assigning it Graphic symbol behavior in the Properties panel. ■

To illustrate the way that symbols can be reused as both graphic content and as mask elements, I have used instances of a symbol as static content on a masked layer and then motion tweened another instance of the same symbol on a mask layer to create an animated oval reveal. Figure 11.27 shows the symbol instance used on the mask layer (on the left), the symbol instances used on the art layer (in the center), and the final mask effect visible when both layers are locked (on the right).

FIGURE 11.27

Instances of one oval symbol combined to create a graphic and a mask effect

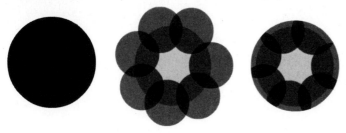

On the CD-ROM

Open the `symbolMask.fla` example from the `MaskLayers` folder inside the `ch11` folder on this book's CD-ROM to see the animated effect. ■

Masking text

Not only can text be masked, but it can also be used to mask other graphics. To mask text, simply set up your mask and art layers, as described in the preceding section, with the text to be masked on the lower layer, and the filled item that you'll use for your aperture on the mask layer, as shown in Figure 11.28.

To use text as a mask, the layers should be set up as described previously. In this situation, the text (which goes on the mask layer) looks as though it were filled by whatever is placed on the lower layer. For this to be effective, a larger point size and fuller, bold letterforms are best, as shown in Figure 11.29.

Caution

Although you can type as much text as you want in a single text box to apply as a mask, you can have only one text box per mask layer. To use multiple text boxes as mask elements, add separate mask layers for each text box. ■

Because the edges of mask letterforms may be hard to discern if the image underneath is not a solid color, it can be helpful to add a drop shadow to make the mask letters more legible. However, a drop shadow or an outline added to the text on the mask layer would not be visible, so you must copy the text onto a normal layer stacked above the mask layer as follows:

1. To keep the text copy aligned with the text mask, use Copy (Ctrl+C/⌘+C) and Paste in Place (Shift+Ctrl+V/Shift+⌘+V) to place a copy of the text into the normal layer exactly on top of the mask text.

2. **After you have copied the text in the mask layer, lock both the mask layer and the masked layer to protect them while you are working on the normal layer.** The solid copied text completely obscures the masked image below, but you can apply a filter and use the Knockout option to drop out the fill of the text characters so that the masked content on the other layers is visible.

3. **Select the copied text, and then use the Filters section in the Properties panel to add a Drop Shadow filter.** The settings that I applied to our example, including the Knockout option, are shown in Figure 11.30. You can adjust the intensity and color of the shadow and the position of the copied (knocked-out) text until you like the end result.

FIGURE 11.28

Masking a text block with a tweened shape (shown on top) and the final reveal effect (shown on the bottom)

FIGURE 11.29

A bitmap pattern (top) placed on the art layer and masked with text (bottom)

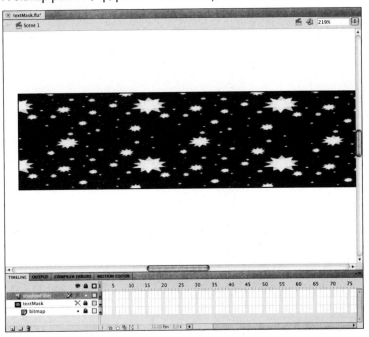

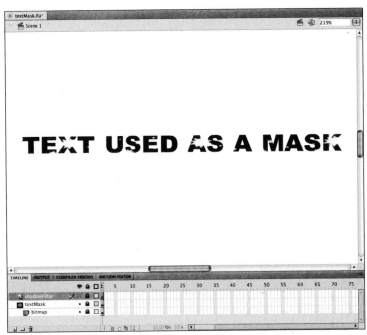

FIGURE 11.30

Apply a Drop Shadow filter with the Knockout option to the copy of your text to add more visual definition to the letter shapes.

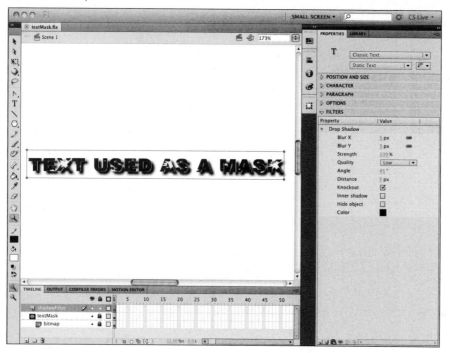

Tip

The Glow Filter works to define the text too, as long as you apply the Knockout option. ■

Of course, you can also animate content on masked layers separately from the content on mask layers. But the endless possibilities for layering masks and masked content starts to get confusing when the additional variable of animation is thrown in. To make the best use of these features, take the extra time to carefully consider the most efficient way to achieve the final effect that you want. First consider what you want to see on the Stage, and then plan any animation of visible elements. The next step should be adding a mask if needed, and finally adding animation to the mask itself. Try to create your effects with the fewest possible animated elements: You will waste less production time and end up with a more optimized file.

Tip

When working on multiple nested layers, it can be visually confusing to work on animation while all layers are displayed. Click the dot in the Eye toggle column to hide or show specific layers in the Timeline so that you can concentrate on only the elements that you are currently editing. Also, to avoid changing the wrong items, lock all layers that you are not currently modifying. ■

Keeping some basic principles in mind as you are working with multiple masks and animated elements will help you to follow the logic of masking in Flash:

- The mask always goes above the item that it reveals.

- Filled items on mask layers function as windows that reveal content on the masked layers nested beneath them.

- The content on mask layers is visible in the authoring environment only if the mask layer is unlocked. For the applied mask to preview properly in the authoring environment, both the mask layer and the masked layer(s) must be locked.

- Mask layers apply only to layers that are nested below them as masked layers. Normal layers or guide layers that may be lower in the layer stack (but not nested with the mask layer) are not affected by the mask.

- Multiple layers can be nested below a single mask layer, but masks cannot be applied to other mask layers, and each mask layer can contain only one masking item (with the exception of multiple primitive shapes or drawing objects).

- Content on mask layers is not visible in the final movie (.swf).

Using Distribute to Layers

The Distribute to Layers command (Shift+Ctrl+D/Shift+⌘+D) is a great time-saver if you're managing multiple elements that you need to move to animate on individual layers. If you've imported several items to the Document window, or you've created a complex graphic that you decide needs to be split up on different layers, you can use this command to do most of the work for you. Instead of having to manually create new layers and copy and paste items one by one, you can select a number of individual items in the Document window and apply Distribute to Layers to have Flash automatically create a layer for each selected item.

To apply Distribute to Layers:

1. **Select the items that you want to have moved to discrete layers.** These items can be symbols, groups, shapes, text blocks, and even bitmaps or video objects.

2. **Choose Modify ➪ Timeline ➪ Distribute to Layers from the application menu, or choose Distribute from the contextual menu.** Strokes and fills for an individual shape are kept together on the same layer, as are items in a group or a multipart symbol. The items you select can be on different source layers, but they must all be on the same frame of the timeline.

3. **When items have been distributed to new layers, you can delete any old layers that have been left empty and rename any new layers that Flash gave awkward names to.**

The auto-created layers are stacked from top to bottom below the currently selected layer in the order that the selected items were created. So the most recently created item should be placed on a layer at the bottom of the stack, just above the layer that was formerly below the selected layer, and the item that was created before the others in the selection is placed at the top of the stack, just below the currently selected layer. If you are completely disoriented by now, have a look at Figure 11.31 to see a file with the layer order before applying Distribute to Layers to the selected items, and look at Figure 11.32 to see how the new layers are stacked and named.

A Flash document with the original layer structure for some bitmaps, symbols, shapes, and a broken-apart text block to be distributed to layers

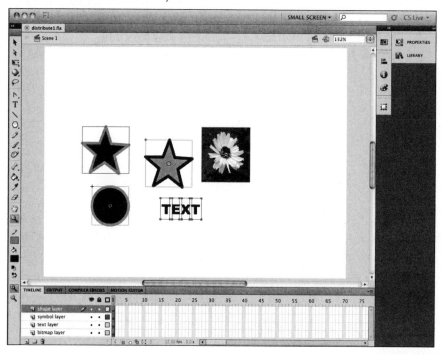

Characters from a broken-apart text block are stacked in layers in the same order that the text block was created (from left to right, right to left, or top to bottom). Flash names auto-created layers with the following conventions:

- A new layer made for any asset stored in the library (a symbol, bitmap, or video clip) is given the same name as the asset.

- A new layer made for a character from a broken-apart text block is named with the text character or letter.

Caution

When you apply Distribute to Layers to text blocks that have not been broken apart, new layers are named with the entire text string. It is best to rename these layers because they usually are difficult to read and may even exceed the 64-character limit for layer names. ■

- A new layer made for a shape (which is not stored in the library) is named in the same numeric sequence as other layers in the current document (Layer 1, Layer 2, and so on).

- A new layer made for a named symbol instance is given the instance name rather than the stored symbol name.

Any layer can always be renamed after it has been created.

The same Flash document after Distribute to Layers has been applied. All selected items have been moved to newly created, auto-named layers, leaving the original layers empty.

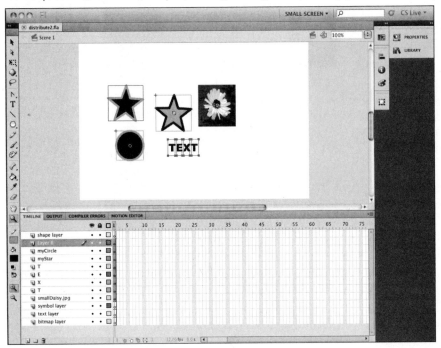

470

Summary

- Filter options in the Properties panel include layering filters and saving presets, without any scripting or special timeline structures required.

- The built-in filters are somewhat limited on their own. The good news is that filters can be combined with blend modes, properties, Transform tools, and tweens to expand their potential well beyond the default settings.

- The options to copy and paste filters from one item to another or save filter settings as presets are time-savers if you want to reuse specific filter effects on multiple elements in your movie.

- Filter properties are included in the Motion Editor for animated elements, making it easier to create or modify custom easing curves to adjust the progression of various properties individually in the same tween.

- Understanding the unique powers of the Adjust Color filter and the Color Effect styles available in the Properties panel gives you many options for controlling the appearance of symbol instances, including the option of using negative values to invert the color or alpha of an element.

- The Blend mode menu in the Properties panel brings some of the power of Photoshop into the Flash authoring environment: Graphics can be blended in subtle and interesting ways.

- The three layer types available in the Flash authoring environment are Normal, Mask, and Guide. A unique layer icon identifies each layer type. Classic motion guides are also still available in Flash CS5, but in most cases you can use the auto-created motion guides created with the optimized motion tween workflow.

- You can assign or modify layer types in the Layer Properties dialog box, which you open by double-clicking any layer icon.

- When you select multiple items on the same layer and use the Distribute to Layers command, they can automatically be moved to new, auto-created layers.

- You use guide layers to hold content that is needed only for reference in the authoring environment, or to speed up movie testing as you develop a project, by temporarily keeping the content on specific layers from being exported with the SWF.

- You can mask any content that you create in a Flash document with a static or animated mask layer.

- You can use filled shapes, text, and symbol instances to define the mask area (or window) on a mask layer, but this content is not visible in the final movie (.swf).

Part IV

Integrating Media Files with Flash

You can create a wide range of graphic elements directly in Flash, but most projects also require imported assets. This section covers the three main media types that you can use to enhance your Flash projects. Chapter 12 introduces the process for importing and controlling sound in Flash. This chapter also covers various compression options and how to edit and export sound from Flash. Learn techniques that help you to get the most bang per byte in your final Flash movies. Chapter 13 addresses the specific workflow and optimization issues related to importing vector and bitmap artwork (and text) from other programs to the Flash authoring environment. Find out how to maintain color consistency and how to preserve layers and vector outlines when moving graphics from other programs, including Adobe Illustrator and Adobe Photoshop. Flash offers a whole range of possibilities for video content. Chapter 14 focuses on the process for optimizing and integrating video, including coverage of the AVC/H.264 video codec, Adobe Media Encoder CS5, and the FLVPlayback component.

Adding Sound

O ne of the more neglected — or perhaps understated — aspects of
multimedia development is sound. Because many people who use
Flash or create multimedia come from graphic arts backgrounds,
it's no surprise that sound is often applied as the last effect to an otherwise
visually stunning presentation — there may be little or no consideration for
the soundtrack in early stages of development. Moreover, it's the one element that is usually taken from a stock source, instead of being the Flash
designer's original work. (Exceptions exist, of course, as Flash designers have
demonstrated time and time again.)

Note
**It goes without saying that as Web projects or applications grow in scope, pro-
duction teams tend to include specific members responsible for unique tasks,
from graphic design to user interface design to sound design. ■**

You can use sound in Flash movies to enhance interactive design with navigation elements, such as buttons, to layer the visitor's experience with a
background soundtrack, to add narration, or for more experimental uses. In
this chapter, I focus on the fundamentals of importing and integrating sound
files into your Flash project. I also discuss the intricacies of controlling audio
output, with particular attention to MP3 bit rates. You learn how to use the
Publish Settings dialog box and compare it with the enhanced control that is
available for customizing compression from within the Sound Properties dialog box of the Library panel. This chapter guides you through using audio
within a Flash document and suggests tips for getting the most bang per byte
in the final Flash movie file (.swf).

Identifying Sound File Import and Export Formats

Flash CS5 can work with a wide variety of sound file formats. In this section, you learn what sound file types you can bring into a Flash document file (.fla) and how Flash can compress audio in a variety of formats in the final Flash movie file (.swf).

Import formats

You can import most sound file formats in either the Windows or Mac version of Flash CS5. All major sound file types, such as MP3 and WAV, are compatible on both versions. After you import a sound file into a Flash document, you can edit the resulting .fla file on either platform.

Flash CS5 can import the following sound file formats:

- **MP3 (MPEG-1 Audio Layer 3):** Among the many advantages of MP3 sound files for Flash users, the most obvious is that they are cross-platform. Flash CS5 can import MP3 files created on either Windows or Mac. This single advantage improves Flash workflow in cross-platform environments. Other advantages are the efficiency of MP3 compression, the increasing availability of MP3 files, as well as the ease of creating MP3 files with common players such as Windows Media Player or Apple iTunes. For more information about MP3s, see the sidebar at the end of the section.

- **WAV (Windows Wave):** Until the relatively recent support for MP3, WAV files reigned for nearly a decade as the standard for digital audio on Windows PCs. Still, the WAV format remains the primary acquisition sound format, the format in which you record sound from a microphone or other sound source on your computer. Flash can import WAV files created in sound applications and editors such as Sound Forge or ACID. The imported WAV files can be either stereo or mono and can support varying bit depths and frequency rates. You can import WAV files directly into Flash CS5 on Mac and PC.

- **AIFF or AIF (Audio Interchange File format):** Much like WAV on the PC, the AIFF format is one of the most commonly used digital audio formats for sound acquisition on the Mac. Flash can import AIFF sounds created in sound applications and editors such as Bias Peak or Adobe Soundbooth CS5. Like WAV, AIFF supports stereo and mono, in addition to variable bit depths and frequency rates. Unassisted, the Windows version of Flash CS5 cannot import this file format. But when QuickTime 4 or later is installed, you can import AIFF files into Flash CS5 on Windows. The Windows version of Flash CS5 recognizes, properly opens, and can edit Flash documents created on the Mac that contain AIFF sounds.

- **Sun AU:** This sound format file (.au) was developed by Sun Microsystems and Next, and it is the native sound format on many Solaris and UNIX systems, just as WAV and AIFF are native to Windows and the Mac, respectively. The Sun AU format is frequently used with sound-enabled Java applets on Web pages.

- **QuickTime:** You can import QuickTime audio files (.qta or .mov) directly into Flash CS5, provided that you have QuickTime 4 or later installed. After you import a QuickTime audio file into a Flash document, the sound file appears in the library just as any other sound would.

- **Sound Designer II:** This proprietary audio file format created by Digidesign is used with its signature professional audio suite, Pro Tools. You can import sounds that you save in this file format into the Mac version of Flash CS5. If you need to use a Sound Designer II file (.sd2 file extension) with the Windows version of Flash CS5, you can import the file directly if you have QuickTime 4 or later installed.

Note

With Flash CS5, you can link proxy sound files to Musical Instrument Digital Interface (MIDI) and Melody For i-mode (MFI) files that can be played back on mobile devices with Flash Lite. For more information, see www.adobe.com/devnet/devices/articles/flashlite_sound_03.html. ∎

Tip

Don't rely upon the imported sound that's embedded in the Flash document file (.fla) as your master or backup sound file. Always retain your original master sound file as a backup or for reuse in other multimedia projects. ∎

These sound file types are structural or "architecture" based, meaning that they simply indicate the wrapper used to encode digital audio. Each of them can use a variety of compression techniques or a variety of audio *codecs*. A codec is a *c*ompression and *dec*ompression module for digital media. Sound and video is encoded (compressed) with a specific technique by an application or device. After it is encoded, it can be played back (decompressed) by a media player that has access to the codec module. In order for a sound file to play on your computer, you must have the audio codec used in that file installed on your system. MP3 files, for example, can be compressed in a variety of bit rates and frequencies, as can WAV and AIF files. After Flash imports a sound file, the wrapper type (AIF, WAV, AU, and so on) is stripped. Flash simply stores the sound file as generic PCM (Pulse Code Modulation) digital audio. Moreover, Flash converts any imported 8-bit sound file into a 16-bit sound file. For this reason, it's best not to use any precompression or low bit depths on your sound files before you bring them into Flash CS5.

Note

You can adjust individual MP3 sound files in the Flash document's Library panel to retain their original compression. This is the sole exception to the rule I just mentioned in the preceding paragraph. As you'll see later in this chapter, however, Flash CS5 may need to recompress all sound files in a Flash movie, depending on their use in the movie's timeline. ∎

Export formats

You can decide which sound encoding to use for audio when publishing Flash document files to Flash movie files (.swf). Although the default publish settings in Flash CS5 is to export all audio with the MP3 format, you can export sound in several other audio formats. I note the benefits and drawbacks of each format in the list that follows.

MP3s Demystified

MP3 is an amazing compression technology as well as a file format. It excels at the compression of a sound sequence — MP3-compressed files can be reduced to nearly a twelfth of their original size without destroying sound quality. MP3 was developed under the sponsorship of the Motion Picture Experts Group (MPEG), using the following logic: CD-quality sound is typically sampled at a bit depth of 16 (16-bit) at sample rate 44.1 kHz, which generates approximately 1.4 million bits of data for each second of sound — but that second of sound includes a lot of data for sounds that most humans cannot hear! By devising a compression algorithm that reduces the data linked to imperceptible sounds, MP3 developers made it possible to deliver high-quality audio over the Internet without excessive *latency* (the delay between loading a sound and playing it). Another way of describing this is to say that MP3 uses perceptual encoding techniques that reduce the amount of overlapping and redundant information that describes sound. As you'll learn later in this chapter, the Flash Player can actually buffer stream sounds (which you can create from any sound file imported into Flash); this means that the sound begins to play in the Flash movie before the sound file has been downloaded in its entirety. Shockwave Audio, the default audio compression scheme for Adobe Director–based Shockwave movies, is actually MP3 in disguise.

Note

Flash CS5 enables you to export device sounds in a Flash movie, for playback on mobile devices that use file formats such as MIDI and MFI. I provide an overview of this feature in this section. ■

Regardless of the format that you choose in your document's publish settings for exporting your sounds, you can individually specify a compression scheme for each sound in the Flash document's library. Furthermore, each format has specific options and settings that I examine later in this chapter.

- **ADPCM (Adaptive Differential Pulse-Code Modulation)**: ADPCM is an audio compression scheme that converts sound into binary information. It is primarily used for voice technologies, such as fiber-optic telephone lines, because the audio signal is compressed, enabling it to carry textual information as well. ADPCM works well because it records only the difference between samples and adjusts the encoding accordingly, keeping file size low. ADPCM was the default setting for older versions of Flash, such as Flash 2 and 3. It isn't as efficient as MP3 encoding, but is the best choice for situations in which compatibility is required with *all* older Flash Players.

- **MP3 (MPEG-1 Audio Layer 3)**: MP3 has become the standard for digital audio distributed on the Internet. Although MP3 compression delivers excellent audio quality with small files, it's much more processor intensive than other compressors. This means that slower computers — and I mean slow, as in Pentium I or pre-PowerMac G3 processors — may gasp when they encounter a high bit-rate MP3 audio while simultaneously processing complex animations. As always, it's wise to know your audience. When in doubt, test your Flash movie with MP3 audio on slower computers. Flash Players 4 and higher support MP3 playback.

Note

Not all versions of the Flash Player support MP3 sound. With Flash Player 6 and higher, you can use ActionScript's `System.capabilities.hasMP3` (ActionScript 2.0) or `flash.system.Capabilities.hasMP3` (ActionScript 3.0) property to determine if the hosting player device supports MP3 audio. You can learn more about this use of ActionScript in the Help documentation that ships with Flash CS5. ■

- **Raw (Raw PCM):** Flash can export sound to SWF files in a raw audio format. If you use this setting, Flash won't compress any audio. However, uncompressed sound makes very large files that would be useless for Internet-based distribution. As uncompressed sound, audio in the imported sound file retains its original fidelity. I recommend that you use the Raw format only for Flash movies that you intend to export as linear animation for output to video-editing applications.

- **Speech (Nellymoser):** This audio codec introduced with Flash Player 6 is specifically designed for audio sources that contain mostly human speech, such as narration or instructional content. Macromedia (before Adobe acquired the company) licensed audio technology from Nellymoser, Inc., which specializes in the development of voice-only audio codecs. All sounds that use the Speech codec are converted to mono sounds. You can see the real power of this codec in live streaming audio delivered by Adobe Flash Media Server, because this codec is incredibly efficient and a fast encoder with a low server and client processor overhead. For example, if you want to use a `NetStream` object in ActionScript to stream live audio from a microphone, the Speech codec optimizes the audio information very efficiently. You must use Flash Player 6 or later to play sounds encoded with this format.

- **Device sound:** With Flash CS5, you can link device sound files to imported sounds in your Flash movie. You use device sounds specifically for playback of Flash movies on mobile devices enabled with Flash Lite, a version of the Flash Player. Because the desktop Flash Player cannot play device sound file formats, you import regular sound files such as MP3s into your Flash document. These sounds are then used in a proxy fashion — you add the sound to event handlers (keyframes, buttons, and so on) just as you would any other sounds. Before you publish the Flash movie file (.swf), however, you change the settings of the sound file in the Library panel to point to a device sound. When the Flash movie is published, the device sound is embedded and used within the Flash movie, not the original imported sound.

Cross-Reference

I examine the specific export options for each audio format later in this chapter. This section will help you determine which format you should use for your specific needs. ■

Table 12.1 shows the compatibility of Flash's audio export formats with various platforms.

TABLE 12.1

Audio Export Formats for Flash Players

Export Format	Flash 3 or Earlier	Flash 4 and 5	Flash 6 or Higher	Comments
ADPCM	Yes	Yes	Yes	Good encoding scheme; compatible with all Flash players; works well for short sound effects such as button clicks
MP3	No	Yes	Yes	Best general-use encoding scheme; ideal for music tracks
Raw	Yes	Yes	Yes	No compression; lossless; large file sizes
Speech	No	No	Yes	Excellent compression for human speech; avoids "tinny" sounds for voices; ideally suited for real-time compression with Flash server-side applications
Device sound	No	No	No	Sound export feature available in Flash CS5; for use with MIDI and MFI files for playback on mobile devices with Flash Lite

Importing Sounds into Flash

In the preceding section, I discussed the various sound formats that Flash CS5 can import and export. In addition to covering the merits of the MP3 and Speech codecs, I also explained the uses of platform-specific AIF (Mac) and WAV (Windows) audio files. But I didn't delve into the process of importing sound into Flash CS5. So, let's get started.

Note
When working with sound, you may encounter some interchangeable terminology. Generally, these terms — sound file, sound clip, and audio file — all refer to the same thing, a single digital file in one of several formats that contains a digitally encoded sound. ∎

Unlike other imported assets, such as bitmaps or vector art, Flash won't automatically insert an imported sound file into the frames of the active layer on the Timeline. In fact, you don't have to select a specific layer or frame before you import a sound file. That's because all sounds are sent directly to the library immediately upon import, regardless of whether you use File ⇨ Import ⇨ Import to Stage or Import to Library. After import, the sound becomes part of the Flash document file (.fla), which may make the file size balloon significantly if the sound file is large. The sound does not become part of the Flash movie file (.swf), nor does it add to the size of the Flash movie *unless* it is assigned to a keyframe, as an instance of that sound, or it is set to export for use in ActionScript.

To import a sound file into the Flash CS5 authoring environment, follow these steps:

1. Choose File ⇨ Import ⇨ Import to Library or Import to Stage (Ctrl+R or ⌘+R). For sound assets, these commands work identically.

2. From the Files of type list (Windows) or Enable list (Mac) in the Import dialog box, select All Sound Formats.

Caution

On the Mac OS X version of Flash CS5, you may need to choose All Files in the Show menu in order to select an appropriate sound file. ■

3. Browse to the sound file that you want to import.

On the CD-ROM

If you're looking for a sample audio file, you can import the atmospheres_1.mp3 or the atmospheres_1_short.mp3 file found in the resources folder of this book's CD-ROM. ■

4. Click Open. The sound file you select is imported into your Flash document file (.fla) and arrives in the document's library with its filename intact. If the Library panel is closed, you can open it by choosing Window ⇨ Library, or by using the keyboard shortcut (Ctrl+L or ⌘+L). With the Library panel open, locate the sound, and click it to highlight the name of the sound file where it appears in the Library list. The waveform appears in the Library preview pane, as shown in Figure 12.1. Click the Play button above the waveform to audition the sound.

FIGURE 12.1

This is a stereo sound in the Flash document's library.

Cross-Reference

Refer to "Fine-Tuning Sound Settings in the Library" later in this chapter for an explanation of how you can specify unique compression settings for each sound in a document's library. ■

How Sound Is Stored in a Flash Movie

Earlier in this chapter, I mentioned that when you import a sound file into a Flash document file (.fla), an entire copy of the sound file is stored within the document. However, when you place a sound on a timeline, a reference is made to the sound in the library. Just as symbol instances refer to a master or parent symbol in the Library panel, sound "instances" refer to the master sound resource in the Library panel.

Throughout this chapter, I use the term "instance" for sound assets with this understanding in mind. When the Flash document is published as a Flash movie, the master sound in the library is compressed and stored *once* in the final movie file (.swf), even though there may be several instances of that sound used throughout the movie (for example, in multiple frames on multiple timelines).

This type of efficient storage, however, applies to event sounds only. Whenever you use stream sounds, the sound file is stored in the Flash movie each time you refer to the sound in a timeline. For example, if you compressed a sound to export from Flash as a 3K sound asset in the final movie file (.swf), you could reuse that sound as an event sound several times without adding significant bytes to the file size. However, that same compressed sound (at 3K) would occupy 12K in the final movie if it was placed four times as a stream sound on keyframes within the movie. I discuss event and stream sounds later in this chapter, so you may want to refer to this sidebar at a later point.

It is also worth mentioning that Flash CS5 must have enough available RAM on the computer system to accommodate imported sound files. For example, if you import a 30MB WAV file into a Flash document, then you must have an additional 30MB of RAM available to the application. On Windows operating systems and Mac OS X, you will not likely experience problems with memory usage, where virtual memory exists alongside the physical RAM within the computer.

You can also import sound files into a Flash document by dragging the sound file from the desktop to the Library panel. On the Mac, you can drag the sound file to the Stage as well. This method can be especially useful when you have searched for a sound file by using the operating system's search tool (Start ➪ Search in Windows, or Spotlight in the Mac OS) and want to quickly bring the sound file into Flash CS5.

Assigning a Sound to a Button

The interactive experience can be enhanced by the addition of subtle effects. The addition of sounds to correspond with the various states of a button is perhaps the most obvious example. Although this effect can be abused, it's hard to overuse an effect that delivers such meaningful user feedback. Here, I show how different sounds can be added to both the Over (rollOver) and the Down (press) states of a button.

Cross-Reference

For more general information about creating the buttons themselves, see Chapter 6, "Symbols, Instances, and the Library," and see Chapter 15, "Understanding Actions and Event Handlers," to learn how to add code to buttons. ∎

Because buttons are stored in the library, and because only instances of a Button symbol are deployed within the Flash movie, sounds that are assigned to a button work for all instances of that Button symbol. However, if different sounds are required for different buttons, a new Button symbol must be created (see the following Tip note for an exception to this "rule"). You can create a new Button symbol from the same Graphic symbols as the previous button (provided it was built out of symbols) or duplicate it in the Library panel by using the Duplicate command in the Library panel's options menu.

To add a sound to the Down state of a button symbol, follow these steps:

1. **Create a new button symbol (Insert ⇨ New Symbol) or choose a symbol from the Buttons Library (Window ⇨ Common Libraries ⇨ Buttons).**

2. **Drag an instance of the button from the Buttons Library panel (or the document's Library panel) to the Stage.**

3. **Edit the Button symbol by double-clicking it on the Stage or in the Library panel.** Both methods transfer the working environment into Edit mode.

4. **Add a new layer to the button's timeline, label the new layer "sound," and then add keyframes to this layer in the Over and Down columns.** Your timeline should look similar to Figure 12.2.

FIGURE 12.2

The timeline for your button should resemble this one.

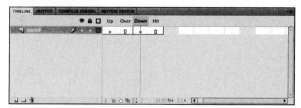

5. **Select the frame of the button state where you want to add a sound for interactive feedback (such as a clicking sound for the Down state), and then access the Properties panel by choosing Window ⇨ Properties (Ctrl+F3 or ⌘+F3).** An

alternative method (with the frame selected) is to simply drag the sound from the Library panel onto the Stage. You should now have the Properties panel open, as shown in Figure 12.3.

FIGURE 12.3

The Properties panel controls the options for sound usage on a given frame.

6. **Choose the sound clip that you want to use from the Sound section's Name menu.** This menu lists all the sounds that have been imported and that are available in the library of the current movie. In this example, I used the `click.wav` sound found in the `resources` folder of the book's CD-ROM.

7. **Use the Sync menu to choose *how* you want the sound to play.** For this lesson, simply use the default, which is the Event option. I'll defer exploration of the other options in the Sync menu to a later section.

You have now added a sound to your button state. Remember that you're still in Edit mode, so to test the button, return to the Scene 1 timeline (that is, the Main Timeline) either by clicking the Scene 1 location label at the upper-left corner of the Document window or by pressing Ctrl+E (⌘+E), and then choose Control ➪ Enable Simple Buttons, or Control ➪ Test Movie.

To add a sound to the Over state of a Button symbol, simply retrace the preceding steps, referencing the Over state of the button wherever appropriate. Remember that different sounds can be assigned to the Up, Over, and Down states of a Button symbol. A sound that is added to the Up state plays whenever the mouse rolls out of a button's hit area.

On the CD-ROM

For a completed example of this button, refer to the Flash movie `button_sound.fla` located in the `ch12` folder on this book's CD-ROM. This movie has a button with sounds attached and was made with the same technique described in this section. ∎

Adding Sound to the Timeline

In addition to the use of sounds to enhance the interactivity of buttons, another popular use for sound in Flash is to provide a background score. The simplest way to achieve this is to place the sound within its own layer in the Main Timeline (Scene 1), at the precise frame in which you want the sound to begin. To do this, you must first import the sound (as described earlier in this chapter) and create a new layer for it.

On the CD-ROM

If you don't have access to sounds, you can use the sample sound `atmospheres_1` to practice. This sound is in the `resources` folder on the CD-ROM. It is available in both WAV and AIF formats. ∎

Tip

Adobe Flash CS5 ships with over 180 sound effects in the Sounds library (Window ⇨ Common Libraries ⇨ Sounds). These sound files have been culled from Adobe Soundbooth CS5's libraries. You can open this library and drag the sounds into your own Flash document's library to use for examples in this chapter. ∎

Adding sound files to a timeline is similar to assigning sound to a button. To add sounds to a timeline, follow these steps:

1. **Add a new layer in the Timeline window and label the layer with the name of the sound.** You can use a name such as "sound" or "background track."

2. **Create a keyframe on the sound layer at the frame where you want the sound to begin.**

3. **With that keyframe selected, open the Properties panel.** Make sure that you have expanded the view to show all the sound attributes.

4. **If you remembered to import the sound that you want to use, you can now choose that sound clip from the Sound section's Name menu.** If you find yourself stuck at this point, review the preceding steps and/or retrace your steps through the methodology for adding sound to a button.

5. **From the Effect menu, choose how Flash should handle the sound.** The Effect menu offers several preset fading and panning treatments, plus Custom, which invokes the Edit Envelope dialog box. For no special effect, choose None. For more about the Effect presets and the Edit Envelope dialog box, refer to the subsequent section "Editing Audio in Flash."

6. **From the Sync menu, choose one of four options — Event, Start, Stop, or Stream — to control how you want the sound to be synchronized.** See the next section, "Organizing Sounds on the Timeline," for a detailed explanation of Sync options.

7. **Specify how many times you want the sound to loop.** To loop the sound indefinitely (for example, as a background track), choose Loop in the second drop-down menu in the Sync parameters. If you want the sound to loop only for a specific number of times, choose Repeat in the menu and enter a number in the text field to the right of the menu. For specific information about looping stream sounds, refer to the next section.

8. Perform any last-minute editing or finessing of the sound file (see "Editing Audio in Flash" later in this chapter).

Your sound is now part of the timeline. Its waveform is visible on the layer to which it was added. Test your sound by pressing Enter on your keyboard, which plays the timeline; or, for sound with a Sync setting of Stream, manually "scrub" the sound by dragging the playhead across the timeline. To perform the most accurate test of the sound, use either Control⇨Test Scene or Control⇨ Test Movie to see and hear it as a Flash movie file (.swf).

Tip

If you sync a sound to a timeline by using the Stream feature, you should test your Flash movie file (.swf) on various platforms and machines with different processor speeds, especially if the timeline is always playing animation. What looks and sounds good on a fast computer might be less impressive on an older legacy machine, like a first- or second-generation Pentium or PowerMac G3 computer. ■

Organizing Sounds on the Timeline

The Flash Player can play several sound layers at once within a Flash movie; each layer functions like a separate sound channel, and Flash mixes them on playback. This capability of Flash might be considered a built-in economy sound mixer. There is, however, a practical limit because each sound layer potentially increases the movie's file size, and the mix of multiple sounds may burden the computer it's being run on.

Tip

Flash Player 8 or later movies can play up to 32 simultaneous sound channels. In older versions of the Flash Player, you are limited to 8 simultaneous sound channels. A stereo sound consumes two channels, and a mono sound consumes one channel. ■

Enhanced viewing of sound layers

Because sound is different from other types of Flash content, some users find that increasing the layer height of the sound layers eases working with multiple sounds in a timeline. That's because a taller layer height provides a better visual cue due to the unique waveforms of each sound. To increase the layer height for individual layers, follow these steps:

1. Right-click (or Control+click on the Mac) the layer in the Timeline window, and then choose Properties from the contextual menu.

2. At the bottom of the Layer Properties dialog box, change the layer height from the default 100 percent to either 200 or 300 percent. Note that these percentages are relative to the settings chosen in the options menu (located at the top-right corner) of the Timeline window.

Cross-Reference

For more information on the Timeline window, see Chapter 4, "Interface Fundamentals." For an actual example of this enhanced viewing, open the file `enhanced_view.fla`, located in the `ch12` folder on the CD-ROM. ■

Tip

Your movie's frame rate, as specified in the Document Properties dialog box (Modify ➪ Document), affects the number of frames that a sound occupies on a timeline. For example, at Flash's default setting of 24 frames per second (fps), a 30-second sound clip extends across 720 frames of the timeline. At 30 fps, the same 30-second clip expands to 900 frames — but in either case, the time length of the sound is unchanged. ■

Organizing sound layers with a layer folder

Flash CS5 offers a great organization tool for layers in any timeline: layer folders. To nest sound layers in a layer folder, create a new layer folder and then drag each of the sound layers to the folder. Each layer you drop on the folder nests within the folder.

Synchronizing Audio to Animations

In film editors' lingo, to *synchronize*, or *sync*, sound means to precisely match picture to sound. In Flash, sound can be synchronized to the visual content of the Timeline. Flash sync affords several options for the manner in which the audio clip is related to graphics or animation on a timeline. Each of these Sync options is appropriate for particular uses, which the following sections discuss.

The Sync options in the sound area of the Properties panel control the behavior of sound in Flash movies, relative to the timeline in which the sound is placed. The Sync option you choose depends on whether your sound is intended to add dimension to a complex multimedia presentation or to add interactivity in the form of button-triggered sound, or whether it is intended to be the closely timed soundtrack of an animated cartoon.

Event

Event is the default Sync option for all sounds in Flash, so unless you change this default to one of the other options, the sound automatically behaves as an event sound. Event sounds begin with the keyframe in which they occur and then play independently of the timeline. If an event sound's duration is longer than the remaining frames of its timeline, it continues to play even though playback on the timeline has stopped. If an event sound requires considerable time to load, the movie pauses at that keyframe until the sound has loaded completely. Event sounds are the easiest to implement and are useful for background soundscapes and other sounds that don't need to be synced. Again, Event is the default Sync setting in the Sound menu of the Properties panel.

Caution

Event sounds can degrade into a disturbing inharmonious round of out-of-tune sound loops. If the timeline holding the event sound loops before the sound has completed, the sound begins again — over the top of the initial sound that has not finished playing. After several loops, the resulting effect can become intolerable. To avoid this effect, use the Start Sync option. ∎

Start

The Start Sync option is similar to an Event option, but with one crucial difference: If any instance of that sound is already playing, then no other instance of that sound can play. In other words, the Start Sync option tells the sound to begin playing only if other instances have finished playing or if it's the first instance of that sound to play. This option is useful if you want to avoid the layering problem discussed in the preceding Caution note for event sounds.

Note

Start sounds are actually a type of event sound. Later in this chapter, when I refer to Audio Stream and Audio Event settings in the Publish Settings dialog box, realize that Start sounds belong to the Audio Event category. ∎

Stop

The Stop Sync option is similar to the Start Sync option, except that any and all instances of the selected sound stop playing when the frame containing the Stop Sync option is played. This option comes in handy when you want to mute a specific sound in a crowd of others. For example, if you created a sound mixer with an arrangement of Button instances, you could assign the Stop Sync option to a mute button for each of the sounds in the mixer.

Stream

Stream sounds are similar to a traditional soundtrack in a video-editing application. A stream sound locks to the timeline and has priority over visual content. When you choose a stream sound, the Flash Player attempts to pace the animation in sync with the sound. However, when animations either get too complex or are run on slower machines, the Flash Player skips — or drops — the frames as needed to stay in sync with the stream sound. A stream sound stops when the playhead reaches the last frame that includes the waveform of the stream sound; likewise, a stream sound pauses if the timeline containing the stream sound is stopped. A stream sound can be *scrubbed*; by dragging the playhead along the layer's frames in the Timeline window, the stream sound plays in direct relationship to the content as it appears, frame by frame. This is especially useful for lip-sync and coordinating the perfect timing of sound effects with visual events.

To use sound effectively, it's important to understand how stream sounds work. When a Flash document is published as a Flash movie file (.swf) and the Sync option for a sound is set to Stream, Flash breaks the sound into chunks that are tied to a timeline. The bytes within the movie are arranged according to the linear order of the Main Timeline (that is, Scene 1). As such, if you have a stream sound that stretches from frames 1 to 100 of the Main Timeline and the movie contains a total of 200 frames, the stream sound's bytes are evenly distributed over the first 50 percent of the file's bytes.

Tip

When adding sounds to a timeline, no matter how many times you tell a stream sound to loop, a stream sound stops playing wherever the visual waveform in the Timeline window ends. To extend a stream sound's duration, add as many frames as necessary to a stream sound's layer. ∎

Stopping Sounds

The default behavior of event sounds is to play through to the end, regardless of the length of the timeline on which they exist. However, you can stop any sound, including event sounds. Place another instance of the same sound at the keyframe where the sound should stop and assign this instance as a Stop Sync option. This Stop setting can be on any layer, and it stops all instances of the specific sound. Let's give this a try.

Stopping an event sound

In this section, I show you how to stop an event sound by using two different methods. The first method uses a Stop sound on a keyframe in the Main Timeline (Scene 1). The second method uses a button instance with a stop sound on its Down state.

1. **Create a Flash ActionScript 3.0 document that has an event sound placed on the first keyframe and has enough frames on the timeline to display the entire waveform of the sound.**

On the CD-ROM

You can use the `enhanced_view.fla` file from this book's CD-ROM as a practice file. If you use this file, change the Sync setting of the sound to Event in the Properties panel. ∎

2. Create a new layer in the Timeline window, and name this layer stop sound.

3. On the stop sound layer, pick a frame that's about five seconds into the sound shown on the original layer.

4. Create a keyframe on this frame in the stop sound layer.

5. With this keyframe selected, open the Properties panel.

6. In the Name menu of the Sound section, choose the same sound file that was used in the original sound layer.

7. **In the Sync menu of the Properties panel, choose Stop.** As a stop sound, this setting tells the Flash Player to stop any and all instances of the sound specified in the Sound menu.

8. **Save your Flash document and test it (Control ⇨ Test Movie).** When the playhead reaches the keyframe with the stop sound, you should no longer hear the Event sound.

Now, I show you how to play and mute an event sound by clicking buttons. You'll place an event sound on one Button symbol instance, and then a stop sound on another Button symbol instance.

1. **In a new Flash ActionScript 3.0 document, create a copy of the Play and Stop buttons from the classic buttons ⇨ Circle Buttons folder in the Buttons Library (Window ⇨ Common Libraries ⇨ Buttons).** To do this, drag each of the buttons from the Buttons Library panel to your document's Stage. Close the Buttons Library when you are done. Rename Layer 1 to buttons. Your document's Stage should resemble Figure 12.4.

2. **Import a sound file to use as your event sound.** You can use the `atmospheres_1.mp3` sound file from the book's CD-ROM.

3. **In the document's Library panel, double-click the Play button to edit the symbol.**

4. **In the Timeline window, create a new layer and name it** sound.

5. **Insert a keyframe on the Down state of the sound layer.**

6. **Select the keyframe made in Step 5 and open the Properties panel.**

FIGURE 12.4

The Play and Stop buttons on the Stage

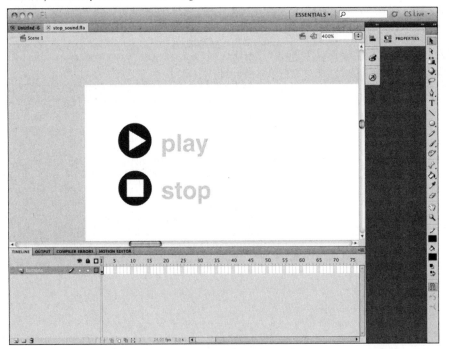

7. **Select the imported sound's name in the Name menu of the Sound section, and leave the Sync menu at the default Event setting.** When you are finished, your document should resemble Figure 12.5.

8. **Double-click the Stop button in the Library panel.**

9. **Repeat Steps 3–7. This time, however, choose Stop in the Sync menu for the atmospheres_1 sound.**

10. **Save your document and test it (Control ⇨ Test Movie).** In Test Movie mode, click the Play button. You should hear the imported sound begin to play. When you click the Stop button, the sound should stop playing.

This sound plays when the Play button is clicked.

You may have noticed that if you click the Play button repeatedly, new instances of the sound begin to play, overlapping with the original playing sound instance. Regardless, the Stop Sync option stops all of them. If you want to prevent the Play button from enabling this type of overlap, go back to the sound keyframe on the Play button and change its Sync option to Start.

On the CD-ROM

You can find a completed example of the Play and Stop buttons exercise as `stop_sound.fla`, located in the `ch14` folder on the CD-ROM. ∎

Stopping a single instance of a stream sound

You can also stop a single instance of a stream sound. To do this, simply place an empty keyframe in the sound layer at the point where the sound should stop.

1. Open the `enhanced_view.fla` file, located in the `ch12` folder of the book's CD-ROM.

2. Switch the layer view of the atmospheres_1 layer back to 100% in the Layer Properties dialog box.

3. Select the first frame of the atmospheres_1 layer.

4. In the Properties panel, switch the Sync option to Stream.

5. Select frame 60 of the atmospheres_1 layer, and insert a blank keyframe (F7). This is the point where the stream sound will stop playing.

6. Save your Flash document and test it (Control ⇨ Test Movie). Notice that the sound stops playing at frame 60. You can open your Bandwidth Profiler (View ⇨ Bandwidth Profiler) in the Test Movie mode to see the playhead move as the movie plays.

The Bandwidth Profiler also reveals something I touched upon earlier: Stream sounds export only the actual portion of the sound that's used within frames of a layer in the Timeline window. In our example, 60 frames' worth of the atmospheres_1 sound was about 12K (at default MP3 compression, 16 kilobits per second, or Kbps).

Stopping all sounds

You can stop the sounds that are playing in all timelines (including Movie Clips) at any point by following these steps in a Flash ActionScript 3.0 document:

1. If there isn't already an actions layer in the Timeline window, add a layer, label it actions, and select the frame that occurs at the point where you want all sounds to stop. Make this frame into a keyframe.

2. With the keyframe selected, open the Actions panel by pressing F9 (or Option+F9 on Mac) or by navigating to Window ⇨ Actions. The title bar of the Actions panel should read Actions — Frame.

3. Click the flash.media booklet in the left pane of the panel. Then click the SoundMixer booklet, followed by the Methods booklet.

4. **Double-click the** `stopAll` **action.** The ActionScript code `SoundMixer.stopAll();` appears in the Script pane of the Actions panel, as shown in Figure 12.6.

FIGURE 12.6

Any sound that's currently playing stops when the movie reaches a keyframe with a `SoundMixer.stopAll ()` action.

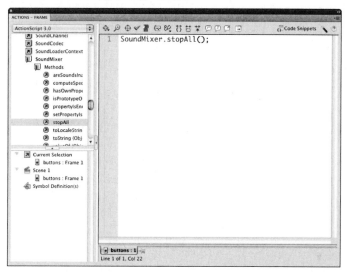

Note

I've updated all ActionScript code in this edition of the book to use ActionScript 3.0. If you need to create ActionScript 2.0 code for legacy projects, refer to previous editions. ■

5. **Save your Flash document and then test it with Control ⇨ Test Movie.** When the movie's playhead reaches the frame with the `SoundMixer.stopAll ()` action, every sound currently playing stops.

The `SoundMixer.stopAll ()` action stops only sounds that are playing at the time the action is executed. It does not permanently mute the sound for the duration of the movie. You can proceed to reinitialize any sounds any time after the `SoundMixer.stopAll ()` action has executed. If you want to stop playback again, you must enable another `SoundMixer.stopAll ()` action or use a stop sound.

Editing Audio in Flash

Although Flash was never intended to perform as a full-featured sound editor, it does a remarkable job with basic sound editing. If you plan to make extensive use of sound in Flash, I recommend that you consider investing in a more robust sound editor. You'll have fewer limitations and greater control over your work.

Sound-editing controls

Flash CS5 has basic sound-editing controls in the Edit Envelope dialog box, which is accessed by clicking the Edit button in the Sound section of the Properties panel. (As you may recall from previous sections, you must first select the keyframe containing the sound, and then view the settings in the Properties panel.) The Time In control and the Time Out control, or Control Bars, in Edit Envelope enable you to change the In (start) and Out (end) points of a sound. You use the envelope handles to create custom Fade-in and Fade-out effects. The Edit Envelope dialog box also enables you to edit each sound channel separately if you are working with a stereo (two-channel) sound.

Note

The edits you apply to a sound file in the Edit Envelope dialog box affect only the specific instance you have assigned to a keyframe. The original file that resides in the Flash document's Library panel is neither changed nor resaved. ■

A sound's In point is where the sound starts playing, and a sound's Out point is where the sound finishes. The Time In control and the Time Out control are used for setting or changing a sound's In and Out points. Here's how to do this:

1. Start by selecting the keyframe of the sound you want to edit, and then access the Properties panel.

2. Click the Edit button in the sound attributes area of the Properties panel to open the Edit Envelope dialog box, as shown in Figure 12.7.

3. Drag the Time In control and Time Out control (located in the horizontal strip between the two channels) to define or restrict which section plays.

4. Use the envelope handles to edit the sound volume by adding handles and dragging them up or down to modulate the volume.

5. Click the Play button to hear the sound as edited before returning to the authoring environment.

6. Rework the sound if necessary.

7. When you've finessed the points and are satisfied with the sound, click OK to return to the Properties panel.

8. Save your Flash document.

FIGURE 12.7

The sound-editing tools and options of the Edit Envelope dialog box, which is accessed from the Properties panel

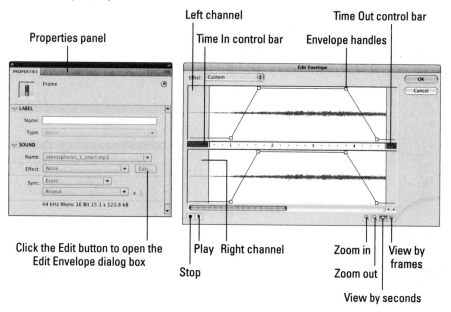

Applying effects from the Effect menu of the Properties panel

You can apply a handful of preset fades and other effects to a sound by selecting the effect from the Effect menu located in the sound attributes area of the Properties panel. For many uses, the Flash presets are more than sufficient, but if you find yourself feeling limited, remember that more subtle effects can be created in an external sound editor. I describe Flash's preset effects in detail here:

- **None:** No effect is applied to either of the sound channels.

- **Left Channel/Right Channel:** Plays only the right or left channel of a stereo sound.

- **Fade Left to Right/Fade Right to Left:** This effect lowers the sound level of one channel while raising the level of the other, creating a panning effect. The effect occurs over the entire length of the sound.

- **Fade In/Fade Out:** Fade In gradually raises the level of the beginning of a sound clip. Fade Out gradually lowers the level at the end of a sound. The default length for either effect is approximately 25 percent of the length of the clip. We've noticed that even if the size of the selection is edited with the control bars, the duration of the Fade In/Fade Out remains the same. (Thus, a 35-second sound clip with an original default Fade In time of 9 seconds still has a 9-second Fade In time even when the selection's length is reduced to, say, 12 seconds.) You can resolve this problem by creating a custom fade.

- **Custom:** Any time you manually alter the levels or audio handles within the Edit Envelope dialog box, Flash CS5 automatically resets the Effect menu to Custom.

Creating a custom Fade-In or Fade-Out

For maximum sound-editing control within Flash, use the envelope handles to create a custom fade or to lower the audio levels (or amplitude) of a sound. In addition to creating custom fades, you can lower the levels creatively to create subtle, low-volume background sounds. Here's how:

1. **Select the keyframe of the sound you want to edit.**
2. **Click the Edit button of the Properties panel to open the Edit Envelope dialog box.**
3. **Click the envelope lines at any point to create new envelope handles.**
4. **After handles have been created, you can drag them around to create your desired volume and fading effects.** The lines indicate the relative volume level of the sound. When you drag an envelope handle downward, the line slopes down, indicating a decrease in the volume level, while dragging an envelope handle upward has the opposite effect. The Edit Envelope control is limited to eight envelope handles per channel (eight for left and eight for right).

Tip
You can remove envelope handles by dragging them outside the Edit Envelope dialog box. ■

Other controls in the Edit Envelope control

Other useful tools in the Edit Envelope dialog box warrant mention. Refer to Figure 12.7 for their locations.

- **Zoom In/Zoom Out:** These tools either enlarge or shrink the view of the waveform, and they are particularly helpful when you're altering the In or Out points or envelope handles.
- **Seconds/Frames:** The default for viewing sound files is to represent time in seconds. But viewing time in frames is advantageous for syncing stream sound. Toggle between viewing modes by clicking either the Seconds or Frames button at the lower right of the Edit Envelope dialog box.

The Repeat/Loop option

This option appears in the Properties panel, yet a measure of its functionality occurs in conjunction with the Edit Envelope dialog box. The Repeat/Loop drop-down menu and field is used to set the number of times that a sound file repeats (or loops indefinitely). You can use a small looping selection, such as a break beat or jazz riff, for a background soundtrack, or loop a short ambient noise for an interesting effect. To test the quality of a looping selection, click the Edit button, which takes you to the Edit Envelope dialog box, where you can click the Play button for a preview of your loop. If the loop isn't perfect or has hiccups, use the In and Out control bars and envelope handles to trim or taper off a blank or adversely repeating section.

Tip

Flash links looped sounds and handles them as one long sound file (although it's really one little sound file played repeatedly). Because this linkage is maintained within the editing environment, the entire expanse of a looped sound can be given a custom effect in the Edit Envelope dialog box. For example, a simple repeating two-measure loop can be diminished over 30 loops. This is a subtle effect that performs well, yet is economical in terms of file size. Note, however, that this applies only to event sounds. ∎

Sound Optimization Overview

You need to be aware of several considerations when preparing Flash sound for export. For Web-based delivery, the primary concern is to find an acceptable middle ground between file size and audio quality. But the concept of acceptability is not absolute; it is always relative to the application. Consider, for example, a Flash site for a record company. In this example, sound quality is likely to be more important than file size because the audience for a record company expects quality sound. In any case, consideration of both your audience and your method of delivery helps you determine the export settings you choose. Luckily, Flash CS5 has capabilities that enhance the user's experience both by optimizing sounds more efficiently and by providing improved programming features to make download delays less problematic.

There are two ways to optimize your sound for export. The quickest, simplest way is to use the Publish Settings dialog box and apply a one-setting-optimizes-all approach. This can work well if all of your sound files are from the same source. For example, if all of your sound material is speech based, then you may be able to use global settings to encode all of your Flash sound. However, if you have a variety of sound sources in your movie, such as a combination of musical scores along with narrative tracks, then the Publish Settings dialog box may not deliver the highest possible level of optimization.

If you demand that your Flash movie has the smallest possible file size, or if your Flash project includes audio from disparate sources, or uses a combination of audio types — such as button sounds, background music, and speech — it's better to fine-tune the audio settings for each sound in the library. This method gives you much better control over output.

Cross-Reference

This chapter discusses only the audio-centric Publish features of Flash CS5. We explain general Publish Settings features in greater detail in Chapter 18, "Publishing Flash Movies." ∎

Publish Settings for Audio

To take a global approach to the control of audio output quality, choose File ➪ Publish Settings (Ctrl+Shift+F12 or Shift+Option+F12 on Mac) to access the Publish Settings dialog box. Then choose the Flash tab of the Publish Settings dialog box, as shown in Figure 12.8. This tab has three areas where the audio quality of an entire Flash movie can be controlled *globally*.

Tip

You can also access the Flash tab of Publish Settings by using the Properties panel. Click the document's Stage or work area, and in the Properties panel, click the Settings button to the right of the Publish label. ■

FIGURE 12.8

The Flash tab of the Publish Settings dialog box has several options to control audio quality.

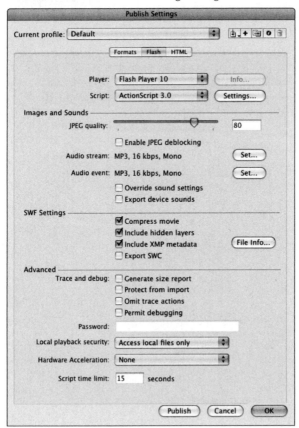

The Flash tab of the Publish Settings dialog box has three options for controlling audio quality:

- **Audio Stream:** Controls the export quality of stream sounds. To customize, click Set. This gives you a number of options, which I describe in the section that follows. Flash supports MP3, which is the optimal streaming format.

- **Audio Event:** Controls the export quality of event sounds. To customize, click Set. This gives you the same number of options as the Set button for Audio Stream. I describe these options in the next section.

- **Override Sound Settings:** If this box is checked, Flash uses the publish settings instead of the individual audio settings that are fine-tuned in the Library panel for the current document. For more information, see "Fine-Tuning Sound Settings in the Library" later in this chapter.

The Set options

Audio stream and Audio event have individual compression settings, which can be specified by their respective Set button options. If you click either Set button on the Flash tab, the same Sound Settings dialog box appears — it is identical for both Audio Stream and Audio Event, which means that the same options are offered for both types of sound. The Sound Settings dialog box, shown in various permutations in Figure 12.9, displays numerous settings related to the control of audio quality and audio file size. The type of compression you select governs the specific group of settings that appear.

FIGURE 12.9

The various options in the Sound Settings dialog box

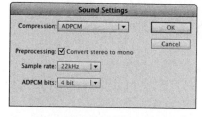
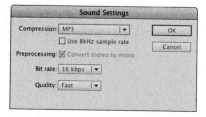

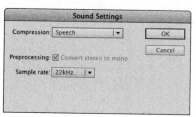

Note

The impact of individual sound settings may be overridden by another setting. For example, a Bit Rate setting of 160 Kbps may not result in high-quality sound if the Quality is set to Fast. Optimal results require attention to all the settings. It's like a set of interlinked teeter-totters: A little experimentation reveals the cumulative or acquired impact of each setting on the others. However, the need to experiment here is hobbled by the lack of a preview mechanism. By contrast, tuning a sound in the library is much more serviceable because there's a sound preview button adjacent to the settings controls. For more about this workflow, refer to "Fine-Tuning Sound Settings in the Library" later in this chapter. ■

The specific options that are available in the Sound Settings dialog boxes are always related to the compression, or audio-encoding scheme, selected in the Compression drop-down menu. That's because different compression technologies support different functionalities:

- **Disable:** This option turns off all sounds that have been assigned in the Properties panel to keyframes in any timeline. If this option is selected, only sound that has been linked and attached for use in ActionScript plays in the movie. All other sound sources assigned in the movie are omitted from the final movie file (.swf). No additional options accompany this setting.

- **ADPCM:** With ADPCM selected in the Compression menu, the following options are available:

  - **Convert Stereo to Mono:** Mixes the right and left channel of audio into one (mono) channel. In sound-engineer parlance, this is known as "bouncing down."

  - **Sample Rate:** Choose from sampling rates of 5, 11, 22, or 44 kHz. Increasing the sample rate of an audio file to something higher than the native sample rate of the imported file simply increases file size, not quality. For example, if you import 22 kHz sounds into the Flash movie, selecting 44 kHz does not improve the sound quality. For more information on sample rates, see Appendix C, "Digital Audio Basics."

  - **ADPCM Bits:** Set the number of bits that ADPCM uses for encoding. You can choose a rate between 2 and 5 bits. The higher the ADPCM bits, the better the audio quality. Flash's default setting is 4 bits.

- **MP3:** If you select MP3 in the Compression menu, you can set the following options:

  - **Convert Stereo to Mono:** Mixes the right and left channels of audio into one (mono) channel. This is disabled at rates below 20 Kbps because the lower bit rates don't allow stereo sound.

  - **Bit Rate:** MP3 measures compression in Kbps. The higher the bit rate, the better the audio quality. Because the MP3 audio compression scheme is very efficient, a high bit rate still results in a relatively small file size. Refer to Table 12.2 for a breakdown of specific bit rates and the resulting sound quality.

- **Quality:** Choose Fast, Medium, or Best quality. These settings determine how well Flash CS5 analyzes the sound file during compression. Fast optimizes the audio file in the shortest amount of time, but usually with less quality. Medium analyzes the sound waveform better than the Fast setting but takes longer to compress. Best is the highest-quality setting, but it takes the longest time to compress the sound file. Note that the file size of the final compressed sound is not affected by any Quality setting — it simply instructs Flash how well it should analyze the sound during compression. The longer Flash takes to analyze a sound, the more likely the final compressed sound captures the high highs and the low lows. If you have a fast computer processor, I recommend that you use the Best setting during your final Flash movie publish. During development and testing, you may want to use Fast to avoid long waits.

- **Raw:** When Raw (also known as Raw PCM audio) is selected in the Compression menu, there are two options:

  - **Convert Stereo to Mono:** Mixes the right and left channels of audio into one (mono) channel.

  - **Sample Rate:** This option specifies the sampling rate for the Audio Stream or Audio Events sounds. For more information on sample rate, refer to Appendix C.

- **Speech:** When the Speech codec is selected in the Compression menu, only one option is available: Sample Rate. Any sound compressed with the Speech codec is converted to mono (one-channel) sound. Even though the Speech codec licensed from Nellymoser was designed for 8 kHz, Flash CS5 "upsamples" this codec to those frequencies the Flash Player supports. See Table 12.3 for an overview of these sampling rates and how they affect sound quality.

TABLE 12.2

MP3 Bit Rate Quality

Bit Rate	Sound Quality	Good For
8 Kbps	Very bad	Best for simulated moonwalk transmissions. Don't use this unless you want horribly unrecognizable sound.
16 Kbps	Barely acceptable	Extended audio files where quality isn't important, or simple button sounds.
20, 24, 32 Kbps	Acceptable	Speech or voice.
48, 56 Kbps	Acceptable	Large music files; complex button sounds.
64 Kbps	Good	Large music files where good audio quality is required.
112–128 Kbps	Excellent	Near-CD quality.
160 Kbps	Best	Near-CD quality.

TABLE 12.3

Speech Sampling Quality

Sample Rate	Sound Quality	Good For
5 kHz	Acceptable	Sound playback over extremely limited data connections, such as 19.2 Kbps wireless Internet modems used by mobile devices.
11 kHz	Good	Standard telephone-quality voice audio.
22 kHz	Excellent	Not recommended for general Internet use. Although this setting produces higher fidelity to the original sound, it consumes too much bandwidth. For comparable sound, I recommend using a midrange MP3 bit rate.
44 kHz	Best	See description for 22 kHz.

Tip

As a general rule, if you use the publish settings to control audio export globally, I recommend choosing MP3 at 20 or 24 Kbps. This results in moderate-to-good sound quality (suitable for most Flash projects), and the ratio of file size to quality gives reasonable performance. A range of 20 to 24 Kbps is an acceptable data rate for speech and short sound effects, while 96 to 128 Kbps is a better data rate for longer sounds and music. ∎

Supporting audio and MP3 playback

Although this is becoming less of an issue with the desktop versions of the Flash Players, it may still be important to consider that MP3 or audio playback may not be supported by all Flash Players, especially device-based players. You can use ActionScript to check the capabilities of the Flash Player installed on a user's system. Using the `flash.system.Capabilities` class, you can check to see whether an MP3 decoder is installed. The specific property is

```
flash.system.Capabilities.hasMP3
```

Tip

In FlashLite 1.1 or later, you can use the `_capMP3` global property at runtime to determine if MP3 playback is supported on a particular device. ∎

More important, though, you can script your movies to check whether the Flash Player has access to general audio output. Some devices with the Flash Player may not have any audio output. This property is

```
flash.system.Capabilities.hasAudio
```

Caution

These class paths of the ActionScript 3.0 language are available only in Flash Player 9 or higher. Earlier versions of the Flash Player simply use `System.Capabilities`, **not** `flash.system.Capabilities`. ∎

Fine-Tuning Sound Settings in the Library

The Publish Settings dialog box is convenient because it permits you to tweak a minimal set of sound adjustments, whereupon Flash exports all of your "noncustomized" stream sounds or event sounds at the same rate and compression. However, if you have many sounds and you are seriously concerned about obtaining the ideal balance of both optimal sound quality and minimum file size, you must export them at different rates and compressions. Consequently, for the fullest level of control over the way in which Flash compresses sound for delivery, I recommend you optimize each sound, individually, in the Library panel. In fact, it would be impossible for us to over-emphasize this bit of sound advice: I *recommend you optimize each sound, individually, in the library.*

Settings for audio in the library

Audio settings in the Library panel are similar to those discussed previously for the Publish Settings dialog box. These settings appear in the Sound Properties dialog box, as shown in Figure 12.10. To access these settings, double-click the icon of the sound in the library; select the sound as it appears in the library and click the Properties button, or choose Properties from the Library panel's options menu; or right-click the sound symbol in the library and choose Properties.

Tip

Flash CS5 also enables you to access the compression settings alone for a sound file by right-clicking (or Control+clicking on the Mac) the sound file in the Library panel and choosing Export Settings from the contextual menu. The options in the Sound Settings dialog box are the same compression settings discussed in this section. ■

FIGURE 12.10

The Sound Properties dialog box enables you to control the compression settings and to precisely balance all other related settings for each individual sound in the library.

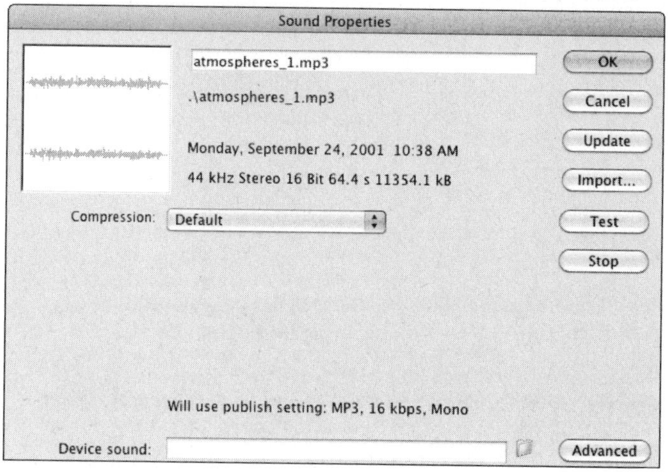

The top half of the Sound Properties dialog box displays status information about the sound file: To the far left is a window with the waveform of the selected audio; to the right of the waveform is an area that displays the name of the file together with its location, date, sample rate, channels, bit depth, duration, and file size.

Note

The file location indicates the full absolute path to the sound file (for example, C:\Inetpub\wwwroot\ mysound.mp3) if you save your Flash document file (.fla) in a volume or hard drive that is different than the location of the sound file. ■

The lower half of the dialog box is titled Export Settings. The first setting is a menu used to select the compression scheme. The Compression options, and the subsequent compression-related options that appear in the other settings, are exactly the same as the sound options of the Publish Settings dialog box discussed earlier in this chapter.

Note

If you imported an MP3 file, the Sound Properties dialog box automatically appears and enables the Use imported MP3 quality check box. The data rate of the imported MP3 file is then used for any event sound compression. However, if you use the MP3 file for stream sounds, the MP3 file is recompressed according to the Stream sound settings in the Publish Settings dialog box. ■

Estimated results appear beneath the Export Settings. Here, the estimated final file size (after compression) of the clip is shown, together with the compression percentage. This is an extremely important tool that is easily overlooked.

Caution

The estimated final file size is just that, an estimate. In our tests, the file size reported in the Sound Properties dialog box was consistently different from the actual file size reported by the size report generated during publishing. You can generate a text file containing detailed information about your final movie by enabling Generate size report in the Flash tab of the Publish Settings dialog box. When enabled, you can view the size report in the Output window in Test Movie mode. ■

The buttons to the right of the Sound Properties dialog box offer the following options:

- **Update:** Click this button to have Flash check for an update of the audio file (if the original MP3, WAV, or AIFF file has been modified), and update it accordingly. Generally, this works only on the machine on which the audio file was originally imported. If you stored your files on a network server, all the members of your Flash production team should be able to use this feature.

- **Import:** This enables you to import another audio file into the Flash environment. The imported audio file overwrites the existing sound appearing in the Sound Properties dialog box, but retains the original sound's name. This feature is useful if you originally imported a placeholder or low-quality sound and need to specify a new file to be used in its place.

- **Test:** This excellent feature enables you to audition the export quality of the sound based on the options that you've selected from the Compression menu (and supporting options in the Export Settings).

- **Stop:** Click this button to stop (silence) the sound that has been auditioned by using the Test button.

Fine-tuning your audio in the Sound Properties dialog box of the Library panel has three benefits. Foremost of these benefits is the ability to set specific compressions and optimizations for each individual sound. Another benefit is the Test button. This is an excellent way to audition your audio file and to know what it will sound like when it is exported with different compression schemes and bit rates — hearing is believing. Finally, the estimated results, which display how each setting will affect the compressed file size, is a powerful tool that helps you obtain the desired balance of quality and file size. In contrast, optimizing sounds with the publish settings is more of a blind process — it is not only more global, it's also more of a painful trial-and-error method.

Combining methods for controlling sounds

One of the coolest things about Flash audio is that you can combine the two methods of controlling sounds, using both the publish settings and the Library panel's Sound Properties dialog box to streamline your workflow while still maintaining a relatively high degree of control over sound quality. (This method works best if you already have some experience with sound behavior in Flash.)

For example, assume that you have three different event sounds in your Flash project. Two of these are simple button sounds. You decide that you won't require specialized compression for the sound used with the buttons. So, based on your prior experience of sound behavior in Flash, you go directly to the publish settings and set event sounds to publish as MP3 at 48 Kbps with Best quality.

Note

I assume that you have left the sounds used for the buttons untouched in the Library panel, leaving the Compression setting in the Sound Settings dialog box at Default. The Default option tells Flash to handle the compression for these sounds with the publish settings. ■

But the third sound is a loop of background jazz music that you want to be heard at near-CD quality. For this sound, you access the Sound Properties dialog box and try a number of combinations — and test each one — until you find a balance between file size and audio quality that pleases your ears. For example, you may decide to assign this sound to export as an MP3, stereo at 64 Kbps, with Quality set to Best.

Final Sound Advice and Pointers

Here are a few final notes about sound and some pointers to more complex sound-related topics that may help you work with sound files in Flash CS5.

VBR (Variable Bit Rate) MP3

Adobe has licensed the Fraunhofer MP3 codec, which supports streaming MP3 with a constant bit rate. However, neither Flash CS5 nor any Flash Player supports Variable Bit Rate (VBR), or VBR MP3, encoding for stream sounds. VBR MP3 is a variant of MP3 that uses specialized algorithms to vary the bit rate according to the kind of sound being compressed. For example, a soprano solo would be accorded a higher bit rate than a crashing drum sequence, resulting in a superior ratio of quality to file size. There are a number of sound applications, such as Apple iTunes and the MP3 creation packs available for Windows Media Player, that export VBR MP3. If you have access to a sound application that exports VBR MP3, you'll be happy to know that you can import your VBR MP3 sound files, which are (theoretically) optimized for file size and quality beyond the compression capabilities of Flash CS5, and that you can maintain the compression of such files by doing the following:

- In the Flash tab of the Publish Settings dialog box, leave the option to Override Sound Settings unchecked.

- In the Sound Properties (or Export Settings) dialog box for each sound in the Library panel, choose MP3 for the Compression option in Export Settings and select the Use imported MP3 quality check box.

- The Sync option (located in the Properties panel) for the sound *cannot* be set to Stream.

If you choose to use VBR MP3 files in your Flash documents, you may need to test the following options of VBR compression in your MP3 creation software:

- **Bit rate:** Test the minimum bit rate that VBR will use for the MP3 file. Regular MP3 files use CBR, or Constant Bit Rate, which keeps the sound's bit rate steady through the entire sound file. With VBR, the bit rate can vary in ranges that you specify. Some higher bit rates, such as 320 Kbps, may not import well into the Flash CS5 authoring tool.

- **Quality:** Most VBR-enabled MP3 software enables you to also pick an arbitrary quality setting for VBR MP3 files. Using terminology like Lowest, Medium Low, and High (and several in between), or percentages (1–100%), you can alter the quality of the bit rate. Note that this "quality" is not necessarily used in the same manner that Flash CS5 refers to quality for MP3 compression.

You may find that Flash CS5 gives you an import error for some VBR- (and CBR-) encoded MP3 files, although I haven't encountered this error with the last two releases of the Flash authoring tool. If a particular setting creates an MP3 file that can't be imported into Flash CS5, try another bit rate and/or quality combination. However, wI have found that Flash has inconsistent behavior when it comes to importing MP3 files. For example, you may find that one VBR setting/combination does not work for a particular sound file but that it works fine for others. Even more strangely, MP3 files that won't import into the Flash authoring environment load just fine into the Flash Player at runtime via ActionScript.

Optimizing sounds for bandwidth usage

It goes without saying that every Internet content creator strives to make every file and data transaction as small and efficient as possible to accommodate the majority of slow network connections in use today. As a Flash designer or developer incorporating sound into your projects, you'll want to properly plan sound usage in an effort to avoid 1MB SWF file downloads.

Table 12.4 explores many of the available network bandwidths that are in use on the Internet. However, as you've likely experienced, it's highly unusual to actually get the full download (or upload) speed out of your network connection. Variables such as network congestion, server load, and phone line conditions affect the quality of your network speed. Using the same formula that Adobe uses to determine approximate download speeds in the Bandwidth Profiler (within Test Movie mode), I calculated estimated bandwidth speeds for the connection speeds shown in Table 12.4. Because Flash CS5 displays compressed sound information in Kbps units, I converted these connection speeds into Kbps bit rates. More important, though, I also provided a 50 percent portion of this bit rate, as you'll likely need to save room for other Flash material, such as vector artwork, bitmap graphics, and animations.

TABLE 12.4

Bit Rates for Flash Movies

Hardware Support	Theoretical Bandwidth	Estimated Bandwidth	Percent of Theoretical	100% Bit Rate	50% Bit Rate
14.4 Kbps	1.8 KB/s	1.2 KB/s	67	9.6 Kbps	4.8 Kbps
19.2 Kbps	2.4 KB/s	1.6 KB/s	67	12.8 Kbps	6.4 Kbps
28.8 Kbps	3.6 KB/s	2.3 KB/s	64	18.4 Kbps	9.2 Kbps
33.6 Kbps	4.2 KB/s	2.8 KB/s	67	22.5 Kbps	11.2 Kbps
56 Kbps	7 KB/s	4.7 KB/s	67	37.6 Kbps	18.8 Kbps
64 Kbps	8 KB/s	5.4 KB/s	67	43.2 Kbps	21.6 Kbps
128 Kbps	16 KB/s	10.7 KB/s	67	85.6 Kbps	42.8 Kbps
256 Kbps	32 KB/s	21 KB/s	67	168 Kbps	84 Kbps
384 Kbps	48 KB/s	32 KB/s	67	256 Kbps	128 Kbps
768 Kbps	96 KB/s	64 KB/s	67	512 Kbps	256 Kbps
1.5 Mbps	192 KB/s	129 KB/s	67	1,032 Kbps	516 Kbps
11 Mbps	1,408 KB/s	943 KB/s	67	7,544 Kbps	3,772 Kbps

Using Table 12.4 as a guide, try to plan your Flash project for your target audience. Actually, you may have more than one target audience. As such, you may need to develop several versions of your sound assets, with each version targeted to a specific connection speed.

After you've decided your target audience(s), you can determine the maximum Kbps that your sound files should use. Table 12.5 shows you the bit rates of Raw, Speech, and ADPCM mono sounds. I don't include MP3 bit rates here because they're already calculated (and available) in the Compression menu of the Sound Properties dialog box: 8, 16, 20, 24, 32, 48, 56, 64, 80, 112, 128, and 160 Kbps. In Table 12.5, I show bit rates that are suitable for analog modem connections (14.4, 28.8, 33.6, and 56 Kbps) in bold.

Note

If you want to see the actual sample rate used by Flash CS5's MP3 compression options, see Table 12.7 later in this chapter. ■

TABLE 12.5

Mono Bit Rates for Streaming Sound

Sampling Rate	Raw	Speech	ADPCM 2-bit	ADPCM 3-bit	ADPCM 4-bit	ADPCM 5-bit
5 kHz	80 Kbps	10 Kbps	10 Kbps	15 Kbps	20 Kbps	25 Kbps
11 kHz	176 Kbps	22 Kbps	22 Kbps	33 Kbps	44 Kbps	55 Kbps
22 kHz	352 Kbps	44 Kbps	44 Kbps	66 Kbps	88 Kbps	110 Kbps
44 kHz	704 Kbps	88 Kbps	88 Kbps	132 Kbps	176 Kbps	220 Kbps

In Tables 12.6 and 12.7, I calculate the file sizes that 1 second of mono (one-channel) sound occupies in a Flash movie file (.swf). Use the values in these tables as multipliers for your sound file's actual length. For example, if you know that you have a 30-second soundtrack file, the final Flash movie file size (containing just the audio) would be about 60K with ADPCM 3-bit, 5 kHz compression. Regardless of the actual content of the digital audio, these encodings produce consistent file sizes based on length and resolution.

TABLE 12.6

File Sizes in Bytes (KB) for One Second of Mono Audio

Sample Rate	Raw	Speech	ADPCM 2-bit	ADPCM 3-bit	ADPCM 4-bit	ADPCM 5-bit
5 kHz	11,037 (10.8)	1,421 (1.4)	1,397 (1.4)	2,085 (2.0)	2,774 (2.7)	3,463 (3.4)
11 kHz	22,061 (21.5)	2,829 (2.8)	2,777 (2.7)	4,115 (4.0)	5,532 (5.4)	6,910 (6.8)
22 kHz	44,109 (43.1)	5,581 (5.5)	5,541 (5.5)	8,296 (8.1)	11,051 (10.8)	13,806 (13.5)
44 kHz	88,205 (86.1)	11,085 (10.8)	11,065 (10.8)	16,576 (16.2)	22,086 (21.6)	27,597 (27.0)

TABLE 12.7

File Sizes in Bytes (KB) for One Second of Mono MP3 Audio

Bit Rate	Size	Output Sample Rate
8 Kbps	1,263 (1.2)	11 kHz
16 Kbps	2,511 (2.5)	11 kHz
20 Kbps	3,135 (3.1)	11 kHz
24 Kbps	3,369 (3.3)	22 kHz
32 Kbps	4,487 (4.4)	22 kHz
48 Kbps	5,605 (5.5)	22 kHz
56 Kbps	5,605 (5.5)	22 kHz
64 Kbps	8,543 (8.3)	44 kHz
80 Kbps	10,716 (10.5)	44 kHz
112 Kbps	14,980 (14.6)	44 kHz
128 Kbps	17,112 (16.7)	44 kHz
160 Kbps	17,112 (16.7)	44 kHz

Note

You may notice that some bit rate settings in Table 12.7 create the same file size for the MP3 compression. This is a known bug of the Flash authoring tool. You may also find that the Convert Stereo to Mono option for MP3 compression does not affect the outcome of some settings. ■

Extracting a sound from a Flash document

Sometime you may be handed a Flash document file (.fla) that has sound embedded within it and be told that the original sounds have either been lost or are no longer available. Here's how to extract a sound from such a file:

1. **Back up the file.** If the original file is named `sound.fla`, you might resave it as `sound_extraction.fla`. If you want to start with an exercise file, save a copy of the `enhanced_view.fla` file, located on the book's CD-ROM. You can skip Steps 2–7 if you are using this file.

2. **Add a new layer in the Timeline window, at the top of the layer stack.**

3. **Label this layer** sound extraction.

4. **With the first frame of this layer selected, open the Properties panel.**

5. **In the Sound section's Name menu, specify the sound file from the Library panel that you want to export.**

6. **Add enough frames to the sound extraction layer so that you can see the entire waveform of the sound file.**

7. **Delete all other layers.**

8. **Open the Library panel and locate the sound that needs to be extracted from the file.** In the example file, the sound is named `atmospheres_1.wav`. Note that any other assets within this file are irrelevant to this process. That's because Flash uses only library items that have actually been used within the movie.

9. **Double-click the sound icon for** `atmospheres_1.wav` **in the Library panel to open the Sound Properties dialog box.**

10. **Set the Compression to Raw.** This ensures that the sound is exported as uncompressed audio.

11. **Select a sample rate that matches the one listed to the right of the waveform display, near the top of the Sound Properties dialog box.** If the sound is specified as a stereo sound, make sure that the Convert Stereo to Mono option is unchecked.

12. **Access the Flash tab of the Publish Settings dialog box, and make sure that the Override Sound Settings check box is** *not* **checked.** Now you're ready to extract the sound file from the Flash document file (.fla). You've created a movie that will ignore all other assets in the library except this sound, and you've told Flash to export the sound with the original sample rate of the sound, as uncompressed (Raw) audio.

13. **Choose File ➪ Export Movie, and specify a file location, name, and file type.** If you're using the Windows version of Flash CS5, choose WAV Audio as the file type. If you're on a Mac, choose QuickTime.

14. **For Windows users, the Export Windows WAV dialog box appears with those sound specifications.** In the Sound Format menu, make sure the audio specifications match those of your audio source in the Library panel; then click OK. For Mac users, the QuickTime Export Settings dialog box appears. Here, click the QuickTime settings button in the lower-left corner. Ignore all the options except Sound Format. In this menu, select the sound setting that matches the specifications of the sound file. For this example, this setting should be 44 kHz 16 Bit Stereo. Click OK.

15. **For Windows users, the process is complete.** You now have a WAV copy of your Flash movie sound asset. For Mac users, you still have a couple of steps to complete:

1. Open the exported QuickTime movie in the QuickTime Player Pro. You must have the Pro version installed.

2. Choose File ⇨ Export.

3. Select Sound to AIFF in the Export menu.

4. Click the Options button, and in the Sound Settings dialog box, set the Compressor to None and choose a sample rate, bit depth, and channel type that match the sound from the Flash document. For this example sound, this should be 44.1 kHz, 16 bit, and Stereo. Click OK.

Note

If you're using Apple QuickTime Pro 7 or later, choose Linear PCM in the Format menu and the sampling settings that match your source audio in the Flash movie. ∎

5. Finally, specify a filename and location for the exported file, and click Save.

Summary

- Flash movie files (.swf) can use four types of audio compression: ADPCM, MP3, Raw, and Speech. ADPCM is compatible with all versions of the Flash Player. MP3 is compatible with most versions of Flash Player 4 and higher. The Speech codec is compatible with Flash Player 6 and higher.

- When sound is imported to a Flash document, it's added and displayed in the Library panel. You can assign sounds from the Library panel to a keyframe on a timeline. You can also use sounds with ActionScript.

- Sounds can be assigned to the Up, Over, and Down states of a Button symbol.

- The Sync options control how a sound plays in relation to the rest of a timeline.

- Use the Loop setting in the Properties panel to multiply the length of the original sound.

- Stream sounds force the Flash Player to keep playback of a timeline in pace with the sound.

- Use a `SoundMixer.stopAll()` action to stop all sounds currently playing in the movie.

- The Effect menu in the Properties panel contains useful presets for sound channel playback. You can perform custom edits with the Edit Envelope dialog box.

- Global audio compression is controlled in the Flash tab of the Publish Settings dialog box.

- Use the Sound Properties dialog box in the Library panel to customize the audio compression schemes of individual sounds.

- The Sound Properties dialog box enables you to test different compression settings and to hear the results. The Export Settings section of this dialog box also provides useful file size information.

- You can bring and export Variable Bit Rate (VBR) MP3 sound files into Flash without degrading the encoding; however, Flash itself cannot encode by using VBR.

Importing Artwork

A lthough Flash gives you powerful options for creating and modifying a variety of graphics, you don't have to limit yourself to the Flash authoring environment. That's because Flash also has the capability of importing artwork from a wide range of sources. You can import both vector and raster graphics, and you can use both formats in a variety of ways.

In this chapter, I discuss the differences between vector graphics and raster or bitmap images. I also show you how to import external artwork so that you can use it in a Flash movie, as well as tell you about the Flash features that you can use to handle imported bitmap images and vector graphics.

I define all the formats that Flash supports and go over some of the issues to consider when preparing artwork for import from various programs. I also introduce some Flash features that are helpful for managing imported assets and give some insight into optimizing your final file size.

Defining Vectors and Bitmaps

In addition to various sound and video formats, Flash supports two types of image formats: vector and bitmap. *Vector* graphic files consist of an equation that describes the placement of points and the qualities of the lines between those points. Using this basic logic, vector graphics tell the computer how to display the lines and shapes, as well as what colors to use, where to put them on the Stage, and at what scale.

Flash is a vector program. Thus, anything that you create with the Flash drawing tools is described in vector format. Vector graphics have some important benefits: They're small in file size and they scale accurately without distortion. However, they also have a couple of drawbacks: Highly complex vector graphics may result in very large file sizes, and vectors aren't really suitable for creating continuous tones, photographs, or artistic brushwork.

Bitmap (also referred to as *raster*) files are described by an arrangement of individual pixels, which are mapped in a grid — like a piece of graph paper with tiny squares. Each square represents a single pixel, and each of these pixels has specific color values assigned to it. So, as the name implies, a bitmap image maps out the placement and color of each pixel on the screen. A line is "drawn" by filling each unique pixel, rather than simply using a mathematical formula to connect two points as is done with vectors.

Note

Do not be confused by the name bitmap. You might already be familiar with the bitmap format used by Windows, which has the file extension .bmp. Although bitmap may refer to that particular image format, it's frequently applied to raster images in general, such as GIF, JPEG, PICT, and TIFF files, as well as many others. ■

Although bitmap images aren't created in Flash, they can be used within Flash projects. To do this, you need to use an external bitmap-editing application and then import the bitmaps into Flash. Figure 13.1 shows a vector image and a bitmap image of the same graphic, scaled at 100 percent.

FIGURE 13.1
_____

A vector image drawn in Flash (left) and the same image imported as a bitmapped GIF graphic (right)

Although these vector and bitmap images are of similar quality at their original size, their differences become more apparent when the same images are scaled to a larger size. Unlike vector graphics, bitmap images become more pixilated as they are scaled larger because there is a finite amount of information in the image and Flash has to spread this information over more pixels. As I explain later in this chapter, Flash is able to interpolate the pixel information by using Smoothing to reduce the jagged appearance of the scaled pixel pattern, but this can also cause the image to look blurred. Figure 13.2 shows the difference between vector and bitmap graphics when scaled in Flash with Smoothing turned off.

FIGURE 13.2

The same vector (left) and bitmap (right) image scaled to 200 percent in Flash to illustrate the difference in image quality

Simple bitmap images are often larger in file size than simple vector graphics, but very complex bitmap images (for example, a photograph) can be smaller and display better quality than vector graphics of equal complexity. Figure 13.3 shows a bitmap image compared to a vector image of equal complexity (created by tracing the bitmap). The original bitmap is a smaller file and better suited for reproducing the photographic image.

FIGURE 13.3

File size comparison of an imported bitmap image (left) and a traced vector image of equivalent complexity (right)

Original bitmap 16 KB   Traced vector image 198 KB

The rule of thumb is to use scalable, bandwidth-efficient vector graphics as much as possible within Flash projects, except for situations in which photographs — or photographic-quality, continuous-tone images — are necessary for special content.

Tip
Most 8-bit raster images are GIFs, and they are most frequently used for images with large areas of solid color, such as logos and text. Rather than use this image type in Flash, consider re-creating or tracing this artwork with Flash drawing tools. The final Flash movie (.swf) will not only be smaller; it will also look cleaner and be scalable. ■

Knowing the File Formats for Import to Flash

You can import a variety of assets (in compatible formats) directly into your Flash project library, or you can import or copy and paste from another application into the Flash Document window. Assets can also be dragged from one Flash Document window or library to another. Files must be a minimum size of 2 pixels by 2 pixels for import into Flash.

Caution
Copying and pasting bitmap images into Flash from other applications does not always transfer transparency settings, so it may not be the best workflow for some assets. Using the Import dialog box and specifying that the artwork be imported as an editable object preserves transparency settings from Fireworks .png files. ■

The import menu (Ctrl+R or ⌘+R) gives you the option to limit imports to a specific format or to choose broad media categories. Unless you find it helpful to have some files grayed out when you dig through lists to find items to import, you will most likely be happy just using the most inclusive menu setting: All Files.

Cross-Reference
For a full discussion of importing and handling sound assets, refer to Chapter 12, "Adding Sound." Flash-compatible video formats are documented in Appendix C, "Digital Video Basics." ■

For now, let's focus on a brief summary of the image formats for Flash import, as shown in Table 13.1.

Note
The QuickTime warning dialog box that would pop up when bitmap images requiring QuickTime support were imported to older versions of Flash no longer appears. Although QuickTime support is still needed for some file types, the warning has been retired to make the process more seamless. ■

TABLE 13.1

Image Formats for Flash Import

File Type	Extension	Description	Platform
Adobe Illustrator (CS5 files are most compatible)	.ai, .eps	Adobe Illustrator files are imported into Flash as vector graphics (unless they contain bitmap images). The importer plug-in is required to import files from Adobe Illustrator 8 and earlier. *To import PDF files to Flash CS3 or CS5, you must first open them in Illustrator and resave in AI (or EPS for Flash CS5) format.*	Windows Mac
AutoCAD DXF	.dxf	Drawing eXchange format is the original inter-program format for AutoCAD drafting software. Because this format does not support fills, it is mainly used for drafting plans or schematic drawings. This format is used by most CAD, 3-D, and modeling programs for transferring drawings to other programs.	Windows Mac
(Windows) Bitmap	.bmp, .dib	Although Bitmap is a Windows format for bitmap images, don't be confused by the format name; not all bitmap images are Windows Bitmaps. Bitmap can be used with all Win and some Mac applications. It allows variable bit depths and compression settings with support of alpha channels and supports lossless compression. It is ideal for high-quality graphics work.	Windows Mac
Enhanced Metafile	.emf	Enhanced Metafile is a proprietary Windows format that supports vectors and bitmaps internally. This format is occasionally used to import vector graphics, but for most professional graphics work, this is not a recommended format.	Windows
Flash movie	.swf, .spl	Flash Player files are exported Flash movies. The movie is flattened into a single layer and scene, and all animation is converted to frame-by-frame animation.	Windows Mac
FreeHand	.fh	This is the vector-based format of FreeHand (v.7 or later).	Windows Mac
Adobe FXG	.fxg	A new XML-based file format used to transfer graphics, text, bitmap filters, and symbols between Adobe applications. Objects Flash supports for editing are preserved to be editable when imported into Flash.	Windows Mac
GIF image or animated GIF	.gif	Graphic Interchange Format (GIF) was developed by CompuServe as a bitmap image type that uses lossless compression. It is limited to a 256-color (or less) palette and is not recommended as a high-quality Flash export format, even for Web use.	Windows Mac

(continued)

TABLE 13.1 *(continued)*

File Type	Extension	Description	Platform
JPEG image	.jpg	Joint Photographic Experts Group (JPEG) is a bitmap type that uses lossy compression. Supports 24-bit RGB color. Recommended for Web-friendly compression of photographic images. Because of small file size, JPEG is often the native format for digital still cameras. No support for alpha channels.	Windows Mac
MacPaint image	.pntg	This is a legacy format for the old MacPaint program.	Windows Mac
PICT image	.pct, .pict	PICT image is compatible with many Win and all Mac applications. It enables variable bit depths and compression settings with support of alpha channels (when saved with no compression at 32 bits), supports lossless compression, and can contain vector or raster graphics. PICT image is ideal for high-quality graphics work.	Windows Mac
PNG image	.png	The Portable Network Graphic (PNG) format is another type of bitmap image that supports variable bit depth (PNG-8 and PNG-24) and compression settings with alpha channels. PNG files imported to Flash from Fireworks or Photoshop as editable objects (unflattened) preserve artwork in vector format. Lossless compression schemes make it ideal for high-quality graphics work. It is the recommended media type for imported images with alpha channels or filter effects.	Windows Mac
Photoshop image (2.5 or later)	.psd	This is the native layered format for most versions of Photoshop.	Windows Mac
QuickTime image	.qtif	This is the static raster image format created by QuickTime. It is not commonly used.	Windows Mac
Silicon Graphics image	.sgi	This is an image format specific to SGI machines.	Windows Mac
TGA image	.tga	The TGA, or Targa, format is a 32-bit format that includes an 8-bit alpha channel. It was developed to overlay computer graphics and live video.	Windows (with QT4) Mac
TIFF image	.tif or .tiff	TIFF is a lossless, cross-platform image type used widely for high-resolution photography and printing.	Windows Mac
Windows Metafile	.wmf	Windows Metafile is a proprietary Windows format that supports vectors and bitmaps internally. This format is generally used to import vector graphics.	Windows

Tip

Although you can export to the GIF format from Flash, this should be considered an option for raw-information transfer only, not as a means for creating final GIF art. For optimal quality and control, export a PNG sequence from Flash that can be brought into Fireworks for fine-tuning and final GIF output. ■

Preparing Bitmaps

Flash is a vector-based application, but that shouldn't stop you from using bitmaps when you *need* them. There are many situations in which either the designs or the nature of the content require that photographic images be included in a Flash project. You can import a wide variety of bitmap image types, including JPEG, GIF, BMP, and PICT by using the methods described in the next section.

Considering that it's a vector-based program, Flash supports bitmap graphics extraordinarily well. However, because the most common use of Flash movies is for Web presentations, you always need to keep file size in mind. Here's what you can do to limit the impact of bitmap images on Flash playback performance:

- Limit the number of bitmaps used in any one frame of a Flash movie.

- Remember that, regardless of how many times the bitmap is placed on the Stage, the actual bitmap (or its compressed version in the .swf file) is downloaded before the first occurrence of the bitmap (or its symbol instance).

- Try spreading out bitmap usage, or hide a symbol instance of the bitmap in an earlier frame before it is actually visible, so that it loads when you need it.

Tip

If you need to include several high-resolution bitmap images in your Flash movie, consider using an ActionScript preloader or try breaking up the project into several linked Flash movies. ■

When you want to bring raster images into Flash documents, you should know what portion of the Flash Stage the image will occupy. Let's assume that you're working with the default Flash document size of 550 × 400 pixels. If you want to use a bitmap as a background image, it won't need to be any larger than 550 × 400 (as long as your movie is not scalable). So, assuming that you're starting with a high-resolution image, you would downscale the image to the largest size at which it will appear in the Flash movie *before* you import it into Flash; for our example, that would be 550 × 400.

Tip

Use an image-editing program such as Fireworks or Adobe Photoshop to downsize the pixel width and height of your source image if necessary. ■

Raster Images: Resolution, Dimensions, and Bit Depth

Resolution refers to the amount of information within a given unit of measurement. Greater resolutions mean better quality (or more image information). With respect to raster images, resolution is usually measured in pixels per inch (when viewed on a monitor) or dots per inch (when output on film or paper).

What is resolution?

The resolution of an original image changes whenever the scale of the image is changed, while the pixel dimensions remain fixed. Thus, if an original photograph is scanned at 300 pixels per inch (ppi) with dimensions of 2 × 2 inches, subsequently changing the dimensions to 4 × 4 inches results in a resolution of 150 ppi. Although a 4-x-4-inch image at 300 ppi could be interpolated from the original image, true resolution is *lost* as an image is scaled larger. When an image is digitally enlarged, the graphics application simply doubles existing pixel information, which can create a softened or blurred image. Reducing the scale of an image has few undesirable side effects — although a much smaller version of an original may lose some fine details.

Because all raster images consist of pixels, and because resolution simply describes how many pixels are arranged in a given area, the most accurate way of referencing raster images is by using the absolute pixel width and height of an image. For example, a 4,000-x-5,000-pixel image could be printed or displayed at any size with variable resolutions. This image could be 4 × 5 inches at 1,000 ppi, or it could be 8 × 10 inches at 500 ppi — without any loss of information. Remember that resolution simply describes how much information is shown per unit. When you reduce the pixel width and height of an image, the resolution is lowered accordingly, and after any pixels are thrown out, discarded, or interpolated, they're gone for good.

Raster images: Bit depth

Bit depth is an important factor that influences image quality and file size. *Bit depth* refers to the amount of information stored for each pixel of an image. The most common bit depths for images are 8-bit and 24-bit, although many others exist. An 8-bit image contains up to 256 colors, while a 24-bit image may contain 16.7 million color values. Depending on their file format, some images can also use an 8-bit alpha channel, which is a multilevel transparency layer. Each addition to an image's bit depth is reflected in a considerable file size increase: A 24-bit image contains three times the information per pixel as an 8-bit image. Mathematically, you can calculate the file size (in bytes) of an image with the following formula (all measurements are in pixels):

```
width×height×(bit depth ÷ 8) = file size
```

Note: You divide bit depth by 8 because there are 8 bits per byte.

When importing 8-bit images in formats such as GIF, BMP, and PICT, it is preferable to use the default Lossless (PNG/GIF) compression setting in Bitmap Properties to avoid adding Flash's default Publish Settings Quality 24-bit JPEG compression. Eight-bit images that use Web-safe color palettes ensure greater display predictability for people viewing your Flash artwork on older systems with 8-bit video cards.

If you mask bitmaps with a mask layer in the Flash timeline, the entire bitmap is still exported. Consequently, before import you should closely crop all images that will be masked in Flash. For example, if all you need to show is a face, crop the image so that it shows the face with as little extraneous background information as possible.

Be aware that Flash doesn't resize (or resample) an image to its viewed or placed size when the Flash movie (.swf) is created. To illustrate how the size of an imported bitmap can affect the size of a final Flash movie (.swf), I compared two different image resolutions used in identical layouts. Using the same source image, I sized the JPEG at two different pixel dimensions, and then placed it in two identical Flash documents (.fla). The first source version of the image had a 400-x-600-pixel dimension, and the second source version had a 200-x-300-pixel dimension — exactly half the size of the first. In both Flash documents, the final image was displayed at 200 × 300 pixels.

In the first Flash document (we'll call it Movie A), I imported the larger JPEG and resized it by 50 percent (using the Info panel) to match the smaller image. In the second Flash document (Movie B), I imported the smaller JPEG and placed it at its original size, occupying the same portion of the Flash Stage as the image in Movie A. Although both Flash movies exported a bitmap of the same display size on the Flash Stage, the resulting SWF files (using the same level of JPEG compression on export) had drastically different file sizes. Movie A was 44.1KB, whereas Movie B was 14.8KB! Movie A is nearly three times larger than Movie B. The difference in image resolution could be seen when a view magnification greater than 100 percent was used within the Flash Player; the larger JPEG in Movie A was much less pixilated than the smaller JPEG in Movie B.

Preserving Bitmap Quality

When you choose to use bitmap images, remember that they do not scale as well as vector drawings in the authoring environment. Furthermore, bitmaps become degraded if the viewer scales your final movie so that the bitmap is displayed larger than its original size. Here are a few points to consider that will help you maintain the quality of your presentation when using bitmaps:

- Know your audience, and design for the largest screen (at the highest resolution) that your audience may have. Or, if you deviate from this, remember that audience members with optimal equipment will see a low-quality version of your work. If you're using ActionScript to load image assets, consider having low-res and high-res versions of the images available.

- Measure your largest hypothetical image dimensions in pixels. One way to determine these dimensions is to use the Flash Info panel to read the size of a placed image or a placeholder shape. Another way is to take a screen capture of your mock-up, and then measure the intended image area in Photoshop.

- Create or resize your bitmap image to the maximum hypothetical dimensions. If there are any rotations or skews required, you may have to do a test to see if the final result is cleaner when the transformation is done in your image-editing program or in the Flash authoring environment.

- Import images into Flash at the maximum required size, and then scale them down to fit into your layout.

The advantage of using this approach is that the movie can be scaled for larger monitors without causing the bitmap image to degrade. The disadvantage is that it requires sending the same large bitmap to all users. A more sophisticated solution is to use JavaScript to detect browser dimensions and then send the appropriately scaled bitmaps to each user. Other workaround solutions that may help preserve the quality of your final presentation without adding file size include the following:

- Restrict scaling capability of your published movie. You can do this by using HTML options in the Publish settings or using ActionScript.

- Set the bitmap's compression to Lossless (GIF/PNG) if it is already optimized in GIF format or if you want to preserve an alpha channel or editable filter effects in a .png or a .psd file.

- Trace the bitmap to convert it to a vector graphic (covered later in this chapter).

- Never apply double JPEG compression to your images. If you have compressed and saved images in JPEG format outside of Flash, be certain to select the Use imported JPEG data check box when importing the images to Flash.

Before sizing and importing bitmaps, you need to consider how you will set the dimensions for the Flash movie (.swf) in the HTML tab of the Publish Settings dialog box. You also need to know whether the bitmap is to be scaled in a motion tween. If the Flash movie scales beyond its original pixel width and height (or if the bitmap is scaled larger in a tween), bitmap images will appear at a lower resolution with a consequent degradation of image quality.

If you're uncertain of the final size that you need for a bitmap in Flash, it may be best to import a temporary low-resolution version of the image — being careful to store your original high-resolution version where you can find it later. Whenever you need to place the bitmap, drag an instance of the symbol onto the Flash Stage. Then during final production and testing, after you've determined the required pixel size for the maximum scale of the final bitmap, create and swap-in a higher-resolution image, as follows:

1. **Double-click the icon of the original low-resolution bitmap in the Flash library to access the bitmap's properties.**

2. **In the Bitmap Properties dialog box, click the Import button and select the new, higher-resolution version of the bitmap.** After import of the high-res image, all instances of the bitmap update automatically, with the scaling, animation, and placement of the image maintained.

Importing and Copying Bitmaps

Flash has the option to import bitmaps directly to the document library, in addition to the standard option of importing to the document Stage. When a bitmap file is imported to the Stage, it is added to the library as well. To import a bitmap into Flash, follow these steps:

1. **If you want to import an item to the Stage, make sure that there's an active, unlocked layer.** If no layer is available for placement of the imported item, the Import to Stage command is dimmed and you can use only the Import to Library option.

2. **Choose File ⇨ Import ⇨ Import to Stage (Ctrl+R or ⌘+R) or File ⇨ Import ⇨ Import to Library.** The Import (or the Import to Library) dialog box opens (shown in Figure 13.4).

3. **Navigate to the file that you'd like to import, select it, and click the Import or Import to Library button.**

The important difference between Import and Import to Library is that the latter option places the asset directly into the document library without placing an instance on the Stage.

Because Flash offers full support for the PNG image format (including lossless compression and multilevel transparency and some Fireworks filters), PNG is an ideal format for images that you intend to import into Flash. The PNG format has two types: PNG-8 and PNG-24. Generally, only PNG-24 images support 24-bit color and an alpha channel, but the file sizes can often be prohibitive. Fireworks makes it possible to create PNG-8 files with transparency for import to Flash.

FIGURE 13.4

The Import dialog box as it appears on Mac OS X. You can import multiple files in the same batch by selecting them from the file list before clicking Import.

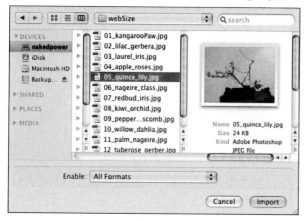

Caution

When you are using bitmap images with transparent areas, display problems can occasionally occur with certain color settings and file types. For troubleshooting assistance, refer to the Adobe TechNote on "Transparency support in Flash" at www.adobe.com/support/flash/ts/documents/transparent_bitmaps.htm. ∎

Importing sequences

When using the Import to Stage option, if you select an image from a series of images in the same storage location that include sequential numbers at the end of their filenames, Flash prompts you to import the files as a sequence. If that's what you want to do, click Yes in the dialog box (shown in Figure 13.5) to have Flash import all the files and place them in numeric sequence on successive keyframes of the current timeline. Otherwise, click No, and only the single file that you've selected is placed on the Stage.

FIGURE 13.5

You can import images in a numbered sequence and place them on successive keyframes automatically by using the Import to Stage option.

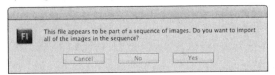

If you are importing a series of stills to be used sequentially to create animation (stills from a video sequence, for example), this feature can save a lot of the time you would spend placing and ordering images manually. The most efficient workflow is to create a Movie Clip symbol before importing the images so that the sequence can be placed directly on the Movie Clip Timeline. This method creates an animated element that can easily be placed anywhere in your Flash project. If you have already imported a sequence to the Main Timeline and decide that it would be more easily managed as a symbol, simply create a Movie Clip, and then cut the images from the Main Timeline and paste them into the Movie Clip Timeline.

Although sequential import is not an option when using Import to Library, it is possible to manually select multiple images for import while using either of the Import dialog boxes. In order to bring more than one file into Flash in the same batch, Shift+click to select multiple items in sequence or use Ctrl+click (or ⌘+click) to select multiple nonsequential items in the file list of the Import dialog box.

Working with layered bitmap files

If you are working with graphic files that go beyond simple, single-layer bitmap images, finding the best way to translate those files to Flash may require some trial and error. Both Fireworks files (PNG) and Photoshop files (PSD) can contain bitmap and vector artwork, as well as text and masks or filters on multiple layers. Fireworks files may also contain frames and guides. You can always opt to flatten elements into a single bitmap file to preserve the exact appearance of the image, or you can choose to preserve editable paths and layers for more flexibility in the Flash authoring environment.

Each layered file imported from Photoshop or Fireworks with editable objects preserved is nested in a new folder in the Flash library that automatically has the same name as the imported file. You can change the default name of these folders and reorganize your Flash library as needed to keep the structure clean. You may find it helpful to create a folder for imported elements and nest all the folders that Flash creates for you so that your library does not get too cluttered.

Tip

Keep in mind that Movie Clip symbols Flash creates to preserve editable files imported from Photoshop or Fireworks are stored along with any bitmaps or other assets in the folders that Flash auto-creates for each file. If you are using a Movie Clip symbol more than once, you may want to rename and move it to a location that is easier to access — such as into the main file list in the Flash library — instead of leaving it in the nested folder. ■

Note

Flash can support some effects and blends created in Fireworks or Photoshop. If an effect is supported in Flash, it is preserved as an editable Flash filter. If an effect is too complex for Flash to preserve, the image can be rasterized to preserve the appearance of the image, but the effect will not be editable in the Flash authoring environment. ■

Importing Photoshop (PSD) files

Flash CS5 offers a detailed import dialog box for layered Photoshop files (shown in Figure 13.6) that makes it easy to control elements of the file to be flattened (as bitmaps) or imported as editable objects.

FIGURE 13.6

Use the import dialog box to choose conversion settings for Photoshop PSD files.

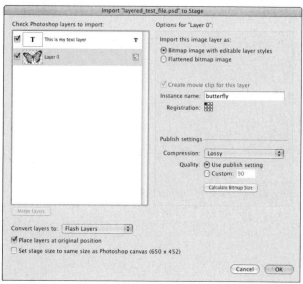

Caution

Although layered Photoshop files can be saved in TIFF or PNG format, these files are flattened on import to Flash, and you do not have the same control over the conversion of specific elements as you do with PSD files. PSD is the only Photoshop file format that can be brought into Flash with the option to keep layers and editable elements intact. ■

When importing images from Photoshop into Flash, you are prompted by the Photoshop Import Settings dialog box to select each layer in the file and make choices for the following import options:

- **Import this image layer as:**
  - **Bitmap image with editable layer styles:** This setting automatically creates a Flash Movie Clip and place the elements onto the Movie Clip Timeline while preserving the image, masks, and other effects (supported by Flash) as editable.
  - **Flattened bitmap image:** This setting flattens the image into a single layer in the main Flash timeline and preserves the appearance of any masks or filters, but they will not be editable in Flash.

- **Import this text layer as:**
  - **Editable text:** Brings the text in as an editable Flash text box, and may require font substitution if you do not have the same font available in Flash. The text is placed on a layer in the Main Timeline or on a Movie Clip Timeline (depending on the other settings you choose).
  - **Vector outlines:** Converts the text to individual letter outlines to preserve the appearance of the characters and the layout. You can modify the text by using Flash drawing tools, but you cannot edit with Flash text tools.
  - **Flattened bitmap image:** Converts the text into a single image to preserve appearance but limits editing options to those that can be applied to bitmaps.

- **Create Movie Clip for this layer:** If you have selected this option (or it has been auto-selected to preserve editable elements), you have the option of assigning an instance name and modifying the registration point.
  - **Instance name:** You only need to assign an instance name if you plan to target the Movie Clip with ActionScript.
  - **Registration:** In most cases, you won't need to worry about changing the default registration point because the convention is to work with the top-left corner as a reference for position and scale.

- **Publish settings:** You have three options:
  - You may opt to import the image without any additional compression (**Lossless**).
  - You may set a custom compression setting for each layer or image as you import it (**Lossy: Custom**).

Tip

Use the Calculate Bitmap Size button to preview the effect of different Custom compression settings before you decide on the final level to apply to your imported image. ■

- Or, you may opt for the default setting, which applies the level of compression you have set globally for your Flash movie in Publish Settings (**Lossy: Use publish setting**).

- **Convert layers to:**
  - **Flash Layers:** Puts the contents of each image layer onto a new layer in the selected Flash timeline (either on the Main Timeline or on a Movie Clip Timeline).
  - **Keyframes:** Puts the contents of each image layer into a new keyframe on a single layer in the selected Flash timeline (either on the Main Timeline or on a Movie Clip Timeline).

Along with the layer-specific settings listed above, there are two handy check boxes at the bottom of the dialog box that enable you to apply two additional (optional) settings for all layers in the file:

- **Place layers at original position:** This setting ensures that the placement of the imported elements is consistent with the original file, relative to the top-left corner of the Stage. If you do not select this check box, the imported elements are just placed in the center of the visible area of the Document window (including the pasteboard) — which usually turns out to be a somewhat random location unless you have been very precise with your zoom setting and your scroll bars to position the Stage within the viewable area of the Document window.
- **Set stage size to same size as Photoshop canvas:** This is very helpful if you are importing an image to a new Flash file and you want to match the sizes, but it may disrupt your layout if you already have other elements placed in the Flash file you are importing to.

If all these options seem like more than you need, you can simplify things by leaving the default settings for each layer as is, or you can select some (or all) of the layers (using Shift+Select or Ctrl+Select) to apply a more limited set of options to all the layers at once.

Tip

Although you have more than one layer selected in the Import dialog box, you may also choose to use the Merge button to flatten the layers into a single bitmap to streamline your file. This preserves the appearance of the layered image but limits your editing options in Flash to those available for simple nonlayered bitmaps.

If you want to fine-tune your import settings without having to make selections each time you see the Photoshop Import dialog box, you can choose your own default settings in the Flash Preferences panel (File ➪ Preferences ➪ PSD File Importer, or on Mac Flash ➪ Preferences ➪ PSD File Importer). You can preset all the available settings for layered PSD files, as shown in Figure 13.7. ■

FIGURE 13.7

Flash Preferences enable you to preset defaults for all the options available with the PSD file importer.

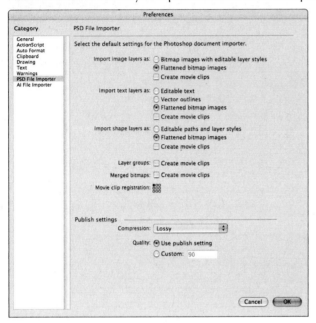

Importing Fireworks (PNG) files

The import dialog box for Fireworks files has fewer options than the import dialog box for PSD files, but it still supports the import of layered, editable files (as shown in Figure 13.8).

FIGURE 13.8

Use this special import dialog box to choose conversion settings for Fireworks PNG files.

Caution

Although Photoshop files saved in PNG format show up in the file list when you browse for PNG files, they do not invoke an import dialog box with options but are flattened into a single-layer bitmap on import. Only PNG files saved from Fireworks enable you to preserve layers and editable shape or text elements on import to Flash. ■

When importing PNG images from Fireworks into Flash, you are prompted by the Fireworks PNG Import Settings dialog box to make selections for the following import options:

- **Import as a single flattened bitmap:** Select this check box to import the PNG as one rasterized image to the current layer on the Main Timeline or to the library. When this option is selected, all other options are unavailable. If you choose this option, you may want to apply Flash JPEG compression to the bitmap image either in Bitmap Properties or in Publish Settings. To edit a flattened image, you can launch Fireworks from inside Flash and edit the original PNG file (including any vector data or text).

- To import more complex files, use these options to control the import structure:

  - **Import:** Page or Layer or Frames — select the option that best describes the location and structure of the Fireworks content you want to bring into Flash.

  - **Into:** Current frame as a Movie Clip to import the PNG file to a new Flash Movie Clip Timeline with all frames and layers intact, or New Layer to import the PNG file into a single new layer in the current Flash document at the top of the stacking order. All Fireworks layers are flattened, but not rasterized unless specified, and any frames in the Fireworks file are included on the new layer.

- Use these settings to control whether content is rasterized or kept editable:

  - **Objects:** Select either Import as bitmaps to maintain appearance to rasterize Fireworks fills, strokes, and effects in Flash as part of a flattened bitmap image, or select Keep all paths editable to preserve vector paths in Flash. Some Fireworks fills, strokes, and effects may be lost on import.

  - **Text:** You can select the same options as those listed for Objects.

As with most files created in external applications, you will find that rasterized and flattened Fireworks artwork and text imports more consistently to Flash, but you also lose all the benefits of having editable vector art and text fields. Although the option for launching Fireworks at any time to edit the original PNG file does make rasterized Fireworks images less limiting than other bitmaps, it is usually worth the little extra time you might need to spend simplifying your artwork to get it to import to Flash with vectors and editable text intact. Any special fills or textures that have been applied to your text in Fireworks are lost if you choose to preserve editable text on import to Flash.

Note

Although gradients imported from FreeHand are converted to raw Flash shapes with gradient fills, gradients imported from Fireworks are converted to Movie Clip symbols that appear in the library in a folder labeled Fireworks Objects. **It is still possible to edit the gradient fill just by opening the symbol in Edit mode (or double-clicking the symbol instance). ■**

Caution

If you import a Fireworks PNG file by cutting and pasting into Flash, all vector elements are rasterized into a flattened bitmap image. ■

Copying and pasting a bitmap into Flash

Here's how to use the Clipboard to import a bitmap into Flash:

1. **Copy the bitmap from your image-editing application to your Clipboard.** (Most programs support the Ctrl+C or ⌘+C shortcut key.)

2. **Return to Flash and make sure that you have an active, unlocked layer that you can paste the bitmap into;** this can be on the Main Timeline or on any symbol timeline.

3. **Paste the bitmap onto the Stage by choosing Edit ⇨ Paste in Center from the menu** (Ctrl+V or ⌘+V).

Caution

When you are pasting a selected area from Photoshop, any transparency (alpha channel) is ignored or renders with unpredictable patterns that you'll have to mask out in Flash. The bitmap name is also replaced with a default numbered asset name. In most cases, results are much more consistent if you import the image file instead of copying and pasting it into Flash. ■

Applying color effects, alpha, and filters to bitmaps

A bitmap has some of the same advantages as the native Flash symbol types: It is automatically added to the library when you import it, and instances can be dragged onto the Stage and even used in motion tweens. However, filters and color (and alpha) effects are not available in the Properties panel when you select a bitmap instance. If you want to change the alpha settings or color tint of an imported image or apply any of the Flash filters, you must first convert the bitmap into a symbol.

Convert the bitmap into a Flash symbol type (F8) — use Movie Clip or Button symbol behavior if you want to use Flash filters. You can use the same name for the symbol instance as the original bitmap image. Filters and Color Effect settings are available in the Properties panel when you select the new (converted) symbol instance. Unfortunately, if you have placed other instances of the raw bitmap in your Flash file before nesting the bitmap in a symbol, not all the instances of the bitmap are automatically linked to the symbol you create, and you cannot use the Swap button to insert a Flash symbol instance in place of a bitmap instance.

Tip

Library folders are very helpful for managing large sequences of images that need to be converted into symbols. I usually create a "Bitmap source" folder and an "Image symbol" folder to make it easy to keep track of where all the assets are. Keep in mind that edits to the bitmap are visible in the Flash symbol, but changes to the Flash symbol do not change the original bitmap. ■

Of course, using an external image-editing program is always an option, too. The features I describe in the next section can assist you if you plan to edit images outside of Flash.

Setting Bitmap Properties

The Bitmap Properties dialog box, shown in Figure 13.9, has several options that are used to control the quality of your imported bitmaps. Settings in the Bitmap Properties dialog box override the default JPEG compression setting for the document that is controlled in the Flash tab of the Publish Settings dialog box (File ➪ Publish Settings).

FIGURE 13.9

The Bitmap Properties dialog box controls the compression settings applied to bitmaps imported into Flash.

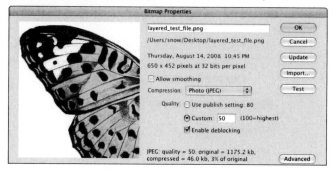

Tip

The Advanced button expands the Bitmap Properties dialog box to show Linkage properties. In addition to importing or exporting for runtime sharing, bitmaps can be set to export for ActionScript. If you decide to enter or modify Linkage properties for a bitmap after it has been imported, you can access these same options by selecting the symbol in the library and choosing Linkage from the contextual menu or from the Options menu. ■

Follow these steps to use the Bitmap Properties dialog box:

1. **Open the Library panel by choosing Window ➪ Library (Ctrl+L or ⌘+L) to access bitmaps in your current project (.fla).**

2. **Double-click one of the bitmap's icons, or use the contextual menu for a selected image to open the Bitmap Properties dialog box.** You can also select Properties from the Library Options menu, or, with the bitmap highlighted, click the Properties button at the bottom of the Library panel.

3. Now, set the properties of your bitmap as needed:

- **Preview window:** This displays the bitmap according to the current settings.

Tip

Although the preview window in the Bitmap Properties dialog box may show only a small portion of your image, you can move the picture around within the preview window by clicking and dragging the image to view different areas. ∎

- **Name:** This is the name of the bitmap, as indicated in the library. To rename the bitmap, highlight the name and enter a new one.

- **Image Path, Date, Dimensions:** Beneath the filename, Flash lists the local path, dimensions, and date information for the source of the imported image (not available if you pasted the image from the Clipboard).

- **Update:** This feature enables you to re-import a bitmap if it's been altered outside of Flash. Flash tracks the original location of the imported bitmap and looks for the original file in that location when the Update button is clicked.

- **Import:** This opens the Import Bitmap dialog box. When using this button, the new imported bitmap replaces the current bitmap (and all instances, if any), while retaining the original bitmap's name and all modifications that have been applied to the image in Flash.

- **Test:** This button updates the file compression information, which appears at the bottom of the Bitmap Properties dialog box and the image in the preview window. Use this information to compare the compressed file size to the original file size after you have selected new settings.

- **Allow smoothing:** Select this check box to enable Flash to anti-alias, or smooth, the edges of an image. Results may vary according to the image. Generally, this is not recommended for non-scaled graphics because it can soften the image. However, smoothing can be beneficial for reducing jagged edges on low-res images scaled in an animation. Figure 13.10 shows the effect of smoothing applied to a GIF image (top) and smoothing applied to a JPEG image (bottom).

- **Use imported JPEG data/Use publish setting:** If the imported image is a JPEG, the first option appears — select this check box to avoid double JPEG compression. If the image is not a JPEG, the second option appears — select this check box to apply the global JPEG Quality setting defined in the Publish Settings dialog box for your current document. To apply a new compression setting for an image, click the Custom radio button and enter a value between 1 and 100. Click the Test button on the right to update the preview window. You will also see compression comparison info at the bottom of the panel. Custom settings are not recommended for imported JPEGs because they result in double JPEG compression. On uncompressed source files, higher-quality settings produce more detailed images but also larger file sizes.

FIGURE 13.10

Compare the images with Flash smoothing (right) to the images with no smoothing (left).

Scale 100

Scale 200

GIF no smoothing   GIF allow smoothing

Scale 100

Scale 200

JPEG no smoothing   JPEG allow smoothing

FIGURE 13.11

Top: A GIF image imported to Flash by using PNG/GIF (Lossless) compression (left) and imported with forced JPEG (Lossy) compression (right). Bottom: A JPEG image imported to Flash by using JPEG (Lossy) compression (left) and imported with forced PNG/GIF (Lossless) compression (right).

- **Enable deblocking:** This new option for smoothing specifically designed to help reduce banding and JPEG artifacts is available when you apply Custom compression (but only if you are targeting Flash Player 10 in your Publish settings). It can almost make double JPEG compression work — but you always get better results if you find a way to avoid recompressing JPEG images.

Note

The Quality settings applied in the Bitmap Properties dialog box are not visible in the authoring environment. The quality for images displayed on the Stage appears the same regardless of the Flash JPEG settings. You will see a difference in the image (and the file size) only when you publish the movie (.swf). You can see smoothing and deblocking in the authoring environment, making it easier to decide which images look better with smoothing applied. ■

Cross-Reference

For specific bitmap compression recommendations for different types of source files, refer to the "Making Sense of Bitmap Compression" section, later in this chapter. ■

Being prepared for common problems

Flash retains existing JPEG compression levels on any imported JPEG image, but if a Custom setting is specified in the Bitmap Properties dialog box, it applies additional JPEG compression (set in the Quality field) when the movie is published or exported. Recompressing an image that has already been compressed usually leads to serious image degradation, due to the introduction of further compression artifacts. When importing JPEGs, you'll note that the Use imported JPEG data radio button is selected by default in the Bitmap Properties dialog box. This is the preferred setting because recompressing a JPEG is generally detrimental to image quality.

Tip

If you import JPEG images, make sure that you either test the results of further JPEG compression or select the Use imported JPEG data radio button in the Bitmap Properties dialog box, which is accessible from the Flash library. ■

You can apply compression settings to each individual bitmap in the library with the Flash Bitmap Properties dialog box to determine the quality that you need before you use the general JPEG settings in the Export Movie or Publish Settings dialog box. Any Quality defined in the Bitmap Properties dialog box overrides the JPEG Quality in Publish Settings. To apply the Publish Settings compression to an image, you must select the Use document default radio button in the Bitmap Properties dialog box.

Cross-Reference

I discuss JPEG export settings for Flash movies (.swf) in greater detail in Chapter 20, "Publishing Flash Movies." ■

Cross-browser consistency

I've received more than a few queries about image formats and Flash's capability to transcend issues of browser inconsistency, so here's the answer. Many image formats, such as PNG, are not supported across all browsers. When you import such an image format into Flash and publish or export to the SWF format, you have accomplished browser independence, because the Flash movie (.swf) is browser independent and the image has been encapsulated within the SWF format. (The image is not being sent to the browser in the imported format and then magically empowered to display.) Conversely, if you export any Flash document (.fla) to PNG or to any other format that's subject to cross-browser inconsistency, browser independence is lost.

Using the Bitmap Buttons in the Properties Panel

When a bitmap is selected in the Document window, the Properties panel displays the bitmap's name, symbol type, current size, and X, Y location. In addition to these basic bitmap properties, the Properties panel offers two useful options: the Swap button and the Edit button.

Swap

The Swap button opens the Swap Bitmap dialog box (shown in Figure 13.12), allowing you to specify a different bitmap from the current project library to replace the bitmap selected in the Document window. This can be considered a localized equivalent of the Import option of the

Bitmap Properties dialog box. Instead of replacing the original bitmap symbol in the library and all instances of the image, the Swap button simply replaces the currently selected bitmap instance without altering the symbols in the library or any of the other instances of the bitmap that may occur in your project. (This feature is also available from the application menu under Modify ➪ Bitmap ➪ Swap bitmap.)

FIGURE 13.12

The Swap Bitmap dialog box lists all the bitmap symbols available in your current project library.

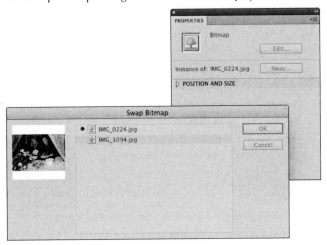

Edit

The Edit button in the Properties panel opens the selected bitmap for editing outside of Flash, either in your default image-editing application or the application that was used to save the bitmap file, if it is installed on your system. After you edit the image and choose Save, it automatically updates in the Flash document. If you prefer to select a specific application for editing a bitmap, select the bitmap in the library before choosing Edit With from the options menu or the contextual menu. The Edit With menu item launches the Select External Editor dialog box that enables you to browse or search for a specific application installed on your system (or network). When you have selected the application of your choice, it launches and the bitmap opens for editing.

Note

Bitmaps imported from Fireworks (as .png) or Photoshop (as .psd) with individual layers specified as editable objects cannot be edited with an external image editor, so the Edit button is not visible in the Properties panel when these items are selected in the Flash authoring environment. ■

Making Sense of Bitmap Compression

Although I did some sample testing to try to show you all the possible image-compression combinations and the final results, the truth is that the optimal settings are entirely dependent on the quality of the original image and the final appearance needed in the context of your design. The main goal when testing various compression strategies should always be to find a balance between image quality and file size. The ideal balance will vary depending on the purpose the image serves in your presentation. For example, when using bitmap images in animation sequences, you may find that you can get away with using higher compression settings because the detail in the image may not be as important as it would be if you used the image in a catalog or some other presentation where the detail and color would be more critical.

The following compression workflows are intended to serve only as general guidelines. You will have to experiment with the specific value settings in each case to find the best results for your particular content and project needs.

24-bit or 32-bit lossless source files

If you have 24-bit (or 32-bit including an alpha channel), high-resolution source images saved without compression in PNG, PICT, PSD, or TIFF format, you have two workflow options:

- **Set JPEG compression in the Bitmap Properties dialog box:** If you want to control the compression applied to each imported image individually, set a Custom JPEG compression (Quality) setting that achieves the best balance of image quality and file size for each imported image in your library. This approach gives you the option of applying more compression to some images than to others.

- **Set JPEG compression in the Publish Settings dialog box:** If your source images have similar color and content, as well as consistent resolution, you may find it more efficient to use the compression settings in the Publish Settings dialog box to apply the same JPEG compression to all of your images. This makes it faster to test different compression settings on all the images in your project at once. If this is the workflow that you choose, make sure that the Use document default quality radio button is selected in the Bitmap Properties dialog box for each imported image. This ensures that the Quality settings in the Publish Settings dialog box are applied when the Flash movie (.swf) is published.

Tip

If you want to test and set different compression settings for individual layers in an imported Photoshop file, you can do this in the Publish settings section of the Import dialog box. Choose Lossy compression and select the Custom button, then enter a value between 0 and 100 in the Quality field. Use the Calculate bitmap size button to apply the compression and check the file size of the image (or layer). This feature enables you to apply different levels of compression to individual layers within a Photoshop image. ∎

The main benefit to importing uncompressed source files is that you are not tied to a specific resolution and thus maintain the option of changing compression settings at any time in the development process. The main drawback is that your project files (.fla) are much larger, and each time you test your movie (.swf), you have to wait for Flash to apply JPEG compression on the images. This might not seem important at first, but the cumulative time loss over the course of developing a project does add up.

Tip

As I mentioned previously, it can be helpful to work with lower resolution placeholder images as you develop a project. You can use the Import option in the Bitmap Properties dialog box to load your high-resolution images in the final stages of the project. ∎

The image formats PNG-24, PSD, PICT, and TIFF also support alpha channels when they're saved with 32-bit color. Alpha channels enable the import of complex masks that might otherwise be difficult to create in Flash. You may be surprised to see that even after you apply Flash JPEG compression to an imported PNG, PSD, PICT, or TIFF image, the transparency is maintained.

Caution

Although Fireworks files are saved with the .png file extension, the options for importing Fireworks PNG files are different from those for importing PNG files saved from Photoshop. For more information about importing Fireworks PNG files, see the section "Importing Vector Artwork," later in this chapter. ∎

8-bit lossless source files

Source files in 8-bit formats are restricted to 256 (or fewer) colors and are optimized to a file size that is Web friendly. These files are usually saved in GIF or PNG-8 format and are best suited for graphics that have simple shapes and limited colors, such as logos or line drawings. PNG-8 and GIF files can still support an alpha channel, but unlike 24-bit images, you will not want to apply any JPEG compression to these files when they're brought into Flash.

Caution

To avoid display problems, when exporting GIF files with transparency for use in Flash, the index color and the transparency color should be set to the same RGB values. If these settings are not correct, transparent areas in the imported GIF may display as solid colors in Flash. For more information on this issue, refer to the Adobe TechNote on Transparency support in Flash at www.adobe.com/support/flash/ts/documents/ transparent_bitmaps.htm. ∎

Applying JPEG compression to 8-bit files generally results in larger files and degraded image quality (refer to Figure 13.7). To preserve the clean graphic quality of 8-bit images, follow these steps:

1. **In the Import dialog box or in the Bitmap Properties dialog box, make sure that Lossless (PNG/GIF) compression is selected.** This is the default for imported 8-bit images, but it never hurts to double-check to ensure that it hasn't been changed by mistake.

2. **Decide whether to leave the default setting for Allow smoothing in Bitmap Properties.** The image will have sharper edges if this option is unchecked, so it is best to make a decision on this setting depending on whether you prefer smoothed edges when the image is scaled larger.

Remember that the JPEG Quality specified in Publish Settings does not apply to imported images that have been set to Lossless compression in the Bitmap Properties dialog box.

Source files with lossy compression

Although JPEG is the native bitmap compression format in Flash, you may want to use an alternative application for optimal JPEG compression on images. In our experience, JPEG compression from Fireworks often produces smaller file sizes and more consistent image quality than JPEG compression applied in Flash. If you have created an optimized Web-ready JPEG by using your preferred lossy compression method or a client has delivered source files in JPEG format, you will want to avoid adding additional compression to these images when importing to Flash.

If you find that a JPEG file size is not reduced enough to fit the parameters of a particular project, it is better to go back to the uncompressed source file to redo the JPEG compression than it is to apply additional compression in Flash. As in all media production, double JPEGing images in Flash produces diminishing returns: By the time you get the file down to a size that you want, it has so many compression artifacts that it is generally unusable. By going back to the uncompressed source file and adjusting your compression settings to produce a new JPEG file, you end up with a cleaner image and a smaller file size than you would by compounding the JPEG compression in Flash.

For optimal results when importing JPEG images to Flash projects, the main settings to consider are the Use imported JPEG data and the Allow Smoothing check boxes in the Bitmap Properties dialog box:

- To maintain the original JPEG compression of your imported image, simply select the check box to Use imported JPEG data from the Bitmap Properties dialog box. When this check box is selected, the original compression is preserved and the JPEG Quality specified in Publish Settings is not added to your imported JPEG image.

- Smoothing is only advised if you will be scaling the JPEG image in Flash and you want to minimize the jagged edges with anti-aliasing. The compromise of Smoothing is that the image also appears slightly blurred — this may or may not be desirable, depending on the detail in the original image.

Although you can clear the Use imported JPEG data check box and choose a setting in the Quality field, remember that this compression is added to the compression on the original image and causes inferior results.

Tip

If you are targeting Flash Player 10, you can take advantage of a smoothing option available in the Bitmap Properties dialog box when you choose to apply Custom compression to imported images. To see if it helps your image look better, select the Enable Deblocking check box and use the Test button to update the image in the preview window. You will notice the benefit of deblocking more clearly if you are using Quality settings below 50. ∎

Converting Rasters to Vectors

Have you ever wanted to take a scan of a "real" pen-and-ink drawing that you made and turn it into a vector graphic? It's not hard to do, and the results are usually pretty close to the original (see Figure 13.13). You can also turn continuous-tone or photographic images into vector art, but unless the image is very high contrast, the converted version will not likely bear much resemblance to the original. However, this can be useful for aesthetic effects.

Compare the raster version (left) of the sketch to its traced vector version (right).

As described in Chapter 9, "Modifying Graphics," bitmap images can be traced in Flash to convert them to vector shapes. Earlier in this chapter, Figure 13.3 illustrated why this is not recommended for complex photographic images — the file size will be huge and the image quality will not be as satisfactory as the original bitmap. However, converting rasters to vectors allows you to create some unique visual effects in Flash. After an image has been traced, you can use any of the Flash tools available for shapes, including the Distort and Envelop options of the Free Transform tool. You can also select parts of the image individually to modify colors, or even add custom gradient or bitmap fills.

The Trace bitmap command is different from using the Break Apart command on a bitmap. When an image is broken apart, Flash perceives it as areas of color that can be modified or sampled for use as a fill in other shapes. Break Apart actually duplicates the automatic conversion handled by the Color panel to show bitmaps from the library in the bitmap fill menu. Although you can modify images that are broken apart with the drawing and painting tools, you cannot select shapes within the image with the Selection tool or apply the Optimization command, Smooth/Straighten options, or Distort and Envelop modifiers as you can with a traced vector image.

To apply Trace Bitmap, select a bitmap image (such as a scanned drawing) that has been imported to Flash (ideally with lossless compression and no Smoothing) and placed on the Stage; then choose Modify ➪ Bitmap ➪ Trace Bitmap from the application menu to open the Trace Bitmap dialog box, as shown in Figure 13.14.

Use the Trace Bitmap dialog box to select settings for converting a raster image into vector shapes.

I detail the settings for the Trace Bitmap command in Chapter 9, but the default settings can be a good place to start. Higher Color Threshold and Minimum Area values reduce the complexity of the resulting Flash artwork, which means smaller file sizes. This process is most effective when applied to simple images with strong contrast. In these cases, tracing a bitmap graphic can actually reduce the file size and improve the appearance of the scaled image. Traced vector images scale seamlessly without any loss of quality.

Tip

The vector lines and fills created by tracing an imported bitmap are not always exact, but you can use the Smooth and Straighten modifiers or any of the other drawing tools to "touch up" the artwork. ∎

In order to get the best results from using Trace Bitmap, I advise reducing the number of colors in the original image before importing it to Flash. Figure 13.15 shows an imported image that was converted to indexed color and reduced to ten colors in Photoshop before saving as a GIF image for import to Flash. After the image is traced, you can simplify the shapes further by applying the Optimize command (Modify ➪ Shape ➪ Optimize), which simplifies the image and reduces the final file size. You can also use any of the drawing tools to further modify the image.

A reduced-color GIF image (left) can be traced and then cleaned up and simplified by using the Optimize command and Eraser tool in Flash (right).

Using External Vector Graphics

All artwork drawn in Flash is vector based; however, not all vector graphics created in other applications import seamlessly to Flash. As shown in Table 13.1, Flash is friendly to external vector formats, including FreeHand and Adobe Illustrator. Some vector graphics may be simple objects and fills, whereas others may include complex blending or paths that add significant weight to a Flash movie. Although most vector graphics are by nature much smaller than raster graphic equivalents, don't assume that they're optimized for Flash use.

Importing vector graphics from other applications is fairly simple and straightforward. However, because most vector graphics applications are geared for print production (for example, publishing documents intended for press), you need to keep some principles in mind when creating artwork for Flash in external graphics applications:

- **Limit or reduce the number of points describing complex paths.**
- **Limit the number of embedded typefaces (or fonts).** Multiple fonts add to the final movie's (.swf) file size. As described later in this chapter, converting fonts to outlines is one way to avoid adding extra fonts to your Flash file.
- **To ensure color consistency between applications, use only RGB colors (and color pickers) for artwork.** Flash can use only RGB color values and automatically converts any CMYK colors to RGB colors when artwork is imported. Color conversions can produce unwanted color shifts.

Note

When Flash imports a vector file with any placed grayscale images, the image is converted to RGB color, which also increases the file size. ∎

- **Unless you're using FreeHand or Fireworks, you may need to replace externally created gradients with Flash gradients, or accept the file size addition to the Flash movie.** Gradients created in other drawing applications are not converted to editable Flash gradients when the file is imported; instead, they are rendered as complex banded graphics with clipping paths or as rasterized, bitmap images.
- **Preserve layers where possible to help keep imported artwork organized.** Some vector formats use layers, and Flash can recognize these layers if the graphic file format is correctly specified. Layers keep graphic elements separate from one another and can make it easier to organize items for use in animation.
- **If the artwork you are importing includes large areas of solid color, such as a plain background, consider excluding those parts of the graphic from import.** They can easily be replaced in Flash after the more complex parts of the artwork are brought in.

Importing Vector Artwork

The import dialog boxes for Adobe Illustrator files (in .ai or .eps format) and Photoshop files (in .psd format) enable fairly precise control of how these files are translated when brought into Flash — including unique settings for each layer, if needed. The other good news is that unlike Flash CS3, Flash CS5 also imports most EPS files. Sadly, PDF workflows that were supported before Flash CS3 are still not an option. Vector graphics from many other applications can be imported into Flash with relative ease by using the Import to Stage or Import to Library command. Browse for files by using the All Files setting or specify Adobe Illustrator, Photoshop, FreeHand, or PNG (Fireworks) file in the Import dialog box. Layered files and files with bitmap and vector elements open an Import Options dialog box with relevant settings. Use these settings to control how your file is handled in the Flash authoring environment. As long as you do *not* choose to import as bitmap, vector graphics are generally imported as editable groups either on the Main Timeline or in a Movie Clip Timeline.

Tip

Flash CS5 supports the import of EPS files created with Adobe Illustrator. However, to import editable graphics from PDF files to Flash CS5, they must still be opened in Illustrator and resaved in AI or EPS format. ■

Note

Simple bitmap files such as single-layer TIFF, GIF, or JPEG files do not require any custom settings and import directly (without opening an Options dialog box), after you browse for the file and choose Import. ■

Vector artwork is saved in the library on import only if it includes clipping paths or gradients that cannot be converted to editable Flash fills. In these cases, Flash automatically adds a folder of nested graphic symbols with masks or bitmap symbols to the library to preserve the appearance of elements that cannot be converted to drawing objects or simple grouped shapes.

You can also copy and paste or even drag and drop artwork from external applications, but this gives you less control over how the vector information is translated in Flash — for example, transparency or special fill types may be lost and any layers are flattened into the currently selected Flash layer.

Because generic numbered layer names, such as Layer 1, may be redundant with layers already present in your Flash document, it is helpful to give layers meaningful names in the original file before importing to Flash. To avoid unexpected color shifts, you should convert your color space to RGB in any external application before saving files that will be imported to Flash.

Caution

You must specify Illustrator 7 or later in the Adobe Illustrator document options when saving AI files to ensure color consistency for artwork imported to Flash. If you choose Illustrator 6 or lower format, RGB values are not saved and color shifts may result. ■

To import a vector file to Flash, simply follow these steps:

1. To import a file to the Stage of your Flash document, make sure that you have an empty, unlocked layer selected, and choose File ⇨ Import ⇨ Import to Stage.

2. In the Import dialog box, choose a file format to browse by using the Files of Type (Win) or Show (Mac) menu.

3. Find the vector file that you want to import and select it from the file list.

4. **Choose Import.** If the application you are importing from includes options for how the artwork will be placed in Flash, you are prompted to make choices from an Import Options dialog box. Depending on your options, the artwork is imported to a single layer or to multiple layers or keyframes in your main Flash timeline or to a Movie Clip symbol timeline after you click OK.

Note

If you choose to rasterize the vector artwork into a bitmap image when importing to Flash, remember to apply JPEG compression by using the Quality setting in the Bitmap Properties dialog box; or if the Use document default quality radio button is selected, set JPEG Quality in the Publish Settings dialog box before exporting your Flash movie (.swf). ■

5. To edit the imported graphic with Flash shape tools, ungroup the elements (Shift+Ctrl+G or Shift+⌘+G) or double-click parts of the group or drawing object until you are able to select strokes and fills in Edit in place mode.

Tip

Double-clicking a grouped item or drawing object takes you into Edit in place mode, but if the item is in a compound group, you may have to continue double-clicking to dive into the nested elements until you are able to isolate the stroke and fill of one part of the group for modification. ■

6. To store elements in the library so that they are reusable, convert them to graphic symbols or Movie Clip symbols.

Tip

If you have imported a layered sequence into multiple Flash keyframes on the Main Timeline, consider cutting and pasting the frames into a new Movie Clip symbol to keep the Main Timeline uncluttered. ■

Although you can scale, move, or rotate the grouped elements, to modify individual parts of the graphic you must either ungroup the elements or dive into Edit mode until you are able to select the strokes and fills of a particular element.

Note

Where possible, imported graphics are interpolated as Flash drawing objects. This makes it easier to edit stroke and fill properties without having to ungroup or click into Edit mode. ■

Any small inconsistencies in fill style are easy to fix after the elements are ungrouped in Flash. Remember that you can delete fills, add strokes, scale, or otherwise modify the imported artwork with any of the Flash tools.

To make the artwork efficient to reuse and update, it is best to convert the whole graphic into a symbol. If you intend to animate parts of the graphic individually, convert these into discrete symbols and place them on separate layers.

Cross-Reference

For more information on working with drawing objects and grouped artwork in Flash, refer to Chapter 9, "Modifying Graphics." For more information on using symbols, refer to Chapter 6, "Symbols, Instances, and the Library." ■

Tip

If you use a program such as FreeHand, Illustrator, or InDesign that enables you to define Flash-compatible symbols and layers in your graphic files, you can save some time when the file is imported to Flash. ■

Copying and pasting a vector image into Flash

Here's how to use the Clipboard to import a vector image into Flash:

1. **Select all vector elements that you want to include.**

2. **Copy the selected items from your vector drawing application to the Clipboard.** Most programs support Ctrl+C or ⌘+C.

3. **Return to Flash and make sure that you have an active, unlocked layer that you can paste the vectors into.** This can be on the Main Timeline or on any symbol timeline.

4. **Paste the graphics onto the Stage by choosing Edit ➪ Paste in Center from the menu (Ctrl+V or ⌘+V).** If you are pasting from Illustrator, you will see the Paste options dialog box (shown in Figure 13.16), which enables you to control how the copied vector artwork is converted when it pastes into Flash. If you are pasting from Fireworks, you see the normal Fireworks Import options dialog box (shown earlier in Figure 13.8) that enables you to select where the artwork is pasted and how it is interpreted in the Flash authoring environment.

5. **You may want to ungroup, regroup, or move parts of the pasted graphic onto new layers in your Flash document for better organization and for animation.**

FIGURE 13.16

The Paste options dialog box for Illustrator artwork enables you to select how graphics are converted when they are pasted into a Flash document.

Importing Adobe Illustrator files

Illustrator is one of the most commonly used applications for transferring vector artwork into Flash. When importing Illustrator files, you can preserve editable vector paths, text fields, and most gradient and pattern fills in addition to named layers and Illustrator symbols. Figure 13.17 shows the options available from the Illustrator Import dialog box, which is opened when importing files with the Illustrator extension (.ai or .eps) into Flash.

The Illustrator Import dialog box is used to specify how the graphics and file structure of an Illustrator (.ai or .eps) file are handled when brought into Flash.

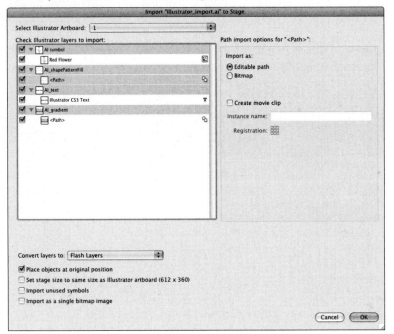

Although Illustrator can export a variety of file formats, including SWF, EPS, and PDF, the native AI format gives you the most editing options for files imported to Flash. As with the Photoshop importer, the default options for the Illustrator importer can be modified in Flash preferences (shown in Figure 13.18), and relevant settings can also be adjusted uniquely on-the-fly for each file that you import.

FIGURE 13.18

Preferences for the Illustrator Import dialog box can be modified in Flash to establish default settings that best match your workflow.

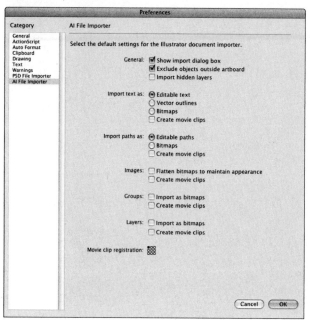

Remember to convert your Illustrator file to RGB color mode. If the file is in CMYK, you are warned with an incompatibility note in the import dialog box. If you proceed to import the file without changing the color settings in Illustrator, the file is converted automatically from CMYK to RGB on import to Flash, and this may cause unexpected color shifts. To ensure seamless translation of Illustrator elements imported into Flash, observe the following guidelines:

- Any placed grayscale elements in Illustrator are converted to RGB color when imported to Flash, which may increase file size.

- Be cautious with compound shapes: When importing overlapping elements that you want to keep intact in Flash, place them on separate layers in Illustrator and import the layers into Flash. If items on a single layer are overlapping when imported, they may be divided or merged at intersection points in the same way as ungrouped shapes created in Flash. Graphics on separate layers are converted into drawing objects on import to Flash and do not accidentally merge unless you break them apart into raw shapes.

- Flash supports up to 15 colors in an imported gradient fill. If a gradient created in Illustrator contains more than 15 colors or special styles (such as contour), Flash uses clipping paths to interpret the gradient. Clipping paths increase file size. To work around this issue, use gradients that contain 15 or fewer colors and use standard gradient styles in Illustrator or replace the imported gradient with a Flash gradient fill as described later in this chapter.

As shown in Figure 13.19, Flash recognizes text and simple gradient or pattern fills imported from Illustrator, making it easy to edit these elements directly in the Flash authoring environment. Effects supported in Flash are also imported and editable. Effects that are not yet available in the Flash authoring environment can either be imported as rasterized bitmaps to preserve their appearance, or they can be sacrificed to preserve the editable content in the file.

FIGURE 13.19

You can edit Illustrator files directly in Flash, but you still need to convert shapes and text elements into symbols to store in the library for reuse. Layer and symbol names from the Illustrator file can also be transferred to the Flash file on import.

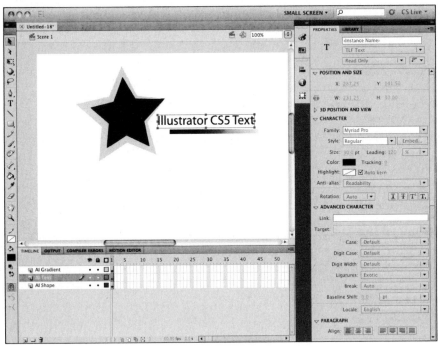

Note

Imported Illustrator symbols are preserved as editable elements, and they are automatically stored in the library in a folder that Flash creates. ∎

Tip

Remember that gradients created in Adobe Illustrator can be directly exported to SWF format as Flash gradients. However, if the gradient contains more than 16 colors or uses special alignment (such as contour gradients), Flash adds clipping paths when it is imported. Also, remember that Flash always interprets FreeHand blends as a series of paths, which can increase file size and sometimes add banding to the blend. ∎

Optimizing Vectors

All vector graphics are made up of paths in one shape or another. A path can be as simple as a straight line with 2 points, a curved line with 2 points, or 500 or more points along an irregular shape or fill. For this reason, vector graphics are best suited for graphic images such as logos, architectural drawings, and clip art that do not include continuous tones. Fonts are also made up of paths. As you've seen with Flash-drawn graphics, you can scale them to any size without any loss of resolution, unlike raster (bitmap) artwork, which cannot scale larger than its original size without loss of resolution.

Note

Vector graphics are eventually rasterized, so to speak. The vector formatting for drawn shapes and text is more of a simplified storage structure that contains a mathematical description (that is, smaller than a bit-for-bit description) of an object or set of objects. When the vector graphic is displayed, especially with anti-aliasing, the video card needs to render the edges in pixels. Likewise, the PostScript RIP (Raster Image Processor) of a laser printer needs to convert the vector information, or an EPS (Encapsulated PostScript) file, into printer "dots." ∎

When you use imported vector graphics in Flash movies, you should minimize the number of points describing curved lines or intricate outlined graphics (for example, "traced" raster images). The problem with creating cool graphics in vector-based applications such as Illustrator, FreeHand, and 3D Studio Max is the large number of points used to describe lines. When these graphics are imported into Flash, animations are slower and harder to redraw (or refresh) on the computer screen. In addition, the file size of the Flash movie grows considerably. Most vector applications include features that enable you to optimize or simplify artwork before importing it to Flash.

There are also a number of ways that you can simplify artwork after it has been imported to Flash. I have discussed many of these Flash features in previous chapters, but I briefly summarize them here.

Interpreting complex vector artwork

Specialized graphics programs, such as Adobe AfterEffects and Autodesk 3ds Max, can create some astonishing vector-based graphics. However, when you import vector versions of those graphics into Flash, they either fall apart (display horribly) or add unrealistic byte chunks to your Flash movie. But this doesn't mean that you can't use these intricate graphics in your Flash movies. You can try several different procedures with intricate vector artwork, including smoothing, as described previously, to make complex graphics more Flash friendly.

Depending on the specific use of the artwork, you may also be able to output small raster equivalents that won't consume nearly as much space as highly detailed vector graphics. However, in some instances, the best solution is a bit more labor intensive. To get just the right "translation" of a complex vector graphic in your Flash movie, you may need to try redrawing the artwork in Flash. Sound crazy and time consuming? Well, it's a bit of both, but some Flash designers spend hour after hour getting incredibly small file sizes from "hand-tracing" vector designs in Flash.

Another approach is to loosen up and make stylized interpretations of complex graphics using fewer lines. For example, if you made a highly detailed technical drawing of a light bulb and wanted to bring it into Flash, you could import the original version of the drawing into Flash, place it on a locked guide layer, and use Flash drawing tools to re-create a stylized sketch version of the object (see Figure 13.20).

Web Resource

Third-party Flash SWF tools can help to speed up the work of optimizing vector artwork — for example, Electric Rain's Swift 3D can simplify 3-D models and output .swf files. Visit their site to learn more about software that can help you with your 3-D Flash work: www.erain.com. ∎

Converting text to outlines

Another aspect of vector graphics that you need to keep in mind — especially when working with other designers — is font linking and embedding. With most vector file formats, such as Illustrator, FreeHand, or EPS, you can link to fonts that are located on your system. However, if you give a design file to someone who doesn't have those fonts installed, he or she won't be able to see or use the fonts. Some formats enable you to embed fonts into the document file, which circumvents this problem. However, whether the fonts are linked or embedded, you may be unnecessarily bloating the size of the vector graphic.

You can break apart imported text in Flash by using the Modify ⇨ Break Apart command (Ctrl+B or ⌘+B). You have to first break the text into letters and then break them apart a second time to get basic shapes.

You can also convert any text into outlines (or *paths*) in most drawing or illustration programs (see Figure 13.21). In FreeHand, select the text as a text block (with the Selection tool, not the Text tool) and choose Text ⇨ Convert to Paths. In Adobe Illustrator, select the text as an object and choose Type ⇨ Create Outlines.

FIGURE 13.20

Compare the original imported vector artwork of the light bulb (left) with the stylized version hand drawn in Flash (right).

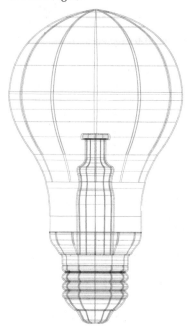 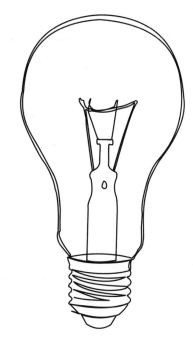

FIGURE 13.21

Make sure that you have finished editing your text before converting it into outlines. The text at the top can be edited, whereas the text at the bottom can be modified only as individual shapes.

Editable text

Editable text

If you have a lot of body text in the graphic, you may want to copy the text directly into a Flash text box and use a _sans, _serif, or other device font. These fonts do not require additional file information (as embedded fonts do) when used in a Flash movie.

Optimizing curves

You can also reduce the complexity of paths within Flash by using the Modify ⇨ Shape ⇨ Optimize command. This has the same effect as the Simplify command in Illustrator or FreeHand, with a couple of extra options. When working with bitmaps or symbols, be sure to use the Modify ⇨ Break Apart command, and if you are working with a group, ungroup it (Modify ⇨ Ungroup) before you use the Optimize command (Alt+Shift+Ctrl+C or Option+Shift+⌘+C) — you can't optimize groups or symbols. Figure 13.22 shows the effect of maximum smoothing on a complex seashell graphic.

FIGURE 13.22

A complex vector graphic simplified with maximum smoothing

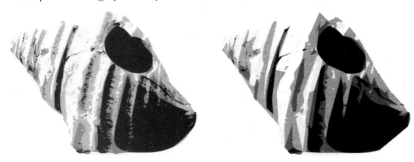

Cross-Reference

For a more detailed description of the Optimize curves options, refer to Chapter 5, "Drawing in Flash." ■

Runtime bitmap caching

Flash 8 introduced *bitmap caching*, a feature designed to improve rendering performance of animation that uses complex vector graphics. The Cache as bitmap option appears as a small check box in the Display section of the Properties panel when a Movie Clip instance is selected in the Flash authoring environment (as shown in Figure 13.23). If bitmap caching is enabled, Flash converts the vector graphic into a bitmap image at runtime. The advantage of using this technique is evident only as you start to build more complex files that require Flash to redraw elements in an animation. If your vector artwork is optimized and uses very few points, converting from vector to bitmap does not offer any performance improvements. However, if you have created a highly detailed vector background that you will use to layer with other animated elements, Flash can dedicate more resources to rendering smooth animation if the background is converted into a cached bitmap. Because the bitmap graphic is rendered only once, the speed and smoothness of your animation are not hindered by Flash having to constantly redraw the points and lines that make up your vector background. These same principles apply if you are using a very complex vector graphic that is motionless but modified with filter effects. Bitmap caching makes it possible for Flash to convert the complex vectors into a simpler pixel surface while it dedicates resources to rendering the filter transformations.

FIGURE 13.23

Bitmap caching can be enabled in the Display section of the Properties panel when a Movie Clip or Button symbol is selected in the authoring environment.

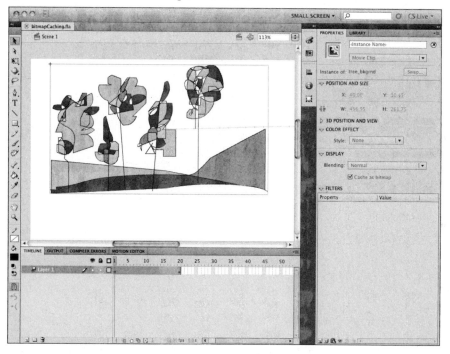

On the CD-ROM

The file shown in Figure 13.23 is included on the CD so you can test the performance difference yourself, even with a simple tween. Open the `bitmapCaching.fla` file in the `ch13` folder and test the movie to preview the animation with Cache as bitmap enabled. Then select the Movie Clip, turn off Cache as bitmap, and test the movie again. You should notice that the graphics look cleaner (less screen redraw) and the animation plays more smoothly when Cache as bitmap is turned on. ∎

There are a few limitations to bitmap caching that you should keep in mind:

- Bitmap caching uses significantly more memory than rendering vectors. Use bitmap caching only when it will noticeably improve the performance (smoothness) of your animation.

- If your animation requires a very close zoom on vector content, it may look pixilated if the cache as bitmap option is enabled for that item.

- Bitmap caching will fail if it is applied to a symbol that is larger than 2,880 pixels tall or wide.

- If the graphic with bitmap caching enabled is nested inside of another symbol that is rotated or scrolled, bitmap caching is ignored for the nested graphic.

- If the Flash Player runs out of memory (producing an error), bitmap caching is canceled.

Working with XFL: The New Flash Format

For many years, the .fla file format used to save Flash project information has been closed to third-party developers. This is why you haven't seen applications that can save or publish in the .FLA format Some applications (from Adobe and from other companies) publish .swf files, but the SWF format is mainly a display format and does not support development and editing like the FLA format does. In a radical move, Adobe has opened the .fla file format to an XML-based file format called XFL. Third-party applications can create .fla files using the XFL specification that works seamlessly with Flash.

AfterEffects CS5 can export XFL files, and Flash can open (not import) these files from Adobe applications and from third-party sources. XFL files, like FLA files, include all the assets used in a project along with the XML information that describes the structure of the file. XFL presents a brand-new opportunity for developers and designers to share files and even create their own tools. The impact of this new file format may be gradual, but if it catches on, it will be the Flash format of the future. For now, most people just need to know that XFL files can be opened in Flash with similar results to opening any other Flash project file.

Tip

The XFL format refers to both a file extension and a specification that works behind the scenes for FLA files. In Flash CS5, .fla files are actually zipped files that include a folder of binary assets (sounds, images, and so on) used in the project and XML files that describe the internal database of the Flash document. To see these files, simply Use the Save As command to save the file as an uncompressed file. ∎

Summary

- Flash can use a variety of external media, which enables you to select the most effective format for various types of content.

- Bitmap smoothing has improved with newer versions of Flash. Even rotated or scaled bitmaps look less jagged on the edges than they did in early versions of Flash.

- Deblocking is a new type of smoothing designed to reduce compression artifacts on bitmap images imported to Flash files targeting Flash Player 10.

- Bitmaps are best suited for photographic images or images that contain detailed shading and/or complex color blends.

- Bitmaps can be converted to vector artwork in a variety of ways. This process works best on simplified bitmap images or when it is used to create special image effects.

- Vector graphics are most often used for logos, line drawings, and other artwork that does not include complex patterns and blends.

- Flash supports the import of layers, editable text, and gradients from some graphics applications, including Photoshop, Fireworks, and Adobe Illustrator. You will need to put some care into preparing files to get the best results, but being able to reuse your file structure and editable elements created in other applications can save you a lot of time.

- Flash CS5 includes preferences for the Illustrator and Photoshop importers that enable you to control how layered files from these applications are translated into Flash.

- Flash has fairly robust support for imported gradients and preserves many Fireworks effects as editable filters in the Flash authoring environment.

- The bitmap caching feature in Flash can greatly improve playback performance in movies that use complex vector graphics as background elements or scrolling content.

- Most graphics applications include their own options for reducing the complexity of vector art. However, using Flash's various tools for optimizing vector artwork can also be an effective way to reduce your final file size.

- XFL is the new open file format used behind the scenes in .fla filesIn Flash CS5, you can open XFL files (created in AfterEffects or InDesign), and save your .fla files in an uncompressed form to view the XML data used to define your document files.

14

Displaying Video

One of the most exciting features introduced with Flash Player 6 was the power to add digital video footage to a Flash movie file (.swf)! Designers and developers alike had long awaited this feature. With Flash Player 6 or later, video encoded with Sorenson Spark codec can be played without relying upon additional browser or system plug-ins such as Apple QuickTime or RealNetworks RealPlayer. Flash Player 7 improved the capabilities and performance of video playback, enabling you to load .flv files directly into Flash movies at runtime from a standard Web server, without the aid of Adobe Flash Media Server. With Flash Player 8, you could take advantage of another video codec, the On2 VP6 codec, which yields better compression (that is, smaller file size) with superior image quality to the Sorenson Spark codec used in Flash Player 6 and 7. With Flash Player 9, the power of full-screen mode was added to present your Flash Video content larger than life! Now, with Flash Player 10, you can deploy video by using the AVC/H.264 video codec and the AAC audio codec — these codecs are among the highest-quality codecs available today.

Note

Adobe added the AVC/H.264 and AAC playback capabilities to Flash Player 9.0.115, also known as Flash Player 9 Update 3. That version was made available to the public between the Flash CS3 and Flash CS4 releases. ■

Adobe has added more tools to make it easier for you to integrate video into your Flash movies. In this chapter, I show you how to perform a wide range of video procedures, from importing a source clip to playing the video clip within the FLVPlayback component.

Integrating Video: The Solutions

In Flash CS5, there are three ways in which you can deploy video content. The following sections provide a high-level overview of these methods.

Note

You can also play Flash-compatible video content in Adobe AIR applications by using any of the methods discussed in the following sections. ■

Loading a Flash Video file at runtime

Starting with Flash Player 7–compatible movies, you can load Flash Video files (.flv) at runtime. When we say "runtime," we mean that you can create a separate Flash Video file (.flv), upload it to your Web server, and use ActionScript code or a component to load the video directly into your Flash movie (.swf) as it plays in the browser. You can create Flash Video files by:

- Importing a video file into a Flash document, and then exporting the Embedded Video symbol from the document's Library panel as a Flash Video file (.flv)

- Encoding a Flash Video file with the Adobe Media Encoder CS5 application, which is part of Flash CS5

- Using a third-party video compression tool designed to export Flash Video files (.flv) such as Sorenson Squeeze, On2 Flix, Telestream Episode Pro, or Rhozet Carbon Coder

Real-time streaming a Flash Video file at runtime

In the previous section, you learned that it's possible to load a Flash Video file directly into a Flash movie file (.swf) as it plays in a browser. However, when you use this type of loading, the Flash Video file is loaded and cached as any other asset accessed at runtime. As such, if you have a large video file but only want to watch the last portion of the video, you'll have to wait until most of the video file has been downloaded.

One way you can offer your users the fastest access to Flash Video files (.flv) is to stream the video in real time with Adobe Flash Media Server (also known in previous editions as Macromedia Flash Communication Server) or a Flash Video Streaming Service provider. With this server technology, a Flash Video file is only temporarily cached on the playback computer. You can more easily protect copyrighted material, and users can seek to any point in the video with minimal wait times.

Note

Adobe Flash Media Server is a specialty server product that works separately from a standard Web server. You can set up and install your own Flash Media Server, or you can purchase hosting from companies such as Influxis.com. ■

Web Resource

For a list of Flash Video Streaming Service providers, see the Flash Video Hosting Providers section at `www.flashsupport.com/links.` ■

Embedding video into a Flash movie

The third method that you can use to view video is to embed the video file in the Flash document file (.fla), where it is then published directly inside the Flash movie file (.swf). This method is compatible with Flash Player 6 or later movies. Adobe Media Encoder CS5 can encode your video with the Sorenson Spark, On2 VP6, or the AVC/H.264 codec (discussed later in this chapter). It's important to understand that these codecs don't require additional plug-ins for playback — the Web user needs only to have Flash Player 6 or later (for Sorenson Spark), Flash Player 8 or later (for On2 VP6), or Flash Player 9.0.115 or later (for AVC/H.264) installed on the browser. Flash-compatible video codecs do not use any system-level video codecs; the codecs are built into the Flash Player plug-in.

When you import a video clip as an Embedded Video object, the video is stored in the library as a Flash Video file (.flv).

Caution

You can only embed .flv files in a Flash document. AVC/H.264 video content cannot be embedded into a Flash document. ■

Tip

You can also use a third-party application to create a Flash movie file (.swf) with embedded video. ■

Importing the Video

Digital video, as with other external media assets that Flash can import, is something that you need to create before working with it in a Flash document. In today's economic climate, you might not only be a Web designer or developer; you might also wear the part-time hat of a videographer. Be sure to read our coverage of video in Appendix D for a primer on shooting and producing better-looking video. The appendix also discusses the various video formats that you can import into Flash CS5.

After you have created a video file in the desired import format, you're ready to prepare the video for use in a Flash movie. This section introduces you to the AVC/H.264, On2 VP6, and Sorenson Spark codec options available for Flash-based video content. In the latter half of this section, we walk you through the process of importing one of the sample files on this book's CD-ROM.

An overview of codec options

Flash Player 9.0.115 and later can play MPEG-4 files that use the AVC/H.264 codec. This codec is one of the best video codecs available today and is used for a number of video deployment applications, from Web-based video to Blu-ray HD content to high-quality consumer video camcorders. The AVC/H.264 codec has been licensed by Adobe from MPEG-LA (www.mpeg-la.com) for noncommercial playback in the Flash Player. Flash Player 8 and later movies have the capability to use another high-quality video codec, On2 VP6. This codec, created by On2 (www.on2.com), has been licensed by Adobe to be used with Flash Player distribution. Both the AVC/H.264 and On2 VP6 codecs feature superior compression and image quality compared to the Sorenson Spark codec introduced with Flash Player 6.

Note

As mentioned in the previous paragraph, Adobe has licensed only a noncommercial usage of the AVC/H.264 codec. MPEG-LA has a summary of licensing options for commercial content on their Web site at www. mpegla.com. ∎

Web Resource

You can view side-by-side comparisons of equivalent bitrate Flash Video files with an example on this book's support site at www.flashsupport.com/bonus/codec_comparison. You can compare the quality of an AVC/H.264, On2 VP6, and Sorenson Spark file. ∎

The AVC/H.264 codec, however, doesn't come without a price. Playback of AVC/H.264 content requires Flash Player 9.0.115 or later. Adoption of Flash Player 9.0.115 is already past the 80 percent mark, as evidenced by recent surveys Adobe has conducted. Furthermore, AVC/H.264 files may require more CPU power and more RAM (memory) to play compared to older Flash-compatible video codecs. Slower machines, such as Apple Power Mac G3 computers and Pentium II computers, may have trouble playing back AVC/H.264 and On2 VP6-encoded files.

Tip

Make sure that you test your Flash Video file's playback on a variety of machines so that you accurately gauge your expectations for the target audience(s) of your Flash content. Larger video frame sizes (greater than 320 × 240) with newer video codecs might tax the CPU of any computer using less than an Intel Core 2 Duo processor. ∎

If you're willing to sacrifice some visual quality of your Flash Video content and want the security of appealing to a larger audience (that is, people who have Flash Player 8 or later), you may want to encode your video content with the On2 VP6 codec. Flash Player 8 is available on over 98 percent of desktop computers in mature markets! You could also opt to use the Sorenson Spark codec, which has the greatest compatibility of all Flash-based video codecs. Sorenson Spark video requires more data rate (or bitrate) than AVC/H.264 or VP6 for equivalent quality. The Sorenson Spark codec is the least processor-intensive codec available in the Flash Player — if you need to target slow devices, you may find that the Sorenson Spark codec is the best codec to use. The quality of Sorenson Spark encoding is not necessarily poor compared to other Web video codecs; however, Adobe Media Encoder CS5 can only encode video in the Basic edition of the codec. You need to use a third-party video encoder to encode video with the higher-quality Pro edition of the Sorenson Spark codec.

Note

Flash Player 8 and later can decode only VP6 video content. If you're broadcasting live camera output from a Flash movie to a Flash Media Server application, Flash Player 6 and later use the Sorenson Spark codec for all live streams. Adobe has released the Flash Live Media Encoder, a stand-alone application that can stream live AVC/H.264 or On2 VP6 video to a Flash Media Server. For more information on this product, go to: `www.adobe.com/products/flashmediaserver/flashmediaencoder.` ■

Video codecs can compress image data in two different ways — temporally and spatially. A temporal compression algorithm, or *interframe compressor*, compares the data between each frame and stores only the differences between the two. A spatial compression algorithm, also known as *intraframe compression*, compresses the data in each frame, just as the JPEG format compresses data in a still image. Most video codecs designed for Web playback, including AVC/H.264, On2 VP6, and Sorenson Spark, do not use a lossless compression technique. Rather, some color and detail information is thrown out in an effort to minimize the amount of data saved with each frame. For example, if the original video source recorded a sunset with 80 shades of orange, the compressed version of the sunset may include only 50 or fewer shades of orange. You may have noticed the extremes of lossy compression in Web videos where a person's face is hardly distinguishable, looking more blocky than human.

Note

Historically speaking, most new codecs developed in the last few years rely upon the ever-increasing computer processor speeds to efficiently decompress each frame of video on playback. For this reason, you may want to test video playback on a number of machines and devices that support your targeted Flash Player version and video decoding. ■

All Flash-based video codecs use interframe (temporal) compression, but they also use intraframe compression when making keyframes. (You will see how tricky keyframes can be in just a moment.) A keyframe in video footage is similar to a keyframe in a Flash timeline. A keyframe defines a moment in time where a significant change occurs. For example, if a section of video has three hard cuts from one scene to another to another, the compressed version of that video should have a keyframe at the start of each scene. A keyframe then becomes the reference for subsequent frames in the video. When the following frame(s) are compared to the keyframe, only the differences are remembered (or stored) in the video file. As soon as the scene changes beyond a certain percentage, a new keyframe is made in the video. Video keyframes are created while the movie is being compressed.

Caution

Video keyframes are the reason you should be careful with special effects or video filter usage in transitions from scene to scene in your video production software. The more frequently your video changes from frame to frame, the more keyframes your video file needs. Keyframes take up more file size than interframes between the keyframes, and if your video data rate can't accommodate the creation of those keyframes, the overall quality of your video degrades. ■

Compressing video with Adobe Media Encoder CS5

Flash CS5 ships with a stand-alone application called Adobe Media Encoders CS5. On Windows, you can find this application at Start Menu ⇨ Programs ⇨ Adobe Media Encoder CS5. On Mac, on your startup disk, look for the Adobe Media Encoder CS5 application in the `Applications/Adobe Media Encoder CS5` folder.

When you run the Flash CS5 Video Encoder application, you see the interface shown in Figure 14.1.

FIGURE 14.1

The Adobe Media Encoder CS5 application

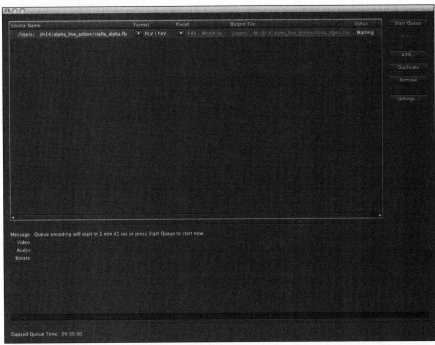

The Adobe Media Encoder CS5 works as a batch processor for the same encoding engine that is used for other CS5 applications such as Adobe Premiere CS5 and Adobe After Effects CS5. You can specify all of your encoding settings in the Adobe Media Encoder CS5 application. Some benefits to using Adobe Media Encoder CS5 include:

- **Adding multiple source video files:** You can drag and drop (or browse to) one or more video source files on your computer or network into the application's queue.

- **Duplicating settings:** After you've specified the settings on one source clip, you can click the Duplicate button to add another entry in the queue with the same clip and its settings. You can then adjust the new duplicate's settings to a different data rate.

- **Saving the queue:** You can save the list of video clips in the queue to resume work in another session. However, you can't save the queue list as an external project file.

- **Deinterlacing capability:** If you have a source clip that is captured from an interlaced video source, such as NTSC footage from a miniDV or DVCAM camcorder, you can de-interlace the footage in Adobe Media Encoder CS5.

- **Cue point import/export:** Adobe Media Encoder CS5 enables you to save your cue point data to an external XML file and create cue point data in an XML file that can be imported directly into the Cue Points tab of the tool.

Note

The encoding options available in Adobe Media Encoder CS5 depend on your installed Adobe CS5 applications. If you only have Flash CS5 installed, your encoding presets are limited to the FLV and F4V file formats. ■

You start the encoding process by dragging a video source file to the queue pane. You can also click the Add button to browse to a video source file on your system. After a source file is added to the queue, you determine how you want to compress the original source clip into the Flash-compatible video file. From the queue pane (shown in Figure 14.2), you can choose from 22 presets as a starting point for your preferred compression options.

The encoding profiles are listed in two formats, FLV (Flash Player 8 or later) and F4V (Flash Player 9.0.115 or later). Each of these formats has three general preset groups:

- **Same as Source:** These presets create an output file whose dimensions and frame rate match that of the source file.

- **HD (High Definition) quality:** The presets labeled with 1080p and 720p create output files with frame rates that match the source file and dimensions that are quarter, half, or full resolution HD. You should only use HD source files with dimensions that match the preset name. For example, if you have a 1080i or 1080p (1920 × 1080, or anamorphic 1440 × 1080) HD source file, you should use the 1080p presets if you want HD quality encoded Flash video. If you have a 720p (1280 × 720) HD source file, you should use the 720p preset for HD quality. 1080p quarter resolution HD is actually a misnomer; if you choose an HD quarter resolution preset, the output size is 480 × 270, which is one-sixteenth the resolution of 1920 × 1080. The 1080p half resolution HD preset is also a misnomer, and is the "real" quarter resolution preset, producing output at 960 x 540.

- **Web quality:** These presets create various resolutions, frame rates, and data rates for deploying Flash-compatible video geared to Internet connection speeds.

FIGURE 14.2

The Preset menu in the queue panel

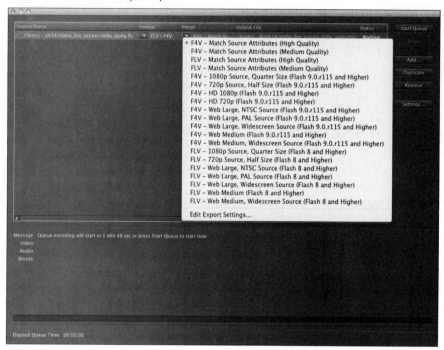

After you have selected a preset, you can customize the encoding settings by clicking the name of the preset in the queue pane. In the following sections, we explore video and audio settings available within a preset. To follow along, add a source video clip to the queue pane, select a preset, and click the underlined preset name.

Tip

If you edit a preset, the preset name changes to Custom. You can save an edited preset as a new preset to reuse within Adobe Media Encoder CS5. ∎

General export settings

On the right-hand side of the Export Settings dialog box (shown in Figure 14.3), you can edit the video and audio compression settings. At the top of the Export Settings section, you can save a customized preset, load a preset, and delete a preset. You can also choose which tracks of the source clip you want to encode. By default, the Export Video and Export Audio boxes are selected.

FIGURE 14.3

The general export settings

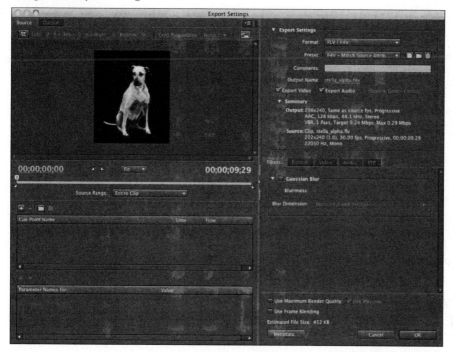

Video tab

Expand the displayed settings by clicking the mode toggle button (the double down-arrow button), shown earlier in Figure 14.3. Click the Video tab (shown in Figure 14.4) to control how the video track of the source file is encoded to the Flash Video (.flv) or the H.264 for Flash (.f4v) format.

The Basic Video Settings section of this tab has the following options:

- **Codec:** This menu selects the codec used for compression. Sorenson Spark is the codec compatible with Flash Player 6 and later, whereas On2 VP6 is available in Flash Player 8 and later. If you choose a F4V preset, the MainConcept H.264 Video codec is automatically selected.

- **Encode alpha channel (FLV only):** This option determines if an alpha channel in the source video file will be compressed and included with a FLV file using the On2 VP6 codec. We discuss the alpha channel encoding capability of the On2 VP6 codec later in this chapter.

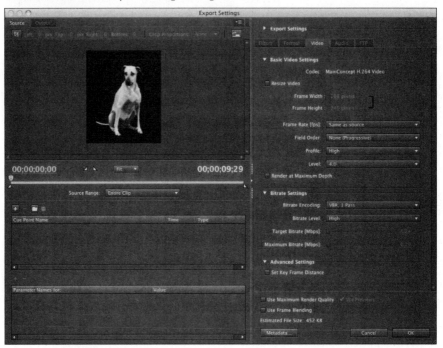

FIGURE 14.4

The Video tab of the Export Settings dialog box

- **Resize Video:** This option resizes the original dimensions of the source video clip. If selected, you can enter a new width and height for the encoded Flash Video clip. If you've captured high-resolution video footage from your DV camcorder (that is, source video with dimensions of 640 × 480 or larger), you may want to reduce the frame size to a more Web-friendly size, such as 320 × 240. You can create smaller video file sizes with a combination of smaller video dimensions and reduced data rates. If you're using DV footage (or any footage with a non-square pixel aspect ratio), be sure to use proper square pixel sizes, such as 160 × 120, 320 × 240, and so on. Unlock the constraints by clicking the chain link button to the right of the width and height fields.

- **Frame Rate:** This menu controls the encoded frame rate of the output video clip. The Same as source option encodes the video clip with the same rate as your original video clip. You can also choose fixed frame rates, from 10 frames per second (very choppy) to 30 frames per second (very smooth).

- **Field Order:** This option enables you to control interlaced output. For Flash-compatible video, you should only choose None (Progressive).

- **Profile and Level:** These options are available only for F4V and H.264 output. The Profile options include Baseline, Main, and High. If you're targeting playback on slower devices such as older Pentium or PowerMac computers, you may want to use the Baseline profile for H.264 because less processing power is required. If you're targeting modern computers, you should use the Main and High profiles. The High profile produces the best quality but requires the most processing power for playback. The Level menu's options conform your video settings to predefined H.264 specifications. Levels are defined from 1.0 to 5.1 — the higher the level, the larger the video dimensions and faster the frame rate.

The Bitrate Settings of the Video tab contain the following options:

- **Bitrate Encoding:** This option, if available for your selected codec, enables you to control how the bitrate of the video track is encoded. CBR, or Constant Bit Rate, encoding is designed for real-time streaming deployment of video. If you plan to use an Adobe Flash Media Server (or equivalent RTMP hosting service) for your video deployment, use CBR encoding. VBR, or Variable Bit Rate, encoding is designed for local or HTTP playback. If you're planning to deploy your video content on a Web server, use VBR encoding.

- **Encoding Passes:** This option determines how well the video track is analyzed during the encoding process. If you choose One, the encoder reads the source file and writes the output file sequentially frame by frame. If you choose Two, the encoder analyzes the source video clip with the first pass, looking for optimization points along the way, and then encodes and outputs the video file on the second pass. You should opt to use a 2-pass encoding setting whenever possible. The only reason you would choose 1-pass encoding is to create your output file more quickly for a draft video.

- **Bitrate:** This slider controls the data rate used by the output video clip. This setting, more than any other, influences the file size and image quality of the encoded clip. The lower the bitrate, the lower overall quality you'll see in your output clip. If your codec selection enables only one bitrate slider, the value indicates the average bitrate for the entire clip. The H.264 codec enables you specify a Target (or average) Bitrate, as well as a Maximum Bitrate. The Maximum Bitrate is available only for VBR encoding. Generally speaking, you should use a bitrate between 300 and 800 Kbps for Web-based video content.

The Advanced Settings section of the Video tab contains the following option:

- **Set Key Frame Displacement:** This option determines how often keyframes within the Flash Video content are created. As discussed earlier in the chapter, keyframes are needed to store differences between frames in the video clip. If you use the default value (deselected), Flash CS5 determines how often a keyframe should be generated. If you enable this option, you can specify your own keyframe interval with the slider. The lower the value you specify, the more frequently the encoder creates keyframes within the output video clip. The higher the value, the less frequently the encoder creates keyframes. Be very careful with custom settings here: If your data rate isn't high enough to support the keyframe interval you specify, the overall image quality is sacrificed to maintain the keyframe interval.

Audio tab

The Audio tab, shown in Figure 14.5, controls the compression settings for the audio track of the source video clip.

The Audio tab of the Encoding screen

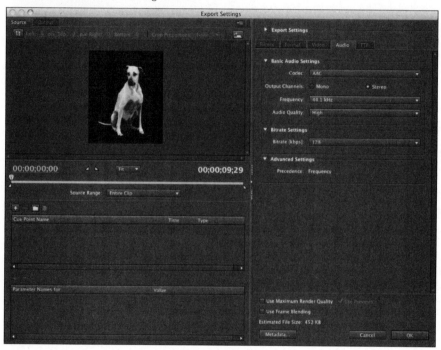

The Basic Audio Settings section of this tab has two options:

- **Codec:** This option controls the audio codec used for the output clip. If you are targeting a .flv file, you can use only the MPEG Layer 3 (MP3) codec. If you are targeting a .f4v file, you can choose variants of the AAC codec, which is the next-generation MP3 codec. AAC + Version 1 and AAC + Version 2 are more complex audio codecs that produce higher-quality audio for equivalent bitrates, at the expense of higher computer processor utilization.

- **Output Channels:** You can choose how the source video's audio track is output in the new compressed file. The Mono option mixes a stereo (dual channel) audio input into one channel. The Stereo option retains left and right channels from the source video clip. Unless your content demands stereo sound, we recommend using a single (mono) channel for audio output.

- **Frequency and Audio Quality:** If you're using the AAC codec, you can choose a sampling rate and quality setting for the audio track. We recommend you use a sampling rate of 44.1 kHz or higher at High quality.

In the Bitrate Settings section of the Audio tab, you can set the following option:

- **Bitrate:** You can modify the data rate of the audio channel, choosing a value between 16 to 256 Kbps (MP3) or 56 to 320 Kbps (AAC). Unless you're encoding high-quality musical scores, an audio data rate between 48 and 64 Kbps is usually adequate.

Note

The audio data rate is separate from the video data rate. As such, you should mentally add both rates to get a clear picture of the total data rate required for the Flash Video clip. For example, if you specify a video data rate of 400 Kbps and an audio data rate of 96 Kbps, the total data rate for the clip is 496 Kbps. ■

Cue Points section

When you view the Export Settings in advanced mode, the cue points section appears at the lower-left side of the dialog box. This section enables you to insert embedded markers within the final output video file. The details of this section are discussed later in this chapter.

Crop tool

The Crop tool is available in the Source tab located at the upper-left corner of the Export Settings dialog box. The Crop tool enables you to change the borders (or cropping) and size of your original source clip before it is encoded.

Tip

Cropping video clips might be necessary if your original footage is letterboxed (that is, black bands are above and below the actual picture area of the clip) or if you captured video with an analog video capture card that retains black borders on the video clip. ■

When you finish specifying the encoding parameters for the clip, you're ready to encode the clip. After you close the Export Settings dialog box, you can click the Start Queue button in the main window of Adobe Media Encoder CS5, and your clip will go start compressing. When the .flv or .f4v file finishes the encoding process, you can use the video file with a Flash file.

Using the Video Import wizard

In Flash CS5, you can import Flash-compatible video files by using the File ⇨ Import ⇨ Import Video command. First, we review the stages of video import. Later in this section, you can follow a step-by-step exercise that shows you how to compress a sample clip on this book's CD-ROM. You can follow along here to familiarize yourself with the process.

Note

If you want to use Flash Video in your Flash document, you must be using Flash Player 6 or later as the tar-geted version in the Publish Settings dialog box (File ➪ Publish Settings). If you want to use the On2 VP6 codec, you must target Flash Player 8 or later. If you want to use the H.264 codec, you must target Flash Player 9.0.115 or later. ∎

Choosing a target Flash Player version

Before you start using the Import Video option, you need to determine which Flash Player you want to target. The Import Video process is optimally geared to preparing output for the FLVPlayback component, available in two versions with Flash CS5. If you create or open a Flash file (ActionScript 2.0) targeting Flash Player 8 or later, the Import Video process can prepare the settings for the ActionScript 2.0 (AS2) version of the FLVPlayback component. If you create or open a Flash file (ActionScript 3.0) targeting Flash Player 9 or later, the Import Video process is enabled to set up the ActionScript 3.0 (AS3) version of the FLVPlayback component.

The options you can use during the video import vary based on the Flash Player version and ActionScript version you have selected in the Flash tab of the Publish Settings dialog box (File ➪ Publish Settings).

Choosing a source clip: The Select Video screen

When you first select the Import Video option from the File ➪ Import menu in Flash CS5, you see the Select Video screen of the Import Video dialog box, as shown in Figure 14.6. On the Select Video screen, you can browse to a Flash-compatible video file. To proceed to the next stage of import, click the Next button.

Note

On the Mac, all Next buttons within the Video Import wizard process are labeled as Continue buttons, as shown in Figure 14.6. ∎

On the CD-ROM

You can find several source clips in the `resource` folder of this book's CD-ROM. ∎

After you select a source clip, you can choose how you want to include the video clip in your Flash movie. With Flash CS5, you have three options:

- **Load external video with playback component:** This option is the default selection, enabling the wizard to automatically configure parameters for the FLVPlayback component. If you are going to deploy your video content with a Web server, choose this option.

- **Embed video in SWF and play in timeline:** This option adds the encoded video clip to the current Flash document's Library panel. Because the audio track of the compressed video clip will be within the Flash movie, you should make sure that you match the encoder's frame rate to that of your Flash movie.

Caution

Only proceed with the Embed video in SWF option if you need to insert short video clips directly into your Flash movie (.swf) file. If you're processing clips longer than a minute in duration, you should proceed with a progressive download or streaming option. ■

- **Import as mobile device video bundled in SWF:** This option inserts a source video file "as is" into the Flash file's library. If you intend to distribute mobile video formats, such as 3GP, with a Flash Lite 2.0 or later movie, you can use this option to create an embedded copy of a video file within the published Flash movie (.swf file). You should bundle only video formats that are supported by the mobile device you are targeting for deployment. (Note that the Flash Video format is not natively supported by current mobile devices running Flash Lite 2.0.)

Note

The other deployment options featured on this screen can be used for video already uploaded to a Web server or Adobe Flash Media Server application. ■

FIGURE 14.6

The Select Video screen

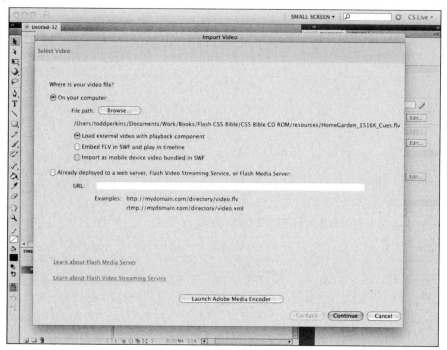

Formatting the embedded video content: The Embedding screen

If, and only if, you selected the Embed FLV in SWF and play in timeline option in the Select Video screen, you determine how you want Flash CS5 to place the encoded video content into the current document. On the Embedding screen (shown in Figure 14.7), you can choose from the following options:

- **Symbol type:** This menu lets you choose how you want the video content to be nested within the Flash document.
  - **Embedded video:** This option simply places the Flash Video clip as an Embedded Video symbol in the Library panel.
  - **Movie clip:** This option places the Flash Video clip inside of a Movie Clip symbol in the Library panel. Note that you still have a separate Embedded Video symbol of the Flash Video clip; this option saves you the step of creating a new Movie Clip symbol and placing the Embedded Video symbol onto its timeline.
  - **Graphic:** This option behaves identically to the Movie clip option, except that the video content is nested within a graphic symbol in the Library panel.
- **Place instance on stage:** This option, if selected, places an instance of the video clip on the current timeline of the Flash document. The instance will be of the symbol type selected in the menu discussed previously.
- **Expand timeline if needed:** This option, if selected, adds more frames to the current timeline of the Flash document to accommodate the length of the video clip. For example, if the timeline had 10 frames and your clip is 100 frames long, 90 new frames would be added to the timeline.
- **Include audio:** This menu controls how the audio track (if it exists) of the video asset is handled. The selected value keeps the audio track bound inside of the embedded video symbol after import. When you use this option, you control the compression of the audio track via the audio stream settings in the Flash tab of the Publish Settings dialog box (File ➪ Publish Settings). If you deselect this option, the audio track is stripped from the video asset; the audio, then, is not imported into the Flash document.

If you click the Next button from the Embedding screen, the wizard goes to the Finish Video Import screen, discussed later in this section.

Controlling the video content: The Skinning screen

If you choose the Load external video with playback component option in the Select Video screen, the next screen in the wizard process is the Skinning screen. This screen enables you to pick a control bar for the FLVPlayback component. You learn more about the options on this screen in the step-by-step exercise that follows this section.

FIGURE 14.7

The Embedding screen

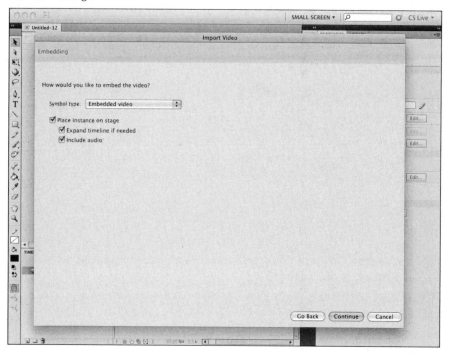

Reviewing your settings: The Finish Video Import screen

After you have taken the care to specify the encoding options you want for your Flash Video clip, you can quickly review some of the presets on the final screen, as shown in Figure 14.8. Click the Finish button to complete the video import process.

Deploying video files with Flash CS5

With Flash CS5, you have several more options for deploying and encoding video content. In this section, you learn about how to deploy an existing .flv or .f4v file that you have uploaded to your Web server. The Flash CS5 Video Import wizard automatically sets up the parameters for a new FLVPlayback component in your Flash document.

FIGURE 14.8

The Finish Video Import screen

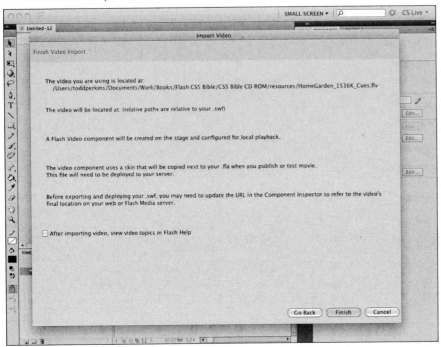

1. **Create a new Flash file.** If you want to use the updated AS3 version of the FLVPlayback component, create a new Flash file (ActionScript 3.0), which targets Flash Player 10. If you want to target Flash Player 8, create a new Flash file (ActionScript 2.0) and change the Flash Player version to 8 in the Publish Settings dialog box.

2. **Choose File ➪ Import ➪ Import Video.** The Select Video screen of the Import Video dialog box (see Figure 14.9) presents you with two options:

   • **On your computer:** This field and Browse button enable you to select a digital video source clip on your local computer or computer network.

   • **Already deployed to a web server, Flash Video Streaming Service, or Flash Media Server:** This option enables you to enter a fully qualified domain name pointing to an existing flv file on a server.

3. **Choose the second radio button option in this screen, and enter the following URL:**

   ```
   http://www.flashsupport.com/video/lizard_112k_vp6.flv
   ```

4. **Click the Next button (or Continue button on Mac) to proceed to the Skinning screen.** After the Select Video screen, the Video Import wizard takes you to the Skinning screen (see Figure 14.10).

FIGURE 14.9

The Select Video screen

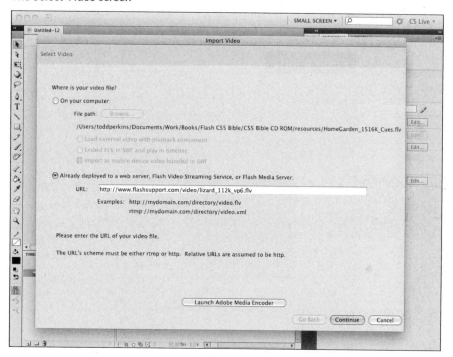

5. **Choose the playback control skin for your video clip.** This skin is used by the FLVPlayback component instance that the Video Import wizard places on to the current document's Stage at the end of the importing process. The skin options vary based on the ActionScript version and Flash Player version specified for the Flash file.

Tip

Full-screen capability is supported in Flash Player 9 or later. The ActionScript 3.0 (AS3) version of the FLVPlayback component includes skin files featuring a full-screen toggle button. Also, the AS3 version of the FLVPlayback component enables you to choose a custom skin background color during the skin selection process. ■

You can select one of several skins in the Skin menu. All these skins are separate swf files included with the Flash CS5 installation. Whichever skin you choose is automatically copied to the location of the current Flash document you're importing the video file into. This .swf skin file must be uploaded along with your Flash document's .swf file to the Web server so that the FLVPlayback component can load the skin into the Flash movie. If you prefer to make your own video playback controls to use with the FLVPlayback component, you can choose None in the Skin menu. You can also choose Custom Skin URL and enter the path (relative or absolute) to the skin .swf file you created for the FLVPlayback component.

FIGURE 14.10

The Skinning screen

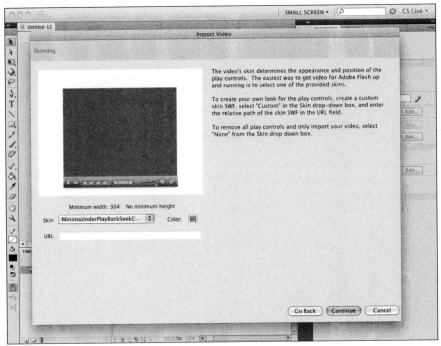

6. **After you pick a skin, click the Next button.** As shown in Figure 14.11, you are taken to the Finish Video Import screen (as described in the earlier coverage of the Video Import wizard). The Finish Video Import screen describes the steps you will need to take after you have finished the import process.

FIGURE 14.11

The Finish Video Import screen

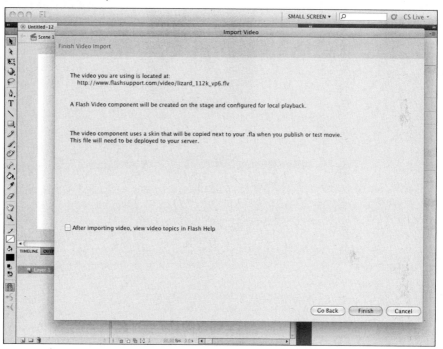

7. **Click the Finish button.** Flash CS5 loads the metadata from the .flv file you specified during the Import Video process. The width and height data from the .flv file are used to size the instance of the FLVPlayback component that Flash CS5 places in the center of your Stage area, as shown in Figure 14.12. Rename Layer 1 to **fp**, short for *FLVPlayback*. In the Properties panel, name the instance `fp` as well.

FIGURE 14.12

The FLVPlayback component

8. **Save the document as** `deploy_http_video.fla`. After you have saved the file, test the movie (Ctrl+Enter/⌘+Enter). When the movie loads, the lizard video clip plays in the FLVPlayback component instance (see Figure 14.13). The skin you selected earlier in this exercise also appears, enabling you to control the playback of the video clip.

On the CD-ROM

You can find the completed file, `deploy_http_video.fla`, in the `ch14` folder of this book's CD-ROM. ■

Tip

If you want to try loading another .flv file into the FLVPlayback instance, you don't have to repeat the Import Video procedure. Instead, select the `fp` instance on the Stage and open the Component Inspector panel (Shift+F7). Select the Parameters tab, and change the `contentPath` value (AS2) or `source` value (AS3) to the new video filename (or location). You can also change the skin file in the Parameters tab.

Also, if you want to test a skin featuring a full-screen togglebutton, be sure to use the Flash Only - Allow Full Screen template in the HTML tab of the Publish Settings dialog box (File ⇨ Publish Settings). Refer to Chapter 18 for more information on publishing Flash movies. ■

FIGURE 14.13

The remote video clip playing in the FLVPlayback component

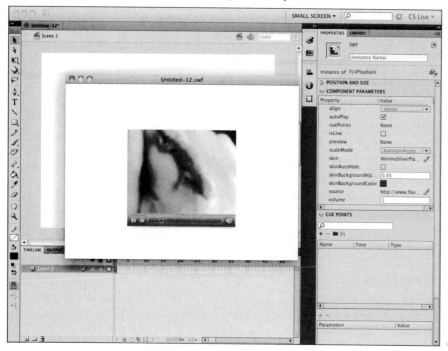

New Feature

The updated FLVPlayback component in Flash CS5 allows you to preview a movie without having to launch the Flash Player. That means you can play, pause, stop, and scrub through your video more quickly and efficiently than ever before. ■

Working with the Component parameters

You don't have to use the Video Import wizard to add an FLVPlayback component instance to your movie. In fact, you can just drag and drop the component from the Components panel (Window ⇨ Components) to the Stage of your Flash file. You can access the following parameters of an FLVPlayback component instance from the Properties panel.

Note

All these parameters can also be used in ActionScript, with the same spelling. For example, if you have an instance of the FLVPlayback component named `fp`, you can set the `autoPlay` parameter to `false` with code: `fp.autoPlay = false;`. ■

- `align`: This parameter determines how the borders of the video clip align to the display area of the FLVPlayback component. The available options are `center`, `top`, `left`, `bottom`, `right`, `topLeft`, `topRight`, `bottomLeft`, or `bottomRight`. The default value is `center`. Alignment values are apparent only if your FLVPlayback instance is sized larger than the native frame size of the video and `noScale` is the value for the `scaleMode` property.

- `autoPlay`: This parameter determines if the video loaded into the component automatically plays (`true`) or loads in a paused state (`false`).

- `cuePoints`: This property specifies the cue points that are linked to the playback of the FLV file. If you create embedded cue points (see our coverage later in this chapter), this property auto-fills within the Properties panel after you select a new FLV file with the `source` property. If you scroll down to the CUE POINTS section of the Properties panel, you can create new ActionScript-based cue points or view embedded cue points. Embedded cue points cannot be changed. We discuss cue points later in this chapter.

- `isLive`: This parameter indicates whether the video is streamed live.

- `preview`: This parameter controls which frame of the Flash Video clip is displayed in the FLVPlayback component while authoring the Flash file. When using the new version of the FLVPlayback component that ships with Flash CS5, this option is grayed out, because the FLVPlayback component uses the new Live Preview feature to allow previewing the whole video while working in Flash.

- `scaleMode`: This parameter controls how video content fits within the display area of the component. If the display area uses an aspect ratio different than that of the video content and this property is set to `exactFit`, the video stretches vertically and/or horizontally to fit the display area. If the property is set to `maintainAspectRatio`, the video content maintains its aspect ratio regardless of the display area's aspect ratio. If the property is set to `noScale`, the Flash Video clip displays at its native size, regardless of the dimensions of the FLVPlayback instance.

- `skin`: This property, when accessed in the Properties panel, opens a dialog box from which you can choose a skin swf file for the component. The values in this menu match the skins available in the Skinning screen of the Video Import wizard.

- `skinAutoHide`: This property controls if the skin .swf used for the component hides itself if the user's mouse cursor is not over the video display area. If set to `false`, the skin is always visible. If set to `true`, the skin disappears when the user's mouse cursor rolls off the component.

- `skinBackgroundAlpha`: This property controls the opacity of the skin background color. The range of values is between 0 and 1, where 1 represents full opacity (no transparency) and 0 represents full transparency (no opacity). You can specify decimal values for partial opacity, such as 0.5, which is 50 percent transparent.

- `skinBackgroundColor`: This property controls the background color of the skin. You can use the color picker for this property's value in the Parameters tab to choose a custom color.

- `source`: This property determines which .flv file is loaded into the component. You can use a relative path (for example, `myVideo.flv`), an absolute path (for example, `/videos/myVideo.flv`), or a fully qualified domain (for example, `www.flash support.com/video/lizard_112k_vp6.flv`).

- `volume`: This property controls the loudness of the .flv file's audio channel, if one exists. You can use a value in the range of 0 to 1, with 0 being absolute silence and 1 being the maximum loudness of the audio channel. You can use decimal values as well to indicate partial loudness. For example, a value of 0.5 indicates half of the original loudness of the audio track.

Using FLVPlayback Custom UI components

With Flash CS5, you can also add custom UI components specifically designed to be used with the FLVPlayback component. In ActionScript, you can tell an FLVPlayback instance to use other components for playback control. The following properties represent component references used with the FLVPlayback component:

- `backButton`: This property specifies the component to seek to cue points prior to the current playhead time.

- `bufferingBar`: This property controls which component displays the buffering status of the video clip.

- `captionButton`: This property controls which component toggles the display of captions for the video.

- `forwardButton`: This property specifies the component to seek to cue points past the current playhead time.

- `fullScreenButton`: This property specifies the component to toggle full-screen mode with the video image area of the FLVPlayback component.

- `muteButton`: This property specifies the component that can toggle the muting of the video's audio track.

- `pauseButton`: This property controls which component can pause the video playback.

- `playButton`: This property controls which component can initiate playback of the video file.

- `playPauseButton`: This property specifies which component can toggle between play and stop states of the video stream.

- `seekBar`: This property specifies the component that displays the scrubbing area and playhead control for the video.

- `stopButton`: This property controls which component stops and resets the stream back to its starting position.

- `volumeBar`: This property specifies the component that controls the volume setting of the video clip.

We show you how to practice using a few custom UI components with an FLVPlayback instance. The following steps introduce you to the process of adding a play/pause button and a seek bar:

1. In Flash CS5, create a new Flash file (ActionScript 3.0) and save it as `flvplay back__as3_custom.fla`.

2. **Rename Layer 1 to** fp. On frame 1 of this layer, drag an instance of the FLVPlayback component from the Video nesting to the Stage.

3. **In the Properties panel, name the instance** fp.

4. **Open the Component Inspector panel and click the Parameters tab.** Double-click the value for the `skin` parameter. In the Select Skin dialog box, set the Skin type to None, as shown in Figure 14.14.

5. **Create a new layer named** custom UI **and place this layer above the fp layer.**

6. **Open the Components panel and expand the Video group.** With frame 1 of the custom UI layer selected, drag an instance of the PlayPauseButton component to the Stage. Place the new instance below the `fp` instance, near the left corner.

FIGURE 14.14

The Select Skin dialog box

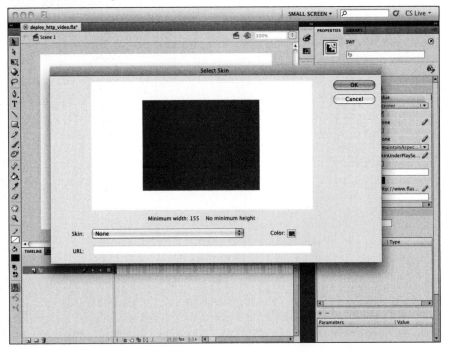

7. **In the Properties panel, name the new instance ppb, as shown in Figure 14.15.**
   Now, you need to link the ppb instance to the fp instance in ActionScript.

The PlayPauseButton component

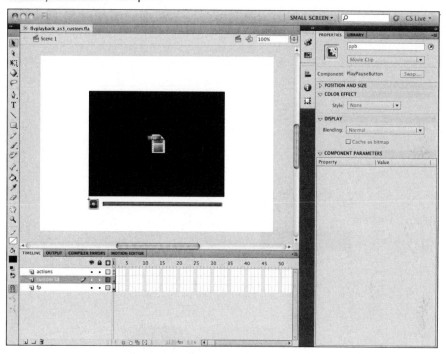

8. **Create a new layer named** actions, **and place it at the top of the layer stack.**

9. **Select frame 1 of the actions layers and open the Actions panel (F9/Option+F9).**
   In the Script pane, add the following actions:

```
//FLVPlayback fp;

fp.playPauseButton = ppb;
fp.source = "stella_raw.flv";
```

Tip

A quick way to see the code hints for an authortime instance in the Actions panel is to use a code comment specifying the data type followed by the instance name. In this code example, the FLVPlayback code hints appear for the `fp` instance because of the `//FLVPlayback fp;` line of code. ∎

10. **Save the Flash document and test it (Ctrl+Enter/⌘+Enter).** The `stella_raw.flv` file automatically plays in the `fp` instance. You can click the `ppb` instance to pause the video, and click it again to resume playback.

11. **Go back to the Flash document.** Let's add another custom UI component. Select frame 1 of the custom UI layer. From the Components panel, drag an instance of the SeekBar component to the Stage, to the right of the PlayPauseButton instance.

12. **Name the SeekBar instance** skb **in the Properties panel.** Optionally, use the Free Transform tool to stretch the width of the SeekBar instance to span the remaining width of the FLVPlayback instance.

13. **Select frame 1 of the actions layer and open the Actions panel.** Add the following bold code to the existing script:

```
//FLVPlayback fp;

fp.playPauseButton = ppb;
fp.seekBar = skb;
fp.source = "stella_raw.flv";
```

14. **Save the Flash document and test it (Ctrl+Enter/⌘+Enter).** You should see the playhead of the SeekBar instance move to the right as the video plays (see Figure 14.16).

FIGURE 14.16

The SeekBar component displaying the current position of the video

You can continue adding other custom UI components from the Components panel and specifying the new instance names to the corresponding property of the `fp` instance in the frame 1 script of the actions layer.

Tip

You can also modify the graphics used by the custom UI components. Open the Library panel to view the skin symbols in the `FLV Playback Skins` folder. ■

On the CD-ROM

You can find the completed file, `flvplayback__as3_custom.fla`, in the `ch14` folder of this book's CD-ROM. Note that this sample links to a relative path for the .flv file, located in the `resources` folder. ■

Adding Cue Points

In general terms, a *cue point* is a specific time within a video clip where something of significance occurs. For example, you might want a cue point at the start of each cut or scene within a video, or when something noteworthy is said within the audio track of a video clip. With Flash-compatible video, you can build systems that work with two types of cue points:

- **Embedded cue points:** Using Adobe Media Encoder CS5, which is included with Flash CS5, you can insert cue points within a video clip before the encoder compresses the clip. The resulting .flv file embeds each cue point on a keyframe in the video track. There are two types of embedded cue points:

  - `navigation`: This type of cue point marks the video frame as a point that the user can seek to, using the forward and back buttons of the FLVPlayback component, or with ActionScript code.

  - `event`: This type of cue point marks the video frame as a point that can be detected with an event handler in ActionScript code. You cannot seek to event cue points unless you modify the functionality of the FLVPlayback component code.

- **ActionScript cue points:** This type of cue point is one that is not embedded with the .flv file. An ActionScript cue point can be added, as its name implies, via ActionScript code. For example, if your .flv file doesn't have cue points, you can create cue points with an XML file specifying the times and names of the cue points. You can load the XML file at runtime, and pass each cue point value to the FLVPlayback component. You can specify ActionScript cue points in the new CUE POINTS section of the Properties panel for an FLVPlayback instance, or use the `FLVPlayback.addASCuePoint()` method.

New Feature

In previous versions of Flash, ActionScript cue points could only be added through the Component Parameters panel. In Flash CS5, you can add, remove, export, and import ActionScript cue points through the CUE POINTS section of the Properties panel. ■

Caution

By default, ActionScript cue points cannot be used as navigation cue points. You need to modify methods of the FLVPlayback instance in order for ActionScript cue points to work with seek buttons. ■

In ActionScript code, you can detect which type of cue point is fired during playback. A cue point object in ActionScript has a `type` property, which is set to a String value of `"navigation"`, `"event"`, or `"actionscript"`. You can also use the `fl.video.CuePointType` class to retrieve constants for these String values.

In the following steps, you learn how to use Adobe Media Encoder CS5 to create cue points for video footage of garden plants. Each plant featured in the video will have a cue point, specifying its name and the location of the name on the screen. The cue points will be used to dynamically create text fields (with drop shadows!) on top of the video. You add both navigation and event cue point types to this footage. The navigation cue points work with the forward/back seek buttons of the FLVPlayback component, and they create the text labels for each plant type. The event cue points remove the text label before the next label fades and blurs onto the Stage.

Tip

You can import and export cue points from Adobe Media Encoder CS5 to an XML file. You can then reuse the cue points with other compression settings or clips, or share the data with other members of your Flash production team. If you don't want to type all the cue point data for this exercise, simply import the `HomeGarden_CuePoints.xml` file from the `resources` folder of this book's CD-ROM into the Cue Points section of Adobe Media Encoder CS5. ■

On the CD-ROM

Make a copy of the `HomeGarden_Full-Res.mp4` file from the `resources` folder of this book's CD-ROM.

1. **Open the Adobe Media Encoder CS5 application.** On Windows, you can find this application shortcut at Start ⇨ Programs ⇨ Adobe Media Encoder CS5. On the Mac, you can find this application here: `[Startup disk]: Applications: Adobe Media Encoder CS5`.

2. **Click the Add button on the right-hand side of the application and browse to your copy of the `HomeGarden_Full-Res.mp4` file.** Add this file to the queue.

3. **In the Preset column for the new video clip, choose FLV – Web Large, NTSC Source (Flash Player 8 or later).**

4. **Click the preset name in the queue to access the Encoding Settings dialog box, as shown in Figure 14.17.** Make sure that the dialog box is toggled to advanced mode.

The Encoding Settings dialog box

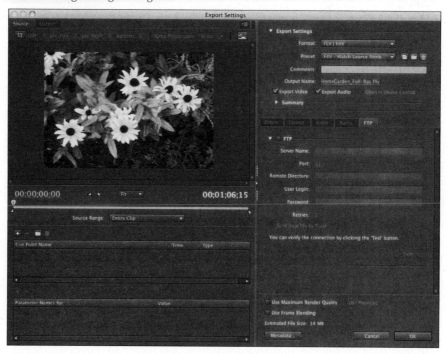

5. **In the Cue Points section, located at the lower left of the dialog box, click the Add (+) button to add a cue point at the start of the video clip.** Change the name of the cue point to **plant_001**. Change the Type menu to Navigation. Under the parameters area of the dialog box, click the Add (+) button to add a new parameter named **label**. For the value, type **Black-eyed susans**. Add another parameter named **position** with a value of **rb**. This position value stands for "right bottom" and it will be used to properly position the label text for the cue point. See Figure 14.18 for these settings.

Caution

Watch your spelling for parameter names and values. You must consistently name your parameters in order for your custom ActionScript code to work. ∎

FIGURE 14.18

The new plant_001 cue point

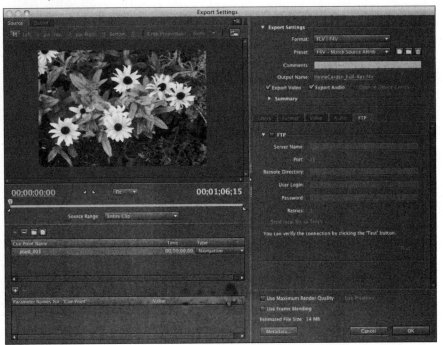

6. **Now, scrub the video playhead below the preview area to the next scene.** The next cue point should be added at 4;17 seconds, as shown in Figure 14.19. Add a cue point by clicking the Add (+) button on the left, and name the cue point **exit_001**. Change the Type to Event. For this exercise, you won't need any parameters for event cue points.

Tip
You can click the playhead marker and nudge it with the Left and Right Arrow keys to finesse the playhead time. ■

7. **Now that you're familiar with the cue point addition process, add the cue points at the approximate times shown in Table 14.1.** (Feel free to choose your preferred values.) When you are finished, your cue point list should resemble Figure 14.20.

FIGURE 14.19

The exit_001 cue point

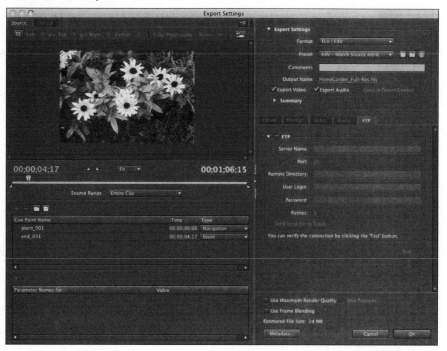

Tip

Double-check the label and position parameters for each cue point before you start the encoding process. Also, if you don't want to type each cue point into the Cue Points tab, you can click the folder icon to import the complete set of cue points, HomeGarden_CuePoints.xml, from the resources folder of this book's CD-ROM. ■

8. **In the Export Settings area of the dialog box, click the Audio tab.** Change the Output Channels to Mono and the Bitrate to 16 Kbps. This particular video clip has an audio track that is silent (meaning, there is an audio track, but it just recorded silence).

Tip

Even if you don't need an audio track, we advise you to include a silent audio track for the clip in your video-editing program. We have found that video playback for larger files is significantly closer to the clip's frame rate if there is an audio track to sync to. ■

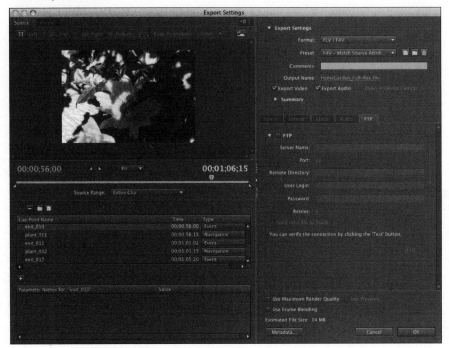

FIGURE 14.20

The complete cue list

9. **Click OK to close the Export Settings dialog box.** Click the Output File value, and type **HomeGarden_1516K_Cues.flv**. This new filename indicates the total bit rate of the FLV file and the presence of cue points.

10. **Click OK to accept all the new encoding settings.** Back in the main application window, click the Start Queue button to begin the encoding process. The lower area of the application window displays the encoding progress, as shown in Figure 14.21.

11. **Before you close the Adobe Media Encoder CS5 application, choose File ⇨ Save Queue.** This option saves your clip's settings (and cue points!) so you can reedit and reencode if you made a mistake.

Tip

You can export cue point data to an XML file in the Cue Points section of the Export Settings dialog box. Click the disk icon in the cue points toolbar to specify an output filename. The cue points file for the sample footage is already saved and included in the `resources` folder of this book's CD-ROM. ■

Now you're ready to build the Flash document to play the .flv file.

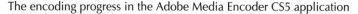

FIGURE 14.21

The encoding progress in the Adobe Media Encoder CS5 application

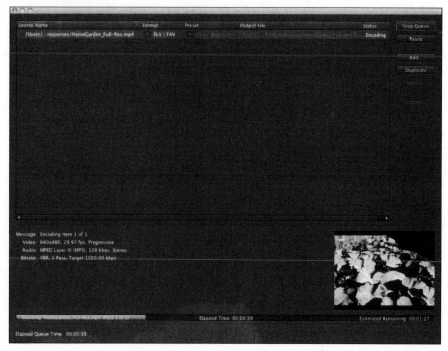

12. **Open Flash CS5 and create a new Flash file (ActionScript 3.0).** Save the document as `cuepoints_embedded_as3.fla`, in the same location as the new .flv file compressed in Step 9.

Tip

You can also use FLV files with embedded cue points with the ActionScript 2.0 version of the FLVPlayback component. ■

13. **Change the dimensions of the Flash document to 800 × 600 in the Modify ➪ Document dialog box.**

14. **Rename Layer 1 to** fp. On frame 1 of this layer, drag an instance of the FLVPlayback component from the Components panel to the Stage. In the Properties panel, name the instance fp.

15. **In the COMPONENT PARAMETERS section of the Properties panel, select a skin for the FLVPlayback instance.** For our example, we used the `MinimalUnderPlay BackSeekCounterVolMuteFull.swf` skin. For the source parameter, browse to the `HomeGarden_1516K_Cues.flv` file created in Step 9.

16. Using the Live Preview of the video on the stage, scrub to the portion of the video that shows strawberries.

17. **In the CUE POINTS section of the Properties panel, add a new ActionScript cue point by clicking the Add ActionScript cue point button.**

18. **Change the name of the new ActionScript cue point to strawberries.** In a later step, we use ActionScript to have a button navigate to this point in the movie.

19. **In the Instance Name field, type vid as the instance name of the FLVPlayback component.** Doing so enables you to communicate to the FLVPlayback component through ActionScript.

20. **On the stage, create two button symbols — one labeled Pumpkin and one labeled Strawberry (Figure 14.22).**

FIGURE 14.22

Button symbols for Pumpkin and Strawberry

21. **Select the Pumpkin button on the main Timeline and set its instance name to pumpkin in the Properties panel, and set the Strawberry button's instance name to strawberry.** This will allow us to connect these buttons to ActionScript code.

22. Select the Pumpkin button and open the Code Snippets panel. The Code Snippets panel is under Window ⇨ Code Snippets.

23. In the Code Snippets panel, expand the Audio and Video folder, and double-click the Click to Seek to Cue Point snippet to add ActionScript code to a new layer in the Timeline.

New Feature

The Code Snippets panel is new to Flash CS5, and offers a simplified way to create ActionScript 3.0 code. In Chapter 15, I discuss the Code Snippets panel in more detail. ∎

24. In the Actions panel, near the bottom of the code generated for you, replace both occurrences of video_instance_name with vid. Remember, vid is the instance name of the FLVPlayback component you set in Step 19.

25. Replace the code that says Cue Point 1 with plant_005. plant_005 is the name of the embedded cue point of the Giant pumpkin, as set earlier in this exercise. You can verify this in the CUE POINTS section of the Properties panel.

26. Repeat Steps 22–25 for the Strawberries button, but instead of typing plant_005 for the cue point name, type strawberries. The name strawberries comes from the ActionScript cue point you added in Step 18 of this exercise.

27. Save the file and test the movie in the Flash Player (Control ⇨ Test Movie). Click the buttons to see them navigate to the appropriate sections of the movie.

On the CD-ROM

You can find the completed file, `cuepoints_embedded_as3.fla`, in the `ch16` folder of this book's CD-ROM. ∎

TABLE 14.1

Cue Points for the HomeGarden_Full-Res.mp4 File

Time	Name	Type	Label	Position
00;00;00;00	plant_001	Navigation	Black-eyed susans	rb
00;00;04;17	exit_001	Event	–	–
00;00;05;01	plant_002	Navigation	Echinacea	rb
00;00;09;24	exit_002	Event	–	–
00;00;10;07	plant_003	Navigation	Dinnerplate dahlia	rt
00;00;14;25	exit_003	Event	–	–
00;00;15;07	plant_004	Navigation	Pumpkin patch	rt
00;00;23;05	exit_004	Event	–	–

(continued)

TABLE 14.1	(continued)			
Time	Name	Type	Label	Position
00;00;23;12	plant_005	Navigation	Giant pumpkin	lb
00;00;28;06	exit_005	Event	–	–
00;00;28;19	plant_006	Navigation	Huckleberry bush	lt
00;00;33;06	exit_006	Event	–	–
00;00;33;13	plant_007	Navigation	Huckleberries	rt
00;00;38;07	exit_007	Event	–	–
00;00;39;08	plant_008	Navigation	Strawberries	rb
00;00;43;07	exit_008	Event	–	–
00;00;44;03	plant_009	Navigation	White roses	lb
00;00;48;21	exit_009	Event	–	–
00;00;49;03	plant_010	Navigation	Mallow	rb
00;00;56;00	exit_010	Event	–	–
00;00;56;13	plant_011	Navigation	Shrub rose	rt
00;01;01;02	exit_011	Event	–	–
00;01;01;15	plant_012	Navigation	Chocolate mint bush	rb
00;01;05;20	exit_012	Event	–	–

Working with Video Alpha Channels

One of the most exciting features of the On2 VP6 codec is its capability to utilize alpha channels within video content. Flash CS5 on its own cannot create a true alpha channel for a video clip: You need to use a dedicated video effects application, such as Adobe After Effects or Adobe Premiere Pro to create a matte for the video track. The process of selecting areas of the video to mask for transparency is known as *keying*. Essentially, you use the video application to select a key color, which is used to create a mask for the video. The accuracy and sharpness of a mask depend on the quality of the keying plug-in. Adobe After Effects offers several keying plug-ins to help you professionally matte your video content.

For the purpose of our coverage in this book, we provide you with the QuickTime .mov files that already have masks created by Adobe After Effects. The general process for keying involves a series of steps:

1. **Acquire video footage.** To successfully mask a subject in the video, you should shoot the subject against an evenly lit green screen or blue screen. You may have seen special effects footage shot on such screens, for action thrillers such as *The Matrix*.

2. **Import the footage into a video effects application.** Using a program such as Adobe After Effects, you can add the footage to a composition. Within the composition, you can add key filters to select the green or blue areas of the content.

3. **Render the footage with an alpha channel.** After you have key filters in place, you can render the footage with an alpha channel. You need to use a video codec that supports alpha channels, such as the Animation codec. In After Effects, make sure you choose RGB + Alpha in the Channels menu of the Video Output settings.

4. **Encode the footage with the On2 VP6 codec.** After you have the rendered QuickTime file, you can process the file with Adobe Media Encoder CS5 or another Flash Video encoding tool. In the Flash Video encoding settings, make sure that you choose the Encode alpha channel check box.

Live action footage

In this section, you learn how to use footage of our dog Stella that was shot against a green screen. The footage already has an alpha channel that was created in Adobe After Effects. You superimpose the footage of Stella on a static .png image imported into a Flash document.

On the CD-ROM

Make a copy of the `stella_alpha.mov` file found in the `alpha_live_action` folder of this book's CD-ROM. ∎

1. In Flash CS5, open the `live_action_starter.fla` from the `ch14/alpha_live_action` folder of this book's CD-ROM. This file is set to publish for Flash Player 10 compatibility, using ActionScript 3.0. Save the document as `live_action.fla`. This document already has a background .png image on the Stage, as well as a masked image of a branch near the trail.

2. Make a copy of the `stella_alpha.flv` file from the `ch14/alpha_live_action` folder of this book's CD-ROM. Move the copy to the same location as the `live_action.fla` file you saved in Step 1.

3. In the Flash document, create a layer named vid, and place it between the bg_mask and bg layers.

4. Open the Library panel (Ctrl+L or ⌘+L). Click the options menu of the panel (in the top-right corner) and choose New Video. In the Video Properties dialog box, choose Video (ActionScript-controlled) as the Type option (see Figure 14.23). Click OK.

5. Drag an instance of the new Video symbol from the Library panel on the Stage, at frame 1 of the vid layer.

6. Select the new Video instance, and in the Properties panel, name the instance vid. Set the width to **152** and the height to **180**. Position the X value at **154** and the Y value at **180**. See Figure 14.24.

Note

The dimension 152 × 180 uses the same aspect ratio as that of the source clip. ∎

FIGURE 14.23

The Video Properties dialog box

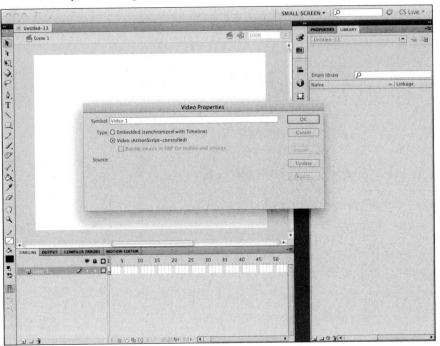

7. **Create a new layer named** actions **and place this layer at the top of the layer stack.**
   Select frame 1 of the actions layer, and open the Actions panel (F9/Option+F9). Add the
   following code. The code creates a new NetStream instance to play the stella_
   alpha.flv file, and attaches the stream to the vid instance.

```
var vid:Video;
var nc:NetConnection = new NetConnection();
nc.connect(null);
var ns:NetStream = new NetStream(nc);
ns.client = this;
ns.play("stella_alpha.flv");
vid.attachNetStream(ns);

function onMetaData(info:Object):void;
```

8. **Save the Flash document and test it (Ctrl+Enter/⌘+Enter).** The footage of Stella
   should be superimposed between the graphic of the branch and the forest background,
   as shown in Figure 14.25.

FIGURE 14.24

The vid instance

FIGURE 14.25

The alpha video footage playing on top of the forest background

On the CD-ROM

You can find the completed files in the `ch14/alpha_live_action` folder of this book's CD-ROM. You can also find another alpha video example in the `ch14/alpha_3D_model` folder of this book's CD-ROM. ■

Summary

- Flash-compatible video can be deployed as .swf files, .flv, or .f4v files. You can load .flv files from a Web server or stream them from a Flash Media Server or Flash Video Streaming Service provider.

- You can compress source video files in Adobe Media Encoder CS5.

- Flash Player 9.0.115 or later is required for .f4v files using the new AVC/H.264 video codec. Flash Player 8 or later is required for .flv files using the On2 VP6 codec. You can use the Sorenson Spark codec with Flash Video content in Flash Player 6 or later.

- The H.264 and On2 VP6 codecs offer superior compression and image quality compared to Sorenson Spark. However, H.264 and VP6 require more computer processing power and memory.

- The Adobe Media Encoder CS5 application can add embedded cue points to an .flv file. These cue points can be detected in ActionScript.

- Flash CS5 has support for Live Preview of videos directly in the Flash environment using the new FLVPlayback component. You can also add, remove, export, and import ActionScript cue points through the Properties panel.

- The On2 VP6 codec supports alpha channels within video content. You can create alpha channels in video applications such as Adobe After Effects.

Part V

Adding Basic Interactivity to Flash Movies

So far you've been learning how to make *things* — drawing shapes, creating symbols, and working with frames and adding special assets. In the next three chapters you learn how to integrate these various elements and how to make things *happen*. In this edition of the *Flash Bible*, you learn ActionScript 3.0 from the ground up! Chapter 15 introduces the concepts you need to understand when adding interactivity to presentations. Chapter 15 also gives you an orientation in the new Flash CS5 Code Snippets panel. Chapter 16 gives you the skills needed to control playback of multiple timelines. Find out how easy it is to use ActionScript to control the display of internal elements in your Flash movies, including nested Movie Clips. If you want to apply these concepts and techniques to real Flash production, Chapter 17 has just what you need — a step-by-step explanation of how to build a basic Flash presentation with a nonlinear interface. The project implements other important features such as components and accessibility options.

Understanding Actions and Event Handlers

Interactivity in a Flash movie can broadly be thought of as the elements that react and respond to a user's activity or input. A user has many ways to give input to a Flash movie, and Flash has even more ways to react. But how does interactivity actually work? It all starts with actions and event handlers.

Actions and Event Handlers

Even the most complex interactivity in Flash is fundamentally composed of two basic parts: the *behavior* (what happens) and the *cause* of the behavior (what makes it happen). Here's a simple example: Suppose you have a looping soundtrack in a movie and a button that, when clicked, turns the soundtrack off. The *behavior* is the sound turning off, and the *cause* of the behavior is the mouse clicking the button. Another example is stopping an animation when it reaches a certain frame on its timeline. When the last keyframe of the animation is played (the *cause*), an action on that keyframe stops the animation (the *behavior*). In Flash, the building blocks of behaviors are referred to as *actions*.

Note

Flash CS5 features an interactive authoring tool called the Behaviors panel. Our usage of the term behaviors in the preceding description should not be confused with this feature. The Behaviors panel can be used only for legacy Flash movies that require ActionScript 2.0. In this edition of the book, I discuss only ActionScript 3.0 code. ∎

The first step in learning how to make interactive movies is becoming familiar with the list of possible actions. However, actions can't act without being told to act *by* something. That something is often the mouse pointer coming

IN THIS CHAPTER

Knowing events and event handlers

Adding interactivity with the Code Snippets panel

Understanding Flash actions

Using the Actions panel with Script Assist

Learning your first Flash actions

Executing actions with event handlers

Using navigateToURL

in contact with a button, but it can also be a keystroke, or simply a command issued from a keyframe. I refer to any occurrence that can cause an action to happen (such as the button click in the preceding example) as an *event*. The mechanism you use to tell Flash what action to perform when an event occurs is known as an *event handler*. This cause-and-effect relationship seems obvious, but it is an extremely important concept.

For the purposes of creating basic interactivity, the difference between an action and the cause of an action is merely a practical detail. As the set of Flash actions, collectively known as *ActionScript*, continues to grow with each release of the Flash authoring tool (and, therefore, the interactive capabilities that they provide), understanding the relationship between actions and the things that cause them can be the key to adding more sophisticated behavior to your movies with traditional programming techniques. Every interactive framework, whether it is Adobe Flash or Adobe Director or Apple DVD Studio Pro, has unique handlers for specific events. Table 15.1 relates interactive events with Flash handlers.

Note

Any ActionScript covered in this chapter refers to ActionScript 3.0. For any examples in this chapter, make sure you choose Flash File (ActionScript 3.0) from the splash screen when you create a new file. ■

TABLE 15.1

Events and Flash Handlers

Event	Type	Event Handler	Example
Playback	Time-based	Keyframes MovieClip instance NetStream instance	Timeline plays until it reaches a certain frame; a MovieClip instance monitors the amount of time that has passed in a movie; when a video stream stops playing, another stream begins playback.
Mouse	User input	SimpleButton instance MovieClip instance Sprite instance Mouse class	A visitor clicks a button; mouse movement is detected over a MovieClip instance.
Key press	User input	SimpleButton instance MovieClip instance Keyboard class	A user presses the Enter key to submit a form; an alert appears if the Caps Lock key is enabled.
Window resize	User input	Stage class	A user clicks the maximize button on a Flash projector or Web browser window and Flash elements respond accordingly.
Microphone or Webcam activity	Audio/video input	Microphone class Camera class	When a user stops talking into a microphone, a graphic turns red; a stream starts to record audio and video when the movement is detected in front of a Webcam.
Data	System-based	URLLoader instance XML instance	Search results appear in the Flash movie when the results have fully loaded.

Although the breadth and depth of ActionScript involved with the interactions described in Table 15.1 may seem overwhelming, don't worry — we're taking it one step at a time. First, you'll learn how to set up the Actions panel, and then we'll look at actions that control movie playback. Later, you'll also learn how to call these actions in various ways with three kinds of event handlers: button manipulation, keyframes, and keystrokes.

What is ActionScript?

Every interactive authoring system uses a language (or code) that enables elements within the system to communicate. Just as there are several languages that people use to speak to one another around the globe, there are hundreds of programming languages in use today. In an effort to make Flash more useable to computer programmers, Flash's scripting language, called ActionScript, strongly resembles JavaScript, a fundamental element for adding advanced interactivity to HTML pages. Right now, I focus on using the most basic Flash ActionScript.

Note

Since Flash Player 9 and Flash CS3 have been released, you can use a completely revamped version of ActionScript called ActionScript 3.0, or AS3. AS3 is more complex than previous versions but is more maintainable and scalable for Flash projects. ActionScript 3.0 will feel more familiar to developers who have used other object-oriented programming languages such as C++ or Java. ■

Navigating the Actions panel

Flash CS5 has a specific interface element that enables you to add interactive commands to Flash movies — the Actions panel. You don't use menus or wizards to add interactive functionality — you type the ActionScript code describing the interactivity in (or out of) the Actions panel. You can open the Actions panel in a number of ways:

- Go to Window ⇨ Actions.
- Press the F9 key/Option+F9.
- Click the ActionScript icon button at the top-right corner of the Properties panel.
- Alt+double-click/Option+double-click a keyframe in the Timeline window.

If you have a keyframe selected in the Timeline window, the Actions panel will be titled Actions – Frame (see Figure 15.1). If you have a Movie Clip symbol instance selected on the Stage, you'll see the name Actions – Movie Clip. If you have a button symbol instance selected on the Stage, the Actions panel will be titled Actions – Button. If you have a component selected, the Actions panel will read Actions – Component. Don't be confused — there is only one Actions panel. Flash CS5 simply lets you know the object to which you are assigning actions.

Tip

The Actions panel in Flash CS5 features a Script Assist mode. Script Assist enables you to code ActionScript by selecting actions and filling in parameters, instead of writing out all the code by hand. ■

FIGURE 15.1

The Actions panel enables you to instantly add, delete, or change Flash movie commands.

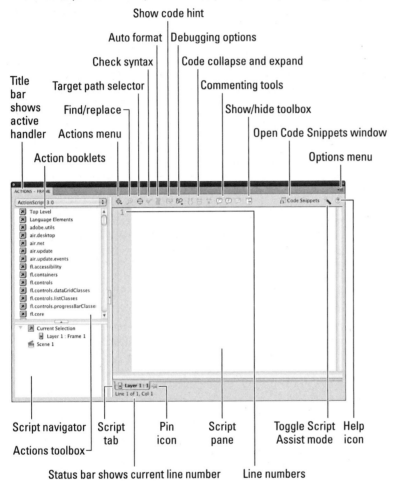

As shown in Figure 15.1, the Actions panel in Flash CS5 has three distinct areas (counterclockwise from the left): the Actions Toolbox, the Script navigator, and the Script pane. The Script Assist area is available within the Script pane. There are two auto-snap dividers, one dividing the Actions toolbox and Script navigator from the Script pane, and another subdividing the Actions Toolbox and Script navigator. You may want to practice opening and closing these dividers, as well as dragging each to your preferred width and height, respectively. Figures 15.1 shows a breakdown of the Actions panel in Flash CS5. The following list details the three areas:

- The Actions Toolbox contains several nested booklets of ActionScript commands. You can select actions to add to the Script pane. The booklets that appear default to the version of ActionScript that your Flash document specifies in the Flash tab of the Publish Settings dialog box (File ⇨ Publish Settings).

Tip

The Actions Toolbox has a booklet selection drop-down menu. The default set of booklets appearing in the Toolbox pertain to ActionScript 1.0, 2.0, and 3.0, but you can switch to other sets of booklets, including various versions of Flash Lite. Each Flash Lite booklet displays only actions compatible with the Flash Lite players that ship on mobile devices and phones. ■

- The Script navigator can jump to any script within your Flash document. When you select a keyframe or object in this pane, any code attached to the item appears in the Script pane.

Tip

The Script navigator shows the actions for the entire document, not just for the current timeline. ■

- The Script pane displays the current code for an item selected on the Stage, a keyframe selected in the Timeline window, or an item selected in the Script navigator. You can type, copy, cut, and paste code into the Script pane, as long as you are not working in Script Assist mode. An options bar is located at the top of the Script pane as well. The options bar contains several buttons to modify, search, debug, or format your code in the Script pane. You can also find most of these options in the panel's options menu, located in the top-right corner of the panel.

Tip

You can click the pin icon at the bottom tab of the script in the Script pane. You can pin multiple scripts in the Script pane, and quickly tab between them. ■

- The Script Assist area within the Script pane enables you to visualize your code with contextual parameters, such as fill-in text fields or drop-down menus, as shown in Figure 15.2. The Script Assist mode is most useful for beginners learning ActionScript for the first time. To enter Script Assist mode, click the Script Assist button on the options bar of the Script pane. Not all actions have the same ease of use within Script Assist; more complex ActionScript code is not well suited for Script Assist mode. When Script Assist mode is enabled, you cannot edit code manually within the Script pane, and you cannot switch the active booklet set.

You can add actions to the Script pane in one of three ways:

- Drag an action from the Actions Toolbox to the Script pane.
- Select an action from the Actions menu, accessed by clicking the plus (+) icon.
- Double-click an action in the Actions pane.

To delete actions, select the action line(s) in the Script pane, and press Delete or Backspace on the keyboard.

FIGURE 15.2

The Script Assist mode displays a more user-friendly interface for controlling action parameters.

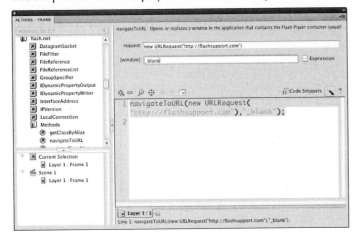

After you have added an action to the Script pane, you can specify parameters (or arguments) for the action. Depending on the action, you may or may not need to type such parameters. By default, Flash CS5 provides code hints as you type actions into the Script pane. The Show Code Hint button enables you to see the parameters for an action, as shown in the `navigateToURL` action in Figure 15.2.

More important, the Script Assist mode makes it much easier for you to add and adjust settings for basic actions, especially those you find in the Timeline Control booklet. You use the Script Assist mode throughout this chapter to learn the basic control actions.

Note

The Script Assist mode is much more useful for legacy ActionScript 1.0 and 2.0 syntax. For ActionScript 3.0 syntax, most actions have limited options revealed in Script Assist mode. ■

You should get in the habit of clicking the Check Syntax button (the blue check mark) to make sure you didn't mistype an action. If you have an error, the Output panel displays some information related to the error, indicating the line number where the syntax error occurs.

A brief primer on code syntax

Some of the most difficult concepts for beginners to understand with code writing are white space, parentheses (( )), semicolons (;), and curly braces ({ }). In the following paragraphs, you learn how each of these affects your ActionScript code.

White space

White space is a collective term referring to any blank areas between lines of code. It includes spaces inserted by the spacebar, indentations inserted with the Tab key, and line returns inserted with the Enter or Return key. When Flash CS5 compiles your ActionScript code into the Flash movie, the white space between your lines of code usually does not generate any errors. For example, the following code works exactly the same:

```
navigateToURL(new URLRequest("http://flashsupport.com"));
```

or

```
navigateToURL(new URLRequest(
        "http://flashsupport.com"
        )
    );
```

or

```
navigateToURL(  new URLRequest( "http://flashsupport.com" ) );
```

However, white space is an issue when it separates the key terms in the action, such as:

```
navigate To URL(new URL Request("http://flashsupport.com"));
```

The spaces between `navigate` , `To`, and `URL` will cause an error when Flash CS5 tries to create the Flash movie.

Tip

To check if your syntax is correct, click the Check Syntax button in the Actions panel. If you do have any white space errors, the Output panel displays information related to the error. Also, if your code has errors, you are prevented from entering the Script Assist mode. ■

Parentheses

Many, but not all, actions require parentheses after the action term, such as `SoundMixer.stop All()`, `navigateToURL()`, or even `play()`. A general rule to remember is that if the action requires a parameter, such as `navigateToURL()`, then parentheses are required as well.

Note

Parameters are also referred to as arguments. ■

However, many actions, such as `play()` and `stop()`, still require parentheses, even though they do not use any arguments. Another rule for parentheses is that any open parenthesis (( ) must eventually be followed by a closing parenthesis ( )). A habit I like to encourage is counting the number of opening parentheses in a script and then counting the number of closing parentheses. If the numbers don't match, you need to review your code to find the place where you forgot to include a parenthesis.

Deprecated and Incompatible Actions: What Are They?

As the ActionScript language of Flash continues to expand and encompass new functionality, older actions coexist with newer and better actions (or methods, properties, event handlers, and functions, which I discuss later). Although Flash Player 10 continues to support ActionScript 2.0 and earlier actions, it's better not to use older actions if the newest version of the Flash Player has a new way of accomplishing the same task. Older actions that have been replaced with a new action (or new way to perform the same task) are called *deprecated actions*. If you switch the Actions Toolbox to ActionScript 1.0 and 2.0, the Actions panel in Flash CS5 houses all deprecated actions in the Deprecated booklet of the Actions pane. Why shouldn't you use these actions? As you'll see in more advanced scripting, ActionScript 2.0 and 3.0 have specific syntax to target Movie Clips and determine whether certain frames have loaded, among other features of the ActionScript "dot syntax" language.

Although you should avoid actions that are highlighted in the Deprecated booklet if possible, Flash Player 10 continues to support them if you're publishing with ActionScript 1.0 or 2.0.

Flash CS5 also lets you know if certain actions are not supported with the Player version that is selected in the Flash format tab of the Publish Settings dialog box (File ➪ Publish Settings). Note that you can also find the Player version setting in the Properties panel when you click an empty area of the Stage or the work area. If an action is not supported by the version you have selected, the action is highlighted in yellow. The following figure shows this type of highlighting in the Actions panel. Notice that the tooltip (or rollover description) indicates which version of the Flash Player supports the action.

Semicolons and curly braces

You've probably already noticed that most actions include a semicolon (;) at the end of the code line. In practice, many coders forget to include semicolons. Usually, Flash is very forgiving if you omit semicolons, but by no means should you be encouraged to omit them. The general rule for semicolons and curly braces is mutually inclusive: If your action doesn't end with a closing curly brace (}), it should end with a semicolon. As with parentheses, all opening curly braces must eventually be followed by a closing curly brace (}). Curly braces are commonly used with `if` and `function` declarations.

Your First Five Actions

Now that you have a general picture of what actions do, let's look at five common actions in detail. At this point, we're describing only the functionality of each action, not how to add an action to your movie. I provide information on adding an action in the next section.

Cross-Reference

You will find coverage of further actions in later chapters. ■

Actions in the Flash interface appear alphabetically sorted from top to bottom. In the following sections, complementary actions are grouped together.

gotoAndPlay() and gotoAndStop()

These "go to" actions change the current frame of the movie to the target frame specified as the action's parameter. There are two variations:

- `gotoAndPlay()`: Changes the current frame to the frame specified, and then executes a `play()` action. `gotoAndPlay()` provides the capability to show animated sequences as preludes to individual content areas. `gotoAndPlay()` also gets frequent use in choose-your-own-adventure style animations, in which the user guides an animated character through different paths in a narrative.

Note

If you use a `gotoAndPlay()` **action to go to a frame that has a** `stop()` **action, the timeline stops at the new frame.** ■

- `gotoAndStop()`: Changes the current frame to the frame specified and then halts playback on that frame. `gotoAndStop()` is often used to produce toolbar-style interfaces where the user clicks buttons to view different areas of content in a movie.

Both actions enable you to jump to certain areas of the Flash movie. The parameters of these actions start with the largest time unit, the scene, and end with the smallest one, the frame.

You can specify frames in other scenes as the target of `goto` actions with the scene parameter. As shown in the following code, you type the name of the scene first, with double quotes around the name, and then the frame number (without quotes) or frame label. In this example, `"Scene 2"` is the name of the scene and `"animate_in"` is the frame label in that scene to jump to.

```
gotoAndPlay("Scene 2", "animate_in");
```

However, if you specify only one parameter in a `gotoAndPlay` or `gotoAndStop` action, the parameter is interpreted as a frame label. For example, the following code tells the current timeline to jump to its `"menu"` frame label:

```
gotoAndStop("menu");
```

There are three methods of specifying the frame to which the movie should go when it receives a `goto` action. The methods for specifying the frame are

- **number:** Specifies the target frame as a number. Frame 1 is the beginning of the movie or scene. Frame numbers should not use surrounding quotes, as frame labels do. The following action tells the current timeline to jump to frame 10 and start playing:

```
gotoAndPlay(10);
```

- **label:** Individual keyframes can be given names via the Label section's Name field in the Properties panel. After a frame is labeled, a goto action can target it by name. To specify a label as the target of a goto action, type the name of the frame as the action's parameter. The following example tells the Flash movie to go to the frame labeled "products" and stop at that frame:

```
gotoAndStop("products");
```

- **ActionScript expression:** Specifies the target frame as an interpreted ActionScript code segment. You use expressions to dynamically assign targets of goto actions. Here's a quick example of a string variable being used as a frame label:

```
var targetLabel = "products";
gotoAndPlay(targetLabel);
```

Notice that the term targetLabel does not use quotes because it is not the actual frame label name. When the Flash Player interprets this action, it looks up the value of targetLabel, which is "products", and inserts that value into the gotoAndPlay action. With strict data typing in ActionScript 3.0, the same action looks like this:

```
var targetLabel:String = "products";
gotoAndPlay(targetLabel);
```

Caution

Using frame numbers to specify the targets of goto actions can lead to serious scalability problems in Flash movies. Adding frames at the beginning or in the middle of a movie's timeline causes the subsequent frames to be renumbered. When those frames are renumbered, all goto actions that use frame numbers must be revised to point to the correct new number of their target frames.

In the vast majority of cases, goto actions that use a frame label to specify target frames are preferable to goto actions that use a frame number to specify target frames. Unlike numbered frame targets, goto actions with labeled frame targets continue to function properly, even if the targeted frame changes position on the timeline. ■

nextFrame() and prevFrame()

The nextFrame() and prevFrame() actions act like a gotoAndStop() action, in that they both transport the timeline to a new position and stop.

- nextFrame(): This action tells the current timeline to move forward one frame and stop playback. nextFrame() can be used in conjunction with prevFrame to quickly set up a slideshow-style walk-through of content, where each of a series of contiguous keyframes contains the content of one "slide." This action does not use any parameters. The following code moves the timeline to the next frame:

```
nextFrame();
```

- `prevFrame()`: This action moves the current timeline backward one frame and stops playback. For example, if the timeline is on frame 20, and the movie runs a `prevFrame()` action, the timeline moves to frame 19. As with the `nextFrame()` action, `prevFrame()` does not use any parameters:

  `prevFrame();`

nextScene() and prevScene()

These actions advance the Flash movie to a new scene. Here's how they work:

- `nextScene()`: This action tells the current timeline to move to the first frame of the next scene. You can use `nextScene()` for more elaborate slide shows or demonstration movies, where each scene contains animated content with a stop action on the last frame. The last frame of the scene then contains a button using the `nextScene()` action. This action does not use any parameters. The following code tells the movie to jump to the next scene:

  `nextScene();`

- `prevScene()`: This action jumps the movie to the previous scene. For example, if the playhead is in Scene 2, the timeline moves to the first frame of Scene 1. As with the `nextScene()` action, `prevScene()` does not use any parameters:

  `prevFrame();`

Note

The `nextScene()` and `prevScene()` actions do not automatically recycle the scenes when the last or first scene is reached, respectively. For example, if you have three scenes and use a `nextScene()` action while the movie is on the last scene, the movie does not jump back to the first scene. ∎

Caution

As I mention earlier, you should avoid the use of multiple scenes in your Flash document. Although you may find it simpler to segment your Flash content across several scenes as you begin to learn Flash, most seasoned Flash designers and developers use only one scene, and separate content across several Movie Clip symbols placed on one or more frames of Scene 1. Scenes are not compatible with standard targeting syntax, as you'll learn in the next chapter. ∎

play() and stop()

These simple actions are the true foundations of Flash timeline control. `play()` sets a movie or a Movie Clip instance in motion. When a `play()` action is executed, Flash starts the sequential display of each frame's contents along the current timeline.

The rate at which the frames appear is measured as frames per second, or fps. The fps rate can be set from 0.01 to 120 (meaning that the `play` action can cause the display of as little as 1 frame every 100 seconds to as many as 120 frames in 1 second, subject to the limitations of the computer's processing speed). In Flash CS5, the default fps is 24.

After `play()` has started, frames continue to appear one after the other, until another action interrupts the flow, or the end of the movie or Movie Clip's timeline is reached. If the end of a movie's timeline is reached, the movie either loops (begins playing again at frame 1, Scene 1) or stops on the last frame.

After the end of the Movie Clip's timeline is reached, playback loops back to the beginning of the clip, and the clip continues playing. To prevent looping, add a `stop()` action to the last frame of your Movie Clip.

Note

A single `play()` action affects only a single timeline, whether that timeline is the main movie timeline or the timeline of a Movie Clip instance. For example, a `play` action executed inside a Movie Clip does not cause the Main Timeline to begin playing. Likewise, any `goto` action on the Main Timeline doesn't migrate to the Movie Clips that reside there. A timeline must be specifically targeted to control playback along that timeline. If there is no specified target, the action is referring to its own timeline. However, this is not the case for animations within graphic symbol instances. An animation in a graphic symbol is controlled by actions on the timeline in which the symbol instance is present — Flash ignores actions on a graphic symbol's timeline. ■

The `stop()` action, as you may have guessed, halts the progression of a movie or Movie Clip that is in a play state. `stop()` is often used with buttons for user-controlled playback of a movie or on frames to end an animated sequence.

Tip

Movie Clip instances placed on any timeline begin to play automatically. Remember to add a `stop()` action on the first frame of a Movie Clip if you don't want it to play right away. ■

navigateToURL()

Want to link to a Web resource from a Flash movie? No problem. That's what `navigateToURL()` is for. For ActionScript 3.0, you can find the `navigateToURL()` action in the flash.net ➪ Methods booklet of the Actions panel. `navigateToURL()` is simply Flash's method of making a conventional hypertext link. It's nearly the equivalent of an anchor tag in HTML (`<a href="…">`), except that Flash's `navigateToURL()` can also send variables for form submission. `navigateToURL()` can be used to link to a standard Web page, an FTP site, another Flash movie, an executable, a server-side script, or anything that exists on the Internet or on an accessible local file system.

Caution

The `navigateToURL()` action can be used only with ActionScript 3.0 content. If you need to publish legacy ActionScript 1.0 and 2.0 content, use the `getURL()` action. ■

`navigateToURL()` has two parameters that are familiar to Web designers and developers (the first one, `url`, is required for this action to work):

- URLRequest: This is the network address of the page, file, script, or resource to which you are linking, formatted within a URLRequest wrapper. Any value is permitted (including ActionScript expressions), but the linked item can be displayed only if the reference to it is correct. The URLRequest value is directly analogous to the HREF attribute of an HTML anchor tag. You can use a relative or absolute URL as well. Examples:

```
http://www.yoursite.com/
ftp://ftp.yoursite.com/pub/documents.zip
menu.html
/cgi-bin/processform.cgi
   /script/form.cfm
```

Tip

You can specify secure domain URLs by using the https protocol for SSL (Secure Sockets Layer) connections. ∎

- window: This is the name of the frame or window in which you want to load the resource specified in the URL setting. The window parameter is directly analogous to the target attribute of an HTML anchor tag. In addition to enabling the entry of custom frame and window names, the window parameter can use the following browser-standard target names:

  - "_self": Loads the URL into the same frame or window as the current movie. If you do not specify a window parameter in the getURL action, this behavior is the default.

  - "_blank": Creates a new browser window and loads the URL into it.

  - "_parent": Removes the current frameset and loads the URL in its place. Use this option if you have multiple nested framesets, and you want your linked URL to replace only the frameset in which your movie resides.

  - "_top": Loads the URL into the current browser and removes all framesets in the process. Use this option if your movie is in a frame, but you want your linked URL to be loaded normally into the browser, outside the confines of any frames.

Note

Frame windows and/or JavaScript windows can be assigned names. You can target these names by manually typing the name in the Window field. For example, if you had a frame defined as <frame name="main"...>, you could load specific URLs into a frame named main from a Flash movie. ∎

Tip

The navigateToURL() action works in the Test Movie environment. Both the Flash stand-alone player and the Test Movie command give you access to external and/or local URLs. ∎

Here are some examples of how you can write a navigateToURL() action. The following code tells the browser to load the URL www.wiley.com into the current browser window:

```
navigateToURL(new URLRequest("http://www.wiley.com"));
```

Alternatively, you can specify a unique target for the loaded URL. The following example loads an HTML document named menu.html into a frame named menu_frame:

```
navigateToURL(new URLRequest("menu.html"), "menu_frame");
```

A more advanced usage of the navigateToURL() action sends variables from the Flash movie to a Web server's script, which is set up to receive the variables. The following code opens a Google.com search results page for the term "Flash Video":

```
var googleURL = new URLRequest("http://google.com/search");
    var searchData = new URLVariables();
    searchData.hl = "en";
    searchData.q = "Flash Video";
    googleURL.data = searchData;
    navigateToURL(googleURL, "_blank");
```

As I mention with the goto actions, you can also use expressions with navigateToURL() actions. Expressions can be used as parameters of any ActionScript action. The following example uses a string variable to specify the URL used by a navigateToURL() action:

```
var siteURL = new URLRequest("http://www.flashsupport.com");
    navigateToURL(siteURL);
```

You should start familiarizing yourself with the ActionScript notation that Flash uses for each action (see Table 15.2). As you use Flash for more advanced interactivity, you'll need to have a firm grasp of code notation.

TABLE 15.2

Common Actions and ActionScript Notation

Action	ActionScript Notation	Arguments
gotoAndStop	gotoAndStop(arguments);	Scene name (frame label, number, or expression)
gotoAndPlay	gotoAndPlay(arguments);	Scene name (frame label, number, or expression)
nextFrame	nextFrame();	None
prevFrame	prevFrame();	None
nextScene	nextScene();	None
prevScene	prevScene();	None
play	play();	None
stop	stop();	None
navigateToURL	navigateToURL(arguments);	URLRequest instance, target frame, or window

Making Actions Happen with Event Handlers

The ten common actions I discuss in the previous sections provide many of the behaviors that you need to make an interesting interactive Flash movie. But those actions can't make your movies interactive on their own. They need to be told when to happen. To tell a Flash movie when an action should occur, you need event handlers. Event handlers specify the condition(s) under which an action can be made to happen. For example, you might want to mouse-click a button to initiate a play() action, or you might want a movie to stop when a certain keyframe in the timeline is reached. Creating interactivity in your movies is simply a matter of deciding what event you want to detect (mouse-click, keystroke, and so on), adding the appropriate event handler to detect it, and specifying the action(s) that should be performed when it happens.

Before I describe each event handler in detail, in the next section I show you an example of exactly how an event handler merges with an action to form a functioning interactive button.

Using the Code Snippets panel

The Code Snippets panel, new in Flash CS5, contains many useful prewritten blocks of code that you can apply in your Flash movies. This panel is found under Window ⇨ Code Snippets. To use Code Snippets, double-click the snippet you would like to apply in the Code Snippets panel, or select a snippet and click the Copy to Clipboard button to copy the code block to the clipboard. Some snippets require an object that is selected on the stage, and some require an instance name for one or more objects. After a code snippet is applied, Flash generates code in a new layer called Actions, and you can modify that code to work in your application.

The Code Snippets panel, shown in Figure 15.3, is the fastest way to use and learn ActionScript 3.0. As you work with the Code Snippets panel and practice modifying the code it generates, try to look at the code to understand how it works. When you have a question about a particular piece of code, highlight it and press F1 on your keyboard to look it up in Flash Help.

FIGURE 15.3

The new Code Snippets panel

Note

The Code Snippets panel also supports custom snippets through its Options flyout menu. ■

Combining an action with an event handler to make a functioning button

Imagine that you have a short, endlessly looping movie in which a wire-frame cube rotates. Now imagine that you want to add a button to your movie that, when clicked, stops the cube from rotating by stopping the playback of the looping movie. Here's what you need to do:

On the CD-ROM

For this exercise, you can use the `rotatingCube.fla` file located in the `ch15` folder on this book's CD-ROM. The finished file is named `rotatingCube_complete.fla`. ■

1. **Open the starter Flash document,** `rotatingCube.fla`. Save this document as `rotatingCube_complete.fla` on your local hard drive.

2. **Make a new layer called** button.

3. **Place a button on the button layer.** You can use Flash CS5's sample Stop button found in the classic buttons➪Circle Buttons folder of the Buttons library (Window➪Common Libraries➪Buttons). See Figure 15.4 to see this button's placement on the Stage.

Tip

Selecting buttons and editing button properties sometimes can be tricky if buttons are enabled in the Flash authoring environment. For easier button manipulation, disable buttons by unchecking Enable Simple Buttons under the Control menu. ■

4. **Select the button instance, and open the Properties panel.** Name the instance **stop-Button**. Button symbol instances must be named to be accessible by ActionScript.

5. With the stopButton instance selected, open the Code Snippets panel (Window➪Code Snippets). In the Timeline Navigation section of the Code Snippets panel, double-click the snippet called Click to Go to Frame and Stop. Doing this adds a block of code to the Timeline and open the Actions panel.

6. **In the Actions panel, find the line of code that has the gotoAndStop() action, and change the line to the following code:**

   ```
   stop();
   ```

Note

In computer programming, a constant is a reserved word with a predefined value. ■

7. Now that you have a button in your Flash movie that stops the movie's playback when it is clicked, save your Flash document (.fla), and test the movie by choosing Control ➪ Test Movie. When you click the button, the rotating cube animation should stop.

FIGURE 15.4

The Stop button on the Stage

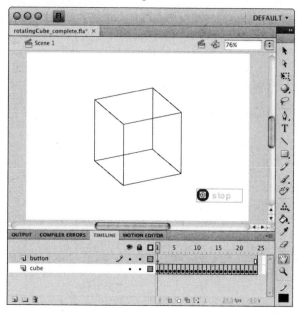

Tip

The Code Snippets panel offers a large amount of prewritten code that you can add to your Flash movies. Try experimenting with the other snippets in the panel to add more functionality to the movie you just created to get practice working with ActionScript 3.0. ■

To make any interactivity in your movies, you simply have to apply the basic principles you used to make the stop button: Decide which action (or actions) you want to happen, and indicate when you want that action to happen with an event handler. Let's look now at more event handlers you can use to make those actions happen.

The Flash event handlers

Three primary event handlers exist in Flash: those that detect mouse activity on button symbol instances (button manipulation), those that recognize when a key is pressed on the keyboard (key presses), and those that respond to the progression of the timeline (keyframes).

Working with mouse events and buttons

Event handlers that occur based on the user's interaction with a button rely entirely on the location and movement of the mouse pointer. If the mouse pointer comes in contact with a button symbol's hit area, the pointer changes from an arrow icon to a finger pointer icon. At that time the mouse is described as "over" the button. If the mouse pointer is not over a button, it is said to be *out* or *outside* of the button. General movement of the mouse *without* the mouse button depressed is referred to as *rolling*. General movement of the mouse *with* the mouse button pressed is referred to as *dragging*.

Cross-Ref

If you don't know how to make a button symbol and its various states, read Chapter 6, "Symbols, Instances, and the Library." ■

Caution

Event handlers and actions for buttons can be placed only on button instances, not on the four frames in the timeline of the original button symbol. One of the features in Flash CS5 is that it does not enable you to place any actions in a button symbol timeline. ■

Here are the mouse-based events for Flash display objects that use the addEventListener() method. Each of these events is case-sensitive when typed in ActionScript 3.0 code.

MouseEvent.MOUSE_DOWN

A single mouse-click can actually be divided into two separate components: the downstroke (the *press*) and the upstroke (the *release*). A MouseEvent.MOUSE_DOWN event occurs when the mouse pointer is over the hit area of a button *and* the downstroke of a mouse-click is detected. This event is best used for control panel–style buttons, especially toggle switches.

Caution

Typically, developers should program reversible decisions for primary navigation so that users can abort their clicks by rolling the cursor away from the hit area before releasing the mouse. For example, a user might click a button for more information and decide he or she would rather not get that information. I do not recommend using the MouseEvent.MOUSE_DOWN event for important user moves such as these because it does not give users an opportunity to abort their moves. ■

MouseEvent.MOUSE_UP and MouseEvent.CLICK

These events occur when the mouse pointer is over the hit area of a button *and* both the down-stroke and the upstroke of a mouse-click are detected. The `MouseEvent.CLICK` event is the standard button-click event.

Tip

If you use the Track as Menu Item behavior for a button instance in the Properties panel, a button responds to a `MouseEvent.MOUSE_UP` event over its Hit state even if the mouse was pressed outside of the button's hit area. ■

MouseEvent.ROLL_OVER

This event occurs when the mouse pointer moves onto the hit area of a button without the mouse button depressed.

Note

To perform standard rollover button effects, such as graphic art changes or sound events, you can insert graphics and sound on to the Over state of the button symbol timeline. ■

MouseEvent.ROLL_OUT

This event occurs when the mouse pointer moves off of the hit area of a button without the mouse button depressed. This event is commonly used for switching an advanced button's graphic state back to its original state when the user rolls off the button.

Capturing time events with keyframes

The keyframe event handler depends on the playback of the movie itself, not on the user. Just about any action can be attached to any keyframe on the timeline. An action attached to a keyframe is executed when the playhead enters the keyframe, whether it enters naturally during the linear playback of the movie or as the result of a `goto` action. So, for example, you may place a `stop` action on a keyframe to pause the movie at the end of an animation sequence.

Note

In ActionScript 3.0 code, button handlers can be defined in keyframes, but the code referenced by a button handler does not execute when the playhead enters the frame where that code exists. ■

In some multimedia applications, keyframe event handlers can differentiate between the playhead *entering* a keyframe and *exiting* a keyframe. Flash has only one kind of keyframe event handler (essentially, on enter). Hence, as a developer, you do not need to add keyframe event handlers explicitly — they are a presumed element of any action placed on a keyframe.

Tip

Complex movies can have dozens, or hundreds (or even thousands!), of actions attached to keyframes. To prevent conflicts between uses of keyframes for animation and uses of keyframes as action containers, it is highly advisable to create an entire layer solely for action keyframes. Name the layer actions and keep it on top of all your layers for easy access. Remember not to place any symbol instances, text, or artwork on your actions layer. You can also create a labels layer to hold — you guessed it — frame labels. ■

The process for adding an action to a keyframe is as follows:

1. **Create a keyframe on a timeline.** This keyframe can exist in the Main Timeline (that is, Scene 1) or a Movie Clip symbol timeline.

2. **Select the keyframe in the Timeline window, and open the Actions panel.** The Actions panel title should read Actions – Frame.

3. **Type your desired actions in the Script pane.**

In the next section, you get a little more hands-on experience adding actions to both buttons and keyframes.

Creating Invisible Buttons and Using navigateToURL

In this section, you learn how to create an "invisible button" and practice the use of `navigate ToURL()` actions. An invisible button is essentially a button symbol that has only a Hit state defined, with empty Up, Over, and Down states. After you create an invisible button, you can use it to convert any type of Flash element into a button. By dragging an instance of the invisible button on top of another piece of artwork or symbol instance on the Stage, you can add interactivity to that element.

On the CD-ROM

Make a copy of the `themakers_ad_starter.fla` **file, located in the** `ch15` **folder of the book's CD-ROM. This file contains a sample layout of graphics and text for a mock Flash ad, sized for display on a Microsoft Windows Mobile 6 device screen. ■**

With the starter Flash document (.fla) open in Flash CS5, quickly familiarize yourself with the existing content. There are four layers on the Main Timeline (Scene 1). The comments layer indicates what the Flash document is, the border layer contains a black outlined box with no fill, the graphics layer contains a graphic symbol of branding artwork, and the animText layer contains a Movie Clip instance featuring a tweened animation. Go ahead and test this movie (Control⇨Test Movie) to see how these elements currently play. When the animation finishes, you should see the artwork shown in Figure 15.5.

FIGURE 15.5

The artwork of the Flash movie designed for a Windows Mobile screen

In this exercise, you're going to add two invisible buttons to this movie. One is an oval-shaped button that fits over the thumbprint graphic, and another is a rectangular-shaped button that fits over the company's name. The thumbprint button, when clicked, opens the e-mail client to send an e-mail to the company. When the user clicks the name button, a new browser window opens displaying the company's Web page.

1. **In the starter Flash document, create a new layer named** actions. Place this layer just underneath the comments layer.

2. **Save the starter document as** makers_ad.fla. Currently, there is more than one frame on the Main Timeline, and if you were to develop this Flash movie further, you wouldn't want the playhead going past the first frame without some input from the user.

3. **Select the first frame of this layer and open the Actions panel (F9,/Option+F9), and type the following code in the Script pane:**

   ```
   stop();
   ```

4. **With this first frame of the actions layer still selected, open the Properties panel and in the Label section's Name field, type** //stop. This adds a frame comment of //stop to the layer in the Timeline window. This comment provides a quick visual cue about the behavior of this keyframe. Now you're going to make your first invisible button.

5. **Choose Insert ⇨ New Symbol (Ctrl+F8/⌘+F8) and make a new button symbol named** invisibleButton_rect. This button will be the rectangular button that is placed over the company's name. Flash takes you right inside the symbol's workspace as soon as you click the OK button in the Create New Symbol dialog box.

6. **Rename Layer 1 to** hit area graphic. On this layer of the button symbol's timeline, create a keyframe for the Hit state. Move the playhead in the Timeline window to this new keyframe.

7. **Select the Rectangle tool, and draw a uniform square on the symbol's Stage.** The square can be any color, although I prefer red for invisible buttons. If you drew the shape with a stroke, delete the stroke. Select the square, and in the Properties panel, give the square a width and height of **50** pixels. Then using the Align panel, center the square on the Stage. Your button symbol and timeline should now resemble Figure 15.6.

FIGURE 15.6

The square acts as the active area of the button symbol.

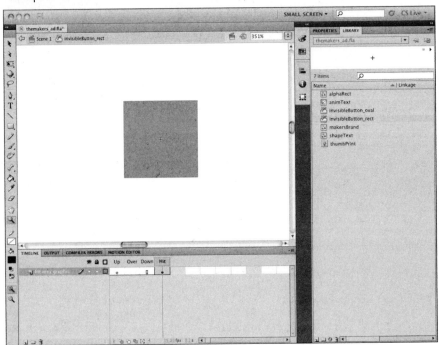

8. **Now, go back to Scene 1 (the Main Timeline), and create a new layer.** Rename this layer **linkButton**, and place it above the graphics layer.

9. **Open the Library panel (Ctrl+L/⌘+L), and drag an instance of the** `invisible Button_rect` **symbol to the Stage.** Place this instance over the company's name. In the Properties panel, name this instance **linkButton**.

10. **Using the Free Transform tool, size the instance to fit the size of the text, without overlapping other elements on the Stage, as shown in Figure 15.7.**

FIGURE 15.7

The linkButton instance resized over the company's name

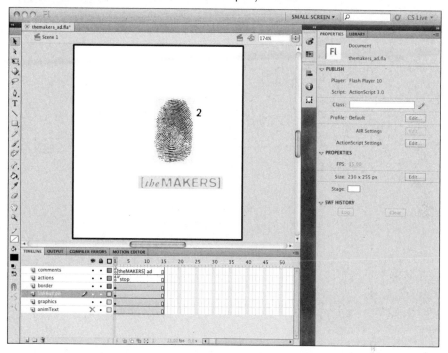

11. **With the Selection tool, select frame 1 of the actions layer, and open the Actions panel (F9,/Option+F9).** Your Action panel title bar should read Actions - Button. In the Script pane, add a button listener for the `MouseEvent.CLICK` event, directing the Web browser to a new Web page when the `linkButton` instance is clicked. Add the following code below the existing `stop()`; action:

```
linkButton.addEventListener(MouseEvent.CLICK, onLinkClick);

function onLinkClick (evt) {
    var siteURL = new URLRequest("http://www.theMakers.com");
    navigateToURL(siteURL, "_blank");
}
```

For this example, I used the URL `http://www.theMakers.com`. When you're linking to domain names, make sure that you specify the transfer protocol (such as `http://`, `ftp://`, and so on). If you are linking to relative URLs, specify the name of the HTML document (or other resource) that you want to access. This `onLinkClick()` handler containing the `navigateToURL()` action directs a button click on this instance to [theMAKERS] Web site, in a new browser window.

12. **Save your Flash document, and test it by using Control ⇨ Test Movie (Ctrl+Enter/ ⌘+Enter).** In the Test Movie window, roll over the company's name in the Flash movie. Notice that this area is an active button. When you click the button, a new browser window opens, displaying the company's Web page.

13. **Now, go back to the Flash document and add another invisible button.** You'll use a different procedure this time. On the Scene 1 timeline, create a new layer and name it **emailButton.** Place this layer above the linkButton layer.

14. **On the first frame of the emailButton layer, select the Oval tool, and draw a perfect circle anywhere on the Stage.** Again, you can use any fill color you want. If the circle has a stroke, delete the stroke. With this circle selected, open the Properties panel and give the circle a width and height of **50** pixels.

15. **With the circle selected, choose Modify ⇨ Convert to Symbol (F8).** In the Convert to Symbol dialog box, make a button symbol named **invisibleButton_oval** and click OK.

16. **Now, edit the new symbol, either by double-clicking the instance on the Stage or by double-clicking its listing in the Library panel.** On this symbol's timeline, rename Layer 1 to **hit area graphic.** Now, select the keyframe for the Up state, and drag it to the Hit state. Note that you may need to click, and then click and drag the keyframe for this method to work properly. When you are finished, your circle shape should be on only the Hit area of the button's timeline.

17. **Go back to the Scene 1 timeline, and you'll notice that your circle button is now an invisible button, just as our rectangular one is.** Move the circular invisible button over the thumbprint graphic, and use the Free Transform tool to shape the circle as an oval that closely matches the shape of the thumbprint, as shown in Figure 15.8. Also, name the instance emailButton in the Properties panel.

18. **Select frame 1 of the actions layer, and open the Actions panel.** Repeat Step 11 of this exercise, referencing the new `emailButton` instance. This time, however, we'll use a `mailto:` URL, as in `"mailto:info@theMakers.com"`. Type this value within a `URLRequest` wrapper. For this `navigateToURL()` action, however, you do not need to specify a window parameter. Add the following code below the existing lines of code:

```
emailButton.addEventListener(MouseEvent.CLICK, onEmailClick);

function onEmailClick (evt) {
    var mailURL = new URLRequest("mailto:info@theMakers.com");
    navigateToURL(mailURL);
}
```

Tip

You can specify subject lines and body text in `mailto:` URLs as well, just as you can with HTML documents. For example, the following code opens a new e-mail message window addressed to `info@theMakers.com`, with a subject line of "Web Feedback" and body text of "Here are my comments." The following code should be typed as one line of code. Do not type the ⊃ character, which indicates a continuation of the same line of code.

```
"mailto:info@theMakers.com? ⊃
    subject=Web%20Feedback&body=Here%20are%20my%20comments%3A"); ■
```

FIGURE 15.8

The thumbprint graphic now has an invisible button on top of it.

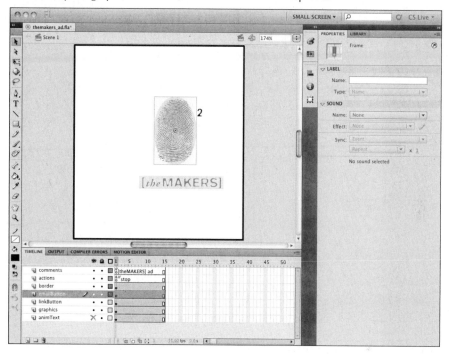

19. **Save your Flash document once again, and test the movie.** When you click the active area over the thumbprint graphic, the default e-mail client on your system should open, displaying a new message window with the To: field predefined to the URL you typed in Step 18.

Tip

You can also change the title and description metadata published with the .swf file by choosing Modify ⇨ Document. This metadata can be included with older .swf formats, including Flash Player 6! If your Flash movie is on a publicly accessible Web page and crawled by a search engine, the metadata can be read by the engine and indexed. ∎

Now you know how to make invisible buttons and add `navigateToURL()` actions to them. In your own work, you may come to realize the true benefit of invisible buttons: You can quickly drag several instances of either invisible button shape (oval or rectangle) to the Stage to create active areas. This offers two benefits: First, you don't have to make button symbols from regular graphics that don't need four button states, and second, you can make "hidden" areas in interactive puzzles or games.

Summary

- ActionScript is Flash's interactive language. It is a set of actions that enables Flash to communicate with internal elements (timelines, symbols, sounds, and so on) and external Web pages and scripts.

- ActionScript 3.0, or AS3, is the newest version of the scripting language for the Flash Player. AS3 is available only in Flash Player 9 or later. You must use ActionScript 1.0 or 2.0 for legacy Flash content playable in Flash Player 8 or earlier.

- Flash CS5 includes a new panel called the Code Snippets panel, which allows you to apply prewritten code to your Flash movies.

- Flash interactivity is based on a relatively simple structure: An event handler waits for something to happen (a playback point being reached or the user providing input), and when that something does happen, it executes one or more actions (which alter the movie's playback, behavior, or properties; load a file; or execute a script).

- All actions need an event handler to activate them. Event handlers include keyframes on a timeline, button clicks, mouse movements, and key presses. More advanced event handlers are discussed in later chapters.

- Invisible buttons enable you to create interactive areas on top of other Flash artwork or symbols.

Building Timelines and Interactions

Unlike most multimedia authoring applications, Flash has the capability to use multiple simultaneous timelines in its movies. So far, most of the examples in this book have only one timeline. You've seen how to add basic actions to your movies to make them interactive. Now you begin exploring the world of multiple movie timelines by using the Movie Clip symbol.

A Brief History of Movie Clips: The Key to Self-Contained Playback

A powerful piece to the Flash movie format is the Movie Clip symbol, introduced in Flash Player 3. Movie Clips enable Flash developers to create complex behaviors by nesting self-contained sequences of animation or interactivity inside each other. These sequences can then be placed as discrete, self-playing modules on the Main Timeline (that is, Scene 1). Initially, the key to the power of Movie Clips was their capability to communicate with and control each other via the `tellTarget` action.

In Flash Player 4, the role of Movie Clips was expanded — they could be used with ActionScript. That capability put Movie Clips at the foundation of advanced interactivity in Flash. In Flash Player 5, when ActionScript matured into a full-blown scripting language that mirrored JavaScript, Movie Clips became the central object of programming. In Flash Player 6, Movie Clips could utilize more compiler directives, which enabled them to become full-blown user-interface components. In Flash Player 7, Movie Clips and components continued to evolve and play a vital role in the organization of a Flash movie's content and interactivity.

In Flash Player 8, Movie Clips gained new filter effects, blend modes, and bitmap-caching optimizations. With Flash Player 9, Movie Clips received a new sibling, the Sprite class, which is available only in ActionScript 3.0. (A sprite instance is essentially a single-frame Movie Clip instance, and is discussed more in the note that follows). With the release of Flash Player 10, the role of Movie Clips remains unchanged. In this chapter, you look at several key features of the Movie Clip symbol.

Note

If you're planning on building projects written in ActionScript 3.0, the role of the `MovieClip` class has changed dramatically. `MovieClip` instances should be used only for multiple-frame timeline-based animations. In ActionScript 3.0, several new classes, including the `Sprite` class, have been introduced to take over most of the functionality that was previously assigned to the `MovieClip` class. Regardless of which version of ActionScript you plan to use, you should understand the fundamentals of the `MovieClip` instances discussed in this chapter and throughout the book. This edition of the Flash Bible includes more coverage of ActionScript 3.0 (AS3). For more comprehensive coverage of ActionScript 3.0, refer to ActionScript 3.0 Bible (Wiley, 2008). ■

How Movie Clips interact within a Flash movie

Previous chapters dealt with Flash movies as a single sequence of frames arranged along a single timeline. Whether the playback along that timeline was linear (traditional animation) or nonlinear (where the playhead jumps arbitrarily to any frame), our example movies have normally comprised only the frames of a single timeline. Ostensibly, a single timeline may seem to provide everything you'd need to create any Flash behavior, but as you get more inventive or ambitious, you'll soon find yourself conceiving ideas for animated and interactive segments that are thwarted by the limits of a single timeline.

Suppose that you want to create a looping animation of a dog with its tail wagging. You decide that the tail should wag every 5 seconds and the dog should bark every 15 seconds. On a single timeline, you'd need a loop of 360 frames to accommodate the timing of the bark (assuming a frame rate of 24 frames per second), and repeating keyframes for the wagging tail artwork every 120 frames. Although animating a dog in that manner would be a bit cumbersome, it wouldn't be impossible — until your dog had to move around the screen as an integrated whole. Making the bark and the wagging tail loop while the whole dog moved around complex paths for extended periods of time would quickly become impractical, especially if the dog was only one part of a larger environment.

Now imagine that you could make the dog by creating two whole separate movies, one for the tail and one for the barking mouth and sound. Could you then place those movies as self-contained, animated objects on the Main Timeline, just like a graphic or a button? Well, you can — that's what Movie Clips are all about. Movie Clips are independent sequences of frames (timelines) that can be defined outside the context of the Main Timeline and then placed onto it as objects on a single frame. You create Movie Clips the same way you create a Graphic symbol in Edit mode. Unlike a graphic symbol, a Movie Clip (as the name somewhat implies) acts in most cases just like a fully functional movie or .swf file, meaning, for example, that frame actions in Movie Clip timelines are functional.

After you have created a Movie Clip as a symbol, you drop instances of it into any keyframe of the Main Timeline or any other Movie Clip timeline. The following are some general Movie Clip principles:

- During playback as a Flash .swf file, a Movie Clip instance placed on a timeline begins to play as soon as the frame on which it occurs is reached, whether or not the Main Timeline (or the clip's parent timeline) is playing.

- A Movie Clip plays back autonomously, meaning that as long as it is present on the Stage it is not governed by the playing or stopping of the Main Timeline.

- Movie Clips can play when the Main Timeline is stopped, or stay halted when the Main Timeline plays.

- Like a Graphic or a Button symbol, Movie Clips can be manipulated on the Stage — you can size them, skew them, rotate them, place effects such as alpha blending on them, or tween them, all while the frames within them continue to play.

Tip

Movie Clip instances can use filter effects and blend modes. You create these effects in real time and set them in the Properties panel or with ActionScript code. ■

- All timelines play at the frame rate specified by the Document Properties dialog box (Modify ➪ Document) or the Properties panel (when the Document window is focused, and all items on the Stage are deselected). However, it is possible to modify playback behavior of a timeline with ActionScript routines.

In our dog wagging and barking example, the tail and head of the dog could be looping Movie Clips, and then those Movie Clips could be nested inside another Movie Clip symbol (representing the entire dog). This "whole" dog clip could then be tweened around the Stage on the Main Timeline to make the dog move. You could use the same principle to move a Movie Clip of a butterfly with flapping wings along a motion path.

One movie, several timelines

Because a Flash movie can have more than one timeline existing in the same space and time, there must be a way to organize Movie Clips within the Main Timeline (Scene 1) of your Flash document. Just as artwork can be placed inside any symbol, symbol instances can be nested within other symbols. If you change the contents of the nested symbol, the parent symbol (the symbol containing the other symbol) is updated as well. Although this may not seem special, it's of extreme importance to Movie Clips and Flash interactivity. Because the playback of each Movie Clip timeline is independent from any other timeline, you need to know how to tell Flash which Movie Clip you want to control.

The Flash movie diagram in Figure 16.1 illustrates multiple timelines. This Flash movie has two layers on the Main Timeline: Layer 1 and Layer 2. Layer 1 has a Movie Clip (instance "A") that exists for 19 frames on the Main Timeline. Layer 2 has a Movie Clip (instance "B") that exists for 10 frames on the Main Timeline, but it also contains a nested Movie Clip (instance "C").

This figure shows one method of diagramming Flash timelines.

Main Timeline

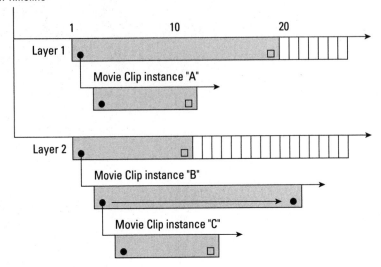

In Figure 16.1, if the Main Timeline has a stop action on the first frame, all three Movie Clips continue to play unless there are stop actions on their first frames or they are told to stop by actions targeted to them. If the Main Timeline plays to frame 20, instance "A" will no longer be on the Stage, regardless of how many frames it may have on its timeline. Figure 16.2 shows a more practical diagram of a timeline hierarchy.

Flash movies can be flow-charted in this fashion. This diagram is similar to the Movie Explorer's method of displaying Flash movie information.

Main Timeline

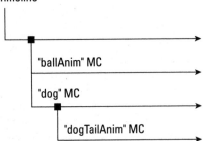

In Figure 16.2, you can see three Movie Clips. Two of them, `ballAnim` and `dog`, occupy space on the Main Timeline. The other one, `dogTailAnim`, is nested within the `dog` Movie Clip. Each Movie Clip instance on any given timeline *must* have a unique name — you can't have two or more Movie Clip instances on the same timeline using the same instance name. The instance name is specified in the Properties panel, as shown in Figure 16.3. To see the settings for a particular instance, you must have the instance selected on the Stage before referencing the Properties panel.

FIGURE 16.3

Among other things, the Properties panel enables you to name each Movie Clip instance that appears on the Stage.

Tip

The suffix `Anim` is the naming convention I use to designate a symbol name (in the library) containing an animation. As you can see in Figure 16.3 I name the instance `dog`, without any naming convention for the data type. You can derive your own naming convention if you'd like as long as you don't use spaces or special characters. You learn more about these concepts later in the chapter. ∎

Now that you understand how multiple timelines can exist within a Flash movie, let's see how you can make Movie Clips communicate with one another.

Targets and Paths Explained

If you already studied Movie Clips in Chapter 6, "Symbols, Instances, and the Library," you probably know that they provide the solution to our animated dog problem. However, you might not have guessed that Movie Clips can also add logic to animation and Flash interfaces. Let's take our animated dog example a little further: When dogs bark, their tails may stop wagging. Our hypothetical dog may look strange if it is barking and wagging at the same time. Suppose I wanted to stop the tail wagging during every bark. We'd have to have some way for the barking head Movie Clip to control the tail Movie Clip so that I could tell the tail to stop wagging when the dog barks, and then tell the tail to return to its wagging loop again when the bark is over.

What Is Dot Syntax?

The Flash 5 authoring tool introduced a new method of writing all ActionScript called *dot syntax*. Earlier versions of Flash used a natural-language scripting environment that was menu-based, in which actions could be read and understood easily and accessed via popup menus and dialog boxes. Although most people prefer easy-to-use scripting environments, the production demands of complex interactive projects are often compromised by such menu-driven scripting environments. Computer programmers prefer to create, edit, and debug scripting with a language they can access and modify easily. Consequently, we see the best of both worlds with Flash CS5.

ActionScript adheres closely to the ECMA-262 specification, the same specification upon which JavaScript is based. JavaScript is the universal scripting language most browsers use for Dynamic HTML (DHTML) documents. Therefore, Flash ActionScript uses a dot syntax, also known as *dot notation*. What does that mean? It means that all actions are written within a standard formula that is common with object-oriented programming (OOP) languages:

```
Object.property = value;
```

or

```
Object.method();
```

The examples beg four things to be defined: objects, properties, methods, and values. An *object* is any element in a program (in this case, the Flash movie) that has changeable and accessible characteristics. Objects can be user-defined (in other words, you create and name them) or predefined by the programming language. Flash has several predefined objects, also called *classes*, meaning that they're already built into the ActionScript language. I look at object types in more detail in later chapters. An important object (and perhaps the easiest to conceptualize) is the `MovieClip` object. Any Movie Clip instance on the Stage is a `MovieClip` object, such as `ballAnim` or `dogTailAnim`. An object has characteristics, or *properties*, that can be updated or changed throughout the movie. An example of a `MovieClip` property is scale, which is referred to as `scaleX` and `scaleY`. Properties always have some data accompanying them. This data is called the property's *value*. Using the previous example, at full size, a `MovieClip` object's `scaleX` is 100 (the scale property uses percent as the unit of measure). For a `MovieClip` object named `ballAnim`, this would be represented in ActionScript syntax as:

```
ballAnim._scaleX = 100;
```

Finally, objects can be enacted upon by procedures that do something to or with the object. These procedures are called *methods*. One method for the `MovieClip` object is the `gotoAndPlay()` method, which was used as a basic action in Chapter 17. In Flash Player 5 or later movies, methods can be created for your own objects or predefined for existing Flash objects. Any `goto` action can be used as a method of any `MovieClip` object, as in:

```
ballAnim.gotoAndPlay("start");
```

The preceding example tells the `ballAnim` instance to direct its playback head to the frame label `start` on its timeline. This chapter helps you understand how to use the `gotoAndPlay()` method for Movie Clips.

Well, you have a few ways to control the tail Movie Clip from the barking head Movie Clip. In Flash Players 3 and 4, the `tellTarget` action was used to let actions on any timeline (including Movie Clip timelines and the Main Timeline) control what happens on any other timeline. How? `tellTarget` simply provided a mechanism for extending basic actions such as `play` and `stop`, enabling them to specify (or *target*) the timeline upon which they should be executed. Targets are any Movie Clip instances that are available at the current "state" of a Flash movie — you can't target a Movie Clip that isn't displayed (or existing) on the Stage. For example, suppose you had two Movie Clips, one on frame 1 and another on frame 10 of the Main Timeline. If the Main Timeline was stopped on frame 1, you couldn't target the Movie Clip on frame 10 because the instance is not on the current frame.

Since Flash Player 5, developers have been able to direct actions to specific timelines by attaching the same actions as *methods* to a `MovieClip` object (I define methods in the sidebar, "What Is Dot Syntax?"). As such, the `tellTarget` action is a deprecated action; it's still supported in current Flash Players, but it's been replaced with more versatile actions and syntax that make its use outdated. For an overview of deprecated actions, see the sidebar on deprecated actions in Chapter 17. In this chapter, you work exclusively with the preferred ActionScript dot syntax to control Movie Clip instances. First, however, you need to understand how targeting works in Flash movies.

Note
If you're new to scripting, read the "What Is Dot Syntax?" sidebar. ■

Tip
If you're building Flash movies for mobile devices with Flash Lite 1.0/1.1, you need to use the `tellTarget` action to control Movie Clip instances. Flash Lite 1.0/1.1 is based on the Flash Player 4 specification. ■

Earlier in this chapter, you found out how multiple Movie Clip timelines appear on the Stage. It's entirely possible to nest several Movie Clip instances within another Movie Clip instances. To understand how Movie Clip instances communicate with one another by using actions, you need to have a firm grasp on Movie Clip paths. A path is simply that — the route to a destination, an address *per se*. If you have a Movie Clip instance named `tailAnim` inside a `dog` Movie Clip instance, how is Flash supposed to know? What if there was more than one `tailAnim` in the entire movie, with others nested in other Movie Clip instances besides the `dog` instance? You can specify a Movie Clip instance's path in an absolute or a relative mode.

Absolute paths

An *absolute path* is the full location information, or target, for a given Movie Clip instance from any other location (or target). Just like your postal address has a street name and number and a ZIP code so that people can find you on a map, all Movie Clip instances have a point of origin: the Main Timeline (that is, Scene 1). Flash CS5 only displays dot notation with absolute and relative paths.

Note

Dot notation and dot syntax are synonymous terms and are used interchangeably throughout this book. ∎

Dot notation follows the ActionScript language conventions. With ActionScript 3.0 dot notation, the Main Timeline becomes

```
root
```

A Movie Clip instance named dog on the Main Timeline (or root) would have an absolute path of

```
root.dog
```

Notice that a period, or dot, separates the term root from dog. The dot denotes a parent-child relationship; the dog instance is a "child" of its parent, root. And, following suit, a Movie Clip instance named tailAnim that is nested within the dog Movie Clip would have the absolute path of

```
root.dog.tailAnim
```

Relative paths

A *relative path* is a contextual path to one timeline from another. From a conceptual point of view, think of a relative path as the relationship between the location of your pillow and the rest of your bed. Unless you have an odd sleeping habit, the pillow is located at the head of the bed. You may change the location of the bed within your room or the rooms of a house, but the relationship between the pillow and the bed remains the same. Another example that can illustrate the difference between absolute and relative references is the postal address example I used earlier. An absolute reference to your residence would use your full street address, city, state, and ZIP code. However, if you're giving directions to a friend of yours who lives nearby, you're more likely to tell your friend, "From your house, walk two blocks down A street, and turn right on B street. I'm five houses down on the left side of the street."

With Flash, relative Movie Clip paths are useful within Movie Clip instances that contain several nested Movie Clip instances. That way, you can move the container (or parent) Movie Clip from one timeline to another and expect the inner targeting of the nested Movie Clip instances to work. To refer to a timeline that is above the current timeline in dot notation, use

```
this.parent
```

Here, the term this refers to the current timeline from where the action is being called, and parent refers to the current timeline's parent timeline. You can use relative dot notation to refer up and down the hierarchy at the same time. For example, if you have two nested Movie Clips, such as tailAnim and barkingAnim, within a larger Movie Clip named dog, you may want to target tailAnim from barkingAnim. The relative dot path for this task is

```
this.parent.tailAnim
```

This path tells Flash to go up one timeline from the current timeline, `barkingAnim`, to its parent timeline (the `dog` timeline), and then look for the instance named `tailAnim` from there.

You can also use successive `parent` references to travel up in the timeline hierarchy multiple times, such as

```
this.parent.parent
```

Using the `dog` instance example again, if you wanted to control the Main Timeline (which is the parent timeline of the `dog` instance) from the `tailAnim` instance, you could use `parent.parent` in the target path of an action executed from the `tailAnim` timeline.

Note

You can directly control the Main Timeline by using the reference `root`. The `root` keyword is specific to ActionScript 3.0. If you're planning to develop with ActionScript 1.0 or 2.0, use the legacy keyword `_root`. This edition of the Flash Bible exclusively covers ActionScript 3.0. For information about ActionScript 1.0 and 2.0, refer to past editions of the Flash Bible (Wiley). ∎

As with absolute paths, I recommend that you become familiar with using the dot notation for relative paths.

Okay, that's enough theory. Now, you're going to practice nesting Movie Clips inside of other Movie Clips, as well as target actions at specific instances by using dot notation.

Targeting Movie Clips in Flash CS5

In this section, you see how to make Movie Clips interact with one another by using dot notation and ActionScript. Specifically, you're going to create the barking and wagging dog example I discuss at the beginning of this chapter. You begin this exercise with a starter Flash document file (.fla) located on the book's CD-ROM.

On the CD-ROM

Open the `stella_starter.fla` file found in the `ch16/stella` folder of this book's CD-ROM. ∎

With the starter file open in Flash CS5, test the movie by using Control ⇨ Test Movie. You'll see that our dog, Stella, is wagging her tail. At timed intervals, she barks. Right now, her tail keeps wagging as she barks. In this exercise, I show you how to stop her tail from wagging while she is barking. Close the Test Movie window and take a look at the Library panel. You'll find the following assets listed:

- `bark.wav`: This is the sound file used for Stella's bark. You will find this sound on the bark layer of the barkAnimClip timeline.
- **BarkAnim:** This Movie Clip symbol contains the animation for Stella's barking head. If you double-click this symbol in the Library panel, you'll see that the timeline has two layers, one for the sound and another for the head animation. This symbol is used in the stellaClip symbol.

- **BodyGraphic:** This graphic symbol is artwork of Stella's body and legs. There is no animation on its timeline. The BodyGraphic symbol is used in the Stella symbol.

- **HeadGraphic:** This Graphic symbol is artwork of Stella's head. You'll find a couple of instances of this symbol in the BarkAnim symbol.

- **Stella:** This Movie Clip timeline contains instances of the BarkAnim, BodyGraphic, and TailAnim symbols.

- **TailAnim:** This Movie Clip symbol contains two instances of the TailGraphic symbol. Each instance is rotated differently to create the wagging effect.

- **TailGraphic:** This Graphic symbol contains the artwork for Stella's tail.

Now, you're going to add some behaviors to the movie. First, you'll need to name the instances in the movie. ActionScript can find a Movie Clip instance only by its instance name. Using the Properties panel, you'll add instance names to all the Movie Clip instances.

After the instances are named, you can then target the instances with ActionScript. In this example, you'll target the `tailAnim` instance from the `barkAnim` instance. When the keyframe containing the barking mouth inside of `barkAnim` is reached, the movie tells `tailAnim` to go to and stop on a specific frame. When the barking is over, `tailAnim` is told to continue playing.

1. **With** `stella_starter.fla` **open in Flash CS5, resave the document as** `stella_absolute.fla`. In this tutorial, you use absolute paths with your targets.

2. **Select the instance of the Stella symbol on the Stage, on the Main Timeline.** Open the Properties panel, and name the instance `dog` in the instance name field, as shown in Figure 16.4.

3. **Double-click the** `dog` **instance on the Stage to edit the Stella symbol in the Library panel.** Select the `BarkAnim` symbol instance, and again, using the Properties panel, name this instance `barkAnim` in the instance name field.

4. **Select the** `TailAnim` **symbol instance located on the tailAnim layer.** Name the instance in the Properties panel, using the name `tailAnim`.

5. **With all the Movie Clip instances named, you can now target actions to specific timelines.** Your first goal is to stop the wagging tail while Stella barks. Double-click the `barkAnim` instance to edit the BarkAnim symbol's timeline.

6. **On the BarkAnim timeline, create a new layer and rename it** `actions`. Place this layer at the top of the layer stack. On frame 14 of this new layer, insert an empty keyframe (F7). Frame 14 is the frame just before the stream sound on the bark layer begins. On frame 14, you want to tell the `tailAnim` instance to stop playing, so give this keyframe a frame comment that indicates this behavior. With the keyframe selected, open the Properties panel and, in the frame label Name field of the Label section, type **stop wagging** and choose Comment in the Type menu, as shown in Figure 16.5.

   After you have assigned a comment on the frame, you're ready to write the ActionScript to perform the described behavior.

FIGURE 16.4

You can name Movie Clip instances in the Properties panel.

7. **With frame 14 selected on the actions layer, open the Actions panel (F9/Option+F9)**
   Make sure that you are not working in Script Assist mode. Click the Target Path selector
   icon (see Figure 15.1 in Chapter 15 for its location). The Insert Target Path dialog box
   opens. Click the plus icon (+) on Windows or the twirl-down arrow on Mac next to the
   dog instance to reveal the nested instances, barkAnim and tailAnim, as shown in
   Figure 16.6. Select the tailAnim instance because it contains the wagging animation
   that you want to stop. Finally, make sure that the Absolute option is selected in the Mode
   setting. Click OK.

   In the Script pane of the Actions panel, you now see the path to the instance
   Object(root).dog.tailAnim.

Note

When you use the Insert Target Path menu, Flash places the word Object before root and wraps root in parentheses. This is called typecasting and is part of the formal best practice for using the root keyword. However,
your code will still work without it, so you can consider it optional. For more information about typecasting,
see ActionScript 3.0 Bible (Wiley, 2008). ∎

FIGURE 16.5

You can use frame comments to describe the actions on a keyframe.

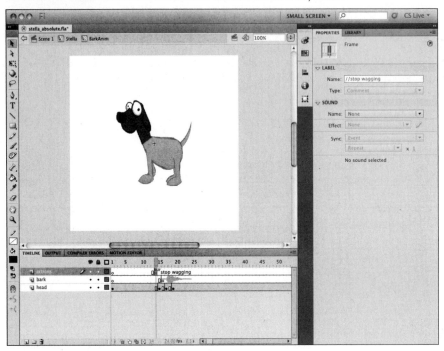

FIGURE 16.6

The Insert Target Path dialog box can help you build the path to a Movie Clip instance.

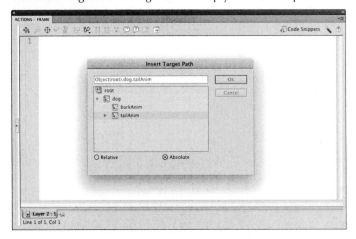

8. **After this name, type** `.stop();`. As described in the last chapter, the `stop()` action halts a playing timeline. When you are finished, the Script pane should contain the following code:

```
Object(root).dog.tailAnim.stop();
```

Tip

You can see code hints if you use ActionScript 3.0 strong data typing with a variable name. To try this technique, delete the line of code from Step 8, and type the following code:

```
var mc:MovieClip = Object(root).dog.tailAnim;
```

After you've declared a variable and its data type, the Actions panel can display code hints for that data type. On line 2, type:

```
mc.
```

As soon as you type the period (.) after the variable name `mc`, the Actions panel displays all the properties and methods of the `MovieClip` class. You can click the entry you want to use, and the Actions panel adds it to the existing line of code. If there are other parameters for the new code, the Actions panel displays code hints for those parameters as well. ■

9. **Use this same technique to tell the** `tailAnim` **instance to start playing again after the bark has ended.** In the BarkAnim symbol timeline, create yet another actions layer. You can make more than one to prevent overlap of your frame comments. Place this new actions layer beneath the original actions layer. On frame 23 of this second actions layer, insert an empty keyframe (F7). Assign a frame comment of **//start wagging** in the Label section of the Properties panel for this keyframe.

10. **Repeat Steps 7 and 8 for the action on this keyframe.** This time, however, type a `.play();` action from the code hints menu in the Actions panel. When you are finished, the following code should be on frame 20 of the actions layer:

```
Object(root).dog.tailAnim.play();
```

11. **Test your movie.** Save the Flash document, and use Control ➪ Test Movie to view your movie. When Stella barks, her tail should stop wagging. When the bark is over, the tail should resume wagging.

On the CD-ROM

This example has shown you how to target Movie Clip instances by using absolute paths built with the Insert Target Path dialog box in the Actions panel. However, you can also try using relative paths to target the instances. In the `ch16/stella` folder of the book's CD-ROM, open the `stella_relative.fla` file to see an example of relative path addressing. Note that this example also uses a `gotoAndStop(4)` action on the `//stop wagging` keyframe to make sure that Stella's tail is pointed down during the bark. You can also find a completed example file for the exercise you just completed, `stella_absolute.fla`. ■

Summary

- Movie Clips are a cornerstone of Flash interactivity for ActionScript projects. Each Movie Clip has its own independent timeline and playback.

- Each Movie Clip instance needs a unique name on any given timeline. You cannot reuse the same name on other Movie Clip instances on a timeline. You can, however, use the same instance name on different timelines.

- There are two types of target paths for Movie Clips: absolute and relative. Absolute paths start from the Main Timeline and end with the targeted instance name. Relative paths start from the timeline that's issuing the action(s) and end with the targeted instance name.

- The Insert Target Path dialog box can help you build the path to a Movie Clip instance to use with another action.

Making Your First Flash CS5 Project

Now that you've learned the basic principles behind Flash actions, you probably want to start creating a presentation to put on a Web site. This chapter integrates several basic production principles and teaches you how to make a simple interactive Flash movie that has basic navigation and text functionality.

Note

In this edition of the *Flash Bible,* we've updated all examples with interactivity to use ActionScript 3.0, which is compatible with Flash Player 9 or later. If you need to create projects with legacy versions of ActionScript (1.0 or 2.0), refer to previous editions of the *Flash Bible* (Wiley). ∎

The Main Timeline As the Site Layout

Before you can start creating a Flash project, you need to know what you're communicating — what is the basic concept of the experience? Is this an all-Flash Web site? Is this a Flash animation that introduces some other type of HTML-based content? For the purposes of this chapter, you create a Flash movie for a basic all-Flash presentation. In a sense, this project is the Flash equivalent of a Microsoft PowerPoint presentation. Let's look at the completed project (shown in Figure 17.1) that you will create in this chapter.

On the CD-ROM

In a Web browser, open the `main.html` document, located in the `ch17/ deploy` folder of this book's CD-ROM. This movie contains two completed sections of the presentation. ∎

FIGURE 17.1

The completed presentation

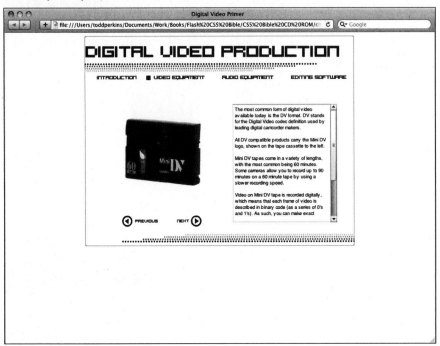

When you load the `main.html` file into a browser with the Flash Player 10 installed, you see the presentation's title, "Digital Video Production," along with four navigation buttons that take you to each section of the presentation. The opening section, Introduction, has scrolling text featuring the TextArea UI component. When you click the Video Equipment button in the navigation bar, a Movie Clip featuring five video items appears along with another instance of the TextArea component. The Next and Previous buttons enable you to browse the video items. Each video item uses a custom component that blurs and fades the item onto the stage.

If you have a screen reader installed and are using the Windows operating system, you will hear the screen reader describe each item in the Introduction section. A screen reader is an application that assists visually impaired computer users by speaking text aloud. The Flash Player 9 ActiveX control works only with screen readers that adhere to the MSAA (Microsoft Active Accessibility) specification built into Windows operating systems. As of this writing, only a handful of screen readers, such as the Window-Eyes screen reader by GW Micro and JAWS from Freedom Scientific, adhere to MSAA. In this chapter, you learn how to add accessibility information to elements in your Flash document.

Creating a plan

When you know what goals you want to achieve with your Flash content, you should map the ideas on paper (or with your preferred project planning or flowchart software). I create a basic presentation for digital video production that has four areas: introduction, video equipment, audio equipment, and editing software. The organizational chart for this site has four discrete areas, as shown in Figure 17.2.

Our organizational chart helps us plan our Flash movie architecture.

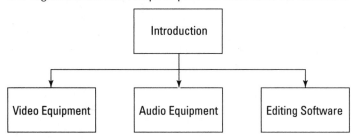

In this chapter, you create the first two sections: introduction and video equipment. If you prefer, you can continue to develop the presentation with graphics provided on the CD-ROM.

Setting up a local folder structure

As described in Chapter 3, an ideal production environment separates your authortime files, such as Flash documents (.fla), from your runtime files, such as Flash movies (.swf) and Web pages (.html). Before you begin creating content in Flash CS5, follow these steps to create suitable folders for your project's content:

1. **Pick a location on your local hard drive to store the files for this chapter.** Create a folder named ch17 in this location.

2. **Inside of the ch17 folder, create two folders:** deploy **and** src. The deploy folder will contain the runtime files, and the src folder will hold the authortime files.

3. **Inside of the src folder, create a folder named** actionscript. Inside of the actionscript folder, create a folder named includes. The includes folder will store ActionScript files (.as) that contain code referenced from the Flash documents (.fla) stored in the src folder.

Now you have the necessary folder structure to begin building the project in this chapter.

Determining Flash movie properties

After you've made your organizational chart, you'll want to determine the frame rate, size, and color of the Flash document. I've skipped much of the "real-life" planning involved with Flash-based Web sites, which are discussed in Chapter 3. For this example, I have made a starter Flash document for you to use that contains all the elements necessary to complete the chapter. This document contains some of the basic graphic elements already positioned on the Stage.

On the CD-ROM
Make a copy of the `main_starter.fla` document, located in the `ch17/src` folder of this book's CD-ROM. ■

Open the starter document in Flash CS5. This document uses a frame size of 640 × 480 (to maintain the aspect ratio of most computer monitors), a standard frame rate of 24 fps (frames per second), and a white background color. These are set in the Document Properties dialog box, shown in Figure 17.3, which is accessed by choosing Modify ➪ Document (Ctrl+J/⌘+J).

FIGURE 17.3

The Flash document properties

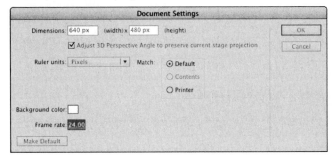

Mapping presentation areas to keyframes

When the Flash document properties have been determined, you can create a Main Timeline structure for the presentation. Because there are four areas in the project (introduction, video equipment, audio equipment, and editing software), you'll have keyframes on the timeline that indicate those sections.

1. **Create a new layer and name it** labels. Place this layer at the top of the layer stack in the Timeline window.

2. **With the Selection tool, select frame 10 of the labels layer, and press the F7 key.** This creates a keyframe on frame 10.

3. **With the keyframe selected, open the Properties panel.** In the Name field of the Label section, type **intro**. After you have typed the text, press Tab (or Enter) to make the name "stick."

4. **Repeat Steps 2 and 3 with frames 20, 30, and 40, with the frame labels video, audio, and software, respectively.**

5. **Select frame 50 of the labels layer, and press F5.** This enables you to read the very last label, software. Your Timeline window should resemble Figure 17.4.

FIGURE 17.4

You use frame labels to differentiate each section of the site.

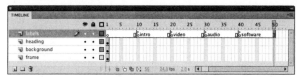

6. **Select frame 50 on all other layers in the Timeline window, and press F5 to extend the content on these layers across the entire timeline, as shown in Figure 17.5.**

FIGURE 17.5

The content in the heading, background, and frame layers will be present throughout the entire movie.

7. **Save your Flash document as** `main_100.fla` **in the** `src` **folder you created earlier in this chapter.**

8. **Make a new layer, and rename it** actions. Place this layer below the labels layer. Add a keyframe on frame 10 of the actions layer, and open the Actions panel (F9/Option+F9). Type the following code into the Script pane:

   ```
   stop();
   ```

9. **Close the Actions panel, and open the Properties panel.** Make sure that frame 10 of the actions layer is selected. In the <Frame Label> field, type **//stop**. The / / characters assign a frame comment rather than a frame label. Although this step isn't necessary for the functionality of the movie, frame comments can provide quick and easy access to the designer's or programmer's notes. Your Timeline window should now look like Figure 17.6.

FIGURE 17.6

Unlike labels, you cannot use frame comments in ActionScript. Comments can provide quick visual references for ActionScript code.

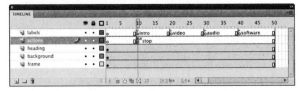

10. Save the Flash document again.

At this point, the Flash document has a skeleton architecture (a blueprint) for your interactive functionality. Now you'll add some content to each section of the movie.

On the CD-ROM

You can find the main_100.fla document in the ch17/src folder of this book's CD-ROM. ∎

Creating content for each area

In this section, you create navigation artwork for each area of the presentation. You also build some content for the video section.

1. **Resave the Flash file you modified in the last section as** main_200.fla. Save the file in the src folder.

2. **Create a new layer named** menu. Place this layer beneath the actions layer. Insert a keyframe on frame 10 of the menu layer.

3. **On frame 10 of the menu layer, use the Text tool to add a static text block with the text** Introduction. For this example, I use the Miniml font hooge 05_53 at 12 points with bold formatting. Use the Properties panel to set these options. Place the text near the left edge of the Stage below the heading, as shown in Figure 17.7.

4. **Repeat Step 3 for the text** Video Equipment, Audio Equipment, **and** Editing Software. Space these text blocks across the Stage beneath the heading, as shown in Figure 17.8. Again, all these text blocks should be on frame 10 of the menu layer. Later, you will convert each of these text blocks to a button symbol.

   Now, you create a graphic that lets the user know which section is currently active. To do this, you add a black square that will appear next to the appropriate text block. When the presentation starts, the black square will be next to the Introduction text. When the user navigates to the Video Equipment section, the black square will appear next to the Video Equipment section. Open the Library panel, and expand the graphics folder. There, you will find a graphic symbol named marker. You will use this symbol in a moment.

FIGURE 17.7

Use the Text tool to add the Introduction text to the Stage.

FIGURE 17.8

Add text that describes each section of the presentation.

5. **Create a new layer on your Main Timeline (that is, Scene 1), and name it** marker. Place this layer underneath the menu layer.

6. **On frame 10 of the marker layer, insert a keyframe.** Drag the marker symbol from the Library panel to the Stage. Position the instance of the marker to the left of the Introduction text, as shown in Figure 17.9.

7. **Insert another keyframe (F6) on frame 20 of the marker layer — make sure you do not insert empty keyframes.** Move the instance of the marker at frame 20 to the left of the Video Equipment text, as shown in Figure 17.10.

8. **Repeat Step 7 from frames 30 and 40 of the marker layer, moving the marker instance to the left of the Audio Equipment and Editing Software text, respectively.** You now have the marker changing its position for all sections of the timeline.

FIGURE 17.9

This marker designates the active section.

FIGURE 17.10

When the user goes to the Video Equipment section, the marker appears next to the Video Equipment text.

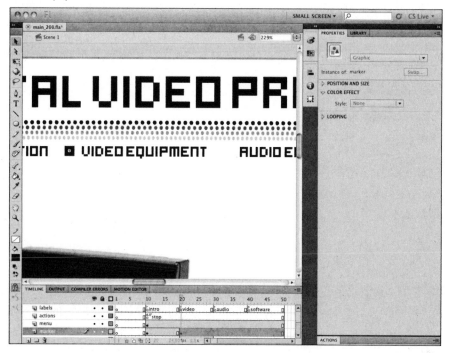

Main Timeline versus Scene Structure

Arguably, you might be wondering why you are using keyframes to delineate each section, rather than new scenes. There are a few reasons to use one scene (in other words, one Main Timeline):

- You can see the entire layout of the site very easily on one timeline.
- You can blend interstitials (transitions between each area of the site) over two sections more easily. It's much easier to have one Movie Clip instance span the area between two section keyframes on the Main Timeline.
- Scenes are not scriptable objects like Movie Clip instances are. You have greater flexibility with Movie Clips than you do with scenes.

Ultimately, the decision is yours. Make sure that you determine your Flash architecture well before you start production within the Flash CS5 authoring environment. It's not a simple task to rearchitect the layout after production has begun.

Now you'll add a slide show of the video equipment that can be used for digital video production. This slide show will appear in the Video Equipment section of the presentation. For this, you create a Movie Clip symbol that has each product graphic on a separate keyframe.

1. **Create a new symbol by using Insert ⇨ New Symbol (Ctrl+F8/⌘+F8).** Make sure that the Type option is set to Movie clip, and give it a name of **videoEquip**.

2. **Flash CS5 automatically switches to Edit mode on the videoEquip timeline.** Rename Layer 1 to **items**.

3. **Add keyframes to frames 2, 3, 4, 5, and 6 of the items layer.** There are six items in the `videoItems` folder of the Library panel, and each item is put on its own keyframe.

4. **Move the playhead to frame 1 of the videoEquip timeline, and drag the dvTape Movie Clip symbol from the `videoItems` folder of the Library panel to the Stage.** When an instance of the symbol is on the Stage, name the instance `tape` in the `<Instance Name>` field of the Properties panel.

5. **Continue moving the playhead to the next frame, dragging another item to the Stage for each frame.** Place cameraLow on frame 2, cameraMid on frame 3, cameraHigh on frame 4, dvDeck on frame 5, and dvCable on frame 6. Make sure that you name each instance in the Properties panel, using the following names: `camLow`, `camMid`, `camHigh`, `deck`, and `cable`. When you're finished, press the < and > keys to review your frames. Check Figure 17.11 to compare your work. You may want to center each graphic on the Stage by using the Align panel (Ctrl+K/⌘+K). As you progress with this exercise, you can adjust the exact placement of each item. Before you proceed to the next step, check that each instance is named in the Properties panel.

6. **Now you need to insert an actions layer for this Movie Clip symbol.** Create a new layer, and rename it **actions**. Select frame 1 of the actions layer, and open the Actions panel. Add a `stop` action to make sure that the items don't automatically loop when the movie loads:

   ```
   stop();
   ```

7. **Return to the Main Timeline (Scene 1) by clicking the Scene 1 tab in the upper-left corner of the document window.**

8. **Create a new layer, and rename it** content. Place this layer underneath the marker layer. Insert a new keyframe on frame 20 of the content layer.

9. **Open the Library panel, and drag the videoEquip symbol from the library to the Stage.** Place it just left of the center of the Stage, as shown in Figure 17.12. In the Properties panel, name this instance `equip`.

10. **Select frame 30 of the content layer, and press the F7 key.** This inserts a blank keyframe. Now, the `equip` instance will show only in the Video Equipment area of the timeline.

11. **Save your Flash document.**

Now you have some content in the Flash document. In the next section, you add navigation controls to the presentation.

FIGURE 17.11

You should have six filled keyframes on the item layers of the videoEquip timeline.

FIGURE 17.12

The equip instance will be present only in the video section of the timeline.

On the CD-ROM

You can find the `main_200.fla` **document in the** `ch17` **folder of this book's CD-ROM.** ■

Adding Navigation Elements to the Main Timeline

In the last section, you created a timeline for a digital video production presentation. You inserted content placeholders for the intro, video, audio, and software sections of the timeline, and you made a Movie Clip with video item graphics to place in the video section. However, the user has no way of actually getting to any section except the intro frame. In this section, you convert the text blocks in the menu to button instances, whose actions control the position of the playhead on the Main Timeline.

Creating text buttons for a menu

In this part of the exercise, you make menu buttons that enable the user to navigate to the different areas of the Flash movie.

1. Resave the `main_200.fla` **file as** `main_300.fla` **in the** `src` **folder.**

2. **On the Main Timeline of the file, select frame 10 of the menu layer.**

3. **With the Selection tool, select the Introduction text block.** Press F8 to convert this text into a symbol. In the Convert to Symbol dialog box, name the symbol **introButton**. Assign it a Button type. Click the top-left corner of the Registration box, as shown in Figure 17.13.

FIGURE 17.13

The introButton symbol settings

---

4. **Select the button instance on the Stage, and at the top field of the Properties panel, type** introBtn **in the Instance name field.** You will target the button in ActionScript 3.0 code you create later in this chapter. Naming your instances is a good habit to get into.

   Now you need to add a Hit state to the introButton timeline. By default, Flash CS5 uses the last frame of a Button symbol timeline for the Hit state, unless content is added to the Hit state keyframe.

5. **Double-click the** introBtn **instance on the Stage to switch to Edit mode.**

6. **On the timeline of the introButton symbol, select the Hit frame of Layer 1.** Press the F7 key to insert an empty keyframe.

7. **Click the Onion Skin Outlines button in the Timeline window toolbar.** This enables you to view the previous frames of the introButton timeline, as shown in Figure 17.14.

8. **Select the Rectangle tool, and draw a filled rectangle that covers the same area of the Introduction text block.** You can use any fill color because the user never sees the Hit state. Make sure you turn off the stroke, or delete the stroke after the shape is drawn. Your button's timeline should resemble the one shown in Figure 17.15.

9. **Select the shape you drew in Step 8, and press F8 to convert it to a graphic symbol named** hitArea. As with the introButton symbol, make sure that the Registration icon is active in the top-left corner. You will reuse this shape for the other buttons in this section.

   Next you add an Over state to the introButton so that the user has a visual indication that it's an active button.

10. **Select the Over frame of Layer 1, and press F6.** This copies the contents of the previous keyframe into the new one. Select the Introduction text block with the Selection tool, and change the fill color to a shade of blue such as #0099CC in the Tools panel or the Properties panel. You can also turn off Onion Skin Outlines at this point.

FIGURE 17.14

Onion skinning enables you to align the contents of several keyframes accurately.

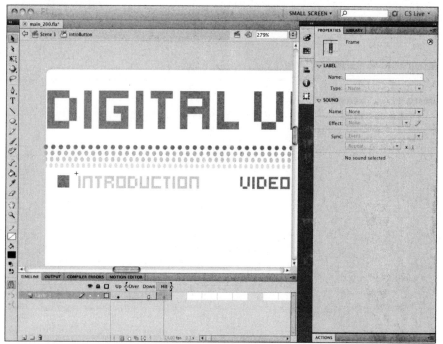

FIGURE 17.15

The Hit state defines the "active" area of the button instance in the movie. When the user's mouse pointer enters this area, the Over frame of the button appears.

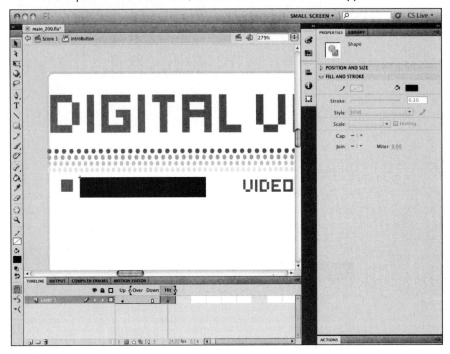

11. **Return to the Main Timeline (that is, Scene 1) of your document, and save your Flash document.** Choose Control ➪ Test Movie to test the states of the introButton. You can also use Control ➪ Enable Simple Buttons to preview the graphical states of a button instance directly on the Stage.

    Now you add ActionScript to the movie to enable interactivity with the introBtn instance. To aid the maintenance of ActionScript code for a project, you can create a separate ActionScript file (.as) to hold the code and use an include directive in the Flash document (.fla) to reference the external code.

12. **Choose File ➪ New.** In the New Document dialog box that appears (Figure 17.16), select ActionScript File and then click OK.

Tip

One of the visual benefits to using an ActionScript file is that you have a much larger document window to write your ActionScript code. With an ActionScript file, you do not use the Actions panel to insert ActionScript code. You can also easily switch to an ActionScript file from another document that is open in Flash CS5. ■

FIGURE 17.16

The New Document dialog box

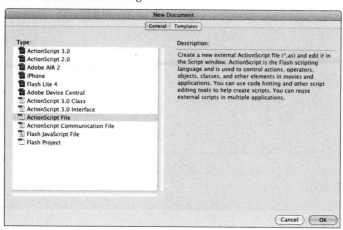

13. **Choose File ⇨ Save, and save the ActionScript file as** main_menu.as **in the** src/
actionscript/includes **folder you created earlier in this chapter.**

14. **In the ActionScript file, type the following code.** Do not type the ⤸ character, which indicates a continuation of the same line of code.

```
//SimpleButton introBtn;

import flash.events.MouseEvent;
import flash.display.SimpleButton;

introBtn.addEventListener(MouseEvent.CLICK, onMenuClick);

function onMenuClick(evt:MouseEvent):void {
   var btn:SimpleButton = evt.currentTarget as SimpleButton;
   var frame:String = btn.name.substring(0, ⤸
      btn.name.indexOf("Btn"));
   this.gotoAndStop(frame);
}
```

The first line of code tells the Flash CS5 authoring environment to display the code hints of the SimpleButton class for the introBtn instance. In ActionScript 3.0, a button symbol belongs to the SimpleButton class.

The import statements tell the ActionScript compiler to reference the MouseEvent and SimpleButton classes that are part of the intrinsic Flash Player classes.

The introBtn.addEventListener() line of code tells the introBtn instance to trigger a function named onMenuClick whenever the user's mouse clicks the introBtn instance. The click event is designated by MouseEvent.CLICK.

The function named `onMenuClick` processes the mouse click event. The first line of code within the function retrieves a reference to the button broadcasting the event. Here, the reference named `btn` refers back to the `introBtn` instance. The second line of code determines which frame the Flash movie should now show by examining the button's name. The `introBtn` instance (`btn.name`) contains the name of the frame to which it belongs, `intro`. The variable named `frame` is then passed to a `gotoAndStop()` action which moves the playhead on the Main Timeline to the proper frame label.

15. Save the `main_menu.as` file, and switch back to the `main_200.fla` document.

16. On the Main Timeline, create a new layer named menu actions, and place this layer above the existing actions layer.

17. Insert an empty keyframe (F7) on frame 10 of the menu actions layer. Select this frame and open the Actions panel (F9,/Option+F9). In the Script pane, type the following line of code. The `include` directive tells the ActionScript compiler to grab the contents of the `main_menu.as` file whenever you test or publish the Flash movie (.swf):

```
include "actionscript/includes/main_menu.as";
```

To make sure that you've typed the path correctly, click the Check Syntax button (designated by a blue check mark) in the toolbar of the Actions panel. If the Output panel reports any errors, make sure that you saved `main_menu.as` in the location stated in Step 15.

If you test your movie at this point, your `introBtn` instance won't do anything — the playhead already stops on the `intro` frame label when the movie starts.

18. Add a button for each section on the site. Repeat Steps 3@nd10 for each section name in your movie. Note that you should reuse the hitArea graphic symbol from Step 9 for the remaining buttons — use the Free Transform tool to size each new instance of hitArea to match the size of the text block in the button symbol. You should end up with four named button instances on the Stage: `introBtn`, `videoBtn`, `audioBtn`, and `softwareBtn`.

Tip

When you're finished making all the buttons, make a folder in the Library panel named `buttons`, and move the button symbols and the hitArea graphic into the new folder. ■

19. Go back to the `main_menu.as` file, and create additional listeners for the new button instances, as shown in the following code:

```
//SimpleButton introBtn;
//SimpleButton videoBtn;
//SimpleButton audioBtn;
//SimpleButton softwareBtn;

import flash.events.MouseEvent;
import flash.display.SimpleButton;

introBtn.addEventListener(MouseEvent.CLICK, onMenuClick);
videoBtn.addEventListener(MouseEvent.CLICK, onMenuClick);
audioBtn.addEventListener(MouseEvent.CLICK, onMenuClick);
softwareBtn.addEventListener(MouseEvent.CLICK, onMenuClick);
```

```
function onMenuClick(evt:MouseEvent):void {
    var btn:SimpleButton = evt.currentTarget as SimpleButton;
    var frame:String = btn.name.substring(0,
        btn.name.indexOf("Btn"));
    this.gotoAndStop(frame);
}
```

20. Save the `main_menu.as` file.

21. Save your Flash document (.fla file) as **main_300.fla** in the src folder and test it (Ctrl+Enter/⌘+Enter).

On the CD-ROM

You can find the `main_300.fla` **document in the** `ch17/src` **folder of this book's CD-ROM. The completed** `main_menu.as` **file is located in the** `ch17/src/actionscript/includes` **folder.** ■

When you test your Flash movie, you should be able to click each button to go to each area of the movie — you should see the square marker move to each category name when you click the name. If a button isn't functioning, double-check the code in the `menu_actions.as` file. Make sure that each button instance is named in the Properties panel. In the next section, you add buttons to the videoEquip Movie Clip symbol so that the user can browse the pictures of the video items.

Browsing the video items

In this section, you go inside the videoEquip symbol and add some navigation buttons for the video items.

1. **Resave the main_300.fla file as** `main_400.fla`.

2. **From the Main Timeline, double-click the** `equip` **instance on frame 20 of the content layer.** Flash CS5 switches to Edit mode.

3. **Make a new layer on the videoEquip timeline, and rename the layer** buttons. Place this layer below the actions layer.

4. **Open the Buttons Library (Window ➪ Common Libraries ➪ Buttons).** In the Buttons Library panel, double-click the classic buttons folder, and then double-click the Circle Buttons folder. Drag the circle button — next instance symbol to the Stage. Place the button instance below and to the right of the `mcTape` instance. Name the new button instance `nextBtn` in the Properties panel.

5. **With the circle button — next instance selected, press Ctrl+D (⌘+D) to duplicate the instance on the Stage.** Name the duplicate instance `prevBtn` in the Properties panel. Move the duplicate instance to the left of the original arrow button. With the Free Transform tool selected, enable the Rotate modifier in the Tools panel. Rotate the duplicated button 180 degrees. Press Shift while rotating, to lock in 45-degree steps.

6. **Select both arrow buttons, and align them horizontally to each other by using the Align panel.** Insert some descriptive text next to the instances, as shown in Figure 17.17.

FIGURE 17.17

Add text to the buttons to describe their functionality.

As discussed in the last section, you can create an external ActionScript file (.as file) to contain code for your Flash document. Start by replacing the existing `stop()` action on frame 1 of the videoEquip timeline with an `include` directive pointing to an ActionScript file.

7. **Select frame 1 of the actions layers, and open the Actions panel (F9/Option+F9).** Delete the `stop();` action, and type the following line of code:

```
include "actionscript/includes/video_equipment.as"
```

You create this new ActionScript file in the next step.

8. **Create a new ActionScript file (File⇨New) and save the file as** `video_equipment.as` **in the** `src/actionscript/includes` **folder you created at the beginning of the chapter.**

9. **In the new script file, type the following code.** This code uses the same event, `MouseEvent.CLICK`, as the main menu buttons. Here, the `onPrevClick()` and `onNextClick()` functions act as listeners, sending the Movie Clip timeline to the previous or next frame, respectively:

```
//SimpleButton prevBtn;
//SimpleButton nextBtn;

import flash.events.MouseEvent;

prevBtn.addEventListener(MouseEvent.CLICK, onPrevClick);
nextBtn.addEventListener(MouseEvent.CLICK, onNextClick);

stop();

function onPrevClick(evt:MouseEvent):void {
    this.prevFrame();
}

function onNextClick(evt:MouseEvent):void {
    this.nextFrame();
}
```

10. **Save the** `video_equipment.as` **file, switch back to your Flash document (.fla file), and test it by choosing Control ⇨ Test Movie (Ctrl+Enter/⌘+Enter).** Click the Video Equipment button, and try the new navigation arrows for your video items catalog.

You can enhance your presentation by adding information in the videoEquip Movie Clip symbol. In the next section, you add a scrolling text window that displays descriptions of the video items.

On the CD-ROM

You can find the `main_400.fla` document in the `ch17/src` folder of this book's CD-ROM. ∎

The topic of Flash usability has received a lot of press, particularly because many Flash interfaces are considered experimental or nonintuitive to the average Web user. Since December 2000, Adobe has maintained a special usability section in its Web site. You can read usability tips and view examples of interface design at `www.adobe.com/devnet/flash/testing_usability.html`.

Closely related to usability is accessibility: How easily can someone with a disability access the content within your Flash movie? I show you Flash movie accessibility options in the final section of this chapter.

Text Scrolling with the TextArea Component

Continuing from the previous Flash movie example with the digital video production presentation, you learn how to create basic scrolling text by using the TextArea component in Flash CS5. You can scroll text in Flash files (ActionScript 3.0) with either the UIScrollBar or the TextArea component. I demonstrate the use of the TextArea component for one item in the videoEquip symbol to get you started.

1. **Resave the** `main_400.fla` **file as** `main_500.fla`.

2. **In the Flash document you created from the previous section, double-click the** `equip` **instance on the Stage, at frame 20 of the content layer.** Flash CS5 switches to Edit mode.

3. **Add a new layer, and rename it** infoArea. Move this layer beneath the buttons layer, and select frame 1 of the infoArea layer. Now, open the Components panel (Ctrl+F7/ ⌘+F7). In the User Interface nesting, drag an instance of the TextArea component to the Stage, to the right of the `tape` instance.

4. **Use the Free Transform tool to stretch the component instance.** This instance should accommodate several lines of text19. The size of the instance should match the size of the text area you want to appear in the scrolling text window. In the Properties panel, name the TextArea instance `infoArea`.

5. **Open the Properties panel, and expand the COMPONENT PARAMETERS section.** With the `infoArea` instance selected on the stage, change the `editable` setting to `false`; the user should not be able to change the contents of the text field at runtime. Your videoEquip timeline should resemble Figure 17.18.

   Now, you'll need to supply some text to the `infoArea` instance. You can specify text directly in the `text` or `htmlText` parameter of the instance in the Properties panel, but for this project you'll learn how to format HTML text that is assigned in ActionScript to the TextArea component. Open the `item_1.rtf` document in a text editor such as WordPad or TextEdit. This file is located in the `ch17/src/text` folder of this book's CD-ROM. Now, open the `item_1_formatted.txt` document on the CD-ROM, and compare it to the `item_1.rtf` version. (You may want to enable word wrapping in your text editor so that you can see all the text in the TXT file.) You'll notice that all the text in the TXT file is specified in one continuous nonbreaking line. Moreover, any carriage returns in `item_1.rtf` have been replaced with `<br/>` tags in the TXT version. Some characters, such as the double quotes around the word "data," have been escaped in the TXT file — that is, the character is preceded by a backslash (\ ). These special formatting characters ensure that ActionScript correctly displays the text.

6. **Select all the text in the** `item_1_formatted.txt` **file, and copy it.** Later in this exercise, you'll paste the text into your own ActionScript code.

7. **On the videoEquip timeline, create a new layer and rename it** actions - text. Place this layer below the existing actions layer.

8. **Select frame 1 of the actions - text layer, and open the Actions panel (F9/Option+F9).** Here, you set a variable named `info` to the text to be displayed in the TextArea instance. In the Script pane, type the following code:

   ```
   info = "";
   ```

9. **Between the pair of double quotes you typed in Step 8, paste (Ctrl+V/⌘+V) the copied text into the Script pane.** Initially, the text should appear on one line, but you can choose Word Wrap in the options menu of the Actions panel to see all the text, as shown in Figure 17.19.

FIGURE 17.18

This text field displays the text associated with the first video item.

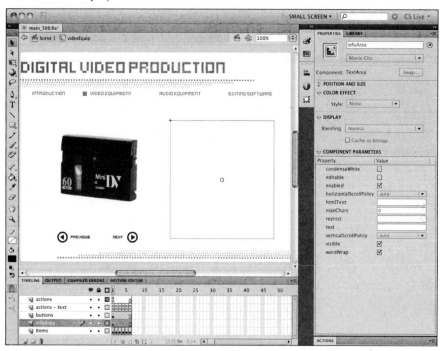

FIGURE 17.19

The Actions panel displaying the code to assign text to the TextArea component

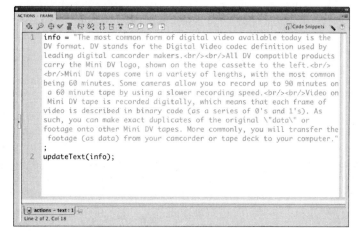

10. After the semicolon (;) at the end of the code you created in Steps 8 and 9, press Enter to start a new line of code. Type the following code:

```
updateText(info);
```

You define the updateText() function in the next step. This function processes the text stored in the info variable and displays it in the infoArea instance.

11. Reopen (or switch back to) the video_equipment.as file you created in the last section. Add the new code shown in bold in the following code block:

```
//SimpleButton prevBtn;
//SimpleButton nextBtn;
//TextArea infoArea;

import flash.events.MouseEvent;

prevBtn.addEventListener(MouseEvent.CLICK, onPrevClick);
nextBtn.addEventListener(MouseEvent.CLICK, onNextClick);

var info:String;

stop();

function onPrevClick(evt:MouseEvent):void {
    this.prevFrame();
}

function onNextClick(evt:MouseEvent):void {
    this.nextFrame();
}

function updateText(val:String):void {
    infoArea.htmlText = val;
    infoArea.verticalScrollPosition = 0;
}
```

This new code declares the info variable as a String variable, which can store text information. The updateText() function processes String data passed to it, setting the htmlText property of the infoArea instance to the new HTML text passed into the function. The vertical scrollbar's scroller is reset to the top of the scrollbar, if the amount of text requires a vertical scrollbar to appear.

12. Save the video_equipment.as file, and switch back to the Flash document (.fla file). Test the Flash document (Ctrl+Enter/⌘+Enter). Click the Video Equipment navigation button, and try the TextArea component. If the text is not appearing or scrolling, go back to the authoring environment and double-check the ActionScript code on frame 1 of the actions - text layer as well as the new code added to the video_equipment.as file. Do not proceed with any steps until the TextArea component is functioning properly.

Now, you're ready to set up the text for the second item on the videoEquip timeline.

13. **Select frame 2 of the actions - text layer, and press F7 to insert an empty keyframe.** Add the same actions and text as shown in Steps 8 and 10, but this time, copy and paste the text from the `item_2_formatted.txt` file (located in the `ch19/src/text` folder of this book's CD-ROM).

14. **Save your Flash document (.fla file) and test it (Ctrl+Enter/⌘+Enter).** When you navigate to the Video Equipment section, you should be able to click the Next button to see the text for item 2.

15. **Repeat Step 13 for frames 3, 4, 5, and 6 of the actions - text layer.** When you are finished, you should have six separate action keyframes, one per item on the timeline.

16. **Save your Flash document again, and test it (Ctrl+Enter/⌘+Enter).** When you go to the Video Equipment section, you should be able to click the Next button to reach each video item's description field, and the field should be scrollable.

The next step in real production would be to finesse the artwork and to add transitional effects between each video item. The next section shows you how to add a custom Fade component that I created for your use in this exercise.

Note

You already added the ActionScript code in Step 11 to reset the scroll bar's position for each new item.

The `verticalScrollPosition` property controls the vertical position of the scroller. Setting it to zero resets the position to the top. So, if the user scrolls to the bottom of one description and presses the Next button, the next item's description reads from the top. ∎

On the CD-ROM

You can find the completed document, `main_500.fla`, in the `ch17/src` folder of this book's CD-ROM. You can also find the finished `video_equipment.as` file in the `ch17/src/actionscript/includes` folder. ∎

Using the Custom BlurFader Component

So far, much of the material and artwork used in this presentation could have been accomplished with a traditional HTML page layout in Adobe Dreamweaver with GIF or JPEG graphics. In this section, you add a fade effect to each of the video items in the videoEquip symbol. I created a custom component that can be applied to any Movie Clip instance on the Stage. This component fades a Movie Clip instance in or out, based on settings in the Component Inspector panel. To see this fade effect in action, open the `main.swf` file from the `ch17/deploy` folder in Flash Player 10. When you go to the Video Equipment section, each item fades and blurs in. In other words, the alpha of each Movie Clip instance animates from 0 to 100 percent while the blur value gradually decreases.

The BlurFader component snaps to Movie Clip instances. Because I built the component for you, you won't find the BlurFader component in the Component panel along with the Flash CS5 components. The BlurFader component is located in the starter document's library and has been saved in each version of the main_ document that you created in previous sections. Here's how to add the BlurFader component to the video items in the videoEquip symbol:

1. **Open your saved Flash document from the previous section, and resave the file as** main_600.fla.

2. **On frame 20 of the content layer, double-click the** equip **instance on the Stage to edit the symbol.**

3. **Select frame 1 of the items layer, and open the Library panel.** Drag the BlurFader component to the tape instance on the Stage. When you release the mouse button, the BlurFader component should snap to the top-left corner of the tape instance, as shown in Figure 17.20. I made a custom icon for this BlurFader component: a little gradient box with the text BF. Select the BlurFader instance and name it bf_1 in the Properties panel.

Note
The BF icon does not show up in the actual Flash SWF file — it appears only in the authoring environment. ■

FIGURE 17.20

The BlurFader component snaps to the top-left corner of the Movie Clip instance.

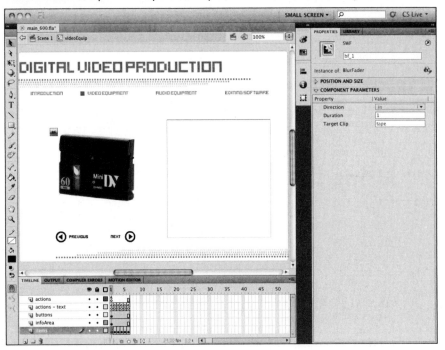

4. **You can view the default settings for the BlurFader component instance in the Properties panel.** Select the component instance at the top-left corner of the `tape` instance, and look in the COMPONENT PARAMETERS section of the Properties panel This component has three options, as shown in Figure 17.20: Direction (*in* to fade in the targeted instance, *out* to fade out the targeted instance), Duration (how long the transition should last, in seconds), and `Target Clip` (the Movie Clip instance that the BlurFader component instance has snapped to).

5. **Save the Flash document, and test it (Ctrl+Enter/⌘+Enter).** When you click the Video Equipment button, the first video item fades into the Stage.

6. **Repeat Step 3 for the other Movie Clip instances on frames 2, 3, 4, 5, and 6 of the items layer.** Make sure that you name each new instance of the BlurFader component, using the frame number as a suffix, such as `bf_2`, `bf_3`, and so on. Otherwise, the blur and fade effect does not execute on the new items.

7. **Save the Flash document again, and test it.** After you click the Video Equipment button, click the Next button. Each video item fades into the Stage.

If you want to use the BlurFader component in other Flash documents that use ActionScript 3.0, simply drag the BlurFader component from one library to another document's library. Alternatively, you can copy and paste the BlurFader component instance from one document to another. Try different Duration values for the BlurFader component (in the Component Inspector panel) to see how the fade animation is affected in the Flash movie.

Note

The BlurFader component adds about 2KB to the file size of your Flash movie file (.swf). ∎

On the CD-ROM

You can find the completed document, `main_600.fla`, in the `ch17/src` folder of this book's CD-ROM. ∎

Making the Movie Accessible

In the final section of this chapter, I show you how to add accessibility information to your Flash presentation. As I mention earlier in this chapter, screen readers on the Windows operating system, working in concert with the Flash Player 6 or later ActiveX control, can read aloud the content inside of Flash movies. Window-Eyes from GW Micro was engineered to work with Flash Player 6 or later through the use of MSAA (Microsoft Active Accessibility) technology. As of this writing, Window-Eyes is one of a limited number of screen readers capable of accessing Flash content.

Note

You can download a demo version of Window-Eyes for the Windows operating system at www.gwmicro.com. This version works only for 30-minute durations — you need to restart your computer to initiate a new session. ∎

I recommend that you review the Accessibility information in the Flash CS5 Help panel. Choose the Help ⇨ Flash Help command in the Flash CS5 application. I provide a quick overview of the Accessibility features of Flash CS5 in this section.

Note

Since Flash MX 2004, Adobe has added accessibility support to the authoring environment as well. This feature enables designers and developers with disabilities to more easily use Flash to author Flash movies. To find out more information about this feature, search with the term "accessibility" in the Help panel. ■

Screen readers access information within the Flash movie differently, depending on the features of the specific screen reader. Here I discuss accessibility options as they relate to Window-Eyes. You will add some content to the Introduction section of the presentation that Window-Eyes can read aloud.

1. Resave the last Flash document you created in the previous section as `main_700.fla`.

2. Insert an empty keyframe at frame 10 of the content layer on the Main Timeline (that is, Scene 1).

3. On frame 10 of the content layer, drag an instance of the TextArea component from the Components panel to the left side of the Stage. In the Component Inspector panel, name this instance `infoArea`. Change the `editable` setting to `false`.

4. Open the `introduction_formatted.txt` document in the `ch17/src/text` folder of this book's CD-ROM. Copy the text in this document. Select the `infoArea` instance in your Flash document, and paste the copied text into the `htmlText` setting of the Component Inspector panel, as shown in Figure 17.21.

FIGURE 17.21

The TextArea component can display HTML formatted text in the authoring environment. The screen reader can read aloud this text field's contents.

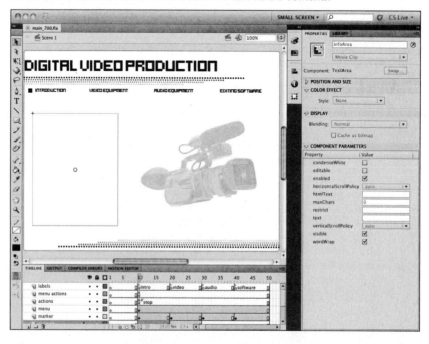

5. **With frame 10 of the content layer active, drag an instance of the cameraHigh Movie Clip symbol (located in the** `videoItems` **folder) from the Library panel to the Stage.** In the Properties panel, change the alpha of this instance to 30 percent. Name the instance `camHigh` as well.

   Now you will use the Accessibility panel to add information to specific elements in the Introduction section of the presentation. You can open the Accessibility panel by choosing Window ⇨ Other Panels ⇨ Accessibility.

   You can add general information about your Flash movie by deselecting all elements on the Stage (you can press the Esc key to do this quickly) and opening the Accessibility panel.

   The Make Movie Accessible option enables the screen reader to see elements inside the Flash movie. If this option is cleared, the screen reader cannot read any elements of the Flash movie.

   The Make Child Objects Accessible option enables the screen reader to access elements other than the current Name and Description in the Accessibility panel.

   Clear the Auto Label option. Auto Labeling tells Flash Player 6 or later to describe buttons and other elements by associating the closest text object to the element. For example, if you had some text underneath a Button instance, Auto Label would assign this text to the Button instance for the screen reader.

   The Name field enables you to assign a title to the Flash movie, and the Description field enables you to add a quick summary about the Flash movie. Window-Eyes reads the Name contents, but not the Description contents. Let's add some general information to the current Flash document.

6. **Deselect all the elements on the Stage, and open the Accessibility panel.** Select the Make movie accessible and Make child objects accessible options, and clear the Auto label option. In the Name field, type the presentation's title: **Digital Video Production**. In the Description field, type the following text: **A primer for digital video equipment and accessories.** (See Figure 17.22.)

7. **Now select the Introduction button on frame 10 of the menu layer.** In the Accessibility option, enter the options shown in Figure 17.23. Note that you do not assign a keyboard shortcut description for this example. The Name and Description for this button are read after the general information you added in the previous step. Window-Eyes says the word "button" before it reads the name. For this example, Window-Eyes says, "Button. Introduction. Access the introduction section of the presentation."

Note

If you do want to have a keyboard shortcut read by the screen reader, then you should type the text for any modifier key or combination including the + character, such as Ctrl+E. You also must add ActionScript to the movie to enable the key press that you described in the Accessibility panel. ■

FIGURE 17.22

The Accessibility panel controls options for the Flash movie and its elements.

FIGURE 17.23

Window-Eyes can read the Name and Description contents for buttons.

8. **Repeat Step 7 for each button instance in the menu layer.**

9. **Select the `infoArea` instance on frame 10 of the content layer, and make sure that the Make movie accessible and Make child objects accessible check boxes are selected in the Accessibility panel.** It is not necessary to add a description to this text field — the text inside of the field is read automatically by the screen reader.

10. **Select the `camHigh` instance on frame 10 of the content layer, and make sure that the Make child objects accessible and Make object accessible options are not selected in the Accessibility panel.** Not all elements need to be read by the screen reader, and this graphic does not need to be revealed to visually impaired users.

11. **Save your Flash document, and preview it in Internet Explorer for Windows.** Make sure that the Window-Eyes application is active. As soon as the movie loads into the browser, Window-Eyes reads the information for the movie and then reads the name and

descriptions of the buttons. Then it reads the text inside of the description text field. After Window-Eyes reads the last Flash element, it speaks the word "bottom," indicating that the end of the Web page has been reached. If you add body text to the HTML document, Window-Eyes reads that text as well.

On the CD-ROM

You can find the completed Flash presentation, `main_700.fla`, in the `ch17/src` folder of this book's CD-ROM. This document contains the first two sections of the presentations — on your own, try adding your content to the remaining sections by using techniques you learned in this chapter. ■

You can continue to add more accessibility information to other elements in the Flash document. You can even add information to elements within Movie Clip symbols. Try adding descriptions to the buttons inside of the videoEquip symbol.

Note

Screen reader technology can interface only with Flash movies played by the Flash Player 6 or later ActiveX control. Screen readers cannot access Flash movies played by the stand-alone Flash Player 6 or later. ■

Summary

- Before you can start to create an interface in Flash, you need to have a plan for your Flash movie timeline. Create an organizational chart outlining the sections of the presentation.

- Determine your Flash movie properties (frame size, frame rate, and background color) before you undergo production in Flash.

- If you don't have final art for a Flash production, you can still create a functional proto-type of the presentation by using placeholder graphics. When the final artwork is ready, replace the placeholder graphics with the final artwork.

- You can create simple slide shows or product catalogs by using sequential keyframes and buttons with `nextFrame()` and `prevFrame()` actions.

- The Hit area of a text-based Button symbol should always be defined with a solid shape.

- You can achieve basic text scrolling by adding the TextArea component to your Flash movie.

- You can apply time-based alpha and blur effects to artwork with the custom BlurFader component.

- You can add accessibility information to Flash movies. Windows-based screen readers designed to work with Flash Player 6 or later, such as GW Micro's Window-Eyes, can read this information.

Part VI

Distributing Flash Movies

When you finally have your project assembled in the Flash authoring environment and you're ready to prepare it for final presentation, this section explains all the options available for delivering Flash content to your audience. Chapter 18 details just about every option and setting in the Publish Settings dialog box for Flash CS5 that controls your final file size and format. This chapter includes tips for optimizing your file sizes for faster downloads and better performance. Chapter 19 covers several HTML techniques relevant to integrating Flash content on Web pages. Learn how to create plug-in and version detection systems for your Flash movies. If you are planning to distribute Flash content offline or you want to avoid plug-in problems, Chapter 20 walks you through the various methods for distributing your Flash movies as self-contained executable applications for CD/DVD-ROMs or other removable storage devices and using the Flash standalone player. Chapter 21 shows how to use Flash to make cross-platform applications using Adobe AIR. In Chapter 22, you will learn how to use Flash to create applications for the iPhone, and how to get those apps on your device.

Publishing Flash Movies

I f you have read Parts I through V of the book, you're probably more than ready to get your Flash movies uploaded to your Web server to share with your visitors. This chapter shows you how to create Flash movies (.swf files) from Flash CS5 so that they can be played with the Adobe Flash Player plug-in or ActiveX Control for Web browsers. I show you how to test your Flash movies, prepare Flash movie options, and adjust other output formats from Flash CS5, such as HTML documents and image formats.

Tip

In this chapter, you also learn how to take advantage of Flash CS5's Flash Player detection option. This feature adds the necessary JavaScript code to your HTML document in order to check the Flash Player plug-in version installed in a user's browser. ■

Testing Flash Movies

You have four ways to test your Flash movies: in the authoring environment by using the Control ⇨ Play command, in the authoring environment by using the Test Movie and Test Scene commands, in a browser by using the Publish Preview command, or in the stand-alone Flash Player by using Flash movie files (.swf) made with the Publish or Export Movie commands. You should test your Flash movie file (.swf) before you transfer Flash movies to your Web server or to the intended delivery medium for several reasons:

- Flash document files (.fla) have much larger file sizes than their Flash movie file (.swf) counterparts. To accurately foretell the network bandwidth that a Flash movie requires, you need to know how large the final Flash movie will be. If the download demand is too overwhelming for your desired Internet connection speed (for example, a 56K modem), you can go back and optimize your Flash document.

- The Control ⇨ Play command in the Flash authoring environment does not provide any runtime information. When you use the Test Movie or Scene command, you can view the byte size of each frame and how long it will take to download the .swf file from the Web server.

- Movie Clip animations and actions targeting Movie Clip instances cannot be previewed by using the standard Control ⇨ Play command (or the Play button on the Controller) in the Flash authoring environment.

Tip

You can temporarily preview Movie Clip symbol instances within the Flash authoring environment (for example, the Timeline window) by changing the symbol instance behavior to Graphic rather than Movie Clip. Do this by selecting the instance, opening the Properties panel, choosing Graphic in the behavior drop-down menu, and setting the Looping section's options menu to Play Once or Loop. However, if you switch the behavior back to Movie Clip, you will have lost the original instance name of the Movie Clip. ■

- Most scripting done with ActionScript cannot be previewed with the Play command. Enabling Simple Frame Actions or Simple Buttons in the Control menu has no effect with most ActionScript 3.0 syntax. You need to use Test Movie to try out most interactive functions in a Flash movie.

Tip

Any actions that require the use of remote server-side scripts, Flash Remoting, or Adobe Flash Media Server connections to load variables, movies, or XML data work in the Test Movie environment. You do not need to view your .swf files in a browser to test these actions, unless your server-side functionality has IP address restrictions that would prohibit playback from your local machine. ■

- Accurate frame rates cannot be previewed with the Play command (Control ⇨ Play) in the authoring environment. Most complex animations appear jerky, pausing or skipping frames when the Play command is used.

Using the Test Scene or Test Movie command

You can test your Flash movies directly within the Flash CS5 interface by using the Control ⇨ Test Movie or Test Scene command. When you choose one of these commands, Flash CS5 opens your Flash document in a new window as a Flash movie file (.swf). Even though you are "testing" a Flash movie, a new .swf file is actually created and stored in the same location as the Flash document file (.fla). For this reason, always saving your Flash document before you begin testing it is a good idea.

Caution

If your movie is currently titled Untitled-1, Untitled-2, and so on in the application title bar, it usually indicates that the document has not yet been saved. Make sure that you save your Flash movie with a distinct name before testing it. ■

Tip

Flash CS5 opens all tested movies in a separate nontabbed window. On the Windows version of Flash CS5, the Test Movie window hosts the playback and debugging commands. On the Mac version of Flash CS5, the application menu bar changes depending on which type of tab or window was focused (authoring document versus movie file). ■

Before you use the Test Scene or Test Movie command, you can specify the settings of the resulting Flash swf file. The Test Scene or Movie command uses the specifications outlined in the Publish Settings dialog box to generate .swf files. I discuss the Publish Settings dialog box later in this chapter. For the time being, you can use the Flash CS5 default settings to explore the Test Scene and Movie commands.

Test Movie

When you choose Control ⇨ Test Movie (Ctrl+Enter/⌘+Enter), Flash generates a .swf file of the entire Flash document that is currently open. If you have more than one Flash movie open, Flash CS5 creates an .swf file for the one that is currently in the foreground and that has "focus."

Tip

You can publish multiple .fla files at the same time by using the Project panel. To learn more about the Project panel, read Chapter 3, "Planning Flash Projects." ■

Test Scene

If you are working on a lengthy Flash document with multiple scenes, you may want to test your scenes individually. You can do this by using Control ⇨ Test Scene (Ctrl+Alt+Enter/⌘+Option+Enter). The process of exporting large movies via Test Movie may require many minutes to complete, whereas exporting one scene requires a significantly smaller amount of time. Movies that require compression for several bitmaps and MP3 sounds usually take the most amount of time to test. As you'll see in the next section, you can analyze each tested scene (or movie) with the Bandwidth Profiler.

Tip

You can use the Test Scene command while in Edit mode to export an .swf file that contains the current symbol timeline. The movie won't contain anything else from your Flash document. Note that the symbol's center point becomes the top-left corner of the playback stage. ■

One Reason to Use Imported MP3 Files

If you have imported raw audio files such as .wav or .aif files into your Flash document, you may notice lengthy wait times for the Test Movie or Publish commands to complete. Why? The default MP3 encoding process consumes much of the computer processor's power and time.

Flash CS5 has three MP3 compression qualities: Fast, Medium, or Best. Fast is the default MP3 quality setting — this is by far the fastest method of encoding MP3 sound. Because MP3 uses perceptual encoding, it compares a range of samples to determine how best to compress the sound. Fast compares a smaller range of samples than either Medium or Best. As you increase quality, the sampling range increases.

This process is similar to building 256-color palettes for video files; it's best to look at all the frames of the video (instead of just the first frame) when you're trying to build a palette that's representative of all the colors used in the video. Although MP3 doesn't quite work in this fashion, the analogy is appropriate. So, at Best quality, the MP3 encoding scans more of the waveform to look for similarities and differences. However, it's also more time intensive.

As strange as it may seem, the quality does not affect the final size of the Flash movie file (.swf). The bitrate of the MP3 sound is the same regardless of the quality setting. Again, we'll use an analogy — consider the file sizes generated by three different digital cameras that have the same number of pixels in the pictures. The best camera, which has the highest-quality lens and recording mechanism, produces better-looking pictures that capture detail *and* produces the same file size as the others. This is one of the few times where it's not about the amount of information stored in the compressed file — it's a matter of the accuracy and quality of the information within that quantity.

If you want to avoid the wait for Flash CS5 to publish Flash movies that use MP3 compression, I recommend that you compress your source audio files to the MP3 format (including support for VBR — Variable Bit Rate — compression) and import those MP3 files into Flash CS5. Unless the MP3 sound file is used for Stream Sync audio, Flash CS5 exports the audio in its original MP3 compressed format.

For more information on sound in Flash movies, read Chapter 12, "Adding Sound."

Note

As I mention earlier in this book, I highly discourage the use of multiple scenes in a Flash document (.fla file). Scenes are a legacy structural unit for Flash content and should be used only for long-form animation destined for broadcast use, such as video production for television or film. ■

Using the Bandwidth Profiler

Do you want to know how long it will take for a 56 kilobits per second (Kbps) modem to download your Flash movie or scene? How about a cable modem? The Bandwidth Profiler enables you to simulate any download speed.

On the CD-ROM

See the `ch18` folder of this book's CD-ROM for a Flash document named `bandwidth.fla`. We use that Flash document for this section. ■

To use the Bandwidth Profiler, you first need to create a movie or scene to test. When you create a Flash movie with the Control ⇨ Test Movie or Scene commands, Flash opens the .swf file in its own window.

View menu

The Test Movie or Test Scene viewing environment opens your Flash movie in a dedicated window with its own View and Control menus.

Note

On the Mac, the View and Control menus appear in the application menu bar, not in the Test Movie window. ■

The first three commands in the View menu are the same as those of the Flash Player plug-in viewing controls, while the others are specific to the testing environment:

- **Zoom In:** Selecting this option enlarges the Flash movie. The shortcut key for this command is Ctrl+=/⌘+=.

- **Zoom Out:** Selecting this option shrinks the Flash movie. The shortcut key for this command is Ctrl+-/⌘+-.

- **Magnification:** This submenu enables you to change the zoom factor of the movie. The Flash movie appears at the original pixel size specified in the Modify ⇨ Document dialog box when 100 percent (Ctrl+1/⌘+1) is the setting. For example, if the movie size is 500 × 300 pixels, it takes up 500 × 300 pixels on your monitor. If you change the size of the viewing window, the movie may be cropped. The lower section of this submenu enables you to change the viewable area of the Flash movie.

Note

In the Test Movie environment, only the 100% and Show All options are enabled in the View menu. The other magnification options are enabled in the authoring environment. ■

- **Bandwidth Profiler:** To view the Bandwidth Profiler in this new window, use View ⇨ Bandwidth Profiler (Ctrl+B/⌘+B). The viewing window expands to accommodate the Bandwidth Profiler. Here's a breakdown of each section of the profiler:
  - The left side of the profiler displays three sections: Movie, Settings, and State. Movie indicates the dimensions, frame rate, size (in KB and bytes), duration, and preload (in number of frames and seconds). The Settings area displays the current selected connection speed (which is set in the View ⇨ Download Settings menu). State shows you the current frame playing and its byte requirements. If you're using the Simulate Download feature (discussed later in this section), the State section displays the percent of the movie that has loaded.

- The larger right section of the profiler shows the timeline header and graph. The lower red line beneath the timeline header indicates whether a given frame streams in real time with the current modem speed specified in the Control menu. For a 28.8 Kbps modem, any frame above 200 bytes may cause delays in streaming for a 12 frames per second (fps) movie. Note that the byte limit for each frame is dependent on frame rate. For example, a 24 fps movie has a limit of 120 bytes per frame for a 28.8 Kbps modem connection.

- When the Bandwidth Profiler is enabled, two other commands are available in the View menu: Streaming Graph (Ctrl+G/⌘+G) and Frame By Frame Graph (Ctrl+F/⌘+F).

- **Streaming Graph:** By default, Flash opens the Bandwidth Profiler in Streaming Graph mode. This mode indicates how the Flash movie streams into a browser (see Figure 18.1). Alternating light and dark gray blocks represent each frame. The size of each block indicates its relative byte size. For our `bandwidth.swf` example, all the frames will have loaded by the time our playhead reaches frame 13 when the movie is played over a 56 Kbps connection. The shortcut key for Streaming Graph is Ctrl+G/⌘+G.

FIGURE 18.1

The Streaming Graph indicates how a movie will download over a given modem connection. Shown here is our `bandwidth.swf` as it would download over a 56 Kbps modem.

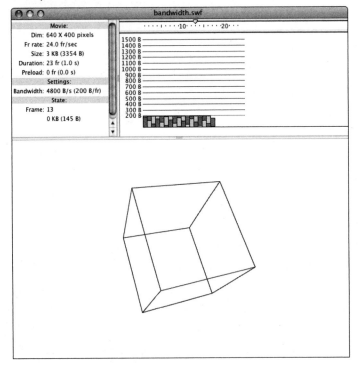

- **Frame By Frame Graph:** This second mode available to the Bandwidth Profiler lays each frame side by side under the timeline header (see Figure 18.2). Although the Streaming Graph enables you to see the real-time performance of a Flash movie, the Frame By Frame Graph enables you to more easily detect which frames are contributing to streaming delays. If any frame block goes beyond the red line of the graph (for a given connection speed), the Flash Player halts playback until the entire frame downloads. In the `band width.swf` example, frame 1, weighing in at 420 bytes, is the only frame that may cause a very slight delay in streaming when the movie is played over a 28.8 Kbps connection. The remaining frames are right around 200 bytes each — right at the threshold of 200 bytes per frame for a 28.8 Kbps modem connection playing a 12 fps Flash movie. The shortcut key for Frame By Frame Graph is Ctrl+F/⌘+F.

Note

If you use Flash CS5's new XMP metadata feature in the Publish Settings dialog box (discussed later in this chapter), you add bytes to the first frame of your Flash movie. Depending on the amount of information you specify, you shouldn't see much more than a few hundred bytes added to your overall .swf file size. ■

FIGURE 18.2

The Frame By Frame Graph shows you the byte demand of each frame in the Flash movie.

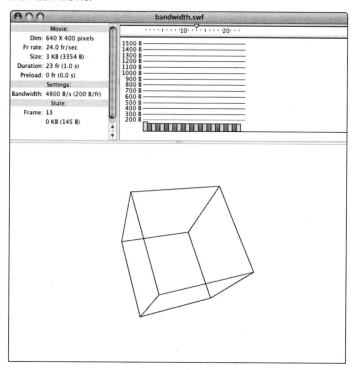

- **Simulate Download:** When the Simulate Download option is enabled, the Bandwidth Profiler emulates the chosen modem speed (in the View ➪ Download Settings menu) when playing the Flash movie. The Bandwidth Profiler counts the bytes downloaded (displayed in the Loaded subsection of the State heading) and shows the download/play progress via a green bar in the timeline header.

Tip

The Simulate Download command also applies to loaded runtime assets, such as SWF, JPEG, and MP3 files. For example, when a `loadMovie()` action begins to load another file, the left side of the Bandwidth Profiler shows the progressive download at the simulated download speed. This feature applies only to assets that are loaded locally, from your system, and not over an Internet connection. ∎

- **Download Settings:** The View menu also features a submenu of connection speeds, which work in tandem with the Streaming and Frame By Frame Graphs:

  - **14.4, 28.8, 56K, DSL, T1:** These settings determine what speed the Bandwidth Profiler uses to calculate estimated download times and frame byte limitations. Notice that these settings use more practical expectations of these modem speeds. For example, a 28.8 modem can theoretically download 3.5 kilobytes per second (denoted as KB/s in the Download Settings menu), but a more realistic download rate for this modem speed is 2.3 kilobytes per second.

  - **User Settings 6, 7, and 8:** These are user-definable speed settings. By default, they are all 2.3 KB/s.

  - **Customize:** To change the settings for any of the modem speeds listed previously, use the Customize command to input the new value(s).

- **Quality:** The Quality submenu controls the visual appearance of graphics within the Flash movie. By default, all graphics are displayed at High quality. You can choose from Low, Medium, or High quality in this menu.

- **Show Redraw Regions:** This option enables you to see which areas of the Flash movie are being updated on the screen. For example, if you have a Graphic symbol animation playing in the movie, a red outline frame appears around that portion of the Stage. Any and all redraw regions are bounded by such a red frame. You can use this feature to determine how much work the Flash Player is doing to redraw the Stage — many performance and playback issues are the direct result of too much screen redrawing.

Control menu

Use the Control menu to play (Enter key) or rewind (Ctrl+Alt+R/⌘+Option+R) the test movie. Rewinding pauses the `bandwidth.swf` movie on the first frame. Use the Step Forward (. or > key) and Step Backward (, or < key) commands to view the Flash movie frame by frame. If a Flash movie doesn't have a `stop()` action on the last frame, the Loop command forces the player to infinitely repeat the Flash movie.

You can use the Disable Keyboard Shortcuts command to turn off the shortcut keys for all the commands available in Test Movie mode. This is especially useful if you have enabled interactive key presses within ActionScript for your movie. For example, enabling the Return or Enter key for a button conflicts with the Play command (Control⇨Play). As such, when you press Enter while you test your movie, the movie plays to the next frame and the button actions are ignored.

Debug menu

The Debug menu contains List Objects and List Variables commands. List Objects can be used to show the names of Movie Clip instances or ActionScript objects in the Output window, and the List Variables command displays the names and values of any currently loaded variables, ActionScript objects, and XML data.

Using the size report

Flash also lets you view a text file summary of movie elements, frames, and fonts called a size report. In addition to viewing Frame By Frame Graphs of a Flash movie with the Bandwidth Profiler, you can inspect this size report for other "hidden" byte additions such as font character outlines. You can enable the size report to be created by accessing the Publish Settings dialog box (File⇨Publish Settings), clicking the Flash tab, and checking the Generate size report option. When it is enabled, you can view the size report in two ways:

- After you publish, publish preview, or export a Flash movie, go to the folder where the SWF file was created. In that folder, you'll find a text file accompanying the Flash movie. This file is named after your Flash movie's name, followed by "Report" and the TXT file extension, as in `bandwidth Report.txt`.

- When you test your Flash movie by using the Control⇨Test Movie command, the Output panel opens automatically in front of the Test Movie window. The report automatically loads into the Output panel.

On the CD-ROM

A sample size report, called `bandwidth Report.txt`, is included in the `ch18` folder of this book's CD-ROM. ■

A Word About the Export Movie Command _____

Even though Flash streamlines the process of creating Flash movies with the Publish commands (discussed in the next section), it is worth mentioning that the File ⇨ Export Movie command provides another route to creating an .swf file. Although the Publish command is the quickest way to create HTML-ready Flash movies, the Export Movie command can be used to create updated .swf files that have already been placed in HTML documents. In practice, I find that I rarely use the Export Movie command. If you don't need HTML documents published with your Flash movie, simply clear the HTML option in the Formats tab of the Publish Settings dialog box.

Publishing Your Flash Movies

After you've made a dazzling Flash movie complete with motion tweens, 3-D simulations, and ActionScripted interactivity, you need to make the Flash movie useable for the intended delivery medium — the Web or a CD- or DVD-ROM, to name a couple. As mentioned in the introduction to this book, you need the Flash CS5 application to open .fla files. Because the Flash Player plug-in uses .swf files, you must export or publish your .fla file in a format that your audience can use. More important, Flash documents are authoring documents, while Flash movies are optimized for the shortest delivery times and maximum playback performance.

You can convert your Flash document files (.fla) to Flash movie files (.swf) by using either the File ➪ Export Movie, Control ➪ Test Movie, or File ➪ Publish/Publish Settings command. You can specify just about all file format properties in one step by using the File ➪ Publish Settings command. After you've entered the settings, the File ➪ Publish command exports any and all file formats with your specified parameters in one step — all from the Flash CS5 application.

Three commands are available with the Publish feature: Publish Settings, Publish Preview, and Publish. I discuss each of these commands in the following sections.

Publish Settings

The Publish Settings command (File ➪ Publish Settings) is used to determine which file formats are exported when the File ➪ Publish command is invoked. By default, new Flash documents created with Flash CS5 use Publish Settings that export a Flash movie file (.swf) and an HTML file with the proper markup tags to utilize the Flash Player 10 plug-in or ActiveX control. If you want to customize the settings of the exported file types, you should familiarize yourself with the publish settings before you attempt to use the Publish command.

Tip

The Publish Settings dialog box has many features that were introduced in Flash MX 2004 and Flash CS3, with some updates in Flash CS5. You should be aware that the default ActionScript language version is AS2 or AS3 for new Flash documents in Flash CS5. ■

Selecting formats

Choose File ➪ Publish Settings to access the Publish Settings dialog box, which is nearly identical for both the Windows and Mac versions of Flash CS5. The dialog box opens to the Formats tab, which has check boxes to select the formats in which your Flash document will be published (see Figure 18.3). For each Type that is checked, a tab appears in the Publish Settings dialog box (with the exception of the Windows and Mac projector options). Click each type's tab to specify settings to control the particulars of the movie or file that will be generated in that format.

If you click the Use Default Names button, all the File fields fill in with the name of your Flash document, followed by the file format's suffix. For example, if your movie is named `sample.fla` and you click the Use Default Names button, this is the base from which the names are generated in publishing. Thus, `sample.swf`, `sample.html`, `sample.gif`, and so on would result.

Tip

You can enter nonversion-specific filenames for Flash documents that you incrementally save as you work. For example, if you have a Flash document named `main_100.fla`, **set the Flash movie filename to** `main.swf`, **and then every new Flash document version you save (for example,** `main_101.fla`, `main_102.fla`, **and so on) still produces a** `main.swf` **file. This way, you can consistently refer to one Flash movie file (.swf) in your HTML code and incrementally save your Flash documents. However, if you work on large Flash projects with a team of Flash designers and developers, you should consider using version control software, such as SVN (Subversion), CVS (Concurrent Versioning System), or Microsoft SourceSafe. With version control software, you don't need to resave files with new names; rather, you check in your changes to the version control system, which keeps track of each file version. I briefly discuss version control in Chapter 3, "Planning Flash Projects." ■**

FIGURE 18.3

The Formats tab of the Publish Settings dialog box enables you to select the published file formats and use default or custom names for these published files.

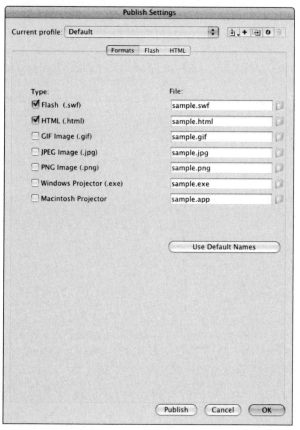

Tip

You can specify which folder a publish document is created and stored in. All the file formats have a folder icon to the right of the File field. If you click the folder icon, you can browse to a specific location where your published file will be created. You can use relative or absolute paths with the filenames in the Formats tab. ■

Using the Flash settings

The primary and default publishing format of Flash CS5 documents is the Flash movie .swf format. Only Flash movies retain full support for Flash actions and animations. To control the settings for the Flash movie, choose the Flash tab of the Publish Settings dialog box, as shown in Figure 18.4.

FIGURE 18.4

The Flash tab of the Publish Settings dialog box controls the settings for a movie published in the Flash format.

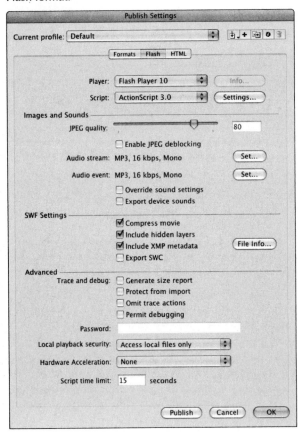

Here are your options in the Flash tab:

- **Player:** This drop-down menu provides the option to publish movies in any of the Flash movie formats. To ensure complete compatibility with all the new Flash CS5 features, select Flash Player 10. Each release of the Flash Player has added specific features and capabilities. If in doubt, you should test your choice of version in that version's Flash Player.

Tip

Flash CS5 has Flash Lite options in the Version menu. Flash Lite 1.0/1.1 is the most common Flash Player shipping with some mobile phones, such as DoCoMo phones in Japan. Newer phones may have Flash Lite 2.0, 2.1, or 3.0 installed. If one of these options is selected, make sure that you are using a Stage size that is compatible with the screen size of the mobile handset on which the movie will be deployed. Several templates are available for devices in the Global Phones, Japanese Phones, and PDA categories of the Template tab of the File ⇨ New dialog box. The new Adobe Device Central application that ships with Flash CS5 can help you find the right Flash document settings for a wide range of mobile devices. For more information on Device Central, read Chapter 20, "Using the Flash Player and Projector." ∎

- **Script:** This option controls how ActionScript is compiled in a Flash movie file (.swf). You can choose ActionScript 1.0, ActionScript 2.0, or ActionScript 3.0. By default, ActionScript 2.0 is selected if you created your Flash document with the Flash file (ActionScript 2.0) option. ActionScript 3.0 is selected if you chose Flash file (ActionScript 3.0). Use ActionScript 2.0 or 3.0 only if you use the ActionScript 2.0 or 3.0 coding features, or if you use components that ship with Flash CS5, such as the FLVPlayback component or the UI components. If you code ActionScript the same way that you did in Flash MX or Flash 5, choose ActionScript 1.0.

Tip

Flash CS5 can compile ActionScript 2.0 code so that it is compatible with Flash Player 6. If you choose ActionScript 2.0 and set the Version menu to Flash Player 6, Flash CS5 automatically compiles ActionScript 2.0 in a format that Flash Player 6 understands. Also, keep in mind that ActionScript 1.0 or 2.0 code is case-sensitive if it is published for Flash Player 7 or later. In Flash Player 7 or later movies, variables, instance names, and other terms in ActionScript are case-sensitive. For example, if you accidentally refer to a variable named myName as myname, Flash Player 7–compiled movies are not as forgiving as Flash Player 6–compiled movies. ∎

- **JPEG quality:** This slider and text-field option specifies the level of Joint Photographic Experts Group (JPEG) compression applied to bitmapped artwork in the Flash movie. The value can be any value between (and including) 0 to 100. Higher values apply less compression and preserve more information of the original bitmap, whereas lower values apply more compression and keep less information. The value entered here applies to all bitmaps that enable the Use document default quality option, found in the Bitmap Properties dialog box for each bitmap in the document's Library panel. Unlike the audio settings discussed in a moment, no "override" option exists to disregard settings in the library.

- **Enable JPEG deblocking:** This feature reduces the visual artifacts that appear in JPEG images within your Flash movie (.swf file) when you use a low JPEG quality value. This feature is available only in Flash Player 10.

- **Audio stream:** This option displays the current audio compression scheme for stream audio. By clicking the Set button, you can control the compression applied to any sounds that use the Stream Sync setting in the Sound area of the Property inspector (when a sound keyframe has focus). Like the JPEG quality option discussed previously, this compression value is applied to any stream sounds that use the Default compression in the Export Settings section of each audio file's Sound Properties dialog box in the document's library. See Chapter 12, "Adding Sound," for more information on using stream sounds and audio compression schemes.

- **Audio event:** This setting behaves exactly the same as the Audio Stream option, except that this compression setting applies to Default compression-enabled event sounds. See Chapter 12, "Adding Sound," for more information on event sounds.

Tip

Flash CS5 supports imported MP3 audio that uses Variable Bit Rate (VBR) compression. However, Flash cannot compress native sounds in VBR. If you use any imported MP3 audio for Stream Sync audio, Flash recompresses the MP3 audio on export. ■

- **Override sound settings:** If you want the settings for Audio stream and Audio event to apply to all stream and event sounds, respectively, and to disregard any unique compression schemes specified in the document's library, check this option. This is useful for creating multiple .swf file versions of the Flash movie (hi-fi, lo-fi, and so on) and enabling the Web visitor to decide which one to download.

- **Export device sounds:** In Flash CS5, you have the option of exporting device sounds with your Flash movie. You use this option only if you are using one of the Flash Lite options in the Version menu. To learn more about the use of this feature, use the search phrase "device sound" in the Help panel (Help ➪ Flash Help) in Flash CS5.

- **Compress movie:** This option compresses Flash Player 6 or later movies only. When enabled, this compression feature greatly reduces the size of text- or ActionScript-heavy Flash movies. However, you may see little or no size difference on other Flash elements, such as artwork and sounds. Compression cannot be used on Flash Player 5 or earlier movies.

- **Include hidden layers:** This option enables you to control hidden layers with your SWF file. For example, if you hide a layer in a Movie Clip symbol, that layer does not export with the SWF file if this option is unchecked in the Flash tab. By default, hidden layers export with the SWF file.

- **Include XMP metadata:** This feature in Flash CS5 allows you to employ Adobe's eXtensible Metadata Platform (XMP) to classify and describe your Flash content. XMP information can be added to just about any file format created by Adobe tools. This option is enabled by default with new Flash files created in Flash CS5 and automatically includes the file creator (Adobe Flash CS5 Professional) and creation date information with the published Flash movie (.swf file). Click the File Info button to modify the metadata included with your content. Note that you can view a SWF file's metadata in Adobe Bridge CS5, included with the default installation of Adobe Flash CS5.

- **Export SWC:** If you've built a document class file for your Flash document, you can export the class as a precompiled component, or SWC file. This option is available only if you use Flash Player 9 or later and ActionScript 3.0.

- **Generate size report:** As discussed earlier in this chapter, the size report for a Flash movie can be very useful in pinpointing problematic bandwidth-intensive elements, such as font characters. When this option is checked, the Publish command exports a text (.txt) file. You can view this document separately in a text-editor application such as Notepad or TextEdit.

- **Protect from import:** This option safeguards your Flash movies on the Internet. When enabled, the .swf file cannot be imported into the Flash CS5 authoring environment or altered.

Caution

The Protect from import option does not prevent a Web browser from caching your .swf files. Also, Adobe Director can import and use protected Flash movies. Flash utilities such as SWF Decompiler from www. sothink.com **can break into any .swf file and extract artwork, symbols, video clips, and sounds. There's even an application called ActionScript Viewer from** www.buraks.com/asv **that can extract ActionScript from your .swf files! For this reason, you should always use server-side scripts to verify sensitive data such as password entries in Flash movies, rather than internal ActionScripted password checking with** if/else **conditions. Don't store sensitive information such as passwords in your source files!** ■

- **Omit trace actions:** If this option is selected, Flash CS5 removes any trace() actions used in your Flash document's ActionScript code. trace() actions open the Output panel in Test Movie mode for debugging purposes. In general, if you used trace() actions, you should omit them from the final Flash movie — they can't be viewed from the standard version of the Flash Player anyway. trace() actions add to the final Flash movie (.swf) file size. For final production and live deployment, you should enable the Omit trace actions option to reduce the overall file size.

- **Permit debugging:** If this option is selected, you can access the Debugger panel from within the Debug Movie environment, or from a Web browser that is using the Flash Debug Player plug-in or ActiveX control. To install the Flash Debug Player plug-in or ActiveX control, go to the Players folder in your Adobe Flash CS5 application folder. There, you find a Debug folder. With your browser applications closed, run one (or more) of the following files:

  - **Install Flash Player 9 ActiveX.msi** to install the ActiveX control for Internet Explorer on Windows 98/ME/2000/XP/Vista/7.

  - **Install Flash Player 9 Plugin.msi** to install the plug-in for Mozilla-compatible browsers such as Firefox or Netscape on Windows 95/98/ME/NT/2000/XP/Vista/7.

  - **Install Flash Player 9 UB** to install the plug-in for Mozilla-compatible browsers such as Apple Safari or Mozilla Firefox on Macs running OS X 10.1 or greater.

- **Password:** If you selected the Permit debugging option, you can enter a password to access the Debugger panel. Because you can debug movies over a live Internet connection, you should always enter a password here if you intend to debug a remote Flash movie. If you leave this field empty and check the Permit debugging option, Flash CS5 still prompts you for a password when you attempt to access the Debugger panel remotely. Simply press Enter when this prompt appears if you left this field blank.

- **Local playback security:** This feature enables you to control the access to local or networked assets from the published Flash movie. In older releases of the Flash Player, a Flash movie file (.swf) could potentially access local files, representing a security hole. A Flash movie, for example, had the capability to load text files on the local computer and transmit the contents of that file to a remote server. Now, local Flash files are able to accept data from both local and network sources. However, if you choose to send data to a network source, you are able to receive only from a network source, with no data available locally. For more information on this feature, search the Help panel in Flash CS5 with the term "local playback security." Note that a Flash projector can potentially read local files and transmit information to other networks.

- **Hardware Acceleration:** This feature in Flash CS5 allows you to control whether the SWF file can take advantage of the user's hardware to enhance playback of the Flash content. You have three options in this menu:

  - **None:** This value disables the use of any direct communication from the Flash Player to graphics hardware on a user's computer. The Web browser (or host environment for the Flash Player runtime engine) handles all graphics processing. By default, this value is selected.

  - **Level 1 - Direct:** This value enables the Flash Player to directly draw graphics to the screen instead of delegating the responsibility to the host environment, such as a Web browser.

  - **Level 2 - GPU:** This value offloads all graphics drawing directly to the Graphics Processing Unit (GPU), better known as your computer's video graphics card. If you are targeting users with modern-day computers (Core 2 Duo) with fast video graphics capabilities, this option improves graphics rendering and video playback. The level of performance varies based on the power of the user's video graphics card.

  For most Flash content, the default value of None is acceptable. If animation and video playback within your Flash content seems to behave slower than expected on modern computer systems, try using the Level 1 or Level 2 options to improve performance.

- **Script time limit:** This option enables you to specify a timeout value for script execution. For example, if you create complex ActionScript code that temporarily bogs down the Flash Player, you can specify a longer time out value in this box. If a script executes longer than the time limit, the Flash Player presents a "script running slowly" dialog box to the user, enabling the user to abort the script.

When you are finished entering the settings for the Flash movie, you can proceed to other file type settings in the Publish Settings dialog box; or you can click OK to return to the authoring environment of Flash CS5 so that you can use the newly entered settings in the Test Movie or Scene environment. You can also export a Flash movie (and other file formats currently selected in Publish Settings) by clicking the Publish button in the Publish Settings dialog box.

Using the HTML settings

HTML is the language in which most Web pages are written. The HTML tab of the Publish Settings dialog box (see Figure 18.5) has a number of settings that control the way in which Flash CS5 publishes a movie into a Web page with HTML tags specifying the Flash Player.

Tip

The Flash Player detection in the HTML publish settings uses a single HTML file with an embedded JavaScript code library called SWFObject. Using the SWFObject library in various ways is discussed in Chapter 19, "Integrating Flash Content with Web Pages." ■

FIGURE 18.5

The HTML tab controls flexible Flash movie options — you can change these options without altering the actual Flash movie (.swf file).

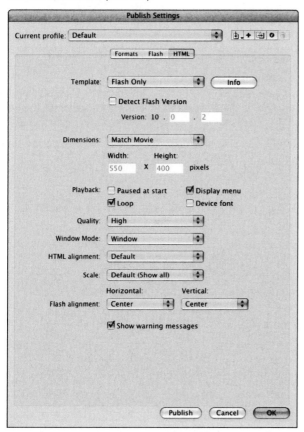

The settings available in the HTML tab include:

- **Template:** Perhaps the most important (and versatile) feature of all publish settings, the Template setting enables you to select a predefined set of HTML tags to display your Flash movies. To view the description of each template, click the Info button to the right of the drop-down list. All templates use the same options listed in the HTML tab — the template simply places the values of those settings into HTML tags scripted in the template. You can also create your own custom templates for your own unique implementation of Flash movies.

  You can view the "source" of each template in the HTML folder found inside the en/ FirstRun/HTML folder (Windows or Mac) of the Flash CS5 application folder. These template files have .html extensions, and you can use Adobe Dreamweaver, Notepad (Windows), TextEdit (Mac), or any text editor to view and edit the files. All the preinstalled templates include HTML tags to create an entire Web page, complete with <head>, <title>, and <body> tags. The following templates are available in the HTML tab:

  - **Flash For Pocket PC 2003:** With this template, Flash creates an HTML document that can display the Flash movie within the Pocket IE application running on a Pocket PC. This template also creates the necessary tags to display the same Flash movie in the regular desktop versions of Internet Explorer. At the time of this writing, Flash Player 7 was the latest public release available for the Pocket PC.

Note

If you are designing Flash movies for the Pocket PC, be sure to check out the PDA document templates. Choose File ⇨ New, click the Templates tab, and choose the PDA category. The Windows Mobile templates work with the screen dimensions of most Pocket PCs. ∎

  - **Flash HTTPS:** This template looks nearly identical to the Flash Only template (discussed next). The only difference with this template is that the download locations for the ActiveX control and plug-in page use https:// rather than http://. If you are loading your Flash movie file (.swf) from a secure URL and page, it's recommended that any and all URLs used within that document use secure URLs as well. A secure URL always starts with https://.

  - **Flash Only:** This default template inserts the <object> and <embed> tags for a Flash movie. It does not perform any browser or plug-in detection. If the user does not have the Flash Player plug-in or ActiveX control, the browser may produce an error message, a missing plug-in icon, or a prompt to download the latest plug-in or ActiveX control, depending on the browser configuration. The HTML this template produces may allow an earlier Flash Player (such as Flash Player 4) to attempt playback of your newer Flash movie. Keep in mind that any version of the Flash Player tries to render any Flash movie file. However, you may get unpredictable results when a newer-version Flash movie loads into an older player.

Note

The Flash Only template includes JavaScript code to create the <object> and <embed> tags. ∎

- **Flash Only - Allow Full Screen:** This template behaves like the Flash Only template but also inserts the necessary tag attributes to enable full-screen playback of Flash movies in Flash Player 9 r28 or later. This feature allows Flash movies to "take over" the entire screen and play outside of the browser window.

- **Flash with AICC Tracking:** Use this template if you are creating Flash movies that incorporate components from the Learning Interactions Library (Window⇨Other Panels⇨Common Libraries⇨Learning Interactions). Use it also if you want the components in the Flash movie to comply with the Aviation Industry CBT Committee (AICC) training guidelines. The template creates JavaScript/VBScript functions that can work with the ActionScript of the learning components. For more information on AICC guidelines, see www.aicc.org. Note that this template functions only in Web browsers that support the fscommand() action from Flash movies.

- **Flash with Named Anchors:** If you are using named anchors in the Main Timeline of your Flash document, you should use this template for your published HTML document. This template creates the necessary JavaScript to enable the Back button on your Web browser with named anchors within your Flash movie. Named anchors allow you to designate specific keyframes (and scenes) that register in the browser's history when played. This feature works in Internet Explorer for Windows, but not in Mozilla-based browsers such as Firefox or Safari.

- **Flash with SCORM 1.2 Tracking:** This template creates the HTML and JavaScript/VBScript functions to enable communication between Flash movies that use the components from the Learning Interactions Library and the HTML page. SCORM, which stands for Shareable Content Object Reference Model, is a set of guidelines for learning systems created by the U.S. Department of Defense Advanced Distributed Learning (ADL) Initiative. Both SCORM and AICC guidelines aim to promote interoperability among learning and training systems. Note that this template functions only in Web browsers that support the fscommand() from Flash movies.

- **Flash with SCORM 2004 Tracking:** This template has the same functionality as the last template, except that the codebase has been updated to support SCORM 2004 features.

- **Image Map:** This template does not use or display any Flash movie. Instead, it uses a GIF, JPEG, or PNG image (as specified in the Publish Settings dialog box's Format tab) as a client-side image map, via an <img> tag with a USEMAP attribute. Use a frame label of #map in the Flash document file (.fla) to designate which frame is used as the map image. See the section, "Using the GIF settings," later in this chapter for more details.

- **Detect Flash Version:** This updated feature of Flash CS5 enables you to add version detection to your Flash content. For the most basic use, simply select this check box and leave the default versions. The version appearing in the HTML tab reflects the version of the Flash Player you selected in the Flash tab of the Publish Settings dialog box. For more advanced use, you can specify major and minor versions of the currently selected Flash Player version. The Detect Flash Version feature creates all the necessary JavaScript to detect the Flash Player on modern browsers. The options for this feature include two fields:

- **Minor Revision:** This text field controls the minor version revision number you want to require. Note that, to date, there have been no minor revisions to any publicly released Flash Players — Adobe has released only incremental revisions.

- **Incremental Revision:** This text field displays the incremental revision number of the Flash Player you want to require. You can edit this value directly in the dialog box. For example, if you want to require the Flash Player 6 r65 option in the Flash tab, you can enter the number **65** in this field. The detection script would then check for r65 or later.

Tip

The Detect Flash Version feature does not create an alternate HTML content page. With Flash CS5, the alternate content HTML is specified in the JavaScript using SWFObject. To include your own custom alternate content, you can edit the JavaScript in Adobe Dreamweaver or your preferred text editor. You learn more about SWFObject in Chapter 19. ∎

- **Dimensions:** This setting controls the `width` and `height` values of the `<object>` and `<embed>` tags. The dimension settings here do not change the original Flash movie; they simply create the area through which your Flash movie is viewed on the Web page. The way that the Flash movie "fits" into this viewing area is determined with the Scale option (discussed later). Three input areas exist: a drop-down menu and two text fields for width and height. The options here are

  - **Match Movie:** If you want to keep the same width and height that you specified in the Document Properties dialog box (Modify ➪ Document), use this option in the drop-down menu.

  - **Pixels:** You can change the viewing size (in pixel units) of the Flash movie window by selecting this option and entering new values in the Width and Height text fields.

  - **Percent:** This option scales the movie to the size of the browser window — or a portion of it. Using a value of 100 on both Width and Height expands the Flash movie to fit the entire browser window. If Percent is used with the proper Scale setting (see the description of the Scale setting later in this chapter), the aspect ratio of your Flash movie is not distorted.

Tip

The ActionScript `Stage` class and its supporting methods enable you to disable or override automatic scaling of the Flash movie. For example, the following action added to frame 1 of your Flash movie disables scaling: `Stage.scaleMode = "noScale";`. If you want to center your Flash movie's Stage in a browser window, you can set the size to Percent in the HTML tab, and the Scale setting to No scale. ∎

- **Width and Height:** Enter the values for the Flash movie width and height here. If Match Movie is selected, you shouldn't be able to enter any values. The unit of measurement is determined by selecting either Pixels or Percent from the drop-down menu.

- **Playback:** These options control how the Flash movie plays when it is downloaded to the browser. Each of these options has `<object>` and `<embed>` attributes if you want to control them outside of Publish Settings. Note that these attributes are not viewable within the Publish Settings dialog box — you need to load the published HTML document into a text editor to see the attributes.

- **Paused at start:** This is equivalent to adding a `stop()` action on the first frame of the first scene in the Flash movie. By default, this option is off — movies play as soon as they stream into the player. A button with a `play()` action can start the movie, or the Play command can be executed from the Flash Player shortcut menu (by right-clicking or Control+clicking the movie). Attribute: `play="true"` or `"false"`. If `play="true"`, the movie plays as soon as it is loaded.

- **Loop:** This option causes the Flash movie to repeat an infinite number of times. By default, this option is on. If it is not checked, the Flash movie stops on the last frame unless some other ActionScripted event is initiated on the last frame. Attribute: `loop="true"` or `"false"`.

- **Display menu:** This option controls whether the person viewing the Flash movie in the Flash Player environment can access the shortcut menu via a right-click (Windows) or Control+click (Mac) anywhere within the movie area. If this option is selected, the visitor can select Zoom In/Out, 100 percent, Show All, High Quality, Play, Loop, Rewind, Forward, and Back from the menu. If this option is not selected, the visitor can select only About Flash Player from the menu. Attribute: `menu="true"` or `"false"`.

- **Device font:** This option applies to Flash movies played only in the Windows version of the Flash Player. When enabled, this option replaces fonts that are not installed on the Player's system with anti-aliased system fonts. Attribute: `devicefont="true"` or `"false"`.

- **Quality:** This menu determines how the Flash artwork in a movie renders. Although it would be ideal to play all Flash movies at high quality, slower processors may not be able to redraw anti-aliased artwork and keep up with the frame rate. The options for this setting include the following:

  - **Low:** This setting forces the Flash Player to turn off anti-aliasing (smooth edges) completely. On slower processors, this may improve playback performance. Attribute: `quality="low"`.

  - **Auto Low:** This setting starts in Low quality mode (no anti-aliasing) but switches to High quality if the computer's processor can handle the playback speed. Attribute: `quality="autolow"`.

  - **Auto High:** This setting is the opposite of Auto Low. The Flash Player starts playing the movie in High quality mode, but if the processor cannot handle the playback demands, it switches to Low quality mode. For most Web sites, this is the optimal setting to use because it favors higher quality first. Attribute: `quality="autohigh"`.

  - **Medium:** This quality produces anti-aliased vector graphics on a 2 × 2 grid (in other words, it smoothes edges over a 4-pixel square area), but it does not smooth bitmap images. Artwork appears slightly better than the Low quality, but not as smooth as the High setting. Attribute: `quality="medium"`. This quality setting works only with the Flash Player 5 or later.

- **High:** When this setting is used, the Flash Player dedicates more of the computer's processor to rendering graphics (instead of playback). All vector artwork is anti-aliased on a 4 × 4 grid (16-pixel square area). Bitmaps are smoothed unless they are contained within an animation sequence such as a motion tween. By default, this setting is selected in the HTML tab of the Publish Settings dialog box. Attribute: `quality="high"`.

- **Best:** This mode does everything that High quality does, with the addition of smoothing all bitmaps — regardless of whether they are in motion tweens. This mode is the most processor-intensive. Attribute: `quality="best"`.

- **Window Mode:** The Window Mode setting works only with any version of the Flash ActiveX control on Internet Explorer for Windows 95/98/ME/NT/2000/XP/Vista/7 or with Flash Player 6 r65 and later for Mozilla-compatible browsers on Windows or Mac OS X. If you intend to deliver to one of these browsers and/or this version of the Flash Player, you can animate Flash content on top of DHTML content. One of the following values can be selected from this menu:

  - **Window:** This is the "standard" player interface, in which the Flash movie plays as it would normally, in its own rectangular window on a Web page. Attribute: `wmode="window"`.

  - **Opaque Windowless:** Use this option if you want the Flash movie to have an opaque (that is, nontransparent) background and have DHTML or HTML elements behind the Flash movie. Attribute: `wmode="opaque"`.

  - **Transparent Windowless:** This option "knocks out" the Flash background color so that other HTML and DHTML elements can show through. You have likely seen this type of Flash movie and effect used on several commercial Web sites, where Flash ads animate across the screen on top of the HTML document. Note that the Flash movie's frame rate and performance may suffer on slower machines when this mode is used because the Flash movie needs to composite itself over other non-Flash material. Attribute: `wmode="transparent"`.

- **HTML alignment:** This setting works much like the `ALIGN` attribute of `<img>` tags in HTML documents, but it's used with the `ALIGN` attribute of the `<OBJECT>` and `<embed>` tags for the Flash movie. Note that these settings may not have any effect when used within a table cell (`<td>` tag) or a DHTML layer (`<div>` or `<layer>` tag). The options for this setting include the following:

  - **Default:** This option left-justifies the Flash movie in the browser window. If the browser window is smaller than a Flash movie that uses a Pixel or Match Movie dimensions setting (see the Dimensions setting earlier in this section), the Flash movie is cropped.

  - **Left, Right, Top, and Bottom:** These options align the Flash movie along the left, right, top, or bottom edge of the browser window, respectively.

- **Scale:** This setting works in tandem with the Dimensions setting discussed earlier in this section, and it determines how the Flash movie appears on the HTML page. Just as big-screen movies must be cropped to fit the aspect ratio of a TV screen, Flash movies may need to be modified to fit the area prescribed by the Dimensions setting. The settings for the Scale option include the following:

- **Default (Show all):** This option fits the entire Flash movie into the area defined by the Dimensions setting without distorting the original aspect ratio of the Flash movie. However, borders may appear on two sides of the Flash movie. For example, if a 300-x-300-pixel window is specified in Dimensions and the Flash movie has an aspect ratio of 1.33:1 (for example, 400 × 300 pixels), a border fills the remaining areas on top of and below the Flash movie. This is similar to the "letterbox" effect on wide-screen video rentals. Attribute: `scale="showall"`.

- **No border:** This option forces the Flash movie to fill the area defined by the Dimensions setting without leaving borders. The Flash movie's aspect ratio is not distorted or stretched. However, this may crop two sides of the Flash movie. Using the same example from Show All, the left and right sides of the Flash movie are cropped when No Border is selected. Attribute: `scale="noborder"`.

- **Exact fit:** This option stretches a Flash movie to fill the entire area defined by the Dimensions setting. Using the same example from Show All, the 400 × 300 Flash movie is scrunched to fit a 300 × 300 window. If the original movie showed a perfect circle, it now appears as an oval. Attribute: `scale="exactfit"`.

- **No scale:** This option prevents the Flash movie from scaling beyond its original size as defined in the Document Properties dialog box (Modify ➪ Document). The Flash Player window size (or the Web browser window size) has no effect on the size of the Flash movie. Attribute: `scale="noscale"`.

- **Flash alignment:** This setting adjusts the `salign` attribute of the `<object>` and `<embed>` tags for the Flash movie. In contrast to the HTML Alignment setting, Flash alignment works in conjunction with the Scale and Dimensions settings and determines how a Flash movie is aligned within the Player window. This setting has the following options:

  - **Horizontal:** These options — Left, Center, and Right — determine whether the Flash movie is horizontally aligned to the left, center, or right of the Dimensions area, respectively. Using the same example from the Scale setting, a 400-x-300-pixel Flash movie (fit into a 300 × 300 Dimension window with `scale="noborder"`) with a Flash Horizontal Alignment setting of Left crops only the right side of the Flash movie.

  - **Vertical:** These options — Top, Center, and Bottom — determine whether the Flash movie is vertically aligned to the top, center, or bottom of the Dimensions area, respectively. If the preceding example used a Show All Scale setting and had a Flash Vertical Alignment setting of Top, the border would occur only below the bottom edge of the Flash movie.

- **Show warning messages:** This useful feature alerts you to errors during the actual Publish process. For example, if you selected the Image Map template and didn't specify a static GIF, JPEG, or PNG file in the Formats tab, Flash returns an error. By default, this option is enabled. If it is disabled, Flash suppresses any warnings during the Publish process.

Using the GIF settings

The Graphics Interchange File (GIF) format, developed by CompuServe, defined the first generation of Web graphics and is still quite popular today, despite its 256-color limitation. In the context of the publish settings of Flash CS5, the GIF format is used to export a static or animated image that can be used in place of the Flash movie if the Flash Player or plug-in is not installed. Although the Flash and HTML tabs are specific to Flash movie display and playback, the settings of the GIF tab (see Figure 18.6) control the characteristics of a GIF animation (or still image) that Flash CS5 publishes.

FIGURE 18.6

You can finesse every subtle aspect of a GIF animation or still image with these settings of the GIF tab of the Publish Settings dialog box.

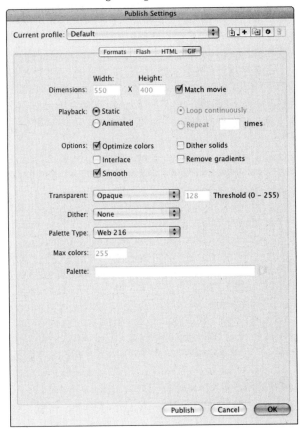

The settings in the GIF tab include the following:

- **Dimensions:** This setting has three options: Width, Height, and Match movie. As you might have guessed, Width and Height control the dimensions of the GIF image. These fields are enabled only when the Match movie check box is unchecked. With Match movie checked, the dimensions of the GIF match those of the Flash movie that is being published.

- **Playback:** These radio buttons control what type of GIF image is created and how it plays (if Animated is chosen):

  - **Static:** If this button is selected, Flash exports the first frame of the Flash movie as a single still image in the GIF format. If you want to use a frame other than the first frame, use a frame label of #Static on the desired frame. Alternatively, you could use the File ⇨ Export Image command to export a GIF image from whatever frame the Current Frame Indicator is positioned over.

  - **Animated:** If this button is selected, Flash exports the entire Flash movie as an animated GIF file (in the GIF89a format). If you don't want to export the entire movie as an animated GIF (indeed, a GIF file for a Flash movie with more than 100 frames would most likely be too large to download easily over the Web), you can designate a range of frames to export. Use a frame label of #First on the beginning frame of a given range of frames. Next, add a frame label of #Last to the ending frame of the desired sequence of frames. Flash actually is pretty good at optimizing animated GIFs by saving only areas that change over time in each frame rather than the entire frame.

  - **Loop continuously:** When the Animated radio button is selected, you can specify that the animated GIF repeats an infinite number of times by selecting the Loop continuously radio button.

  - **Repeat _ times:** This option can be used to set up an animated GIF that repeats a given number of times. If you don't want the animated GIF to repeat continuously, enter the number of repetitions here.

- **Options:** The options in the Options settings control the creation of the GIF's color table and how the browser displays the GIF:

  - **Optimize colors:** When you are using any palette type other than Adaptive, this option removes any colors preexisting in the Web 216 or custom palettes that the GIF image does not use. Enabling this option can only save you precious bytes used in file overhead — it has no effect on the actual quality of the image. Most images do not use all 216 colors of the Web palette. For example, a black-and-white picture can use only between 3 and 10 colors from the 216-color palette.

  - **Interlace:** This option makes the GIF image download in incrementing resolutions. As the image downloads, the image becomes sharper with each successive "scan." Using this option is typically a personal preference. Some people like to use it for image maps that can provide basic navigation information before the entire image downloads.

  - **Smooth:** This option anti-aliases the Flash artwork as it exports to the GIF image. Text may look better when it is anti-aliased, but you may want to test this option for your particular use. If you need to make a transparent GIF, smoothing may produce unsightly edges.

- **Dither solids:** This option determines whether solid areas of color (such as fills) are dithered. In this context, this type of dithering would create a two-color pattern to mimic a solid color that doesn't occur in the GIF's color palette. See the discussion of dithering later in this section.

- **Remove gradients:** Flash gradients do not translate or display very well in 256 or fewer colors. Use this option to convert all Flash gradients to solid colors. The solid color is determined by the first color prescribed in the gradient. Unless you developed your gradients with this effect in mind, this option may produce undesirable results.

- **Transparent:** This setting controls the appearance of the Flash movie background, as well as any Flash artwork that uses alpha settings. Because GIF images support only one level of transparency (that is, the transparent area cannot be anti-aliased), exercise caution when using this setting. The Threshold option is available only if Alpha is selected. The options for this setting include the following:

  - **Opaque:** This option produces a GIF image with a solid background. The image has a rectangular shape.

  - **Transparent:** This option makes the Flash movie background appear transparent. If the Smooth option in the Options setting is enabled, Flash artwork may display halos over the background HTML color.

  - **Alpha and Threshold:** When the Alpha option is selected in the drop-down menu, you can control at what alpha level Flash artwork becomes transparent by entering a value in the Threshold text field. For example, if you enter 128, all alphas at 50 percent become completely transparent. If you are considering an animated GIF that has Flash artwork fading in or out, you probably should use the Opaque transparent option. If Alpha and Threshold were used, the fade effect would be lost.

- **Dither:** *Dithering* is the process of emulating a color by juxtaposing two colors in a pattern arrangement. Because GIF images are limited to 256 colors (or fewer), dithering can often produce better-looking images for continuous-tone artwork such as gradients. However, Flash's dithering seems to work best with the Web 216 palette. Dithering can increase the file size of a GIF image.

  - **None:** This option does not apply any dithering to the GIF image.

  - **Ordered:** This option applies an intermediate level of dithering with minimal file size overhead.

  - **Diffusion:** This option applies the best level of dithering to the GIF image, but with larger file size overhead. Diffusion dithering has a noticeable effect only when the Web 216 palette is chosen in Palette Type.

- **Palette Type:** As I mention earlier in this section, GIF images are limited to 256 or fewer colors. However, this grouping of 256 is arbitrary: Any set of 256 (or fewer) colors can be used for a given GIF image. This setting enables you to select predefined sets of colors to use on the GIF image. See Chapter 7, "Applying Color," for more information on the Web color palette. The options for this setting include:

- **Web 216:** When this option is selected, the GIF image uses colors only from the limited 216 Web color palette. For most Flash artwork, this should produce acceptable results. However, it may not render Flash gradients or photographic bitmaps very well.

- **Adaptive:** With this option selected, Flash creates a unique set of 256 colors (or fewer, if specified in the Max colors setting) for the GIF image. However, these adapted colors fall outside of the Web safe color palette. File sizes for adaptive GIFs are larger than Web 216 GIFs, unless few colors are chosen in the Max colors setting. Adaptive GIFs look much better than Web 216 GIFs, but they may not display very well with 8-bit video cards and monitors.

- **Web Snap Adaptive:** This option tries to give the GIF image the best of both worlds. Flash converts any colors close to the 216 Web palette to Web safe colors and uses adaptive colors for the rest. This palette produces better results than the Adaptive palette for older display systems that use 8-bit video cards.

- **Custom:** When this option is selected, you can specify a palette that uses the ACT file format to be used as the GIF image's palette. Macromedia Fireworks and Adobe Photoshop can export color palettes (or color look-up tables) as ACT files.

- **Max colors:** With this setting, you can specify exactly how many colors are in the GIF's color table. This numeric entry field is enabled only when Adaptive or Web Snap Adaptive is selected in the Palette Type drop-down menu.

- **Palette:** This text field and the folder browse button are enabled only when Custom is selected in the Palette Type drop-down menu. When enabled, this dialog box is used to locate and load a palette file from the hard drive.

Using the JPEG settings

The Joint Photographic Experts Group (JPEG) format is just as popular as the GIF format on the Web. Unlike GIF images, however, JPEG images can use much more than 256 colors. In fact, JPEG files must be 24-bit color (or full-color RGB) images. Although GIF files use lossless compression (within the actual file itself), JPEG images use lossy compression, which means that color information is discarded in order to save file space. However, JPEG compression is very good. Even at its lowest-quality settings, JPEG images can preserve quite a bit of detail in photographic images.

Another significant difference between GIF and JPEG is that GIF images do not require nearly as much memory (for equivalent image dimensions) as JPEG images do. You need to remember that JPEG images "uncompress" when they are downloaded to your computer. Although the file sizes may be small initially, they still open as full-color images in the computer's memory. For example, even though you may get the file size of a 400-x-300-pixel JPEG image down to 10KB, it still requires nearly 352KB in memory when it is opened or displayed.

Flash publishes the first frame of the Flash movie as the JPEG image, unless a #Static frame label is given to another frame in the Flash movie. The limited settings of the JPEG tab of the Publish Settings dialog box (see Figure 18.7) control the few variables of this still photo-quality image format:

- **Dimensions:** This setting behaves the same as the GIF Dimensions setting. Width and Height control the dimensions of the movie. But these fields are enabled only when the Match movie check box is unchecked. With Match movie checked, the dimensions of the JPEG match those of the Flash movie.

- **Quality:** This slider and text field work exactly the same way as the JPEG Quality setting in the Flash tab of Publish Settings. Higher values apply less compression and result in better quality, but they create images with larger file sizes.

- **Progressive:** This option is similar to the Interlaced option for GIF images. When enabled, the JPEG image loads in successive scans, becoming sharper with each pass.

FIGURE 18.7

The settings of the JPEG tab are limited because JPEGs are still images with relatively few variables to address.

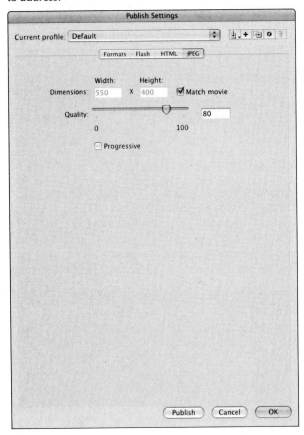

Using the PNG settings

The Portable Network Graphic (PNG) format is another still-image format. The PNG specification was developed in 1996 by the W3C (World Wide Web Consortium), and the format is an improvement over both the GIF and JPEG formats in several ways. Much like JPEG, it is excellent for transmission of photographic quality images. The primary advantages of PNG are variable bit depths (images can be 256 colors or millions of colors), multilevel transparency, and lossless compression. However, some browsers do not offer full support for all PNG options without some kind of additional plug-in. When in doubt, test your PNG images in your preferred browser.

The settings of the PNG tab (see Figure 18.8) control the characteristics of the PNG image that Flash publishes.

FIGURE 18.8

The settings found on the PNG tab closely resemble those on the GIF tab. The PNG was engineered to have many of the advantages of both the GIF and JPEG formats.

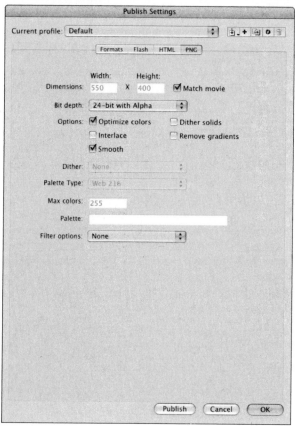

The PNG tab options are

- **Dimensions:** This setting works just like the GIF and JPEG equivalents. When Match movie is checked, you cannot alter the Width and Height of the PNG image.

- **Bit depth:** This setting controls how many colors are created in the PNG image:

  - **8-bit:** In this mode, the PNG image has a maximum color palette of 256 colors, similar to the palette function of GIF images. When this option is selected, the Options, Dither, Palette Type, Max Colors, and Palette settings can be altered.

  - **24-bit:** When this option is selected, the PNG image can display any of the 16.7 million RGB colors. This option produces larger files than 8-bit PNG images, but it renders the Flash artwork most faithfully.

  - **24-bit with Alpha:** This option adds another 8-bit channel to the 24-bit PNG image for multilevel transparency support. This means that Flash treats the Flash movie background as a transparent area so that information behind the PNG image (such as HTML background colors) shows through. Note that, with proper browser support, PNG can render anti-aliased edges on top of other elements, such as HTML background images!

Note

Flash CS5's PNG export or publish settings do not reflect the full range of PNG options available. PNG can support transparency in both 8-bit and 24-bit flavors, but Flash enables transparency only in 24-bit with Alpha images. ■

- **Options:** These options behave the same as the equivalent GIF publish settings.

- **Dither, Palette Type, Max colors,** and **Palette:** These settings work the same as the equivalent GIF publish settings. Because PNG images can be either 8- or 24-bit, these options apply only to 8-bit PNG images. If anything other than 8-bit is selected in the Bit depth setting, these options are disabled. Refer to the previous section for more information.

- **Filter options:** This drop-down menu controls what type of compression sampling or algorithm the PNG image uses. Note that this does not apply an art or graphic "filter effect" as the filters in Adobe Photoshop do, nor does it throw away any image information — all filters are lossless. It simply enables you to be the judge of what kind of compression to use on the image. You need to experiment with each of these filters on your Flash movie image to find the best filter-to-file-size combination. Technically, the filters do not actually look at the pixel data. Rather, they look at the byte data of each pixel. Results vary depending on the image content, but here are some guidelines to keep in mind:

  - **None:** When this option is selected, no filtering is applied to the image. When no filter is applied, you usually have unnecessarily large file sizes.

  - **Sub:** This filter works best on images that have repeated information along the horizontal axis. For example, the stripes of a horizontal American flag filter nicely with the sub filter.

- **Up:** The opposite of the sub filter, this filter works by looking for repeated information along the vertical axis. The stripes of a vertical American flag filter well with the up filter.

- **Average:** Use this option when a mixture of vertical and horizontal information exists. When in doubt, try this filter first.

- **Path:** This filter works like an advanced average filter. When in doubt, try this filter after you have experimented with the average filter.

- **Adaptive:** This filter provides the most thorough analysis of the image's color and creates the most accurate color palette for the image. However, it usually provides the largest file sizes for the PNG format.

Creating Windows and Mac projectors

To export a Mac stand-alone projector, check the Macintosh Projector option in the Formats tab. To publish a Windows stand-alone projector, check the Windows Projector option in the Formats tab.

Note

The Mac Projector published by Flash CS5 is designed for playback on Mac OS X (10.1) and later. If you want to publish a projector compatible with Mac OS 9.x or earlier, you must use Flash MX 2004 or earlier. ■

Publish Preview and Publish Commands

After you have entered the file format types and specifications for each in the Publish Settings dialog box, you can proceed to preview and publish the file types you selected.

Using Publish Preview

The Publish Preview submenu (accessible from File ➪ Publish Preview) lists all the file types currently enabled in the Publish Settings dialog box. By default, HTML is the first file type available for preview. In general, the first item enabled in the Formats tab of the Publish Settings dialog box is the first item in the submenu and can be executed by pressing Ctrl+F12/⌘+F12. Selecting a file type in the Publish Preview menu launches your default browser and inserts the selected file type(s) into the browser window.

Using Publish

When you want Flash to export the file type(s) selected in the Publish Settings dialog box, choose File ➪ Publish (Shift+F12). Flash creates the new files wherever the Flash movie was last saved. If you have selected an HTML template in the HTML tab of the Publish Settings dialog box, you may receive a warning or error message if any other necessary files were not specified. That's it! After you've tested the files for the delivery browser and/or platforms of your choice, you can upload the files to your Web server.

Using Publish Profiles

Flash CS5 includes a profile feature in the Publish Settings dialog box. You can save the settings from all the enabled format tabs in Publish Settings to a custom profile. You can create as many profiles as you need. The profiles that you create are document-specific. They are saved with the Flash document file (.fla), and by design, you cannot access the profiles of one document directly from another. However, you can export a profile from a Flash document and import it into another.

To choose, create, modify, or delete profiles, open the Publish Settings dialog box (File ➪ Publish Settings). At the top of the dialog box, you will find the Profile features available in Flash CS5. See Figure 18.9 and the following description list.

- **Profile Name:** This drop-down menu displays the currently active profile. Every new Flash CS5 document has a Default profile. If you open a Flash document from an earlier version of Flash (such as Flash MX 2004 or Flash 8) in Flash CS5 and resave it as a Flash CS5 document, the original document publish settings are stored in a Flash MX, Flash MX 2004, Flash 8, or Flash CS3 Settings profile.

- **Import/Export Profile:** If you click this button, you can choose Import or Export from this option's menu. If you want to use one document's publish settings in another document, you need to first export the current profile. Profiles are exported as XML documents. In the other document, you can then import the XML profile document.

- **Create New Profile:** This button adds a new profile name to the Profile Name menu, using the current profile's settings as a starting point. If you click this button, the Create New Profile dialog box appears, prompting you to enter a new profile name.

- **Duplicate Profile:** This button makes a copy of the currently active profile. If you click this button, the Duplicate Profile dialog box appears, prompting you to enter a new profile name for the copy.

- **Profile Properties:** This button opens a dialog box wherein you can change the name of the currently active profile. No other properties are associated with a profile.

- **Delete Profile:** Clicking this button removes the currently active profile from the document.

Changes to profiles do not need to be saved. When you choose a profile from the Profile Name menu, any settings that you change, enable, and so on are automatically saved to the current profile as long as you click OK to close the Publish Settings dialog box. If you click the Cancel button, any changes you make are not saved to the current profile.

FIGURE 18.9

The Profile features in the Publish Settings dialog box

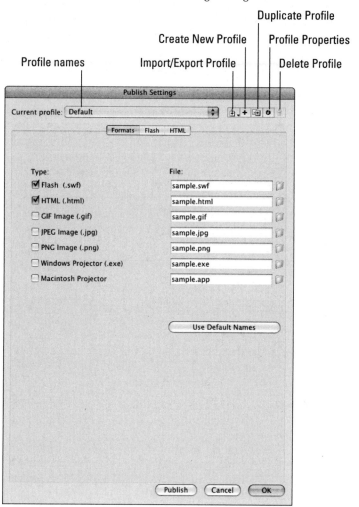

Summary

- To minimize your wait during publishing or testing Flash movies, you may want to use MP3 files for all of your Event Sync sounds.

- Test your Flash movies and scenes within the Flash authoring environment. The Bandwidth Profiler can provide vital information about frame byte requirements and can help you find problematic streaming areas of the Flash movie.

- The size report that can be generated from the Export Movie or Publish commands for Flash movies lists detailed information related to individual elements, such as audio, fonts, and frame byte size.

- The Publish Settings dialog box enables you to pick any number of file formats to export at one time. You can control just about every setting imaginable for each file type and use HTML templates to automate the insertion of Flash movies into your Web pages.

- Flash movies published from Flash CS5 can have specific local playback security options, preventing unscrupulous Flash content creators from accessing private information on another person's computer.

- Flash CS5 offers a Flash Player version detection feature in the Publish Settings dialog box. With this feature, you can create an HTML page that detects which version of the Flash Player a user has and direct him or her to appropriate content on your site.

- The profiles feature in Flash CS5 enables you to quickly load publish presets that you can apply to one or more Flash documents.

Integrating Flash Content with Web Pages

I f you're not one for automated HTML production by using templates, this chapter is for you. In this chapter, I teach you the ins and outs of the `<object>` and `<embed>` tags, as well as some tips on how to check for the Flash Player with Flash CS5's detection features or SWFObject. At the end of this chapter, I examine how Flash movies can interact with JavaScript and DHTML (Dynamic HTML) by using the new `ExternalInterface` actions from Flash.

Note

Many thanks to Geoff Stearns for his ongoing commitment to provide one of the best open source Flash Player detection scripts, SWFObject, to the Flash community. You can find more information about SWFObject later in this chapter. ■

Writing Markup for Flash Movies

In Chapter 18, you learn how to use the Publish feature, which included automated HTML templates. These templates created the necessary HTML tags to display Flash movies on Web pages. In this section, I discuss the use of Flash movies in your handwritten HTML documents. You can also use this information to alter HTML documents created by the Publish feature.

Note

In the following code examples, I use an asterisk (*) when displaying optional parameters that are not in the default options that are enabled in the Flash Only HTML template. I also use the term plug-in to mean both the Mozilla-compatible plug-in and the ActiveX control for Flash Player 10. ■

IN THIS CHAPTER

Defining HTML tags and attributes for the Flash Player

Detecting the Flash Player plug-in or ActiveX control with SWFObject

Sending commands with the `ExternalInterface` API to JavaScript

You can use two tags to place Flash movies on a Web page (such as an HTML document): <object> and <embed>. You need to include both of these plug-in tags in HTML documents, as each tag is specific to a browser: <object> for Internet Explorer (IE) on Windows and <embed> for Mozilla-compatible browsers on Windows and Mac. Each tag works similarly to the other, with some slight differences in attribute names and organization. Remember that if both sets of tags are included with the HTML, only one set of tags is actually read by the browser, depending on which browser is used to view the Web page. Without these tags, the browser cannot display Flash movies with other HTML elements such as images and text.

Using the <object> tag

Microsoft Internet Explorer for Windows and any browser that adheres to the HTML 4.01 specification from the World Wide Web Consortium (W3C) use this tag to enable the Flash Player ActiveX control (Internet Explorer for Windows) or plug-in. You can use the <object> tag to specify where in your HTML document layout you want a Flash movie (.swf file) to appear.

Caution

The implementation of the <object> tag discussed in this section is oriented to Internet Explorer for Windows implementation. I strongly encourage you to use the SWFObject JavaScript library discussed later in this chapter for the best method of Flash content integration with HTML content. ■

Note

Flash Player 6 introduced a Stage class that enables you to control or override many of the same properties that the Player HTML tags specify. For more details on the Stage class, refer to the Flash ActionScript Bible series (Wiley). ■

```
A. <object
B.       classid="clsid: clsid:d27cdb6e-ae6d-11cf-96b8- ⤶
         444553540000"
C.       codebase="http://download.macromedia.com/pub/ ⤶
         shockwave/cabs/flash/swflash.cab#version=10,0,0,0"
D.       width="550" height="400"
E.       id="home"
F.       align="middle">
G.       <param name="allowScriptAccess" value="sameDomain" />
H.       <param name="allowFullScreen" value="false" />
I.       <param name="movie" value="home.swf" />
J.       <param name="play" value="false" />
K.       <param name="loop" value="false" />
L.       <param name="menu" value="false" />
M.       <param name="quality" value="high" />
N.       <param name="scale" value="noborder" />
O.       <param name="salign" value="LT" />
P.       <param name="wmode" value="transparent" />
Q.       <param name="devicefont value="true" />
R.       <param name="bgcolor" value="#FFFFFF" />
```

```
S.        <param name="flashvars" value="title=My%20Movie" />
T.        <param name="base" value="." />
U.  </object>
```

Note

Flash CS5's HTML templates use XHTML-compliant code. Notice that all the tags use lowercase, and that all `<param>` tags end with a `/>`. ■

A. `<object`: This is the opening tag containing the ID code and locations of the ActiveX control for the Flash Player. Note that this opening tag includes the attributes lettered B through F.

B. `classid`: This lengthy string is the unique ActiveX identification code. If you are inserting the `<object>` tag by hand in a text editor, make sure that you copy this ID string exactly.

C. `codebase`: Like the `codebase` attribute of a Java `<applet>` tag, this attribute of the `<object>` tag specifies the location of the ActiveX control installer file (.cab) as a URL. Notice that the `#version=10,0,0,0` portion of the URL indicates that the Flash Player version 10 should be used. You can also specify specific minor releases, such as `#version=6,0,65,0`, which would require Flash Player 6.0 r65 ActiveX control or later. If the visitor doesn't have the ActiveX control already installed, Internet Explorer automatically downloads the control from this URL.

Tip

If you want to make a secure Web page with Flash content, make sure that the `codebase` URL uses `https://` rather than `http://`. ■

D. `width` **and** `height`: These attributes control the actual width and height, respectively, of the Flash movie as it appears on the Web page. If no unit of measurement is specified, these values are in pixels. If the `%` character is added to the end of each value, the attribute adjusts the Flash movie to the corresponding percent of the browser window. For example, if 100 percent was the value for both `width` and `height`, the Flash movie fills the entire browser, except for the browser gutter. See Colin Moock's tutorial at the Web archive for this book to learn how to minimize this gutter thickness.

E. `id`: This attribute of the `<object>` tag assigns a JavaScript/VBScript identifier to the Flash movie so that it can be controlled by DHTML JavaScript/VBScript functions. By default, this attribute's value is the name of the actual .swf file, without the .swf extension. Each element on a DHTML page should have a unique `id` or `name` attribute. I discuss the `name` attribute in the next section.

F. `align`: This attribute of the `<object>` tag determines how the Flash movie aligns on the HTML document. The acceptable values for this attribute are `left`, `right`, `top`, `bottom`, or `middle`. As with `<img>` tags in HTML, the `align` attribute gives very loose layout control. It's likely that you'll want to rely on other HTML tags and cascading style sheets (CSS) to position a Flash movie with other HTML elements.

G. `<param name="allowScriptAccess" value="sameDomain" />`: This is the first set of `<param>` subtags within the `<object></object>` tags. Each parameter tag has a unique `name=` setting, not to be confused with JavaScript names or `ids`. `allowScriptAccess` controls how the Flash movie can access JavaScript or VBScript functions contained within the HTML document. A Flash movie can try to invoke a JavaScript or VBScript function by using an ActionScript `fscommand()` or `getURL()` line of code. There are three values supported: `always`, `never`, and `sameDomain`. The value `always` enables the Flash movie to access scripts on the page, and `never` prohibits the Flash movie from accessing scripts. The value `sameDomain`, which is the default value, enables a Flash movie to access scripts on the page *only* if the Flash movie resides on the same domain as the HTML page containing the movie. The `allowScriptAccess` attribute is supported by Flash Player 6 r40 and later.

H. `<param name="allowFullScreen" value="false" />`: This parameter specifies if the Flash movie can utilize full screen mode when playing in a Web browser window. If set to `false`, a Flash movie cannot play outside of the browser in full screen mode. If set to `true`, a Flash movie's stage can take over the entire desktop screen area and play outside of a Web browser window. You must script full screen capability within your Flash movie to use this feature. The ActionScript 3.0 version of the FLVPlayback component in Flash CS5, for example, includes a full screen feature. The `allowFullScreen` attribute is supported only by Flash Player 9 r28 or later.

I. `<param name="movie" value="home.swf" />`: This parameter determines which Flash movie file (.swf) is loaded into the document. The `value` attribute specifies the filename of the Flash movie, as a relative or absolute URL. Note that you can pass Flash variables to the movie directly by specifying them after the filename. For example, `home.swf?firstName=Jeremy` passes a variable named `firstName` with a string value of `Jeremy` to the `root` timeline (that is, `_level0`). You can use the newer `flashvars` (item S) HTML attribute to do this type of data transfer as well.

Note

In ActionScript 3.0, variables declared with the `flashvars` attribute are accessed through the `parameters` property of the `LoaderInfo` class on the `root` instance. ∎

J. `<param name="play" value="false" />`: This optional parameter tells the Flash Player whether it should start playing the Flash movie as it downloads. If `value` equals `false`, the Flash movie loads in a "paused" state, just as if a `stop()` action was placed on the first frame. If the `value` equals `true`, the Flash Player starts playing the movie as soon as it starts to stream into the browser. If this tag is omitted, the Flash Player behaves as if `play` equals `true`.

Note

If you do have a `stop()` action on the first frame of your movie, setting `play` to `true` does not override the `stop()` action. ∎

K. `<param name="loop" value="false" />`: This optional setting tells the Flash Player whether the Main Timeline should repeat when the playhead reaches the last frame. If `value` equals `false`, the playhead does not loop. If `value` equals `true`, the playhead loops. If this parameter tag is omitted, the Flash Player by default loops playback of the Main Timeline.

Note

If you have a `stop()` action on the last frame of the Main Timeline, the Flash movie does not loop, regardless of the HTML loop value. ■

L. `<param name="menu" value="false" />`: This setting controls the display of the Flash Player contextual menu that can be invoked by right-clicking (Windows) or Control+clicking (Mac) the Flash movie in the Web browser. If you set this option to `false`, the menu displays the options shown in Figure 19.1. If you set this option to `true`, all the options are available to the end user, as shown in Figure 19.2. Also, the player's Settings option is available in both modes of the menu.

FIGURE 19.1

The Flash Player menu with control options disabled

Note

The default Play, Stop, and Rewind options that were available in Flash Player 6 and earlier are no longer available in Flash Player 7 or later. ■

Note

If you have installed the Debugger version of Flash Player 10, the contextual menu displays a Debugger option in both modes of the `menu` attribute (`true` and `false`). Figure 19.2 shows the Debugger option. For more information on using the Debugger, read Adobe's DevNet article at `www.adobe.com/devnet/flash/articles/as3_debugger.html`. ■

Note

Flash Player 7 and later supports additional items that you can script into the contextual menu, using the `ContextMenu` class. For more detailed information on the usage of this class, refer to the Flash CS5 Help panel and the Flash ActionScript Bible series (Wiley). ■

FIGURE 19.2

The Flash Player menu with control options enabled

M. `<param name="quality" value="high" />`: This parameter controls how the Flash movie's artwork renders within the browser window. `value` can be `low`, `autolow`, `autohigh`, `high`, or `best`. Most Flash movies on the Web use the `high` value because this setting forces the Flash Player to render the movie elements anti-aliased. For a full description of each of the `quality` settings, refer to Chapter 20, "Publishing Flash Movies."

N. `<param name="scale" value="noborder" />`: This optional parameter controls how the Flash movie scales in the window defined by the `width` and `height` attributes of the opening `<object>` tag. Its value can be `showall`, `noborder`, `exactfit`, or `noscale`. If this entire subtag is omitted, the Flash Player treats the movie as if the `showall` default setting was specified. The `showall` setting fits the Flash movie within the boundaries of the `width` and `height` dimensions without any distortion to the original aspect ratio of the Flash movie. Again, refer to Chapter 18 for a complete description of the `scale` settings and how they work within the dimensions of a Flash movie.

O. `<param name="salign" value="lt" />`: This parameter controls the alignment of the Flash movie within the space allocated to the viewing area of the movie in the browser window. For example, if you size your Flash movie to use 100 percent of the width and height of the browser window, a `value` of `lt` aligns the Flash movie to the left and top of the browser window. The acceptable values for this parameter are shown in the following list. For more information, refer to our coverage in Chapter 18, "Publishing Flash Movies."

- `l` : left edge, centered vertically
- `r` : right edge, centered vertically
- `t` : top edge, centered horizontally
- `b` : bottom edge, centered horizontally
- `lt` : left and top edges
- `rt` : right and top edges
- `lb` : left and bottom edges
- `rb` : right and bottom edges

P. `<param name="wmode" value="transparent" />`: This Player option works with all versions of the Flash Player if you are using Internet Explorer (version 3 or later) for Windows, or with Flash Player 6 r65 or later on Internet Explorer, Netscape, and most Mozilla-based browsers. If you are targeting an audience that uses these browsers, you can control how the Flash movie's background color appears on top of the HTML or DHTML elements on the Web page. There are three acceptable values:

- `window`: This value is the default appearance of movies playing in the Flash Player on Web pages. With this value, movies play within the area specified by the `width` and `height` attributes (discussed in item D), and the background color of the Flash movie's stage (as defined by Document Properties, or item Q, later in this section) appears.

- `opaque`: This value provides the same visual appearance of the movie's stage as `window` does. However, if you want to animate other DHTML objects in front of or behind a layer containing the Flash movie, it is recommended that you use the `opaque` value.

- `transparent`: This value enables the stage of the Flash movie to act like an alpha channel. When enabled, the Flash movie appears to float on the HTML page, without any background color to reveal the corners of the Flash movie's stage. Again, although this feature is somewhat extraordinary, it functions only with specific browsers and later versions of the Flash Player plug-in. Also, because the browser must anti-alias the Flash artwork on top of other HTML elements, playback of Flash animations may suffer.

Q. `<param name="devicefont" value="true" />`: This feature controls how Flash text appears in the browser window and works only on the Windows operating system. Like the device fonts with the Flash authoring environment (_sans, _serif, and _typewriter), this option can display any and all embedded text to system fonts such as Times and Arial. To do this, set `value` to `true`. To disable device font rendering in this fashion, set `value` to `false`. If this tag is omitted from the HTML, the `value` defaults to `false`. Finally, the rules of Flash device fonts apply to system device fonts as well. For example, device or system fonts cannot be masked, rotated, or manipulated with the Transform panel or the Property inspector.

Note

This seldom-used setting does not work predictably from use to use. In our tests, I could not get `devicefont` to work consistently from movie to movie, nor could I propose any reasonable use for it. It's likely that this is a legacy setting, meaning that it was made available for machines that had slow video or computing performance when the Flash Player was first introduced to the market. ∎

R. `<param name="bgcolor" value="#FFFFFF" />`: This parameter name, `bgcolor`, controls the background color of the Flash movie. If you published an HTML document via the Publish command, the `value` is automatically set to the background color specified by the Modify ⇨ Document command in Flash. However, you can override the Movie setting by entering a different value in this parameter tag. Note that this parameter, like all HTML tags and attributes concerning color, uses hexadecimal code to describe the color. For more information on color, see Chapter 7, "Applying Color."

S. `<param name="flashvars" value="title=My%20Flash%Movie" />`: This Flash Player 6 and later attribute enables you to declare variables within the Flash movie when it loads into the Web browser. `flashvars` stands for "Flash Variables." This feature enables you to circumvent the browser URL length limitation for declaring variables in the Flash movie's filename, as I discuss in item I of this list. For example, you can use client-side (for example, JavaScript) or server-side (for example, ColdFusion, ASP, PHP) scripting to dynamically write the `value` for this tag in your HTML, passing information from databases into the Flash movie at load time.

Tip

If you use Flash Remoting services with your Flash movie, be sure to declare the `gatewayUrl` variable in `flashvars`. The `gatewayUrl` variable specifies the location of the Flash Remoting gateway, such as `<param name="flashvars" value="gatewayUrl=http://mydomain.com/flashservices/ gateway" />`. ∎

T. `<param name="base" value="." />`: This attribute tells the Flash movie how to interpret any relative paths used with ActionScript. The default value is `"."`, which means that Flash resolves any relative paths within ActionScript to the same directory that the Flash movie resides in. For example, if `base` is set to `"."`, the following action in ActionScript 3.0 looks for an HTML document named `form.html` in the same directory as the Flash movie file (.swf):

```
navigateToURL(new URLRequest("form.html"));
```

You can use dot notation with the `base` attribute, such as `"../"`, or specify a fully qualified domain name, such as `"http://www.myserver.com/section_1"`, to let the Flash movie know that all relative paths should be resolved from that starting point.

Web Resource

You can read Macromedia's tech notes about the `base` attribute by perusing the links in the "Flash and HTML Tags" category at `www.flashsupport.com/links`. ∎

Caution

In our tests, I only saw the `base` attribute recognized by `getURL()` or `navigateToURL()` actions. Other actions that use URLs, such as `loadMovie()`, `LoadVars`, `XML`, and `NetStream`, did not use the `base` attribute to resolve relative URLs. If you keep your Flash movie files (.swf) in a separate folder from assets that need to be loaded into the Flash movies, you should pass the starting path into the Flash movie with `flashvars` (see item S in this list) and append that value to all of your relative paths in ActionScript. Also, if you use dot notation with the `base` attribute, such as `"../"`, the path is oddly interpreted relative to the HTML document, not the Flash movie. ∎

U. `</object>`: This is the closing tag for the starting `<object>` tag. As I show you later in this chapter, you can put other HTML tags between the last `<param>` tag and the closing `</object>` tag for non-ActiveX-enabled browsers, such as Netscape or Apple Safari. Because Internet Explorer for Windows is the primary browser that currently implements `<object>` tags, most browsers simply skip the `<object>` tag (as well as its `<param>` tags) and read only the tags between the last `<param>` and `</object>` tags.

Tip

I recommend that you consistently apply quotes around names and values, such as `<param name="bgcolor" value="#FFFFFF" />`. This syntax is especially important for the `flashvars` attribute. ∎

Using the <embed> tag

Netscape and Mozilla-based browsers use the `<embed>` tag to display nonbrowser, native file formats that require a plug-in, such as Adobe Flash Player and Shockwave Director or Apple QuickTime. Following is a sample listing of attributes and values for the `<embed>` tag. Again, attributes with an asterisk are generally optional for most Flash movie playback.

Note

The `<object>` tag can be used with most Mozilla-based browsers, but the implementation is somewhat different than that of Internet Explorer for Windows. You learn more about using the `<object>` tag for Mozilla-based browsers in our coverage of SWFObject later in this chapter. ∎

```
A. <embed
B.      src="home.swf"
C.      play="false"
D.      loop="false"
E.      quality="high"
F.      scale="noborder"
G.      salign="lt"
H.      wmode="transparent"
I.      devicefont="true"
J.      bgcolor="#FFFFFF"
K.      width="550" height="400"
L.      swLiveConnect="false"
M.      name="home"
N.      id="home"
O.      align="middle"
P.      allowScriptAccess="sameDomain"
Q.      allowFullScreen="false"
R.      flashvars="name=Lucian"
S.      type="application/x-shockwave-flash"
T.      base="."
U.      pluginspage="http://www.macromedia.com/go/ ⤵
        getflashplayer">
V. </embed>
```

A. `<embed`: This is the opening `<embed>` tag. Note that lines B through T are attributes of the opening `<embed>` tag, which is why you don't see the > character at the end of line A.

B. `src`: This stands for *source,* and it indicates the filename of the Flash movie. This attribute of `<embed>` works exactly like the `movie` parameter of the `<object>` tag.

C. `play`: This attribute behaves in the same manner as the `play` parameter of the `<object>` tag. If you omit this attribute in your HTML, the Flash Player assumes that it should automatically play the Flash movie.

D. `loop`: This attribute controls the same behavior as the `loop` parameter of the `<object>` tag. If you omit this attribute in your HTML, the Flash Player automatically loops playback of the movie's Main Timeline.

E. `quality`: This attribute controls how the Flash movie's artwork appears in the browser window. Like the equivalent `quality` parameter of the `<object>` tag, its value can be `low`, `autolow`, `autohigh`, `high`, or `best`.

F. `scale`: This attribute of `<embed>` controls how the Flash movie fits within the browser window and/or the dimensions specified by `width` and `height` (item K). Its value can be `showall` (default if attribute is omitted), `noborder`, `exactfit`, or `noscale`.

G. `salign`: This attribute controls the internal alignment of the Flash movie within the viewing area of the movie's dimensions. See the description for the `salign` parameter of the `<object>` tag for more information.

H. `wmode`: This attribute controls the opacity of the Flash movie's background color and works only with specific browser and Flash Player version combinations. See the `wmode` parameter description in the `<object>` tag for more details.

I. `devicefont`: This attribute controls the appearance of any text within a Flash movie and functions correctly only on the Windows operating system. See the description for `devicefont` in the `<object>` tag section.

J. `bgcolor`: This setting controls the Flash movie's background color. Again, this attribute behaves identically to the equivalent `<param>` subtag of the `<object>` tag. See that tag's description in the preceding section.

K. `width` and `height`: These attributes control the dimensions of the Flash movie as it appears on the Web page. Refer to the `width` and `height` descriptions of the `<object>` tag for more information.

L. `swLiveConnect`: This is one attribute that you won't find in the `<object>` tag. This unique tag enables Netscape's LiveConnect feature, which enables plug-ins and Java applets to communicate with JavaScript. By default, this attribute is set to `false`. If it is enabled (the attribute is set to `true`), the Web page may experience a short delay during loading. The latest versions of Netscape don't start the Java engine during a browsing session until a Web page containing a Java applet (or a Java-enabled plug-in such as the Flash Player) is loaded. Unless you use `fscommand()` actions in your Flash movies, it's best to omit this attribute or set its value to `false`.

M. `name`: This attribute works in tandem with the `swLiveConnect` attribute, enabling the Flash movie to be identified in JavaScript. The value given to the `name` attribute is the Flash movie object name that can be used within your JavaScript programming.

N. `id`: This attribute is also used for JavaScript functionality. It's uncertain whether this value is necessary if the name attribute exists, but Flash MX 2004's Flash with FSCommand HTML template (in the Publish Settings dialog box) includes both the `name` and `id` attributes. The `id` attribute should use the same value as the `name` attribute.

O. `align`: This attribute behaves exactly the same as the `align` parameter for the `<object>`. See its description in the preceding section for more information.

P. `allowScriptAccess`: This attribute controls how the Flash movie can access JavaScript from `getURL()` and `fscommand()` actions. See the description of `allowScriptAccess` in the `<object>` tag coverage earlier in this chapter.

Q. `allowFullScreen`: This attribute determines the full screen capability of a Flash movie running in Flash Player 9 r28 or later. See the description of `allowFullScreen` in the `<object>` tag coverage earlier in this chapter.

R. `flashvars`: This attribute assigns variables to the Main Timeline of the Flash movie at runtime. See the description of `flashvars` in the `<object>` tag coverage earlier in this chapter.

S. `type="application/x-shockwave-flash"`: This attribute tells the browser what MIME (Multipurpose Internet Mail Extension) content-type the embedded file is. Each file type (TIF, JPEG, GIF, PDF, and so on) has a unique MIME content-type header, describing what its content is. For Flash movies, the content-type is `application/x-shockwave-flash`. Any program (or operating system) that uses files over the Internet handles MIME content-types according to a reference chart that links each MIME content-type to its appropriate parent application or plug-in. Without this attribute, the browser may not understand what type of file the Flash movie is. As a result, it may display the broken plug-in icon when the Flash movie downloads to the browser.

T. `base="."`: This attribute tells the Flash movie how to resolve relative paths used in the movie's ActionScript code. See the description of `base` in the `<object>` tag coverage earlier in this chapter.

U. `pluginspage`: Literally "plug-in's page," this attribute tells the browser where to go to find the appropriate plug-in installer if it doesn't have the Flash plug-in already installed. This is not equivalent to a JavaScript-enabled auto installer or detection page. It simply redirects the browser to the URL of the Web page where the appropriate software can be downloaded.

V. `</embed>`: This is the closing tag for the original `<embed>` tag in line A. Some older or text-based browsers such as Lynx are incapable of displaying `<embed>` tags. You can insert alternate HTML (such as a static or animated GIF image with the `<img>` tag) between the `<embed>` `</embed>` tags for these browsers. Some browsers may require that you insert these alternate tags between a `<noembed></noembed>` set of tags within or after the `<embed></embed>` tags.

Detecting the Flash Player

What good is an awesome Flash experience if no one can see your Flash movies? Because most Flash content is viewed with a Web browser, it's extremely important to make sure that your HTML pages check for the existence of the Flash Player plug-in before you start pushing Flash content to the browser. There are a variety of ways to check for the Flash Player, and this section provides an overview of the available methods.

Plug-in versus ActiveX: Forcing content without a check

The Flash Player is available for Web browsers in two forms: the Flash Player plug-in (as a Netscape-compatible, or Mozilla-compatible, plug-in) and the Flash Player ActiveX control (for use only with Microsoft Internet Explorer on Windows 98/ME/2000/XP/Vista/7).

If you directly insert a Flash movie into a Web page with the `<embed>` tag (for Mozilla browsers), one of two scenarios happens:

- The browser has the Flash Player plug-in and loads the Flash movie.
- The browser does not have the Flash Player plug-in and displays a broken plug-in icon.

If the second scenario occurs and the `pluginspage` attribute of the `<embed>` tag is defined, the user can click the broken plug-in icon and go to the Adobe site to download the Flash Player plug-in. If the `pluginspage` attribute is not specified, clicking the broken plug-in icon takes you to a generic plug-in page provided by the browser vendor.

If you insert a Flash movie into an HTML document with the `<object>` tag (for Internet Explorer on Windows only), one of two scenarios happens:

- The browser has the Flash Player ActiveX control and loads the Flash movie.
- The browser does not have the Flash Player ActiveX control and auto-downloads and installs the ActiveX control file from the Adobe site.

Note

Newer versions of Windows XP (that is, with Service Pack 2 or SP2 installed) will likely get an additional warning represented as a strip across the top of the Web page attempting to initiate the installation of a new ActiveX control. The user must also click this strip and accept the download of the ActiveX control. ■

The ActiveX control auto-downloads and installs only if the `classid` and `codebase` attributes of the Flash movie's `<object>` tag are correctly specified. Depending on the user's security settings, the user needs to grant permission to a Security Warning dialog box to commence the download and install process.

Although using the `<object>` and `<embed>` tags by themselves is by far the simplest method for integrating Flash content into a Web page, it's not the most user-friendly method of ensuring that the majority of your Web visitors can view the Flash content. Flash CS5 uses an updated JavaScript detection mechanism, replacing the older JavaScript approach used in Flash CS3.

Note

Since Flash Player 4 was released, many seasoned Flash developers have used small Flash movies known as sniffers to detect the presence of the Flash Player in a user's Web browser. Sniffers are virtually hidden from the visitor to a Web site, and they direct an entry HTML page to a new location (using a `getURL()` action) where the real Flash content (or site) exists. If the Player is not installed, the sniffer movie cannot play and directs the HTML page to a new location. If this happens, a special `<meta>` tag in the `<head>` of the HTML document directs the browser location to a screen that informs the visitor to download the plug-in or ActiveX control. However, page redirection mechanisms are not ideal for search engine optimization — I recommend using SWFObject as discussed later in this chapter. ■

Detecting the Flash Player with Flash CS5

In Flash CS5, Adobe has made the process of using a sniffer methodology incredibly simple. In the following steps, you learn how to use the Detect Flash Version feature to properly direct a user to Flash Player 6 r65 content.

Note

You can check for Flash Player 4 or later with the Detect Flash Version feature. For demonstration purposes, I chose Flash Player 6 r65 because Flash MX 2004 introduced a new optimization feature for .swf files generated for this version (or later) of Flash Player 6. ■

Caution

If you used the Detect Flash Version in older versions of Flash such as Flash MX 2004, be sure to review this section. The feature no longer uses three HTML pages for the detection process. Everything from the detection to the content display to the alternate content display occurs on one HTML page. ■

1. **Create a new Flash document by choosing File ➪ New.** In the New Document dialog box, choose Flash File (ActionScript 3.0) and click OK. Alternatively, open an existing .fla file that you have created and skip to Step 4.

2. **Save the new Flash document as** `detection_test.fla`.

3. **Add some placeholder text to the Stage by using the Text tool.** Because this example is checking for Flash Player 9 r28, you can type **This is Flash Player 9 r28 content.**

4. **Choose File ➪ Publish Settings.** By default, both the Flash and HTML formats are selected in the Formats tab of the Publish Settings dialog box. The filenames for these formats should reflect the current .fla filename, such as `detection_test.swf` and `detection_test.html`, respectively.

5. **To keep the new version settings in a separate profile, click the Create New Profile (+) button at the top of the Publish Settings dialog box.** Name the profile FP9 r28 Detection, as shown in Figure 19.3. Click OK to close the dialog box, but leave the Publish Settings dialog box open.

6. **Click the Flash tab.** In the Version menu, choose Flash Player 9. In the ActionScript version menu, choose ActionScript 3.0 if not already selected. See Figure 19.4 for a review of these settings.

FIGURE 19.3

The Create New Profile dialog box, showing the new profile name.

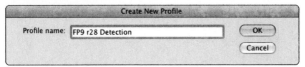

FIGURE 19.4

The Flash Player 9 settings in the Flash tab.

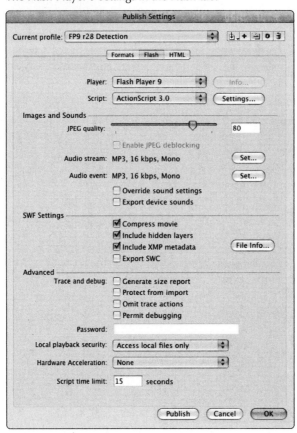

7. **Click the HTML tab of the Publish Settings dialog box and select the Detect Flash Version check box.** The two editable text fields to the right of the Version label should now be enabled. The major version of the Flash Player is fixed to the Player version you chose in the Flash tab. The first of the two editable fields represents a Minor Revision

value; to date, Adobe hasn't released any minor revisions of the Flash Player, but this feature is enabled just in case Adobe does release any minor revision during the life cycle of the Flash CS5 authoring tool. The second field represents the Incremental Revision value. Since Flash Player 4, Adobe has released several incremental revisions of the Flash Player for each player cycle.

Web Resource

To get a sense of how many incremental revisions of Flash Player 7 were released, see the "Flash Player Release Notes" category at `www.flashsupport.com/links.` ■

8. **Type** 28 **in the second field, as shown in Figure 19.5.** If you wanted to check for a different incremental version of Flash Player 9, you could enter that value instead. Click OK to close the dialog box, and go back to the HTML tab of the Publish Settings dialog box.

FIGURE 19.5

The Publish Settings dialog box

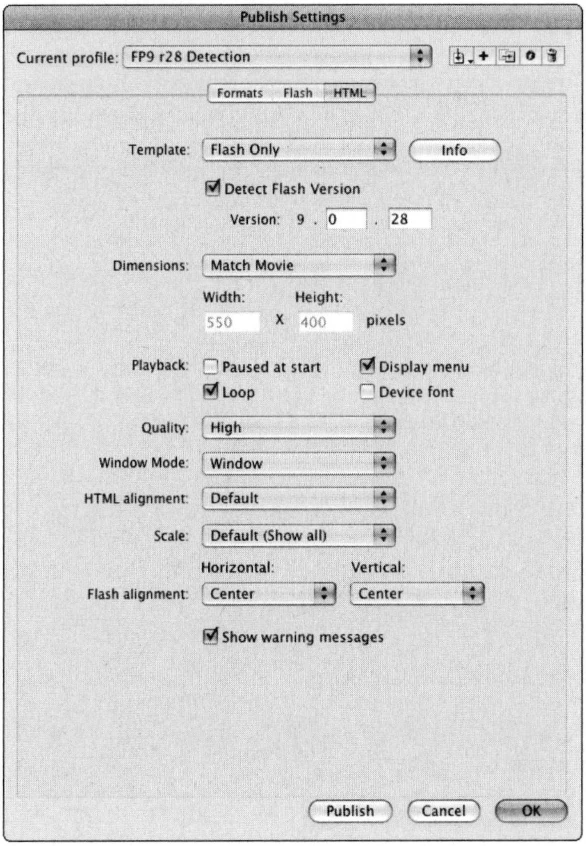

9. **In the Publish Settings dialog box, click the Publish button.** Flash CS5 generates all the necessary JavaScript within the published HTML document to properly detect the Flash Player version. Click OK to close the Publish Settings dialog box.

10. **On your desktop, navigate to the folder where you saved your original .fla file.** If you created the sample document in Step 1, you want to find the location of `detection_test.fla`. In this location, you will see the HTML file created for the detection process.

11. **In your own Web browser, load the `detection_test.html` page.** If your browser has Flash Player 9 r28 or later, the browser should display your `detection_test.swf` movie. This process works because the `detection_test.html` page uses JavaScript to check the installed Flash Player version, if one exists. If you open the HTML document in a text editor such as Adobe Dreamweaver CS5, you'll see that lines 286–291 declare the version numbers you entered in the HTML tab of the Publish Settings dialog box. The JavaScript code compares these values to the version of the Flash Player that loaded the movie. If the Flash Player matches (or exceeds) the version requirements, the Flash content tags (`<object>` and `<embed>`) are written to the HTML page with JavaScript. Otherwise, the alternate content specified on line 330 in the JavaScript code is loaded into the browser window.

Note

Adobe provides generic alternate content that you should replace with your own preferred HTML tags indicating what you want to the user to do if the version of the Flash Player required is not installed. ∎

12. **To accurately test your pages over an Internet connection, upload all the files (except the .fla file) to your Web server and load the `detection_test.html` document from the Web server URL to redo the test.**

On the CD-ROM

You can find all these files created for this detection example in the `ch19/flashCS5_detection` folder of this book's CD-ROM. The JavaScript in the `detection_test_fCS5b.html` version of the document contains additional alternate content that is specified in an `alternate.js` file, also included on the CD-ROM. If you want to find the latest "Get Flash Player" graphics to use in your Web pages, go to `www.adobe.com/macromedia/style_guide/buttons`. ∎

If you want to test the detection mechanism with an older version of the Flash Player, I recommend that you use an older Flash Player installer with a Mozilla-compatible browser. The process of uninstalling an ActiveX control used by Internet Explorer is much more difficult to do.

Web Resource

You can find just about every past version of the Flash Player at `www.adobe.com/cfusion/knowledgebase/index.cfm?id=tn_14266` for testing purposes. As mentioned previously, I recommend that you install the older versions with a Mozilla-compatible browser. If you are using Mac OS X, the first Flash Player released for Mac OS X was version 5. ∎

You can set up your Mozilla-compatible browser's plug-ins folder to accommodate multiple versions of the Flash Player plug-in. When you installed Flash CS5, the latest release of Flash Player 9 should have automatically been installed to your Mozilla-based browser's `Plugins` (or `plugins`) folder. The plug-in file, named `NPSWF32.dll`, can be moved outside of the `Plugins` folder, into a new parent folder that you create. For the following example, we'll use Mozilla Firefox as our test browser.

Web Resource

Mozilla Firefox is a free Web browser that you can download at `www.mozilla.org/products/firefox/`. **Firefox has quickly become the preferred cross-platform browser of many Web developers.** ∎

I prefer to create a `_Flash Players` folder in the `C:\Program Files\Mozilla FireFox` folder, and put each Flash Player version plug-in file into its own folder, as shown in Figure 19.6.

Caution

Regardless of the Flash Player version you install, all Flash Player plug-in files for Mozilla-compatible browsers have the same name on Windows: `NPSWF32.dll`. **For this reason, you must isolate multiple installations of the Flash Player into their own folder.** ∎

FIGURE 19.6

A sample Flash Players folder structure for use with Mozilla Firefox on Windows

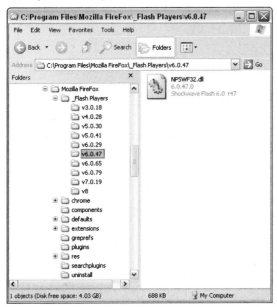

You can do the same procedure on Mac OS X, where all browsers share the same plug-in folders. That's right! Mozilla, Firefox, Internet Explorer, and Apple Safari all refer to the same plug-ins folder. On your boot disk, such as Macintosh HD, browse to the `Library\Internet Plug-Ins\` folder. In this location, you find the `Shockwave Flash NP-PPC` plug-in file. As Figure 19.7 shows, you can create a `Library\Internet Plug-Ins (DISABLED)` folder to store other versions of this plug-in file.

Caution

On Mac OS X, you may need to re-create the same plug-in structure with the `Users\[Your User Name]\ Library\Internet Plug-Ins\` folder. Or, you may just want to remove any Flash Player plug-in files within this folder. Mac OS X should then default to the main `Library\Internet Plug-Ins\` folder. ■

This process takes some time because you have to download and run each installer from the URL I mentioned in the earlier Web Resource note, and move the `NPSWF32.dll` file from the `Plugins` folder to its own folder in the `Flash Players` folder. When you're done, however, you'll have an efficient system for checking your content against older versions of the Flash Player. Simply move the current `NPSWF32.dll` file into its appropriate `_Flash Players` folder, and move the desired test version from its `Flash Players` folder into the `Plugins` folder.

FIGURE 19.7

A sample Flash Players folder structure for use with Mozilla Firefox or Apple Safari on Mac OS X

Tip

If you use Firefox 3.0, you're in luck. Alessandro Crugnola has built Flash Switcher, a free Flash Player plug-in utility that includes past versions of the Flash Player and swaps your installed version of the player with a convenient menu built right into the browser window! For more information, see www.sephiroth.it/ firefox/flash_switcher/. ■

Detecting the Flash Player with SWFObject

Although the Adobe Flash CS5 detection features work wonderfully, you should know about a popular and widely used JavaScript library, SWFObject. This JavaScript code, created by Geoff Stearns, can be downloaded at code.google.com/p/swfobject/. I've included the latest version, 2.2, in the ch19/swfobject/swfobject_2-2 folder on this book's CD-ROM. In this section, you learn how to use SWFObject with Flash content.

Note

SWFObject 2.0 and later supports two methods of publishing Flash content: static and dynamic. In this walkthrough, I use the static method, which is more Web standards–compliant. For more information, visit code. google.com/p/swfobject/wiki/documentation. ■

Reviewing the content

We've included a Flash movie named trafficLightGreen.swf in the ch19/swfobject folder. This file displays a vector graphic of a flashing green traffic light, as shown in Figure 19.8. The SWFObject code displays this movie only if Flash Player 9 r28 is installed, which is required for full screen capability.

FIGURE 19.8

A sample Flash movie

An alternative non-Flash piece of content has also been provided in the ch19/swfobject folder: trafficLightRed.gif, as shown in Figure 19.9.

The HTML document displays this GIF file in the following cases:

- Flash Player 9 r28 or later is not installed.
- JavaScript has been disabled by the user in the Web browser's preferences.

FIGURE 19.9

A sample alternate graphic

Copy both the SWF and GIF files from the CD-ROM to a preferred location on your computer. Be sure to save the HTML file discussed in the next section to the same location.

Creating the HTML document

In this section, you learn how to build an HTML file that uses the SWFObject library to determine which piece of content, the Flash movie or the GIF graphic, to display in the Web browser.

Caution

In the code samples shown in this section and throughout the book, do not type the ⤴ character, which indicates a continuation of the same line of code. ∎

1. **In Adobe Dreamweaver CS5, create a new HTML file by choosing File ➪ New.** In the New Document dialog box, choose Blank Page, and then HTML in the Page Type column, None in the Layout column, and XHTML 1.0 Strict in the Doc Type menu, as shown in Figure 19.10. Click OK to create the file, and assign a document title of **SWFObject Detection**. If you don't have Dreamweaver, create a new HTML file in your preferred HTML editor and insert the code shown in Listing 19.1. If you're using Dreamweaver, switch to code view.

2. **Save the HTML file as** `swfobject_sample.html`.

3. **Copy the** `swfobject.js` **and** `expressInstall.swf` **files from the** `ch19/swfobject/swfobject_2_1` **folder to the same location as your HTML file saved in Step 2.** The `swfobject.js` JavaScript file contains the Flash Player detection code, and the `expressInstall.swf` file is a pre-built Flash movie (swf file) that automatically downloads the latest version of the Flash Player if the required Flash Player version is not available. Note that the `expressInstall.swf` file requires Flash Player 6 r65 or later to be installed to initiate the automated plug-in download-and-install process.

FIGURE 19.10

The New Document dialog box in Adobe Dreamweaver CS5.

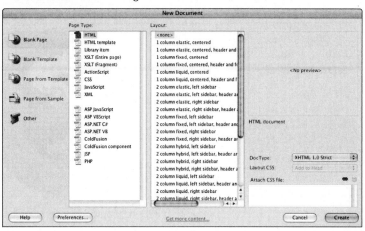

4. **After the closing** `</title>` **tag and before the closing** `</head>` **tag, insert the following code to load the SWFObject code into the HTML document:**

```
<script type="text/javascript" src="swfobject.js"></script>
```

5. **Between the** `<body></body>` **tags, add the code shown in Listing 19.2.** The `<div>` container specifies both the Flash movie (.swf file) that you want to appear on the page as well as the alternate content that you want to appear if the required version of the Flash Player is unavailable. The alternate content is also indexed by search engines.

6. **Go back up to the** `<head>` **section of your HTML document and add the following code.** This code creates a new SWFObject instance in JavaScript. If the required Flash Player version is installed (version 9 r28), the `<div>` content displays the Flash movie specified in the `<object>` tags. Review the code comments to see the parameters required for a new SWFObject instance.

```
<script type="text/javascript">
    swfobject.registerObject("flashContent", "9.0.28", ⤵
    "expressInstall.swf");
</script>
```

7. **Save the HTML file and test the file in a Web browser.** If the browser has Flash Player 9 r28 installed, you should see the green traffic light animation. If the browser has an earlier version of the Flash Player or does not have any version of Flash Player installed, the red traffic light graphic appears.

LISTING 19.1

The HTML Starter Code

```
<!DOCTYPE html PUBLIC "-//W3C//DTD XHTML 1.0 Strict//EN"
    "http://www.w3.org/TR/xhtml1/DTD/xhtml1-transitional.dtd">
<html xmlns="http://www.w3.org/1999/xhtml">
<head>
<meta http-equiv="Content-Type" content="text/html; charset=utf-8" />
<title>SWFObject Detection</title>
</head>

<body>
</body>
</html>
```

LISTING 19.2

The Flash Movie and Alternate Content

```
<div>
    <object id="flashContent" classid="clsid:D27CDB6E-AE6D-11cf-
    96B8-444553540000" width="105" height="185">
        <param name="movie" value="trafficLightGreen.swf" />
        <!--[if !IE]>-->
        <object type="application/x-shockwave-flash"
        data="trafficLightGreen.swf" width="105" height="185">
        <!--<![endif]-->
            <img src="trafficLightRed.gif" width="105" height="185"
            align="left"/>
            <p style="font-family:Verdana, Arial, Helvetica,
            sans-serif; position: relative; top: 50px; width:
            300px;">Please download the <a
            href="http://www.adobe.com/go/getflashplayer">latest
            Flash Player</a> for the best experience.</p>
        <!--[if !IE]>-->
        </object>
        <!--<![endif]-->
    </object>
</div>
```

On the CD-ROM

You can find the finished HTML code in the `ch19/swfobject` folder on this book's CD-ROM. ∎

Using Flash Movies with JavaScript and DHTML

The ActionScripting features of Flash Player 8 or later have increased the range of interactive and dynamic possibilities for Flash movies on the Internet. Prior to Flash Player 4, Flash movies could interact with external HTML or scripts only through the `fscommand()` action. This meant mapping commands and variables to JavaScript, which, in turn, passed information to the document object model of DHTML, Java applets, or CGI (common gateway interface) scripts. Now that Flash movies can directly send and receive data to server-side scripts, just about anything can be done within the Flash movie. If you want to directly communicate with the Web browser or the HTML document, you need to use JavaScript with either `fscommand()` actions or the `External Interface` API (application programming interface) introduced with Flash Player 8.

Tip

The `ExternalInterface` **API is part of the** `flash.external` **package in ActionScript 2.0 and 3.0, and is available in Flash Player 8 or later (AS2) and Flash Player 9 and later (AS3). This new set of actions (collectively known as an API) enables you to communicate directly with the Flash movie's hosting environment. Unlike the older** `fscommand()` **action, the** `ExternalInterface` **API enables you to receive data from the hosting environment immediately, without setting up callback handlers.** ■

A word of caution to Web developers

This section covers the `ExternalInterface` API actions, which, when used in Flash movies on Web pages, are supported by the following browsers:

- Internet Explorer 4.0 and later for Windows 98/ME/2000/XP/Vista/7
- Mozilla 1.7.5 and later
- Mozilla Firefox 1.0 and later
- Opera 9.0 and later
- Apple Safari 1.3 and later

The coverage of the `ExternalInterface` API assumes that you have a working knowledge of JavaScript and Flash ActionScript. If you don't know how to add actions to frames or buttons, read Chapter 15, "Understanding Actions and Event Handlers." If you don't know JavaScript, you can still follow the steps to the tutorials and create a fully functional Flash-JavaScript movie. However, because this isn't a book on JavaScript, I don't explain how JavaScript syntax or functions work.

Understanding how Flash movies work with JavaScript

As I mention earlier, Flash Player has a class called `ExternalInterface`. This class has methods that can invoke commands (passing optional arguments, or parameters) from a Flash movie to its hosting environment, such as JavaScript in a Web browser. What does this mean for interactivity?

The `ExternalInterface` API offers the capability to have any Flash event handler (button instance, frame actions, and so on) initiate an event handler in JavaScript. Although this may not sound too exciting, you can use `ExternalInterface` actions to trigger anything that you would have used JavaScript alone to do in the past, such as updating HTML form text fields, changing the visibility of HTML elements, or switching HTML background colors on the fly. I look at these effects in the next section.

Flash movie communication with JavaScript is not a one-way street. You can also monitor and control Flash movies with JavaScript. Just as JavaScript treats an HTML document as an object and its elements as properties of that object, JavaScript treats a Flash movie as it would any other element on a Web page. Therefore, you can use JavaScript functions and HTML hyperlinks (`<a href>` tags) to control Flash movie playback.

Note

For JavaScript to receive Flash events, you need to make sure that the attribute `allowScriptAccess` for the `<object>` and `<embed>` tags is set to `"sameDomain"` or `"always"`. By default, most Flash CS5 HTML templates have this set to `"sameDomain"`. If you're testing your Flash movies and HTML documents locally, you should temporarily switch the value to `"always"`; otherwise, JavaScript does not receive the events from the Flash movie. ■

Web Resource

This edition of the Flash Bible features coverage of the `ExternalInterface` API in ActionScript 3.0 available in Flash Player 9 or later. If you want to read more about the older `fscommand()` method of sending data to and from the Flash Player and JavaScript, refer to the archived document at `www.flashsupport.com/archive`. ■

Changing HTML attributes

In this section, I show you how to dynamically change the `bgcolor` attribute of the `<body>` tag with an `ExternalInterface` action from a Flash movie while it is playing in the browser window. In fact, the background color changes a few times. Then after that has been accomplished, you learn how to update the text field of a `<form>` tag to display what percent of the Flash movie has been loaded.

On the CD-ROM

Before you start this section, make a copy of the Flash document `countdown_starter.fla` located in the `ch19/ExternalInterface` folder of this book's CD-ROM. This is a starter document to which you will add ActionScript 3.0 code. ■

Adding ExternalInterface actions to a Flash movie

Open the `countdown_starter.fla` Flash document from this book's CD-ROM, and use
Control ➪ Test Movie to play the Flash .swf file. You should notice that the filmstrip countdown
fades to white, and then to near black, and then back to its original gray color. This countdown
continues to loop until the entire first scene has loaded into the Flash Player. When the first scene
has loaded, playback skips to a video clip of a younger Robert swinging around and around.
There's more to the Flash movie, but for now, that's all you need to deal with.

Our goal for this section of the tutorial is to add function calls to specific keyframes in the `count-
down_starter.fla` document. When the Flash Player plays the frame with a function call, the
Player sends a command and argument string to JavaScript. JavaScript then calls a function that
changes the background color to the value specified in the argument string of the function. To be
more exact, you'll create a function named `changeBgColor` in ActionScript. This function, when
invoked (or "called"), invokes a corresponding function named `changeBgColor` in the JavaScript
code created later in this section. You'll add code to invoke the `changeBgColor()` function to
the frames where the color fades to white, black, and gray. When the Flash movie changes to these
colors, JavaScript changes the HTML background colors.

Here's the process:

1. **Select frame 1 of the actions layer, and open the Actions panel (F9,/Option+F9).** In
   the Script pane, add the following code. Make sure that you are not in Script Assist mode.
   This code, written in ActionScript 3.0 syntax, imports the `ExternalInterface` class
   and creates a `changeBgColor()` function that accepts one argument named `color`.
   This argument is passed to the `call()` method of the `ExternalInterface` class. The
   `call()` method takes one or more parameters. The first argument is always the name of
   the method (or function) to call in the hosting environment, and subsequent arguments
   are passed to the called method. In this example, you need to pass only one argument,
   `color`, to the JavaScript host environment.

   ```
   import flash.external.ExternalInterface;

   function changeBgColor(color:String):void {
      ExternalInterface.call("changeBgColor", color);
   }
   ```

2. **On frame 16 of the Main Timeline, add a keyframe on the actions layer.** With the
   keyframe selected, open the Actions panel (F9/Option+F9). Type the following action
   into the Script pane:

   ```
   changeBgColor("#FFFFFF");
   ```

   This action invokes the `changeBgColor()` function you defined on frame 1 in the previous step. The argument string #FFFFFF is passed to that function. The Flash function
   named `changeBgColor()` passes that argument to the hosting environment's
   `changeBgColor()` function as well, changing the HTML background color to white.

3. **On frame 20, add another action to the corresponding keyframe on the actions layer.** With frame 20 selected, open the Actions panel and type the following code:

   ```
   changeBgColor("#333333");
   ```

   The argument `"#333333"` is used to change the HTML background color to a dark gray.

4. **On frame 21 of the actions layer, follow the same instructions as you did for Step 3, except use `"#9E9E9E"` for the argument string.** This changes the HTML background color to the same color as the Flash movie countdown graphic.

5. **On frame 66 of the actions layer, add another action invoking the `changeBgColor()` function.** (Add this action after the existing action on this frame.) This time, use an argument string of `"#000000"`, which changes the HTML background color to black.

6. **Now that you've added several actions, try them out in the browser.** Save the document as `countdown_100.fla`, and open the Publish Settings dialog box (for more information on publish settings, refer to Chapter 20, "Publishing Flash Movies"). In the Formats tab, make sure that only the Flash format check box is selected. Change the Flash filename to `countdown.swf`. Click OK to close the Publish Settings dialog box. Choose the File ⇨ Publish command to export the Flash movie.

Next, you build the JavaScript code that is added to the HTML file Flash publishes.

Enabling JavaScript for Flash movies

In this section, you add the necessary JavaScript to make the `ExternalInterface.call()` action work in the browser. Remember, you added this action to the `changeBgColor()` function on frame 1 of the Flash movie. What follows in Listing 19.3 is the JavaScript code that defines the custom function `changeBgColor` that I have created for you.

Make a copy of the `countdown_swfobject_starter.html` file from the `ch21/ExternalInterface` folder of this book's CD-ROM. Copy the file to the same location as the `countdown.swf` file published in the last section. Add the code in Listing 19.3 to the `countdown_swfobject_starter.html` file.

Note

The line numbers reflect the actual line numbers in the HTML document. Also, remember that the ⤵ indicates a continuation of the same line of code. Do not insert this character into your HTML document. ∎

LISTING 19.3

The JavaScript Code to Enable the ExternalInterface Actions

```
10.    <script type="text/javascript" language="javascript">
11.    <!--
12.    function changeBgColor(hexColor){
```

```
13.        document.bgColor = hexColor;
14.    }
15.    //-->
16.    </script>
```

The following is a line-by-line explanation of the code:

10: This HTML tag initializes the JavaScript code.

11: This string of characters is standard HTML comment code. By adding this after the open-ing `<script>` tag, non-JavaScript browsers ignore the code. If this string wasn't included, text-based browsers such as Lynx might display JavaScript code as HTML text.

12: This is where the function `changeBgColor()` is defined. Remember that the `change BgColor()` function in the Flash ActionScript specifies `"changeBgColor"` in the `ExternalInterface.call()` method. There is one argument defined for the func-tion: `hexColor`, representing the hexadecimal color value passed from the Flash movie.

13: This line of code passes the argument `hexColor` to the `document.bgColor` property, which controls the HTML background color.

14: This line of code ends the function defined in line 12.

15: This end comment closes the comment started in line 11.

16: The closing `</script>` tag ends this portion of JavaScript code.

That's it! I also added `<center>` tags around the `<div>` tag to center the Flash movie on the HTML page, and I added the `allowScriptAccess` parameter in the `<object>` tag, respec-tively, to `"always"`. After you've manually added the custom lines of JavaScript code, you can load the HTML document into either Internet Explorer or a Mozilla-compatible browser (see the caveats mentioned at the beginning of this section). When the Flash Player comes to the frames with `changeBgColor()` actions, the HTML background should change along with the Flash movie. Next, you add a `<form>` element that displays the percentage of the Flash movie that has loaded into the browser window.

On the CD-ROM

You can find this version of the `countdown_100.fla` **document in the** `ch19/ExternalInterface` **folder on this book's CD-ROM. You will also find** `countdown.swf` **and a fully JavaScripted HTML document called** `countdown_swfobject_100.html`. ∎

Adding a percentLoaded() method

With Flash Player 8 or later and the `ExternalInterface` API, JavaScript can also communicate back to the Flash movie. In the Flash movie, you need to define callback handlers by using the `ExternalInterface.addCallback()` method. This method lets you set up custom func-tions that are exposed to the hosting environment.

In this section, you create a JavaScript `percentLoaded()` method to display the Flash movie's loading progress update as a text field of a `<form>` element. First, you add the necessary `ExternalInterface` action and custom function to the Flash movie, next you add HTML `<form>` elements, and then you add the appropriate JavaScript.

1. **Open the `countdown_100.fla` file that you modified in the previous section.** Select frame 1 of the actions layer, and open the Actions panel (F9/Option+F9). Add the code shown in Listing 19.4 after the first import statement but before the `changeBg-Color` function declaration. Do not type the ⟲ character because it denotes a continuation of the same line of code.

   The `import flash.display.LoaderInfo;` statement makes ready the `LoaderInfo` class necessary for accessing the Flash movie's percent-loaded information. The `import flash.sysem.Security;` statement makes available the `Security` class that defines which Web domain can access content with the Flash movie (.swf file).

   The `Security.allowDomain("*");` action allows JavaScript to access the Flash movie's methods and properties. Use the "*" value only when testing the file locally. If you intend to upload a live example to your Web server, specify the Web server's domain name.

   The next block of code uses an `if` statement to check whether the `ExternalInterface` capabilities are available in the current host environment, such as a Web browser. If `ExternalInterface` is available, an ActionScript function named `getPercent Loaded` is exposed to JavaScript with the `ExternalInterface.addCallback()` method. This method takes two arguments: the name you want to use in JavaScript to call the Flash function (`"getPercentLoaded"`, although you could specify a different name here to use in JavaScript if you preferred), and the Flash function name that is invoked when JavaScript calls the function named as the first argument (`getPercentLoaded`). The `catch` statements are invoked only if an error is encountered when the Flash movie tries to access JavaScript with the `addCallBack()` method. The `throw new Error()` actions display an error dialog at runtime to alert the user to an error encountered during playback.

   The function `getPercentLoaded()` does not use any arguments. The purpose of the `getPercentLoaded()` function is to return the percent loaded of the Flash movie file (.swf).

2. **Save your Flash document as `countdown_complete.fla`, and publish your Flash movie.**

3. **In a text editor such as Adobe Dreamweaver, Notepad, or TextEdit, open the `countdown_swfobject_100.html` document from the previous section.** Immediately resave this document as `countdown_swfobject.html`.

4. **Add the following HTML after the** `<object>` **and** `<embed>` **tags:**

```
<form method="post" action="" name="flashPercent" ⤸
   style="display:show">
 <input type="text" name="labelField" size="5" ⤸
 style="display:show" />
</form>
```

The code in Step 4 uses two `name` attributes so that JavaScript can recognize them. Also, the DHTML `style` attribute assigns a `display:show` value to both the `<form>` and `<input>` tags.

5. **Add the JavaScript code shown in Listing 19.5 to your HTML document after the** `changeBgColor()` **function.** The following `percentLoaded` function tells the browser to update the `<form>` text field with the percent of the Flash movie currently loaded. When the value is greater than or equal to 100, then the text field reads 100 percent and disappears after two seconds. This code also declares a `thisMovie()` function, which returns a reference to the Flash object in the `<object>` tag. The `thisMovie()` function is used in the `percentLoaded()` function to call the Flash movie's `getPercentLoaded()` function you wrote in Step 1 of this section, to retrieve the loaded percent of the Flash movie. After the `percentLoaded()` function is declared in JavaScript, you use the `setInterval()` function in JavaScript to continuously invoke the `percentLoaded()` function, every 100 milliseconds. This interval is cleared when the Flash movie is fully loaded. (The ⤸ indicates a continuation to the same line of code. Do not type this character in your code.)

Note

The `thisMovie()` **function code is a slightly modified version of an example taken directly from Adobe's** `ExternalInterface` **API example code shown in the documentation that is accessed through the Help panel. Also, you might notice that JavaScript has some of the same function names that Flash ActionScript does. Both JavaScript and ActionScript have a** `setInterval()` **function to enable you to call a function continuously at a specific interval.** ■

6. **Save the HTML document and load it into a browser.** If you run into errors, check your JavaScript syntax carefully. A misplaced `;` or `}` can set off the entire script. Also, the function names specified in the Flash ActionScript code and the JavaScript code are case-sensitive and must be exactly the same. If you continue to run into errors, compare your document to the `countdown_swfobject.html` document on this book's CD-ROM. I also recommend that you test the preloading functionality from a remote Web server. If you test the file locally, the Flash Player may throw a security error dialog box.

LISTING 19.4

The ActionScript Code for the percentLoaded() Function

```
import flash.external.ExternalInterface;
import flash.display.LoaderInfo;
import flash.system.Security;

Security.allowDomain("*");

if (ExternalInterface.available) {
   try {
      ExternalInterface.addCallback("getPercentLoaded", getPercentLoaded);
   }
   catch (error:SecurityError) {
      throw new Error(error.message);
   }
   catch (error:Error) {
      throw new Error(error.message);
   }
} else {
   throw new Error("ExternalInterface not available for this host ⤶
   environment.");
}

function getPercentLoaded():Number {
   var li:LoaderInfo = this.loaderInfo;
   var lb:Number = li.bytesLoaded;
   var tb:Number = li.bytesTotal;
   return Math.floor((lb/tb)*100);
}
```

LISTING 19.5

The JavaScript Code for the percentLoaded() Function

```
function thisMovie(movieName) {
   var isIE = navigator.appName.indexOf("Microsoft") != -1;
   return (isIE) ? window[movieName] : ⤶
   document.getElementById(movieName);
}
```

```
function percentLoaded(){
   try {

      var movie = thisMovie("countdown");

      var pl = movie.getPercentLoaded();


   if(pl >= 100 ){

         document.flashPercent.labelField.value= "100 %";

         setTimeout("document.flashPercent.labelField.style.⊃
      display = 'none'", 2000);

         clearInterval(checkID);

      } else {

         document.flashPercent.labelField.value = pl + " %" ;

      }

   }

   catch(err){

      alert("Can't determine percent loaded... Aborting..");

      document.flashPercent.labelField.style.display = 'none';

      clearInterval(checkID);
   }
}
var checkID = setInterval(percentLoaded, 100);
```

Caution

Remember that this type of interactivity won't work on all browsers, and it requires the use of Flash Player 8 or later. ■

Okay, that wasn't the easiest task in the world, and, admittedly, the effects might not have been as spectacular as you may have thought. Now that you know the basics of Flash and JavaScript interactivity, however, you can take your Flash movie interactivity one step further.

Summary

- You can customize many Flash movie attributes by adjusting the attributes of the `<object>` and `<embed>` tags in an HTML document. Scaling, size, quality, and background color are just a few of the Flash movie properties that can be changed within HTML without altering the original .swf file.

- Flash CS5 includes a Detect Flash Version feature in the publish settings. This feature automatically creates an HTML document with the appropriate JavaScript and HTML tags to check for a version of the Flash Player that you specify.

- The SWFObject JavaScript library is a clean and concise method for adding Flash content to HTML pages, as well as detecting and requiring a specific version of the Flash Player.

- Flash movies can interact with JavaScript and HTML elements on a Web page. This type of interactivity, however, is limited to the 4.0 or later versions of Internet Explorer (on 32-bit Windows versions) and more current versions of Mozilla-compatible browsers.

- Flash Player 8 or later can receive events and data from JavaScript. For example, JavaScript can query a Flash movie to determine how much of it has downloaded to the browser.

Using the Flash Player and Projector

T his chapter explores alternative means of distributing your Flash movies as self-contained executable applications for CD/DVD-ROMs or other removable storage devices. I also look at the broad support available for the Flash Player plug-in for Web browsers.

Using the Stand-Alone Flash Player and Projector

The stand-alone Flash Player and projector enable you to take your Flash right off the Web and onto the desktop without having to worry whether users have the plug-in. In fact, you don't even need to worry about them having browsers! Stand-alone players and projectors have similar properties and limitations, although they're slightly different.

- **Stand-alone player:** This is an executable player that comes with Flash CS5. You can open any SWF file in this player. The stand-alone player can be found in the `Adobe/Flash CS5/ Players/Release` folder (Windows) or the `Adobe Flash CS5:Players:Release` folder (Mac) on the volume where you installed Flash CS5.

- **Projector:** A projector is an executable copy of your movie that doesn't need an additional player or plug-in to be viewed. It's essentially a movie contained within the stand-alone player. The projector is ideal for distribution of Flash applications on CD-ROMs or DVD-ROMs. Figure 20.1 shows a Flash movie played as a projector on Windows.

IN THIS CHAPTER

Creating a Flash projector

Distributing the Flash Player

Third-party utilities for Flash stand-alones

FIGURE 20.1

A movie playing as a projector

For the sake of simplicity, I refer to both projectors and movies played in the stand-alone Flash Player as *stand-alones* in this discussion. Because both the projector and stand-alone player have similar properties and limitations, you can apply everything discussed here to either one you choose to use.

Note

Due to the differences in operating systems, Flash stand-alones on Mac have the application menu listed in the system bar at the top of the Mac desktop area. On Windows, the application menu bar is part of the stand-alone window, as shown in Figure 20.1. ■

Creating a projector

When you have finished producing a Flash movie, it's fairly simple to turn it into a projector. You have two ways to create a stand-alone projector. Turning your Flash movies into Flash Player 10 stand-alone projectors typically adds 4MB (Windows projectors) or 13MB (Mac projectors) to the final file size.

Method 1: Using the Publish command

The simplest way to make a Flash projector file is to use the Publish feature of Flash CS5. In three short steps, you can have a stand-alone Flash movie presentation.

1. **Choose File ⇨ Publish Settings from the application menu.**
2. **When the Publish Settings dialog box opens, select the Formats tab and check the projector formats.** Publish both Windows and Mac projectors by using this method. Figure 20.2 shows the Publish Settings dialog box with the appropriate formats selected.

Be sure to select the Flash tab to control how your Flash movie is compiled (Flash Player version, ActionScript version, and so on).

Select the projector formats in the Publish Settings dialog box.

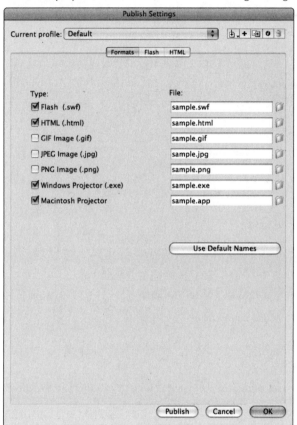

3. **Click the Publish button in the Publish Settings dialog box, and your Flash movie will be published in all the formats (for example, .swf, .gif, .jpg, and projector formats) specified with Publish Settings.**

Method 2: Using the stand-alone Flash Player

You can also create a Flash projector file by using the stand-alone Flash Player executable file that ships with Flash CS5. You can find the stand-alone Flash Player in the `Players/Release` folder of the Flash CS5 application folder.

Note

If you use this method to create a projector, you can make a projector for the current platform only. Thus, if you are using the Windows version of the stand-alone Flash Player, you can create a Windows projector only. ■

1. Export your Flash movie as an SWF file by using File ➪ Export Movie. Alternatively, you can use the Publish feature to create the SWF file.

2. Open the exported Flash movie file (.swf) in the stand-alone Flash Player.

3. Choose File ➪ Create Projector from the stand-alone player's application menu, as shown in Figure 20.3.

FIGURE 20.3

Choose File ➪ Create Projector from the stand-alone player menu.

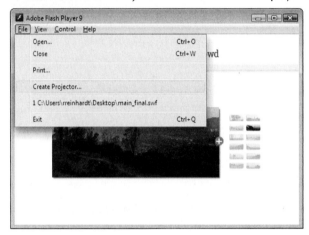

4. When the Save As dialog box opens, name the projector and save it.

Distribution and licensing

Distribution of stand-alone projectors or the Flash Player is free; you don't have to buy a license to distribute either the stand-alone Flash Player or projector. However, according to Adobe, you need to follow specific guidelines for distributed Flash Players and projectors. You can download the runtime license agreement and Adobe logos from the Adobe Web site. For more information, check out www.adobe.com/products/players/fpsh_distribution1.html.

Distribution on CD-ROM or DVD-ROM

The Flash platform has become increasingly popular for use on multimedia CD-ROMs or DVD-ROMs, especially as embedded SWF files in larger Adobe Director projectors. Stand-alones can be used as front ends for installations, splash screens for other programs, or even as complete applications. When you combine the good looks of a Flash interface with a few `fscommand` actions (see the next section for more information) and put them together on a CD-ROM (or DVD-ROM) that's programmed to start automatically on insertion, you have a first-class product.

Caution

As a general rule, don't try to send projector files (EXE files) as attachments to e-mail messages. Most current e-mail clients, such as Microsoft Outlook, do not allow you to open an e-mail containing an executable file, protecting you against computer virus infections. ■

Stand-Alone Limitations and Solutions

When you create a stand-alone, the task may not be as simple as taking your Flash document and exporting it as a projector. This section briefly discusses issues that may affect the performance of your projector.

When you distribute your Flash movies as stand-alones, you may think that you won't have to worry about streaming and download. As a consequence, stand-alones are often made considerably larger than a typical Flash movie — which can be a mistake! Very large movies (5MB or more) may not play well on slower computers with Pentium III (or PowerMac G4) or older processors. Remember that Flash movies require the computer processor to compute all those vector calculations, especially for rich animation. When you try to give a slower computer a large Flash movie to load, it may not be able to handle it.

Tip

One way to get around this limitation is to break your movies into several smaller movies. You can use the `loadMovie`/`unloadMovie` **actions to open and close other movies within the original movie. You should use these actions in your stand-alones. ■**

You should also test your movies on a variety of computers, especially if you plan to put a lot of development time and money into distributing them on CD-ROM. Some processors handle the movies better than others, and you often have to decide which processor you want to target as the lowest common denominator.

Using the Flash Player Plug-In for Web Browsers

Flash movies can be played only in Web browsers that have the Flash Player plug-in or ActiveX control installed. Macromedia has made huge strides in making the plug-in prepackaged with newer Web browsers and operating system installation programs, eliminating the need for users to manually download and install the plug-in themselves. Unfortunately, the Flash Player 9 version of the plug-in will likely only be included in future releases of Web browsers and operating systems. Remember that earlier versions of the plug-in can *try* to play Flash movies published for Flash Player 9; however, new features in Flash Player 9–based movies (such as ActionScript 3.0, full-screen movie sizes, and so on) will not be available.

Note

For up-to-date information on the Flash Player plug-in, see Adobe's download page at `www.adobe.com/ shockwave/download/alternates.` ∎

Supported operating systems

Since Flash 3, Adobe has greatly expanded its platform support for the Flash Player plug-in. At the time of this writing, you can download Flash Players for Windows 95/98/ME/NT/2000/XP/Vista/7 , for Power PC and Intel Macs, and for Linux *x*86. At conferences worldwide, Adobe has demonstrated that Flash graphics can be ported to a variety of GUIs (graphical user interfaces) and operating systems. We've also seen Flash graphics showing up in add-on applications for entertainment consoles such as the Sony PlayStation and set-top boxes from Motorola.

Supported browsers

The Flash Player plug-in works best with Mozilla-compatible and Internet Explorer browsers. Any browser compliant with Netscape Navigator 2.0's plug-in specification or Internet Explorer's ActiveX technology can support the Flash Player plug-in or ActiveX control, respectively. Note that Mac versions of Internet Explorer or Apple Safari use a Netscape plug-in emulator to use the Flash Player plug-in rather than an ActiveX control.

For AOL subscribers, any version of AOL's 3.0 through 9.0 browsers (except for the earliest 3.0 release that used a non-Microsoft Internet Explorer shell) supports Adobe plug-ins.

For a comprehensive list of supported browsers (and Flash compatibility), see the Adobe tech note at `www.adobe.com/support/flash/ts/documents/browser_support_matrix.htm`.

Plug-in and Flash movie distribution on the Web

Anyone can download the Flash Player plug-in for free from the Adobe Web site. You can direct visitors of your Web sites to Adobe's Flash Player download page, `www.adobe.com/go/getflash player`. In fact, according to Adobe's licensing agreement, if you're publishing Flash movies on your Web site, you need to display the "Get Shockwave Player" logo or "Get Flash Player" logo on your Web site. This logo should link to Adobe's download page, which I just listed. However, you can't distribute the plug-in installer yourself — you need to license the right to distribute any plug-in installer from Adobe. For more details on licensing, see `www.adobe.com/licensing/`.

The Flash Player on Mobile Devices

The development for the Flash Player is so demanding that Macromedia dedicates an entire department's worth of resources to the job. The Flash Player has been made available for Pocket PC devices using the Pocket PC 2002/2003 and Windows Mobile 5 and 6 operating systems from Microsoft. Computer hardware manufacturers such as Hewlett-Packard/Compaq and Casio currently manufacture a wide range of PDAs (personal digital assistants) that can use the Flash Player via the Pocket Internet Explorer Web browser or a stand-alone player. At the time of this writing, Flash Player 7 was available for most Pocket PCs and devices running Windows Mobile 5 and 6. As the computer processing power of Palm, Handspring, and Sony devices (that implement the Palm OS) increases, I see Flash Player support being extended to these devices.

Nokia and DoCoMo have released phones in Japan that can play full-color Flash animations as well! These phones use a version of the Flash Player called Flash Lite. With version 1.0/1.1 of this player, you can create Flash movies that use Flash 5 objects and Flash 4 ActionScript. For more information on Flash Lite, visit the following page on Adobe's site:

`www.adobe.com/products/flashlite/`

It's no surprise that the Flash Player is being adopted so widely by computer and device manufacturers. The SWF format allows rich media such as animation, sound, and video to be transmitted over incredibly slow (or congested) networks. Until high-speed wireless access becomes more available, we'll likely need to keep wireless connection speeds such as 19.2 Kbps (CDPD-based networks) or 25 to 60 Kbps (GPRS-based networks) in mind while developing Flash movies that a universal audience can access.

If you plan to deploy Flash content to Flash Lite, be sure to check out Adobe Device Central CS5, which is included with Adobe Flash CS5 Professional. This application enables you to create Flash content specifically sized and published for a wide variety of mobile devices.

You can find the official Adobe button graphics at:

`www.adobe.com/macromedia/style_guide/buttons/`

Plug-in installation

In Chapter 18 I discuss the Publish feature of Flash CS5 and the use of preformatted HTML templates to deliver your Flash movies to your Web site. The template and/or handwritten HTML that you use for your Flash-enabled Web pages determines the degree of difficulty your visitors will have upon loading a Flash movie.

Adobe has also officially named the auto-update experience of the Flash Player plug-in as Express Install. This feature refers to the nearly pain-free process of upgrading from Flash Player 6 or later to the latest version of the Flash Player. Flash Player 7 was released with an auto-update feature, enabling new versions of the plug-in to download without the hassle of installing an updated ActiveX control or downloading a plug-in installer application.

Web Resource

You can change the auto-update preferences of your Flash Player installation by visiting the following Adobe Web page:

`www.adobe.com/support/documentation/en/flashplayer/help/settings_manager05.html`

By default, the Flash Player checks for an updated version of the plug-in every 30 days. You can change the time interval to as little as 7 days. ■

Using the Settings in Flash Player 6 and Later

Flash Player 6 introduced the Settings option from the Flash Player's contextual menu, which can be accessed by right-clicking (or Control+clicking on Mac) a Flash movie. When you choose the Settings option, the Macromedia Flash Player Settings dialog box opens. This dialog box has four tabs, which are discussed in the following sections.

Privacy

This tab, shown in Figure 20.4, controls the access of the current Flash movie to your Webcam and microphone. Whenever a Flash movie tries to access your Webcam or microphone, the Flash Player opens this tab to ask you for permission. You can choose Allow, which gives the Flash movie access to your camera and microphone, or Deny, which stops the Flash movie from gaining access to these devices. You can also select the Remember check box so that the Flash Player remembers the choice you made, preventing the dialog box from opening during subsequent visits to the same Flash movie (or Web site hosting the Flash movie). If you click the Advanced button in the Privacy tab, a new Web browser opens and loads the help page for the Settings options on Macromedia's site.

Note

Flash movies can stream live audio and video to Flash Media Server applications by using the `Camera`, `Microphone`, **and** `NetStream` **objects. ■**

The Privacy option applies to any and all Flash movies hosted on the domain listed in the Privacy tab.

Web Resource

For the most up-to-date information on the Privacy tab, refer to the following page on Macromedia's site:

`www.adobe.com/support/flashplayer/help/privacy/`

You can also access the Global Settings manager on Adobe's site, which enables you to control the privacy settings for all sites you have visited. Go to the following URL:

`www.adobe.com/support/flashplayer/help/settings/global_privacy.html` ■

FIGURE 20.4

The Privacy tab

Local Storage

As shown in Figure 20.5, the Local Storage tab controls how much information can be stored on your computer from the Flash Player. Since Flash Player 6, Flash movies can be engineered to store data on the user's machine, with the use of local Shared Objects. The SharedObject class in ActionScript enables you to store customized information on a user's machine, just like cookies can store information from a Web application.

FIGURE 20.5

The Local Storage tab

By default, a Web site and Flash movies hosted on that site can allocate as much as 100K of data on a user's machine. If a Flash movie hosted from a Web site requests more than this amount, the Flash Player automatically opens this tab asking for the user's permission to store more data. You can click the Never Ask Again option to prevent the Flash Player from automatically opening this tab when a site requests to store more data than its allotted amount.

Web Resource

You can find the latest information about the Local Storage tab at:

www.macromedia.com/support/documentation/en/flashplayer/help/help02.html. ∎

Cross-Reference

To learn more about using the `SharedObject` class, read the Flash ActionScript Bible series (Wiley). ∎

Microphone

The Microphone tab, shown in Figure 20.6, controls the source of audio input to a Flash movie. Depending on your computer system, you may have several audio capture devices listed in this tab's menu. If you don't have an audio capture device on your system, then you may not see any options available in this panel. You can use this tab to control the sensitivity of the microphone (or capture device) by adjusting the slider position. The tab provides real-time audio monitoring with a bar graph. You can click the Reduce Echo check box to minimize the echo or feedback from a speaker that is located near your microphone.

FIGURE 20.6

The Microphone tab

Web Resource

For more information on Microphone settings, see www.adobe.com/support/flashplayer/help/microphone. ∎

Camera

The Camera tab, shown in Figures 20.7 and 20.8, controls the camera source used by the Flash Player. If your computer does not have a camera (or digital video capture card, which includes FireWire, or IEEE 1394, cards), then you may not see a camera source listed in this tab. If you have multiple video capture sources, you can use this tab to control which source is used for live streams going out of the Flash movie into a Flash Media Server application.

FIGURE 20.7

The default view of the Camera tab

You can click the camera icon in the Camera tab to see live video from your chosen capture source, as shown in Figure 20.8. If you do not see any picture in this area after you click the camera icon, you may have a problem with your capture driver, or the Flash Player may be incompatible with the driver.

FIGURE 20.8

An active preview of a camera's output in the Camera tab

Web Resource

For more information on the Camera tab and its settings, see the following page on Macromedia's site: www. adobe.com/support/flashplayer/help/camera. ■

Player Utilities

You can also reformat and modify stand-alones for both Windows and Mac. A few software companies create applications specifically designed to modify Flash movies and stand-alones. Here is a list of Web site URLs for those companies:

- www.flashjester.com
- www.multidmedia.com
- www.northcode.com
- www.screentime.com
- www.alienzone.com/screensaver_features.htm
- www.goldshell.com

Some of these companies offer more than just one utility for Flash movie development, such as the JTools of FlashJester. For updates to this list, check out this book's Web site, listed in the preface of this book.

Tip

You can find directories of Flash utilities at www.flashmagazine.com **and** graphicssoft.about.com/cs/flashtools. ∎

One of our favorite utilities is Versiown, created by Goldshell Digital Media. This handy utility allows you to modify the properties of a Flash (or Director) projector file, specifically EXE versions for Windows. With Versiown, you can:

- Add or modify the version information that shows up in the Properties dialog box, accessible by right-clicking the .exe file and choosing Properties.
- Add a custom icon for the .exe file of the projector. Together with an icon utility such as IconBuilder from Iconfactory (which is a filter plug-in for Adobe Photoshop), you can make custom .ico files to be used as icons for your Flash projectors.

You can download trial versions of Versiown at www.goldshell.com/versiown. A trial of IconBuilder is available at www.iconfactory.com/ib_home.asp.

Note

You can use the Get Info dialog box (Mac OS X) on Mac files to easily replace the icon image for Flash projector files on Mac. Open the .ico file made from IconBuilder in an image editor such as Adobe Photoshop, use Edit ⇨ Select All to select the entire image, copy it to the Clipboard (Edit ⇨ Copy), and paste it into the picture area of the Get Info dialog box. ∎

Summary

- Flash movies can be viewed in Web pages with the Flash Player plug-in or ActiveX control. You can also play Flash movie files (.swf) with the stand-alone Flash Player included with the Flash CS5 application, or you can publish a Mac or Windows projector that packages the stand-alone Flash Player and .swf file into one executable file.

- You can freely distribute a Flash movie projector or stand-alone Flash Player as long as you adhere to the guidelines outlined at Adobe's Web site.

- Flash movies can be distributed with other multimedia presentations such as Macromedia Director projectors. Your Flash movies can be distributed on a CD-ROM or DVD-ROM.

- You can enhance your Flash movies with third-party tools such as FlashJester's JTools for Flash.

Creating Adobe AIR Applications Using Flash CS5

A dobe AIR allows you to publish Flash applications as native desktop applications on Windows or Mac. This means you can use the skills you have learned in Flash to create applications that install and run just like any other native applications on your operating system. In this chapter, you will learn how to create AIR applications and distribute them through a variety of means.

Understanding Adobe AIR

Adobe Integrated Runtime, AIR, is a growing platform that allows developers to deploy Rich Internet Applications (RIAs) created using HTML, JavaScript, and/or ActionScript to the desktop. Applications currently seen through Web browsers can also be deployed as native applications for Windows or Mac, without having to modify any code. Using Adobe Dreamweaver, Flash Builder, and Flash Professional, applications created for the Web can be published as AIR applications after a few minor adjustments.

Learning security differences between standard Flash Player and AIR

AIR applications are desktop applications and require a security model different from what is used on the Web. People who install desktop applications give the apps a degree of trust that is not commonly given to applications deployed through a Web browser. For example, desktop applications are allowed to access, create, delete, and update files on the user's computer, whereas Web applications are not given that same permission.

As you develop AIR applications, keep in mind that some things that are common and acceptable in Web applications, like loading remote data, can create security risks in a desktop application.

For more information about security in AIR, see www.adobe.com/devnet/air/articles/ introduction_to_air_security.html.

Creating a simple AIR application

Creating and testing an AIR application is essentially the same as creating any other Flash application. In this section, you create a simple Web browser using AIR.

   1. In Flash, choose File ➪ New to create a new Adobe AIR 2 Flash file (Figure 21.1).

Creating an Adobe AIR 2 file

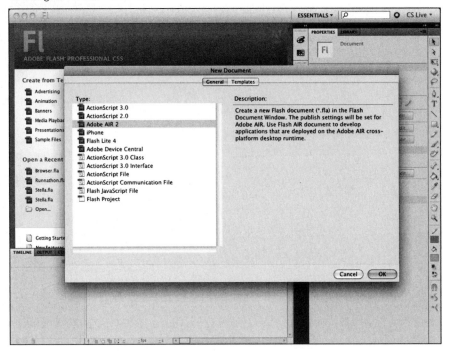

2. Save the file as Browser.fla.

3. In the Properties section of the Properties panel, click the Edit button to edit the stage size, and then change the stage size to 800 × 600 (Figure 21.2).

4. Open the Components panel, and drag a Text Input component onto the stage.

5. Drag a Button component onto the stage from the Components panel and close the Components panel (Figure 21.3).

6. **Place the Button component at the top right of the stage, and place the Text Input component at the top left of the stage.** You can use the Align panel to make sure they are aligned vertically.

FIGURE 21.2

Adjusting the Document Properties to change the size of the stage

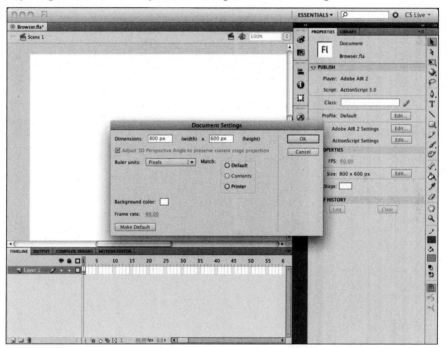

FIGURE 21.3

The Text Input and Button components on the stage

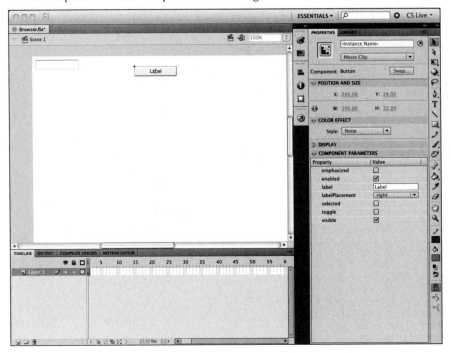

Select the Button component, and in the Component Parameters section of the Properties panel, edit the value of the label field to display Go instead of Label (Figure 21.4).

Editing the label of the button

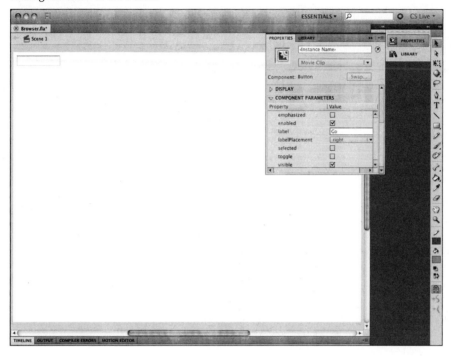

7. In the Properties panel, click in the Instance Name field and set the instance name of the button to go_btn (Figure 21.5).

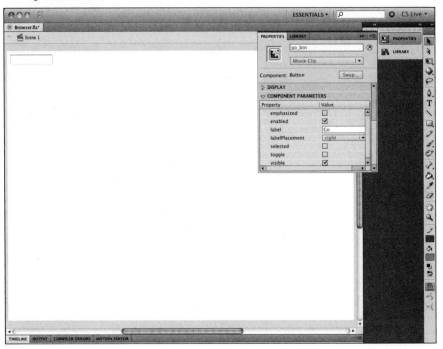

FIGURE 21.5

Adding an instance name to the button

8. Using the Free Transform tool, scale the Text Input component horizontally to fill the space between it and the Button (Figure 21.6).

9. With the Text Input component selected, click in the Instance Name field in the Properties panel and type `url_txt` for the instance name.

10. In the Timeline, create a new layer named Actions.

11. Select the first keyframe of the Actions layer and open the Actions panel by choosing Window > Actions from the Flash menu.

12. In the Actions panel, type the following code to create the ActionScript object that will load and display Web pages:

```
var loader:HTMLLoader = new HTMLLoader();
```

Note

If Flash automatically generated an extra line of code for you, you can delete it if you want. It is not essential for this exercise, but will not cause any errors either. ■

Scaling the Text Input component

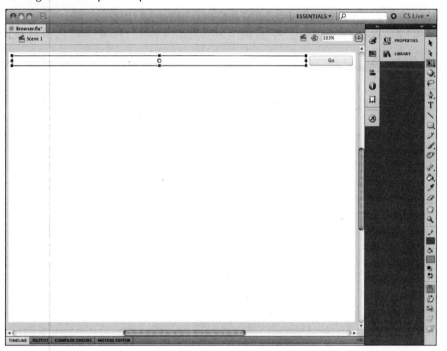

13. Below the line of code you just wrote, add the following code, which places the HTMLLoader on the stage:

    ```
    addChild(loader);
    ```

14. Next, set the vertical position of the HTMLLoader to display below the Text Input and Button components by setting its y property to 37 pixels from the top of the stage:

    ```
    loader.y = 37;
    ```

15. **Because the default visible area for an HTMLLoader object is 0 × 0 pixels, you need to define a width and height using ActionScript in order to see the loaded Web pages.** For the width, set the width property equal to the width of the stage:

    ```
    loader.width = stage.stageWidth;
    ```

16. **For the height property, set the value to go to the bottom of the stage.** To do this, subtract the amount the HTMLLoader is offset from the top of the stage (37 pixels, as defined in Step 15) from the total height of the stage using the following code:

    ```
    loader.height = stage.stageHeight - loader.y;
    ```

17. Make sure your code matches the following:

```
var loader:HTMLLoader = new HTMLLoader();
addChild(loader);
loader.y = 37;
loader.width = stage.stageWidth;
loader.height = stage.stageHeight - loader.y;
```

18. **Next, make sure your code is correct by testing the HTMLLoader to make sure it's working properly**. To do that, write the following code to make the HTMLLoader load the URL http://labs.adobe.com:

```
loader.load(new URLRequest("http://labs.adobe.com"));
```

19. **Test the movie using Control ⇨ Test Movie to preview your AIR application (Figure 21.7)**. After a few seconds, you should see the Adobe Labs Web site load into the HTMLLoader. If you don't see the Web site, or you see error messages, check your code to make sure each character is correct.

FIGURE 21.7

Viewing a Web site in the AIR application

20. **Now, I will make the HTMLLoader load the Web site when the Button component is clicked.** Above the last line of code you wrote, add the following code:

```
go_btn.addEventListener(MouseEvent.CLICK, showSite);
```

This line of code tells the Button component on the stage, which is referenced by its instance name go_btn, to respond to a mouse click. When the button is clicked, Flash will run a block of code called showSite, which I will define in the next step.

21. **Below the code you wrote in the previous step, add the following code:**

```
function showSite(event:MouseEvent):void
{
```

Note

This code definies a block of code called a function, which is contained in curly braces. The function is named showSite, and the code within the curly braces will run when the button on the stage is clicked (see Step 21 for more information). ■

22. **At the bottom of all your code, add a closed curly brace (}).** Your code should now look like this:

```
var loader:HTMLLoader = new HTMLLoader();
addChild(loader);
loader.y = 37;
loader.width = stage.stageWidth;
loader.height = stage.stageHeight - loader.y;
go_btn.addEventListener(MouseEvent.CLICK, showSite);
function showSite(event:MouseEvent):void
{
loader.load(new URLRequest("http://labs.adobe.com"));
}
```

23. **Test the movie again (Control ➪ Test Movie) to preview the application.** The Web site should now load only after you click the button. Again, you may have to wait a few seconds for the site to load before it displays on your screen.

24. **Complete the simple Web browser application by modifying the second to last line of code to look like this (note there are no longer quotes):**

```
loader.load(new URLRequest(url_txt.text));
```

25. **Test the movie once more to preview your Web browser (Figure 21.8).** In the text field, type in a URL (make sure to include the beginning http://) and then click the button to see the browser load the Web site.

26. **Save and close the file.**

FIGURE 21.8

Viewing the finished application

Note

Though this browser is limited in features, it is possible to add additional functionality, such as bookmarking, history, and back and forward buttons, using code provided by the AIR API. For more information, see the HTMLLoader class in Flash Help. ∎

Understanding additional AIR APIs

In the last exercise, you used an ActionScript class called HTMLLoader to load Web pages into your Web browser app. The HTMLLoader class is not available in the standard Web Flash Player, but is only available when publishing to AIR. AIR has several other classes, or Application Programming Interfaces (APIs) that are not available when working with the standard Flash Player. For the entire list, see Adobe's ActionScript 3.0 Language and Components Reference at www.adobe.com/livedocs/flash/9.0/ActionScriptLangRefV3/. Table 21.1 is a list of some the most commonly used AIR APIs:

TABLE 21.1

Commonly Used AIR APIs

Class	Package	Description
Clipboard	flash.desktop	Can be used to copy and paste data to and from the system's clipboard
DockIcon	flash.desktop	Allows control over changing the appearance of Mac OSX dock icons
File	flash.filesystem	Used to access files in the user's computer for reading and writing
HTMLLoader	flash.html	Used to render HTML data, including text, images, and Flash content
NativeApplication	flash.desktop	Allows access to application-wide properties and methods
NativeMenu	flash.display	Allows definition of the application's native operating system menus
NativeWindow	flash.display	Gives access to native operating system windows
SQLConnection	flash.data	Used to create and access local SQL databases
StorageVolume	flash.filesystem	Allows access to external storage devices, including USB hard drives (AIR 2.0 and above only)
SystemTrayIcon	flash.desktop	Can control appearance of the application's Windows system tray icon
Updater	flash.desktop	Used to update the application to a newer version

Publishing and Sharing AIR Applications

Once you have created your AIR application, there are only a couple more steps to get your app out into the world. You have to publish your application, and then you can distribute it. In this section, you learn how to publish AIR applications and distribute them through several different means.

Preparing to publish an AIR app

Before you can distribute your AIR applications, you will need to publish them to get the necessary distributable files. In Flash, you can define settings for publishing your AIR files and publish them through the Application & Installer Settings window (File ⇨ Adobe AIR 2 Settings). In that menu, there are four tabs: General, Signature, Advanced, and Icons.

General settings

The General settings tab allows you to control general settings for your application. The top half holds your app's output name, full name, Application ID, version number, description, and copyright information. It also allows you to choose whether to output a special installer for easier installation on a Mac (a DMG file). Other than the App ID field, these fields are essentially self-explanatory. The App ID field should be a unique string of text, as shown in the example com. yourdomain.appname. Because domain names must be unique, following this reversed domain structure and placing your application's name at the end ensures that your application's identifier is unique.

The bottom half of the General settings tab allows you to set the window style, device profiles, and files included in your application. Window style can be set to the default operating system style (System Chrome) or the AIR app can use your artwork in Flash as the background of your application (Custom Chrome). If you choose the transparent Custom Chrome option, areas where there is no artwork in Flash will be transparent (surprise!), revealing the operating system's desktop or open windows. The Profiles section allows you to define what types of devices are supported for this AIR application. Unless you have explicit reasons for not allowing your app on a certain platform, you are safe leaving all of these boxes checked. Included files are for any files that will be loaded into your SWF file at runtime, so if you are using the Loader class to load images that are stored in the same folder as your FLA file, you should include all necessary files and folders here. Bitmaps stored in the Library panel of your Flash file do not need to be included here, since they are automatically embedded into your output file.

Signature settings

To publish an AIR application, you need to give the app a digital signature. This gives some degree of authenticity to your app. You can click the New button to create one in Flash, along with an accompanying password, or you can purchase a certificate from a recognized certificate authority (CA).

Note

The advantage to purchasing a certificate is that when someone opens your AIR application they will see your name or your business' name, and you will have a greater degree of trust placed in your app because the certificate can be traced back to you, the developer. If your application is not signed by a trusted certificate authority, but created by you in Flash, the person opening the app will see that the signer of the certificate is unknown or unverified and will have less trust in your app. ■

Putting a timestamp on your file gives you power to distribute your application, even after your certificate is expired, providing the application was created and time stamped prior to the expiration of the certificate. Without a timestamp, the expired certificate will disallow installation of your app if a person tries to install your app after the certificate's expiration date.

Alternatively, you can create an AIR Intermediate file that can be signed later, but the file must still be signed in the future before distribution.

Advanced settings

The Advanced settings tab allows you to control what file types are associated with your app, the size and positioning of your app, and its resizing settings. You can also choose where the app will install by default and whether you want to use a custom user interface for updating it.

Icons

The Icons tab lets you define the various sized icons of your application. These icons should be images in PNG format and can have transparent backgrounds. Each icon must be the appropriate pixel dimensions.

Publishing an AIR application

Here is an example of publishing your AIR app through Flash Professional:

1. **Open the saved version of Browser.fla you created in the last exercise.**

2. **Choose File ⇨ Adobe AIR 2 Settings to launch the Application & Installer Settings window (Figure 21.9).**

FIGURE 21.9

The Application and Installer Settings window

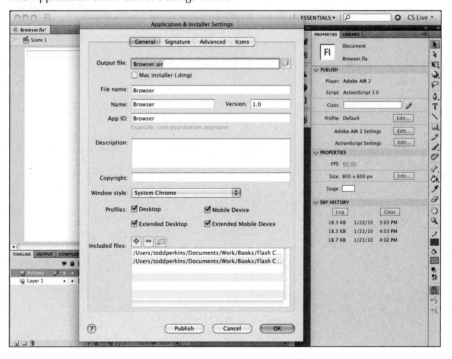

3. **In the General tab, set the App ID to com.wiley.simplebrowser.**

4. **Add a simple description of your application.**

5. **In the Signature tab, click the New button to create a new signature file.**

6. **Fill in the necessary fields to create the certificate, and save the file.**

7. **Click OK to create the certificate and return to the Signature tab.**

8. **Enter the password you created for your certificate.** You may want to check Remember password for this session, so you don't have to enter your password again if you close this window before publishing your file.

9. **In the Icons tab (Figure 21.10), select the icon 16x16 option and click the folder icon to browse for the file icon16x16.png in the Chapter 21 folder.**

10. **Repeat Step 9 for the remaining icons.**

11. Click Publish to create the AIR file.

Setting icons for the application

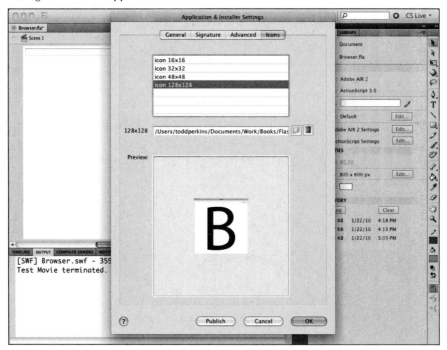

Distributing an AIR Application

After you have published an AIR app, you have your application ready to distribute, bundled in a single file. AIR applications can be distributed through several different means. Because AIR files are not directly connected to any one storefront, the files can be distributed in the same way as any other files may be distributed. They can be transferred over the Web through FTP software, standard Web file downloads, or on plug-and-play hard drives or discs. Adobe has also recently launched a program called Shibuya (`http://labs.adobe.com/technologies/shibuya/`), currently in beta, which allows developers to monetize AIR applications. This program acts as a storefront, handling the money collection for you, and even offers your applications in a "try before you buy" system.

Summary

- AIR allows you to leverage your Flash and ActionScript 3.0 knowledge to create fully functioning desktop applications, so you don't have to learn any other programming languages or even create entirely new apps to reach a whole new audience.

- AIR applications are as easy to create and distribute as any other Flash applications.

- With Shibuya, you even have a platform to monetize your AIR apps.

Using Flash to Create iPhone Applications

P erhaps the most exciting addition to Flash CS5 Professional is the ability to create iPhone applications that can be used on your iPhone. Given the popularity of both iPhone and Flash, the marriage of the two technologies is exciting, because you can now leverage the graphical, animation, and interactivity tools you're already familiar with in Flash to create native iPhone applications without having to learn the complex code normally required to do so.

Throughout this chapter, I explore using Flash to develop iPhone applications, including an explanation of how the technology works, as well as how to get Flash applications on your iPhone for testing.

Caution

Recent statements from Apple appear to indicate that Apple will reject apps submitted to the app store that were developed with Flash. This news was received sadly by the Adobe community. Adobe will still be including the Export to iPhone feature in Flash Professional CS5, so I am going to discuss its use. But please be aware that apps built with this feature may not make it onto the app store under Apple's new policy. ■

Note

This chapter discusses many details of programming in ActionScript 3.0. While you do not need to know ActionScript to create the iPhone application I will build in this chapter, some of the content discussed in this chapter may be more useful to you if you have a working knowledge of the ActionScript 3.0 language. If you are unfamiliar with ActionScript 3 and would like a more comprehensive understanding than what is shown in this book, see *ActionScript 3.0 Bible* **(Wiley, 2008).** ■

Understanding Flash on the iPhone

As you may know, Apple has never allowed a Flash Player on the iPhone, but today, I can use Flash to create iPhone applications. In this section, I will discuss how that is possible, and some of the differences between standard Flash apps and those created for deployment on the iPhone.

Learning how it works

You need to understand some important aspects of how Flash works on the iPhone. First of all, the iPhone does not have a Flash Player like what you would find on a computer or other mobile devices. Restrictions from Apple prohibit the use of code that is interpreted while an application is running, so processing ActionScript code in the same way the Flash Player does on a computer, for example, is not possible.

On a computer with the Flash Player, ActionScript code is processed by using a browser plug-in and a virtual machine. This allows for code to be processed "just in time," which means the code is not precomplied as code is in other languages, like Objective-C, which is the native language of the iPhone.

iPhone applications created using Flash Professional CS5 are compiled by Flash into native iPhone applications. Therefore, they are not Flash applications at all — they are iPhone applications, created by Flash. The way this is done involves Flash translating ActionScript 3 code into languages compatible with iPhone, and compiling the code completely to output an application that an iPhone can interpret.

Differences when working with Flash for iPhone development

Flash iPhone applications can be created by using ActionScript 3 and are essentially identical to regular Flash applications, with the exception of size restrictions and some different code that can or cannot be used. For example, the following ActionScript APIs (Application Programming Interfaces) do not work on iPhone:

Accessibility

DockIcon

DRMManager

EncryptedLocalStore

HTMLLoader

LocalConnection

NativeApplication.menu

NativeApplication.isSetAsDefaultApplication()

NativeApplication.startAtLogin

NativeMenu

NativeProcess

NativeWindow

NativeWindow.notifyUser()

PDF support

PrintJob

Shader

ShaderFilter

StorageVolumeInfo

XMLSignatureValidator

In addition to these APIs, note that ActionScript code cannot be processed "just in time" as in the Flash Player on a computer. Therefore, if you load an external SWF file into your app, ActionScript code will be ignored.

Along with code that cannot be used in Flash-created iPhone applications, the following APIs are specific to Flash iPhone applications:

MediaLibrary

DisplayObject.cacheAsSurface

Accelerometer

AccelerometerEvent

Geolocation

GeolocationEvent

GestureEvent

GesturePhase

MultiTouch

MultitouchInputMode

TouchEvent

TransformGestureEvent

Stage.orientation

StageOrientationEvent

Preparing to Develop iPhone Apps

Believe it or not, the easy part of creating Flash iPhone applications is, well, creating Flash iPhone applications. Because Flash iPhone apps are essentially identical to regular Flash apps, all you need to learn to create Flash iPhone apps is the ActionScript code that is unique to the iPhone. The more difficult portion of developing Flash iPhone apps is getting your apps on a device. Once your device is ready to run your iPhone applications, you will be able to create Flash iPhone apps and test them on your own device. Here are the things you need to do to get your Flash iPhone applications onto your iPhone. In the following sections, I look at each of these necessary steps in detail.

- Join the iPhone Developer Program (http://developer.apple.com/iphone/program/)
- Obtain your device's ID
- Request a development certificate from Apple
- Download your development certificate
- Create a provisioning profile for your device
- Connect your development certificate to your provisioning profile
- Create an application identifier
- Create a Flash iPhone app in Flash
- Publish an IPA file from Flash
- Open the IPA file in iTunes
- Put your Flash iPhone app on your iPhone through iTunes

Note

It costs $99 to join Apple's Developer Program. Joining the program is the only way to get your apps onto an iPhone. Also, it may take time to enroll in the program. Usually, it takes less than a week, but I have heard stories of Apple taking up to three months to accept enrollment. If you apply for the Developer Program and do not hear a response for a few days, try e-mailing Apple. Giving them a nudge could speed up the process and help you get your apps on your iPhone sooner. ■

Joining the Developer Program

The first step in getting ready for testing and deployment of your Flash iPhone apps is joining Apple's Developer program. For information about the program, and to sign up, go here- `http://developer.apple.com/iphone/program/`. There are three different types of iPhone developers: Individuals, Businesses, and Enterprises. Individuals are single-person development teams, and as such cannot have application testers. With an individual account, you will make, test, and deploy apps to the App Store- just not apps created with Flash. Businesses allow for a development team, meaning a business can have multiple people testing the app in different locations while the app is in development. A Business account requires a business license, and it generally takes longer for Apple to respond than when you set up an Individual account. Enterprise accounts allow you to distribute apps within a business, instead of through the App Store.

If you're wondering whether you should get a Business or Individual account, I recommend going with Individual to start out with, because you can always upgrade to a business account for free later on. That way, you can test applications on your iPhone while you are waiting on a response to your business account application.

Obtaining your device's ID

In order to move forward in getting your Flash applications on your iPhone, you will need your device's ID. There are a few different ways to obtain your iPhone's ID number, but perhaps the easiest way is to plug your iPhone into your computer and access the ID through iTunes. Here are the steps:

1. Make sure iTunes is open and your device is connected.

2. Select your iPhone from the Devices section on the left side of the iTunes window.

3. Click on Serial Number in the top section of the main iTunes window.

4. Your ID number is then revealed where the Serial Number appeared before.

Requesting a development certificate

The next step is to obtain a development certificate from Apple. To get the certificate, you will need to create a certificate request. The process of requesting a development certificate varies significantly depending on your operating system. In this section, you will learn how to request a development certificate on a Mac and a PC.

Requesting a development certificate on a Mac

On a Mac, this process is explained in detail in the iPhone Developer Portal on Apple's Web site (`http://developer.apple.com/iphone`). Through Apple's Developer Portal, you can watch videos and read detailed instructions about obtaining your developer certificate.

Requesting a development certificate on Windows

If you're on a PC, the process is a little more complicated than it is on a Mac. You will have to create the certificate request through your computer's command line and send the request through Apple's Developer Program portal. Here are the steps to create the certificate request:

Note

These steps use the Windows command line utility, which can be found by going to the Start menu and choosing Run. Type cmd in the Run text field, and click the button to run the application. ■

Caution

Using the Windows command line can do serious damage to your computer if you type the wrong commands, because the command line has access to nearly all of the data on your computer. When using the command line, make sure you follow each of these steps perfectly, and you should have no risk of harming data on your machine. ■

1. Install OpenSSL on your Windows computer. (Go to `http://www.openssl.org/related/binaries.html`.)

2. Open a Windows command session, and CD to the OpenSSL bin directory (the default directory is c:\OpenSSL\bin\).

   cd c:\OpenSSL\bin

3. Create the private key by entering the following in the command line. Save this private key file. You will use it later.

   openssl genrsa -out mykey.key 2048

Caution

When using OpenSSL, do not ignore error messages. If OpenSSL generates an error message, it may still output files. However, those files may not be useable. If you see errors, check your syntax and run the command again. ■

4. Create the CSR file by entering the following in the command line. Replace the e-mail address, CN (certificate name), and C (country) values with your own.

   ```
   openssl req -new -key mykey.key -out CertificateSigningRequest.
       certSigningRequest -subj
   "/emailAddress=yourAddress@example.com, CN=John Doe, C=US"
   ```

5. Upload the CSR file to Apple at the iPhone developer center site.

Downloading your development certificate

After you request a certificate from Apple, there may be a waiting period before you can download your certificate. To find out if your certificate is ready, check your Apple Developer account at `http://developer.apple.com/iphone` to see if your request was approved. Once your certificate is ready, you can download it from the iPhone Developer Portal.

Creating a provisioning profile for your device

A provisioning profile allows you to test applications you created. You can create a provisioning profile through the iPhone Developer Portal and open the profile in iTunes to get the profile onto your iPhone.

Creating a .p12 version of your certificate

The file format that you get from Apple as your development certificate, .cer, is not an acceptable certificate file format in Flash. You will need to convert this certificate to a .p12 file in order for it to work properly. This is another part of the process that differs on Mac and Windows.

Creating a .p12 file on a Mac

On a Mac, you need to open up Keychain Access (\Applications\Utilities\Keychain Access) and locate the private key for your certificate. Right-click the private key and choose Export to export the file as a .p12 file. When you do this, you will be prompted to enter a password to protect the file, which you will need to remember when you go to publish your iPhone application from Flash.

Creating a .p12 file on Windows

You will need to use the Windows command line to generate the .p12 certificate file. Before you begin these steps, make sure you have downloaded your developer certificate from Apple and that it is in the OpenSSL bin directory.

1. **Convert the developer certificate file you receive from Apple into a PEM certificate file. Run the following command line statement from the OpenSSL bin directory:**

    ```
    openssl x509 -in developer_identity.cer -inform DER -out
        developer_identity.pem -outform PEM
    ```

2. **You can now generate a valid P12 file, based on the key and the PEM version of the iPhone developer certificate:**

    ```
    openssl pkcs12 -export -inkey mykey.key -in developer_identity.pem
        -out iphone_dev.p12
    ```

Creating an application identifier

Each application you create needs to have an App ID. You can create identifiers for your applications in the App ID section of the iPhone Developer Portal. When you create applications for release in the App Store, each application should have a unique identifier. If you are creating applications for testing, as you're doing in this chapter, it is acceptable to use the same identifier for multiple testing applications. As a generic identifier for testing, you can simply use an asterisk (*).

After you've created an App ID, you can associate it with a provisioning profile, and associate your provisioning profile with your device through the Developer Portal. When you view your App IDs through the Developer Portal, you will see the App ID listed as a string of characters followed by a dot (example: B123455.com.yourwebsite.yourappid). The information after the first dot is what Flash is referring to when it asks for your App ID. If you use an asterisk to create a generic ID, you will see something like B123455.*. In that case, you can use any text you'd like in Flash for the App ID, since the asterisk represents a wildcard character, which means any string of text characters is acceptable.

Publishing a IPA file from Flash

The next step is to create the iPhone application file, or IPA file, through Flash's Publish Settings. In Flash, you can open the iPhone Publish Settings window through File ⇨ iPhone Settings. To publish your IPA file, you will need your App ID, your .p12 file and its password, and your provisioning profile. All of this information is entered through the General tab of the iPhone Settings window in the IPA file section. The rest of the information entered in this window allows you to provide icons for your app, as well as some other information about your application, such as a description. This information is useful, but for this example it is not necessary. Click the Publish button to create the IPA file. It may take a few minutes, but if you give Flash some time you'll have a nice IPA file before long.

Using a default loading image

After a user taps your app's icon to launch it from their iPhone or other compatible device, the app will begin to load. Typically, this process takes a few seconds. While your app is loading, you can display a loading screen that shows your app's name, logo, or any other information you would like to display. To set a default loading image for your app, you need to create a file called Default. png that is 320 pixels wide and 480 pixels high, regardless of whether your app is portrait or landscape. If your app is set for landscape orientation, you can create an image that's 480 pixels wide and 320 pixels high, and then rotate the image 90 degrees clockwise so it will appear at the correct orientation. The Default.png file must be named Default.png (make sure to use a capital "D"), be in the same directory as your FLA file, and you must tell Flash to include that file in the iPhone application settings window.

Getting the IPA file on your iPhone

Once you've created the IPA file, you can open the file in iTunes and it will load in as an application. From there, you can plug your iPhone into your computer and put the app on your iPhone just like any other application.

Building a Flash iPhone Application

Earlier in this chapter, I mentioned that a Flash iPhone application was essentially the same as a regular Flash application. This makes developing iPhone applications in Flash fairly straightforward. In this section, I will walk through the process of creating a Flash iPhone application. The application shows an animation of a dog that barks when you tap on it. This section demonstrates how to convert a mouse click in Flash to a tap on the iPhone. Follow these steps:

1. **Open Stella.fla from the stella_start folder. Notice that the file contains a premade animation.** You can create an iPhone FLA file from scratch by choosing File ➪ New ➪ iPhone from the window menu in Flash (see Figure 22.1).

FIGURE 22.1

The Stella.fla file

2. **Browse through the file to understand its structure**. Notice that the instance of to Movie Clip Stella on the Main Timeline has an instance name of dog. Inside the Stella Movie Clip, notice that the instance of BarkAnim on the barkAnim layer has an instance name of barkAnim. In the barkAnim Movie Clip, notice that there is an animation, and a stop() action in the actions layer on frame 1.

3. **On the Main Timeline, select the instance of Stella and open the Code Snippets panel by choosing Window ➪ Code Snippets from the menu.**

4. **In the Audio/Video section of the Code Snippets panel, double-click Click to Play/ Stop Sound**. Code is then added to a new layer called Actions, and the code can be viewed through the Actions Panel (see Figure 22.2).

5. **In the generated code, delete lines 24 through 28**. This code does not apply to the application you are creating.

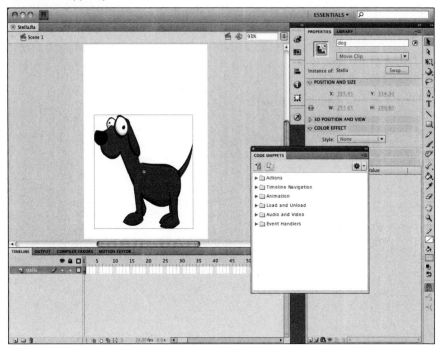

FIGURE 22.2

The Code Snippets panel

6. **On line 21, change the text in quotes to Bark.mp3**. This code now loads the barking sound when the dog is clicked.

7. **Test the movie (Control ➪ Test Movie) and click on the dog to hear it bark**. If you do not hear the dog barking, look back over the previous steps to make sure you did everything correctly.

8. **Below line 21, create a new line and add the following code**: dog.barkAnim.play();

9. **Test the movie again, and click on the dog to watch the barking animation play as you hear the barking sound**.

10. **Above all the code already written in the Actions Panel, create a new line and add the following code**: import flash.events.*; (see Figure 22.3). Also, see Listing 22.1.

11. **Choose File ➪ iPhone Settings to launch the iPhone Settings window and go to the General tab**. The General tab contains areas for you to define name, version, orientation, and rendering method for your application.

FIGURE 22.3

Viewing the application in the Flash Player

12. **In the General tab, choose GPU for the Rendering option.** This will put the graphics processing for your app on the video card, enhancing performance.

13. **Above the Included Files section in the General tab, click the + icon to add a file to include, and choose the file Bark.mp3 in the stella_start folder.**

14. **Repeat Step 13 to add the Default.png image.** This image will display as your app is loading, and it must be set to be included in your published app in order to appear on a device.

15. **In the Certificate section of the Deployment tab, click the folder icon to browse for your .p12 certificate file.**

16. **In the password field, enter the password for your .p12 certificate.** You can check Remember password for this session if you want Flash to save your password until you close the FLA file you are working with.

17. **In the App ID field, enter the identifier for your app.** This identifier can be created and accessed through the iPhone Developer Program Portal on Apple's Web site. Once logged in, you can find your Application Identifiers in the App IDs page under the Description heading. Make sure you only use the string of characters after the first period, or any text if you used the wildcard asterisk when creating your App ID.

18. **In the iPhone deployment type section, make sure Quick publishing for device testing is selected.**

19. **Select the Icons tab in the iPhone Settings window.**

20. **Select icon 29x29, and click the folder icon to browse for the file 29x29.png.** These icon files should be PNG files and can be created in Flash using the File ⇨ Export ⇨ Export Image menu command, or by using any other application that can create PNG files, such as Adobe Photoshop (see Figure 22.4).

LISTING 22.1

```
import flash.events.*;

/* Click to Play/Stop Sound
Clicking on the symbol instance plays the specified sound.
Clicking on the symbol instance a second time stops the sound.

Instructions:
1. Replace "http://www.helpexamples.com/flash/sound/song1.mp3" below with
   the desired URL address of your sound file. Keep the quotation marks
   ("").
*/

dog.addEventListener(MouseEvent.CLICK, fl_ClickToPlayStopSound_2);

var fl_SC_2:SoundChannel;

//This variable keeps track of whether you want to play or stop the sound
var fl_ToPlay_2:Boolean = true;

function fl_ClickToPlayStopSound_2(evt:MouseEvent):void
{
    if(fl_ToPlay_2)
{
    var s:Sound = new Sound(new URLRequest("Bark.mp3"));
    dog.barkAnim.play();
    fl_SC_2 = s.play();
}

}
```

FIGURE 22.4

Setting the application's icons

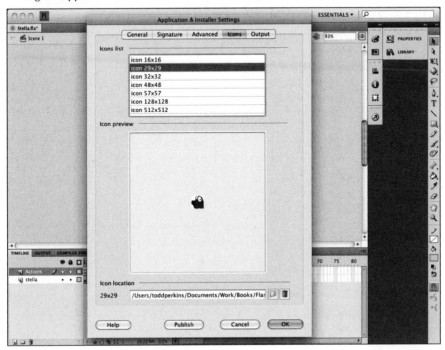

21. Repeat the previous step for the 57x57 and 512x512 icons.

22. **Click Publish to create your Flash iPhone application.** This process can take a few minutes.

23. **Use iTunes to open the IPA file created by Flash.** This step adds the application you created to your other applications managed through iTunes.

24. **Connect your iPhone or iPod touch to your computer and click the Sync button to add the application you created to your device.**

25. **Open the application on your device.** Notice the Default.png file shows the static image of the dog until the app is loaded. You can tell the app is loaded when the dog's tail starts wagging.

Understanding performance in Flash iPhone applications

Performance in Flash iPhone applications is one of the most important things to consider when you create iPhone apps in Flash. Consider the following — the processing power on an iPhone is significantly less than that of a PC or a Mac. You also have less RAM to work with, as well as a less powerful video card. In addition to those things, the capabilities of the devices vary greatly (i.e. the first-generation iPhone has about half the RAM of the third generation iPhone). Needless to say, your applications should ideally perform well on the lowest common denominator, which would be the first-generation iPhone. Here are some tips to remember when creating your apps.

Test on as many devices as possible

Ideally, your Flash iPhone apps will have the same performance on each compatible device. To ensure this, test the app on as many devices as you can. This can make a significant difference in the success of your apps. Many of the people who download apps from the App Store are using a first-generation iPhone and will not give your app positive reviews if it does not work on their iPhone, regardless of whether you mention on your app's page that it is optimized for a particular device. The best way around this is to make sure it works on every device through rigorous testing.

Using methods to enhance performance

There are a few APIs that Flash has for you to optimize your iPhone applications. Mainly, it is wise to cache display objects that move. This can put the processing load on the iPhone's GPU instead of its CPU or RAM, which can greatly enhance performance. To set the app to use GPU rendering, make sure that option is selected in the Rendering section of the General tab in the iPhone Settings window.

Using the right types of image assets can enhance performance in Flash iPhone apps as well. Avoid using filters and blend modes as much as you can, as this is highly taxing on the iPhone's resources. Instead, try to use PNG images with transparency if you want to have filter effects, like drop shadows or bevels. It is also a good idea to use bitmap images instead of using gradients on vector shapes.

When using assets that are animated, it is best to cache them to save resources. The best way to do this for iPhone development is to use the `DisplayObject.cacheAsBitmapMatrix()` method, which is similar to the `DisplayObject.cacheAsBitmap()` method, with the exception that the `DisplayObject.cacheAsBitmapMatrix ()` method also caches transformations, including scaling and rotation.

The way that events are handled in Flash is also taxing on the iPhone's resources, so listening for events at the object level is better than listening for events at the parent level. This is because as events "bubble" up, resources are being consumed. It is best to listen for the event at the child object level, and then stop bubbling via the `Event.stopPropagation()` method.

Summary

- Flash CS5 can be used to publish iPhone applications. These apps can be developed just like any other Flash applications but are packaged by Flash to use iPhone-native code rather than ActionScript.

- Applications created by Flash are mostly for testing on your own iPhone, and will likely be rejected if submitted to the App Store.

- In order to publish an iPhone app created by Flash, you must register as an iPhone developer with Apple. This can be done at `http://developer.apple.com/iphone`.

- On a Mac, all the necessary iPhone development files can be obtained by following the instructions in Apple's iPhone Developer Program Portal.

- On Windows, you will need to use the command line utility to generate a certificate signing request and a .p12 file.

- Flash-created iPhone apps can be optimized using GPU rendering and several ActionScript methods.

- More information about iPhone development in Flash can be found at `http://www.adobe.com/iphone`.

Part VII

Appendixes

If you're wondering what the CD-ROM included with this book is for and how to make the most of it, refer to Appendix A. To learn more about the Flash talent that provided expert tutorials for this edition of the book, browse their bios and visit their URLs listed in Appendix B. The experts who have provided e-mail addresses would be glad to hear from you, but we cannot guarantee that they will reply right away — they are all kind people but they are busy, too.

Audio and video are both complex topics to which many other books are dedicated. We have done our best to include key information in Appendix C and Appendix D. This material will get you off on the right foot when you start creating and editing audio and video to enhance your Flash projects. Hopefully, this will help you to avoid common pitfalls and keep your media assets looking and sounding as good as your Flash content.

Using the CD-ROM

This appendix provides information on the contents of the CD-ROM that accompanies this book and the system requirements for using the sample files and trial applications that enhance the text content of the book.

Note

For the latest version of this appendix, including any late-breaking updates, refer to the ReadMe file located in the root directory of the CD-ROM. ■

Caution

If your CD-ROM is missing from the book when you purchase it, return it to the store where you bought it and get a copy of the book that has a CD-ROM included. If you lose or damage your CD or it gets stolen, your best option is to contact the publisher (Wiley) and tell them your story — they may be able to help you, but there are no guarantees that you'll get a free replacement. The phone and e-mail contact info for Wiley Publishing is provided at the end of this appendix. ■

Here is what you will find on the CD-ROM:

- Source .swf and .fla files for step-by-step exercises
- Reusable ActionScript
- A listing of relevant applications and software trials

Before loading the CD-ROM, make sure that your computer meets the minimum system requirements listed in this section. If your computer doesn't match up to most of these requirements, you may have a problem using the contents of the CD-ROM.

For Windows 2000/XP/Vista/Windows 7:

- PC with a Pentium 4 or faster processor, including Intel Centrino, Intel Xeon, or Intel Core Duo (or compatible) processor
- Windows XP with Service Pack 3 or Windows Vista with Service Pack 1 (certified for 32-bit editions) or Windows 7
- At least 1GB of total RAM installed on your computer (note that you need additional RAM to open other programs with Flash)
- 2.5GB available hard-disk space (additional required during CS5 installation)
- 16-bit color monitor capable of 1024 × 768 display recommended
- A CD-ROM drive (DVD-ROM drive required for Creative Suite installer discs)

For Macs:

- PowerPC G5 or later running OS X 10.4.9 and later, running at 1 GHz or faster
- 1GB of RAM
- 2.5GB available hard-disk space required during installation
- 1,024 × 768 monitor resolution
- A CD-ROM drive (DVD-ROM drive required for Creative Suite installer discs)

CS5 applications also require an Internet or phone connection for product activation.

Note
Some features of Flash CS5 require the latest version of QuickTime. During the installation of QuickTime, select the "Recommended" installation type to install the components Flash requires. To download a trial or purchase the latest version of QuickTime, go to www.apple.com/quicktime. ■

Reviewing Example .swf and .fla Files

Many of the examples I discuss in the text and in step-by-step tutorials are included in the relevant chapter folder on the CD-ROM. Opening the Flash movie (.swf) is the quickest way to see how the finished example is supposed to look. The fonts should display correctly, and as long as you haven't moved the file to a new location, any loaded assets should also work.

When you open a Flash document (.fla), you may get a warning about missing fonts. This warning simply means that you do not have the same fonts installed on your machine as the original author of the file. Select a default font and you will be able to review and edit the Flash document on your machine. However, without the proper fonts installed, the layout may not appear as it was originally designed.

Installing and Using Plug-Ins and Applications

To download the Mac and Windows trial versions of Flash CS5, go to www.adobe.com/downloads. Additional plug-ins and trial versions of applications discussed in this book can also be found online, in most cases. The links.html file included on the CD-ROM is a good reference for finding these Web resources.

Source Files and Applications

The CD-ROM included with this book aids you with many examples and tutorials by providing relevant files, including the following:

- Custom components for image loading and effects, scripted by Robert Reinhardt and integrated with project examples in Chapter 17
- Just about every .fla and .swf file that is discussed in the book, including many shown in examples from guest experts

Web Resource
Other applications or utilities discussed in the book can be found online. For a list of relevant Web links, refer to the links.html **document included in the main directory of the CD-ROM.** ∎

Shareware programs are fully functional, trial versions of copyrighted programs. If you like particular programs, register with their authors for a nominal fee and receive licenses, enhanced versions, and technical support. *Freeware programs* are copyrighted games, applications, and utilities that are free for personal use. Unlike shareware, these programs do not require a fee or provide technical support. *GNU software* is governed by its own license, which is included inside the folder of the GNU product. See the GNU license for more details.

Trial, demo, or *evaluation versions* are usually limited either by time or functionality (such as being unable to save projects). Some trial versions are very sensitive to system date changes. If you alter your computer's date, the programs "time out" and are no longer functional.

Troubleshooting

If you have difficulty installing or using any of the materials on the companion CD-ROM, try the following:

- **Turn off any antivirus software that you may have running.** Installers sometimes mimic virus activity and can make your computer incorrectly believe that it is being infected by a virus. (Be sure to turn the antivirus software back on later.)

- **Close all running programs.** The more programs you're running, the less memory is available to other programs. Installers also typically update files and programs; if you keep other programs running, installation may not work properly.

- **Reference the ReadMe:** Please refer to the `ReadMe` file located at the root of the CD-ROM for the latest product information at the time of publication.

Customer Care

If you have trouble with the CD-ROM, call the Wiley Product Technical Support phone number at 800-762-2974. Outside the United States, call 1-317-572-3994. You can also contact Wiley Product Technical Support at `http://support.wiley.com`. John Wiley & Sons provides technical support only for installation and other general quality-control items. For technical support on the applications themselves, consult the program's vendor or author.

To place additional orders or to request information about other Wiley products, call 877-762-2974.

Guest Experts' Information

Brown, Scott
Los Angeles, California, USA
sbrown@artcenter.edu
www.spicybrown.com
* Tutorial: "Designing for Usability" in Chapter 3

Lott, Joey
Valley Village, California, USA
joey@person13.com
* Tutorial: "Adding New Tools to Flash," in Chapter 4

Winkler, Tom
Hollywood, California, USA
tomwink@earthlink.net
www.doodie.com
* Animation examples in Chapter 10

Digital Audio Basics

I f you plan carefully and pay attention to technical detail, sound can add dimension to your Flash projects. That's because sound introduces another mode of sensory perception. Coordinated with visual form and motion, sound deepens the impact and can even enhance the ease of use of your Flash creation.

Cross-Reference
For detailed information on adding sound to your Flash productions, refer to Chapter 12, "Adding Sound." Chapter 12 explains how to work with imported sound in Flash CS5, covering topics from codecs and compression to syncing to behaviors. ■

IN THIS APPENDIX

Audio sampling and quality basics

Production tips

Understanding the Basics of Sampling and Quality

Before you begin integrating sound with your Flash project, it's important to understand the basics of digital audio. To help you with this, this appendix is dedicated to sampling, bit resolution, and file size.

What is sound?

Hearing is one of our five senses; it's the sense that's produced when vibrations in the air strike the aural receptors located within your ears. When you hear a sound, the volume of the sound is determined by the intensity of the vibrations, or sound waves.

The *pitch* that you hear — meaning how high (treble) or low (bass) — is determined by the frequency of those vibrations (waves). The frequency of sound is measured in hertz (abbreviated as Hz). Theoretically, most humans have the ability to hear frequencies that range from 20 to 20,000 Hz. The frequency of the sound is a measure of the range of the sound — from the highest high to the lowest low. It's important to note here that, when starting to work with sound, the most common error is confusing the frequency of the sound with the recording sample.

What affects the quality and size of sound files?

When you add sound to a Flash movie, a number of factors affect the final quality of the sound and the size of the sound file. The quality of the sound is important because it determines the aesthetic experience of the sound. The file size is important because it determines how quickly (or slowly) the sound arrives at the end user's computer. The primary factors that determine the quality and size of a sound file are sample rate and bit resolution.

Sample rate

The sample rate, measured in hertz (Hz), describes the number of times an audio signal is sampled when it is recorded digitally. In the late 1940s, Harry Nyquist and Claude Shannon developed a theorem which said that, for optimal sound quality, a sampling rate must be twice the value of the highest frequency of a signal. Thus, the higher the sample rate, the better the audio range. Generally, higher sample rates result in a richer, more complete sound. According to Nyquist and Shannon, in order for the audible range of 20 to 20,000 Hz to be sampled correctly, the audio source needs to be sampled at a frequency no lower than 40,000 Hz, or 40 kHz. This explains why CD audio, which closely resembles the source sound, is sampled at 44.1 kHz.

Note

A sound sample refers to one "analysis" of a recorded sound, whereas a sound file refers to the entire collection of samples recorded, which comprise a digital recording. ■

The less a sound is sampled, the further the recording will deviate from the original sound. However, this tendency toward loss of the original quality of the sound yields one advantage: When the sample rate of a sound file is decreased, the file size drops proportionally. For example, a 300KB, 44.1 kHz sound file would be 150KB when saved as a 22.05 kHz file. See Table C.1 for more details on how sample rates affect quality.

TABLE C.1

Audio Sample Rates and Quality

Sample Rate	Quality Level	Possible Uses
48 kHz	Studio quality	Sound or music recorded to a digital medium such as miniDV, DAT, DVCam, and so on
44.1 kHz	CD quality	High-fidelity sound and music
32 kHz	Near-CD quality	Professional/consumer digital camcorders
22.050 kHz	FM radio quality	Short, high-quality music clips
11.025 kHz	Acceptable for music	Longer music clips; high-quality voice; sound effects
5 kHz	Acceptable for speech	"Flat" speech; simple button sounds

Because the native playback rate of most common audio cards is 44.1 kHz, sound that is destined for playback on any computer should be a multiple of 11.025. Thus, I recommend sample rates of 44.1 kHz, 22.05 kHz, and 11.025 kHz for *any* use on computers. (Although sample rates that deviate from the rule of 44.1 may sound fine on your development platform, and may sound fine on many other computers, some may have problems. This simple rule goes a long way toward reducing complaints of popping and distorted sound.) These standard rates become more important with Flash. When Flash imports sounds that are not multiples of 11.025, the sound file is resampled, which causes the sound to play at a lower or higher pitch than the original recording. This same logic applies to sound export, which I discuss in Chapter 12. Finally, although Flash menus list sample rates as 11, 22, and 44, these are abbreviations for the truly precise sample rates of 11.025, 22.05, and 44.1 kHz.

Note

Although the Flash Player can play a wide range of sampling rates with runtime assets, the Flash Player resamples all audio to 44.1 kHz during playback. You may want to make sure that all external assets that you intend to play at runtime use 44.1 kHz for consistency. ■

Bit resolution

The second key factor that influences audio quality is bit resolution (or bit depth). *Bit resolution* describes the number of bits used to record each audio sample. Bit resolution is increased exponentially, meaning that an 8-bit sound sample has a range of 28, or 256, levels, whereas a 16-bit sound sample has a range of 216, or 65,536, levels. Thus, a 16-bit sound is recorded with far more information than an 8-bit sound of equal length. The result of this additional information in a 16-bit sound is that background hiss is minimized, while the sound itself is clearer. The same sound recorded at 8-bits will be noisy and washed out.

A 16-bit sound file is twice the size of the same file saved at 8-bit quality. This is due to the increase in the amount of information taken to record the higher-quality file. So, if your sound is too big, what can you do? Well, a sound that's been recorded at a higher bit resolution can be converted to a lower bit resolution, and a sound with a high sample rate can be converted to a lower sample rate. Although a professional studio might perform such conversions with hardware, you can do either of these conversions with software.

Tip

If you're having difficulty understanding the significance of bit depths, yet are familiar with the intricacies of scanning photographic images, consider the difference between an 8-bit grayscale image and a 24-bit color image of equivalent dimensions. The file size for the 8-bit grayscale image (such as a black-and-white photograph) is much smaller than the 24-bit color image (such as a color photograph). The grayscale image doesn't have as much tonal information — only 256 levels of gray — yet the 24-bit color image records a range of 16.7 million colors. Unlike photographs, sound samples don't require anything close to a range of 16.7 million values. Also, 16-bit sound samples deliver a dynamic range of over 64,000 values, which is more than the human ear can detect. ■

Table C.2 lists the various bit depths of sound along with their quality levels and possible uses.

TABLE C.2

Audio Bit Resolution and Quality

Bit Depth	Quality Level	Possible Uses
16-bit	CD quality	High-fidelity sound and music
12-bit	Near-CD quality	Professional/consumer digital camcorder audio
8-bit	FM radio quality	Short, high-quality music clips
4-bit	Acceptable for music	Longer music clips; high-quality voice; sound effects

Note

As hardware technology improves, we're seeing even better audio bit resolution beyond the 16-bit and 44 kHz range. The DVD-Audio format, for example, offers audio bit resolutions of 16, 20, or 24, and sampling rates of 48, 96, or 192 kHz. Obviously, these extraordinarily high fidelity recordings are appreciated by extreme audiophiles who have superior playback devices and speakers. Don't worry if your multimedia presentations don't use such extremes — trust me when I say that 16-bit 44 kHz audio is more than enough quality for average computer-audio devices and speakers. ■

See Figures C.1 and C.2 for a comparison of the differences between sounds at different sample rates and bit depths. Both figures show a waveform derived from the same original sound file, differing only in their sample rates and bit depths. The waveform of the 16-bit 44.1 kHz sound has twice as many *points* — or samples of information — as the 8-bit 11.025 kHz sound. Because the 16-bit 44.1 kHz sound has more samples, the gap between each sample isn't as large as the gaps of the 8-bit 11.025 kHz sound. More samples result in a much smoother, cleaner sound.

Tip

A common mistake novices make with sound is the assumption that 8-bit audio is acceptable, especially because it ought to result in a much smaller file than 16-bit sound. This is wrong for at least two reasons. First, 8-bit is unacceptable because it sounds far worse than 16-bit sound. Second, the horrible sound does not pay for itself in diminished file size because most audio compression codecs (especially those used by Flash) won't work with 8-bit sound. ■

FIGURE C.1

A waveform of a sound sampled at 44.100 kHz with a 16-bit resolution, as displayed in a high-end sound application

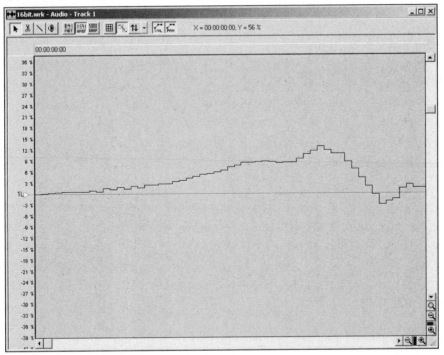

FIGURE C.2

The same sound that is shown in Figure C.1, but it's down-sampled to 11.025 kHz with an 8-bit resolution

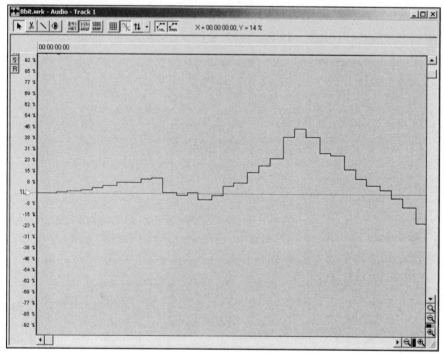

Channels

Audio files are either mono (single channel) or stereo (dual channel: left and right). Stereo files are twice the size of mono files because they have twice the information. Most audio-editing applications offer the option to mix the two stereo channels together and either save or export a stereo sound to a one-channel mono sound. Most audio applications also have the capability to save the right or left channel of a stereo sound separately as a .wav or .aif file.

With the more robust, multitrack-editing applications such as Deck, ProTools, Sound Forge, or Cool Edit Pro, it's not unusual to work with eight or more audio tracks — limited only by your system configuration. As you may imagine, these applications give the sound artist greater control over the final sound mix. For use in Flash, these multitrack audio project files need to be "bounced" or mixed down to a stereo or mono file in order to be saved as .wav or .aif files.

Getting Tips on Production

The primary goal of sound optimization for limited delivery networks (such as the Internet) is to deliver an acceptable quality without a large file-size "cost." You should be concerned about the file size of your audio clips for several reasons:

- Sound files require a large amount of drive space.

- Managing large sound files and importing them into Flash can be cumbersome and slow.

- Download times for large, elaborate sound clips (even when heavily compressed upon export from Flash) can be detrimental to the appreciation of your Flash project (even if your target audience has what may be considered a high-speed Internet connection).

When you're working with audio clips, it's important to create the shortest audio clips possible. That means trimming off any excess sound that you don't need, especially any blank lead-in or lead-out *handles* (also called in and out points) at either the beginning or the end of a clip.

Cross-Reference

I discuss trimming excess sound briefly in Chapter 12, with reference to Flash's sound tools. ∎

If you plan to have a background music track in your Flash project, it's a good idea to use a small audio clip that can be looped.

Cross-Reference

I describe looping audio clips in Chapter 12. ∎

Here is a simple formula to determine the file size, in bytes, of a given audio clip:

Seconds of audio × sample rate × # of channels × (bit depth ÷ 8) = file size

Note

In the preceding formula, the sample rate is expressed in Hz (hertz), not kHz (kilohertz). The bit depth is divided by 8 because there are 8 bits per byte. ∎

Thus, a 20-second stereo audio loop at 8 bits, 11 kHz would be calculated like this:

20 sec × 11,025 Hz × 2 channels × (8 bits ÷ 8 bits/byte) = 441,000 bytes = 430KB

There are two schools of thought regarding the ideal quality of sound files for import into Flash. These schools are pretty much divided into those who have high-end sound-editing tools and those who don't. In an effort to delineate the best path for each group, we've noted the following:

- If you don't have high-end sound tools available, you may be among those who always prefer to start with audio source files of the highest possible quality (16-bit, 44.1 kHz is ideal), and then use the Flash sound settings to obtain optimal compression upon export.

Cross-Reference
See Chapter 12 for detailed information on the sound export settings for Flash movies. ■

- If you do have high-end sound tools available, you may prefer to compose most of your clients' music from scratch and may very rarely work with the MP3 format before importing into Flash. You may also disagree with those who advise you to bring sound into Flash at the highest quality before optimizing. This workflow difference may be attributable to the plethora of options available to those with high-end sound tools. I know of one sound engineer who converts all of his audio to 16-bit, 22.1 kHz mono files, "with major bass reduction," before importing into Flash.

You should always keep in mind that Flash can retain imported MP3 compression settings only with those MP3 files that will be used for non-Stream sync options. Anytime you set a sound to use Stream sync on a timeline, Flash needs to recompress the file with the Stream export settings found in the Publish Settings dialog box.

Finally, all linked sounds, or those set to export from the Library and played back via ActionScript, are treated as non-Stream sounds. If you use linked sounds, you may find it useful to import precompressed MP3 files at your preferred bit rate. Flash does not recompress the MP3 file upon export to a .swf file.

Digital Video Basics

A s you begin to create more complex Flash presentations that include digital video, you need to know how to achieve the highest-quality image and playback. In this appendix, you learn how to prepare a digital video file for use in a Flash CS5 document.

Cross-Reference

After you have successfully created a digital video file, you can learn how to import and use digital video files within a Flash CS5 document by reading Chapter 14, "Displaying Video." ■

Before you consider importing digital video footage into Flash CS5 or exporting your video with Adobe Media Encoder CS5, you need to plan how the video will be used within the Flash movie (or Web site). Will you be using several video clips for product demonstrations, interviews, or prerecorded events? Will you be using video for special effects such as a time-lapse effect of moving clouds or the sun setting? The more footage you plan to use, the more important it is to make sure that you're acquiring the footage properly — you wouldn't want to redo all your footage after you've seen the results in the Flash movie! This appendix provides tips for making sure that you have the best possible video quality for your Flash presentations.

Garbage In, Garbage Out: Controlling Video Quality

You may have heard this phrase before, which means that you can't get something from nothing. Ever tried making a soup with bad ingredients, thinking it would still taste good? The same principle holds true for video production. Four primary factors influence the quality of your video footage: source format, image quality, sound quality, and subject matter.

Source format

The source format is the container in which the video is stored, whether it's a digital recording encoded on miniDV or DVCAM tape, an analog recording on VHS or Hi8 tape, or a file recorded on your digital camera. Each recording medium has inherent resolution limitations — some formats can store more information than others. The more information the medium stores, the higher the quality of the recording.

The following list outlines the resolution capacities of common recording mediums. For the purposes of our discussion, this list is restricted to video formats and excludes film formats, such as 35mm or 16mm motion picture film. The video formats are compared by *line resolution,* which is the number of horizontal scan lines the format can capture. Line resolution is not the definitive attribute for video quality, but it does measure the capacity of potential visual information captured by the camera or recording device. The most important factor to remember when comparing line resolutions is that video is primarily targeted at television screens that, in North America, display 525 lines of resolution.

Note
Practically speaking, standard definition (SD) television sets display a maximum of 483 lines of visible resolution — the remaining lines convey other information such as the sync pulse. High-Definition TV (HDTV) is capable of displaying up to 1,080 lines of resolution, and many multimedia producers are using HD cameras to record video. ■

- **VHS, VHS-C, or 8mm videotape:** These tape formats, especially VHS, are common video formats in use by consumers today. The average household VCR records video in VHS format. These tape formats can record about 240 lines of resolution. This resolution is less than half of the potential scan lines that can be shown on a TV screen, which is why the VHS recordings of your favorite TV shows don't exactly match the live broadcasts. These tape formats are analog in nature — the signal they record is not digital and can deteriorate from copy to copy. To translate this tape format into digital video for use in a multimedia production, you need to capture the footage with an analog video capture card.

- **S-VHS or Hi8 videotape:** S-VHS and Hi8 video use the same tape sizes as their VHS and 8mm equivalents, but they capture up to 400 lines of resolution. This resolution capacity comes very close to the 525 lines of resolution that a television can display. You probably won't encounter many S-VHS camcorders anymore, but Hi8 video camcorders are still popular and in use today. Although the video quality is a noticeable improvement, the video signal is still analog, so as with VHS, you must capture it with an analog video capture card.

- **miniDV, Digital8, or DVCAM tape:** A popular breed of video recording devices for consumer, prosumer, and professional use is the DV (Digital Video) format. DV formats use the DV codec to digitally record video, while storing audio at near-CD or CD-quality sampling rates. The native resolution for the DV format is 525 lines, but the actual resolution a DV camcorder records varies from model to model. Most high-end DV camcorders are considered broadcast quality, meaning the video image is good enough to use on a television show such as the evening news. Many computer systems today ship with an IEEE 1394 (also known as FireWire or iLink) port to capture digital video from DV recording devices. When video is transferred digitally from a camera to a computer over an IEEE 1394 connection, there is no loss of quality.

- **HDV tape:** One of the newer video recording formats is HDV, or High-Definition Video. HDV content is recorded on the same tape cassette used by miniDV cameras. HDV content uses the same bit rates as miniDV content but uses MPEG-2 compression to store a much larger frame size — usually 1920 × 1080. Most HDV camcorders record content at 1440 × 1080, but on playback, the content is stretched to 1920 × 1080 with the proper 16:9 aspect ratio. Host HDV camcorders can also record or down-convert HD content to regular standard definition (SD) video, on the fly. Video is transferred from an HDV camcorder or player to a computer by using an IEEE 1394 (also known as FireWire or iLink) cable. Newer HDV camcorders can record directly to an internal hard drive on the camera, enabling videographers to more easily transfer recorded content over USB or FireWire.

- **Betacam SP, Digital Betacam:** These tape formats are for serious video professionals who work in the television industry. Betacam SP has been the industry standard for network television for more than 30 years. Although Betacam SP is an analog format, Digital Betacam (also known as DigiBeta) records video with a proprietary Sony codec. Both formats capture 550 or more lines of resolution.

- **MPEG file recording:** Many digital cameras and camcorders can record MPEG video at various sizes and resolutions. Most digital still cameras use an MPEG codec. Many MPEG recording devices can only capture at line resolutions equal to or less than VHS quality. The popular AVC/H.264 codec, part of the MPEG-4 family of codecs, is becoming more widely used in consumer and professional camcorders. This codec can be used to record incredibly high-quality video with much less bit rate than other codecs and is commonly used with HD frame sizes such as 1280 × 720 or 1920 × 1080.

As a general guideline, I recommend using the highest-quality camcorder available with your resources to record video that you intend to use for multimedia presentations within a Flash movie. Several factors beyond the recording format affect the quality of any recording. In the next two sections, I discuss variables that influence the visual and audio portions of a recording.

Web Resource

If you're a beginner videographer and want to know more about video resolution, check out the following links:

```
www.bealecorner.com/trv900/respat
http://en.wikipedia.org/wiki/Display_resolution ■
```

Image quality

Regardless of the source format that you use for your video recording, the recording device may have other limitations. The recorded resolution of your camera may be significantly lower than the upper limit of your recording format's line resolution. For example, the DV format is capable of storing 525 lines of resolution. However, your specific DV camcorder may have an effective resolution of 490 lines. The following variables can affect the quality of the picture recorded by the camera. Note that this list is by no means exhaustive for the professional videographer — I chose these topics as a general summary to guide you in your video production.

- **Optics:** The characteristics of the lens (or lens system) that your camera uses are known as the optics. The optical quality of video camcorders varies wildly. Many camcorders boast Carl Zeiss lenses, which are known for their precision and accuracy. Some lenses are constructed of plastic, whereas others are glass. Neither lens type is necessarily better than the other, but the only way to accurately judge the optical system of your camera is to conduct extensive testing with a resolution target.

- **CCD or CMOS:** The CCD, or charged-coupled device, is the electronic plate that captures the image that the camera's lens renders. Newer video cameras are offering a CMOS () chip rather than a CCD, for longer battery life and better color sampling. You can think of the CCD or CMOS as the digital film that's being exposed to the light coming through the lens. Imaging chips come in a variety of sizes, ranging from ¼ inch to 1 inch. Although these sizes may sound incredibly small, even ¼-inch chips can capture amazing detail. The larger a chip is, however, the more information it can capture. Most cameras only have one chip, but some cameras have three chips — one for each color of the RGB (red, green, and blue) spectrum. These are known as three-chip cameras, and they have better color fidelity than single-chip cameras. Color fidelity, simply put, is the measure of how closely the recorded color of an image matches the original colors of the subject.

- **Tape quality:** The quality of the tape on which you record the video can also affect the quality of the overall image. Each tape brand has unique characteristics, such as the type of metal particles that are magnetized onto the tape. Some brands (or stocks) are more durable and can withstand the rigors of repeated recordings. In general, you should always record on a fresh tape — and preferably one listed as premium or high quality.

Tip

Make sure that you use the same brand and model of tape consistently throughout a shoot. There are slight color variations and differences in quality in each brand and tape type. Preferably, all the tapes used for a shoot should be manufactured from the same batch, and as such, you should buy bulk boxes of your preferred tape brands and formats. ■

- **Shutter mechanism:** The shutter mechanism is the device that controls how quickly the imaging chip samples the image rendered by the lens. Most camcorders have shutters that record interlaced video, which records two interwoven fields (or separate halves of a picture) to create one frame of video. Have you ever noticed how the image on your TV flickers when you pause a VHS recording? You're seeing the two fields of the frame alternating. Computer monitors do not display interlaced video. Rather, they use progressive scanning to minimize a flicker effect. Some higher-end camcorders have progressive scan shutters that record the image with higher apparent resolution. I discuss de-interlacing video later in this appendix.

- **Exposure:** You should make every effort to shoot your video footage with the correct exposure. Exposure refers to the amount of light captured by the imaging chip and the shutter mechanism. Some camcorders do not allow you to control the exposure — it's all automatic. The biggest pitfall for most videographers is underexposing video footage or shooting in low light. When you try to record a poorly lit subject, you tend to get noise in the darkest areas of the image. Video noise is a random pattern of dots that shows up on the image. Finally, make every effort to properly white-balance your shot to suit the color temperature of the dominant light source — some camcorders enable you to control the color temperature. You'll notice the effects of color temperature in the video samples on the CD-ROM. You learn more about white balance later in this appendix.

So what do all these variables boil down to? In a nutshell, I recommend that whenever possible, you should shoot video with a camcorder that has a superior optical system with three imaging chips, use high-quality tapes, and properly control your exposure. Avoid shooting in low light, unless you are shooting with a particular effect in mind, such as infrared lighting.

Sound quality

Every videographer should consider how audio is recorded during production. Most video camcorders have a decent built-in stereo microphone, but professional videographers equip themselves with accessories beyond those that ship with the camera. Review the following guidelines for capturing sound with your video recording:

- **External microphones:** To achieve the best audio recording, put an external microphone as close as possible to the source of the sound. If you want to record a person talking, an external microphone, such as a wireless Lavaliere mic that's pinned to the person's shirt, collar, or tie, produces a much cleaner recording than the microphone on the camera.

- **Balanced versus unbalanced audio:** Most microphones you find at electronics stores use a stereo or mono 3.5mm mini-adapter that plugs into the microphone jack on your camcorder. These microphones are considered "unbalanced" audio sources, due to the nature of their internal wiring. For many video shoots, this may not pose a problem. However, professional audio engineers use balanced audio for all sound sources. The cabling for balanced audio tends to be a heavier gauge than that of the consumer variety. Many balanced microphones have a three-pin XLR connector, and most camcorders require an XLR adapter to connect these sources to the mini microphone jack. Many professional video cameras have built-in XLR jacks.

- **Sampling rate and bit depth:** Unless you're using a DV format camcorder, you likely have little or no control over the specific sampling rate and bit depth used to record audio on the camera. DV camcorders enable you to record with either 32 kHz or 48 kHz: 32 kHz audio is recorded at 12-bit, which is suitable for recording dialog and live action; 48 kHz is recorded at 16-bit, which is suitable for recording live musical performances or any other scene requiring high fidelity.

- **Audio levels:** One of the most overlooked aspects of video production is monitoring the audio levels of your source while recording. Most camcorders record audio only with AGC, or Automatic Gain Control. This "feature" allows the camcorder to determine how much an audio signal should be boosted or minimized during recording. Professional audio engineers prefer to manually monitor and adjust sound levels while the recording is taking place. Undesirable side effects of using AGC include amplified background noise during silent periods, audio distortion, and sudden jumps or drops in audio levels. Whenever possible, listen to your audio source through headphones connected to the camera.

- **Unwanted noise:** Do your best to minimize any background noise when you are recording. The microphone(s) connected to your camera pick up more noise than you may realize. Each microphone has a different "pick-up" pattern, determining the range and direction of sound that it receives.

In summary, you should record audio as close as possible to the source, using balanced microphones and monitoring the audio feed with headphones connected to the camera. For most video recording, either the 32 kHz or 48 kHz sampling rates yield superior audio reproduction.

Subject matter

Last, but by no means least, the type of subject matter you are shooting can influence the results of video compression in video deployed to the Flash platform. When it comes to video compression, the most important factor to remember is variability from frame to frame. That is, how much and how often does your subject matter change? Are you recording the Indy 500, panning race cars accelerating at incredibly fast speeds? Or, are you recording a time lapse of a flower slowly blooming? In general, you will achieve the best results with video compression if the subject matter does not move randomly or quickly.

Here are some general guidelines when choosing and shooting your subject matter:

- **Use a tripod:** One of the most common mistakes amateur videographers make is to handhold the video camcorder. Unless you need to freely move with your camera or intentionally want to introduce shakiness to your video image, always mount your camera on a tripod.

- **Avoid quick and jerky movements:** If you need to follow your subject matter by panning the head on the tripod, practice the movement a few times before recording. Try to be as slow and fluid as possible. The more quickly you pan a video camera while recording, the more likely you'll see compression artifacts show up in your final video in the Flash movie.

- **Avoid zooming:** Although it may be tempting, do not zoom the lens while recording your subject matter. It's better to use the zoom to frame the shot before you record. Of course, you may intentionally want to use wild zooming effects to re-create the next *Blair Witch* mockumentary, but be aware that any rapid movement from zooming the lens will likely compress very poorly in the Flash movie.

- **Lock focus:** All camcorders can auto-focus the lens. If you plan to record a stationary object, you may want to switch to manual focus. If your subject matter moves away from the camera's focus "spot," the camera may refocus on areas behind the subject matter. This type of focus drifting may yield very unpleasant compression artifacts in the Flash video.

- **Watch white balance:** White balance refers to how the camera interprets color. You might notice that your skin looks much less appealing under fluorescent light than it does under an incandescent or soft white indoor light bulb. The human eye can "correct" the perception of a light source's color (or color temperature) with greater ease than an automatic setting on your camera. Be sure to match the white-balance setting on your camcorder to the predominant light source in your video composition. Most cameras have at least two white-balance settings: indoor (for tungsten light) and outdoor (for daylight). Some cameras enable you to perform a custom white balance. To set a custom white balance, focus the entire viewing area on a solid field of white and engage the white-balance lock on your camera.

Another factor to consider is the area of the video composition that changes from frame to frame. In a previous example, I mention panning a race car. In that example, the entire picture changes in every frame. Compression works best on video footage with the least amount of movement per pixel in the frame. For example, if you mount your camera on a tripod and keep the camera motionless, you can record the motion of a single subject, such as the flight of a bee between flowers. In such an example, the video compression with the Sorenson Spark codec is much more effective than it would be in the example of the race car.

Tip

Although I mention these general rules for better-looking video shoots, it is also crucial to develop a look and feel for whatever you are shooting. Establish a set of rules that apply to everything in the shoot. For example, perhaps you want to shoot everything handheld, rack the focus regularly, underexpose the image slightly, dutch the angle on all wide shots, and so on. With today's cutting-edge video and film effects, it is more important to develop a style and operate to achieve a consistent look than to worry excessively over conventional dos and don'ts. ∎

Editing Footage

After you have recorded the video with your camcorder, it's time to start editing the footage in a digital video editor such as Adobe Premiere or Apple Final Cut Pro.

It's beyond the scope of this book to fully explain the process of editing video footage, but I offer the following pointers to maximize the compression benefits of the video codecs that the Flash Player uses:

- **Watch transitions and filter effects:** Keep the general rule in mind that I mentioned previously — refrain from global changes to the entire frame. Some effects and transitions, such as cross-fades and slow dissolves, introduce rapid changes to successive frames of video. These changes require more keyframes to retain quality, and these keyframes add significant weight to the file size of the compressed video. Otherwise, if you don't want the extra weight, you'll have to accept less quality in the overall image.

- **Minimize duration:** The shorter you make your finished video clip, the smaller the file size of your Flash movie (.swf). Although you can stream video content just like any Flash content, you should keep in mind the data rate of your target audience.

When you finish editing your video, make a master version that can serve other purposes beyond your Flash movie presentation. You may even want to output a final version of the edited footage to DV tape. In the next section, I discuss what output format to use for your edited footage. Later, this output format will be compressed and embedded in the Flash document.

Choosing an Import Format

After you complete the editing phase for your video footage, you're ready to output a final version of your video project that you can use with your Flash document. The following checklist should help you determine how to get the most effective use out of the Flash Player's video codecs, Sorenson Spark, On2 VP6, or AVC/H.264. Just as you don't want to re-JPEG a JPEG (that is, save a JPEG file again with more JPEG compression), you will find that it's best to retain as much original quality from the video as possible before you bring it into Flash.

- **Frame size:** Most video sources are captured and edited at full-frame NTSC sizes, such as 640 × 480 and 720 × 480. It's unlikely that you'll want to expend the bandwidth required to display this full-frame size. A starting frame size should be 320 × 240; work your way up or down from there. If you are targeting Web users with dial-up connection speeds such as 28.8 or 56 Kbps, you may want to consider a frame size of 160 × 120. Remember, when you scale down a bitmap-based element in the Flash authoring environment, you don't actually throw away any pixels — the full size of the graphic is retained in the final Flash movie file (.swf).

- **Frame rate:** When you capture video from your camcorder to your desktop video-editing application, the video has a frame rate of 29.97 fps (NTSC) or 25 fps (PAL). This frame rate, as with regular video frame sizes, requires more bit rate to play with equivalent quality than a lower frame rate. As a general rule, keep your video frame rate as close as possible to (or lower than) the frame rate of your Flash movie, as defined in the Document Properties dialog box (Modify ⇨ Document). Most video on the Internet has a frame rate of 15, 24, or 30 fps.

Note

As fast broadband Internet connections become more predominant, you'll find more and more sites featuring Flash Video that uses video clips with 24, 29.97, or 30 fps. If you plan to load .flv files at runtime into Flash movies with Flash Player 7 or later, the video content's frame rate can differ from the host Flash movie without any conflict. Slower processors, such as Pentium III or older PowerBook G3 computers, however, may have a more difficult time decoding Flash Video that uses high frame rates such as 24, 29.97, or 30 fps. ∎

- **Video compression:** Use a lossless video codec for your final video file that you export from your video editing software. If you're outputting a QuickTime file, use the Animation codec set to Best (100%) quality. You can also use the Uncompressed option (available in Apple QuickTime Player Pro or any video-editing application such as Adobe Premiere or Apple Final Cut Pro) when you save your final video file.

- **Audio compression:** Follow the same guidelines for video compression. DV-formatted video stores audio uncompressed.

- **De-interlacing:** I mention earlier in this chapter that video recorded by camcorders is interlaced. However, computer monitors (and the graphics appearing on them) are progressively scanned and do not require interlacing. (You may notice how "soft" your DV footage appears in most desktop video-editing applications; this is due to the even and odd "interlaces" being multiplied to accommodate the progressive scanning of computer video.) The general rule of thumb is to use a de-interlace filter (or export option) on any video footage that you intend to use for computer playback. However, if you resize your video to 320 × 240 or smaller and decrease the frame rate from its original rate, you effectively de-interlace the video footage. Usually, you do not see any difference enabling a de-interlace filter on top of these reductions.

After you have gone through this checklist for your video footage, export a final video file that you can compress with Adobe Media Encoder. Most video applications (including Apple QuickTime Player Pro) can resave a finished video file with a new frame size, frame rate, video and audio compressions, and other options such as de-interlacing. Adobe Media Encoder can import a variety of video file formats, listed in Table D.1.

TABLE D.1

Video Import Formats for Adobe Media Encoder

Format	Platform	Required Drivers	Description
AVI (.avi) Audio Video Interleaved	Windows Mac	DirectX 7 or later, or QuickTime 4 or later	Standard Windows video format; usually the format in which video is captured on Windows; can use any combination of video and audio codecs
DV (.dv) Digital Video stream	Windows Mac	QuickTime 4 or later	Format saved from applications such as Adobe Premiere or Apple QuickTime Player Pro; uses the DV codec for video and uncompressed audio
MPEG (.mpg, .mpeg) Motion Picture Experts Group	Windows Mac	DirectX 7 or later, or QuickTime 4 or later	Precompressed video in the MPEG-1, MPEG-2, or MPEG-4 codec; a format used by many digital cameras that save to media formats such as Compact Flash (CF) and Memory Stick
QT (.mov) Apple QuickTime	Windows Mac	QuickTime 4 or later	Standard video format on the Mac; usually the format in which video is captured on the Mac; can use any combination of video and audio codecs
WMV (.wmv, .asf) Windows Media files	Windows	DirectX 7 or later	Precompressed video in a modified MPEG-4 codec developed by Microsoft to use with the Windows Media Player

Of the formats listed in Table D.1, I recommend that you import formats that don't apply any recompression to the original source format of your video. If you can avoid using compressed video such as Windows Media and MPEG files, you can prevent the video codecs available in the Flash Player from introducing further artifacts into the video. *Compression artifacts* are areas in the video frame where detail is lost. The process of compressing a file already using compression is known as *recompression*.

Caution

If you try to import MPEG files into the Mac version of Adobe Media Encoder, you may not be able to convert the audio track in the final output file. Only Windows' DirectX driver successfully converts both the video and audio tracks in most MPEG files to a format useable in the final video file. To import an MPEG via QuickTime on the Mac, you may need to use an application such as MPEG Streamclip (www.squared5.com) to convert the MPEG to a QuickTime movie that uses another codec. ■

Index

Index

Index

Index

Index

Index

J

JavaScript
    detecting Flash Player with, 725–729
    <embed> tag attributes for, 716, 717
    generating within HTML pages, 722
    <object> tag attributes for, 709, 710, 714
    support for, 28
    using Flash movies with, 729–737
JavaScript Flash (.jsfl) files, 66
join settings for shapes, 119–120
Jordan, Eric (contributor)
    "Interface Design" tutorial, 48
JPEG quality option, Publish Settings, 685
.jpg files
    importing, 518, 534–535
    publish settings for, 686, 699–700
.jsfl files, 66

K

kerning for text, 276
Key press event, 602
Keyboard class, 602
keyboard shortcuts, 74–76
keyframe-based tweened animation. *See* tweened animation
keyframes
    adding, 362–363, 644–646
    blank keyframes, 99, 103–104
    described, 99
    editing, 105
    erasing, 131
    as event handler, 602
    events for, 619–620
    inserting, 103–104
    property keyframes, 99, 395–396
    viewing, 386
keys, shortcut, for Timeline, 93
Knockout setting, filters, 433
Kuler panel, importing colors from, 244–245
Kuler Web site, from Adobe Labs, 239

L

label for keyframes, 100
label text, 270
languages supported
    Font Embedding options for, 279
    locale setting for text, 267, 277
    right-to-left text option, 266–267

Lasso tool, 154–156
Layer blend mode, 450
layer folders
    adding, 97
    deleting, 108
    described, 95, 100
    expanding and collapsing, 108
    inserting, 108
    moving layers in and out of, 107
Layer Properties dialog box, 108
Layer section, Timeline window, 92, 93, 95
layered bitmap graphics, 524–525
layers
    active, setting, 96
    adding, 97
    deleting, 97, 107
    display features for, 100
    distributing items to, 468–470
    guide layer, 100, 107, 455–458
    hidden, 96–97, 107, 686
    inserting, 107
    locking and unlocking, 97, 107
    mask layer
        animating, 467–468
        converting another layer to, 108, 455
        described, 100, 458–459, 468
        displaying, 108
        filled shape used for, 460–462
        grouped shapes used for, 463
        symbol instance used for, 463–464
        text used for, 464–468
    motion guide layer, 107
    motion tween layer, 108
    organizing, 106–107
    outlines of, toggling, 97
    pose layers, 369, 415–419
    rearranging, 107
    scrolling through, 96
    showing, 107
    structure of, 107
    view options for, 97
Layers contextual menu, 107–108
layout flowchart, 37
leading for text, 275
libraries
    Common Libraries, 187–189, 190
    Document Libraries
        conflicts between assets in, 196
        described, 186–187

Index

Index

R

radial gradients, 252–253
raster graphics. *See* bitmap graphics
Raw (Raw PCM) format, 479, 480, 501
raw shapes
    converting to drawing objects, 197, 370
    described, 196
    scaling, 320–321
    shape tweening for. *See* shape tweens
read-only text, 264
RealPlayer, 26–27
Real-Time Messaging Protocol (RTMP), 21
real-time video streaming, 558–559
Recognize Lines setting, Pencil tool, 125
Recognize Shapes setting, Pencil tool, 125
Rectangle Primitive tool, 114, 115, 118–119
Rectangle tool, 118–119
red box in text field, 281
Redo command, Edit menu, 171
Reflect overflow style, 317
Registration grid, 167
relative paths, 634–635
Remove gradients option, Publish Settings, 698
Rename option, Library panel, 193
Repeat command, Edit menu, 171
Repeat overflow style, 317
Replace Colors option, Swatches panel, 243
resolution
    bit resolution, for sound, 795–798, 806
    color resolution, 234
    of images, 520, 702
    printer resolution, 141, 309, 321
    screen resolution, 85, 788
    video resolution, 802–805
resources. *See* books and publications; help; Web site resources
RGB color, 233–234
Rich Internet Applications, 30
right-click (contextual) menus, 71
right-to-left text, 266–267
RTMP (Real-Time Messaging Protocol), 21
rulers, in Document window, 89
runtime bitmap caching, 425, 552–554
runtime files, 14
runtime sharing
    described, 190, 227
    font symbols with, 294–299

S

`salign` attribute, `<embed>` tag, 716
`salign` parameter, `<object>` tag, 712
sampling sounds, 793–795
Saturation setting, Adjust Color filter, 444
Save as Default option, Swatches panel, 243
Save Colors option, Swatches panel, 243
Scalable Vector Graphics (SVG), 26
`scale` attribute, `<embed>` tag, 716
Scale option, Publish Settings, 694–695
`scale` parameter, `<object>` tag, 712
Scene panel, 86–88
Scene Stage. *See* Stage area, Document window
scenes
    actions for, 611, 614
    editing, 88
    multiple, not recommended, 676
    navigating, 88, 89
    testing. *See* Test Scene command
    uses of, 86–87
Screen blend mode, 450
screen readers, 666–669
screen resolution, 85, 788
Script Assist mode, Actions panel, 603, 605–606
Script option, Publish Settings, 685
Script time limit option, Publish Settings, 688
scripts. *See* ActionScript; JavaScript
scrubbing
    sound, 486, 488
    timeline, 95, 201, 377
    video, 588
search engines, indexing movie content for, 24
seekBar property, FLVPlayback component, 581
Select All command, Edit menu, 171
Select Unused Items option, Library panel, 194
selectable text, 264
Selection tool, 147–154
selections
    deselecting items, 148
    drag-selections, 148
    duplicating items with, 149
    of freeform areas, 154–155
    hiding edge selection patterns, 90, 147
    highlight indicating, 147, 148
    Lasso tool, 154–156
    mesh pattern indicating, 147, 148
    moving items with, 150–151

Index

Index

Index